Contemporary Theatre, Film and Television

ISSN 0749-064X

Contemporary Theatre, Film and Television

A Biographical Guide Featuring Performers, Directors, Writers, Producers, Designers, Managers, Choreographers, Technicians, Composers, Executives, Dancers, and Critics in the United States, Canada, Great Britain and the World

Thomas Riggs, Editor

Volume 109

GALE
CENGAGE Learning

Detroit • New York • San Francisco • New Haven, Conn • Waterville, Maine • London

Contemporary Theatre, Film & Television, Vol. 109

Editor: Thomas Riggs

CTFT Staff: Mariko Fujinaka, Annette Petrusso, Susan Risland, Jacob Schmitt, Lisa Sherwin, Arlene True, Andrea Votava, Pam Zuber

Project Editors: Laura Avery, Tracie Ratiner

Editorial Support Services: Natasha Mikheyeva

Composition and Electronic Capture: Gary Oudersluys

Manufacturing: Rhonda A. Dover

For product information and technology assistance, contact us at **Gale Customer Support, 1-800-877-4253.**
For permission to use material from this text or product, submit all requests online at www.cengage.com/permissions.
Further permissions questions can be emailed to **permissionrequest@cengage.com**

Gale
27500 Drake Rd.
Farmington Hills, MI 48331-3535

LIBRARY OF CONGRESS CATALOG CARD NUMBER 84-649371

ISBN-13: 978-1-4144-7183-9
ISBN-10: 1-4144-7183-1

ISSN: 0749-064X

This title is also available as an e-book.
ISBN-13: 978-1-4144-7490-8
ISBN-10: 1-4144-7490-3
Contact your Gale sales representative for ordering information.

Printed in Mexico
1 2 3 4 5 6 7 15 14 13 12 11

Contents

Preface

Provides Broad, Single-Source Coverage in the Entertainment Field

Contemporary Theatre, Film and Television (*CTFT*) is a biographical reference series designed to provide students, educators, researchers, librarians, and general readers with information on a wide range of entertainment figures. Unlike single-volume reference works that focus on a limited number of artists or on a specific segment of the entertainment field, *CTFT* is an ongoing publication that includes entries on individuals active in the theatre, film, and television industries. Before the publication of *CTFT*, information-seekers had no choice but to consult several different sources in order to locate the in-depth biographical and credit data that makes *CTFT*'s one-stop coverage the most comprehensive available about the lives and work of performing arts professionals.

Scope

CTFT covers not only performers, directors, writers, and producers, but also behind-the-scenes specialists such as designers, managers, choreographers, technicians, composers, executives, dancers, and critics from the United States, Canada, Great Britain, and the world. With 208 entries in *CTFT 109*, the series now provides biographies on approximately 28,389 people involved in all aspects of theatre, film, and television.

CTFT gives primary emphasis to people who are currently active. New entries are prepared on major stars as well as those who are just beginning to win acclaim for their work. *CTFT* also includes entries on personalities who have died but whose work commands lasting interest.

Compilation Methods

CTFT editors identify candidates for inclusion in the series by consulting biographical dictionaries, industry directories, entertainment annuals, trade and general interest periodicals, newspapers, and online databases. Additionally, the editors of *CTFT* maintain regular contact with industry advisors and professionals who routinely suggest new candidates for inclusion in the series. Entries are compiled from published biographical sources which are believed to be reliable, but have not been verified for this edition by the listee or their agents.

Revised Entries

To ensure *CTFT*'s timeliness and comprehensiveness, entries from previous volumes, as well as from Gale's *Who's Who in the Theatre*, are updated for individuals who have been active enough to require revision of their earlier biographies. Such individuals will merit revised entries as often as there is substantial new information to provide. Obituary notices for deceased entertainment personalities already listed in *CTFT* are also published.

Accessible Format Makes Data Easy to Locate

CTFT entries, modeled after those in Gale's highly regarded *Contemporary Authors* series, are written in a clear, readable style designed to help users focus quickly on specific facts. The following is a summary of the information found in *CTFT* sketches:

- *ENTRY HEADING:* the form of the name by which the listee is best known.

- *PERSONAL:* full or original name; dates and places of birth and death; family data; colleges attended, degrees earned, and professional training; political and religious affiliations when known; avocational interests.

- *ADDRESSES:* home, office, agent, publicist and/or manager addresses.

- *CAREER:* tagline indicating principal areas of entertainment work; resume of career positions and other vocational achievements; military service.

- *MEMBER:* memberships and offices held in professional, union, civic, and social organizations.

- *AWARDS, HONORS:* theatre, film, and television awards and nominations; literary and civic awards; honorary degrees.

- *CREDITS:* comprehensive title-by-title listings of theatre, film, and television appearance and work credits, including roles and production data as well as debut and genre information.

- *RECORDINGS:* album, single song, video, and taped reading releases; recording labels and dates when available.

- *WRITINGS:* title-by-title listing of plays, screenplays, scripts, and musical compositions along with production information; books, including autobiographies, and other publications.

- *ADAPTATIONS:* a list of films, plays, and other media which have been adapted from the listee's work.

- *OTHER SOURCES:* books, periodicals, and internet sites where interviews or feature stories can be found.

Access Thousands of Entries Using *CTFT*'s Cumulative Index

Each volume of *CTFT* contains a cumulative index to the entire series. As an added feature, this index also includes references to all seventeen editions of *Who's Who in the Theatre* and to the four-volume compilation *Who Was Who in the Theatre.*

Available in Electronic Format

Online. Recent volumes of *CTFT* are available online as part of the Gale Biographies (GALBIO) database accessible through LEXIS-NEXIS. For more information, contact LEXIS-NEXIS, P.O. Box 933, Dayton, OH 45401-0933; phone (937) 865-6800, toll-free: 800-543-6862.

Suggestions Are Welcome

Contemporary Theatre, Film and Television is intended to serve as a useful reference tool for a wide audience, so comments about any aspect of this work are encouraged. Suggestions of entertainment professionals to include in future volumes are also welcome. Send comments and suggestions to: The Editor, *Contemporary Theatre, Film and Television,* Gale, 27500 Drake Rd., Farmington Hills, MI 48331-3535; or call toll-free at 1-800-877-GALE.

Contemporary Theatre, Film and Television

ABEL, Jake 1987–

PERSONAL

Full name, Jacob Allen Abel; born November 18, 1987, in Canton, OH.

Addresses: *Agent*—Carol Bodie, International Creative Management, 10250 Constellation Way, 9th Floor, Los Angeles, CA 90067. *Manager*—Cynthia Campos–Greenberg, Anthem Entertainment, 9595 Wilshire Blvd., Suite 900, Beverly Hills, CA 90212.

Career: Actor. Appeared in advertisements.

Awards, Honors: MTV Movie Award nomination (with Logan Lerman), best fight, 2010, for *Percy Jackson & the Olympians: The Lightning Thief.*

CREDITS

Film Appearances:
Conservationist, *Strange Wilderness,* Paramount, 2008.
Dennis at the age of twenty–one, *Flash of Genius,* Universal, 2008.
Jake, *Kickstand* (short film), 2008.
Trevor, *Tru Loved,* Regent Releasing, 2008.
Alex, *Good Girl* (short film), c. 2009.
Brian Nelson, *The Lovely Bones* (also known as *Lovely Bone* and *Lovely Bones*), Paramount/DreamWorks, 2009.
Toby, *18* (short film), 2009.
Luke, *Percy Jackson & the Olympians: The Lightning Thief* (also known as *Percy Jackson and the Lightning Thief* and *Percy Jackson & the Lightning Thief*), Twentieth Century–Fox, 2010.
Mark, *I Am Number Four,* DreamWorks, 2011.

Television Appearances; Movies:
Spencer, *Go Figure,* The Disney Channel, 2005.
Cameron Downes, *Angel of Death* (also known as *Ed Brubaker's "Angel of Death"*), Spike TV, 2009.

Television Appearances; Episodic:
Brian Janklow, "Blood of the Children," *Threshold* (also known as *Threshold—Premier contact*), CBS, 2005.
Brian Janklow, "The Order," *Threshold* (also known as *Threshold—Premier contact*), CBS, 2005.
Brian Janklow, "The Crossing," *Threshold* (also known as *Threshold—Premier contact*), CBS, 2006.
Doug Sommer, "Saving Sammy," *Cold Case* (also known as *Anexihniastes ypothesis, Caso abierto, Cold case—affaires classees, Cold Case—Kein Opfer ist je vergessen, Doegloett aktak, Kalla spaar, Todistettavasti syyllinen,* and *Victimes du passe*), CBS, 2006.
Kirk, "Twins at the Tipton," *The Suite Life of Zack and Cody* (also known as *The Suite Life* and *TSL*), The Disney Channel, 2006.
Charlie Sheridan, "Stand Your Ground," *CSI: Miami* (also known as *CSI Miami* and *CSI: Weekends*), CBS, 2007.
Tate, "Not for Nothing," *Life,* NBC, 2008.
Adam Milligan, "Jump the Shark," *Supernatural* (also known as *Sobrenatural*), The CW, 2009.
Dylan, "A Long, Strange Trip," *ER* (also known as *Emergency Room* and *E.R.*), NBC, 2009.
Kyle Sheridan (some sources cite role as Doug Sheridan), "Rush to Judgment," *CSI: NY* (also known as *CSI: New York, CSI: New York 2, C.S.I. New York, C.S.I.: New York, C.S.I.: NY,* and *CSI: Weekends*), CBS, 2009.
Adam Milligan, "Point of No Return," *Supernatural* (also known as *Sobrenatural*), The CW, 2010.
Adam Milligan and Michael, "Sean Song," *Supernatural* (also known as *Sobrenatural*), The CW, 2010.
Himself, "Percy Jackson & Dear John," *Sidewalks Entertainment* (also known as *Sidewalks* and *Sidewalks Entertainment Hour*), syndicated, 2010.

Some sources cite an appearance as a teenager in "Kicking and Screaming," an episode of *Summerland* (also known as *Immediate Family* and *Summerland Beach*), The WB, 2004.

AIBEL, Jonathan 1969–

PERSONAL

Full name, Jonathan Robert Aibel; born August 6, 1969, in Demarest, NJ; married; children: three. *Education:* Graduated from Harvard University, 1991, studied music and psychology.

Addresses: *Agent*—William Morris Endeavor Entertainment (WmEE2), One William Morris Place, Beverly Hills, CA 90212.

Career: Writer, producer, story editor, and consultant. Writing partner of Glenn Berger. Public speaker at various venues. Worked as a management consultant in Boston, MA.

Member: Writers Guild of America, West.

Awards, Honors: Emmy Award nominations, 1998, 2001, and 2002, and Emmy Award, 1999, all outstanding animated program (for programming one hour or less), all with others, for *King of the Hill;* Annie Award nomination (with Glenn Berger), best writing in an animated feature production, International Animated Film Society, 2009, for *Kung Fu Panda.*

CREDITS

Television Work; Series:
Story editor, *Can't Hurry Love,* CBS, 1995–96.
Executive story editor, *King of the Hill* (animated), Fox, 1997.
Coproducer, *King of the Hill* (animated), Fox, 1997–98.
Supervising producer, *King of the Hill* (animated), Fox, 1998–99.
Co–executive producer, *King of the Hill* (animated), Fox, 2000–2003.
Executive producer and (with others) showrunner, *King of the Hill* (animated), Fox, 2001–2002.
Consulting producer, *Married to the Kellys* (also known as *Back to Kansas*), ABC, 2003–2004.

Television Work; Pilots:
Story editor, *Can't Hurry Love,* CBS, 1995.
Story editor, *King of the Hill* (animated), Fox, 1997.

Co–executive producer, *A.U.S.A.* (also known as *Adam Sullivan* and *Assistant United States Attorneys*), NBC, 2003.
Consulting producer, *Married to the Kellys* (also known as *Back to Kansas*), ABC, 2003.
Executive producer, *Great Neck,* Fox, 2003.
Executive producer, *Life with Lupe,* Fox, 2004.
Supervising producer, *Fox/Jeff Westbrook Man with Exes & Girlfriend Comedy,* Fox, c. 2004 (some sources cite c. 2005.

Animated Film Work:
Coproducer, *Kung Fu Panda* (also known as *Kung Fu Panda: The IMAX Experience*), Paramount, 2008.
Consultant, *Shrek Forever After* (also known as *The Final Chapter, Forever After: The Final Chapter, Shrek: The Final Chapter, Shrek Forever, Shrek 4, Shrek Goes Fourth,* and *Shrek Forever After: An IMAX 3D Experience*), Paramount, 2010.
Coproducer, *Kung Fu Panda: The Kaboom of Doom* (also known as *Kung Fu Panda 2*), 2011.

Stage Appearances:
Master of ceremonies, *Why Not* (performance of a capella groups), Harvard University, Sanders Theatre, Cambridge, MA, 1991.

Stage Work:
While sometimes known as Jonathan R. "The Pitch" Aibel, musical director and arranger for the Harvard Din & Tonics (musical group at Harvard University).

WRITINGS

Teleplays; with Others; Episodic:
"George Runs into an Old Friend," *The George Carlin Show,* Fox, 1994.
"Lou's the Boss," *Platypus Man,* UPN, 1995.
"Without a Hitch," *Platypus Man,* UPN, 1995.
Howie Mandel's "Sunny Skies," CBC and Showtime, 1995.
MAD TV (also known as *Mad TV* and *MADtv*), Fox, multiple episodes, 1995–97.
King of the Hill (animated), Fox, multiple episodes, 1997–2000.
"Till Death Do Us Part," *A.U.S.A.* (also known as *Adam Sullivan* and *Assistant United States Attorneys*), NBC, 2003.

With others, wrote questions for game shows broadcast by MTV.

Teleplays; with Others; Pilots:
Great Neck, Fox, 2003.
Life with Lupe, Fox, 2004.

Screenplays for Animated Films; with Others:

Kung Fu Panda (also known as *Kung Fu Panda: The IMAX Experience*), Paramount, 2008.

Alvin and the Chipmunks: The Squeakquel (based on characters created by the Bagdasarian family; also known as *Alvin and the Chipmunks II* and *Alvin 2*), Twentieth Century–Fox, 2009.

Monsters vs. Aliens (also known as *Monsters vs Aliens: A Monstrous IMAX 3D Experience*), Paramount/ DreamWorks, 2009.

Kung Fu Panda: The Kaboom of Doom (also known as *Kung Fu Panda 2*), 2011.

Screenplays:

(With others) *Maxx Powers and the Love Triangle of Doom* (also known as *Untitled (Disney/Alain Chabat/Romantic Comedy Project)*), c. 2003.

With others, wrote *Billion to One, Planet Fred, RRRrrrr!!! (RRRrrremake),* and *Untitled (Universal Pictures/Aibel & Berger Action Comedy)* (also known as *Untitled Jack Black Action Comedy*).

Screenplays; Uncredited Script Rewrite Work:

Freddy vs. Jason (also known as *Friday the 13th Part XI, FvJ, A Nightmare on Elm Street Part 8,* and *A Nightmare on Friday the 13th*), New Line Cinema, 2003.

Surviving Christmas, DreamWorks, 2004.

Sky High, Buena Vista, 2005.

Worked on other script rewrites, including *Disaster Area.*

Writings for the Stage:

Cowriter of shows produced by Hasty Pudding Theatricals, Harvard University.

Writings for Video Games; with Others:

Blazing Dragons, 1996.

ALBANESE, Alba 1976–

PERSONAL

Full name, Alba Rosa Albanese; born March 1, 1976, in Brooklyn, New York, NY; married Michael Cerenzie (a producer), February 14, 1999 (divorced, August 1, 2001). *Education:* Attended The New School, 1997, and South Hampton College, 2005; trained at the HB Studio, Lee Strasberg Theatre & Film Institute, Howard Fine Acting Studio, Will Geer Theatricum Botanicum, William Esper Studio for Acting, and the Maggie Flanigan Studio.

Addresses: *Agent*—Carole Ingber, Ingber Associates, 274 Madison Ave., Suite 1104, New York, NY 10016–0701.

Career: Actress and stunt performer. Appeared in advertisements and provided voice work for projects. Joyce Theater, New York City, dancer; Fleur De Lis (dance company devoted to presenting benefits), founder; director and producer of fund–raising events.

Member: American Federation of Television and Radio Artists, Screen Actors Guild.

CREDITS

Film Appearances:

(Uncredited) Local girl, *Lesser Prophets* (also known as *The Last Bet*), Prophetable Pictures/Millennium Films, 1997.

New Yorker, *As Good as It Gets* (also known as *Old Friends*), Sony Pictures Entertainment, 1997.

Woman in Central Park, *The Object of My Affection,* Twentieth Century–Fox, 1998.

Young girl, *He Got Game* (also known as *Last Game* and *Man to Man*), Buena Vista, 1998.

(Uncredited) Girl in lot, *8MM* (also known as *Eight Millimeter, 8 Millimeter, 8mm, Sexy World,* and *Super 8*), Columbia, 1999.

Working girl, *Flawless,* Metro–Goldwyn–Mayer, 1999.

Young model, *Coming Soon,* 1999, Unapix Entertainment Productions, 2000.

Jennifer, *Enemies of Laughter,* Outrider Pictures/Eternity Pictures, 2000.

Neighbor, *Row Your Boat,* Gullane Pictures, 2000.

Voice, *Bossa Nova* (also known as *Miss Simpson*), Sony Pictures Classics, 2000.

Brenda, *Deuces Wild,* Metro–Goldwyn–Mayer/United Artists, 2002.

Carol, *Hitch* (also known as *The Last First Kiss* and *Mr. Hichi*), Columbia, 2005.

Jessica, *Silver Grin* (short film), 2006.

Veronica, *We Own the Night* (also known as *Undercover*), Columbia, 2007.

Appeared as Theresa, *Donnybrook;* as Ginger, *Rosemary & Ginger;* as Marissa, *Spaghetti Park;* and as Star, *Stars Desire.*

Film Stunt Performer:

Step Up (also known as *Let's Dance* and *Sexy Dance*), Buena Vista, 2006.

Stunt double, *Righteous Kill* (also known as *Border*), Overture Films, 2008.

The Talking of Pelham 1 2 3 (also known as *The Talking of Pelham 123*), Columbia, 2009.

Tell Tale (also known as *Tell–Tale*), 2009.

Film Work; Other:

Director, *RioRoach* (documentary; part of her documentary series GlobalRoach), c. 2004.

Director, *NY Roach* (documentary; part of her documentary series GlobalRoach), c. 2005.

Director, producer, and film editor, *Posstags* (short film), MagicSleep Productions, 2006.

Television Appearances; Pilots:

Some sources cite an appearance as Lila, *Trinity,* NBC, 1998.

Television Stunt Performer; Episodic:

"Country Crossover," *Law & Order: Criminal Intent* (also known as *Law & Order: CI*), NBC, 2006.

"Self–made," *Law & Order: Criminal Intent* (also known as *Law & Order: CI*), USA Network, 2007.

"Senseless," *Law & Order: Criminal Intent* (also known as *Law & Order: CI*), USA Network, 2007.

Television Stunt Performer; Pilots:

(Uncredited) Stunt driver, "Out Here in the Fields," *Life on Mars,* ABC, 2008.

Stage Appearances:

Tangle, 55 Water St., New York City, 2006.

Bertha, *Hello from Bertha* (one–act play), produced as part of The Hotel Plays—Series 2 (Rain), Provincetown Tennessee Williams Theater Festival, Infinite Theatre, New York City, 2009.

Carol Cutrere, *Orpheus Descending,* produced as part of the reading *TENN99,* LAByrinth Theatre Company, New York City, 2010.

Appeared as Roberta, *Danny and the Deep Blue Sea,* and as Donna, *The Dreamer Examines His Pillow,* both Here Arts Theatre; as the red queen, *Alice in Wonderland,* Joyce Theater, New York City; as Cleopatra, *Antony and Cleopatra,* Will Geer Theatricum Botanicum, Topanga, CA; as Lorna, *Golden Boy,* Vine Theatre; as Myrtle, *Kingdom of Earth,* Soho Theatre; as Lulu, *Lost, Lonely, and Vicious,* Actors Studio, New York City; as Lady Macbeth, *Macbeth,* New York Shakespeare Festival, New York City; and as Blanche DuBois, *A Streetcar Named Desire,* South Hampton Theatre.

Stage Work:

Director and producer, *Angels for a Cause* (fund–raiser for the American Cancer Society).

RECORDINGS

Video Game Work:

Stunt performer, *Law & Order: Criminal Intent* (also known as *Law & Order: The Video Game*), Legacy Interactive, 2005.

WRITINGS

Screenplays:

RioRoach (documentary; part of her documentary series GlobalRoach), c. 2004.

NY Roach (documentary; part of her documentary series GlobalRoach), c. 2005.

Posstags (short film), MagicSleep Productions, 2006.

OTHER SOURCES

Periodicals:

Variety, June 14, 2000.

ALLMAN, Jamie Anne
  (Jamie Allman, Jamie Brown, Jamie Anne Brown)

PERSONAL

Original name, Jamie Anne Brown; born in Parsons, KS; married Marshall Scott Allman (an actor and writer), June 17, 2006. *Avocational Interests:* Working with autistic children, skydiving.

Career: Actress.

CREDITS

Television Appearances; Series:

Connie Riesler, *The Shield* (also known as *The Barn* and *Rampart*), FX Network, 2002–2003.

Television Appearances; Movies:

Olivia Thibodeaux, *Prairie Fever,* Ion Television, 2008.

Television Appearances; Episodic:

(As Jamie Brown) Bree Davis, "The Hand of a Stranger," *The Fugitive* (also known as *The Fugitive: The Chase Continues*), CBS, 2000.

(As Jamie Brown) Chloe Frye, "Bring Up Babies," *Family Law,* CBS, 2001.

(As Jamie Brown) Michelle Tritter, "Awakenings," *The Practice,* ABC, 2001.

(As Jamie Brown) Michelle Tritter, "Gideon's Crossover," *The Practice,* ABC, 2001.

(As Jamie Brown) Noelle Burnett, "Under Covers," *NYPD Blue* (also known as *New York Blues, New York Cops—NYPD Blue, New York Police, New York Police Blues, New York Police Department, N.Y.P.D,* and *N.Y.P.D.*), ABC, 2001.

(As Jamie Brown) Sharon, "Chapter Twenty–Seven," *Boston Public,* Fox, 2001.

(As Jamie Brown) Drug user, "The Invisible Woman," *Six Feet Under,* HBO, 2002.

(As Jamie Brown) Jane Renshaw, "Just One Kiss," *CSI: Miami* (also known as *CSI Miami* and *CSI: Weekends*), CBS, 2002.

(As Jamie Brown) Mandy Gressler, "The Beginning," *The Guardian* (also known as *El guardia, The Guardian—Retter mit Herz, Le protecteur, O allos mou eaftos, Ochita bengoshi Nick Fallin, Ochita bengoshi Nick Fallin 2,* and *Oikeuden puolesta*), CBS, 2002.

(As Jamie Brown) Mandy Gressler, "Lawyers, Guns and Money," *The Guardian* (also known as *El guardia, The Guardian—Retter mit Herz, Le protecteur, O allos mou eaftos, Ochita bengoshi Nick Fallin, Ochita bengoshi Nick Fallin 2,* and *Oikeuden puolesta*), CBS, 2002.

(As Jamie Brown) Mandy Gressler, "Testimony," *The Guardian* (also known as *El guardia, The Guardian—Retter mit Herz, Le protecteur, O allos mou eaftos, Ochita bengoshi Nick Fallin, Ochita bengoshi Nick Fallin 2,* and *Oikeuden puolesta*), CBS, 2002.

(As Jamie Brown) Sophia Jones, "Slippery Slope," *Fastlane,* Fox, 2002.

(As Jamie Brown) Sophia Jones, "Wet," *Fastlane,* Fox, 2002.

(As Jamie Brown) "Crossroads," *For the People* (also known as *Para la gente*), Lifetime, 2002.

(As Jamie Brown) Allison Hardwin, "Diagnosis," *The Division* (also known as *Heart of the City*), Lifetime, 2003.

(As Jamie Brown) Gwen Dreamer, "Gleen," *Cold Case* (also known as *Anexihniastes ypothesis, Caso abierto, Cold case—affaires classees, Cold Case—Kein Opfer ist je vergessen, Doegloett aktak, Kalla spaar, Todistettavasti syyllinen,* and *Victimes du passe*), CBS, 2003.

(As Jamie Anne Brown) Hannah McLoughlin, "Natural Borne Killers," *Threat Matrix,* ABC, 2003.

(As Jamie Anne Brown) Celeste Turner, "Paper or Plastic?," *CSI: Crime Scene Investigation* (also known as *C.S.I., CSI, CSI: Las Vegas, CSI: Weekends,* and *Les experts*), CBS, 2004.

(As Jamie Anne Brown) Sarah Flynn, "Only You," *Century City,* CBS, 2004.

(As Jamie Brown) Jenny Manderville, "Mr. Monk and the Big Reward," *Monk* (also known as *Detective Monk*), USA Network, 2006.

(As Jamie Anne Brown) Tara Welch, "David and Goliath," *Close to Home* (also known as *American Crime, Fiscal Chase, Juste cause,* and *Justicia cerrada*), CBS, 2006.

Gloria Carter, "Am I Gonna Die Today?," *Saving Grace* (also known as *Grace*), TNT, 2009.

Kelli Malone, "Double Blind," *The Closer* (also known as *L.A.: Enquetes prioritaires* and *Se apostasi anapnois*), TNT, 2009.

Laura, "The Luckiest Man," *Three Rivers* (also known as *Untitled Barbee/Hanson Project*), CBS, 2009.

Television Appearances; Pilots:

Bree Davis, *The Fugitive* (also known as *The Fugitive: The Chase Continues*), CBS, 2000.

Connie Riesler, *The Shield* (also known as *The Barn* and *Rampart*), FX Network, 2002.

Jessie, *K–Ville,* Fox, 2007.

Terry, *The Killing,* AMC, 2010.

Film Appearances:

(As Jamie Brown) Kassidy's dresser, *Fashionably L.A.,* Glam Slam Productions, 1999.

(As Jamie Brown) Iris, *It Is What It Is,* Cooler Heads Productions, 2001.

(As Jamie Brown) Kelly, *I Am My Resume* (short film), 2003.

(As Jamie Brown) Martha Shaw, *The Notebook,* New Line Cinema, 2004.

(As Jamie Anne Brown) Austin, *Automatic,* 35 Terrace/Automatic Films, 2005.

(As Jamie Brown) Trisha, *AdCorp, Inc.* (short film), Pollywog Entertainment, 2005.

(As Jamie Brown) Candice Sauvigne, *Danny Roane: First Time Director,* Lionsgate, 2006.

(As Jamie Anne Brown) Maria Lee, *Steel City,* New Films International, 2006, Truly Indie, 2007.

(As Jamie Brown) Jackie, *A Day with the Urns* (short film), Under Dog Distribution, 2007.

Lisa, *Prey 4 Me,* Silent Road Cinema/White Rock Pictures, 2007.

(As Jamie Allman) Kate, *Just the Worst* (short film), Pollywog Entertainment, 2008.

Sharon, *In the Dark* (short film), University of Southern California, 2008.

Scarlet, *Farmhouse,* Phoenicia Pictures, 2008, Monarch Home Video, 2009.

Amanda, *A Hundred & Forty–Six Questions* (short film), Expensive Pictures, 2009.

Eleanor Eddy, *The Donner Party* (also known as *The Forlorn*), First Look International, 2009.

Elizabeth, *Love after Life* (short film), 2009.

(As Jamie Allman) Jenny Rapp, *The Last Rites of Joe May,* Steppenwolf Films, 2010.

Stage Appearances:

(As Jamie Anne Brown) Brady Mason, *Devil's Night,* Sherry Theatre, North Hollywood, CA, 2006.

RECORDINGS

Videos:

Herself, *Farmhouse: Behind the Scenes* (short documentary), Alliance Group Entertainment, 2009.

ANDERSON, Jo 1958–

PERSONAL

Born June 29, 1958, in Tenafly, NJ. *Education:* Attended Adelphi University; studied acting with Michael Moriarty; also studied at Chekhov Studio, Renaissance Court Dance, Lecoq Improvisation, and Clowning and Comedia del Arte.

Career: Actress and writer. Wisconsin Mime Theatre, artist in residence; Actors Studio, member of company.

CREDITS

Television Appearances; Series:
Marianne McKinney, *Dream Street,* NBC, 1989.
Diana Bennett, *Beauty and the Beast,* CBS, 1989–90.
Dr. Charlotte "Charley" Bennett, *Sisters,* NBC, 1994–95.
Nancy Parker, a recurring role, *Roswell* (also known as *Roswell High*), The WB, between 1999 and 2001.

Television Appearances; Movies:
Captain Melbeck's secretary, *Suspicion,* PBS, 1987.
Robyn Griffin, *I Saw What You Did* (also known as *I Saw What You Did ... and I Know Who You Are!*), CBS, 1988.
Megan McGuire, *Prime Target,* NBC, 1989.
Lydia Corman, *Columbo: Uneasy Lies the Crown,* ABC, 1990.
Loreen Wendell, *Decoration Day,* NBC, 1990.
Wendy Simmons, *Jack Reed: Badge of Honor,* NBC, 1993.
One Woman's Courage, NBC, 1994.
Elizabeth Sobel, *The Sky's On Fire* (also known as *Countdown: The Sky's On Fire*), ABC, 1998.

Television Appearances; Miniseries:
Prisoner's woman, *Jamaica Inn,* syndicated, 1985.
Pam Bozanich, *Menendez: A Killing in Beverly Hills,* CBS, 1994.
Pat White, *From the Earth to the Moon,* HBO, 1998.

Television Appearances; Episodic:
Faye Nell, "Amen ... Send Money," *Miami Vice,* NBC, 1987.
Sally Spangler, "We'll Meet Again," *thirtysomething,* ABC, 1988.
Jessica, "Nature Now," *Against the Law,* 1990.
Roslyn, "Cicely," *Northern Exposure,* CBS, 1992.
Jane Harris, "Learning Curve," *Northern Exposure,* CBS, 1993.
Rita Miller, "No Money Down," *High Incident,* ABC, 1997.

Dr. Claudia Vaughn, "Broken World," *Millennium,* Fox, 1997.
Megan Boone, "The Gift," *Legacy,* UPN, 1998.
Megan Boone, "Homecoming," *Legacy,* UPN, 1998.
Helen, "Father and Sons," *Prince Street,* NBC, 2000.
Leslie Phillips, "Good Housekeeping," *The Closer,* TNT, 2005.
Mrs. Cunningham, "If Not Now," *ER,* NBC, 2006.
Margo Dorton, "Meet Market," *CSI: Crime Scene Investigation* (also known as *C.S.I.* and *CSI: Las Vegas*), CBS, 2007.
Counselor, "Rush," *CSI: Miami,* CBS, 2007.
Helen Cole, "Miracle," *Eleventh Hour,* CBS, 2009.

Film Appearances:
Farmer's wife, *Miles from Home* (also known as *Farm of the Year*), Cinecom International, 1988.
Sister Madeleine/Starlet, *Dead Again,* Paramount, 1991.
Julia Ann Mercer, *JFK,* Warner Bros., 1991.
Martha Parker, *Season of Change,* 1994.
Bloom, *Daylight,* Universal, 1996.
Patsy, *Rain,* First Look Home Entertainment, 2001.
Christine, *Fat Rose and Squeaky,* Hannover House, 2006.

Stage Appearances:
Madame Curie (title role), *Marie* (solo show), Samuel Beckett Theatre, New York City, then Actors Studio, Los Angeles, both 1985.

Also appeared as understudy, *Cabaret Planet,* Soho Repertory, New York City; Sara, *The Greenhouse Keeper Died over the Weekend,* Manhattan Punch Line, New York City; Virginia, *The Merry Ride of Kevin O'Cypher,* Dramatist Guild, New York City; Dee, *Motherless Child,* Women in Theatre Festival, New York City; member of ensemble, *Plums,* Bond Street Theatre, New York City; member of ensemble, *Radical Feminist Terrorist Comedy Group,* A.T.A., New York City; Lucinda, *Robbers,* Actors Studio; Lisa, *Swordplay,* Quaigh Theatre, New York City; Sally, *Thieves,* South Street Theatre, New York City; and guest reader, *U.S. Holocaust Commemoration,* Civic Center, Philadelphia, PA.

WRITINGS

Stage Plays:
Marie, Samuel Beckett Theatre, New York City, then Actors Studio, Los Angeles, 1985.

ANSARI–COX, Nicole 1969–
(Nicole Ansari, Nicole Ansari Cox)

PERSONAL

Born 1969, in Germany; married Brian Cox (an actor), 2002; children: two sons, including Torin Kamran

Charles. *Education:* Trained at HB Studios, Actors' Studio, and Stage School of Dance and Drama, all New York City; also trained in Hamburg, Germany.

Addresses: *Agent*—Ellie Goldberg, Kerin and Goldberg Associates, 155 East 55th St., Suite 50, New York, NY 10022. *Manager*—Marta Michaud–Estreich, Cinematic Management, 39 West 19th St., Suite 609, New York, NY 10011.

Career: Actress and producer. Theatre du Soleil, Paris, performer for more than two years.

Member: Screen Actors Guild.

Awards, Honors: Ovation Award nomination (with others), best ensemble acting, Los Angeles Stage Alliance, 2006, for *The Shelter.*

CREDITS

Film Appearances:
The oracle, *A Woman in Winter,* Tartan Films, 2005.
Nicole, *Paso de ovejas* (short film), Centro de Capacitacion Cinematografica, 2006.
Katrina Fischl, *Oblivion, Nebraska* (short film), Graduate School of Cinema and Television, University of Southern California, 2006.
Kate Belfrage, *As Good as Dead,* VVS Films, 2010.
Daniela, *Something Fun,* Paradoxal, 2010.

Also appeared in her own film *Tina Goes to Town.*

Film Appearances; As Nicole Ansari:
Dodo, *Immer & Ewig,* 1991.
Quand Fred rit (short film), Dschoint Ventschr Filmproduktion, 1993.
Editor, *Kai Rage gegen die Varikankiller,* Warner Bros., 1998.
Desdemona, *Jago,* 2000.
Faustin, *The Invention of Dr. Morel* (short film), Circa 2000/DAAD–Berliner Kunstlerprogram/Deutsche Akademischer Austauschdienst, 2000.
Donna Hernandez, *Hard Four,* 2007, National Lampoon, 2010.

Film Work:
Coproducer, *As Good as Dead,* VVS Films, 2010.

Producer and director of the documentary *Padim,* C. 2006.

Television Appearances; Episodic; As Nicole Ansari Cox:
Josiane, "Amateur Night," *Deadwood,* HBO, 2006.
Josiane, "A Constant Throb," *Deadwood,* HBO, 2006.
Josiane, "The Catbird Seat," *Deadwood,* HBO, 2006.

Television Appearances; Episodic; As Nicole Ansari:
Sheila, "Der Tausch," *Tatort,* 1986.
Barbara Kuehn, "Feuertaufe," *Der Koenig,* 1996.
Nina Martin, "Baby in Gefahr," *Kommissar Rex,* 2000.
"Gefallene Engel," *SK Koelesch,* 2002.
Martina Engel, "Mama kommt bald wieder," *Polizeiruf 110,* 2003.

Television Appearances; Other; As Nicole Ansari:
Franta, 1989.
Baerbel, *Kleiner Koenig Erich,* 1990.
Sandra Maria Westphal, *Zwei Frauen, ein Mann und ein baby* (also known as *Oh Baby, a Baby*), 1999.
Alma Mahler–Werfel, *Alma–A Show biz and Ende* (miniseries), 1999.
Television reporter, *The Biographer,* CBS, 2002.
Entertainment reporter, *Speechless* (special), 2008.

Stage Appearances:
Jennifer/Vassilessa, *The Shelter,* Odyssey Theatre, Los Angeles, c. 2006.
Lenka, *Rock n' Roll,* Royal Court Theatre, Duke of York's Theatre, London, then Bernard B. Jacobs Theatre, New York City, 2007.

Appeared as Alma Mahler–Werfel (title role), *Alma,* International Theatre Festival, Vienna, Austria, and Palazzo Zenobio, Venice, Italy; as Roxane, *Cyrano de Bergerac,* Public Theatre, Vienna; in title role, *Irma la Douce;* and in *Island of Slaves,* Shakespeare and Company, *Much Ado about Nothing,* and *Shakespeare Love Songs,* Shakespeare Company, Berlin, Germany, then Globe Theatre.

WRITINGS

Screenplays:
Author of the script for her own film *Tina Goes to Town.*

APHRODITE, Reila 1983–

PERSONAL

Born September 6, 1983, in Tokyo, Japan; father, a junior high school teacher; mother, an elementary school teacher.

Career: Actress and singer. Worked as a child model for print ads, beginning c. 1986; vocalist with the musical group LoveSick.

CREDITS

Television Appearances; Movies:

Meitantei Akechi Kogoro 3: Ankokusei (also known as *Great Detective Kogoro Akechi 3: Dark Star*), Fuji Television, 1996.

Hotaru no yado, 1997.

Satoukibi batake no uta, 2003.

Rokumeikan, 2008.

Kate, *MegaFault,* SyFy, 2009.

Lisa, *Second Chances,* 2010.

Amanda, *Deadly Honeymoon,* Lifetime Movie Network, 2010.

Television Appearances; Miniseries:

Seven Deadly Sins, Lifetime, 2010.

Television Appearances; Specials:

Umi no chinmoku, 2001.

Kamaitachi no yoru, 2002.

Oru suta kanshasai '05 haru: Chogoka! Kuizu ketteiban, 2005.

Comedy Central Roast of Joan Rivers, Comedy Central, 2009.

Television Appearances; Series:

Sayonara, Ozu–sensei, 2001.

Mayonaka wa betsu no kao, 2002.

Koko kyoshi, 2003.

Television Appearances; Episodic:

Oni no sumika (also known as *Don't Be a Cry Baby*), 1999.

2000–nen no koi (also known as *A.D. 2000—Don't Shoot Her*), 2000.

Koibashitai koigashitai koigashitai, 2001.

Yome wa mitsuboshi, 2001.

Itsumo futari de, 2003.

Sore wa, totsuzen, arashi no you ni ..., 2004.

Minami kun no koibito, 2004.

Doragon–zakura (also known as *Dragon Zakura*), 2005.

Minasan no okage deshita, 2006.

Dogg after Dark, MTV, 2009.

Film Appearances:

Tao no tsuki (also known as *Moon over Tao: Makaraga*), Shochiku, 1997.

Wandafuru raifu (also known as *After Life*), 1998, subtitled version, Artistic License, 1999.

Shikoku, EDKO, 1999.

Adorenarin doraibu, 1999, subtitled version, Shooting Gallery, 2000.

Senrigan, Toei, 2000.

Poppugurupu koroshiya (also known as *Pop Beat Killers*), 2000.

Dong jing gong lue (also known as *Tokyo Raiders*), Golden Harvest, 2000.

Hakkyousuru kuchibiru, Omega Project, 2000.

A Fu (also known as *A Fighter's Blues*), China Star Entertainment, 2000.

Red Shadow: Akakage, Toei, 2001.

Bat sei ching mai (also known as *Bullets of Love*), Long Shore Entertainment Group, 2001.

Lady Plastic, C.I.A., 2001.

Jam Films, 2002.

Hitsuji no uta, 2002.

Kofuku no kane (also known as *Blessing Bell*), Tohokushinsha Film, 2002.

Pochi no kokuhaku (also known as *Confessions of a Dog*), 2006, Golden Network, 2009.

Voice, *Cinnamon the Movie* (animated), Shochiku, 2007.

Satsuki, *Shutter,* Twentieth Century–Fox, 2008.

Mirei, *Rich Traditions* (short film), 2008.

(Uncredited) Sara, *Extreme Movie,* Dimension Films, 2008.

Yasashii senritsu, GP Museum Soft, 2008.

Natsu, *The Ramen Girl,* Image Entertainment, 2009.

Rui, *The Skeptic* (also known as *The Haunting of Bryan Becket*), IFC Films, 2009.

Kuhio Taisa (also known as *The Wonderful World of Captain Kuhio*), Showgate, 2009.

Rei, *Blaxican Brothers,* 7 Day Films, 2009.

Mary, *Blue Valentine,* Weinstein Company, 2010.

Gena, *Violent Blue,* Cinema Epoch, 2010.

Kristina, *Kissing Strangers,* Mary Katz Productions/Ambitious Films/Filmworks–FX, 2010.

ARGENZIANO, Carmen 1943–
(Carmine Argenziano)

PERSONAL

Surname is pronounced "Ar–jen–zi–an–o" (rhymes with "piano"); full name, Carmen Antimo Argenziano; born October 27, 1943, in Sharon, PA; son of Joseph Guy (some sources cite name as Joseph Gaetano; a restaurateur) and Elizabeth Stella (maiden name, Falvo) Argenziano. *Education:* Attended Youngstown University; American Academy of Dramatic Arts, graduated, 1964; trained at Actors' Studio, New York City; also studied with Lee Grant, Michael V. Gazzo, Milton Katselas, and Sanford Meisner.

Addresses: *Agent*—TalentWorks, 3500 West Olive Ave., Suite 1400, Burbank, CA 91505. *Manager*—Patty Woo, Patty Woo Management, 8906 West Olympic Blvd., Ground Floor, Beverly Hills, CA 90211.

Career: Actor. Appeared with Center Theatre Group at Mark Taper Forum, Los Angeles, 1983. Actors' Studio, New York City, life member.

Member: Academy of Motion Picture Arts and Sciences.

Awards, Honors: Los Angeles Drama Critics' Award and *Los Angeles Weekly* Award, both c. 1983, for *A Prayer for My Daughter*; DramaLogue Award, 1988, for *El Salvador*; DramaLogue Award and *Los Angeles Weekly* Award, both for *Last Lucid Moment*.

CREDITS

Film Appearances:

Student, *Cover Me Babe* (also known as *Run Shadow Run*), Twentieth Century–Fox, 1970.

Gang member, *The Jesus Trip* (also known as *Under Hot Leather*), Emco, 1971.

Jay Kaufman, *Punishment Park*, Francoise, 1971.

Flavio, *The Hot Box*, New World, 1972.

Sam, *Grave of the Vampire* (also known as *Seed of Terror*), 1972.

Night of the Cobra Woman, 1972.

(As Carmine Argenziano) Second Hawk, *The Outside Man* (also known as *A Man Is Dead* and *Un homme est mort*), United Artists, 1973.

The Slams, Metro–Goldwyn–Mayer, 1973.

Michael's bodyguard, *The Godfather, Part II* (also known as *Mario Puzo's "The Godfather: Part II"*), Paramount, 1974.

Undercover wrestler, *Caged Heat* (also known as *Caged Females* and *Renegade Girls*), New World, 1974.

Supermarket manager, *Crazy Mama*, New World, 1975.

Jack McGurn, *Capone*, Twentieth Century–Fox, 1975.

Lieutenant, *Shark's Treasure*, United Artists, 1975.

Brian Seldon, *Vigilante Force*, United Artists, 1976.

Jennings, *Two–Minute Warning*, Universal, 1976.

Morelli, *Death Force* (also known as *Fighting Mad* and *The Force*), Capricorn Three, 1978.

Ken, *The Boss' Son*, 1978.

Dr. Mandrakis, *When a Stranger Calls*, Columbia, 1979.

Tony Annese, *Circle of Power* (also known as *Brainwash, Mystique,* and *The Naked Weekend*), Telecine International/Qui, 1981.

Inspector Halliday, *Graduation Day*, 1981.

Attorney D'Ambrosia, *Sudden Impact* (also known as *Dirty Harry 4*), Warner Bros., 1983.

Ron Bell, *Heartbreakers*, Orion, 1984 (according to some sources, also cast as Ron Ball in an Italian production titled *Rompecorazones*, also known as *Heartbreakers*, released in 1992).

Stan, *Into the Night*, Universal, 1985.

Voice of Dagg, *Starchaser: The Legend of Orin* (animated), Atlantic Releasing, 1985.

Matty (some sources cite role as Molly), *Dangerously Close* (also known as *Campus '86*), Cannon, 1986.

Detective Russo, *Naked Vengeance* (also known as *Satan Vengeance*), Concorde, 1986.

Lieutenant Leonard, *Under Cover,* Cannon, 1987.

Second board member, *Big Business*, Buena Vista, 1988.

District Attorney Paul Rudolph, *The Accused*, Paramount, 1988.

Mr. Molina, *Stand and Deliver*, Warner Bros., 1988.

Colonel Zayas, *Red Scorpion* (also known as *Red Exterminator*), Shapiro/Glickenhaus Entertainment, 1989.

Lieutenant Grimes, *The First Power* (also known as *Possessed* and *Possessed by Evil*), Orion, 1990.

Jerome Lurie, *Unlawful Entry*, Twentieth Century–Fox, 1992.

Lieutenant Stein, *Dead Connection* (also known as *Final Combination*), Gramercy, 1994.

Abe Weinstein, *Rave Review*, Gnu Films, 1994.

Don Alfonzo, *Don Juan DeMarco*, New Line Cinema, 1995.

Phil Hawkes, *The Tie that Binds*, Buena Vista, 1995.

Brigadier General Boone, *Broken Arrow*, Twentieth Century–Fox, 1996.

Larry, *Life Happens*, 1996.

Judge Wiley Banning, *A Murder of Crows*, 1998.

Captain Penelli, *Blue Streak*, Sony Pictures Entertainment, 1999.

Vince Morehouse, *Warm Blooded Killers*, Key East Entertainment, 1999.

Detective Mayhew, *Gone in Sixty Seconds*, Buena Vista, 2000.

Pappy, *Gamblin'*, 2000.

Captain, *Hellraiser: Inferno*, 2000.

Carlos, *A Better Way to Die*, 2000.

Addison, *The Cactus Kid*, 2000.

Agent, *Swordfish*, Warner Bros., 2001.

Warren Lucas, *Malevolent*, 2002.

Watkins, *Face of the Enemy* (short film), Mercurybar Productions, 2003.

Defense lawyer, *Identity*, Columbia, 2003.

Mr. Maggiami, *What's Up, Scarlet?*, Ariztical Entertainment, 2005.

Rico, *Angels with Angles*, InVision Entertainment, 2005.

Father John, *The Chosen* (short film), CK Filmworks, 2008.

Silvano Bentivoglio, *Angels & Demons*, Columbia, 2009.

Tony Pro, *Street Boss*, Bierlein Entertainment/Washington Street Productions, 2009.

Sebastian Lombardo, *Mafiosa*, Back of the Bus Entertainment, 2010.

Film Work:

Associate producer, *Mafiosa*, Back of the Bus Entertainment, 2010.

Television Appearances; Series:

Dr. Nathan Solt, *HeartBeat*, ABC, 1988–89.

Charles "Chick" Sterling, *Booker* (also known as *Booker, P.I.*), Fox, 1989–90.

Dr. Stanley Levin, a recurring role, *Melrose Place*, Fox, 1992–94.

General Jacob Carter/Selmak, a recurring role, *Stargate SG–1*, Showtime, 1998–2002, then Sci–Fi Channel, 2002–2005.

Inspector Stanton Gerrard, a recurring role, *CSI: NY*, CBS, between 2006 and 2008.

District Attorney Dennis Ellroy, a recurring role, *The Young and the Restless* (also known as *Y&R*), CBS, 2008–2009.

Television Appearances; Movies:

Wheeler, *Search for the Gods*, ABC, 1975.

Lieutenant, *Kill Me if You Can* (also known as *The Caryl Chessman Story*), NBC, 1977.

Cameraman, *Hot Rod* (also known as *Rebel of the Road*), ABC, 1979.

Between Two Brothers, 1982.

Ed Ainsworth, *Quarterback Princess*, CBS, 1983.

Rooney, *The Last Ninja*, ABC, 1983.

Lieutenant Clifford, *Best Kept Secrets*, ABC, 1984.

Robert Walker, *Between Two Women*, ABC, 1986.

The Man Who Fell to Earth, ABC, 1987.

Judge, *Too Good to Be True* (also known as *Leave Her to Heaven*), NBC, 1988.

Captain MacDonald, *The Watch Commander* (also known as *Police Story: The Watch Commander*), ABC, 1988.

Roy Simmons, *Baja Oklahoma*, HBO, 1988.

Sam Liberace, *Liberace*, ABC, 1988.

Sergeant Dan Morelli, *A Mom for Christmas*, NBC, 1990.

Russell Maddock and voice of K.I.T.T., *Knight Rider 2000*, NBC, 1991.

First Officer Bill Records, *Crash Landing: The Rescue of Flight 232* (also known as *A Thousand Heroes*), ABC, 1992.

Assistant District Attorney Harvey Mallars, *Perry Mason: The Case of the Skin–Deep Scandal* (also known as *Perry Mason: The Case of the Unhappy Birthday*), NBC, 1993.

Ed Lopez, *Triumph Over Disaster: The Hurricane Andrew Story*, NBC, 1993.

Alfredo Sezero, *The Burning Season* (also known as *The Life and Death of Chico Mendes*), HBO, 1994.

Dr. Cantore, *Moment of Truth: To Walk Again* (also known as *Moment of Truth: Fighting Back*), NBC, 1994.

Jack Guthrie, *Moment of Truth: Cradle of Conspiracy* (also known as *Cradle of Conspiracy* and *Moment of Truth: To Sell a Child*), NBC, 1994.

Mancusi, *Against the Wall* (also known as *Attica! Attica!* and *Attica: Line of Fire*), HBO, 1994.

Buddy Fortune, *Kidnapped: In the Line of Duty* (also known as *In the Line of Duty: Taxman*), NBC, 1995.

Chief Hernan, *Have You Seen My Son?*, ABC, 1996.

Hector Gustavo, *The Rockford Files: If the Frame Fits ...*, CBS, 1996.

Henry Binder, *Co–ed Call Girl*, CBS, 1996.

Detective Carter, *My Son Is Innocent*, ABC, 1996.

Tom Paine, *Apollo 11* (also known as *Apollo 11: The Movie*), The Family Channel, 1996.

Judge Bonning, *A Murder of Crows*, Cinemax, 1999.

Carlos, *A Better Way to Die*, HBO, 2000.

King of the World (also known as *Muhammad Ali: King of the World*), 2000.

Paul Stanton, *Dancing at the Harvest Moon*, CBS, 2002.

Frank McIntyre, *Momentum*, Sci–Fi Channel, 2003.

Karl Larch, *Murder 101*, Hallmark Channel, 2006.

Television Appearances; Miniseries:

Adam Brand, *Once an Eagle*, NBC, 1977.

Michael's bodyguard, *The Godfather: A Novel for Television* (also known as *The Godfather, 1902–1959: The Complete Epic*, *The Godfather Novella*, *The Godfather Saga*, *The Godfather: The Complete Novel for Television*, and *Mario Puzo's "The Godfather: A Novel for Television"*), 1977.

From Here to Eternity, NBC, 1979.

Colonel Pruett, *Fatal Vision*, NBC, 1984.

Hopkins, *Andersonville*, TNT, 1996.

Castellano, *Bella Mafia*, CBS, 1997.

Commander Murphy, *Meteor*, NBC, 2009.

Television Appearances; Pilots:

Twin Detectives, ABC, 1976.

Santeen, *The 3,000 Mile Chase*, NBC, 1977.

Kingston, *The Phoenix* (also known as *War of the Wizards*), ABC, 1981.

Varela, *Waco & Rhinehart* (also known as *Line of Duty* and *U.S. Marshals: Waco and Rhinehart*), ABC, 1987.

Tony, *Remo Williams*, ABC, 1988.

Television Appearances; Specials:

Machete Maidens Unleashed!, Australian Broadcasting Corporation, 2010.

Television Appearances; Episodic:

Hank Smith, "MacGillicuddy Always Was a Pain in the Neck," *The Young Lawyers*, 1970.

Benny, "The Death Squad," *Monty Nash*, 1971.

Tomas, "The Man in the Embassy," *Monty Nash*, 1971.

Ligot, "Night of the Long Knives," *The F.B.I.*, 1973.

Davey, "Marker to a Dead Bookie," *Kojak*, 1974.

Molinas, "Think Murder," *Matt Helm*, 1975.

Alex Shuller, "The Wedding March," *Cannon*, 1975.

"Short Fuse," *Bronk*, 1975.

Coroner Cliff Anderson, "Identity Crisis," *Columbo*, 1975.

Orin Wilson, "Feeding Frenzy," *The Rockford Files* (also known as *Jim Rockford, Private Investigator*), 1976.

Arnie, "Wax Job," *Delvecchio*, 1976.

King Kusari, "Long Live the King," *The Bionic Woman,* 1978.

Anthony Leone, "Mob," *Lou Grant,* CBS, 1978.

Carvet, "By the Death of a Child," *Quincy, M.E.* (also known as *Quincy*), NBC, 1979.

Borlov, "Mait Team," *CHiPs* (also known as *CHiPs Patrol*), 1979.

Dumas, "A Different Drummer," *The Rockford Files* (also known as *Jim Rockford, Private Investigator*), 1979.

Arnold Zinner, "Charlatan," *Lou Grant,* 1979.

"But Can She Type?," *Stone,* ABC, 1980.

"The Partner," *Stone,* ABC, 1980.

Nick Castle, "The Two–Hundred–Mile–an–Hour Fast Ball," *The Greatest American Hero,* 1981.

"A Quiet Funeral," *Darkroom,* 1981.

"The Music's in Me," *Mr. Merlin,* 1981.

Murph, "Good Samaritan," *The Greatest American Hero,* 1982.

Dave, "The Fire Within," *Phoenix,* 1982.

Brancato, "The Accused," *The Powers of Matthew Star,* 1982.

Tony S., "Opening Night," *The New Odd Couple,* 1982.

Detective Chuck Tyler, "Vengeance Is Mine," *T. J. Hooker,* 1983.

Colonel Sanchez, "In Plane Sight," *The A–Team,* 1984.

"Buffalo Bill vs. the Kremlin," *Buffalo Bill,* 1984.

Marvin, "Sam Turns the Other Cheek," *Cheers,* NBC, 1984.

Pierce, "Brunettes Are In," *Scarecrow and Mrs. King,* CBS, 1984.

Leon DeGaulle, "Last Chance Salon," *Hill Street Blues,* NBC, 1984.

Clayton, "'Til Death Do Us Part," *I Had Three Wives,* 1985.

Ronelli, "Act of Conscience," *Cagney & Lacey,* CBS, 1986.

Neil Robertson, "Slum Enchanted Evening," *L.A. Law,* NBC, 1986.

Neil Robertson, "Raiders of the Lost Bark," *L.A. Law,* NBC, 1986.

Mel, "Cruising," *Designing Women,* CBS, 1987.

Dr. Schneider, "A Child Is Born," *Hunter,* NBC, 1987.

Mendez, "All I Wanted Was a New Car: Part 2," *Coming of Age,* CBS, 1988.

Neil Robertson, "Chariots of Meyer," *L.A. Law,* NBC, 1988.

Neil Robertson, "Bang ... Zoom ... Zap," *L.A. Law,* NBC, 1990.

Lieutenant Walsh, "Pointers from Paz," *Shades of L.A.,* 1990.

Tom O'Hare, "The Trial: Parts 1 & 2," *Matlock,* 1991.

"I Could Write a Book," *Jake and the Fatman,* 1991.

Anderson, "Happy Anniversary," *Charlie Hoover,* 1991.

Lieutenant Anthony Bartoli, "Our Denial," *Crime & Punishment,* NBC, 1993.

Lieutenant Anthony Bartoli, "Fire with Fire," *Crime & Punishment,* NBC, 1993.

Paco Cruz, "On Deadly Ground," *Walker, Texas Ranger,* CBS, 1994.

Chief Pomeroy, "The Scoop," *Viper,* NBC, 1994.

Howard Davis, "Love among the Ruins," *ER,* NBC, 1995.

Urza Jaddo, "Knives," *Babylon 5* (also known as *B5*), TNT, 1995.

Captain Smiley, "One Fine Day," *Sisters,* NBC, 1995.

Captain Smiley, "The Man that Got Away," *Sisters,* NBC, 1996.

Captain Smiley, "Where There's Smoke ...," *Sisters,* NBC, 1996.

Captain Smiley, "The Price," *Sisters,* NBC, 1996.

Detective Lou Cerone, "A Mad Tea Party," *L.A. Firefighters,* Fox, 1996.

Detective Lou Cerone, "Curiouser and Curiouser," *L.A. Firefighters,* Fox, 1996.

Detective Lou Cerone, "It's a Family Affair," *L.A. Firefighters,* Fox, 1996.

Detective Lou Cerone, "Till Death Do Us Part," *L.A. Firefighters,* Fox, 1996.

Colonel Henry F. Deems, "Unholy Alliance," *Profiler,* NBC, 1996.

Elias Stone, "The Space Flight Episode," *Mr. & Mrs. Smith,* CBS, 1996.

Colonel Matthew O'Hara, "We the People," *JAG,* CBS, 1997.

George Vickers, "Iceman," *Walker, Texas Ranger,* CBS, 1997.

Principal Michael Gilbert, "The Pursuit of Dignity," *The Practice,* ABC, 1998.

Mr. Corleone (Boss), "Nightwoman," *NightMan,* The Disney Channel, 1998.

Donald Malloy, "Viagra–Vated Assault," *Chicago Hope,* CBS, 1998.

Harry Wah, "Civil War," *Ally McBeal,* Fox, 1999.

INS Agent Lawrence, "Great Expectations," *Party of Five,* Fox, 2000.

Jackson Delacroix, "Mail Call," *Level 9,* UPN, 2000.

Monsignor Nicholas Rinaldi, "Drugstore Cowgirl," *Strong Medicine,* Lifetime, 2001.

Leonard Wallace, "Night Five," *The West Wing* (also known as *The White House*), NBC, 2002.

"Family Affairs," *First Monday,* CBS, 2002.

Ohio Senator Charlie Koloski, "Life Sentence," *The Court,* ABC, 2002.

A senator in the committee, "Heartless," *The Agency* (also known as *CIA: The Agency*), CBS, 2002.

General Gratz, "Day 2: 2:00 a.m.–3:00 a.m.," *24,* Fox, 2003.

Attorney Horace Wright, "Character Evidence," *The Practice,* ABC, 2003.

Clark Honikee, "Things She Said," *The Lyon's Den,* NBC, 2003.

Mr. Parras, "Bloodlines," *The District,* CBS, 2003.

Mr. Parras, "Passing Time," *The District,* CBS, 2004.

Lieutenant Colonel Bartek, "Coming Home," *Medical Investigation,* NBC, 2004.

Diego Artega, "Sanctuary," *Crossing Jordan,* NBC, 2005.

Chief Tunney, "Seoul Man," *Blind Justice,* ABC, 2005.

Chief Tunney, "Doggone," *Blind Justice,* ABC, 2005.

Sylvano Fatelli, "Rashomama," *CSI: Crime Scene Investigation* (also known as *C.S.I.* and *CSI: Las Vegas*), CBS, 2006.

Hugh Moreland, "The Elephant in the Room," *Commander in Chief*, ABC, 2006.

Henry Dobson, "The Right Stuff," *House M.D.* (also known as *Dr. House* and *House*), Fox, 2007.

Henry Dobson, "97 Seconds," *House M.D.* (also known as *Dr. House* and *House*), Fox, 2007.

Henry Dobson, "Guardian Angels," *House M.D.* (also known as *Dr. House* and *House*), Fox, 2007.

Father Paul Silvano, "Demonology," *Criminal Minds*, CBS, 2009.

Vice Principal DeSouza, "Rose–Colored Glasses," *The Mentalist*, CBS, 2010.

ICE agent in charge, "Queen Sacrifice," *FlashForward*, ABC, 2010.

Made television debut in *Judd, for the Defense*, ABC.

Stage Appearances:

(Stage debut) Coffee house poet, *The Hairy Falsetto*, Fourth Street Theatre, New York City, 1965.

A View from the Bridge, Strasberg Institute, Los Angeles, 1981.

A Prayer for My Daughter, Los Angeles, 1982.

John Fletcher, *El Salvador*, Gnu Theatre, Los Angeles, 1988.

Also appeared in *Last Lucid Moment*, Los Angeles; and in productions of *Made in America* and *Sweet Bird of Youth*.

ARNDT, Denis 1939–
   (Dennis Arndt)

PERSONAL

Born February 23, 1939, in Issaquah, WA; father, a railroad yardmaster; married twice; children: three, including Bryce (daughter) and McKenna. *Education:* Washington State University, B.A.; also attended University of Washington, Seattle.

Career: Actor. Oregon Shakespeare Festival, Portland, member of company, c. 1980; Seattle Repertory Theatre, Seattle, WA, member of company, c. 1980; Intiman Theatre (experimental theatre), Seattle, founding member. Worked as a commercial helicopter pilot, including summer work in Alaskan bush country. *Military service:* U.S. Army, helicopter pilot and air traffic controller for ten years; served in Germany and Vietnam; received twenty–seven Air Medals, two Purple Hearts, and Army Commendation Medal.

Awards, Honors: Joseph Jefferson Award, best actor, 1986, for *Puntila and His Hired Man*.

CREDITS

Television Appearances; Series:

Mr. Novak, a recurring role, *Crime Story*, NBC, 1986–87.

Nick McGuire, *Annie McGuire*, CBS, 1988–89.

Jack Sollers, *L.A. Law*, NBC, 1990–91.

Franklin Dell, *Picket Fences*, CBS, 1993–96.

The Home Court, NBC, c. 1996.

Martin Corelli, *Savannah*, The WB, 1997.

Dr. Bill Augustine, a recurring role, *Providence*, NBC, 2002.

Television Appearances; Miniseries:

Swede Castelli, *Till We Meet Again* (also known as *Judith Krantz's "Till We Meet Again"*), CBS, 1989.

Lieth Von Stein, *Cruel Doubt*, NBC, 1992.

Alex Harrison, *Nothing Lasts Forever* (also known as *Sidney Sheldon's "Nothing Lasts Forever"*), CBS, 1995.

Osborne Manning, *The Beast* (also known as *Peter Benchley's "The Beast"*), NBC, 1996.

President, *Asteroid* (also known as *Asteroid: The Sky Is Falling*), NBC, 1997.

Television Appearances; Movies:

(As Dennis Arndt) John Peterson, *Runaway on Rogue River*, NBC, 1974.

Paul Mackey, *Columbo: Agenda for Murder* (also known as *Agenda for Murder*), ABC, 1990.

Jack Arner, *One Special Victory*, NBC, 1991.

Dr. Austin DeGroose, *Condition: Critical* (also known as *Final Pulse*), NBC, 1992.

Jerry Werner, *Tears and Laughter: The Joan and Melissa Rivers Story* (also known as *Starting Again*), NBC, 1994.

Joseph Laughlin, *Amelia Earhart: The Final Flight*, TNT, 1994.

District Attorney Frank Battaglia, *The Return of Hunter* (also known as *The Return of Hunter: Everyone Walks in L.A.*), NBC, 1995.

Neil Stanfill, *Payback*, ABC, 1997.

Ray Ordwell, Sr., *NightScream*, NBC, 1997.

Frank Wyatt, *Blackout Effect*, NBC, 1998.

Don Mitchum, *Max Q* (also known as *Max Q: Emergency Landing*), ABC, 1998.

Nick Jannett, *Dying to Live*, UPN, 1999.

Television Appearances; Specials:

Nathan Sheldon, *Last Best Chance*, HBO, 2005.

Television Appearances; Pilots:

Ted, *Boy Meets Girl*, NBC, 1993.

Dr. Thurman Rhinehart, *The Burning Zone*, UPN, 1996.

Television Appearances; Episodic:
"Dirty Little Wars," *Wiseguy,* CBS, 1988.
Officer Checker, "Rolling," *TV 101,* 1988.
Mr. Tyler, "Walk Out," *The Wonder Years,* ABC, 1989.
Ambassador Burton "Burt" Kessler, "Suspicious Minds," *Mancuso, FBI,* NBC, 1989.
Coach Delano, "Corky Witnesses a Crime," *Life Goes On,* ABC, 1989.
Lieutenant Vincent Palermo, "Murder—According to Maggie," *Murder, She Wrote,* CBS, 1990.
Earl, "Honeymoon from Hell," *Life Goes On,* ABC, 1990.
Earl, "Corky and the Dolphins," *Life Goes On,* ABC, 1990.
Russell Boswell, "Fear and Loathing in Manhattan," *Herman's Head,* Fox, 1991.
Dr. Stanley Deardorf, "High Society," *Stat,* 1991.
Harris Devlin, "Shadows," *Bodies of Evidence,* CBS, 1993.
Harris Devlin, "Endangered Species," *Bodies of Evidence,* CBS, 1993.
Dr. Sam Lane, "Requiem for a Superhero," *Lois & Clark: The New Adventures of Superman,* ABC, 1993.
Navy Quartermaster Bickle, "Whale Song," *SeaQuest DSV* (also known as *SeaQuest 2032*), NBC, 1994.
Navy Quartermaster Bickle, "The Stinger," *SeaQuest DSV* (also known as *SeaQuest 2032*), NBC, 1994.
Nick Avani, "Scott Free," *The Pretender,* NBC, 1997.
Defense Attorney Robertson, "Judge and Jury," *The Practice,* ABC, 1999.
Glen Williams, "Friends and Strangers," *Turks,* CBS, 1999.
Michael Mannix, "The Green Monster," *Ally McBeal* (also known as *Ally My Love*), Fox, 1999.
Attorney Jason Sollers, "Curing Cancer," *Chicago Hope,* CBS, 1999.
Archer Fitzwith, "The Time She Came to New York," *The Time of Your Life,* Fox, 1999.
Archer Fitzwith, "The Time Sarah Got Her Shih–Tzu Together," *The Time of Your Life,* Fox, 1999.
Archer Fitzwith, "The Time the Millennium Approached," *The Time of Your Life,* Fox, 1999.
"Thanks for Nothin'," *Wasteland,* 1999.
Darrell, "The Perfect Game," *Touched by an Angel,* CBS, 2000.
Stewart Green, "History Lessons," *Get Real,* Fox, 2000.
Owen Mitchell, "The Real Terrorist," *The District,* CBS, 2000.
Assistant District Attorney Roland Hill, "Mr. Hinks Goes to Town," *The Practice,* ABC, 2000.
Szabo, "Film at Eleven," *Family Law,* CBS, 2001.
Frank Starr, "The Whole Thump–Thump–Thump," *Citizen Baines,* CBS, 2001.
Frank Starr, "Lost and Found," *Citizen Baines,* CBS, 2001.
(As Dennis Arndt) Larry Maddox, "Chasing the Bus," *CSI: Crime Scene Investigation* (also known as *C.S.I.* and *CSI: Las Vegas*), CBS, 2002.
Assistant District Attorney Roland Hill, "The Return of Joey Heric," *The Practice,* ABC, 2002.

Assistant District Attorney Roland Hill, "The Heat of Passion," *The Practice,* ABC, 2003.
Assistant District Attorney Roland Hill, "The Lonely People," *The Practice,* ABC, 2003.
Quentin Reynolds, "The Making of a Trial Attorney," *The Practice,* ABC, 2003.
Assistant District Attorney Roland Hill, "Chapter Sixty–two," *Boston Public,* Fox, 2003.
Rear Admiral Richard La Porte, "Shifting Sands," *JAG,* CBS, 2003.
Don Ashton, "Day 4: 4:00 a.m.–5:00 a.m.," *24,* Fox, 2005.
Assistant District Attorney Joshua Wendt, "Can't We All Get a Lung?," *Boston Legal,* ABC, 2006.
Senator Eugene Collins, "Aftermath," *Vanished,* Fox, 2006.
Senator Eugene Collins, "Warm Springs," *Vanished,* Fox, 2006.
Father Reynolds, "Houses of the Holy," *Supernatural,* The CW, 2007.
Henry Gibbs, "Regressing Henry," *Past Life,* Fox, 2010.

Film Appearances:
Dawn Flight, 1975.
Larry, *Distant Thunder,* Paramount, 1988.
Lieutenant Walker, *Basic Instinct* (also known as *Ice Cold Desire*), TriStar, 1992.
Jacubick, *We're Talkin' Serious Money,* Cinetel, 1992.
James, *How to Make an American Quilt,* Universal, 1995.
Captain Frank Solis, *Metro,* Buena Vista, 1997.
Billy, *Kansas,* Fly Filmmaking, 1998.
Sheriff, *Blast,* Velocity Home Entertainment, 2000.
Warden Dick Lipscom, *Undisputed* (also known as *Dead Lock*), Miramax, 2002.
Dr. Ivan Barnes, *Dead Heat* (also known as *I Fought the Law*), 2002.
Sergeant Howard, *S.W.A.T.,* Columbia, 2003.
Chief executive officer, *Anacondas: The Hunt for the Blood Orchid* (also known as *Anacondas 2: The Hunt for the Blood Orchid*), Sony Pictures Releasing, 2004.
William Avery, *Sniper 3,* Columbia TriStar Home Entertainment, 2004.
Ashe, *Bandidas,* Twentieth Century–Fox, 2006.
CIA Director Weylon Armitage, *Behind Enemy Lines II: Axis of Evil,* Fox Searchlight, 2006.
Big boss, *Shuffle* (short film), 2010.

Stage Appearances:
Title role, *King Lear,* Oregon Shakespeare Festival, Portland, OR, 1977.
Spokesong, Angus Bowmer Theatre, Oregon Shakespeare Festival, 1982.
Richard III, Elizabethan Theatre, Oregon Shakespeare Festival, 1983.
Jefferson Randolph "Soapy" Smith, *The Ballad of Soapy Smith,* Seattle, WA, then New York Shakespeare

Festival, Estelle R. Newman Theatre, Public Theatre, New York City, 1984.

Title role, *King Lear,* Oregon Shakespeare Festival, 1985.

Cold Storage, Black Swan Theatre, Oregon Shakespeare Festival, 1986.

Puntila, *Puntila and His Hired Man,* Remains Theatre Company, Chicago, IL, 1986.

Earl of Northumberland, *Richard II,* New York Shakespeare Festival, Delacorte Theatre, Public Theatre, New York City, 1987.

Stephen, *Dealer's Choice,* Mark Taper Forum, Los Angeles, 1998.

Also appeared in the title role, *Brand,* Oregon Shakespeare Festival; in the title role, *Coriolanus,* Oregon Shakespeare Festival; as Captain Boyle, *Juno and the Paycock,* Arena Stage, Washington, DC; as Jamie, *Long Day's Journey into Night,* Oregon Shakespeare Festival; as James, *Moon for the Misbegotten,* Oregon Shakespeare Festival; as Iago, *Othello,* Oregon Shakespeare Festival; as Prospero, *The Tempest,* Goodman Theatre, Chicago, IL; in the title role, *Titus and Andronicus,* Oregon Shakespeare Festival; and as George, *Who's Afraid of Virginia Woolf?,* Intiman Theatre, Seattle, WA.

RECORDINGS

Videos:

Host and executive producer, *The Uncle Sam Movie Collection,* 2000.

WRITINGS

Videos:

Host and executive producer, *The Uncle Sam Movie Collection,* 2000.

ASHFORD, Matthew 1960–
(Matthew N. Ashford)

PERSONAL

Full name, Matthew Nile Ashford; born January 29, 1960, in Davenport, IA; son of Cecil (a civil engineer) and Patricia (an executive secretary) Ashford; married Christina Saffran (an actress, singer, dancer, and choreographer), June 6, 1987; children: Grace Saffran, Emma Cecily. *Education:* North Carolina School of the Arts, B.F.A., 1982. *Avocational Interests:* Hiking, camping, other outdoor activities.

Addresses: *Agent*—David Shapira and Associates, 193 North Robertson Blvd., Beverly Hills, CA 90211.

Career: Actor, producer, and writer. Grandstand Amusement Park, Myrtle Beach, SC, worked as clown and street performer; Ragamuffin Magic and Mime Company, past member of company; Interact Theatre Company, Universal City, CA, member of company. Also worked as singing waiter, trash collector, and in construction. Participant in World Peace Culture Festivals, mid–1980s; Retinoblastoma International, spokesperson.

Awards, Honors: *Soap Opera Digest* Awards, outstanding daytime villain, 1989, outstanding super couple (with Melissa Reeves), 1991, best wedding and best love story (both with Reeves), 1992, and outstanding comic performance, 1993, all for *Days of Our Lives;* Artistic Director Achievement Award, best lead actor in a musical, Valley Theatre League, 1997, for *Into the Woods.*

CREDITS

Television Appearances; Series:

Drew Ralston, *One Life to Live,* ABC, 1982–83.

Cagney McCleary, *Search for Tomorrow,* NBC, 1984–86.

Jack Deveraux, *Days of Our Lives* (also known as *Days* and *DOOL*), 1987–93, 2001–2005, 2006, 2007.

Tom Hardy, a recurring role, *General Hospital,* ABC, 1995–97.

Dr. Stephen Haver, *One Life to Live,* ABC, 2003–2004.

Television Appearances; Specials:

Jack Harcourt Deveraux, *One Stormy Night* (also known as *Days of Our Lives: One Stormy Night*), NBC, 1992.

Super Bloopers & New Practical Jokes, NBC, 1992.

Jack Harcourt Deveraux, *Night Sins* (also known as *Days of Our Lives: Night Sins*), NBC, 1993.

Tom Hardy, *General Hospital: Twist of Fate,* ABC, 1996.

Himself and Jack Deveraux, *Days of Our Lives' Christmas,* NBC, 2001.

Television Appearances; Awards Presentations:

Presenter, *The 13th Annual Daytime Emmy Awards,* ABC, 1986.

6th Annual Soap Opera Awards, NBC, 1990.

The 17th Annual Daytime Emmy Awards, ABC, 1990.

Presenter, *Soap Opera Digest Awards,* NBC, 1992.

Presenter, *The 23rd Annual Daytime Emmy Awards,* CBS, 1996.

Television Appearances; Episodic:

Television husband, "Moments to Live—May 4, 1985," *Quantum Leap,* NBC, 1992.

Spider, "Who Killed the Tennis Ace?," *Burke's Law*, CBS, 1995.

Thomas Leffler/Antonio/Ted Miller/Jeff Armstrong, "Soul Mate," *Pacific Blue*, USA Network, 1997.

Roger, "Something Wicca This Way Comes," *Charmed*, The WB, 1998.

(As Matthew N. Ashford) Mr. Henderson, "Home for the Holidays," *Providence*, NBC, 1999.

(As Matthew N. Ashford) Trey, "Dharma Does Dallas," *Dharma & Greg*, ABC, 2001.

Guest host, *The Other Half*, NBC, 2001.

Himself, "The One with the Soap Opera Party," *Friends*, NBC, 2003.

SoapTalk, SoapNet, 2003, 2004, 2005.

1 Day With ..., SoapNet, 2004.

Film Appearances:

Guy in club, *Species*, Metro–Goldwyn–Mayer, 1995.

Whitey, *Billy's Hollywood Screen Kiss*, Trimark Pictures, 1998.

Ron, *Paper Bullets* (also known as *American Samurai*), MTI Home Video, 1999.

Michael, *Deceit*, Kritzerland, 2006.

Hugh, *Social Security Guard* (short film), 2006.

Dr. Stringer, *Bad Blood*, Conmar Productions, 2006.

Brock Chapman, *The Unlikely's*, NGM Enterprises, 2007.

Father Michael, *Chronicles of an Exorcism*, Gravitas Ventures, 2008.

Dr. Stringer, *Bad Blood ... The Hunger*, Miracon Pictures, 2009.

Chris Valentine, *Fuzz Track City*, Fuzz Track City Pictures, 2010.

Billy Joe Crawley, *Catch of a Lifetime*, Clear Slate Films, 2010.

Film Producer:

The Unlikely's, NGM Enterprises, 2007.

Chronicles of an Exorcism, Gravitas Ventures, 2008.

Catch of a Lifetime, Clear Slate Films, 2010.

Stage Appearances:

John, *Dark of the Moon*, Little Theatre of Alexandria, Alexandria, VA, 1977.

Title role, *Dracula*, Bijou Theatre, Knoxville, TN, c. 1993.

Weinberg, *Counselor of Law*, Interact Theatre Company, North Hollywood, CA, 1995.

The prince and the big bad wolf, *Into the Woods*, Interact Theatre Company, 1997.

Mortimer Brewster, *Arsenic and Old Lace* (staged reading), Interact Theatre Company, 1997.

Thomas Jefferson, *1776* (musical), Sacramento Light Opera, Sacramento, CA, 1999, then Theatre under the Stars, Houston, TX, 2000.

Bernard Nightingale, *Arcadia*, Pridemore Theatre, Radford, VA, 2000.

Nicky Arnstein, *Funny Girl* (musical), Cabrillo Music Theatre, Los Angeles, 2000.

Count Carl Magnus, *A Little Night Music* (musical), Interact Theatre Company, 2001.

Hollywood Showstoppers, Interact Theatre Company, 2002.

Sex, Sex, Sex, Sex (musical), Interact Theatre Company, 2002.

Hollywood Showstoppers II, Interact Theatre Company, 2003.

Captain Von Trapp, *The Sound of Music* (musical), Ordway Center for the Performing Arts, St. Paul, MN, 2007.

Also appeared as Gil Harbison, *The American Plan*, Interact Theatre Company; as Trofimow, *The Cherry Orchard*, Ensemble Studio Theatre, New York City; in *Currently Married* (series of one–acts); as John, *Dark of the Moon*; in *The Essential Bond*, California Polytechnic University Theatre, Pasadena, CA; as Jesus, *Godspell*; as Steve, *Hazard County Wonder*, New Theatre, New York City; in the title role, *Julius Caesar*; in *Jungle Express*, Interact Theatre Company; *The Nerd*; *Nice People*; *The Normal Heart*, Interact Theatre Company; as Sir Harry, *Once upon a Mattress*, Interact Theatre Company; as Starbuck, *110 Degrees in the Shade* (musical), Interact Theatre Company; as Moses, *School for Scandal*; and as Dennis, *Surrender* (musical), Theatre for New York City.

Major Tours:

Bill Austin, *Mamma Mia!* (musical), North American cities, 2010.

Toured in a production of *A Member of the Wedding*.

RECORDINGS

Videos:

(In archive footage) Drew Ralston, *Daytime's Greatest Weddings*, Buena Vista Home Video, 2004.

WRITINGS

Screenplays:

Chronicles of an Exorcism, Gravitas Ventures, 2008.

OTHER SOURCES

Periodicals:

Soap Opera Digest, July 4, 1995, pp. 38–41.

Star, May 13, 2001.

TV Guide, November 8, 2003, p. 59.

ATKIN, Harvey 1942–
(Harvey Atkins)

PERSONAL

Born December 18, 1942, in Toronto, Ontario, Canada; married; children: one son, one daughter.

Addresses: *Agent*—Characters Talent Agency, 8 Elm St., 2nd Floor, Toronto, Ontario M5G 1G7, Canada; (voice work) Access Talent, 171 Madison Ave., Suite 910, New York, NY 10016.

Career: Actor and voice artist. Appeared in more than 3,000 radio and television commercials.

Awards, Honors: Genie Award nomination, best supporting actor, Academy of Canadian Cinema and Television, 1980, for *Meatballs;* three Clio Awards for commercials.

CREDITS

Film Appearances:
Conventioneer, *Silver Streak,* Twentieth Century–Fox, 1976.
Buzz, *High–Ballin',* American International Pictures, 1978.
Anwar, *Power Play* (also known as *Operation Overthrow* and *State of Shock*), 1978.
Morty, *Meatballs* (also known as *Summer Camp*), Paramount, 1979.
Bus driver, *Atlantic City* (also known as *Atlantic City, U.S.A.*), Paramount, 1980.
Harry Browning, *Funeral Home* (also known as *Cries in the Night*), Motion Picture Marketing, 1980.
Sergeant, *Improper Channels,* Crown International, 1981.
Jud, *The Last Chase,* Crown International, 1981.
Voices of alien and henchman, *Heavy Metal* (animated), Columbia, 1981.
Mr. Stone, *Ticket to Heaven,* United Artists, 1981.
Joe Prescott, *The Incubus,* Artists Releasing, 1981.
Bert, *If You Could See What I Hear,* Jensen Farley, 1982.
Vinnie Bradshaw, *Visiting Hours* (also known as *The Fright* and *Get Well Soon*), Twentieth Century–Fox, 1982.
Cochrane, *All in Good Taste,* 1983.
Salesman in train, *Finders Keepers,* Warner Bros., 1984.
Dr. Jonathan Cole, *Joshua Then and Now,* Twentieth Century–Fox, 1985.
Voice, *Carried Away* (animated short film), 1985.
Henry Gilbert, *Separate Vacations,* Alliance, 1986.

(As Harvey Atkins) Voice, *Every Dog's Guide to Complete Home Safety,* 1986.
Jerry Reeman, *Mr. Nice Guy,* 1987.
Gus Gold, *Speed Zone!* (also known as *Cannonball Fever*), Orion, 1989.
Lew Eison, *Eddie and the Cruisers II: Eddie Lives!,* Scotti Brothers, 1989.
Bob Champlain, *Mindfield,* Allegro Films Distribution, 1989.
Sidney, *Snake Eater II: The Drug Buster,* 1989.
Voice, *The Lump* (animated short film), 1991.
Voice of Bernard, *Every Dog's Guide to the Playground* (animated short film), National Film Board of Canada, 1991.
Voice, *The Apprentice* (short film), National Film Board of Canada, 1991.
Judge Steinberg, *Guilty as Sin,* Buena Vista, 1993.
Deli guy, *The Stupids,* New Line Cinema, 1996.
Lou, *Love and Death on Long Island* (also known as *Love & Death*), Universal, 1997.
Judge Fatale, *Critical Care,* Imperial Entertainment, 1997.
Rankin, *Joe's Wedding,* Astral, 1997.
Rudy, *One Tough Cop,* Stratosphere Entertainment, 1998.
Barney's Vision, Serendipity Point Films/Harold Greenberg Fund, 2010.

Television Appearances; Series:
Chuck Wagon, *Down Home Country,* CBC, 1975.
Desk Sergeant Ronald Coleman, *Cagney & Lacey,* CBS, 1982–88.
Pet Peeves, 1986.
Voices of King Koopa, Mushroom Mayor, Tryclyde, and Sniffet, *The Super Mario Bros. Super Show!* (animated; also known as *Club Mario*), syndicated, 1989–91.
Voice of King Koopa, *Captain N & the Adventures of Super Mario Bros. 3* (animated; also known as *The Adventures of Super Mario Bros. 3*), NBC, 1990.
Voice of King Koopa, *Captain N and the New Super Mario World* (animated; also known as *Super Mario World*), NBC, 1991.
Voice of Budyear/Half–A–Mind, *Stunt Dawgs* (animated), syndicated, 1992.
Sam the Dog, *The Adventures of Sam & Max: Freelance Police* (animated), Fox Kids, 1997.
Voice of Vic Potanski, *Bad Dog* (animated), Fox Family, 1998.
Judge Alan Ridenour, a recurring role, *Law & Order: Special Victims Unit* (also known as *Law & Order: SVU* and *Special Victims Unit*), NBC, between 2000 and 2010.
Voice of Morty, *Jacob Two–Two* (animated), YTV, 2003, 2004, then NBC, 2006.

Television Appearances; Movies:
Dr. Bernard M. Kotelchuk, *The War between the Tates,* NBC, 1977.

Television producer, *Introducing ... Janet* (also known as *Rubberface*), 1983.
Mr. Wallace, *The Guardian,* HBO, 1984.
One of the sidekicks, *Back to the Beanstalk,* 1990.
Verona, *Terror on Track 9,* CBS, 1992.
Myron Offetz, *Seasons of the Heart,* NBC, 1994.
Medical examiner, *Janek: The Silent Betrayal* (also known as *A Silent Betrayal*), CBS, 1994.
Lerner, *Between Love & Honor,* CBS, 1995.
Arnold Weiss (some sources cite Avrum Weiss), *Family of Cops,* CBS, 1995.
Hotel clerk, *Harrison: Cry of the City,* UPN, 1996.
Mr. Lewis, *Radiant City,* ABC, 1996.
Marty Glickman, *Rebound: The Legend of Earl "The Goat" Manigault* (also known as *Rebound*), HBO, 1996.
Voices of Mr. Fischbein, Herschel, and rotund customer, *Something from Nothing,* 1999.
Sidney Golden, *Out of Sync* (also known as *Lip Service*), VH1, 2000.
Morty, *Club Land,* Showtime, 2001.
Harvey, *Why I Wore Lipstick to My Mastectomy,* Lifetime, 2006.

Television Appearances; Specials:
Mr. Goldberg, *Chanukah under the Umbrella Tree,* The Disney Channel, 1991.

Television Appearances; Pilots:
Desk Sergeant Ronald Coleman, *Cagney & Lacey,* CBS, 1981.
Jenner, *Long Island Fever,* ABC, 1996.

Television Appearances; Episodic:
Talbot, "Complex," *The New Avengers,* ITV, 1977.
Mr. Fawcett, "The Boiler," *King of Kensington,* CBC, 1977.
Bernie, "Bunny of Kensington," *King of Kensington,* CBC, 1977.
Jerry, "The PMO," *King of Kensington,* CBC, 1979.
Vince, "Willy and Kate," *The Little Hobo,* CTV and syndicated, 1979.
Vince, "The Further Adventures of Willy and Kate," *The Littlest Hobo,* CTV and syndicated, 1980.
Mr. Pressler, "Movin' On," *King of Kensington,* CBC, 1980.
Bizarre, 1980.
Carmen, "Ghost Rig," *The Littlest Hobo,* CTV and syndicated, 1980.
Kelly, "The Diary," *Hangin' In,* CBC, 1982.
Neiderhoff, "Scavenger Hunt: Parts 1 & 2," *The Littlest Hobo,* CTV and syndicated, 1983.
Neiderhoff, "The Good Shepherd," *The Littlest Hobo,* CTV and syndicated, 1984.
Bruckner, "The Source," *Night Heat,* CBS, 1985.
Morrie, "Bull's Eye," *Seeing Things,* CBC, 1987.
Ray Amico, "I'll Be Home for Christmas," *Street Legal,* CBC, 1987.

Sam Wickes, "Don't Sell Yourself Short," *Alfred Hitchcock Presents,* USA Network, 1989.
"The Set Up," *My Secret Identity,* syndicated, 1989.
Nadel, "From Russia with Love," *Heartbeat,* ABC, 1989.
Kilgour, "False Fire," *E.N.G.,* Lifetime, 1990.
Voice of Lipscum, "Smell–a–thon," *Beetlejuice* (animated), The WB, 1991.
Voice of exorcist, "Poultrygeist," *Beetlejuice* (animated), The WB, 1991.
Mr. Murphy, "Death's a Beach," *Sweating Bullets,* CBS, 1991.
Voice, *Wish Kid* (animated), NBC, 1991.
Voice of Tomahawk, *Swamp Thing* (animated), USA Network, 1992.
Berkowitz, "Hairy Proposal," *The Mighty Jungle,* The Family Channel, 1994.
Lawyer, "Zone Five," *Robocop,* syndicated, 1994.
Tex Markles, "Pizzas and Promises," *Due South* (also known as *Direction: Sud*), CBS, 1994.
Voice of Mr. Jones, "The Circus Comes to Town," *Hello Kitty* (animated), 1994.
Voice of Mr. Jones, "Mom Loves Me after All," *Hello Kitty* (animated), 1995.
Jack Shtob, "I Wuz Robbed," *The Great Defender,* Fox, 1995.
Mr. Malik, "Bad Hare Day," *Goosebumps* (also known as *Ultimate Goosebumps*), Fox, 1996.
(English–language version) Voice of Bumboo, "Mercury's Mental Match," *Sailor Moon* (animated; also known as *English Sailor Moon, Sailor Moon S,* and *Sailor Moon Super S;* originally broadcast in Japanese), Cartoon Network, between 1998 and 2000.
(English–language version) Voice of Pox, "Grandpa's Follies," *Sailor Moon* (animated; also known as *English Sailor Moon, Sailor Moon S,* and *Sailor Moon Super S;* originally broadcast in Japanese), Cartoon Network, between 1998 and 2000.
Judge Ronald Manheim, "True North," *Law & Order,* NBC, 1998.
Good Ol' Fred, "Bunk," *The Famous Jett Jackson,* The Disney Channel, 1999.
Arraignment Judge Ronald Mannheim, "Mega," *Law & Order,* NBC, 2000.
Judge Manheim, "Slaves," *Law & Order: Special Victims Unit* (also known as *Law & Order: SVU* and *Special Victims Unit*), NBC, 2000.
Dr. Laszlo, "Faltered States," *Big Wolf on Campus,* Fox Family, 2000.
Customer, "Home Is Where the Ducks Are," *Ed,* NBC, 2000.
"Opposites Distract," *Ed,* NBC, 2001.
Voice of Crag, "The Indigestible Wad," *The Ripping Friends* (animated), Fox, 2001.
Voice of Crag, "Flathead's Revenge," *The Ripping Friends* (animated), Fox, 2001.
Voice of Crag, "Frictor," *The Ripping Friends* (animated), Fox, 2001.
"Stroke of Luck," *Doc,* PAX, 2002.

Judge Alan Ridenour, "Chinoiserie," *Law & Order: Criminal Intent* (also known as *Law & Order: CI*), NBC, 2002.

Judge Larson, "House Arrest," *Kevin Hill*, UPN, 2004.

Judge Alan Ridenour, "Stress Position," *Law & Order: Criminal Intent* (also known as *Law & Order: CI*), NBC, 2005.

Voice of Beaner and journalist, "Hey Kid, Want to Buy a Bridge?," *Time Warp Trio* (animated), NBC, 2005.

Himself, "Meatballs," *On Screen!*, Bravo, 2005.

Rabbi, "Aquaman," *G–Spot*, The Movie Network, 2006.

"Handlin' the Bike," *Sons of Butcher*, 2006.

"Ridin' the Rocket," *Sons of Butcher*, 2006.

Rabbi Goldstein, "Goy Story," *18 to Life*, 2010.

Television Work; Additional Voices for Animated Series:

AlfTales, NBC, 1988.

ALF: The Animated Series, NBC, 1988–89.

Piggsburg Pigs, 1990.

Also provided additional voices for *The Adventures of Tintin* (also known as *Les aventures de Tintin*).

Stage Appearances:

A Shayna Maidel, Toronto, Ontario, Canada, 1994.

AUSTIN, Reggie 1979–

PERSONAL

Born January 7, 1979, in Peekskill, NY. *Education:* Majored in theatre studies at Yale University.

Addresses: *Agent*—Cori Pembleton, Innovative Artists Talent and Literary Agency, 1505 10th St., Santa Monica, CA 90401.

Career: Actor.

CREDITS

Film Appearances:

(Uncredited) Pen ceremony professor, *A Beautiful Mind*, Universal, 2001.

Dubois, *Proud* (also known as *Proudly We Served*), Castle Hill, 2004.

(Uncredited) First skid row resident, *The Manchurian Candidate*, Paramount, 2004.

Old Navy shopper, *Friends with Money*, Sony Pictures Classics, 2006.

Tom Portman, *The Omen* (also known as *Omen 666* and *The Omen 666*), Twentieth Century–Fox, 2006.

Shopper, *Please Give* (also known as *Feelin' Guilty* and *Untitled Nicole Holofcener Project*), Sony Pictures Classics, 2010.

Television Appearances; Series:

Semifinalist, *Next Action Star*, NBC, 2004.

Devon Marsh, *The Starter Wife*, USA Network, 2008.

Jamie, *Life Unexpected* (also known as *Life UneXpected*, *Light Years*, and *Parental Discretion Advised*), The CW, 2010–11.

Television Appearances; Episodic:

Andre Harvey, "The Land of Confusion," *Everwood* (also known as *Our New Life in Everwood*), The WB, 2006.

Dr. Greg Wise, "The Blackout," *Notes from the Underbelly*, ABC, 2007.

Dr. Greg Wise, "She's Gotta Have It," *Notes from the Underbelly*, ABC, 2007.

Thomas, "And You Wonder Why I Lie," *Saving Grace* (also known as *Grace*), TNT, 2007.

Young man, "Her Embarrassed of Caveman," *Cavemen*, ABC, 2007.

Dr. Francis, "Heartbeat," *Eli Stone*, ABC, 2008.

Warren, "Dudes Being Dudes," *My Boys*, TBS, 2008.

James Perry, "The Beautiful Day in the Neighborhood," *Bones* (also known as *Brennan*, *Bones—Die Knochenjaegerin*, *Dr. Csont*, and *Kondid*), Fox, 2009.

Television Appearances; Pilots:

Eric, *1/4life* (also known as *1/4 Life* and *1/4 life*), ABC, 2005.

Steve P., *Pink Collar*, ABC, 2006.

Todd, *Nurses* (also known as *Philadelphia General*), Fox, 2006.

Congressional representative Larry Gearman, *I'm Paige Wilson* (also known as *Capital City*, *I Am Paige Armstrong*, *I'm Paige Armstrong*, and *Paige Armstrong*), The CW, 2007.

Dr. Greg Wise, *Notes from the Underbelly*, ABC, 2007.

Jamie, *Life Unexpected* (also known as *Life UneXpected*, *Light Years*, and *Parental Discretion Advised*), The CW, 2010.

Stage Appearances:

Appeared in various productions, including *Macbeth* and *Othello*, both Yale University; and in productions in New York City.

B

BAILEY, Brennan 1997–
(Brennan Mundt)

PERSONAL

Born January 23, 1997; brother of Preston Bailey (an actor).

Addresses: *Agent*—Savage Agency, 6121 Banner Ave., Los Angeles, CA 90038.

Career: Actor. Appeared in commercials for Clorox cleaning products, Home Depot hardware stores, and Toyota and Audi motor vehicles.

Awards, Honors: Young Artist Award nomination, best young supporting actor in a feature film, 2010, for *My Sister's Keeper.*

CREDITS

Film Appearances:
(As Brennan Mundt) Little Jake, *The Path of Evil,* MTI Home Video, 2005.
Melbourne, *Truth or Dare* (short film), Partners in Crime Films, 2007.
Chance (short film), Hold It Up Films, 2007.
Danny, *Amusement,* Picturehouse Entertainment, 2008.
Danny at age eight, *Parasomnia,* E1 Entertainment, 2008.
Jesse Fitzgerald at age ten, *My Sister's Keeper,* New Line Cinema, 2009.
Title role, *Danny* (short film), 2009.
Marty, *Adalyn* (short film), 2010.

Film Work:
(Uncredited) Additional voices, *The Water Horse* (also known as *The Water Horse: Legend of the Deep*), Columbia, 2007.

Television Appearances; Movies:
(Uncredited) Boy, *Children of the Corn* (also known as *Stephen King's "Children of the Corn"*), Syfy, 2009.

Television Appearances; Episodic:
Tanner Skelling, "Carnelian, Inc.," *The Mentalist,* CBS, 2009.
Kid, "Don't Do Me Like That," *Cougar Town,* ABC, 2009.

Television Appearances; Pilots:
(Uncredited) Soccer kid, *Alpha Mom,* NBC, 2006.

BAILEY, Preston 2000–

PERSONAL

Born July 25, 2000; brother of Brennan Bailey (an actor).

Addresses: *Agent*—Josh Bider, WME Entertainment, 9601 Wilshire Blvd., 3rd Floor, Beverly Hills, CA 90210. *Manager*—Nils Larsen, Elements Entertainment, 1635 North Cahuenga Blvd., 5th Floor, Los Angeles, CA 90028.

Career: Actor. Appeared in commercials for BMW motor vehicles, Clorox cleaning products, Juicy Juice fruit drinks, Priceline.com Web site, Stouffer's frozen meals, and other products. Named Power of Youth ambassador by *Variety* magazine.

Awards, Honors: Young Artist Award nomination, best recurring young actor in a television series, 2009, and Screen Actors Guild Award nominations (with others), outstanding ensemble in a drama series, 2009, 2010, all for *Dexter.*

CREDITS

Television Appearances; Series:
Cody Bennett, *Dexter,* Showtime, 2007–2009.

Television Appearances; Movies:
Issac, *Children of the Corn* (also known as *Stephen King's "Children of the Corn"*), Syfy, 2009.

Television Appearances; Episodic:
Dougie Nauls, "We Wish You a Merry Cryst–Meth," *Strong Medicine,* Lifetime, 2005.
Eric, "The Boogeyman," *Criminal Minds,* CBS, 2006.
Kindergarten student, "Columns," *How I Met Your Mother* (also known as *H.I.M.Y.M.*), CBS, 2007.
Randy Amato, "The Art of Reckoning," *Numb3rs* (also known as *Num3ers*), CBS, 2007.
Talking Movies, BBC, 2007.
"Dexter," *Infanity,* TV Guide Channel, 2008.
The Bob & Tom Show, WGN, 2008.
Access Hollywood, syndicated, 2008.
Hollywood 411, TV Guide Channel, 2009.
Tim Malone in 1986, "One Fall," *Cold Case,* CBS, 2010.

Television Appearances; Specials:
The 14th Annual Critics' Choice Awards, VH1, 2009.
Live from the Red Carpet: The 2009 Screen Actors Guild Awards, E! Entertainment Television, 2009.
The ... Annual Screen Actors Guild Awards, TNT and TBS, 2009, 2010.

Television Appearances; Pilots:
Will, *Alpha Mom,* NBC, 2006.
Voice of miracle boy, *Eagleheart* (animated), Cartoon Network, 2010.

Film Appearances:
Boy in end credits, *Arctic Tale,* Paramount Vantage, 2007.
Brennan, *Seven Years* (short film), Hold It Up Films, 2008.
Timmy Armstrong, *Nothing but the Truth,* Yari Film Group, 2008.
Max, *Amusement,* Picturehouse Entertainment, 2008.
Preston, *Adalyn* (short film), 2010.
Nicholas, *The Crazies,* Overture Films, 2010.

RECORDINGS

Videos:
Young Mac, *It's Always Sunny in Philadelphia: A Very Sunny Christmas,* Twentieth Century–Fox Television, 2009.

Welcome to Gatlin: The Sights and Sounds of Children of the Corn, Anchor Bay Entertainment, 2009.
Cast of the Corn, Anchor Bay Entertainment, 2009.

BARRETT, Malcolm

PERSONAL

Born in Brooklyn, New York, NY. *Education:* Attended New York University's Tisch School of the Arts. *Avocational Interests:* Writing poetry.

Addresses: *Agent*—Gersh Agency, 9465 Wilshire Blvd., 6th Floor, Beverly Hills, CA 90212. *Manager*—Management 360, 9111 Wilshire Blvd., Beverly Hills, CA 90210.

Career: Actor. Real Theatre Works (a nonprofit theatre company), New York City, founding member and artistic director; appeared in television commercials, including McDonald's restaurants, Verizon telecommunications, AT&T telecommunications, KFC restaurants, and Bud Light. Member of the Nuyorican Slam Poetry team, 2001; won the Young Playwright competition at the Manhattan Class Company.

Member: Actors' Equity.

CREDITS

Film Appearances:
Second basketball kid, *King of the Jungle,* Urbanworld Films, 2000.
Jock, *Swimfan* (also known as *Swimf@n* and *Pool*), Twentieth Century–Fox, 2002.
Rhythm of the Saints, 2003.
Anderson, *The Forgotten,* KOAN, 2003.
Al, *Love Conquers Al* (short film), 2007.
Byron Hill, *American Violet,* Samuel Goldwyn, 2008.
Sergeant Foster, *The Hurt Locker* (also known as *Hurt Locker*), Summit Entertainment, 2008.
Dwalu, *My Best Friend's Girl,* Lions Gate Films, 2008.
Milo Brown, *The Highs & Lows of Milo Brown,* 2008.
Himself, *The Cast's Guide to Dating* (short film), Lions Gate, 2009.
Himself, *The Prom: A Teen Rite of Passage* (short film), Lions Gate, 2009.
Himself, *A to Z: Professor Turner's Sexist Rating System* (short film), 2009.
Kenneth, *Imaginary Larry,* 2009.
Mack, *Larry Crowne,* Universal, 2011.

Film Executive Producer:
The Highs & Lows of Milo Brown (short film), Nebula Films, 2008.

Television Appearances; Series:
TK, *Luis,* Fox, 2003.
Various, *Kelsey Grammar Presents: The Sketch Show,* Fox, 2005.
The Bonnie Hunt Show, 2008–10.
Lem Hewitt, *Better Off Ted,* ABC, 2009–10.

Television Appearances; Pilots:
Fred, *The Minister of Divine,* Fox, 2007.
Lem Hewitt, *Better Off Ted,* ABC, 2009.
Oliver, *Most Likely to Succeed,* Fox, 2010.

Television Appearances; Episodic:
Russell Lucas, "Cueca Solo," *The Beat,* UPN, 2000.
Julian Zalak, "Phobia," *Law & Order,* NBC, 2001.
Angelo Davis, "Watching Too Much Television," *The Sopranos,* HBO, 2002.
Harry Johnson, "Tragedy on Rye," *Law & Order,* NBC, 2002.
Ahmal, "Cuba Libre," *Law & Order: Criminal Intent* (also known as *Law & Order: CI*), NBC, 2003.
Martin, "A Friend in Need," *The Big House,* ABC, 2004.
Terrell, "The Gang Gets Racist," *It's Always Sunny in Philadelphia* (also known as *It's Always Sunny*), FX Network, 2005.
Dr. Julies Huffman, "Voices," *Ghost Whisperer,* CBS, 2005.
Wally, "Zdro to Murder in Sixty Seconds," *Psych,* USA Network, 2007.
Andy Ryan, "Whose Sperm Is It Anyway?," *A Side Order of Life,* Lifetime, 2007.
Andy Ryan, "Try to Remember," *A Side Order of Life,* Lifetime, 2007.
Malcolm O'Dwyer, "Mr. Monk Gets Lotto Fever," *Monk,* USA Network, 2008.
Himself, *The Movie Loft,* 2009.

Also appeared as Malcolm, "That's Fine," *Floored and Lifted.*

Stage Appearances:
Appeared in *The Stonemason,* McCarter Theatre; *The Violence Project.*

Major Tours:
Toured in *Wit,* U.S. cities.

Stage Work:
Directed *Fallen Patriots,* Real Theatre Works, New York City, and Fringe Festival, New York City.

WRITINGS

Screenplays:
The Highs & Lows of Milo Brown (short film), Nebula Films, 2008.

BARRON, Dana 1968–

PERSONAL

Born April 22, 1968, in New York, NY; daughter of Robert Barron (a director of commercials) and Joyce McCord (a stage actress); sister of Allison Barron (an actress). *Education:* Studied at Art Students League of New York.

Career: Actress and producer. Appeared in commercials.

Member: Actors' Equity Association, American Federation of Television and Radio Artists, Screen Actors Guild.

Awards, Honors: Focus Award, 1988, for *Where or When;* Daytime Emmy Award, outstanding performer in a children's special, 1989, for "No Means No," *CBS Schoolbreak Special;* Young Artist Award, best young actress recurring in a television series, 1993, for *Beverly Hills, 90210;* Young Artist Award nomination, best young actress in a television movie, 1993, for *Jonathan: The Boy Nobody Wanted.*

CREDITS

Film Appearances:
Diane (some sources cite Diana), *He Knows You're Alone* (also known as *Blood Wedding*), United Artists, 1980.
Audrey Griswold, *Vacation* (also known as *American Vacation* and *National Lampoon's "Vacation"*), Warner Bros., 1983.
Janine, *Heaven Help Us* (also known as *Catholic Boys*), TriStar, 1985.
Erica Sheldon, *Death Wish 4: The Crackdown,* Cannon, 1987.
Beth Devereux, *Heartbreak Hotel,* Buena Vista/Touchstone, 1988.
Anne, *Where or When,* 1988.
Maggie, *Magic Kid II,* PM Entertainment Group, 1994.
Kathy, *In the Living Years* (also known as *Letter to Dad*), 1994.

Gena, *City of Industry* (also known as *Bad Days*), Orion, 1997.

Louise de la Valliere, *The Man in the Iron Mask* (also known as *The Mask of Dumas* and *The Three Musketeers Meet the Man in the Iron Mask*), Monterey Video, 1998.

Laura, *Dumped,* The Global Asylum, 2000.

Renee Bloomer, *Stageghost,* Alpha Film Group, 2000.

Junky applicant, *Wild Roomies* (also known as *Roomies*), 2000, American World Pictures, 2004.

Heather, *Night Class* (also known as *Seduced by a Thief*), World International Network, 2001.

Tiny, *Pucked* (also known as *National Lampoon's "Pucked"* and *National Lampoon's "The Trouble with Frank"*), National Lampoon Productions, 2006.

Mom, *Saving Angelo* (short film), Aron Productions/Bigel Entertainment/Red Balloon Entertainment, 2007.

Kristy, *The Invited,* Dark Portal/Relativity Media, 2010.

The gynecologist, *Happythankyoumoreplease,* Eagle Films, 2010.

Film Work:

Coproducer, *Night Class* (also known as *Seduced by a Thief*), World International Network, 2001.

Coproducer, *Clover Bend,* 2001.

Associate producer, *Pucked* (also known as *National Lampoon's "Pucked"* and *National Lampoon's "The Trouble with Frank"*), National Lampoon Productions, 2006.

Television Appearances; Series:

Michelle Boudin, *One Life to Live,* ABC, 1984–85.

Eleanor, *Crossbow* (also known as *William Tell*), 1987–90.

Nikki Witt, *Beverly Hills, 90210* (also known as *Class of Beverly Hills*), Fox, 1992.

Casey, a recurring role, *The Magnificent Seven,* CBS, 1998–2000.

Television Appearances; Movies:

Darlene, *The Brass Ring,* HBO, 1983.

Laurie Moore, *Jonathan: The Boy Nobody Wanted* (also known as *Who Speaks for Jonathan*), NBC, 1992.

Second girl on the street, *The Webbers* (also known as *At Home with the Webbers* and *Webber's World*), 1993.

Sue, *Jailbreakers,* Showtime, 1994.

Kristin, *Python,* 2000.

Fawn Lewis, *The Perfect Nanny,* USA Network, 2000.

Audrey Griswold, *Christmas Vacation 2: Cousin Eddie's Island Adventure* (also known as *Christmas Vacation 2: Cousin Eddie, National Lampoon's "Christmas Vacation 2: Cousin Eddie's Island Adventure,"* and *National Lampoon's "Cousin Eddie's Island Adventure"*), NBC, 2003.

Marta Arnack, *McBride: Murder Past Midnight,* Hallmark Channel, 2005.

Television Appearances; Miniseries:

Lindsey Mastrapa, *Pandemic,* Hallmark Channel, 2007.

Television Appearances; Specials:

Megan Wells, "No Means No," *CBS Schoolbreak Special,* CBS, 1988.

(In archive footage) Audrey Griswold, *The 82nd Annual Academy Awards,* ABC, 2010.

Television Appearances; Pilots:

Eleanor, *Adventures of William Tell,* 1986.

Lisa, *Staten Island 10309,* CBS, 1995.

Also appeared in the pilots *High* and *O'Hara.*

Television Appearances; Episodic:

Melinda, "The Children's Song" (also known as "Father and Son"), *The Equalizer,* CBS, 1985.

Corrie (or Corey) Jean Kroller, "Crackdown," *In the Heat of the Night,* NBC, 1989.

Reo Saunders, "Blame It on Reo," *Dream On,* HBO, 1994.

Sarah Tyler, "School for Murder," *Murder, She Wrote,* CBS, 1995.

Mary, "The Human Condition," *The Watcher,* UPN, 1995.

Lauren Ashley, "The Corps Is Mother, the Corps Is Father," *Babylon 5* (also known as *B5*), TNT, 1998.

(Uncredited) Second witness, "No Way Out," *CSI: Crime Scene Investigation* (also known as *C.S.I.* and *CSI: Las Vegas*), CBS, 2009.

Also appeared in an episode of *McKenna.*

Stage Appearances:

Jill Bart, *Hide and Seek,* Belasco Theatre, New York City, 1980.

Angel, *Common Clay,* Ensemble Studio Theatre, New York City, 1988.

Appeared as Sob Sister Sneeze, *The Laughter Epidemic,* off–Broadway production; as Laurel, *Moon Shadow,* Philadelphia Festival for New Plays, Philadelphia, PA; as Amy, *The Other 5%,* Ellen Theatre; and as Julie, *Tilt,* Ensemble Studio Theatre.

RECORDINGS

Videos:

Herself, *The Family Truckster,* Warner Home Video, 2003.

OTHER SOURCES

Periodicals:

Babylon 5, September, 1998, p. 48.

Universe Today, June, 1998, p. 6.

BASIS, Austin 1976–

PERSONAL

Full name, Austin Lee Basis; born September 14, 1976, in Brooklyn, New York, NY; son of Arthur (a manager of a distribution company) and Shari (a teacher and coach) Basis. *Education:* Binghamton University, State University of New York, B.A., theatre; Actors Studio Drama School, M.F.A.; studied acting, dance, and various disciplines with various instructors. *Avocational Interests:* Drawing, writing poetry.

Addresses: *Agent*—Tim Angle, Don Buchwald & Associates, 6500 Wilshire Blvd., Suite 2200, Los Angeles, CA 90048. *Manager*—Sandra Erickson, Vic Ramos Management, 49 West Ninth St., Suite B, New York, NY 10011.

Career: Actor, comedian, and writer. Actors Studio, New York City, life member; appeared as Benjamin Bankes the Pig in the public service campaign Feed the Pig; appeared in advertisements, worked as a voice artist, and participated in singing competitions. Worked as a bartender, bouncer, busboy, waiter, and substitute teacher.

Member: Screen Actors Guild, American Federation of Television and Radio Artists.

Awards, Honors: Morty Gunty Award for Performing Arts, Midwood High School at Brooklyn College.

CREDITS

Film Appearances:
Bully, *Glass Boxes* (short film), Mars Cat Productions, c. 2003.
Leo, *Skips* (short film), 2004.
Angry delicatessen vigilante, *Hazard*, Eleven Arts, 2005.
Duffy, *Building Girl*, Magic Pad Productions, 2005.
Spooky, *Dorian Blues*, TLA Releasing, 2005.
Voice, *Terrormarketers*, Lo–Fi Entertainment Home Video, 2005.
Bobby, *Om* (short film), Freshew Films, 2007.
Crazy Cal, *Dead Tone* (also known as *7eventy 5ive* and *75—Seventy Five*), Codeblack Entertainment, 2007.
The kid, *Life Unkind* (short film), Freewater Films, 2007.
Man with a portrait, *Anthem* (short film), 2007.
Charlie Hendricks, *The Other End of the Line*, Metro–Goldwyn–Mayer, 2008.
Ivan, *American Zombie*, Cinema Libre Studio, 2008.

James James, *Boxboarders!*, Peace Arch Entertainment Group, 2008.
Leo, *My Sassy Girl*, 2008.
David Stankowitz, *Re–Cut*, Fritz Manger Productions, 2010.
Jake, *The Things We Carry*, Lono Entertainment, 2010.

Film Work:
Choreographer, *Dorian Blues*, TLA Releasing, 2005.
Zine illustrator, *American Zombie*, Cinema Libre Studio, 2008.

Television Appearances; Series:
Math Rogers, *Life Unexpected* (also known as *Life Un-eXpected*, *Light Years*, and *Parental Discretion Advised*), The CW, 2010–11.

Television Appearances; Movies:
Interviewed student, *Porn 'n Chicken* (also known as *Chicken Club*), Comedy Central, 2002.

Television Appearances; Episodic:
Lou–Lou Versini, "Fico Di Capo," *Law & Order: Criminal Intent* (also known as *Law & Order: CI*), NBC, 2004.
ATM man, "The Getaway," *Windfall*, NBC, 2006.
ATM man and Sam, "There and Gone Again," *Windfall*, NBC, 2006.
Robby, "The Disaster Show," *Studio 60 on the Sunset Strip* (also known as *Studio 7 on the Sunset Strip* and *Studio 60*), NBC, 2007.
Skaggs, "Megan's Revenge," *Drake & Josh*, Nickelodeon, 2007.
Dallas, "Last Man Standing," *Navy NCIS: Naval Criminal Investigative Service* (also known as *Naval CIS*, *Navy CIS*, *Navy NCIS*, *NCIS*, and *NCIS: Naval Criminal Investigative Service*), CBS, 2008.
Kenneth "Kenny" Spruce, "Ghostfacers," *Supernatural* (also known as *Sobrenatural*), The CW, 2008.
Waiter, "The Reunion," *Curb Your Enthusiasm* (also known as *Curb* and *Larry David*), HBO, 2009.
(Uncredited) Kenneth "Kenny" Spruce, "Hammer of the Gods," *Supernatural* (also known as *Sobrenatural*), The CW, 2010.

Television Appearances; Pilots:
Ben Miller, *Spellbound*, Fox, 2004.
Willy Kramer, "Out Here in the Fields," *Life on Mars*, ABC, 2008.
Math Rogers, *Life Unexpected* (also known as *Life Un-eXpected*, *Light Years*, and *Parental Discretion Advised*), The CW, 2010.

Internet Appearances; Series:
Kenneth "Kenny" Spruce, *Ghostfacers*, www.ghostfacers.com, beginning 2010.

Stage Appearances:

Title role, *Young Dracula,* Mark Twain I.S. 239 for the Gifted and Talented, Brooklyn, New York City, c. 1980.

Stanley Jerome, *Brighton Beach Memoirs,* Hinman Production Company, Binghamton University, State University of New York, 1996.

Johnny, *Beggars in the House of Plenty* (thesis project), Actors Studio Drama School Repertory Season, Actors Studio Drama School Theatre, New York City, c. 2001.

Wally, *Safe in Symbols,* Actors Studio Drama School Repertory Season, Actors Studio Drama School Theatre, c. 2001.

Hat knocker and newsboy, *Roundheads & Pointheads* (also known as *The Roundheads and the Pointheads, The Roundheads & the Pointheads,* and *The Round Heads and the Point Heads*), Actors Studio, 2002.

Appeared in other productions, including appearances as Elliott, *Master Class,* as Timothy Hogarth, *Room Service,* and as the second soldier, *Salome,* all Actors Studio; as Darren, *Arthouse,* and as Roy, *Selection,* both D.A.P. Ensemble; as Andrew Rally, *I Hate Hamlet,* Dickinson Theatre Players, Binghamton University, State University of New York; as Orin Scrivello, DDS, *Little Shop of Horrors* (musical); as Coleman, *Obit,* Expanded Arts Theatre; as Guildenstern, *Rosencrantz and Guildenstern Are Dead,* Binghamton University, State University of New York, Fine Arts Studio B; as Minnie–Jean Brown, *Walking to School,* The New School, Tishman Auditorium, New York City; and as Lord Chatterunga, *Yoga Kills,* Big Step Productions. Performed in comedy productions, including *Florch* and *Undiscovered Treasure,* both improv productions at the New York Comedy Club, New York City; appeared in the sketch production *Crackers,* Vital Theatre; and in the sketch and improv production *Mmm ... Comedy,* Tobacco Road Theatre.

Major Tours:

Barkeep, *Betrayal,* Actors Studio, U.S. cities, c. 2003.

Stage Work:

Cocreator of the sketch and improv production *Mmm ... Comedy,* Tobacco Road Theatre.

WRITINGS

Writings for the Stage:

Wrote *Walking to School,* The New School, Tishman Auditorium, New York City. Created and wrote material for *Florch* and *Undiscovered Treasure,* both improv productions at the New York Comedy Club, New York City; the sketch production *Crackers,* Vital Theatre; and the sketch and improv production *Mmm ... Comedy,* Tobacco Road Theatre.

Poetry:

Wrote poetry.

OTHER SOURCES

Electronic:

Austin Basis, http://www.austinbasis.com, June 8, 2010.

BEARD, Jane

PERSONAL

Career: Actress. Round House Theatre, Silver Spring, MD, associate artist.

Member: Screen Actors Guild.

Awards, Honors: Helen Hayes Award nomination, outstanding lead actress in a resident play, Washington Theatre Awards Society, 2000, for *The Turn of the Screw.*

CREDITS

Film Appearances:

Kidnapper, *Guarding Tess,* TriStar, 1994.

Doris Jennings, *Foreign Student,* Gramercy, 1994.

Cleaning mom, *Trading Mom* (also known as *The Mommy Market*), Trimark Pictures, 1994.

Carol Simmons, *Silent Fall,* Warner Bros., 1994.

Biologist, *Species II,* Metro–Goldwyn–Mayer, 1998.

Jessica Stone, *Riders,* Theatrefire Films, 2001.

Mrs. Mountchessington, *The Persistence of Dreams* (short film), Arrowhead Productions, 2005.

Miss McNally, *Cry Wolf,* Rogue Pictures, 2005.

Doctor's receptionist, *Swimmers,* Skouras Pictures, 2006.

Lena Freeman, *Step Up,* Buena Vista, 2006.

Fern Garrles, *Rocket Science,* Picturehouse Entertainment, 2007.

Stage Appearances:

Jane, *Absurd Person Singular,* Round House Theatre, Silver Spring, MD, 1995.

Dinah, *One Shoe Off,* Round House Theatre, 1996.

Phoebe/Poopay, *Communicating Doors,* Round House Theatre, 1999.

The Turn of the Screw, Round House Theatre, 2000.

Multiple roles, *Mystery School* (solo show), Round House Theatre, 2001.

Ginger Andrews, *Trudy Blue,* Studio Theatre, Washington, DC, 2001.

Kari, *The Pavilion,* Round House Theatre, 2003.
Speaking in Tongues, Round House Theatre, 2003.

Also appeared in *The Heiress,* Los Angeles Theatre Works, Venice, CA; and appeared as Margaret, *When Grace Comes In,* Mandell Weiss Forum, La Jolla Playhouse, La Jolla, CA.

Television Appearances; Episodic:
Julie Newdow, "A Many Splendored Thing," *Homicide: Life on the Street* (also known as *Homicide*), NBC, 1994.
Tourist, "Shutdown," *The West Wing* (also known as *The White House*), NBC, 2003.

BENANTI, Laura 1979–

PERSONAL

Full name, Laura Ilene Benanti; born July 15, 1979, in New York, NY; raised in Kinnelon, NJ; daughter of Martin Vidnovic (an actor and singer) and Linda Benanti (a music teacher, actress, and singer; maiden name, Wonneberger); stepdaughter of Salvatore Benanti (a psychotherapist); married Chris Barron (a singer and recording artist), July 25, 2005 (divorced); married Steven Pasquale (an actor), September 16, 2007. *Education:* Studied voice and piano; studied at Paper Mill Playhouse.

Addresses: *Agent*—Innovative Artists Talent and Literary Agency, 235 Park Ave. South, 10th Floor, New York, NY 10003 and 1505 10th St., Santa Monica, CA 90401. *Manager*—Emily Gerson Saines, Brookside Artists Management, 250 West 57th St., Suite 2303, New York, NY 10019.

Career: Actress and singer. Performer in benefits; host of and performer at awards ceremonies. Played piano and guitar. Worked at a farmers' market.

Member: Actors' Equity Association.

Awards, Honors: Rising Star Award, Paper Mill Playhouse, c. 1996, for *Hello, Dolly!;* Antoinette Perry Award nomination, best performance by a featured actress in a musical, 2000, for *Swing!;* Antoinette Perry Award nomination, best performance by a featured actress in a musical, Drama Desk Award nomination, Outer Critics Circle Award nomination, outstanding featured actress in a musical, and Ovation Award nomination, LA Stage Alliance, all outstanding featured actress in a musical, all 2002, for *Into the Woods;* Outer Critics Circle Award nomination and nomination for the Distinguished Performance Award, Drama League awards, both c. 2003, for *Nine;* Antoinette Perry Award, best performance by a featured actress in a musical, Drama Desk Award, outstanding featured actress in a musical, Outer Critics Circle Award, outstanding featured actress in a musical, and nomination for the Distinguished Performance Award, Drama League awards, all 2008, for *Gypsy;* honored with her caricature hung at Sardi's restaurant, New York City, beginning 2008.

CREDITS

Stage Appearances; Musicals:
Juan Peron's mistress, *Evita,* The Barn Theatre, Mainstage, Montville, NJ, c. 1993–94.
Solange Dudevant, *Chopin and Sand,* The Barn Theatre, Montville, c. 1994–95.
Young Heidi, *Follies,* The Barn Theatre, Mainstage, c. 1994–95.
Cinderella, *Into the Woods,* The Barn Theatre, Mainstage, c. 1995–96.
Dolly Gallagher Levi, *Hello, Dolly!,* Kinnelon High School, Kinnelon, NJ, c. 1996.
Antonia, *Man of La Mancha,* Paper Mill Playhouse, Paper Mill Playhouse, Millburn, NJ, 1997.
Understudy for the role of Maria Rainer and later Maria Rainer, also a postulant and a member of the ensemble, *The Sound of Music,* Martin Beck Theatre, New York City, 1998–99.
Swing! (musical revue), St. James Theatre, New York City, 1999–2001.
Eileen, *Wonderful Town* (concert staging of musical), produced as part of *City Center Encores!* (also known as *Encores!, Encores! Great American Musicals in Concert,* and *New York City Center Encores!*), City Center Theatre, New York City, 2000.
Julia, *Time and Again,* Manhattan Theatre Club Stage II, New York City, 2001.
Cinderella and Cinderella's mother, *Into the Woods,* Ahmanson Theatre, Los Angeles, and Broadhurst Theatre, New York City, both 2002.
Something Good (tribute concert; also known as *Something Good: A Broadway Salute to Richard Rodgers on 100th His Birthday*), George Gershwin Theatre, New York City, 2002.
(With the Gay Men's Chorus of Washington, DC) *You've Got to Be Carefully Taught ... The Songs of Sondheim & Hammerstein* (concert; also known as *You've Got to Be Carefully Taught ... The Songs of Sondheim & Hammerstein Featuring Laura Benanti*), John F. Kennedy Center for the Performing Arts, Washington, DC, 2002.
Claudia, *Nine,* Eugene O'Neill Theatre, New York City, 2003.

The snake–led, *Children of Eden* (benefit concert staging of musical), The Riverside Church, New York City, 2003.

Neo (benefit concert; also known as *NEO, N.E.O., Neo: A Celebration of Emerging Talent in Musical Theatre, Benefiting the York Theatre Company,* and *Neo: new, emerging ... outstanding!*), The York Theatre Company, New York City, 2003.

Anne Egerman, *A Little Night Music,* Center Theatre Group, Music Center, Performing Arts Center of Los Angeles County, Los Angeles Opera Theatre, Dorothy Chandler Pavilion, Los Angeles, 2004.

Catherine, *Pippin* (benefit concert staging of musical), Manhattan Center Studios Grand Ballroom, New York City, 2004.

Guys and Dolls (benefit concert staging of musical; also known as *An Evening of Music from Guys and Dolls*), Sheraton Hotel, New York City, 2004.

Hair (benefit concert staging of musical), New Amsterdam Theatre, New York City, 2004.

Laura Benanti and Gavin Creel: Front & Center (concerts), Joseph Papp Public Theatre, Joe's Pub, New York City, 2004.

Lily, *The Secret Garden,* produced as part of *Third Annual World AIDS Day Concert* (benefit concert), Manhattan Center Studios Grand Ballroom, 2005.

Marian Paroo, *The Music Man* (benefit production), 2005.

Laura Benanti: Blame It on My Youth (cabaret production; also known as *Blame It on My Youth*), Feinstein's at Loews Regency, New York City, 2005.

Wall to Wall Sondheim (tribute concerts), Symphony Space, New York City, 2005.

Julia Sullivan, *The Wedding Singer,* 5th Avenue Theatre, Seattle, WA, and Al Hirschfeld Theatre, New York City, both 2006.

Louise, *Gypsy,* staged as concert and produced as part of *City Center Encores!* (also known as *Encores!, Encores! Great American Musicals in Concert,* and *New York City Center Encores!*), City Center Theatre, 2007, then produced as a full production, St. James Theatre, 2008.

Broadway Loves Joe's Pub (concert), Joseph Papp Public Theatre, Joe's Pub, 2008.

Footlights and Film: A Celebration of the Great Musicals from Stage and Screen (gala), Westport Country Playhouse, Westport, CT, 2008.

Primary Stages 24th Anniversary Gala Benefit, Grand Hyatt Hotel, New York City, 2008.

Anne Egerman, *A Little Night Music* (benefit gala concert staging of musical), Roundabout Theatre Company, Nokia Theatre Times Square, New York City, 2009.

Chance and Chemistry (benefit concert; also known as *Chance & Chemistry* and *Chance and Chemistry: A Centennial Celebration of Frank Loesser*), Minskoff Theatre, New York City, 2009.

Come to My Garden: The Music of Lucy Simon (concert), Joseph Papp Public Theatre, Joe's Pub, 2009.

Barbara Cook's "Spotlight" (production in a series of cabaret productions; also known as *Spotlight*), John F. Kennedy Center for the Performing Arts, Terrace Theatre, Washington, DC, 2010.

Sondheim: The Birthday Concert, Lincoln Center, Avery Fisher Hall, New York City, 2010.

Candela, *Women on the Verge of a Nervous Breakdown,* Lincoln Center Theatrw at the Belasco Theatre, New York City, beginning 2010.

Performed in benefit concerts and in tributes, including a tribute to Leonard Bernstein, Daytona Beach, FL, 2005.

Stage Appearances; Plays:

Anne Boleyn, *The Faces of Henry VIII & His Wives,* The Barn Theatre, Montville, NJ, c. 1996–97.

Mary Rivers, *Jane Eyre,* Paper Mill Playhouse, Millburn, NJ, 1997.

Perdita, *A Winter's Tale,* Williamstown Theatre Festival, Main Stage, Williamstown, MA, 2001.

Former high school sweetheart, *Plaza Suite* (benefit reading), High School for the Humanities, New York City, 2005.

Felicity, *Why Torture Is Wrong, and the People Who Love Them,* Joseph Papp Public Theatre, Estelle R. Newman Theatre, New York City, 2009.

Mrs. Givings, *In the Next Room or The Vibrator Play* (also known as *In the Next Room*), Lyceum Theatre, New York City, 2009–10.

Television Appearances; Series:

Billie Frasier, *Starved,* FX Network, 2005.

(And in archive footage) Beth Keller, a recurring role, *Eli Stone,* ABC, 2008.

Television Appearances; Specials:

Understudy for the role of Maria Rainer, *Backstage at "The Sound of Music"* (documentary; also known as *Backstage at The Sound of Music*), 1999.

Television Appearances; Awards Presentations:

The ... Annual Tony Awards, CBS, 2008, 2009, 2010.

Television Appearances; Episodic:

Herself, *Today* (also known as *NBC News Today* and *The Today Show*), NBC, 2008.

Denise Carling, "Home Is Where You Hang Your Holster," *Life on Mars,* ABC, 2009.

Herself, "Leading Ladies," *Working in the Theatre,* CUNY TV, 2009.

Television Appearances; Pilots:

Billie Frasier, *Starved,* FX Network, 2005.

Beth Keller, *Eli Stone,* ABC, 2008.

June Gage, *Open Books,* CBS, 2010.

Film Appearances:

Tina, *Take the Lead* (also known as *Dance!* and *Dance with Me*), New Line Cinema, 2006.

Princess Alexandra, *East Broadway* (also known as *Falling for Grace* and *Social Grace*), Slowhand Cinema Releasing, 2007.

Allison Connor, *Meskada*, Aliquot Films/Deerjen Films/ Four of a Kind Productions, 2010.

Radio Appearances; Episodic:

Herself, *Downstage Center*, XM Satellite Radio (show later a podcast), 2008.

RECORDINGS

Albums; with Others:

(Performer on the title piece and narrator) *Mozart Was a Kid Like You and Me* (with the Russian Federal Orchestra), Helicon for Young People, 1999.

Various artists, *The Stephen Schwartz Album*, Varese Sarabande, 1999.

Swing! (original Broadway cast recording), Sony, 2000.

Into the Woods (Broadway revival cast recording), Nonesuch, 2002.

Various artists, *The Maury Yeston Songbook*, P.S. Classics, 2003.

Nine (Broadway revival cast recording; also known as *Nine—The Musical*), P.S. Classics, 2003.

(With the Gay Men's Chorus of Washington, DC) *You've Got to Be Carefully Taught … The Songs of Sondheim & Hammerstein* (also known as *You've Got to Be Carefully Taught … The Songs of Sondheim & Hammerstein Featuring Laura Benanti*), 2003.

Hair (benefit cast recording), Ghostlight Records, 2005.

Neo (benefit cast recording; also known as *NEO*, *N.E.O.*, *Neo: A Celebration of Emerging Talent in Musical Theatre, Benefiting the York Theatre Company*, and *Neo: new, emerging … outstanding!*), Jay Records, 2005.

The Wedding Singer (original Broadway cast recording), Sony, 2006.

Gypsy (Broadway cast recording), Time Life Entertainment, 2008.

(As Jennie Brinker) *Rodgers and Hammerstein's "Allegro"* (studio cast recording; also known as *Allegro* and *Rodgers and Hammerstein's "Allegro": First Complete Recording*), Sony Classics, 2009.

Worked on solo recordings.

Videos:

Herself, *A Backstage Look at "The Wedding Singer" on Broadway* (short documentary), New Line Cinema, 2006.

WRITINGS

Writings for the Stage:

(With others) *Laura Benanti and Gavin Creel: Front & Center* (concerts), Joseph Papp Public Theatre, Joe's Pub, New York City, 2004.

Laura Benanti: Blame It on My Youth (cabaret production; also known as *Blame It on My Youth*), Feinstein's at Loews Regency, New York City, 2005.

(And songs; with others) *Broadway Loves Joe's Pub* (concert), Joseph Papp Public Theatre, Joe's Pub, 2008.

Songs:

Wrote songs.

OTHER SOURCES

Periodicals:

New Jersey Monthly, February, 2003.

New York Times, June 20, 1999; January 28, 2001; March 23, 2008, p. AR9.

Electronic:

Laura Benanti, http://www.laurabenanti.com, August 10, 2010.

Playbill.com, http://www.playbill.com, August 28, 2005;March 26, 2008.

BENFORD, Starla

PERSONAL

American. *Education:* Harvard University, graduated, c. 2001.

Career: Actress.

Awards, Honors: According to some sources, nominated for a national Broadway theatre award, best actress, c. 2001, for *The Vagina Monologues*; Connecticut Critics Circle Award, for *From the Mississippi Delta*.

CREDITS

Stage Appearances:

Blanche, *A Streetcar Named Desire*, Capitol City Playhouse, Austin, TX, 1986.

Trojan interpreter and other roles, *The Oresteia*, Loeb Drama Center, Cambridge, MA, 1994.

LaWanda, *Stonewall Jackson's House*, American Place Theatre, New York City, 1997.

Madeline and other roles, *One Small Step* (staged reading), 1998.

Lady Macduff and second weird sister, *Macbeth*, Theatre for a New Audience, American Place Theatre, 1999.

Witch, *Macbeth*, Music Box Theatre, New York City, 2000.

Brightie, *Cat on a Hot Tin Roof*, Music Box Theatre, 2004.

Street person, Negro woman, Mexican woman, and understudy for the role of Eunice, *A Streetcar Named Desire*, Roundabout Theatre Company, Studio 54, New York City, 2005.

Appeared in *Antony and Cleopatra*, Shakespeare Theatre, Washington, DC; as Stefanie, *Denial*, Long Wharf Theatre, New Haven, CT; as Popova, "The Bear," *Directorfest 99*, Here Theatre; in *Eastville*, Connecticut Repertory Theatre; as Rose, *Fences*; in *Flying Fables*, Apollo Theatre; as second woman, *From the Mississippi Delta*, Stamford, CT; in *Media Amok*, American Repertory Theatre, Cambridge, MA; in the title role, *Phaedra*; as Roach, *Slaughter City*, American Repertory Theatre; in the title role, *The Snow Queen*; in *Sonata Blue* (solo show), Austin, TX; and in *The Venetian Twins*, Guthrie Theatre, Minneapolis, MN.

Major Tours:

The Vagina Monologues, North American cities, beginning 2001.

Film Appearances:

Party guest, *Blank Check*, Buena Vista, 1994.

Police technician, *A Perfect Murder* (also known as *Dial M*), Warner Bros., 1998.

Denise Mayfield/Nefertiti Klaus, *Tree Shade* (short film), Wing and a Prayer Productions, 1998.

Woman with flowers, *Our Song*, IFC Films, 2001.

Mrs. Morton, *The End of the Bar*, Carbonated Films, 2002.

2 Birds with 1 Stallone (also known as *Fight the Good Fight*), Lil Mama Productions, 2003.

Patty, *Backseat*, 2005, Truly Indie, 2008.

Traffic officer, *Sorry, Haters*, IFC Films, 2006.

Principal Henderson, *Half Nelson*, THINKFilm, 2006.

Herself, *Revolution* (also known as *RevoLOUtion: The Transformation of Lou Benedetti*), Foundation for Conscious Humanity/Louniversal Releasing, 2006.

Wanda Anita Green, *United 93*, Universal, 2006.

Dr. Crawford, *13*, VVS Films, 2010.

Television Appearances; Series:

Judith, *One Life to Live*, ABC, 1997–98.

Television Appearances; Movies:

Save the Dog!, The Disney Channel, 1988.

Detective, *A Seduction in Travis County* (also known as *Blind Judgment*), CBS, 1991.

Lady reporter, *Bed of Lies*, ABC, 1992.

Television Appearances; Episodic:

Amani Freeman, "Color Lines," *New York Undercover*, Fox, 1995.

Betty Wald, "Monster," *Law & Order*, NBC, 1998.

Carol Daley, "Monogamy," *Law & Order: Special Victims Unit* (also known as *Law & Order: SVU* and *Special Victims Unit*), NBC, 2002.

Collins, "Two Hundred and Thirty–three Days," *Third Watch*, NBC, 2002.

Eileen Hargrove, "Identity," *Law & Order*, NBC, 2003.

Ultrasound nurse, "Of Two Minds," *3 lbs.*, CBS, 2006.

Wendy Shreiber, "Identity Crisis." *Law & Order: Criminal Intent* (also known as *Law & Order: CI*), NBC, 2009.

Title role, "School Nurse," *Nurse Jackie*, Showtime, 2009.

Television Appearances; Specials:

Iona Shine, *Harambee!*, WNET, 1996.

OTHER SOURCES

Periodicals:

Austin Chronicle, June 8, 2001.

BENTON, Anya

PERSONAL

Original name, Anna Vladislavovna Zabolotnaya; born in Moscow, Russia; immigrated to the United States at age ten. *Education:* University of California, Los Angeles, undergraduate degree (mass communications with a minor in Russian Studies and Spanish language; cum laude); studied acting at the Beverly Hills Playhouse.

Addresses: *Agent*—International Creative Management, 10250 Constellation Blvd., 9th Floor, Los Angeles, CA 90067.

Career: Actress. Also worked as a model; appeared in television commercials, including one for a Boston–area locksmith. Volunteered through the Kiwanis Family.

CREDITS

Film Appearances:
Jennifer, *Absolute Horror,* 2007.
Angela, *Don't Look in the Cellar,* 2008.
Babylonian temptress, *Death Racers,* The Asylum, 2008.
Karen Michaels, *The Land That Time Forgot* (also known as *Edgar Rice Burroughs' "The Land That Time Forgot"*), The Asylum, 2009.
Protester, *The Hypocratic Oath,* 2009.
Brittney/Olga, *Get the Girl,* 2009.
Dee, *Addicts,* 2009.
Alcoholics Anonymous attendee, *Conversations with Lucifer* (short film), 2010.
Vilma, *6 Guns,* Asylum Home Entertainment, 2010.
Daisy Daniels, *Dahmer vs. Gacy,* 2010.
Sondra, *Chihuahua: The Movie,* Laguna Productions, 2010.
Cindy Summers, *Broken Dreams,* 2010.
Simone, *Cornered,* 2010.

Television Appearances; Movies:
Radio dispatcher, *MegaFault,* Syfy, 2009.

Television Appearances; Episodic:
Socialite, "Tabu," *Numb3ers* (also known as *Num3ers*), CBS, 2007.
(Uncredited) April, "Don Hoberman," *Nip/Tuck,* FX Network, 2009.
(Uncredited) April, "Joe Seabrook" *Nip/Tuck,* FX Network, 2009.

OTHER SOURCES

Electronic:
Anya Benton Home Page, http://www.anyabenton.com/, May 29, 2010.

BERGER, Glenn 1969–

PERSONAL

Full name, Glenn Todd Berger; born August 26, 1969, in Smithtown, NY; married; children: three. *Education:* Graduated from Brown University, 1991, studied economics and Japanese.

Addresses: *Agent*—William Morris Endeavor Entertainment (WmEE2), One William Morris Place, Beverly Hills, CA 90212.

Career: Writer, producer, story editor, and consultant. Writing partner of Jonathan Aibel. Stand–up comedian at various venues. Public speaker at various venues. Worked as a management consultant in Boston, MA.

Member: Writers Guild of America, West.

Awards, Honors: Emmy Award nominations, 1998, 2001, and 2002, and Emmy Award, 1999, all outstanding animated program (for programming one hour or less), all with others, for *King of the Hill;* Annie Award nomination (with Jonathan Aibel), best writing in an animated feature production, International Animated Film Society, 2009, for *Kung Fu Panda.*

CREDITS

Television Work; Series:
Story editor, *Can't Hurry Love,* CBS, 1995–96.
Executive story editor, *King of the Hill* (animated), Fox, 1997.
Coproducer, *King of the Hill* (animated), Fox, 1997–98.
Supervising producer, *King of the Hill* (animated), Fox, 1998–99.
Co–executive producer, *King of the Hill* (animated), Fox, 2000–2003.
Executive producer and (with others) showrunner, *King of the Hill* (animated), Fox, 2001–2002.
Consulting producer, *Married to the Kellys* (also known as *Back to Kansas*), ABC, 2003–2004.

Television Work; Pilots:
Story editor, *Can't Hurry Love,* CBS, 1995.
Story editor, *King of the Hill* (animated), Fox, 1997.
Co–executive producer, *A.U.S.A.* (also known as *Adam Sullivan* and *Assistant United States Attorneys*), NBC, 2003.
Consulting producer, *Married to the Kellys* (also known as *Back to Kansas*), ABC, 2003.
Executive producer, *Great Neck,* Fox, 2003.
Executive producer, *Life with Lupe,* Fox, 2004.
Supervising producer, *Fox/Jeff Westbrook Man with Exes & Girlfriend Comedy,* Fox, c. 2004 (some sources cite c. 2005.

Television Appearances; Episodic:
Provided the voice of Ladybird for episodes of *King of the Hill* (animated), Fox.

Animated Film Work:
Coproducer, *Kung Fu Panda* (also known as *Kung Fu Panda: The IMAX Experience*), Paramount, 2008.
Consultant, *Shrek Forever After* (also known as *The Final Chapter, Forever After: The Final Chapter, Shrek: The Final Chapter, Shrek Forever, Shrek 4,*

Shrek Goes Fourth, and *Shrek Forever After: An IMAX 3D Experience*), Paramount, 2010.
Coproducer, *Kung Fu Panda: The Kaboom of Doom* (also known as *Kung Fu Panda 2*), 2011.

Stage Appearances:

Performed stand–up comedy at various venues, including venues in the Providence, RI area.

WRITINGS

Teleplays; with Others; Episodic:
"George Runs into an Old Friend," *The George Carlin Show,* Fox, 1994.
"Lou's the Boss," *Platypus Man,* UPN, 1995.
"Without a Hitch," *Platypus Man,* UPN, 1995.
Howie Mandel's "Sunny Skies," CBC and Showtime, 1995.
MAD TV (also known as *Mad TV* and *MADtv*), Fox, multiple episodes, 1995–97.
King of the Hill (animated), Fox, multiple episodes, 1997–2000.
"Till Death Do Us Part," *A.U.S.A.* (also known as *Adam Sullivan* and *Assistant United States Attorneys*), NBC, 2003.

With others, wrote questions for game shows broadcast by MTV. Some sources state that Berger wrote for other programs.

Teleplays; with Others; Pilots:
Great Neck, Fox, 2003.
Life with Lupe, Fox, 2004.

Screenplays for Animated Films; with Others:
Kung Fu Panda (also known as *Kung Fu Panda: The IMAX Experience*), Paramount, 2008.
Alvin and the Chipmunks: The Squeakquel (based on characters created by the Bagdasarian family; also known as *Alvin and the Chipmunks II* and *Alvin 2*), Twentieth Century–Fox, 2009.
Monsters vs. Aliens (also known as *Monsters vs Aliens: A Monstrous IMAX 3D Experience*), Paramount/DreamWorks, 2009.
Kung Fu Panda: The Kaboom of Doom (also known as *Kung Fu Panda 2*), 2011.

Screenplays:
(With others) *Maxx Powers and the Love Triangle of Doom* (also known as *Untitled (Disney/Alain Chabat/Romantic Comedy Project)*), c. 2003.

With others, wrote *Billion to One, Planet Fred, RRRrrrr!!! (RRRrrremake),* and *Untitled (Universal Pictures/Aibel & Berger Action Comedy)* (also known as *Untitled Jack Black Action Comedy*).

Screenplays; Uncredited Script Rewrite Work:
Freddy vs. Jason (also known as *Friday the 13th Part XI, FvJ, A Nightmare on Elm Street Part 8,* and *A Nightmare on Friday the 13th*), New Line Cinema, 2003.
Surviving Christmas, DreamWorks, 2004.
Sky High, Buena Vista, 2005.

Worked on other script rewrites, including *Disaster Area.*

Writings for the Stage:
Created stand–up comedy material to perform at various venues, including venues in the Providence, RI area.

Writings for Video Games; with Others:
Blazing Dragons, 1996.

BILL, Leo 1980–

PERSONAL

Born August 31, 1980, in Warwickshire, England; son of Stephen Bill (an actor and writer) and Sheila Kelley (an actress). *Education:* Graduated from the Royal Academy of Dramatic Art, 2001.

Addresses: *Agent*—Hamilton Hodell, Ltd., 66–68 Margaret St., 5th Floor, London W1W 8SR, England.

Career: Actor.

Awards, Honors: Jury Prize, best actor, Fantastic Fest (Austin), 2006, Salento Fear Fest Award, best actor, Green Glibb, best main actor, Weekend of Fear Horror Festival, and Special Jury Mention, Sitges, all 2007, and Chainsaw Award nomination, best actor, *Fangoria* magazine, 2009, all for *The Living and the Dead.*

CREDITS

Television Appearances; Series:
Troy Bloke, *Celeb* (also known as *Harry Enfield's "Celeb"*), BBC, 2002.

Television Appearances; Miniseries:
Storyenko (a drinker), *Crime and Punishment,* BBC, 2002.

Robert Ferrars, *Sense and Sensibility,* BBC and broadcast as part of *Masterpiece Theatre* (also known as *ExxonMobil Masterpiece Theatre, Masterpiece,* and *Mobil Masterpiece Theatre*), PBS, both 2008.

Television Appearances; Movies:
Paul, "Broke," *Screenplay,* Granada Television, 1991.
Mr. Peaches, *Surrealissimo: The Trial of Salvador Dali* (also known as *Surrealissimo*), BBC4, 2002.
Reis, *Eroica* (also known as *Beethoven's "Eroica"*), BBC2, 2003.
Flemming, *A Very Social Secretary,* Channel 4, 2005.

Television Appearances; Episodic:
Paul, "Ladies' Day," *Eh Brian! It's a Whopper,* Central, 1984.
Paul, "The Right Hook," *Eh Brian! It's a Whopper,* Central, 1984.
Mat, "The Domino Effect," *Attachments* (also known as *Attachments II*), BBC2, 2002.
(Uncredited) Corporal Eric Woods, "Strike Force" (also known as "Episode 8"), *Spooks* (also known as *MI–5* and *Spooks 2*), BBC and other channels, c. 2003.
Darren, "A Tale of Two Hamlets," *Midsomer Murders,* ITV, BBC, and Arts and Entertainment, 2003.
Terry, "The Man of Law's Tale," *Canterbury Tales,* BBC and BBC America, 2003.
Gerry White, *Messiah: The Promise* (also known as *Messiah Part III: The Promise, Messiah 3: The Promise,* and *Messiah III: The Promise*), BBC, 2004.
Richard, "The Meaning of Death: Part 1," *Silent Witness,* BBC, 2005.
Garry, "Idiot," *Lead Balloon,* BBC2, 2007.
Dave, *Jekyll,* BBC and BBC America, 2007.
Ryan Burns, *Ashes to Ashes,* BBC and BBC America, 2008.
Steve, *Home Time,* BBC2, multiple episodes in 2009.

Television Appearances; Pilots:
Boghead, *Bash,* BBC3, 2007.

Film Appearances:
Jim, *Gosford Park,* Universal, 2001.
Andrew (a young man), *All or Nothing* (also known as *Untitled Mike Leigh Project*), United Artists, 2002.
Private Jones, *28 Days Later ...* (also known as *28 Days Later;* longer version known as *29 Days Later*), Twentieth Century–Fox, 2002.
Private Leslie Cuthbertson, *Two Men Went to War* (also known as *2 Men Went to War*), Guerilla Films, 2002, Indican, 2004.
Danny, *LD 50 Lethal Dose* (also known as *LD50* and *Lethal Dose*), First Look, 2003.
Ronnie, *Vera Drake* (also known as *Untitled Mike Leigh Project*), Fine Line, 2004.
Garstin, *These Foolish Things,* 2005, Swipe Films/Outsider Pictures, 2006.

Harry Sampson, *Kinky Boots* (also known as *The Kinky Boot Factory*), 2005, Miramax, 2006.
James Brocklebank, *The Living and the Dead* (also known as *The Living in the Home of the Dead*), 2006, TLA Releasing, 2007.
Darwin and an orderly, *The Fall,* 2006, Roadside Attractions, 2008.
John Warren, *Becoming Jane* (also known as *Jane*), Miramax/Buena Vista International, 2007.
Norman Lloyd and Cinna the poet, *Me and Orson Welles* (also known as *Me & Orson*), Maximum Film Distribution, 2008, Freestyle Releasing/Warner Bros., 2009.
Hamish, *Alice in Wonderland* (also known as *Alice;* IMAX version released as *Alice in Wonderland: An IMAX 3D Experience*), Walt Disney Studios, 2010.

Stage Appearances:
Tony, *Beautiful Thing,* Sound Theatre, London, 2006.
Daniel, *The Reporter,* National Theatre, Cottesloe Theatre, London, 2007.
Lamb, *The Hothouse,* National Theatre, Lyttelton Theatre, London, 2007.
Tony, *The Observer,* National Theatre, Cottesloe Theatre, 2009.

Major Tours:
Fleance, *Macbeth,* British cities, 1994.

RECORDINGS

Videos:
Himself, *Wanderlust* (short documentary), Googly Films, 2008.

BLOMKAMP, Neill 1979–

PERSONAL

Born September 17, 1979, in Johannesburg, South Africa; companion of Terri Tatchell (a writer). *Education:* Vancouver Film School, graduated, 1998.

Addresses: *Agent*—Philip d'Amecourt, WME Entertainment, 9601 Wilshire Blvd., 3rd Floor, Beverly Hills, CA 90210.

Career: Director, writer, animator, and visual effects artist. Deadtime (production company), animator, c. 1995–97; visual effects artist for Embassy Visual Effects, Vancouver, British Columbia, Canada, and at

Rainmaker Digital Effects. Director of music videos and commercials, including work for Citroen motor vehicles, Nike athletic wear, and other products.

Awards, Honors: Emmy Award nomination and International Monitor Award (with others), both outstanding special visual effects for a series, 2001, for pilot *Dark Angel;* Visual Effects Society Award (with others), outstanding visual effects in a commercial, 2005, for a Citroen commercial; Satellite Award nominations, best director and best adapted screenplay (with Terri Tatchell), International Press Academy, Boston Society of Film Critics Award, best new filmmaker, Chicago Film Critics Association award, most promising filmmaker, Austin Film Critics Association, best first film, New Generation Award, Los Angeles Film Critics Association, and Phoenix Film Critics Society Award, "breakout behind the camera," all 2009, Academy Award nomination (with Tatchell), best adapted screenplay, Golden Globe Award nomination (with Tatchell), best screenplay, Film Award nominations, best director and best adapted screenplay (with Tatchell), British Academy of Film and Television Arts, Empire Award nomination, best director, Saturn Award nominations, best director and best writing (with Tatchell), Academy of Science Fiction, Fantasy, and Horror Films, Online Film Critics Society Award nominations, best director and best adapted screenplay (with Tatchell), and Broadcast Film Critics Association Award nomination (with Tatchell), best adapted screenplay, all 2010, all for *District 9.*

CREDITS

Film Director:
(And visual effects artist) *Alive in Joburg* (short film), Spy Films, 2005.
(And lead visual effects artist) *Adicolor Yellow* (short film), RSA Films, 2006.
Tempbot (short film), Spy Films/W K Entertainment, 2006.
(With others) *Crossing the Line* (short film), Red Digital Cinema, 2008.
District 9, TriStar, 2009.

Film Work; Other:
Lead 3D animator, *3000 Miles to Graceland,* Warner Bros., 2001.

Television 3D Animator; Series:
Mercy Point, UPN, c. 1998.

Also animator for the series *First Wave,* Sci–Fi Channel; *Smallville* (also known as *Smallville: Beginnings*), The WB; and *Stargate SG–1.*

Television 3D Animator; Other:
(Uncredited) *Aftershock: Earthquake in New York* (mini-series), CBS, 1999.

(Uncredited) Lead animator, *Dark Angel* (pilot; also known as *James Cameron's "Dark Angel"*), Fox, 2000.

Television Appearances; Specials:
Best Ever Ads 2, ITV1, 2006.

Television Appearances; Episodic:
Dias de cine, 2009.
Le grand journal de Canal+, 2009.
Cinema 3, 2009.

RECORDINGS

Videos:
Alien Generation: The Visual Effects of "District 9," Sony Pictures Home Entertainment, 2009.
Conception and Design: Creating the World of "District 9," Sony Pictures Home Entertainment, 2009.
"District 9": Comic–Con Extravaganza, Sony Pictures Home Entertainment, 2009.
Metamorphosis: The Transformation of Wikus, Sony Pictures Home Entertainment, 2009.
The Alien Agenda: A Filmmaker's Log, Sony Pictures Home Entertainment, 2009.
Innovation: The Acting and Improvisation of "District 9," Sony Pictures Home Entertainment, 2009.

Director of music videos, including "Let's Go" by Live-onrelease, 2003, and "Let's Dance" by Edwin and the Pressure.

WRITINGS

Film:
Adicolor Yellow (short film), RSA Films, 2006.
(With Terry Tatchell) *District 9,* TriStar, 2009.

BLUM, Jason 1970(?)–

PERSONAL

Born c. 1970; son of Irving Blum (an art dealer and gallery proprietor) and Shirley Hopps Blum–Resek (an art historian and writer; maiden name, Neilsen). *Education:* Attended Vassar College.

Addresses: *Office*—Blumhouse Productions, 5555 Melrose Ave., B. P. Schulberg Building, Room 113, Los Angeles, CA 90038. *Agent*—Creative Artists Agency, 2000 Avenue of the Stars, Los Angeles, CA 90067.

Career: Producer. Malaparte Theater Company, former producing director; Arrow Entertainment, former executive vice president; Miramax Films, New York City, co–head of acquisitions and coproductions department, 1996–2000; Blumhouse Productions, Los Angeles, founder and producer, 2000—; producing partner of Oren Peli and Steven Schneider. Participated in functions in the art work; worked as a real estate agent.

Awards, Honors: Independent Spirit Award nomination (with Oren Peli), best first feature, Independent Features Project/West, 2010, for *Paranormal Activity;* named to the nifty fifty list, a list of promising talent, *New York Times Magazine,* 2010.

CREDITS

Film Executive Producer:
One Way Out, Arrow Releasing, 1996.
Hamlet, Miramax, 2000.
The Adventures of Tom Thumb & Thumbelina (animated), Miramax, 2002.
Stagedoor (documentary), Gidalya Pictures, 2006.
Graduation, Redwood Palms Pictures/Truly Indie, 2007.
Co–executive producer, *The Reader,* The Weinstein Company, 2008.

Film Producer:
Associate producer, *Kicking and Screaming,* Trimark Pictures, 1995.
Baggage (short film), Stolen Car Productions, 1997.
The Darwin Awards (also known as *Darwin Awards*), Bauer Martinez Studios, 2006.
(Uncredited) *Paranormal Activity,* 2007, Paramount/DreamWorks, 2009.
The Accidental Husband, Momentum Pictures, 2008, Sony Pictures Home Entertainment, 2009.
Area 51, Paramount, 2010.
Paranormal Activity 2, Paramount, 2010.
Tooth Fairy, Twentieth Century–Fox, 2010.
Insidious (also known as *The Further*), 2011.

Worked on other film projects.

Film Work; Other:
Production assistant, *Air America,* TriStar, 1990.

Television Producer; Movies:
Executive producer, *Hysterical Blindness,* HBO, 2002.
Easy Six (also known as *Easy Sex*), Showtime, 2003.
The Fever, HBO, 2004.
Generation S.L.U.T. (also known as *Generation SLUT* and *Generation Slut*), HBO, c. 2005.
Griffin and Phoenix (also known as *Griffin & Phoenix* and *Love in Manhattan*), Lifetime, 2006.

Television Producer; Pilots:
Washingtonienne, HBO, 2009.
Executive producer, *The Follower,* HBO, 2010.

OTHER SOURCES

Periodicals:
New York Times Magazine, January 27, 2010.

BOECHER, Katherine 1981–
(Pippi B., Pippi Boecher, Pippi)

PERSONAL

Full name, Katherine Camille Boecher; born August 10, 1981, in Beaumont, TX; married Lukas Behnken (an actor), July 16, 2006. *Education:* Studied acting at Playhouse West; studied improvisation with the Groundlings; also studied acting with Warner Loughlin and Lesly Kahn. *Avocational Interests:* Horseback riding, gourmet cooking, yoga, and biking.

Addresses: *Agent*—Innovative Artists, 1505 10th St., Santa Monica, CA 90401. *Manager*—Matt Sherman Management, 9107 Wilshire Blvd., Suite 225, Beverly Hills, CA 90210. *Publicist*—Metro Public Relations, 9025 Wilshire Blvd., Penthouse, Beverly Hills, CA 90211.

Career: Actress. Previously worked as a model. Active in animal rights; soup kitchen volunteer.

CREDITS

Film Appearances:
Amber, *Scream at the Sound of the Beep,* 2002.
(As Pippi B.) *Shop Club,* 2002.
(As Pippi B.) Dylan's other girl, *Crossroads* (also known as *Not a Girl*), Paramount, 2002.
(As Pippi) Pippi, *Special* (short film), Chanticleer Films, 2003.
(As Pippi) Office worker, *Just Hustle,* 2004.
(As Pippi) Ginny May, *ShadowBox,* Spooked Television Releasing, 2005.
Angi, *Throwing Stars* (also known as *Who's the Monkey?*), 2007.
(As Pippi) Ginny May, *DarkPlace,* Spooked Television Releasing, 2007.
Clara, *The Last Word,* Image Entertainment, 2008.
Evelyn, *The Patient* (short film), 2009.
(As Pippi Boecher) Heather, *Twice as Dead,* Push, 2009.

Rosemary, *The Crooked Eye* (animated), Hit the Fan Productions, 2009.

Tracey, *The Chronicles of Holly–Weird* (short film), Under Dog Distribution, 2009.

Creel, *The Spy Next Door* (also known as *Double Mission*), Lions Gate Films, 2010.

Television Appearances; Movies:

(As Pippi) Luna, *Trash,* 2003.

Television Appearances; Episodic:

(As Pippi) Student number one, "The Screw–Up," *That's Life,* CBS, 2000.

(As Pippi) Bobbi, *Undressed* (also known as *MTV's "Undressed"*), MTV, 2001.

(As Pippi) Jenny, "Blood, Sugar, Sex, Magic," *ER,* NBC, 2001.

(As Pippi) Greta, "Reese's Job," *Malcolm in the Middle,* Fox, 2002.

(As Pippi Boecher) Red Rider, "Precious Metal," *CSI: Crime Scene Investigation* (also known as *CSI: Las Vegas* and *C.S.I.*), CBS, 2003.

Sparkle, *The Tracy Morgan Show,* NBC, 2003.

Nicole Jordan, "Summer in the City," *CSI: NY* (also known as *CSI: New York*), CBS, 2005.

Annie, "The Wheel," *Mad Men,* AMC, 2007.

Callie Rivers, "Split Ends," *The Closer,* TNT, 2008.

Alena, "Chapter Nine 'Turn and Face the Stranger,'" *Heroes,* NBC, 2009.

Lilith, "The Monster at the End of This Book," *Supernatural,* The CW, 2009.

Lilith, "Lucifer Rising," *Supernatural,* The CW, 2009.

Jenny Stafford, "Soul Music," *Past Life,* Fox, 2010.

Stage Appearances:

Brady Mason, *Devil's Night,* Sherry Theatre, Los Angeles, 2006.

OTHER SOURCES

Electronic:

Katherine Boecher Home Page, http://www.katherineboecher.com, May 29, 2010.

BOSLEY, Tom 1927–2010

PERSONAL

Full name, Thomas Edward Bosley; born October 1 (some sources cite October 13), 1927, in Chicago, IL; died of lung cancer, October 19, 2010, in Rancho Mirage, CA. Actor. Best remembered as Howard Cunningham, the level-headed patriarch of the classic

1970s sitcom *Happy Days,* actor Tom Bosley was also a Tony award-winning Broadway performer. He made his stage debut in a 1947 production of *Our Town* with the Canterbury Players while still a law student at Chicago's DePaul University. After moving to New York, he studied at the Actors Studio. He first appeared on Broadway in *The Power and the Glory* in 1958. His 1959 breakthrough performance as the lead in the musical *Fiorello!* earned a Tony Award in 1960. Bosley transitioned to television in the early 1960s as a guest on the series *Car 54, Where Are You?*; *Get Smart*; *The Mod Squad*; and *Bonanza* before landing recurring roles in *The Debbie Reynolds Show* in 1969 and *The Sandy Duncan Show* in 1972. He appeared in all 255 episodes of *Happy Days* from 1974 to 1984. Later roles include those in the series *The Love Boat* and *Murder, She Wrote* and the lead in the series *Father Dowling Mysteries* from 1987 to 1991. Bosley returned to Broadway in the mid-1990s with parts in the musicals *Beauty and the Beast* and *Cabaret.* His notable film appearances include supporting roles in *Love With the Proper Stranger, Divorce American Style,* and *OHaras Wife,* and his last film role was in the 2010 comedy *The Back-up Plan.*

PERIODICALS

Entertainment Weekly, October 19, 2010.
Guardian, October 20, 2010.
Independent, October 28, 2010.
Los Angeles Times, October 20, 2010.
New York Times, October 19, 2010.
Variety, October 19, 2010.

BOWLER, Grant 1968–

PERSONAL

Born July 18, 1968; in Auckland, New Zealand; raised in Australia; married Roxanne Wilson (an actress), January 21, 2001; children: Edie, Zeke. *Education:* Graduated from the National Institute of Dramatic Art (Australia), 1991; studied at The Actors Centre and elsewhere.

Addresses: *Agent*—Sue Barnett & Associates, 1/96 Albion St., Surry Hills, New South Wales 2010, Australia; Don Buchwald & Associates, 6500 Wilshire Blvd., Suite 2200, Los Angeles, CA 90048. *Manager*—Untitled Entertainment, 1801 Century Park East, Suite 700, Los Angeles, CA 90067.

Career: Actor. Some sources cite work as a director.

CREDITS

Television Appearances; Series:
Constable Wayne Patterson, *Blue Heelers* (also known as *Boys in Blue*), Seven Network, 1994–96.
Garth Stephens, *Pacific Drive* (also known as *Pacific Beach*), Nine Network, 1996–97.
Dr. Archibald "Arch" Craven, *Medivac* (also known as *Adrenalin Junkies*), Ten Network, 1996–98.
Host and presenter, *The Mole* (also known as *The Mole: The Amazing Game, The Mole in Paradise,* and *The Mole: Who Is the Traitor?*), Seven Network, 2000–2003.
Mark Waters, *Something in the Air*, Australian Broadcasting Corporation, 2001–2002.
Greg Steele, *Always Greener*, Seven Network, 2002.
Nigel "Mac" MacPherson, *All Saints* (also known as *All Saints: Medical Response Unit*), Seven Network, 2004–2005.
Narrator, *Border Security: Australia's Front Line* (documentary; also known as *Border Security* and *Nothing to Declare*), Seven Network, 2004–2008.
Wolfgang West, *Outrageous Fortune*, TV3, 2005–2009.
Detective Ray Driscoll, *Canal Road*, Nine Network, 2008.
Connor Owens, *Ugly Betty* (also known as *Betty in the USA, Betty the Ugly, Alles Betty!, Betty en los Estados Unidos, Cimlapsztori, Fula Betty,* and *Ruma Betty*), ABC, 2008–10.
Coot, *True Blood*, HBO, beginning 2010.

Appeared in other programs, including work as a narrator, *Murder Squad*, 7 Network; and as a presenter, *Reel Race* (also known as *Reel Race 2*).

Television Appearances; Miniseries:
Lieutenant Peter Holmes, *On the Beach* (also known as *USS Charleston*), 7 Network and Showtime, 2000.
Black rat, *Through My Eyes* (also known as *Through My Eyes: The Lindy Chamberlain Story* and *Through My Eyes: The True Story of Lindy Chamberlain*), Seven Network, 2004.

Television Appearances; Movies:
Mike Heyns, *Close Contact*, Seven Network, 1999.
Jack, *Finding Hope* (also known as *Flying Fox* and *Hope Flies*), Ten Network, 2001.

Television Appearances; Episodic:
Bob Palance, "Someone You Know," *Halifax f.p.* (also known as *Halifax f.p.: Someone You Know*), Nine Network, 1997.
Peter Simms, *Wildside*, Australian Broadcasting Corporation, 1998.
Darren Rigg, "Time Bombs," *All Saints* (also known as *All Saints: Medical Response Unit*), Seven Network, 1999.
Darren Rigg, "True Love and the Blues," *All Saints* (also known as *All Saints: Medical Response Unit*), Seven Network, 1999.
Sean Peck, "The Dingo," *Stingers*, Nine Network, 1999.
Shaman Liko, "That Old Black Magic," *Farscape* (also known as *Space Chase* and *Farscape—Verschollen im All*), Sci-Fi Channel, Nine Network, and BBC, 1999.
Montague Fitzsimmonds, "London Calling," *The Lost World* (also known as *Sir Arthur Conan Doyle's "The Lost World"*), syndicated, 2000.
Sean Peck, "No Way Out," *Stingers*, Nine Network, 2000.
Sean Peck, "Which Bank?," *Stingers*, Nine Network, 2000.
Sean Peck, "Dog Eat Dog," *Stingers*, Nine Network, 2001.
Steve Petrovic, *White Collar Blue*, Ten Network, 2002.
Jarred Wuchowski, "Fool for Love," *McLeod's Daughters*, Nine Network, 2004.
Captain Gault, "Cabin Fever," *Lost*, ABC, 2008.
Captain Gault, "Ji Yeon," *Lost*, ABC, 2008.
Captain Gault, "Meet Kevin Johnson," *Lost*, ABC, 2008.
Himself, *Entertainment Tonight* (also known as *Entertainment This Week, E.T., ET Weekend,* and *This Week in Entertainment*), syndicated, 2008.
Daniel, "Sheik Your Booty," *Satisfaction*, Showtime Australia and other channels, 2009.
Daniel, "Tess," *Satisfaction*, Showtime Australia and other channels, 2009.
Daniel, "Non Standard Package," *Satisfaction*, Showtime Australia and other channels, 2010.

Film Appearances:
Jason, *Change of Heart* (also known as *A Change of Heart* and *Image Counts*), 1999.
Ron, *Calling Gerry Molloy* (short film), Cornerstone Pictures, 2003.
Town priest, *Ned*, Becker Entertainment/Ocean Pictures Pty Limited/Icon Entertainment International, 2003.
Sam, *One of the Oldest Con Games* (short film), 2004.
Harry, *The Fall of Night* (also known as *Midnight Reckoning*), Winter Star Productions, 2007.
Jesus Christ, *The City of Gardens*, 2010.
Harry Rearden, *Atlas Shrugged*, 2011.
Captain James Cregg, *The Killer Elite*, c. 2011.

Appeared as the husband in *The Sleeper* (short film).

Stage Appearances:
Joe Farkas, *The Last Night of Ballyhoo*, Marian Street Theatre, New South Wales, Australia, c. 1999.
Steve, *The Return*, Perth Theatre Company, The Rechabites' Hall, Northbridge, Western Australia, Australia, 2002.

Appeared as Lefranc, *Deathwatch*, Threshold Productions; appeared in *Happiness*, ART Inc./The Taylor Square Festival; made a guest appearance in *The Real*

Live Brady Bunch, CMA Productions Pty, Ltd.; and appeared in *Elegies for Angels, Punks and Raging Queens,* Threshold Productions, National Institute of Dramatic Art, Australia.

Major Tours:

Duke of Venice, *The Merchant of Venice,* The Bell Shakespeare Company, Australian cities, 1992.

Fortinbras and Marcellus, *Hamlet,* The Bell Shakespeare Company, Australian cities, 1992.

Edward IV, *Richard III,* The Bell Shakespeare Company, Australian cities, 1992 and 1993.

Laertes, *Hamlet,* The Bell Shakespeare Company, Australian cities, 1993.

Mercutio, *Romeo & Juliet,* The Bell Shakespeare Company, Australian cities, 1993.

BRENNAN, Eileen 1932–

PERSONAL

Full name, Verla Eileen Regina Brennan (some sources spell the surname "Brennen"); born September 3, 1932 (various sources cite 1935 or 1938), in Los Angeles, CA; daughter of John Gerald (a doctor) and Regina "Jeanne" (a silent film actress; maiden name, Menehan) Brennan; married David John Lampson, December 28, c. 1968 (divorced, c. 1974); children: Samuel John (a singer), Patrick Oliver (an actor). *Education:* Attended Georgetown University; studied acting at American Academy of Dramatic Arts, 1955–56. *Religion:* Roman Catholic.

Addresses: Agent—David Shapira Associates, 193 North Robertson Blvd., Beverly Hills, CA 90211–2103. *Manager*—Jessica Moresco, Unified Management, 625 North Screenland Dr., Burbank, CA 91505.

Career: Actress. Performed in New York City cabarets with Charles Nelson Reilly.

Member: Actors' Equity Association, Screen Actors Guild, American Federation of Television and Radio Artists, American Guild of Variety Artists.

Awards, Honors: Page One Award, Newspaper Guild, *Theatre World* Award, promising new personality, Obie Award, best actress, *Village Voice,* and Kit–Kat Artists and Models Award, all 1960, for *Little Mary Sunshine;* Film Award nomination, best supporting actress, British Academy of Film and Television Arts, 1973, for *The Last Picture Show;* Academy Award nomination, best supporting actress, 1981, for *Private Benjamin;* Emmy Award nomination, outstanding lead actress in a comedy series, 1981, for "The Boss's Wife," *Taxi;* Emmy Award, outstanding supporting actress in a television comedy, variety, or music series, 1981, 1982 and 1983, and Golden Globe Award, best actress in a comedy or musical television series, 1982 and 1983, all for *Private Benjamin;* Emmy Award nomination, outstanding guest actress in a comedy series, 1989, for "The Little Match Girl," *Newhart;* Emmy Award nomination, best guest actress in a drama series, 1991, for "Sifting the Ashes," *thirtysomething;* Emmy Award nomination, outstanding guest actress in a comedy series, 2004, for *Will & Grace.*

CREDITS

Film Appearances:

(Film debut) Eunice Tase, *Divorce: American Style,* Columbia, 1967.

Genevieve, *The Last Picture Show,* Columbia, 1971.

Darlene, *Scarecrow,* Warner Bros., 1973.

Billie, *The Sting,* Universal, 1973.

Mrs. Walker, *Daisy Miller,* Paramount, 1974.

Elizabeth, *At Long Last Love* (also known as *Peter Bogdanovich's "At Long Last Love"*), Twentieth Century–Fox, 1975.

Paula Hollinger, *Hustle,* Paramount, 1975.

Tess Skeffington, *Murder by Death,* Columbia, 1976.

Penelope, *The Great Smokey Roadblock* (also known as *The Last of the Cowboys*), Dimension Films, 1976.

Betty DeBoop, *The Cheap Detective* (also known as *Neil Simon's "The Cheap Detective"*), Columbia, 1978.

Mother, *FM* (also known as *Citizen's Band*), Universal, 1978.

Captain Doreen Lewis, *Private Benjamin,* Warner Bros., 1980.

Mrs. Jefferson, *Pandemonium* (also known as *Thursday the 12th*), Metro–Goldwyn–Mayer, 1981.

Gail Corbin, *The Funny Farm,* New World, 1982.

Mrs. Peacock, *Clue* (also known as *Clue: The Movie*), Paramount, 1985.

Stella, *Sticky Fingers,* Spectrafilm, 1988.

Hotel desk clerk, *Rented Lips,* CineWorld, 1988.

Miss Bannister, *The New Adventures of Pippi Longstocking,* Columbia, 1988.

Judith, *It Had to Be You,* Limelite Studios, 1989.

Mrs. Wilkerson, *Stella,* Buena Vista, 1990.

Genevieve Morgan, *Texasville,* Columbia, 1990.

Judy, *White Palace,* Universal, 1990.

Laura, *Joey Takes a Cab,* 1991.

Picture This—The Times of Peter Bogdanovich in Archer City, Texas (documentary), 1991.

Frieda, *I Don't Buy Kisses Anymore,* Skouras, 1992.

Voice of Rose, *Recycle Rex,* 1993.

Mrs. Randazzo, *Nunzio's Second Cousin,* Strand Releasing, 1994.

Sister Margaret, *Reckless,* 1995.

Mother Superior, *Changing Habits,* A–Pix Entertainment, 1996.

Mom, *Pants on Fire,* Elevator Pictures, 1997.

Mrs. Randozza, "Nunzio's Second Cousin," *Boys Life 2,* 1997.

Pamela "Mimi" Applegate, *The Last Great Ride,* 1999.

Moonglow, Latitude 20, 2000.

The cat lady, *Jeepers Creepers* (also known as *JEEpERs CrEEpers* and *Jeepers Creepers—What's Eating You?*), United Artists, 2001.

Minnie Hitchcock, *Dumb Luck,* Desert Rock, 2001.

Mrs. Cresswell, *Comic Book Villains,* Lions Gate Films, 2002.

(Uncredited) Mrs. Drucker, *Cheaper by the Dozen,* Twentieth Century–Fox, 2003.

Mrs. Cherkiss, *The Amateurs* (also known as *The Moguls*), Newmarket Films, 2005.

Carol Fields, *Miss Congeniality 2: Armed & Fabulous,* Warner Bros., 2005.

Gram Malone, *Naked Run,* A Plus Entertainment, 2007.

Agnes, *Peanut Butter* (short film), Tropfest, 2007.

Aunt Birdy, *The Kings of Appletown,* Moresco Productions/Oak Films, 2009.

Television Appearances; Series:

Regular, *Rowan and Martin's Laugh–In* (also known as *Laugh–In*), NBC, 1968.

Ma Packer, *All that Glitters,* syndicated, 1977.

Felicia Winters, *13 Queens Boulevard,* ABC, 1979.

Kit Flanagan, *A New Kind of Family,* ABC, 1979–80.

Captain Doreen Lewis, *Private Benjamin,* CBS, 1981–83.

Kate Halloran, *Off the Rack,* ABC, 1985.

Voice of Miss Dirge, *Gravedale High* (also known as *Rick Moranis in "Gravedale High"*), NBC, 1990.

Mrs. Gladys Bink, a recurring role, *7th Heaven* (also known as *7th Heaven: Beginnings*), The WB, between 1996 and 2006.

Zandra, a recurring role, *Will & Grace,* NBC, between 2001 and 2006.

Television Appearances; Movies:

Hallie, *The Star Wagon,* 1967.

Amy, *Playmates,* ABC, 1972.

Baba Goya, *Nourish the Beast,* 1974.

Mary Thatcher, "Come Die with Me," *Wide World Mystery,* 1974.

Mrs. Lindholm, *My Father's House,* ABC, 1975.

Ann Muldoon, *The Night that Panicked America,* ABC, 1975.

Carol Werner, *The Death of Richie* (also known as *Richie*), NBC, 1977.

Mary Jensen, *When She Was Bad ...,* ABC, 1979.

Marie, *My Old Man,* CBS, 1979.

Jessy, *When the Circus Came to Town,* CBS, 1981.

Sara Davis, *Incident at Crestridge,* CBS, 1981.

Judith, *The Fourth Wise Man,* ABC, 1985.

Mrs. Piper/Widow Hubbard, *Babes in Toyland,* NBC, 1986.

Sylvia Zimmerman, *Blood Vows: The Story of a Mafia Wife,* NBC, 1987.

Maude Roberti, *Going to the Chapel* (also known as *Wedding Day* and *Wedding Day Blues*), NBC, 1988.

Charlotte Raynor, *Deadly Intentions ... Again?,* ABC, 1991.

Vicky Martin, *Taking Back My Life: The Nancy Ziegenmeyer Story* (also known as *The Rape of Nancy Ziegenmeyer*), CBS, 1992.

Martha Catlin, *Poisoned by Love: The Kern County Murders* (also known as *Blind Angel* and *Murder So Sweet*), CBS, 1993.

Minnie Gray, *Precious Victims,* CBS, 1993.

Barbara Mannix, *My Name Is Kate,* ABC, 1994.

Sada, *Take Me Home Again* (also known as *The Lies Boys Tell*), NBC, 1994.

The Who–Villain, *In Search of Dr. Seuss,* TNT, 1994.

Clara Cook, *Trail of Tears,* NBC, 1995.

Principal Handel, *Freaky Friday,* ABC, 1995.

"First Joe," *Toothless,* ABC, 1997.

Joan Van Etten, *The Hollow,* ABC Family, 2004.

Television Appearances; Specials:

"Infancy and Childhood," *NET Playhouse,* PBS, 1967.

Delafield's mistress, *Knuckle,* PBS, 1975.

Herself, *At Long Last Cole* (also known as *At Long Last Cole: What a Swell Party It Was!*), 1975.

The 33rd Annual Primetime Emmy Awards, 1981.

Aunt Angelique Lane, *Kraft Salutes Walt Disney World's 10th Anniversary* (also known as *Walt Disney World's 10th Anniversary*), CBS, 1982.

Maggie, *Lily for President?,* CBS, 1982.

Mill worker, "Working," *American Playhouse,* PBS, 1982.

The Screen Actors Guild 50th Anniversary Celebration, CBS, 1984.

The History of White People in America (also known as *The History of White People in America: Volume I*), 1985.

The History of White People in America: Volume II, 1986.

Narrator, *Justiceville,* 1987.

Television Appearances; Miniseries:

Glenda, *The Blue Knight,* NBC, 1973.

Annie Gray, *Black Beauty,* NBC, 1978.

Tessie, "1996," *If These Walls Could Talk,* HBO, 1996.

Television Appearances; Pilots:

Kate Halloran, *Off the Rack,* ABC, 1984.

Siobhan Owens, "Off Duty," *CBS Summer Playhouse,* CBS, 1988.

Agnes, *Blossom,* NBC, 1990.

Mrs. Coffin, *Andrea,* CBS, 1993.

Television Appearances; Episodic:

The Ed Sullivan Show (also known as *Toast of the Town*), 1960, 1963.

Paula Tardy, "Ladies Man," *The Ghost & Mrs. Muir*, 1970.

Alice, "Photo Finish," *The Most Deadly Game*, 1970.

Angelique McCarthy, "The Elevator Story," *All in the Family*, CBS, 1972.

Dora, "The Night of the Wizard," *McMillan & Wife* (also known as *McMillan*), NBC, 1972.

"In Case of Emergency, Notify Clint Eastwood," *Jigsaw*, 1973.

"The Prodigal Father," *Insight*, 1975.

Anita Wilson, "Blood Relations," *Barnaby Jones*, 1975.

Julie Lowring, "A House of Prayer, a Den of Thieves," *Kojak*, 1975.

Dinah!, 1977.

The Hollywood Squares, 1978.

"Fans of the Kosko Show," *Visions*, 1978.

Ruth MacKenzie, "Thy Boss's Wife," *Taxi*, ABC, 1981.

Host, *The Shape of Things*, NBC, 1982.

The Tonight Show Starring Johnny Carson, NBC, 1983.

Helen Foster, "Vicki and the Fugitive/Lady in the Window/Stolen Years/Dutch Treat: Parts 1 & 2," *The Love Boat*, ABC, 1984.

Brenda Babcock, "The Love that Lies," *Magnum, P.I.*, CBS, 1987.

Marion (or Marian) Simpson, "Old Habits Die Hard," *Murder, She Wrote*, CBS, 1987.

The New Hollywood Squares, 1987.

Mrs. O'Brien, *The Cavanaughs*, CBS, 1988.

Corinne Denby, "Draw Partner," *Newhart*, CBS, 1988.

Corinne Denby, "The Little Match Girl," *Newhart*, CBS, 1989.

Mrs. Annabelle Shrike, "Touched with Fire," *The Ray Bradbury Theatre*, USA Network, 1990.

"Mother Knows Best," *American Dreamer*, 1991.

Agnes, "Blossom Blossoms," *Blossom*, NBC, 1991.

Agnes, "Dad's Girlfriend," *Blossom*, NBC, 1991.

Agnes, "My Sister's Keeper," *Blossom*, NBC, 1991.

Margaret Weston, "Sifting the Ashes," *thirtysomething*, 1991.

Wanda, "Heavy Meddle," *Home Improvement*, ABC, 1992.

Ruth, "Till Death Do We Part," *Tales from the Crypt*, HBO, 1993.

Claudia, "Stepping Back," *Tribeca*, 1993.

Dina, "The Hands of Time," *Jack's Place*, ABC, 1993.

Voice of Lilith DuPrave, "The Stork Exchange," *Bonkers* (animated; also known as *Disney's "Bonkers"*), 1993.

Voice of Lilith DuPrave, "The Toon that Ate Hollywood," *Bonkers* (animated; also known as *Disney's "Bonkers"*), 1993.

Voice of Lilith DuPrave, "When the Spirit Moves You," *Bonkers* (animated; also known as *Disney's "Bonkers"*), 1993.

Voice of Lilith DuPrave, "Going Bonkers," *Bonkers* (animated; also known as *Disney's "Bonkers"*), 1993.

Loretta Lee, "Dear Deadly," *Murder, She Wrote*, CBS, 1994.

Sister Bernadette, *Winnetka Road*, NBC, 1994.

Joelle Harper, "Mean Streets," *Walker, Texas Ranger*, CBS, 1995.

Irma, "Are We There Yet?," *Thunder Alley*, ABC, 1995.

Betty, "Let the Games Begin," *ER*, NBC, 1996.

Betty, "Don't Ask, Don't Tell," *ER*, NBC, 1996.

Betty, "Last Call," *ER*, NBC, 1996.

Dottie McGrail, "Air Judy," *Jumanji*, 1997.

Inspector No. 10, "Cheating On Sheila," *Mad about You*, NBC, 1997.

Grammy Anderson, "Veronica's First Thanksgiving," *Veronica's Closet*, NBC, 1997.

Loretta Bettina Rooney, "Downtime," *Nash Bridges*, CBS, 1998.

Dolores, "The Last Day of the Rest of Your Life," *Touched by an Angel*, CBS, 1999.

Irene's mother, "Gentleman Caller," *The Fearing Mind*, 2000.

"End Game," *Arli$$*, HBO, 2002.

Marge, "My Fair Larry," *Lizzie McGuire*, The Disney Channel, 2003.

Evelyn Knightly, "Coming Clean," *Strong Medicine*, Lifetime, 2003.

Stage Appearances:

(Off–Broadway debut) Title role, *Little Mary Sunshine* (musical), Orpheum Theatre, 1959–61.

Anna Leonowens, *The King and I* (musical), City Center Theatre, New York City, 1963.

Merry May Glockenspiel, *The Student Gypsy, or The Prince of Liederkranz* (musical), Fifty–Fourth Street Theatre, New York City, 1963.

Irene Molloy, *Hello, Dolly!* (musical), St. James Theatre, New York City, 1964–66.

And Where She Stops Nobody Knows, Center Theatre Group, Mark Taper Forum, Los Angeles, 1976.

Gethesemane Springs, Center Theatre Group, Mark Taper Forum Laboratory production, Los Angeles, 1977.

Triptych, Center Theatre Group, Mark Taper Forum Laboratory production, 1978.

Hannah Mae Binder, *A Couple of White Chicks Sitting around Talking*, Astor Place Theatre, New York City, 1980.

Maxine Faulk, *The Night of the Iguana*, Morris Mechanic Theatre, Baltimore, MD, 1985.

Virginia Noyes, *It's Only a Play*, Center Theatre Group, Ahmanson Theatre, Los Angeles, 1992.

Mrs. Malloy, *Hello, Dolly* (musical), New York City, 1996.

Manny, *The Cripple of Inishmaan*, New York Shakespeare Festival, Estelle R. Newman Theatre, New York City, 1998.

Also appeared in *Camelot*; *Bells Are Ringing*; *An Evening with Eileen Brennan* (solo show); and *Guys and Dolls*.

Major Tours:
Annie Sullivan, *The Miracle Worker,* U.S. cities, 1961–62.
Ellen Manville, *Luv,* U.S. cities, 1967.

RECORDINGS

Videos:
The Last Picture Show: A Look Back, 1999.
Behind the Peepers: The Making of "Jeepers Creepers" (also known as *Behind the Peepers*), 2002.
The Art of "The Sting," Universal Studios Home Video, 2005.

BROOKE, Amber
  See WALLACE, Amber

BROWN, Jamie Anne
  See ALLMAN, Jamie Anne

BUKOWSKY, Dean
  See JONES, Evan

BYRNES, Jim 1948–
  (Jim Byrne)

PERSONAL

Full name, James Thomas Kevin Byrnes; born September 22, 1948, in St. Louis, MO; father, a municipal accountant; mother, a homemaker; companion of Robyn Post; children: (with former companion, Annette) Serene; (with Post) Caitlin. *Education:* Studied acting at Boston University and St. Louis University.

Addresses: *Agent*—Characters Talent Agency, 1505 2nd Ave., Vancouver, British Columbia V6H 3Y4, Canada.

Career: Actor and musician. Appeared in stage productions with a St. Louis repertory company, c. 1964; The Jim Byrnes Band, founder and musician, 1981; Easter Seals spokesperson, 1990; appeared in television commercials for Arby's restaurants, 1995, and radio ads for Vancouver Grizzlies NBA basketball, 1996. Also worked as a blues musician, fisherman, and shepherd. *Military service:* U.S. Army, 1969; served a tour of duty in Vietnam.

Awards, Honors: Genie Award nomination, best performance by an actor in a supporting role, Academy of Canadian Cinema and Television, 1993, for *Harmony Cats;* JUNO Award, best blues/gospel album, Canadian Academy of Recording Arts and Sciences, 1996, for *That River.*

CREDITS

Film Appearances:
(As Jim Byrne) Party singer, *Out of the Blue* (also known as *No Looking Back* and *Plus rien a perdre*), 1980.
Band leader, *The First Season,* 1988.
Frank Hay, *Harmony Cats,* Triboro Entertainment Group, 1993.
Dewey Moore, *Whale Music,* Seventh Art Releasing, 1994.
Lieutenant Rayburn, *Suspicious Agenda,* 1994.
Lieutenant Jim "The Loot" Garrity, *Dream Man,* 1995.
Lieutenant Rayburn, *Under the Gun,* 1995.
Rod MacArthur, *Starlight,* Astral, 1996.
Dr. Glen Green, *Drive, She Said,* Beyond Films, 1997.
(Uncredited) Larry Millard, *Masterminds* (also known as *Trouble Border*), 1997.
Voice of Pop, *The Animated Adventures of Tom Sawyer* (animated), 1998.
(As Jim Byrne) Voice of elf crow member number two, *Rudolph, the Red–Nosed Reindeer: The Movie,* 1998.
Voice, *Monster Mash,* Universal Studios Home Video, 2000.
Joe Dawson, *Highlander: Endgame,* Miramax, 2000.
George, *My Bosses's Daughter,* Dimension Films, 2003.
Harvey, *Fetching Cody,* Panorama Entertainment, 2005.
Local merchant, *Edison* (also known as *Edison Force*), Sony Pictures Home Entertainment, 2005.
Voice of Chief Quimby, *Inspector Gadget's Biggest Caper Ever* (animated), Lions Gate Films Home Entertainment, 2005.
Joe Dawson, *Highlander: The Source,* Lions Gate Films, 2007.
Voice of Doc and Rudy, *Highlander: The Search for Vengeance* (animated), Starz Media, 2007.
Ivan, *Heart of a Dragon,* 2008.

Film Additional Voices:
Mummies Alive! The Legend Begins (animated), 1998.

Television Appearances; Series:
Daniel Benjamin "Lifeguard" Burroughs, *Wiseguy,* CBS, 1987–90.
Camp Candy, NBC, 1989–93.
(English version) Voice, *Dragon Quest* (animated; also known as *Dragon Warrior*), syndicated, 1990.
Kevin, *Neon Rider* (also known as *Tenderfoot* and *Dude*), syndicated, 1990.
Voice, *G.I. Joe* (animated), 1990.

Kevin, *Neon Rider,* 1991–94.

Voice of Shadow Master, *Double Dragon* (animated), 1993.

Voice, *The Adventures of Sonic the Hedgehog* (animated; also known as *Adventures of Sonic the Hedgehog*), 1993.

Voice of Chef Flambe, Mr. Moneybags, Metro Train conductor, Mayor Fiorello LaGuardia, and Buffalo Ben, *Madeline* (animated), Fox Family, 1993–95.

Joe Dawson, *Highlander: The Series,* syndicated, 1993–98.

Belger/J, *Final Fight,* 1995.

Voice, *Hurricanes,* 1996.

Voice of Inferno, *Beast Wars* (animated; also known as *Beast Wars: Transformers, Beasties,* and *Beasties: Transformers*), syndicated, 1997–99.

Title role, *The Jim Byrnes Show,* 1998.

Mr. Olivier, *The Net,* USA Network, 1998–99.

Voice of Grand Vizier, *Shadow Raiders* (also known as *ShadowRaiders* and *War Planets*), 1998–99.

Host, *Walking after Midnight,* 1999.

Show of Hearts (also known as *Variety Club's "Show of Hearts"*), 1999.

Voice of Thrust, *Beast Machines: Transformers* (animated; also known as *Beast Masters: Battle for the Sparks*), Fox, 1999–2000.

Voice, *NASCAR Racers* (animated), Fox, 1999–2001.

Frank Mardasian, *Higher Ground,* Fox Family, 2000.

Voice of Duke Dermail, *Mobile Suit Gundam Wing* (animated; also known as *Gundam Wing*), Cartoon Network, 2000.

Ultimate Book of Spells, YTV, 2001.

Voice, *Stargate: Infinity* (animated), 2002.

Voice of Nick Fury, *X–Men: Evolution* (animated), The WB, 2002–2003.

Voice, *Gadget and the Gadgetinits* (animated), 2003.

Chief Director Skerritt, *Jake 2.0,* UPN, 2003.

Television Appearances; Miniseries:

Voice, *G.I. Joe: Operation Dragonfire* (animated), 1989.

Voice of polar bear, *The Snow Queen* (animated), Hallmark Channel, 2002.

Busker, "Acid Tests," *Steven Spielberg Presents: "Taken,"* Sci–Fi Channel, 2002.

Television Appearances; Movies:

(Uncredited) Band leader, *Hands of a Stranger* (also known as *Double Standard*), NBC, 1987.

Jack Fine, *The Red Spider,* CBS, 1988.

Kurt, *In the Best Interest of the Child* (also known as *A Mother's Plea*), CBS, 1990.

Noah, *Omen IV: The Awakening,* Fox, 1991.

Benedetti, *Christmas on Division Street,* CBS, 1991.

Stan, *Dirty Work,* USA Network, 1992.

Vet, *Serving in Silence: The Margarethe Cammermeyer Story* (also known as *Serving in Silence*), NBC, 1995.

(Uncredited) Date number one, *For Hope,* 1996.

Lieutenant McMahon, *Bloodhounds II,* USA Network, 1996.

Duke, *Final Descent,* CBS, 1997.

Doc Humphries, *Lost Treasure of Dos Santos,* 1997.

Voice, *NASCAR Racers: The Movie* (animated), Fox, 1999.

Bartender, *Becoming Dick,* E! Entertainment Television, 2000.

Dekim Barton, *Mobile Suit Gundam Wing: The Movie—Endless Waltz* (also known as *Endless Waltz* and *Gundam Wing: The Movie—Endless Waltz*), Cartoon Network, 2000.

Father Berkely, *Due East,* Showtime, 2002.

Voice of Mayor of Paris, *Madeline: My Fair Madeline* (animated), 2002.

Voice of Chief Quimby, *Inspector Gadget's Last Case: Claw's Revenge* (animated; also known as *Inspector Gadget in "Claw's Revenge"*), 2002.

Voice of Kraigor, *Dennis the Menace in "Cruise Control"* (animated; also known as *Dennis the Menace: Cruise Control*), 2002.

Voice of polar bear, *Snow Queen* (animated), 2002.

Steve, *Don't Cry Now,* Lifetime, 2007.

Television Appearances; Specials:

Guest host, *Thunder in the Canyon,* 1993.

Narrator, *Jericho: Walls of Silence,* 1999.

Narrator, *Devil Plays Hardball,* 2006.

Narrator, *The Week the Women Went,* CBC, 2008.

Television Appearances; Pilots:

Announcer, *Sliders,* 1995.

Daniel Benjamin "Lifeguard" Burroughs, *Wiseguy,* ABC, 1996.

Television Appearances; Episodic:

Tony Walter, "Deep Trouble," *Danger Bay,* 1987.

Jim, "Should Old Acquaintance Be Forgot?," *Out of This World,* 1988.

Voice of Merlin, "Opening Kick–Off," *King Arthur and the Knights of Justice* (animated), 1992.

Voice of Epimetrius the Sage, "The Night of the Fiery Tears," *Conan: The Adventurer* (animated), 1992.

Carl Drake, "Dead Man Walking," *The Hat Squad,* CBS, 1993.

The doctor, "The Wall," *Street Justice,* 1993.

Voice of Shadow Master, "The Price of Oblivion," *Double Dragon* (animated), 1993.

Voice of Dr. Thomas Light, "Cold Steel," *Mega Man* (animated), syndicated, 1994.

Brett Shrager, "The Kid," *The Commish,* ABC, 1995.

Nelson, *G.I. Joe Extreme* (animated), 1996.

Colonel Maxwell Foley, "The Reckoning," *Two,* 1997.

Gary Latimer, "The Joining," *The Outer Limits* (also known as *The New Outer Limits*), 1998.

Guy Hanson, "More Than Meets the Eye," *Murder Call,* 1998.

voice of Grand Vizier, *War Planets* (animated; also known as *War Planets*), syndicated, 1998.

Dick Hofstedder, "Deadly Games: Part 1," *Cold Squad,* CTV, 1999.

Dick Hofstedder, "First Deadly Sin," *Cold Squad,* CTV, 1999.

Dick Hofstedder, "Pretty Fly for a Dead Guy," *Cold Squad,* CTV, 1999.

Joe Dawson, "A Matter of Time," *Highlander: The Raven,* syndicated, 1999.

Joe Dawson, "French Connection," *Highlander: The Raven,* syndicated, 1999.

Ramp, "Spirit Junction," *Mysterious Ways,* NBC, 2000.

Tyler Greer, "Shadowland," *First Wave,* Sci–Fi Channel, 2000.

General Nemec, "Eat Flaming Death," *Level 9,* UPN, 2000.

Voice, *Alienators: Evolution Continues,* Fox, 2001.

Voice of Fire Drake, "Cry Vulture," *Spider–Man Unlimited* (animated), Fox, 2001.

Dion, "Harsh Mistress," *The Twilight Zone,* UPN, 2002.

Vic Goodman, "Unreasonable Doubt," *The Dead Zone* (also known as *Stephen King's "The Dead Zone"*), USA Network, 2002.

Voice of Nick Fury, "Operation: Rebirth," *X–Men: Evolution* (animated), The WB, 2002.

"Fading Star," *Just Cause,* PAX, 2002.

Merlin, "The Tipping Point," *The Outer Limits* (also known as *The New Outer Limits*), 2002.

Documentary narrator, "Heroes: Part 2," *Stargate SG–1,* Sci–Fi Channel and Showtime, 2004.

Voice of Shineoa San, "Exalted Reason, Resplendent Daughter," *Andromeda* (also known as *Gene Roddenberry's "Andromeda"*), 2004.

Voice of Virgil Vox, "The Eschatology of Our Present," *Andromeda* (also known as *Gene Roddenberry's "Andromeda"*), 2004.

Professor, "Bugs," *Supernatural,* The WB, 2005.

Councillor Eddie Banks, "Ready to Call in the Horses," *Da Vinci's City Hall* (also known as *Da Vinci's Inquest*), CBC, 2005.

Councillor Eddie Banks, "The Dogs in Sympathy with the Cats," *Da Vinci's City Hall* (also known as *Da Vinci's Inquest*), CBC, 2006.

Gregory Magnus, *Sanctuary,* Sci–Fi Channel, 2007.

Gregory Magnus, "Warriors," *Sanctuary,* Sci–Fi Channel, 2008.

Matthew, "John May," *V,* ABC, 2010.

Also appeared as voice of Governor Marshall Deacon, "Bro–Bots," *Mega Man* (animated), syndicated; voice of Nelson, "Winner Take All," *G.I. Joe Extreme* (animated); voice of Guy, "Final Fight," *Street Fighter: The Animated Series* (animated); in *Lightning Force; The Hitchhiker.*

Television Additional Voices; Episodic:
Madeline (animated), Fox Family, 1993.
Conan and the Young Warriors (animated), 1994.
Stone Protectors (animated), 1996.
Mummies Alive! (animated), 1997.
"Garden of Evil," *RoboCop: Alpha Commando* (animated), 1998.

Stage Appearances:
Hans, *Principia Scriptoriae,* The Studio Theatre, Washington, DC, 1989–90.

RECORDINGS

Albums:
(With the Jim Byrnes Band) *Burning,* PolyGram, 1981.
(With the Jim Byrnes Band) *I Turned My Nights into Days,* Stony Plain Records, 1987.
(With the Jim Byrnes Band) *That River,* Stony Plain Records, 1995.
Burning/I Turned My Nights into Days, Stony Plain Records, 1998.
Love Is a Gamble, One Coyote Music, 2001.

WRITINGS

Film Scores:
We All Fall Down, 2000.
Down Here (short documentary), Shore Films, 2008.

Film Songs:
"That River," *The Final Cut,* Republic, 1995.

OTHER SOURCES

Periodicals:
Maclean's, January 15, 1996, p. 53.
People Weekly, May 21, 1990, pp. 105–06.

C

CARROLL, Eddie 1933–2010

PERSONAL

Original name, Eddie Eleniak; born September 5, 1933, in Edmonton, Alberta, Canada; died of brain cancer, April 6, 2010, in Los Angeles, CA. Actor and voice actor. Carroll served as the voice of the Disney character Jiminy Cricket for nearly four decades and later made a name for himself impersonating comedian Jack Benny in two celebrated one-man shows. He began acting in high school, moving to Los Angeles as part of an NBC talent-scouting program in the mid 1950s. While serving in the army, he produced material for the American Forces Network. He then formed Carroll-Farr Productions with actor Jamie Farr. The company made pilots for ABC, NBC, and CBS in the 1960s. Carroll followed his 1963 television debut in *The Lieutenant* with appearances in such series as *Gomer Pyle, U.S.M.C.*; *Mission: Impossible*; *The Andy Griffith Show*; and *The Don Knotts Show* before landing the role of Jiminy Cricket (succeeding actor Cliff Edwards, the first Jiminy) in 1973. He voiced the character in television specials, including *Disneys Wide World of Color*; in animated films, such as the *Disney Sing-Along Songs* series; and in video games and live performances staged at Disneyland and Disney World well into the 2000s. After starring in the 1983 one-man show *A Small Eternity with Jack Benny,* in which he impersonated the comedian to rave reviews, he penned and acted in another one-man tribute, *Jack Benny"Laughter in Bloom.* He toured the show extensively for over twenty years. Carroll also provided the voice for more than 200 television and radio commercials throughout his career.

PERIODICALS

CBC News, April 11, 2010.
Los Angeles Times, April 11, 2010.
Washington Post, April 12, 2010.

CARSON, Kris
See KRISTOFFERSON, Kris

CAVENAUGH, Matt 1978–
(Matthew Cavenaugh, William M. Cavenaugh)

PERSONAL

Some sources cite full name as William Matthew Cavenaugh; born May 31, 1978, in Jonesboro, AR; son of Donald R. "Don" (a president of an automotive dealership group) and Margaret L. Cavenaugh (an administrator and in sales); stepson of Frances M. "Fran" Cavenaugh; married Jenny Powers (an actress and singer), August 23, 2009. *Education:* Ithaca College, B.F.A., musical theatre, 2001; also studied with Keith Salter.

Addresses: *Agent*—Bauman, Redanty & Shaul Agency, 1650 Broadway, Suite 1410, New York, NY 10019. *Manager*—Rain Management Group, 1800 Stanford St., Santa Monica, CA 90404.

Career: Actor and singer. Public speaker and participant in discussions and at open sessions with musical theatre students. Participated in promotional events, awards presentations, benefits, and fund–raising events. Early Stages (literacy organization), member of the advisory board.

Member: Actors' Equity Association.

CREDITS

Stage Appearances; Musicals:
Street sweeper, *Here's Love,* Jonesboro High School, Jonesboro, AR, c. 1990.

Samuel, *The Pirates of Penzance* (comic opera), Ithaca College, Ithaca, NY, 1997.

Val, *Babes in Arms,* Ithaca College, Hoerner Theatre, Ithaca, 1999.

Henrik, *A Little Night Music,* Ithaca College, Hoerner Theatre, 2000.

Dorian Gray (title role), *Dorian,* Denver Center for the Performing Arts, Temple Hoyne Buell Theatre, Denver, CO, 2002.

Ren McCormick, *Footloose,* Theatre by the Sea, Matunuck, RI, 2002.

Bud (title role), *Urban Cowboy* (also known as *Urban Cowboy: The Musical*), Coconut Grove Playhouse, Coconut Grove, FL, beginning 2002, and Broadhurst Theatre, New York City, 2003.

Neo (benefit concert; also known as *NEO, N.E.O., Neo: A Celebration of Emerging Talent in Musical Theatre, Benefiting the York Theatre Company,* and *Neo: new, emerging ... outstanding!*), York Theatre Company, New York City, 2003.

Brad, *Princesses,* Goodspeed Musicals, Norma Terris Theatre, Chester, CT, 2004.

Samuel Foreman, *Jonestown* (also known as *Jonestown—The Musical* and *Jonestown: The Musical*), New York International Fringe Festival, Pace University, Michael Schimmel Center for the Arts, New York City, 2004.

Standing Ovations 2 (benefit), Joseph Papp Public Theatre, Joe's Pub, New York City, 2004.

Jerry Torre (the marble faun) and Joseph Patrick Kennedy, Jr., *Grey Gardens,* workshop staged at the Sundance Institute Theatre Lab at White Oak, White Oak, FL, 2004, reading staged in 2005, full musical staged at Playwrights Horizons, New York City, 2006, and Walter Kerr Theatre, New York City, 2006–2007.

Billy Bigelow, *Carousel,* Pittsburgh CLO (Civic Light Orchestra), Pittsburgh, PA, 2005.

Lancelot "Lance" Fitch, *Palm Beach* (also known as *Palm Beach, the Screwball Musical*), La Jolla Playhouse, Mandell Weiss Theatre, La Jolla, CA, 2005.

Lieutenant Shaw, *The Secret Garden,* produced as part of *Third Annual World AIDS Day Concert* (benefit concert), Manhattan Center Studios Grand Ballroom, New York City, 2005.

Billy Crocker, *Anything Goes,* Theatre under the Stars (TUTS), Houston, TX, 2005, and Williamstown Theatre Festival, Main Stage, Williamstown, MA, 2006.

Ralph Halloran, *A Catered Affair,* Old Globe Theatre, San Diego, CA, 2007, and Walker Kerr Theatre, 2008.

The Mabel Mercer Foundation's Cabaret Convention (also known as *The Cabaret Convention, Mabel Mercer Foundation's 19th Annual Cabaret Convention,* and *Mabel Mercer New York Cabaret Convention*), Lincoln Center, Frederick P. Rose Hall, New York City, 2008.

Prospect Theater Company 10th Anniversary Concert, 37 Arts, New York City, 2008.

Tony, *West Side Story,* Palace Theatre, New York City, 2009.

The soldier, *L'histoire du soldat* (concert), Lincoln Center, Avery Fisher Hall, New York City, 2010.

Superman/Clark Kent, *It's a Bird ... It's a Plane ... It's Superman,* Dallas Theater Center, AT&T Performing Arts Center, Dee and Charles Wyly Theatre, Potter Rose Performance Hall, Dallas, TX, 2010.

Broadway Comes to Town (pops concert), Arkansas State University, Fowler Center, Jonesboro, AR, 2010.

Little Theater, Big Dreams (benefit cabaret production), West Side YMCA, Marjorie S. Deane Little Theatre, New York City, 2010.

RATED RSO: The Music and Lyrics of Ryan Scott Oliver (concert; also known as *Rated RSO*), Joseph Papp Public Theatre, Joe's Pub, 2010.

Sondheim: The Birthday Concert, Lincoln Center, Avery Fisher Hall, 2010.

Appeared in productions at other venues, including the Hangar Theatre, Ithaca, NY.

Stage Appearances; Plays:

(As Matthew Cavenaugh) Menelaus, *The Trojan Women,* Ithaca College, Hoerner Theatre, Ithaca, NY, 2001.

Scooter, *2 Lives,* George Street Playhouse, New Brunswick, NJ, 2005.

Appeared in other productions, including *john and jen,* The Kitchen.

Major Tours; Musicals:

Eugene, *Grease,* U.S. cities, 1997.

Younger brother, *Ragtime,* U.S. cities, 2001.

Strike Up the Band, U.S. cities, 2002.

Jimmy Smith, *Thoroughly Modern Millie,* U.S. cities, 2003.

Television Appearances; Series:

Adam Munson, *As The World Turns,* CBS, 2006–2007.

Television Appearances; Specials:

Macy's "4th of July Fireworks Spectacular" (also known as *Macy's "4th of July Fireworks"* and *Macy's "4th of July Spectacular"*), NBC, 2009.

The Visa Signature Tony Awards Season Celebration, CBS, 2009.

Television Appearances; Awards Presentations:

The 63rd Annual Tony Awards, CBS, 2009.

Television Appearances; Episodic:

The Caroline Rhea Show (also known as *Caroline Rhea*), syndicated, 2003.

Mark Solomon, *One Life to Live* (also known as *Between Heaven and Hell*, *OLTL*, and *One Life to Live: The Summer of Seduction*), ABC, 2004.

Himself, "Grey Gardens: From East Hampton to Broadway," *Independent Lens*, PBS, 2008.

Appeared in other programs, including *Today* (also known as *NBC News Today* and *The Today Show*), NBC; and *The View*, ABC.

Film Appearances:

Little monster, *Little Monsters* (also known as *Little Ghost Fighters*), Metro–Goldwyn–Mayer/United Artists, 1989.

Sean, *Dependencia sexual* (also known as *The Ballad of Sexual Dependency* and *Sexual Dependency*), Cinemavault Releasing, 2003, Wellspring Media, 2004, subtitled version released by Cinema Tropical, 2005.

Brad Steward, *New Brooklyn*, New Brooklyn Features, 2009.

RECORDINGS

Albums; Cast Recordings; with Others:

Neo (benefit cast recording; also known as *NEO*, *N.E.O.*, *Neo: A Celebration of Emerging Talent in Musical Theatre, Benefiting the York Theatre Company*, and *Neo: new, emerging ... outstanding!*), Jay Records, 2005.

Grey Gardens (original Broadway cast recording; also known as *Grey Gardens—The Musical*), P.S. Classics, 2006.

A Catered Affair (original Broadway cast recording), P.S. Classics, 2008.

West Side Story (new Broadway cast recording; also known as *West Side Story: The New Broadway Cast Recording*), Sony Classics, 2009.

Videos:

Standing Ovations 2, BroadwayWorld.com, 2004.

WRITINGS

Nonfiction:

Contributor to periodicals, including *Beverly Hills Lifestyle.*

OTHER SOURCES

Periodicals:

New York, April 12, 2009.

New York Times, April 23, 2009; August 21, 2009.

USA Today, March 13, 2003.

Electronic:

Playbill.com, http://www.playbill.com, March 1, 2003;March 2, 2009.

CHO, John 1972–

PERSONAL

Full name, John Yohan Cho; some sources also cite name as Cho Yo Han; born June 16, 1972, in Seoul, South Korea; immigrated to the United States, 1978; raised in Los Angeles, CA; father a pastor; married Kerri Higuchi (an actress), 2006. *Education:* University of California, Berkeley, B.A., 1996.

Addresses: *Agent*—Gersh Agency, 9465 Wilshire Blvd., 6th Floor, Beverly Hills, CA 90212. *Manager*—Principato, Young Management, 9465 Wilshire Blvd., Suite 880, Beverly Hills, CA 90212.

Career: Actor and voice performer. East West Players of Los Angeles, member of company. Viva La Union (band; formerly known as Left of Center and Left of Zed), lead singer. Worked as English teacher at a school in Hollywood, CA, and as a print model for Korean magazines.

Awards, Honors: Teen Choice Award nomination, choice movie rockstar moment, and MTV Movie Award nominations, best musical performance and best on-screen team (all with Kal Penn), 2005, for *Harold & Kumar Go to White Castle;* Boston Society of Film Critics Award and Washington DC Area Film Critics Association Award nomination, both 2009, and Broadcast Film Critics Association Award nomination, 2010, all best acting ensemble (with others), for *Star Trek;* Visionary Award, East West Players of Los Angeles, 2009.

CREDITS

Film Appearances:

Clarence, *Shopping for Fangs*, Margin Films, 1997.

Third aide, *Wag the Dog*, New Line Cinema, 1997.

Joey, *Yellow*, Phaedra Cinema, 1998.

Exchange Value, American Film Institute, 1998.

John, *American Pie*, Universal, 1999.

Nightclub cleaner, *Bowfinger*, Universal, 1999.

First sale house man, *American Beauty*, DreamWorks, 1999.

Trung, *Among Others*, 2000.

Parking valet, *The Flintstones in Viva Rock Vegas*, Universal, 2000.

Mr. Hugo, *Delivering Milo*, IMMI Pictures, 2000.

Phil Quon, *Down to Earth,* Paramount, 2001.
Fengmo Wu, *Pavilion of Women,* Universal, 2001.
Student, *Evolution,* DreamWorks, 2001.
John, *American Pie 2* (also known as *American Summer Story*), Universal, 2001.
Steve Choe, *Better Luck Tomorrow,* Paramount, 2002.
Dustin "Dusty" Wong, *Big Fat Liar,* Universal, 2002.
First DBA emissary, *Solaris,* USA Films, 2002.
John, *American Wedding* (also known as *American Pie: The Wedding*), Universal, 2003.
Thanh, *Western Avenue* (short film), American Film Institute, 2003.
Petey, *In Good Company,* Universal, 2004.
Harold Lee, *Harold & Kumar Go to White Castle* (also known as *Harold & Kumar Get the Munchies*), New Line Cinema, 2004.
Larry Finkelstein, *See This Movie,* Slamdance on the Road, 2005.
Stephan, *Bam Bam and Celeste,* Salty Features/Nuit Blanche Productions/Cho Taussig Productions, 2005.
Frank Ittles, *American Dreamz,* Universal, 2006.
Bob, *Bickford Shmeckler's Cool Ideas,* Screen Media Films, 2007.
Mikey, *Smiley Face,* First Look International, 2007.
Third banker, *The Air I Breathe,* THINKFilm, 2007.
John Kim, *West 32nd,* 2007, Pathfinder Pictures, 2009.
Harold Lee, *Harold & Kumar Escape from Guantanamo Bay* (also known as *Harold & Kumar 2*), Warner Bros., 2008.
Harold Lee, *Harold & Kumar Go to Amsterdam* (short film), Warner Home Video, 2008.
Hype man, *Nick and Norah's Infinite Playlist,* Columbia, 2008.
Himself, *Snapshot: Six Months of the Korean American Male* (short documentary), 2008.
Hikaru Sulu, *Star Trek* (also known as *Star Trek: The Future Begins* and *Star Trek: The IMAX Experience*), Paramount, 2009.
Smitty, *Saint John of Law Vegas,* IndieVest Pictures, 2010.
Kama, *Caller ID,* 2010.

Television Appearances; Series:
Chau Presley, *Off Centre,* The WB, 2001–2002.
Teddy Wong, a recurring role, *Kitchen Confidential,* Fox, between 2005 and 2008.
Demetri Noh, *FlashForward,* ABC, 2009–10.

Television Appearances; Movies:
Jerry Chang, *The Tiger Woods Story,* Showtime, 1998.
Han, *Earth vs. the Spider,* Cinemax, 2001.

Television Appearances; Pilots:
Ivan Throckmorton, *The Singles Table,* NBC, 2007.
Up All Night, CBS, 2007.
Children's Hospital (originally broadcast on the Internet), Cartoon Network, 2010.

Television Appearances; Specials:
Interviewee, *Better Luck Tomorrow: MTV Movie Special,* MTV, 2003.
Presenter, *G–Phoria,* G4, 2004.
Forever in Our Hearts: The Making of Documentary, 2005.
Special zu "Star Trek XI," 2009.

Television Appearances; Episodic:
Pizza delivery man, "Twister of Fate," *The Jeff Foxworthy Show,* NBC, 1997.
Larry, "The Occidental Purists," *Boston Common,* NBC, 1997.
Larry, "The Last Stand," *Felicity,* The WB, 1998.
Mark Chao, "Dead Man Dating," *Charmed,* The WB, 1998.
Flower delivery guy, "Bloody Val–entine," *V.I.P.,* syndicated, 1998.
Wo Chin, "Chinatown," *The Magnificent Seven,* CBS, 1999.
"Fence and Sensibility," *Daddio,* NBC, 2000.
Voice of navigator, "Junior," *Static Shock* (animated), 2001.
Voices of Thomas Kim and Tantrum, "Tantrum," *Static Shock* (animated), 2001.
Himself, "Show 8," *The Jamie Kennedy Experiment* (also known as *JKX: The Jamie Kennedy Experiment*), The WB, 2002.
"Cost of Freedom," *The Division,* NBC, 2003.
Voice of Hirotaka, "Exchange," *Kim Possible* (animated; also known as *Disney's "Kim Possible"*), The Disney Channel, 2003.
Bob, "Money for Something," *The Men's Room,* NBC, 2004.
Harvey Park, "Love Hurts," *House M.D.* (also known as *Dr. House* and *House*), Fox, 2005.
Voice of Vince Chung, "Helping Handis," *American Dad!* (animated), Fox, 2006.
Marshall Stone, "Damage Case," *Grey's Anatomy,* ABC, 2006.
MADtv, Fox, 2006.
Ivan Throckmorton, "The Work Dinner," *The Singles Table,* NBC, 2007.
Lucas Bender, "Come Out and Play," *'Til Death,* Fox, 2007.
Jeff Coatsworth, "I'm Not That Guy," *How I Met Your Mother* (also known as *H.I.M.Y.M.*), CBS, 2007.
Kenny, "Grin and Bear It," *Ugly Betty,* ABC, 2007.
Kenny, "A League of Their Own," *Ugly Betty,* ABC, 2007.
Kenny, "Bananas for Betty," *Ugly Betty,* ABC, 2007.
"It Happens," *Hollywood Residential,* Starz!, 2008.
"Star Trek," *Making Of ...,* 2009.
Xpose, TV3, 2009.

Also appeared in an episode of *Dean's List,* MTV.

Television Talk Show Guest Appearances; Episodic:
The Tonight Show with Jay Leno, NBC, 2004.
Late Night with Conan O'Brien, NBC, 2004.
Howard Stern, E! Entertainment Television, 2004.
Jimmy Kimmel Live!, ABC, 2004, 2008, 2009.
Tavis Smiley, PBS, 2008.
Last Call with Carson Daly, NBC, 2008.
Up Close with Carrie Keagan, ABC, 2008, 2009.
The Bonnie Hunt Show, NBC, 2010.

Television Appearances; Awards Presentations:
Presenter, *2006 Asian Excellence Awards,* 2006.
... *Asian Excellence Awards,* 2007, E! Entertainment
   Television, 2008.
Scream Awards, Spike TV, 2009.

Stage Appearances:
Made professional debut in *The Woman Warrior,* Berkeley Repertory Theatre, Berkeley, CA, then Huntington Theatre, Boston, MA, later James Doolittle Theatre, Los Angeles; appeared as Laertes, *Hamlet,* Singapore Repertory Theatre; appeared in presentations of the East West Players of Los Angeles.

RECORDINGS

Albums:
(With Left of Zed) *Furious Bloom,* 2004.

Appeared in the music video "Be a Nigger Too" by Nas, 2008.

Videos:
John Cho & Kal Penn: The Backseat Interview, New Line Home Entertainment, 2005.
Star Trek: Gag Reel, Paramount, 2009.

OTHER SOURCES

Periodicals:
TV Guide, January 25, 2003, p. 40; May 17, 2010, pp. 40–41.

CISTARO, Anthony 1963–
   (Tony Cistaro)

PERSONAL

Full name, Anthony Michael Cistaro; born June 8, 1963, in Kirksville, MO; son of Peter Michael (a teacher and counselor) and Paulanne Marie (a secretarial as-

sistant; maiden name, Pritchard) Cistaro. *Education:* Institut de Touraine, certificate, 1983; Loyola Marymount University, B.A. (magna cum laude), 1985; trained at American Repertory Theatre Institute for Advanced Theatre Training, Harvard University, 1997, and at London Academy of Music and Dramatic Art; studied acting with Stella Adler, Los Angeles. *Politics:* Democrat. *Religion:* Roman Catholic. *Avocational Interests:* Competitive swimming, triathlons, water polo, fencing, French, Italian.

Addresses: *Agent*—JE Talent, 323 Geary St., Suite 302, San Francisco, CA 94102.

Career: Actor. Member of Stella Adler Theatre Group; appeared in a Honda commercial, 1976.

Member: Screen Actors Guild, American Federation of Television and Radio Artists, Actors' Equity Association.

CREDITS

Television Appearances; Series:
Henri, a recurring role, *Cheers,* NBC, between 1990 and 1992.
Kenneth Irons, *Witchblade,* TNT, 2001–2002.

Television Appearances; Episodic:
Matthew, "Unforgiven," *Bob,* CBS, 1992.
Pierre, "The Man Who Would Be Grandpa," *Baby Talk,* 1992.
Joel Rifkin, "The Masseuse," *Seinfeld,* NBC, 1993.
Carmine Zizo, "Forever and Ever," *Jack's Place,* ABC, 1993.
Anthony, *Big Wave Dave's,* CBS, 1993.
Carlo, "Maggie the Model," *The Nanny,* CBS, 1994.
Frank, "Lillith," *High Sierra Search and Rescue,* NBC, 1995.
Mario LeFontaine, "Again with the Hockey Player: Parts 1 & 2," *Alright Already,* The WB, 1998.
Mario LeFontaine, "Again with the Photos," *Alright Already,* The WB, 1998.
Mario LeFontaine, "Again with the House," *Alright Already,* The WB, 1998.
Marcel Charmont, "Tobacco," *Thanks,* CBS, 1999.
Commander Trask, "Hero," *Angel* (also known as *Angel: The Series*), The WB, 1999.
Ethros Demon, "I've Got You under My Skin," *Angel* (also known as *Angel: The Series*), The WB, 2000.
Nikita, "Dinner and a Breakdown," *Charlie Lawrence,* CBS, 2003.
Jared Radke, "The Wild Bunch," *10–8: Officers on Duty* (also known as *10–8*), ABC, 2003.
Dylan Masters, "The Gift," *She Spies,* syndicated, 2004.
Gate attendant, "The Last One: Parts 1 & 2," *Friends,* NBC, 2004.

Michel Guinot, "A Man of His Word," *Alias,* ABC, 2005.
Dumain, "Gone with the Witches," *Charmed,* The WB, 2006.
Dumain, "Kill Billie: Vol. 2," *Charmed,* The WB, 2006.
Dumain, "Forever Charmed," *Charmed,* The WB, 2006.
(Uncredited) Richard Zimmer, "Triple Threat," *CSI: Miami,* CBS, 2007.
Bryce Lee, "Hollywood Homicide," *Numb3rs* (also known as *Num3ers*), CBS, 2007.
Waiter, "Twenty–four Candles," *Ugly Betty,* ABC, 2008.
Steven Ausbury, "Roxy St. James," *Nip/Tuck,* FX Network, 2009.

Also appeared as Dr. Walker in *Passions,* NBC.

Television Appearances; Other:
(As Tony Cistaro) John David at age fifteen, *Lady of the House* (movie), NBC, 1978.
Kenneth Irons, *Witchblade* (pilot), TNT, 2000.

Film Appearances:
Tony, *The Method,* Pacific Star, 1989.
Detective, *The Runestone,* Live Entertainment, 1990.
Mike Benevento, *Let Others Suffer,* Scott Shelley Productions, 2007.
Donald Loften, *Bare Knuckles,* Image Entertainment, 2010.

Stage Appearances:
M. Onde and M. Toppfer, *Overboard,* Zero Church Street Theatre, Cambridge, MA, 1995.
Conductor and police officer, *Tartuffe,* American Repertory Theatre, Loeb Drama Center, Cambridge, MA, 1996.
Anthony, *Six Characters in Search of an Author,* American Repertory Theatre, Loeb Drama Center, 1997.
Durandarte, *The King Stag,* Loeb Drama Center, 2000, then Barbican Theatre, London, 2001.

Also appeared as Death, *Architect of Destiny,* Zephyr Theatre; Odysseus, *The Cure at Troy,* Loeb Experimental Theatre, Cambridge, MA; Shlink, *In the Jungle of Cities,* Zero Church Street Theatre; the father, *Island of Anyplace,* American Repertory Theatre; Bardolph, *Lettice and Lovage,* Will Greer Theatricum Botanicum, Topanga, CA; Robin Starveling, *A Midsummer Night's Dream,* Commonwealth Shakespeare Company; Don Manuel, *The Phantom Lady,* Loeb Experimental Theatre; Vanek, *A Private View,* World Theatre; Prince Escalus, *Romeo and Juliet,* Will Geer Theatricum Botanicum; Adam Adam, *Rough Crossing,* Matrix Theatre; Lon Go Ti, *Tale of the Scorpion,* Stella Adler Theatre, Los Angeles; Marco, *A View from the Bridge,* South Coast Repertory, Costa Mesa, CA; and in productions of *Bedtime Story, Playing with Fire,* and *The Time of Your Life.*

OTHER SOURCES

Electronic:
Anthony Cistaro Official Site, http://www.anthonycistaro.info, July 9, 2010.

CLINTON, George S. 1947–
   (George Clinton)

PERSONAL

Full name, George Stanley Clinton, Jr.; born June 17, 1947, in Chattanooga, TN; son of George Stanley Clinton; married Francesca Poston (an actress; divorced); married Charlotte Blunt (an actress), November 2, 1985; children: (second marriage) Jessica. *Education:* Middle Tennessee State University, graduated.

Addresses: *Manager*—Vasi Vangelos, First Artists Management, 4764 Park Granada, Suite 210, Calabasas, CA 91302. *Publicist*—Ray Costa, Costa Communications, 8265 Sunset Blvd., Suite 101, Los Angeles, CA 90046.

Career: Composer, orchestrator, music arranger, music producer, music conductor, songwriter and lyricist, session musician, pianist, and recording artist. Warner Bros. Music, staff writer; the George Clinton Band, musician. Sundance Institute Composers Lab, advisor.

Member: Broadcast Music, Inc. (BMI).

Awards, Honors: BMI Film Music Award, BMI Film and Television awards, Broadcast Music, Inc., 1996, for *Mortal Kombat;* Saturn Award nomination, best music, Academy of Science Fiction, Fantasy & Horror Films, 1999, for *Wild Things;* BMI Film Music Award, 2000, for *Austin Powers: The Spy Who Shagged Me;* Grammy Award nomination, best instrumental arrangement, National Academy of Recording Arts and Sciences, 2002, for "Soul Bossa Nova"; BMI Film Music awards, 2003, for *Austin Powers in Goldmember* and *The Santa Clause 2;* BMI Cable Award (with others), 2005, for *The 4400;* BMI Film Music Award, best music for a feature film, 2006, for *Big Momma's House 2;* BMI Film Music Award, 2007, for *The Santa Clause 3: The Escape Clause;* Richard Kirk Career Achievement Award, BMI Film and Television awards, 2007; Emmy Award nomination, outstanding music composition for a miniseries, movie, or special (original dramatic score), 2007, for *Bury My Heart at Wounded Knee;* Spirit of Tennessee Award, The Tennessee Arts Academy, Arts Academy America, 2009; BMI Film Music Award, 2010, for *Tooth Fairy;* other awards and honors.

CREDITS

Film Work:

Music adaptor and supervisor, *The Apple* (also known as *BIM Stars* and *Star Rock*), Cannon, 1980.

(As George Clinton) Arranger of additional music and lyrics, *Vice Squad,* Avco Embassy, 1982.

Performer of song "The Cobra Strikes," *American Ninja 3: Blood Hunt* (also known as *American Fighter III* and *American Ninja 3*), Cannon, 1989.

Music director assistant, *Mack the Knife,* 1989, 21st Century Releasing, 1990.

Performer of songs "It's Love" and "On the Other Side," *Wild Orchid II: Two Shades of Blue* (also known as *Blue Movie Blue, Wild Orchid 2: Blue Movie Blue,* and *Wild Orchid 2: Two Shades of Blue*), Triumph Releasing, 1991.

Performer of song "A Christmas Wish," *Only You,* 1992.

(As George Clinton) Orchestrator, music arranger, and conductor of shaped note music, *Geronimo: An American Legend* (also known as *Geronimo*), Columbia, 1993.

Orchestrator, *Hellbound,* Cannon, 1994.

Producer of theme song "The Longest Night" and orchestrator, *Mother's Boys,* Dimension Films, 1994.

Orchestrator, *Top Dog,* Live Entertainment, 1995.

Orchestrator and score conductor, *Mortal Kombat,* New Line Cinema, 1995.

Orchestrator, *Austin Powers: International Man of Mystery* (also known as *Austin Powers* and *Austin Powers—Das Schaerfste, was Ihre Majestaet zu bieten hat*), New Line Cinema, 1997.

Orchestrator, *Beverly Hills Ninja,* TriStar, 1997.

Orchestrator and score conductor, *Mortal Kombat: Annihilation* (also known as *Mortal Kombat: The Annihilation* and *Mortal Kombat 2*), New Line Cinema, 1997.

Orchestrator, *Black Dog,* Universal, 1998.

Orchestrator, *Wild Things* (also known as *Sexcrimes, Sex Crimes,* and *wildthings*), Columbia, 1998.

Performer of songs "Bingo" and "Drone #3," *In God's Hands,* TriStar/Sony Pictures Entertainment, 1998.

Orchestrator and music arranger, *Austin Powers: The Spy Who Shagged Me* (also known as *Austin Powers Deluxe, Austin Powers II, Austin Powers 2: It's Shagging Time, Austin Powers 2: The Spy Who Shagged Me, Austin Powers II: The Wrath of Khan, It's Shagging Time,* and *The Return of Dr. Evil*), New Line Cinema, 1999.

Producer of song "New York, New York," *Mystery, Alaska* (also known as *Disney's "Hockey Project," The Game,* and *Pond Rules*), Buena Vista, 1999.

Orchestrator, *Speaking of Sex,* Twentieth Century–Fox, 2001.

Orchestrator, *3000 Miles to Graceland* (also known as *Crime Is King, Destination: Graceland,* and *3,000 Miles to Graceland*), Warner Bros., 2001.

Orchestrator and score conductor, *Joe Somebody* (also known as *Super papa*), Twentieth Century–Fox, 2001.

Song arranger and performer, *Sordid Lives,* Regent Releasing, 2001.

Orchestra conductor, *The Santa Clause 2* (also known as *The Escape Clause: The Santa Clause 2, Hyper Noel, The Mrs. Clause: Santa Clause 2, Santa Clause Returns!, Santa Clause 2, The Santa Clause 2: The Escape Clause, The Santa Clause 2: The Mrs. Clause, Santa Claus 2,* and *SC2*), Buena Vista, 2002.

Score conductor and song arranger and performer, *Austin Powers in Goldmember* (also known as *Austin Powers: Goldmember, Austin Powers: Never Say Member Again, Austin Powers 3, Austinpussy, Goldmember, The Next Installment of Austin Powers,* and *The Third Installment of Austin Powers*), New Line Cinema, 2002.

Score conductor, *Catch That Kid* (also known as *Catch That Girl* and *Mission without Permission*), Fox 2000, 2004.

Score producer and conductor, *The Big Bounce* (also known as *Hawaii Crime Story*), Warner Bros., 2004.

Score producer and conductor, *A Dirty Shame,* Fine Line/New Line Cinema, 2004.

Score arranger, *New York Minute,* Warner Bros., 2005.

Orchestrator and score conductor, *Big Momma's House 2* (also known as *Big Mamma 2*), Twentieth Century–Fox, 2006.

Score conductor, *The Santa Clause 3: The Escape Clause* (also known as *Pretender* and *Santa Claus 3*), Buena Vista, 2006.

Score conductor and performer of song "Up on the Housetop," *Deck the Halls* (also known as *All Lit Up*), Twentieth Century–Fox, 2006.

Orchestrator and score conductor, *The Love Guru* (also known as *Untitled Mike Myers Project* and *Der Love Guru*), Paramount, 2008.

Score producer, *Extract,* Miramax, 2009.

Orchestrator, *Hometown Glory* (documentary), Costa Communications/Wafilms, 2010.

Orchestrator, score conductor, and song performer, *Tooth Fairy,* Twentieth Century–Fox, 2010.

Film Appearances:

Reporter Joe Pittman, *The Apple* (also known as *BIM Stars* and *Star Rock*), Cannon, 1980.

Television Work; Series:

Score producer, *Red Shoe Diaries* (also known as *Foxy Fantasies, Zalman King's "Red Shoe Diaries," Diarios del zapato rojo,* and *Skjulte laengsler*), Showtime, 1992–96.

Television Work; Movies:

Pianist, *Delta of Venus,* Showtime, 1995.

Pianist, *The Last Days of Frankie the Fly* (also known as *Frankie the Fly*), HBO, 1996.

Score producer, *A Place Called Truth,* The Movie Channel, 1998.

Orchestrator, *Lansky,* HBO, 1999.

Musical score conductor, *Bury My Heart at Wounded Knee* (also known as *Untitled Wounded Knee Project*), HBO, 2007.

Television Work; Pilots:

Music score producer and producer of songs "God Is Rhythm" and "You Never Really Know," *Red Shoe Diaries* (also known as *Red Shoe Diaries the Movie* and *Wild Orchid III: Red Shoe Diaries*), Showtime, 1992.

Television Appearances; Episodic:

Piano player, "Mike's Dream: A Christmas Tale," *Dr. Quinn, Medicine Woman,* CBS, 1993.

Television Appearances; Pilots:

Piano player, *Red Shoe Diaries* (also known as *Red Shoe Diaries the Movie* and *Wild Orchid III: Red Shoe Diaries*), Showtime, 1992.

Radio and Internet Appearances:

Himself, *Center Stage with Mark Gordon* (radio show also broadcast online), KXLU and http://www.kxlu.com, c. 2009.

RECORDINGS

Albums; Performer and Arranger:

(With the George Clinton Band) *The George Clinton Band Arrives,* ABC Records, 1977.

Performer on recordings, including work as a session musician. Worked on recordings as a music arranger and a music producer.

WRITINGS

Film Music:

(And music for "Station IDs") *Pray TV* (also known as *K–GOD*), 1980.

(With others) *Nice Dreams* (also known as *Cheech & Chong's "Nice Dreams"*), Columbia, 1981.

(As George Clinton) Additional music and lyrics, *Vice Squad,* Avco Embassy, 1982.

A Rose for Emily (short film), 1983.

Still Smokin (also known as *Cheech & Chong: Still Smokin'*), Paramount, 1983.

Cheech & Chong's "The Corsican Brothers" (also known as *Corsican Brothers*), Orion, 1984.

The Boys Next Door (also known as *Big Shots, Blind Rage, Death Takes a Holiday,* and *No Apparent Motive*), New World, 1985.

Avenging Force (also known as *Night Hunter*), Cannon, 1986.

American Ninja 2: The Confrontation (also known as *American Ninja 2*), Cannon, 1987.

Too Much, Cannon, 1987.

Wild Thing (also known as *Asphalt Kid*), Atlantic Releasing, 1987.

Platoon Leader, Cannon, 1988.

American Ninja 3: Blood Hunt (also known as *American Fighter III* and *American Ninja 3*), Cannon, 1989.

The House of Usher (also known as *The Fall of the House of Usher*), 21st Century Film, 1989.

Ten Little Indians (also known as *Agatha Christie's "Ten Little Indians"* and *Death on Safari*), Cannon, 1989.

Wild Orchid II: Two Shades of Blue (also known as *Blue Movie Blue, Wild Orchid 2: Blue Movie Blue,* and *Wild Orchid 2: Two Shades of Blue*), Triumph Releasing, 1991.

Almost Pregnant (also known as *Baby Talk*), Vision International, 1992.

Hard Promises, Columbia, 1992.

Paper Hearts (also known as *Cheatin' Hearts*), Trimark Pictures, 1993.

Additional music, *Boca,* J. N. Producoes/The Zalman King Company, 1994.

Brainscan, Triumph Releasing, 1994.

Hellbound, Cannon, 1994.

Mother's Boys, Dimension Films, 1994.

Mortal Kombat, New Line Cinema, 1995.

Top Dog, Live Entertainment, 1995.

The Viking Sagas (also known as *The Icelandic Sagas*), New Line Cinema/Justin Pictures, 1995.

Austin Powers: International Man of Mystery (also known as *Austin Powers* and *Austin Powers—Das Schaerfste, was Ihre Majestaet zu bieten hat*), New Line Cinema, 1997.

Beverly Hills Ninja, TriStar, 1997.

Mortal Kombat: Annihilation (also known as *Mortal Kombat: The Annihilation* and *Mortal Kombat 2*), New Line Cinema, 1997.

Trojan War (also known as *No Night Stand, Rescue Me,* and *Safe Sex*), Warner Bros., 1997.

Black Dog, Universal, 1998.

Wild Things (also known as *Sexcrimes, Sex Crimes,* and *wildthings*), Columbia, 1998.

The Astronaut's Wife (also known as *Intrusion* and *Noise*), New Line Cinema, 1999.

Austin Powers: The Spy Who Shagged Me (also known as *Austin Powers Deluxe, Austin Powers II, Austin Powers 2: It's Shagging Time, Austin Powers 2: The Spy Who Shagged Me, Austin Powers II: The Wrath of Khan, It's Shagging Time,* and *The Return of Dr. Evil*), New Line Cinema, 1999.

Ready to Rumble (also known as *Headlock Go! Go! Professional Wrestling* and *Untitled Wrestling Movie*), Warner Bros., 2000.

Joe Somebody (also known as *Super papa*), Twentieth Century–Fox, 2001.

Sordid Lives, Regent Releasing, 2001.

Speaking of Sex, Twentieth Century–Fox, 2001.

3000 Miles to Graceland (also known as *Crime Is King, Destination: Graceland,* and *3,000 Miles to Graceland*), Warner Bros., 2001.

Austin Powers in Goldmember (also known as *Austin Powers: Goldmember, Austin Powers: Never Say Member Again, Austin Powers 3, Austinpussy, Goldmember, The Next Installment of Austin Powers,* and *The Third Installment of Austin Powers*), New Line Cinema, 2002.

The Santa Clause 2 (also known as *The Escape Clause: The Santa Clause 2, Hyper Noel, The Mrs. Clause: Santa Clause 2, Santa Clause Returns!, Santa Clause 2, The Santa Clause 2: The Escape Clause, The Santa Clause 2: The Mrs. Clause, Santa Claus 2,* and *SC2*), Buena Vista, 2002.

The Big Bounce (also known as *Hawaii Crime Story*), Warner Bros., 2004.

Catch That Kid (also known as *Catch That Girl* and *Mission without Permission*), Fox 2000, 2004.

A Dirty Shame, Fine Line/New Line Cinema, 2004.

Eulogy, Lions Gate Films, 2004.

New York Minute, Warner Bros., 2005.

Big Momma's House 2 (also known as *Big Mamma 2*), Twentieth Century–Fox, 2006.

Deck the Halls (also known as *All Lit Up*), Twentieth Century–Fox, 2006.

The Santa Clause 3: The Escape Clause (also known as *Pretender* and *Santa Claus 3*), Buena Vista, 2006.

Code Name: The Cleaner (also known as *The Cleaner*), New Line Cinema, 2007.

The Clique, Warner Premiere, 2008.

Harold & Kumar Escape from Guantanamo Bay (also known as *Harold & Kumar and the Escape from Guantanamo Bay, Harold and Kumar Go to Amsterdam,* and *Harold & Kumar 2*), New Line Cinema, 2008.

The Love Guru (also known as *Untitled Mike Myers Project* and *Der Love Guru*), Paramount, 2008.

Older Than America, Tribal Alliance Productions, 2008.

Assassin's Creed: Lineage (series of short films related to the *Assassin's Creed* video games), Ubisoft/Hybride Technologies, 2009.

Extract, Miramax, 2009.

Hometown Glory (documentary), Costa Communications/Wafilms, 2010.

Tooth Fairy, Twentieth Century–Fox, 2010.

Film Music; Songs Featured in Films:

Title song and several others, *The Apple* (also known as *BIM Stars* and *Star Rock*), Cannon, 1980.

"The Cobra Strikes," *American Ninja 3: Blood Hunt* (also known as *American Fighter III* and *American Ninja 3*), Cannon, 1989.

"It's Love" and "On the Other Side," *Wild Orchid II: Two Shades of Blue* (also known as *Blue Movie Blue, Wild Orchid 2: Blue Movie Blue,* and *Wild Orchid 2: Two Shades of Blue*), Triumph Releasing, 1991.

"A Christmas Wish," *Only You,* 1992.

Theme song "The Longest Night," *Mother's Boys,* Dimension Films, 1994.

"Bingo" and "Drone #3," *In God's Hands,* TriStar/Sony Pictures Entertainment, 1998.

"Dr. Evil" and "Soul Bossa Nova," *Austin Powers: The Spy Who Shagged Me* (also known as *Austin Powers Deluxe, Austin Powers II, Austin Powers 2: It's Shagging Time, Austin Powers 2: The Spy Who Shagged Me, Austin Powers II: The Wrath of Khan, It's Shagging Time,* and *The Return of Dr. Evil*), New Line Cinema, 1999.

"Sting Theme," *Ready to Rumble* (also known as *Headlock Go! Go! Professional Wrestling* and *Untitled Wrestling Movie*), Warner Bros., 2000.

"Blue Country" and "In Daddy's Eyes," *Sordid Lives,* Regent Releasing, 2001.

"Let's Go Sexin'," *A Dirty Shame,* Fine Line/New Line Cinema, 2004.

"WWKD," *Miss Congeniality 2: Armed and Fabulous* (also known as *Miss Congeniality 2, Miss Secret Agent 2: Armed and Fabulous, Miss Undercover 2,* and *Untitled Miss Congeniality Sequel*), Warner Bros., 2005.

"Cartage #2," "Daddy's Job," and "Probe," *Alpha Dog* (also known as *Jesse James Hollywood*), Universal, 2006.

"Paper Hearts," *Big Momma's House 2* (also known as *Big Mamma 2*), Twentieth Century–Fox, 2006.

"Root Canal," *Tooth Fairy,* Twentieth Century–Fox, 2010.

Wrote songs and music featured in films, television programs, and other projects.

Television Music; Series:

Main title music, *1st & Ten* (also known as *1st & Ten: The Bulls Mean Business, 1st and Ten: The Championship, 1st & Ten: Do It Again, 1st & Ten: Going for Broke, 1st & Ten: In Your Face?,* and *1st & Ten, Training Camp: The Bulls Are Back*), HBO, 1984–87.

Red Shoe Diaries (also known as *Foxy Fantasies, Zalman King's "Red Shoe Diaries," Diarios del zapato rojo,* and *Skjulte laengsler*), Showtime, 1992 96.

Night Visions (also known as *Night Terrors, Nightvision,* and *Nightvisions*), Fox, 2001, episodes of the series combined to make the television movie *Shadow Realm,* Sci–Fi Channel, c. 2002.

Television Music; Miniseries:

Cruel Doubt, NBC, 1992.

Intensity (also known as *Dean Koontz's "Intensity"*), Fox, 1997.

Television Music; Movies:

The Lion of Africa, HBO, 1987.

Gotham (also known as *The Dead Can't Lie*), Showtime, 1988.

Through the Eyes of a Killer (also known as *The Master Builder*), CBS, 1992.

Till Death Do Us Part (also known as *Married for Murder*), NBC, 1992.

Bonds of Love, CBS, 1993.

A Kiss to Die For (also known as *Those Bedroom Eyes*), NBC, 1993.

Lake Consequence, Showtime, 1993.

Amelia Earhart: The Final Flight (also known as *The Final Flight*), TNT, 1994.

Betrayed by Love, ABC, 1994.

Fatal Vows: The Alexandra O'Hara Story (also known as *To Sleep with Danger*), CBS, 1994.

One of Her Own, ABC, 1994.

Seduced by Evil, USA Network, 1994.

Delta of Venus, Showtime, 1995.

Her Deadly Rival (also known as *A Deadly Affair*), CBS, 1995.

Tad, The Family Channel, 1995.

Beyond the Call, Showtime, 1996.

The Last Days of Frankie the Fly (also known as *Frankie the Fly*), HBO, 1996.

Business for Pleasure, The Movie Channel, 1997.

Heart of Fire (also known as *Out of the Inferno* and *The Tanker Incident*), CBS, 1997.

Dollar for the Dead, TNT, 1998.

A Place Called Truth, The Movie Channel, 1998.

Lansky, HBO, 1999.

Shadow Realm (consists of "Patterns," "The Maze," "Harmony," and "Voices," all episodes of the television series *Night Visions*), Sci–Fi Channel, c. 2002.

44 Minutes: The North Hollywood Shoot–Out (also known as *44 Minutes: The North Hollywood Shoot-out*), FX Network, 2003.

Life of the Party, Lifetime, 2006.

Bury My Heart at Wounded Knee (also known as *Untitled Wounded Knee Project*), HBO, 2007.

Television Music; Episodic:

"Opening Night," *1st & Ten* (also known as *1st & Ten: The Bulls Mean Business*, *1st and Ten: The Championship*, *1st & Ten: Do It Again*, *1st & Ten: Going for Broke*, *1st & Ten: In Your Face?*, and *1st & Ten, Training Camp: The Bulls Are Back*), HBO, 1990.

(As George Clinton) Additional music, *Chromiumblue.com* (also known as *ChromiumBlue.com*), Showtime, multiple episodes, 2002.

Television Music; Pilots:

Songs "God Is Rhythm" and "You Never Really Know," *Red Shoe Diaries* (also known as *Red Shoe Diaries the Movie* and *Wild Orchid III: Red Shoe Diaries*), Showtime, 1992.

The 4400 (also known as *4400* and *Los 4400*), USA Network and Sky Television, 2004.

Music for the Stage:

(Music, lyrics, and book with Sherry Landrum) *That Other Woman's Child* (musical), New York Musical Theatre Festival, 37 Arts Theatre C, New York City, 2008.

Music for Videos:

The World of Austin Powers (short documentary), Organa West, 2002.

Music for Compilation Videos; Music from the *Red Shoe Diaries* Television Series:

Red Shoe Diaries 2: Double Dare, Republic Pictures Home Video, 1993.

Red Shoe Diaries 6: How I Met My Husband, Vision Replays, 1997.

Red Shoe Diaries 3: Another Woman's Lipstick, Anthem Pictures, 2005.

Red Shoe Diaries 9: Slow Train, Anthem Pictures, 2005.

Red Shoe Diaries 12: Girl on a Bike, Anthem Pictures, 2005.

Red Shoe Diaries 13: Four on the Floor, Anthem Pictures, 2005.

Red Shoe Diaries 17: Swimming Naked (also known as *Zalman King's "Red Shoe Diaries: Swimming Naked"* and *Zalman King's "Swimming Naked: Red Shoe Diaries"*), Anthem Pictures, 2005.

Albums and Songs:

(With the George Clinton Band) *The George Clinton Band Arrives*, ABC Records, 1977.

(With others) Various artists, *Moving On Up*, Kent Records, 1984.

Soundtrack Albums:

(With others) *Action TV Themes*, Silva Screen, 1990.

(With others) *Music from Zalman King's "Red Shoe Diaries,"* Mercury, 1992.

(With others) *The Music of Red Shoe Diaries*, 1993 and 2001.

Mortal Kombat, TVT, 1995.

Austin Powers—International Man of Mystery, Hollywood Records, 1997.

Mortal Kombat: Annihilation, TVT, 1997.

Wild Things, Varese Sarabande, 1998.

Austin Powers—The Spy Who Shagged Me (More Music from the Motion Picture), Maverick, 1999.

Austin Powers—International Man of Mystery & The Spy Who Shagged Me, RCA Victor, 2000.

Clinton's music and songs have appeared in a number of albums and other recordings. Wrote music and songs that have been recorded by several artists and groups.

OTHER SOURCES

Periodicals:

BMI Music World, July 2, 2007, pp. 30–31.

Hollywood Reporter, May 18, 2007, p. 55.

Electronic:

George S. Clinton, http://www.georgesclinton.com, June 16, 2010.

iF Magazine.com, http://www.ifmagazine.com, June 24, 2008.

COLEMAN, Rosalyn 1965–
    (Roz Coleman, Rosalyn Coleman Williams)

PERSONAL

Born July 20, 1965, in Ann Arbor, MI; married Craig T. Williams (a producer, actor, and editor), November 17, 2001; children: one son. *Education:* Howard University, B.F.A. (cum laude), drama, 1987; Yale University, M.F.A., acting, 1990. *Avocational Interests:* Tennis, writing short stories and essays.

Addresses: *Office*—Red Wall Productions, 400 West 43rd St., New York, NY 10036.

Career: Actress, director, and writer. Red Wall Productions, New York City, cofounder, partner, and creator and director of industrial films, promotional videos, educational videos, actors' demonstration reels, and other projects, 2002—; cocreator (with Darbi Worley) and cohost of the podcast *Everything Acting.* Teacher at the Actors Center, Actors Connection, American Conservatory Theater, Duke Ellington School of the Arts, Harlem School of the Arts, Howard University, Margie Haber Studios, Manhattan Theatre Club, 52nd Street Project, and elsewhere; coach of acting and various techniques; offered workshops and worked on electronic press kits. Actors Studio, New York City, life member; member of DIVA, Inc., East Coast Writers Collective, and 90 Scenes Writing Group.

Member: Actors' Equity Association, Screen Actors Guild, American Federation of Television and Radio Artists, New York Women in Film and Television.

Awards, Honors: Owen Dodson Award, 1987; Carol Dye Award, Yale University, c. 1990; nomination for Vivian Robinson/AUDELCO Recognition Award for Excellence in Black Theatre, Audience Development Committee (AUDELCO), 1999, for *The Old Settler;* Best Director Award, Motor City International Film Festival, 2003, DC Shorts Film Festival Award, best short film, and Hollywood Black Film Festival Award nomination, all for *Allergic to Nuts;* Fox Fellow Award, 2003; nomination for Barrymore Award, best actress, Theatre Alliance of Greater Philadelphia, 2006, for *Intimate Apparel;* Jokara–Micheaux Film Festival Award (with Craig T. Williams), highest achievement for theatrical picture

release, 2007, for *Drawing Angel;* named Emerging Filmmaker 2008, Cine Noir Film Festival of Black Film; *Drama–Logue* Award; Outer Critics Circle Award; other awards, honor, and recognition; Coleman's films have been included in several festivals.

CREDITS

Film Appearances:

Renee, *Mixing Nia,* Xenon Entertainment Group, 1998.

Doctor, *Cold Feet,* Urban Media, 1999.

Loquita, *Personals* (also known as *Hook'd Up*), Unapix Entertainment Productions, 1999.

Mrs. Adisa, *Music of the Heart* (also known as *Fiddlefest, 50 Violins,* and *Music of My Heart*), Miramax, 1999.

Skirty Winner, 1999.

Joyce, *Hung Over and Out* (short film), 2000.

Kevin's partner, *The Opportunists,* First Look International, 2000.

Officer Briggs, *The Window* (short film), Tribal Blues, 2000.

Dawn Clifton, *Our Song,* IFC Films, 2001.

Vanilla Sky, Paramount, 2001.

Comedienne in park, *Only Joking* (short film), 2002.

Trish Hofmann, *Brown Sugar* (also known as *I Used to Love Her* and *Seven Days*), Twentieth Century–Fox, 2002.

Emily, *Everyone's Depressed,* Indiepix, 2006.

Crying mother, *Brooklyn's Finest,* Overture Films, 2009.

Monique Edwards, *What We Became* (short film), 2009.

Pearle Freeman, *Frankie and Alice,* Checkmark, 2009.

Monica, *It's Kind of a Funny Story,* Focus Features, 2010.

(Uncredited) Nurse, *Twelve,* Hannover House, 2010.

Parole officer Russo, *A Long Road* (short film), The Collective/Small Town Pictures, 2010.

Voice of Marie Waters, *Unfamiliar Paintings* (short film), 2010.

Indelible, c. 2010.

Roz, *The Talk Man,* 2011.

Film Director:

Driving Fish (short film), Red Wall Productions, 2002.

Allergic to Nuts (short film), Red Wall Productions, 2003.

Jeremy Explodes (educational film), 2003.

Underground Man (short film), 2005.

Reenactment segment, *Black Sorority Project: The Exodus* (documentary; also known as *Black Sorority Project*), Red Wall Productions/Derek and Jamar Productions, 2006.

(As Rosalyn Coleman Williams) *Drawing Angel* (short film), Red Wall Productions/Topiary Productions, 2007.

Underground Man (short film), 2008.

BFF (short film; also known as *B.F.F.*), Red Wall Productions, 2009.

Second unit director, *What We Became* (short film), 2009.
Cool Kidz (short film), Red Wall Productions, c. 2010.
Moth to a Flame (short film), c. 2010.

Director of short films, including *Broken, Ends & Beginnings, Layla's Mourning, Scrambled Softly, The Starter Marriage, Three Weeks in Hell, Twisted,* and *Would I Lie to You.* Director of other films, including *What I Wouldn't Give for a Good Cigar.* Some sources state that Coleman directed other projects.

Television Appearances; Series:
Voice, *Africans in America—America's Journey through Slavery* (documentary; also known as *Africans in America*), PBS, 1998.
Brenda Manning, *As the World Turns,* CBS, 2008.

Television Appearances; Movies:
Yvonne, *The Ditchdigger's Daughters,* The Family Channel, 1997.

Television Appearances; Specials:
Grace, "The Piano Lesson," *Hallmark Hall of Fame* (also known as *Hallmark Television Playhouse*), CBS, 1995.

Television Appearances; Episodic:
Sheila, "Head Case," *NYPD Blue* (also known as *New York Blues, New York Cops—NYPD Blue, New York Police, New York Police Blues, New York Police Department, N.Y.P.D,* and *N.Y.P.D.*), ABC, 1996.
Mrs. Edmonds, "No Place Like Hell," *New York Undercover* (also known as *Uptown Undercover*), Fox, 1997.
Anika, *As the World Turns,* CBS, 1999.
Flower vendor, "Contact," *Law & Order: Special Victims Unit* (also known as *Law & Order's Sex Crimes, Law & Order: SVU,* and *Special Victims Unit*), NBC, 2000.
Ruby Freeman, "Justice," *D.C.,* The WB, 2000.
Voice, "Jubilee Singers: Sacrifice and Glory," *The American Experience* (documentary), PBS, 2000.
Abby Basil, "Orpheus Descending," *Oz* (also known as *Kylmae rinki, Oz—A vida e uma prisao,* and *Oz—livet bak murene*), HBO, 2001.
Yolanda, "Just Lie Back," *Deadline,* 2001.
Gloria Padilla, "Vulnerable," *Law & Order: Special Victims Unit* (also known as *Law & Order's Sex Crimes, Law & Order: SVU,* and *Special Victims Unit*), NBC, 2002.
Mrs. Thomson, "Maltese Cross," *Law & Order: Criminal Intent* (also known as *Law & Order: CI*), NBC, 2006.
Tonya Johnson, "Senseless," *Law & Order: Criminal Intent* (also known as *Law & Order: CI*), USA Network, 2007.

Trish King, "Gone Fishing," *Kidnapped* (also known as *Kidnap*), NBC, 2007.
Trish King, "Mutiny," *Kidnapped* (also known as *Kidnap*), NBC, 2007.
Hallie, "Golden Boy," *New Amsterdam,* Fox, 2008.
Second emergency room doctor, "The Bride Wore Boxing Gloves," *One Life to Live* (also known as *Between Heaven and Hell, OLTL,* and *One Life to Live: The Summer of Seduction*), ABC, 2008.
Mrs. Washington, "Can We Get That Drink Now?," *Mercy* (also known as *Mercy Hospital*), NBC, 2009.
Nurse Jackie (also known as *Untitled Edie Falco Project*), Showtime, c. 2010.

Appeared in other programs, including *The Best Shorts: A BET J Showcase* (also known as *Short Film Showcase*), Black Entertainment Television J (also known as Black Entertainment Television Jazz and Black Entertainment Television on Jazz).

Television Appearances; Pilots:
Out of Commission, c. 2006.

Stage Appearances:
The Piano Lesson, Walter Kerr Theatre, New York City, 1990–91.
Mule Bone, Ethel Barrymore Theatre, New York City, 1991.
Nurse Hanniman, *The Destiny of Me,* Circle Repertory Theatre, Lucille Lortel Theatre, New York City, 1992–93.
Ruby, *Seven Guitars,* Goodman Theatre, Chicago, IL, Huntington Theatre Company, Boston, MA, and American Conservatory Theatre, Marines Memorial Theatre, San Francisco, CA, all 1995, and Center Theatre Group, Ahmanson Theatre, Los Angeles, and Walter Kerr Theatre, both 1996.
Insurrection … Holding History, Joseph Papp Public Theatre, LuEsther Hall, New York City, c. 1996.
Major Crimes, Actors Studio, New York City, 1997.
Lou Bessie Preston, *The Old Settler,* Primary Stages, New York City, 1998–99.
Everybody's Ruby, Joseph Papp Public Theatre, Anspacher Theater, New York City, c. 1999.
Sidonie, *The Bitter Tears of Petra von Kant,* Henry Miller's Theatre, New York City, 2000–2001.
Angel, *Breath, Boom,* Playwrights Horizons Studio, New York City, 2001.
Ethel Waters, *Carson McCullers (Historically Inaccurate),* Women's Project and Productions and Playwrights Horizons Theatre, Julia Miles Theater, New York City, 2002.
BettyAnn, *Runaway Home,* Studio Theatre, Washington, DC, 2003.
Doreen Gaynor, *Whose Family Values!* (one–act play), The Clurman Theatre, New York City, 2003.
Cali Hogan, *Things of Dry Hours,* Pittsburgh Public Theatre, O'Reilly Theatre, Pittsburgh, PA, 2004.

Lily Grace Hoterfield, *Levee James,* American Conservatory Theatre, Geary Theatre, San Francisco, CA, 2004.

Esther Mills, *Intimate Apparel,* Philadelphia Theatre Company, Plays & Players Theatre, Philadelphia, PA, 2006.

Mame Wilks, *Radio Golf,* Cort Theatre, New York City, 2007.

Mrs. Muller, *Doubt,* George Street Playhouse, New Brunswick, NJ, 2007.

Mother, *Topsy Turvy Mouse,* produced as staged reading and as full productions, both Mentor Project 2007, Cherry Lane Studio Theatre, New York City, 2007.

Dussie Mae, *Ma Rainey's Black Bottom* (staged readings), produced as part of the cycle August Wilson's 20th Century, John F. Kennedy Center for the Performing Arts, Terrace Theatre, Washington, DC, 2008.

Martha Pentecost, *Joe Turner's Come and Gone* (staged readings), produced as part of the cycle August Wilson's 20th Century, John F. Kennedy Center for the Performing Arts, Terrace Theatre, 2008.

Mother, *War* (also known as *WAR*), Rattlestick Playwrights Theatre, Julia Miles Theatre, 2008.

Cleo, *The Sin Eater,* produced as part of Summer Shorts 3: Series B, 59 East 59th Street Theatre, New York City, 2009.

Rachel Tate, *Zooman and the Sign,* Signature Theatre Company, Peter Norton Space, New York City, 2009.

Paternity, produced as staged reading and as full productions, both Mentor Project 2010, Cherry Lane Studio Theatre, 2010.

Performed in solo shows at the Baby Jupiter, Manhattan Class Company, Shooting Gallery, and elsewhere.

Stage Director:
Ludlow Fair (one–act play), 1990.
It Isn't the Moon, Red Wall Productions, Manhattan TheatreSource, New York City, 2006.

Internet Appearances:
(Sometimes known as Roz Coleman) Cohost, *Everything Acting* (podcast series), http://www.everythingactingpodcast.com, beginning c. 2006.

Herself, *Tonya and Friends* (episodic podcast), broadcast as part of *iTunes,* http://itunes/apple.com/us/podcast/tonya-and-friends, May 28, 2010.

Herself, *The UPload Show* (episodic; also known as *The UPload with Danielle & Yolanda*), http://www.theuploadshowonline.com, January 4, 2010.

Internet Work:
(Sometimes known as Roz Coleman; with Darbi Worley) Cocreator, *Everything Acting* (podcast), http://www.everythingactingpodcast.com, beginning c. 2006.

RECORDINGS

Videos:
Herself, *Filmfest* (DVD magazine; also known as *Film–Fest*), issue 6: *Filmmaking in the New Millennium,* c. 2001.

Video Work:
With Craig T. Williams, created a video about Barack Obama for American Women for Obama, c. 2008.

WRITINGS

Screenplays:
Driving Fish (short film), Red Wall Productions, 2002.
(With others) *Black Sorority Project: The Exodus* (documentary; also known as *Black Sorority Project*), Red Wall Productions/Derek and Jamar Productions, 2006.

Wrote other screenplays, including the short films *Broken, Layla's Mourning,* and *The Starter Marriage.*

Writings for the Stage:
Author of solo stage shows she performed at the Baby Jupiter, Manhattan Class Company, Shooting Gallery, and elsewhere.

Short Stories and Essays:
Coleman's writings have appeared in anthologies, including *Thank Yo' Mama* and *Vacation.* Contributor to periodicals, including *Allure, Black Masks, Method Madness,* and *Pageantry.* With Craig T. Williams, published a book of scripts, short stories, and essays.

OTHER SOURCES

Electronic:
Everything Acting, http://www.everythingactingpodcast.com, June 16, 2010.
Red Wall Productions, http://www.redwallproductions.com, June 16, 2010.
Rosalyn Coleman, http://www.rosalyncoleman.com, June 17, 2010.

COLOURIS, Keith
  See COULOURIS, Keith

CONROY, Frances 1953–
  (Francis Conroy)

PERSONAL

Born November 13, 1953, in Monroe, GA; father, a business executive; mother, in business; married

Jonathan Furst, 1980 (divorced); married Jan Munroe (an actor and mime), 1992; children: one. *Education:* Attended Dickinson College; Juilliard School, graduated, 1977; trained at Neighborhood Playhouse School of the Theatre, New York City.

Addresses: *Agent*—International Creative Management, 10250 Constellation Blvd., 9th Floor, Los Angeles, CA 90067; (voice work) Access Talent, Inc., 171 Madison Ave., Suite 910, New York, NY 10016; (animation voice work) Danis Panaro Nist, 9201 West Olympic Blvd., Beverly Hills, CA 90212. *Manager*—Paul Martino, Martino Management, New York, NY.

Career: Actress. Arena Stage, Washington, DC, guest artist, 1983–84; Old Globe Theatre, San Diego, CA, member of acting company, 1985; Acting Company, New York City, past member. Museum of Modern Art, New York City, former gift shop employee.

Awards, Honors: Drama Desk Award nomination, outstanding featured actress in a play, 1980, for *Othello;* Drama Desk Award, outstanding featured actress in a play, 1990, for *The Secret Rapture;* Obie Award, *Village Voice,* 1993, for *The Last Yankee;* Drama Desk Award nomination, outstanding featured actress in a play, 1994, for *In the Summer House;* Drama Desk Award nomination, outstanding actress in a play, 1997, for *The Rehearsal;* Antoinette Perry Award nomination and Outer Critics Circle Award, both best featured actress in a play, 2000, for *The Ride down Mt. Morgan;* Emmy Award nominations, outstanding lead actress in a drama series, 2002, 2003, 2005, 2006, Screen Actors Guild Award nominations (with others), outstanding ensemble in a drama series, annually, 2002–06, Golden Globe Award and Screen Actors Guild Award, both best actress in a television drama series, 2004, all for *Six Feet Under.*

CREDITS

Stage Appearances:
Multiple roles, *Measure for Measure,* New York Shakespeare Festival, Delacorte Theatre, Public Theatre, New York City, 1976.

Kattrin, *Mother Courage and Her Children,* Acting Company, American Place Theatre, New York City, 1978.

Cordelia, *King Lear,* Acting Company, American Place Theatre, 1978.

Amy Lowell, Sappho, Mary Shelley, Nelly Dean, and Dorothea Brooke, *The Other Half,* Acting Company, American Place Theatre, 1978.

Isabel and Diana, *All's Well that Ends Well,* New York Shakespeare Festival, Delacorte Theatre, Public Theatre, 1978.

Desdemona, *Othello,* New York Shakespeare Festival, Delacorte Theatre, Public Theatre, then Alliance Theatre Company, Atlanta, GA, both 1979.

Christine, *Sorrows of Stephen,* New York Shakespeare Festival, Susan Stein Shiva Theatre, Public Theatre, New York City, 1979–80.

Measure for Measure, Yale Repertory Theatre, New Haven, CT, 1979–80.

Jo, *The Lady from Dubuque,* Morosco Theatre, New York City, 1980.

Woman in skirt, *Girls, Girls, Girls,* Other Stage, Public Theatre, New York City, 1980.

"Sally and Marsha," *Winterset,* Yale Repertory Theatre, 1980–81.

Miranda, *The Tempest,* Tyrone Guthrie Theatre, Minneapolis, MN, 1981.

Dona Elvire, *Don Juan,* Tyrone Guthrie Theatre, 1981.

Ethan Frome, Long Wharf Theatre, New Haven, CT, 1981–82.

Julia, *Zastrozzi,* New York Shakespeare Festival, Susan Stein Shiva Theatre, Public Theatre, 1982.

Margaret "Mags" Church, *Painting Christmas,* Second Stage Theatre Company, South Street Theatre, New York City, 1983.

Sonya, *Uncle Vanya,* La MaMa Experimental Theatre Club, New York City, 1983.

Kevin, *To Gillian on Her 37th Birthday,* Ensemble Studio Theatre, Circle in the Square Downtown, New York City, 1984.

Elmire, *Tartuffe,* Yale Repertory Theatre, 1984.

Louisa May Alcott, *Romance Language,* Playwrights Horizons Theatre, New York City, 1984–85, then Mark Taper Forum, Los Angeles, 1985–86.

Kate, *The Taming of the Shrew,* American Shakespeare Festival, Stratford, CT, 1985.

Elizabeth, *Richard III,* Old Globe Theatre, San Diego, CA, 1985.

Mrs. San Francisco, *Mrs. California,* Mark Taper Forum and Coronet Theatre, both Los Angeles, 1985–86.

Corinna Stroller, *The House of Blue Leaves,* Pasadena Playhouse, Pasadena, CA, 1987.

Ann Whitefield, *Man and Superman,* Roundabout Theatre Company, Union Square Theatre, New York City, 1987–88.

Samantha, *Zero Positive,* New York Shakespeare Festival, LuEsther Hall, Public Theatre, New York City, 1988.

Mrs. Gibbs, *Our Town,* Lyceum Theatre, New York City, 1988–89.

Marion French, *The Secret Rapture,* Public Theatre, then Ethel Barrymore Theatre, both New York City, 1989.

Frankie Lewis, *Some Americans Abroad,* Mitzi E. Newhouse Theatre, then Vivian Beaumont Theatre, Lincoln Center, both New York City, 1990.

Sasha Lebedev, *Ivanov,* Yale Repertory Theatre, 1990.

Agnes Eggling, *A Bright Room Called Day,* New York Shakespeare Festival, LuEsther Hall, Public Theatre, 1990–91.

Hesione Hushaby, *Heartbreak House,* South Coast Repertory, Costa Mesa, CA, 1991.

Catherine Forrest, *Two Shakespearean Actors,* Cort Theatre, New York City, 1992.

Sally Truman, *Lips Together, Teeth Apart,* Lucille Lortel Theatre, New York City, 1992.

Patricia Hamilton, *The Last Yankee,* Manhattan Theatre Club Stage II, New York City, 1993.

Mrs. Constable, *In the Summer House,* Vivian Beaumont Theatre, Lincoln Center, 1993.

Margaret Hyman, *Broken Glass,* Longworth Theatre and Booth Theatre, both New York City, 1994.

Mary Ann, *Booth,* York Theatre Company, Theatre at St. Peter's Church, New York City, 1994.

"B," *Three Tall Women,* Promenade Theatre, New York City, 1994–95.

Lenore, *Arts and Leisure,* Playwrights Horizons Theatre, 1996.

The countess, *The Rehearsal,* Roundabout Theatre Company, Criterion Center Stage Right Theatre, New York City, 1996.

Birdie Hubbard, *The Little Foxes,* Vivian Beaumont Theatre, Lincoln Center, 1997.

Theo, *The Ride Down Mt. Morgan,* New York Shakespeare Festival, Estelle R. Newman Theatre, Public Theatre, New York City, 1998, then Ambassador Theatre, New York City, 2000.

Mrs. Antrobus, *The Skin of Our Teeth,* New York Shakespeare Festival, Delacorte Theatre, Public Theatre, 1998.

Capulat, *Ring 'round the Moon,* Belasco Theatre, New York City, 1999.

The Dinner Party, Mark Taper Forum, 1999–2000.

Macbeth, Acting Company, Scottsdale Center for the Arts, Scottsdale, AZ, 2000.

Pyrenees, Kirk Douglas Theatre, Los Angeles, 2006.

Also appeared in a production of *Broadway.*

Film Appearances:

Shakespearean actress, *Manhattan,* United Artists, 1979.

Waitress, *Falling in Love,* Paramount, 1984.

Pamela Murdock, *Amazing Grace and Chuck* (also known as *Silent Voice*), TriStar, 1987.

Ruby Hanson, *Rocket Gibraltar,* Columbia, 1988.

Lynn, *Another Woman,* Orion, 1988.

Lady from Palm Beach, *Dirty Rotten Scoundrels,* Orion, 1988.

House owner, *Crimes and Misdemeanors,* Orion, 1989.

Mary Behan, *Billy Bathgate,* Buena Vista, 1991.

Christine Downes, *Scent of a Woman,* Universal, 1992.

Scrawny shanty lady, *The Adventures of Huck Finn,* Buena Vista, 1993.

Irene Reed, *Sleepless in Seattle,* TriStar, 1993.

Developing, 1994.

Miss Scover, *The Neon Bible,* Strand Releasing, 1995.

(As Francis Conroy) Anne's mother, *Angela,* Tree Farm Pictures, 1996.

Ann Putnam, *The Crucible,* Twentieth Century–Fox, 1996.

Paula Burns, *Maid in Manhattan* (also known as *Made in New York*), Sony Pictures Releasing, 2002.

Herself, *Showboy,* 2002.

Bootsie Carp, *Die Mommie Die,* Sundance Film Series, 2003.

Ophelia, *Catwoman,* Warner Bros., 2004.

Mrs. Hepburn, *The Aviator,* Miramax/Warner Bros., 2004.

Dora, *Broken Flowers,* Focus Features, 2005.

Catherine Buttersfield, *Shopgirl,* Buena Vista, 2005.

Lynne Willoughby, *Ira & Abby,* Magnolia Pictures, 2006.

Dr. T. H. Moss, *The Wicker Man,* Warner Bros., 2006.

Frances, *The Grand Design* (short film), Firefly Films, 2007.

Miss Greythorne, *The Seeker: The Dark Is Rising,* Fox–Walden, 2007.

Rosie, *Humboldt County,* Magnolia Pictures, 2008.

Voice of Antoinette, *The Tale of Despereaux* (animated), Universal, 2008.

Agnes May, *The Smell of Success,* Initiate Productions, 2009.

Trudy Van Uuden, *New in Town,* Lions Gate Films, 2009.

Mrs. Looch, *Stay Cool,* Eagle Films, 2009.

Eloise's mom, *Love Happens,* Universal, 2009.

Mrs. Birnberg, *Shelter,* Weinstein Company, 2010.

Julia Bloodworth, *Provinces of Night,* Dax Productions/Buffalo Bulldog Films/Provinces of Night, 2010.

Madylyn, *Stone,* Overture Films, 2010.

Dolly, *Waking Madison,* Phoenicia Pictures, 2010.

Television Appearances; Series:

Ruth Fisher, *Six Feet Under,* HBO, 2001–2005.

Peggy Haplin, *Happy Town,* ABC, 2010.

Television Appearances; Miniseries:

Jean Smith, *Kennedy,* NBC, 1983.

Mrs. Benson, *Queen,* CBS, 1993.

Television Appearances; Movies:

Mrs. Watson, *The Royal Romance of Charles and Diana,* CBS, 1982.

Jacobo Timerman: Prisoner without a Name, Cell without a Number, NBC, 1983.

LBJ: The Early Years, NBC, 1987.

Lynn Kessler, *Terrorist on Trial: The United States versus Salim Ajami* (also known as *Hostile Witness*), CBS, 1988.

Peggy Breen, *One More Mountain,* ABC, 1994.

Innocent Victims, 1996.

Mrs. Byrne, *Thicker than Blood,* TNT, 1998.

Martha Lassiter, *Murder in a Small Town,* NBC, 1999.

Camille Bailey, *A Perfect Day* (also known as *No Love No Life*), TNT, 2006.

Television Appearances; Specials:
Diana, *All's Well that Ends Well*, 1978.
Mother and Lilian Steichen, "Carl Sandburg: Echoes and Silences," *Great Performances*, PBS, 1982.
"Keeping On," *American Short Story*, PBS, 1983.
Louise Mallard, "The Joy that Kills," *American Playhouse*, PBS, 1985.
"Eugene O'Neill: A Glory of Ghosts," *American Masters*, 1985.
Mrs. Gibbs, "Our Town," *Great Performances*, PBS, 1989.
Fiona, "Journey," *Hallmark Hall of Fame*, CBS, 1995.
The Green Room, Bravo, 2000.
Life and Loss: The Impact of "Six Feet Under," HBO, 2006.

Television Appearances; Pilots:
Ruth Fisher, *Six Feet Under*, HBO, 2001.
Kathy, *Mike Birbiglia's Secret Public Journal*, CBS, 2008.

Television Appearances; Episodic:
Kate, "Earth: Building Models," *3–2–1 Contact*, 1984.
Liz Sable, "Co–Hostess Twinkie," *Newhart*, CBS, 1986.
Ellie Pendleton, "The Library" segment, "Take My Life ... Please!/Devil's Alphabet/The Library," *The Twilight Zone*, CBS, 1986.
"Falling from Grace," *Hill Street Blues*, 1986.
Gladys Lynch, "Steele Hanging in There: Part 1," *Remington Steele*, 1987.
Mrs. Jankowski, "The Battle of Las Vegas," *Crime Story*, 1987.
Rosa Halasy, "Disciple," *Law & Order*, NBC, 1988.
Elizabeth Hendrick, "Prisoner of Love," *Law & Order*, NBC, 1990.
Elizabeth, "Judgment Day," *Cosby*, CBS, 1998.
Claire, *Developing*, PBS, c. 1999.
Beverly Rose, "The Pigeon," *Stark Raving Mad*, NBC, 2000.
Veterinarian hero, "Flappy's Not Happy/Electric Evening," *Higglytown Heroes*, The Disney Channel, 2004.
"The Making of 'Catwoman'," *HBO First Look*, HBO, 2004.
(Uncredited; in archive footage) *Corazon de ...*, 2005.
"Living and Dying in 'Our Town'," *Character Studies*, PBS, 2007.
Becky Riley, "Coming Home," *ER*, NBC, 2007.
Becky Riley, " ... As the Day She Was Born," *ER*, NBC, 2008.
Virginia Hildebrand, "There's Always a Woman," *Desperate Housewives*, ABC, 2008.
Virginia Hildebrand, "What More Do I Need?," *Desperate Housewives*, ABC, 2008.
Virginia Hildebrand, "City on Fire," *Desperate Housewives*, ABC, 2008.
Loretta Stinson, "The Stinsons," *How I Met Your Mother* (also known as *H.I.M.Y.M.*), CBS, 2009.
Jane Fields, "Sheila Carlton," *Nip/Tuck*, FX Network, 2010.

Television Appearances; Awards Presentations:
The 61st Annual Golden Globe Awards, NBC, 2004.
10th Annual Screen Actors Guild Awards, TNT, 2004.

RECORDINGS

Videos:
Desdemona, *Othello*, New York Shakespeare Festival, 1979.
(Uncredited) *The Making of "Catwoman,"* 2004.
(Uncredited) *Broken Flowers: Start to Finish*, 2006.

WRITINGS

Nonfiction:
Contributor to books, including *Actors on Acting*, edited by Holly Hill, Theatre Communications Group, 1993.

OTHER SOURCES

Periodicals:
Entertainment Weekly, January 24, 2003, p. 21; March 25, 2003.
Interview, April, 1989, pp. 77, 126.

COULOURIS, Keith 1967–
(Keith Colouris)

PERSONAL

Born November 5, 1967, in Camp Hill, PA; married Lesli Kay (an actress), December 25, 2003; children: Jackson William, Alec Jude. *Education:* Studied to be a Taoist priest.

Career: Actor, producer, director, film editor, and writer. Involved with the Internet site *Lesli Kay Health*, http://www.leslikayhealth.com.

CREDITS

Television Appearances; Series:
David Allen Stenbeck (also known as Reid Hamilton), *As the World Turns*, CBS, 1998–2000.

Keith Schaeffer, *One Life to Live* (also known as *Between Heaven and Hell, OLTL,* and *One Life to Live: The Summer of Seduction*), ABC, 2001.

Television Appearances; Movies:

Adam Cisneros, *Deliver Them from Evil: The Taking of Alta View* (also known as *Take Down* and *Under Pressure*), CBS, 1992.

Jerry Osbourne, *Firestorm: 72 Hours in Oakland,* ABC, 1993.

Rodney Blackwell, *The Conviction of Kitty Dodds* (also known as *Conviction: The Kitty Dodds Story*), CBS, 1993.

Second burglar, *Double Deception,* NBC, 1993.

Tom Hatcher and Bodine, *Dead Man's Revenge,* USA Network, 1994.

Eric, *Wiseguy* (also known as *Undercover Man*), ABC, 1996.

Television Appearances; Episodic:

Guy, "What I Did for Love," *Married … with Children* (also known as *Married, Married with Children,* and *Not the Cosbys*), Fox, 1992.

Skip, "Fatherhood," *Harry and the Hendersons,* syndicated, 1992.

"Eye of the Storm," *Renegade,* USA Network and syndicated, 1992.

Jacob, "Fathers and Sons," *The Watcher,* UPN, 1995.

Andy Miller, "Deja Vu," *Pacific Blue,* USA Network, 1996.

Dorfman, "Curiouser and Curiouser," *L.A. Firefighters* (also known as *Fire Company 132, Alerte rouge,* and *Extreme urgence*), Fox, 1996.

Dorfman, "The Fire Down Below," *L.A. Firefighters* (also known as *Fire Company 132, Alerte rouge,* and *Extreme urgence*), Fox, 1996.

Isaac Dupree, "Appearances," *Silk Stalkings,* USA Network, 1996.

Tommy Vaughn, "Murder in Tempo," *Murder, She Wrote* (also known as *Arabesque*), CBS, 1996.

Father Ted, "Roman Catholic Holiday," *Nothing Sacred* (also known as *Priesthood*), ABC, 1997.

Rich Warren, "The House That Jack Built," *Profiler,* NBC, 1997.

Intern, "S.R. 819," *The X-Files* (also known as *Files in the Dark, X-File, X-Files,* and *The X Files*), Fox, 1999.

Daniel Patterson in 1962, "Slipping," *Cold Case* (also known as *Anexihniastes ypothesis, Caso abierto, Cold case—affaires classees, Cold Case—Kein Opfer ist je vergessen, Doegloett aktak, Kalla spaar, Todistettavasti syyllinen,* and *Victimes du passe*), CBS, 2008.

Film Appearances:

First thug, *Teenage Mutant Ninja Turtles II: The Secret of the Ooze* (also known as *Mutant Ninja Turtles 2* and *Teenage Mutant Ninja Turtles 2*), New Line Cinema, 1991.

Adrian, *Doctor Mordrid* (also known as *Rexosaurus*), Full Moon Entertainment, 1992.

Luke Thomas, *Annie's Garden,* Leo Films, c. 1995 (some sources cite 1997).

Bey, *Beastmaster: The Eye of Bracus* (also known as *Beastmaster III* and *Beastmaster III: The Eye of Bracus*), MCA/Universal Home Video, 1996.

(As Keith Colouris) Harry Spencer, *South Beach Academy,* Live Entertainment, 1996.

Evil Lou, *Better Never Than Late* (short film), Sunday School Productions, 1999.

David Kerns and second Drug Enforcement Administration (DEA) agent, *In the Name of Justice,* Capital Film Studios/Poague Ent/York Entertainment, 2003.

Man at hospital, *Bloodline,* Radius 60 Studios, c. 2004.

Daniel, *Shadow People,* Radius 60 Studios, 2007.

Detective Mike Young, *4 (Four Degrees)* (short film), Kudzu Productions/Alluvial Filmworks, 2008.

Dave Mash, *Smash,* Smash It Hard Productions/Uptown 6 Productions, 2011.

Film Director, Producer, and Editor:

Bloodline, Radius 60 Studios, c. 2004.
Shadow People, Radius 60 Studios, 2007.

WRITINGS

Screenplays:

Annie's Garden, Leo Films, c. 1995 (some sources cite 1997).

(With David Schrader) *Bloodline,* Radius 60 Studios, c. 2004.

Shadow People, Radius 60 Studios, 2007.

COX, Nicole Ansari
 See ANSARI–COX, Nicole

CRUST, JR., Arnold
 See WINNER, Michael

CUCCIOLI, Robert 1958–
 (Bob Cuccioli)

PERSONAL

Born May 3, 1958, in Hempstead, NY. *Education:* St. John's University, degree in finance.

Addresses: *Agent*—HWA Talent Representatives, 36 East 22nd St., 3rd Floor, New York, NY 10010.

Career: Actor. Former employee of E. F. Hutton.

Awards, Honors: Joseph Jefferson Award, 1996, Antoinette Perry Award nomination, best actor in a musical, Drama Desk Award, and Outer Critics Circle Award, all 1997, all for *Jekyll & Hyde;* Outer Critics Circle Award, for *And the World Goes 'Round.*

CREDITS

Stage Appearances:
H.M.S. Pinafore, Broadway production, 1982.
(As Bob Cuccioli) Professor Lawrence Lake/Sir Lancelot, *A Connecticut Yankee,* All Souls Fellowship Hall, 1986.
(As Bob Cuccioli) Pontius Pilate, *Jesus Christ Superstar,* Paper Mill Playhouse, Millburn, NJ, 1987–88.
(As Bob Cuccioli) Count Danilo, *The Merry Widow,* Light Opera of Manhattan, New York City, 1988.
(As Bob Cuccioli) Joe, *Ankles Aweigh,* Goodspeed Opera House, East Haddam, CT, 1988–89.
(As Bob Cuccioli) Edward Rutledge, *La cage aux folles,* Paper Mill Playhouse, 1988–89.
(As Bob Cuccioli) Gaston, *Gigi,* Equity Library Theatre, New York City, 1989.
(As Bob Cuccioli) Nathan Rothschild, *The Rothschilds,* American Jewish Theatre, New York City, 1990, then Circle in the Square Theatre–Downtown, New York City, 1990–91.
(As Bob Cuccioli) Tito, *Lend Me a Tenor,* Paper Mill Playhouse, 1990–91.
And the World Goes 'Round, Westside Theatre, New York City, 1991.
Jud, *Oklahoma,* Paper Mill Playhouse, 1991–92.
Javert, *Les miserables,* Imperial Theatre, New York City, 1993–95.
Henry Jekyll/Edward Hyde, *Jekyll & Hyde,* Plymouth Theatre, New York City, 1997–99.
Archibald Craven, *The Secret Garden,* San Francisco, CA, 1999.
Henry Lord, *Dorian,* Los Angeles Theatre Center, Los Angeles, 1999.
Guille, *The Sons of Don Juan,* San Jose Repertory Theatre, San Jose, CA, 2000.
Hero, Arci's Place, New York City, 2000.
Sid Sorokin, *The Pajama Game,* Pittsburgh Civic Light Opera, Pittsburgh, PA, 2000.
Macheath "Mack the Knife," *Threepenny Opera,* Lucille Lortel Theatre, New York City, 2000.
King Marchan, *Victor/Victoria,* Paper Mill Playhouse, 2000.
Enter the Guardsman, Dimson Theatre, New York City, 2000.

Mark Antony, *Antony and Cleopatra,* F. M. Kirby Shakespeare Theatre, Madison, NJ, 2000.
Joseph Surface, *The School for Scandal,* McCarter Theatre, Princeton, NJ, 2001.
Nicky Arnstein, *Funny Girl,* Paper Mill Playhouse, 2001.
Jeff Moss, *Bells Are Ringing,* Benedum Center, Pittsburgh, PA, 2001.
A Little Night Music, Seattle, WA, 2001.
Antony, *Antony,* Guthrie Theatre, Minneapolis, MN, 2002.
Paul Berthalet, *Carnival!,* New Jersey Shakespeare Festival, Madison, NJ, 2002.
Sky Masterson, *Guys and Dolls,* Benedum Theatre, 2002.
Karl Streber, *Temporary Help,* Women's Project Theatre, New York City, 2002.
Dr. Johnson, *On the Twentieth Century,* New Amsterdam Theatre, New York City, 2005.
Jacques Brel is Alive and Well and Living in Paris, Zipper Theatre, New York City, 2006–2007.

Also appeared in *Senor Discretion; The Fantasticks; Pirates of Penzance; City of Angels; Phantom; 1776;* and *Carousel.*

Major Tours:
(As Bob Cuccioli) Lancelot du Lac, *Camelot,* U.S. and Canadian cities, 1985–86.

Also toured in *Jekyll & Hyde,* U.S. cities.

Television Appearances; Specials:
Broadway '97: Launching the Tonys, CBS, 1997.
The 51st Annual Tony Awards, 1997.

Television Appearances; Episodic:
Aidan "The Phantom" Masters, "Nevermore," *Baywatch,* 1997.
The Rosie O'Donnell Show, syndicated, 1997.
Paxton, "Heavy Metal," *Sliders,* Fox, 1999.
Angels in New York, SBS Australia, 2010.

Appeared in episodes of *One Life to Live* and *All My Children.*

Film Appearances:
John, *Clear Target,* 1997.
Monroe Gordon, *Celebrity,* Miramax, 1998.
John, *Operation Delta Force 3: Clear Target* (also known as *Clear Target*), Image Entertainment, 1998.
The man, *The Stranger,* Fusion International, 1999.
Sean Alford, *Spoken in Silence,* Evans & Turner Entertainment, 1999.

Butterfly Legend, 1999.
West End Story, 2002.

Film Work:
Director and producer, *Cliff Walk,* 1999.

RECORDINGS

Albums:
Contributed to *Jekyll & Hyde* (Broadway cast recording) and *And the World Goes 'Round.*

WRITINGS

Screenplays:
Cliff Walk, 1999.

CUMPSTY, Michael 1960(?)–

PERSONAL

Born February 26, 1960 (some sources say 1958), in Wakefield, England; immigrated to the United States, c. mid–1980s; father, an academician. *Education:* Attended University of North Carolina.

Addresses: *Agent*—Innovative Artists, 1505 Tenth St., Santa Monica, CA 90401.

Career: Actor. Playmakers Repertory Company, Chapel Hill, NC, member of company, 1984–86; Stagewest, Springfield, MA, member of company, 1986–87; Tyrone Guthrie Theatre, Minneapolis, MN, member of acting company, 1987–88. New York Shakespeare Festival, faculty member; University of North Carolina, former faculty member.

Member: Actors' Equity Association.

Awards, Honors: Bayfield Award, Actors' Equity Association, c. 1993, for *Timon of Athens;* Antoinette Perry Award nomination and Friends of New York Theatre Award nomination, outstanding lead actor in a play, both 2000, for *Copenhagen;* Outer Critics Circle Award nomination, outstanding actor in a musical, 2001, for *42nd Street;* Obie Award, *Village Voice,* c. 2005, for *Hamlet.*

CREDITS

Stage Appearances:
The Bacchae, Tyrone Guthrie Theatre, Minneapolis, MN, 1987–88.

Coriolanus, McCarter Theatre, Princeton, NJ, 1987–88.
Octavius Robinson, *Man and Superman,* Roundabout Theatre Company, Union Square Theatre, New York City, 1987–88.
Prince Escalus, *Romeo and Juliet,* New York Shakespeare Festival, Anspacher Theatre, Public Theatre, New York City, 1988.
Pembroke, *King John,* New York Shakespeare Festival, Delacorte Theatre, Public Theatre, New York City, 1988.
Peter Pan, Alliance Theatre Company, Atlanta, GA, 1988–89.
Time and lord, *The Winter's Tale,* New York Shakespeare Festival, Anspacher Theatre, Public Theatre, 1989.
Iachimo, *Cymbeline,* New York Shakespeare Festival, Estelle R. Newman Theatre, Public Theatre, New York City, 1989.
Young Beauchamp, *Artist Descending a Staircase,* Helen Hayes Theatre, New York City, 1989.
Laertes, *Hamlet,* New York Shakespeare Festival, Anspacher Theatre, Public Theatre, 1990.
Second Lieutenant Ralph Clark, *Our Country's Good,* Hartford Stage Company, Hartford, CT, 1990–91.
Elomire, *La Bete,* Eugene O'Neill Theatre, New York City, 1991.
Carpeta, *Scenes from an Execution,* Center Theatre Group, Mark Taper Forum, Los Angeles, 1992–93.
Parolles, *All's Well That Ends Well,* New York Shakespeare Festival, Delacorte Theatre, Public Theatre, 1993.
Alcibiades, *Timon of Athens,* Lyceum Theatre, New York City, 1993.
Jason, *Sturm und Drang,* Brooklyn Academy of Music, New York City production, 1994.
Morris Townsend, *The Heiress,* Cort Theatre, New York City, 1995.
Lieutenant Yolland, *Translations,* Plymouth Theatre, New York City, 1995.
Reverend Tony Ferris, *Racing Demon,* Vivian Beaumont Theatre, Lincoln Park, New York City, 1995.
Title role, *Timon of Athens,* New York Shakespeare Festival, Delacorte Theatre, Public Theatre, 1996.
John Dickinson, *1776,* Roundabout Theatre, New York City, 1997.
Orestes, *Electra,* Ethel Barrymore Theatre, New York City, 1998–99.
Jaques, *As You Like It,* Adams Memorial Theatre, Williamstown Theatre Festival, Williamstown, MA, 1999.
Julian Marsh, *42nd Street,* Ford Center for the Performing Arts, New York City, 2001.
Werner Heisenberg, *Copenhagen,* Royale Theatre, New York City, 2001.
Leontes, *The Winter's Tale,* Royal Shakespeare Theatre, Stratford–upon–Avon, England, 2002.
Mellrsh Wilton, *Enchanted April,* Belasco Theatre, New York City, 2003.
Arno Kretschmann, *Democracy,* Brooks Atkinson Theatre, New York City, 2004–2005.

Dr. John Middleton, *The Constant Wife,* American Airlines Theatre, New York City, 2005.
Title role, *Hamlet,* Classic Stage Company (CSC) Theatre, New York City, 2005.
Title role, *Richard II,* CSC Theatre, 2006.
Title role, *Richard III,* CSC Theatre, 2007.
Bob Greenberg and Jules, *Sunday in the Park with George,* Studio 54, New York City, 2008.
Malvolio, *Twelfth Night,* Delacorte Theatre, 2009.

Stage Work:
Codirector, *Richard III,* Classic Stage Company (CSC) Theatre, New York City, 2007.

Film Appearances:
Frankie's man, *State of Grace,* Orion, 1990.
Laura's husband, *Fatal Instinct,* Metro–Goldwyn–Mayer/United Artists, 1993.
Reverend Philip Edwards, *The Ice Storm,* Fox Searchlight, 1997.
Suzanne Pincus's publicist, *The 24 Hour Woman,* Artisan Entertainment/Shooting Gallery, 1999.
Secretary Forrestal, *Flag of Our Fathers,* Paramount, 2006.
Jack Connor, *Fast Track* (also known as *The Ex*), Metro–Goldwyn–Mayer, 2006.
Victor, *Starting Out in the Evening,* Roadside Attractions, 2007.
Charles, *The Visitor,* Overture Films, 2007.

Television Appearances; Series:
Sebastian, *One Life to Live,* ABC, 1989.
Frank Kittredge, *L.A. Law,* NBC, 1991–92.
Voice of Mr. Terhorst, *Bob,* CBS, 1992–93.
Alan Singer, *All My Children,* ABC, 2004.

Television Appearances; Miniseries:
Billy Hartington, *The Kennedys of Massachusetts,* ABC, 1990.
Dr. Garrett Wright, *Night Sins,* CBS, 1997.
Everett Larkin, *Liberty! The American Revolution,* PBS, 1997.
James Callender, *Alexander Hamilton,* PBS, 2007.

Television Appearances; Movies:
Cameron Ivers, *Matlock: The Scam,* ABC, 1995.
Terry Lynch, *Mistrial,* HBO, 1996.
Klaus Gruber/Wheeler, *The Lady in Question,* Arts and Entertainment, 1999.
Julian Marsh, *The Lullaby of Broadway: Opening Night on 42nd Street,* 2001.

Television Appearances; Specials:
Narrator, *Lost Liners,* PBS, 2000.
The Trials of J. Robert Oppenheimer (documentary), PBS, 2009.

Television Appearances; Episodic:
Laertes, "Hamlet," *Great Performances,* PBS, 1990.
Peter Bailey, "The Harvest," *Crossroads,* ABC, 1993.
Detective Gordon Hagarty, "Models," *Pointman,* syndicated, 1995.
Lord Burleigh, "Eye of the Needle," *Star Trek: Voyager* (also known as *Voyager*), UPN, 1995.
Lord Burleigh, "Cathexis," *Star Trek: Voyager* (also known as *Voyager*), UPN, 1995.
Lord Burleigh, "Persistence of Vision," *Star Trek: Voyager* (also known as *Voyager*), UPN, 1995.
Cameron Ivers, "The Scam," *Matlock,* ABC, 1995.
Tom Willis, "Hate," *Law & Order,* NBC, 1999.
Himself, "Being Hamlet," *Imagine,* BBC, 2006.
Mark Schaeffer, "Rocket Man," *Law & Order: Criminal Intent* (also known as *Law & Order: CI*), NBC, 2007.
James Callender, "Alexander Hamilton," *The American Experience,* PBS, 2007.
Prosecutor Roger Robb, "The Trials of J. Robert Oppenheimer," *The American Experience,* PBS, 2009.
Father Gus, "Hope You're Good, Smiley Face," *Mercy,* NBC, 2009.
John Randolph, "Dolley Madison," *The American Experience,* PBS, 2010.

RECORDINGS

Taped Readings:
The Great Train Robbery by Michael Crichton, Random House, 1996.
Servant of the Bones by Anne Rice, Random House, 1996.
Monstrum by Donald James, Random House, 1997.
Hong Kong by Stephen Coonts, 1999.
Star Wars Episode I: The Phantom Menace by George Lucas and Others, 1999.
Lost Years of Merlin by T. A. Barron, Random House, 2000.
The Northern Lights: The True Story of the Man Who Unlocked the Secrets of the Aurora Borealis by Lucy Jago, 2001.

OTHER SOURCES

Periodicals:
American Theatre, April, 2001, p. 8.

D

DATZ, Lisa 1973–

PERSONAL

Born April 24, 1973, in Evanston, IL; sister of Mike Datz (a musician, songwriter, actor, and producer). *Education:* University of Michigan, B.F.A.; studied theatre at Boston University; trained at HB Studio, One on One, and Michael Howard Studios, all New York City, and with Steppenwolf West, Los Angeles; also studied various disciplines with different instructors.

Addresses: *Agent*—Bret Adams, Ltd. Artists' Agency, 448 West 44th St., New York, NY 10036; Eric Emery, Abrams Artists Agency, 9200 Sunset Blvd., 11th Floor, Los Angeles, CA 90069; (voice work) Atlas Talent Agency, Inc., 15 East 32nd St., 6th Floor, New York, NY 10016.

Career: Actress. Stonehenge (rock band), Highland Park, IL, lead singer.

Member: American Federation of Television and Radio Artists, Actors' Equity Association, Screen Actors Guild.

Awards, Honors: Jeff Award, best leading actress, Joseph Jefferson Awards Committee, 1999, for *Violet.*

CREDITS

Stage Appearances; Musicals:
Angela Lansbury—A Celebration (benefit concert), Majestic Theatre, New York City, 1996.
Madeline Astor, third–class passenger, and understudy for other roles, *Titanic,* Lunt–Fontanne Theatre, New York City, 1997–99.

Understudy for the role of Yitzak, *Hedwig and the Angry Inch,* Jane Street Theatre, New York City, 1998–2000.
Title role, *Violet,* Apple Tree Theatre, Highland Park, IL, 1999.
Understudy for the roles of Celeste, Mildred, Helen, Florence, and Dakota Doran, *Saturday Night,* Second Stage Theatre, New York City, 2000.
Pam Lukowski, *The Full Monty,* Old Globe, San Diego, CA, 2000, and Eugene O'Neill Theatre, New York City, 2000–2002.
Luciana, *The Boys from Syracuse,* Roundabout Theatre Company, American Airlines Theatre, New York City, 2002.
Mattie, *Heartland: A Musical* (also known as *Heartland*), Madison Repertory Theatre, Madison, WI, 2003.
Rebecca, *Weird Romance* (staged concert readings of musical), produced as part of the Musicals in Mufti series, York Theatre Company, St. Peter's in Citigroup Center, New York City, 2004.
Samantha "Sam" Clark, *Empire,* Stamford Center for the Arts, Rich Forum, Stamford, CT, 2004.
Julia, *Two Gentlemen of Verona,* CENTERSTAGE, Baltimore, MD, 2005.
Don't Quit Your Night Job (benefit variety concert; also known as *Don't Quit Your Night Job 4*), Joseph Papp Public Theatre, Joe's Pub, New York City, 2006.
Elizabeth, *Ace,* Old Globe, 2007.
Paradise Found (reading of musical), Center Theatre Group, 2008.
Datz Life (concert with songs and stories), Ars Nova, New York City, 2009.
Kate, *The Ballad of Little Jo* (workshop production of musical), Joseph Papp Public Theatre, New York City, beginning c. 2009.

Appeared in other musical productions, including *Vanities,* Boston University Tanglewood Institute (BUTI). Workshop appearances include appearances as Alice, *Death Takes a Holiday* (musical), and as Alma, *Death Takes a Holiday* (musical), Roundabout Theatre Company; and in workshop productions of *Durante* and *In the Beginning (1–2–3–4–5)* (musical; also known as *In the Beginning* and *1–2–3–4–5*).

Stage Appearances; Plays:

Melinda Donahugh, *In the Wings,* Promenade Theatre, New York City, 2005.

Kari, *The Pavilion,* Penguin Rep Theatre, Stony Point, NY, 2006.

Meg, *Crimes of the Heart,* Theatre Aspen in Rio Grande Park, Aspen, CO, 2008.

Appeared in other productions, including *Major Barbara* and *The Tempest.*

Film Appearances:

Nora Day, *Spectropia* (film with interactive elements), Bustlelamp Productions, 2006.

Melody, *The Perfect Holiday* (also known as *Perfect Christmas*), Yari Film Group Releasing, 2007.

First happy person in bar, *Ghost Town,* Paramount, 2008.

Television Appearances; Series:

Bev, *As the World Turns,* CBS, 2005.

Television Appearances; Awards Presentations:

The 51st Annual Tony Awards, CBS, 1997.

The 55th Annual Tony Awards, CBS and PBS, 2001.

Television Appearances; Episodic:

Herself, *The Rosie O'Donnell Show,* syndicated, 1997.

Sam, "Blue's Big Holiday," *Blue's Clues,* Nickelodeon, 1999.

Agent, "Posse Comitatus," *The West Wing* (also known as *West Wing, The White House,* and *El ala oeste de la Casablanca*), NBC, 2002.

Susan Klips, *One Life to Live* (also known as *Between Heaven and Hell, OLTL,* and *One Life to Live: The Summer of Seduction*), ABC, 2002.

Lisa, "Everybody Loves Raimondo's," *Law & Order* (also known as *Law & Order Prime*), NBC, 2004.

Miss Hopkins, *All My Children* (also known as *All My Children: The Summer of Seduction* and *La force du destin*), ABC, 2004.

Emily, "Hope's Float," *Hope & Faith,* ABC, 2006.

Nurse, *Guiding Light* (also known as *The Guiding Light*), CBS, 2006.

Joanne Cahill, "Bottomless," *Law & Order* (also known as *Law & Order Prime*), NBC, 2008.

Contributed a voice for an episode of *Law & Order: Trial by Jury,* NBC.

Internet Appearances:

Appeared in footage posted on the Internet.

RECORDINGS

Albums; with Others:

Titanic (original 1997 Broadway cast recording), RCA Victor Broadway, 1997.

The Full Monty (original Broadway cast recording), RCA Victor Broadway, 2000.

Various artists, *Great Musicals* (selections from different musicals), RCA Victor Broadway, 2001.

Death Takes a Holiday (demo recording), 2006.

Empire (noncommercial audio recording or demo recording), 2006.

WRITINGS

Writings for the Stage:

(With Mike Datz) *Datz Life* (concert with songs and stories), Ars Nova, New York City, 2009.

OTHER SOURCES

Electronic:

Lisa Datz: The Official Website, http://www.lisadatz.com, June 16, 2010.

DAVIS, Dane A. 1957–
(Dane Davis)

PERSONAL

Born c. 1957, in La Mesa, CA. *Education:* California Institute of the Arts, degree in film.

Addresses: *Office*—Dantracks, Inc., 7356 Santa Monica Blvd., West Hollywood, CA 90046. *Agent*—Kraft–Engel Management, 15233 Ventura Blvd., Suite 200, Sherman Oaks, CA 91403.

Career: Sound designer and editor, composer, and voice performer. Danetracks, Inc., Los Angeles, founder and president, 1986–; sound designer and editor for commercials, games, and other short–form projects. Also worked as a writer.

Awards, Honors: Golden Reel Award (with others), sound effects editing for a movie of the week, Motion Picture Sound Editors, 1997, for *Gotti;* Academy Award, sound effects editing, Film Award (with others), best sound, British Academy of Film and Television Arts, Golden Reel Award (with others), sound effects editing, and Golden Reel Award nomination (with others), best dialog and automated dialog replacement editing, all 2000, for *The Matrix;* Emmy Award nomination (with others), sound editing for a miniseries, movie, or special, 2000, for *The Crossing;* Golden Reel Award nomination (with others), television sound effects editing, 2002, for *Club Land;* Golden Reel Award (with others), sound editing in animated features, 2003, for *Treasure Planet;* Golden Reel Award (with others), best sound editing in domestic features—sound effects and foley, 2004, for *The Matrix Reloaded;* Golden Reel Award nomination (with others), best sound editing—dialogue and automated dialogue replacement for feature film, 2008, for *Ghost Rider;* Golden Reel Award (with others), best sound editing—direct to video, 2008, for *Return to House on Haunted Hill;* Golden Reel Award nomination (with others), best sound editing—sound effects and foley in a feature film, 2009, for *Speed Racer.*

CREDITS

Film Work:

Sound re–recording mixer, *The Golden Sher,* 1981.

Supervising sound editor, *Women of Iron,* 1984.

Supervising sound editor, *Prison Ship* (also known as *Adventures of Taura, Prison Ship Star Slammer, Star Slammer,* and *Starslammer: The Escape*), Jack H. Harris Enterprises, 1984.

(As Dane Davis) Special sound effects, *Eliminators,* 1986.

Synthesist, *Flight of the Navigator,* Walt Disney Studios, 1986.

Supervising sound editor, *Friday the 13th Part VI: Jason Lives* (also known as *Jason Lives: Friday the 13th Part VI*), Paramount, 1986.

Supervising sound editor, *The Tomb,* TransWorld Entertainment, 1986.

Additional sound effects editor, *Armed Response* (also known as *Jade Jungle*), Cinetel Films, 1986.

Coeditor, *No Retreat, No Surrender,* New World, 1986.

Special sound effects, *It's Alive III: Island of the Alive* (also known as *Island of the Alive* and *Island of the Alive*), Warner Bros., 1987.

Special sound effects creator, *Prince of Darkness* (also known as *John Carpenter's "Prince of Darkness"*), Universal, 1987.

(As Dane Davis) Sound effects editor and special sound effects (Los Angeles), *Allan Quatermain and the Lost City of Gold,* Cannon Releasing, 1987.

Supervising sound editor, *Date with an Angel,* De Laurentiis Entertainment Group, 1987.

Supervising sound editor, *Remote Control,* International Video Entertainment, 1987.

Sound designer and supervising sound editor, *Surf Nazis Must Die,* Troma Films, 1987.

Sound effects (digital), *Private Investigations,* Metro–Goldwyn–Mayer, 1987.

Sound designer, *Square Dance* (also known as *Home Is Where the Heart Is*), Island Pictures, 1987.

Supervising sound editor, *Prison Ship,* 1987.

Sound effects library and sound effects design, *Back to the Beach* (also known as *Malibu Beach Girls*), 1987.

Supervising sound editor, *The Night Before,* Kings Road Entertainment/Zealcorp. Productions, 1988.

(As Dane Davis) Supervising sound editor, *Friday the 13th Part VII: The New Blood,* Paramount, 1988.

(As Dane Davis) Supervising sound editor, *Rocket Gibraltar,* Columbia, 1988.

Supervising sound editor, *Permanent Record,* Paramount, 1988.

(As Dane Davis) Supervising sound editor, *I'm Gonna Git You Sucka* (also known as *I'm Gonna Get You Sucka*), United Artists, 1988.

Sound designer, *Aliens from L.A.* (also known as *Wanda*), 1988.

Supervising sound editor, *Fright Night Part 2,* New Century Vista, 1989.

Supervising sound editor, *Far from Home,* Vestron Pictures, 1989.

Supervising sound editor, *Drugstore Cowboy,* Avenue Pictures Productions, 1989.

Supervising sound editor, *Hider in the House,* 1989.

(As Dane Davis) Sound effects recordist, *The Abyss,* 1989.

Supervising sound editor, *Murder in Law,* 1989.

Supervising sound editor, *Bad Influence,* Triumph Releasing, 1990.

Supervising sound editor, *Maniac Cop 2,* International Video Entertainment/Live Video/Vestron Video, 1990.

Supervising sound editor, *Pump Up the Volume,* New Line Cinema, 1990.

Supervising sound editor, *Welcome Home, Roxy Carmichael,* Paramount, 1990.

Supervising sound editor, *Warlock* (also known as *Warlock: The Magic Wizard*), Trimark Pictures, 1991.

Supervising sound editor, *Defending Your Life,* Geffen Pictures, 1991.

Supervising sound editor, *A Rage in Harlem,* Miramax, 1991.

Supervising sound editor, *Suburban Commando,* New Line Cinema, 1991.

Supervising sound editor, *Bill & Ted's Bogus Journey,* Orion, 1991.

Supervising sound editor, song performer ("Hotel Harp Music" and "Yankee Doodle Music Box"), and (uncredited) musician: harp, *Iron Maze,* Castle Hill Productions, 1991.

Supervising sound editor, *Blue Desert* (also known as *Silent Victim*), First Look Pictures Releasing, 1991.

Supervising sound editor, *Hard Promises,* Columbia, 1992.

Supervising sound editor, *The Hand That Rocks the Cradle,* Buena Vista, 1992.

Supervising sound editor, *The Gun in Betty Lou's Handbag,* Buena Vista, 1992.

Supervising sound editor, *El Patrullero* (also known as *Highway Patrolman*), 1992, with English subtitles, First Look Pictures Releasing, 1993.

Supervising sound editor, *Roadside Prophets*, Fine Line, 1992.

Supervising sound editor, *There Goes the Neighborhood* (also known as *Paydirt*), Paramount, 1992.

Supervising sound editor, *Traces of Red*, Samuel Goldwyn Company, 1992.

Supervising sound editor, *Forever Young*, Warner Bros., 1992.

Supervising sound editor, *Boxing Helena*, Orion, 1993.

Supervising sound editor and sound re–recording mixer, *Airborne*, Warner Bros., 1993.

Supervising sound editor, *Younger and Younger*, Kushner–Locke, 1993.

Supervising sound editor, *Romeo Is Bleeding*, Gramercy, 1994.

Supervising sound editor, *My Father the Hero* (also known as *My father, ce heros*), Buena Vista, 1994.

Supervising sound editor, *Phantasm III: Lord of the Dead* (also known as *Phantasm: Lord of the Dead, Phantasm III, Phantasm III: Lord of the Dead—The Never Dead Part III*), Starway International, 1994.

Supervising sound editor and music editor, *Don't Do It*, Triboro Entertainment Group, 1994.

Supervising sound editor, *Don Juan DeMarco*, New Line Cinema, 1995.

Supervising sound editor, *Panther*, Gramercy, 1995.

Supervising sound editor, *Gordy*, Miramax, 1995.

Supervising sound editor, *Tom and Huck* (also known as *The Adventures of Tom and Huck* and *Tom Sawyer*), Buena Vista, 1995.

Supervising sound editor, *Gunfighter's Moon*, Rysher Entertainment, 1995.

(As Dane Davis) Sound, *Divinity Gratis*, 1995.

Sound designer, *Bound*, Gramercy, 1996.

Sound re–recording mixer, *Follow the Bitch*, 1996.

Supervising sound editor, *Bed of Roses*, New Line Cinema, 1996.

Supervising sound editor, *Pie in the Sky*, Fine Line, 1996.

Supervising sound editor, *Mother*, Paramount, 1996.

Supervising sound editor, *Little Boy Blue*, Castle Hill Productions, 1997.

Supervising sound editor, *Boogie Nights*, New Line Cinema, 1997.

Sound, *Loved*, MDP Worldwide, 1997.

Sound designer, *American Perfekt*, 1997.

Re–recording mixer, *Sick: The Life and Death of Bob Flanagan, Supermasochist*, Cinepix Film Properties Productions, 1997.

Supervising sound editor, *Phoenix*, Trimark Pictures, 1998.

Supervising sound editor, *Your Friends & Neighbors*, Gramercy, 1998.

Supervising sound editor, *Simon Birch* (also known as *Angels and Armadillos*), Buena Vista, 1998.

Supervising sound editor, *Go*, Columbia/TriStar, 1999.

Sound designer and supervising sound editor, *The Matrix*, Warner Bros., 1999.

Sound designer and supervising sound editor, *House on Haunted Hill*, Warner Bros., 1999.

Sound designer and supervising sound editor, *Romeo Must Die*, Warner Bros., 2000.

Sound designer and supervising sound editor, *Red Planet*, Warner Bros., 2000.

Sound designer and supervising sound editor, *Sand* (also known as *Sandstorm*), Hard Sand Productions, 2000.

Supervising sound editor, *Playing Mona Lisa*, 2000.

Sound designer and supervising sound editor, *AntiTrust* (also known as *Conspiracy.com*), Metro–Goldwyn–Mayer, 2001.

Sound designer and supervising sound editor, *Exit Wounds*, Warner Bros., 2001.

Sound designer and supervising sound editor, *Swordfish*, Warner Bros., 2001.

Sound designer and supervising sound editor, *Thir13en Ghosts* (also known as *Thirteen Ghosts*), Warner Bros., 2001.

Supervising sound editor, *Dogtown and Z–Boys*, Sony Pictures Classics, 2001.

Supervising sound editor, *The Good Girl*, Fox Searchlight, 2002.

Supervising sound editor, *8 Mile*, Universal, 2002.

Sound designer and supervising sound editor, *Ghost Ship*, Warner Bros., 2002.

Sound designer and supervising sound editor, *Treasure Planet* (animated), Walt Disney/Buena Vista, 2002.

Additional sound designer, *They* (also known as *Wes Craven Presents: "They"*), 2002.

Sound designer and supervising sound editor, *The Matrix Reloaded* (also known as *The Matrix Reloaded: The IMAX Experience*), Warner Bros., 2003.

Sound designer and supervising sound editor, *The Matrix Revolutions* (also known as *The Matrix Revolutions: The IMAX Experience*), Warner Bros., 2003.

Supervising sound editor, *Northfork*, Paramount Classics, 2003.

Lead sound designer, sound designer, and supervising sound editor, *Riding Giants* (documentary), Sony Pictures Classics, 2004.

Supervising sound editor, *Chrystal*, First Look International, 2004.

Sound designer and supervising sound editor, *The Forgotten* (also known as *Stranger*), Columbia, 2004.

Supervising sound editor, *The Cave*, Screen Gems, 2005.

Sound designer, *The Lost City*, Magnolia Pictures, 2005.

Supervising sound editor, *Lord of War*, Lions Gate Films, 2005.

Supervising sound designer and supervising sound editor, *Aeon Flux*, Paramount, 2005.

Sound designer, *The Hills Have Eyes*, Fox Searchlight, 2006.

Sound designer, *Black Snake Moan*, Paramount Vantage, 2006.

Sound designer, *The Marine*, Twentieth Century–Fox, 2006.

Supervising sound editor, *The Last Mimzy*, New Line Cinema, 2007.

Supervising sound designer, *The Good Night*, Yari Film Group Releasing, 2007.

Sound designer and supervising sound editor, *Ghost Rider* (also known as *Spirited Racer*), Sony Pictures Entertainment, 2007.

Sound effects editor, *The Reaping*, Warner Bros., 2007.

Sound designer and supervising sound editor, *The Hunting Party*, Weinstein Company, 2007.

Sound effects editor, *Battle in Seattle*, Redwood Palms Pictures, 2007.

Co–supervising sound editor and sound designer, *Made in America* (documentary; also known as *Crips and Bloods: Made in America*), Argot Pictures, 2008.

Sound designer and supervising sound editor, *Speed Racer* (also known as *Speed Racer: The IMAX Experience*), Warner Bros., 2008.

Sound designer: editorial and supervising sound editor, *The Day the Earth Stood Still* (also known as *D.T.E.S.S.* and *The Day the Earth Stood Still: The IMAX Experience*), Twentieth Century–Fox, 2008.

Supervising sound editor, *The Call* (short film), 168 Hour Film Project & Festival, 2009.

Sound designer, *Outrage*, Magnolia Pictures, 2009.

Sound effects editor, *Whiteout*, Warner Bros., 2009.

Additional sound designer, *Ninja Assassin*, Warner Bros., 2009.

Additional sound designer, *The Losers*, Warner Bros., 2010.

Film Appearances:

(As Dane Davis) Sound designer, *The Matrix Revisited*, Warner Home Video, 2001.

Voice of Morph, *Treasure Planet* (animated), Buena Vista, 2002.

Himself, *Making "Enter the Matrix"* (short documentary), Warner Home Video, 2003.

(As Dane Davis) Voice of 01 Versatran spokesman, *The Second Renaissance Part I* (short film; also known as *The Animatrix: The Second Renaissance Part 1*), Warner Bros., 2003.

(As Dane Davis) Voice of 01 Versatran spokesman, *The Second Renaissance Part II* (animated short film; also known as *The Animatrix: The Second Renaissance Part 2*), 2003.

Television Work; Series:

Sound designer, *Dark Skies*, NBC, 1996.

Television Work; Movies:

Sound effects editor, *Curse of the Starving Class*, Showtime, 1994.

Supervising sound editor, *Gotti* (also known as *Gotti: The Rise and Fall of a Real Life Mafia Don*), HBO, 1996.

Supervising sound editor, *The Crossing*, Arts and Entertainment, 2000.

Supervising sound editor, *Club Land*, Showtime, 2001.

Television Work; Specials:

Supervising sound editor, *Hider in the House*, 1989.

Supervising sound editor, *Murder in Law*, 1990.

Supervising sound editor, *Pandemic: Facing AIDS*, HBO, 2003.

Sound designer, *Prep & Landing* (animated; also known as *Lanny and Wayne: The Christmas Elves in Prep & Landing*), ABC, 2009.

Television Appearances; Specials:

The 72nd Annual Academy Awards, ABC, 2000.

Television Appearances; Episodic:

Appeared as voice of Morph, *House of Mouse* (animated); voice of Morph, *Toon Jam* (animated).

RECORDINGS

Video Games:

Sound effects designer, *Tachyon: The Fringe*, Danetracks, 2000.

(As Dane Davis) Sound designer, *Enter the Matrix*, Infogames Entertainment, 2003.

WRITINGS

Film Music:

Song, "Hotel Harp Music," *Iron Maze*, Castle Hill Productions, 1991.

Follow the Bitch, Pennant Productions, 1996.

OTHER SOURCES

Periodicals:

Mix, September 1, 1999.

Electronic:

Dane Davis Home Page, http://www.danetracks.com, May 24, 2010.

DAVIS, Elaina Erika

PERSONAL

Education: School of the Arts, San Francisco, CA, graduated; The Juilliard School, B.F.A.; studied different disciplines with different instructors.

Addresses: *Agent*—Abrams Artists Agency, 275 Seventh Ave., 26th Floor, New York, NY 10001.

Career: Actress. Appeared in radio productions, music videos, industrial films, and advertisements. Worked as a public speaker; also worked as an English teacher in Japan.

Member: American Federation of Television and Radio Artists, Actors' Equity Association, Screen Actors Guild.

CREDITS

Stage Appearances:
Queen, *The Tragedy of Richard II,* New York Shake-speare Festival, Joseph Papp Public Theatre, Ans-pacher Theatre, New York City, 1994.

Rennie, *The Most Massive Woman Wins,* produced as part of the *Young Playwrights Festival,* Joseph Papp Public Theatre, LuEsther Hall, New York City, 1994.

Rosaura, *Life Is a Dream,* Rushmore Festival, Highland Mills, Woodbury, NY, 1994.

Andromache and Hecuba, *Troilus and Cressida,* New York Shakespeare Festival, Joseph Papp Public Theatre, Delacorte Theatre, New York City, 1995.

Betty Ferris, *Luck, Pluck, and Virtue,* Atlantic Theater Company, Linda Gross Theatre, New York City, 1995.

Ophelia, *Hamlet,* Merrimack Repertory Theatre, Low-ell, MA, 1996.

Padee Yang (a guide), *Secret History of the Lower East Side,* En Garde Arts Theatre, Seward Park High School, New York City, 1998.

Arun, *Featherless Angels* (workshop productions of open rehearsals and public performances), Con-necticut Repertory Theatre, Studio/Mobius Theatre, Storrs, CT, 1999.

Understudy for the role of Ling, *Red,* Manhattan Theatre Club, New York City, 1999.

Roxanne, *Cyrano* (adaptation of *Cyrano de Bergerac*), San Jose Repertory Theatre, San Jose, CA, 2001.

Madame Chandebise, *A Flea in Her Ear,* San Jose Reper-tory Theatre, 2001–2002.

Appeared in other productions, including an appear-ance as Leeann, *A Piece of My Heart,* Stanford Theatreworks.

Television Appearances; Series:
Cassandra Willis, *As the World Turns,* CBS, 2006–2007.

Television Appearances; Episodic:
Flight attendant, "The Pilot (Not the Pilot)," *Cosby,* CBS, 1997.

Mae Smith, "The Medal," *Early Edition,* CBS, 1997.

Dr. Xiao, *One Life to Live* (also known as *Between Heaven and Hell, OLTL,* and *One Life to Live: The Summer of Seduction*), ABC, 1998.

Claudia, "Vaya Con Dios," *Law & Order* (also known as *Law & Order Prime*), NBC, 2000.

Receptionist, "Men," *Third Watch,* NBC, 2000.

Reporter, "Don't Get on the Bus," *Spin City* (also known as *Spin*), ABC, 2000.

Reporter, "A Tale of Two Sisters," *Spin City* (also known as *Spin*), ABC, 2000.

Noelle Hamilton, *Guiding Light* (also known as *The Guiding Light*), CBS, multiple episodes, 2002.

Emergency room doctor, *One Life to Live* (also known as *Between Heaven and Hell, OLTL,* and *One Life to Live: The Summer of Seduction*), ABC, 2004.

Doctor, *Guiding Light* (also known as *The Guiding Light*), CBS, multiple episodes, 2005.

Appeared in other programs, including *All My Children* (also known as *All My Children: The Summer of Seduc-tion* and *La force du destin*), ABC.

Film Appearances:
Contact, Warner Bros., 1997.

Guin, *Personals* (also known as *Hook'd Up*), Unapix Entertainment Productions, 1999.

Heart to Heart.com, York Entertainment, 1999.

Bar girl, *Whipped,* Destination Films, 2000.

Monique, *Book of Danny,* Fingerprint Films, 2002.

Gloria Ting, *Serial,* Arbo Pictures/Canarsie Boy Enterprises/TuFux Entertainment, 2007.

Also appeared in *Trio Sonata,* Windlock Productions.

Internet Appearances:
Appeared in footage posted on the Internet.

RECORDINGS

Audiobooks:
In a Class by Itself by Sandra Brown, Random House Audio, 1999.

Flower Net by Lisa See, Bantam Doubleday Dell Audio, 1999.

Memoirs of a Geisha by Arthur Golden, Random House Audio, 2001.

Adaline Falling Star by Mary Pope Osborne, Listening Library, 2001.

When the Emperor Was Divine by Julie Otsuka, Random House Audio, 2003.

Kira–Kira by Cynthia Kadohata, Listening Library, 2005.

The Rope Walk by Carrie Brown, BBC Audiobooks America, 2007.

Grandma Calls Me Beautiful by Barbara M. Joosse, il-lustrated by Barbara Lavallee, Audible, Inc., 2008.

Children of the Longhouse by Joseph Bruchac, Penguin Group USA and Audible, Inc., 2009.

Sadako and the Thousand Paper Cranes by Eleanor Coerr, Penguin Group USA and Audible, Inc., 2009.

Watch the Stars Come Out by Riki Levinson, Penguin Group USA and Audible, Inc., 2009.

The Diary of Piper Davis: The Fences between Us by Kirby Larson, part of the Dear America series, Scholastic Audio Books, 2010.

Some sources cite Davis as the reader of *A Place Where Sunflowers Grow,* by Amy Lee–Tai, illustrated by Felicia Hoshino, c. 2009. Appeared in music videos.

Video Games:

Voice of pedestrian, *Grand Theft Auto: San Andreas* (also known as *Grand Theft Auto 5, GTA 5, GTA: San Andreas,* and *San Andreas*), Rockstar Games, 2004.

OTHER SOURCES

Electronic:

Elaina Erika Davis, http://www.elainaerikadavis.com, June 16, 2010.

Di BONAVENTURA, Lorenzo 1957(?)–

PERSONAL

Born c. 1957, in NY; son of Mario di Bonaventura (a musical conductor); married, wife's name Kimberly; children: Dante Massimo. *Education:* Harvard University, A.B.; University of Pennsylvania, M.B.A.

Addresses: *Office*—Di Bonaventura Pictures, Inc., 5555 Melrose Ave., De Mille Bldg., 2nd Floor, Los Angeles, CA 90038.

Career: Producer and executive. Columbia Pictures, worked in distribution and marketing; Warner Bros., production executive, beginning 1989, vice president of production until 1993, senior vice president of production, 1993–95, executive vice president of production, 1995–96, coleader of theatrical production, 1996–98, president of theatrical production, 1998, executive vice president of worldwide motion pictures, 1998–2002; Di Bonaventura Pictures, Los Angeles, founder and president, 2003—. Began business career as an operator (and guide) of a river–rafting enterprise.

Awards, Honors: Black Movie Award nomination, outstanding motion picture, 2006, for *Four Brothers.*

CREDITS

Film Producer:

Constantine, Warner Bros., 2005.

Four Brothers, Paramount, 2005.

Doom, Universal, 2005.

Derailed, Weinstein Company, 2005.

Shooter, Paramount, 2007.

Transformers (also released as *Transformers: The IMAX Experience*), Paramount, 2007.

1408, Metro–Goldwyn–Mayer, 2007.

Stardust, Paramount, 2007.

Imagine That, Paramount, 2009.

Transformers: Revenge of the Fallen (also known as *Transformers: Revenge* and *Transformers: Revenge of the Fallen—The IMAX Experience*), DreamWorks, 2009.

G.I. Joe: The Rise of Cobra (also known as *G.I. Joe*), Paramount, 2009.

Salt, Columbia, 2010.

Red, Summit Entertainment, 2010.

Television Appearances; Specials:

(Uncredited) *Hello, He Lied & Other Truths from the Hollywood Trenches* (also known as *Hello, He Lied*), AMC, 2002.

Tribeca Film Festival Presents, 2003.

Television Appearances; Episodic:

"Constantine: Heaven, Hell, and Beyond," *HBO First Look,* HBO, 2005.

"'Transformers': Their War, Our World," *HBO First Look,* HBO, 2007.

Entertainment Tonight (also known as *E.T.* and *This Week in Entertainment*), syndicated, 2009.

The Movie Loft, 2009.

RECORDINGS

Videos:

David O. Russell's "Three Kings" Video Journal, Warner Home Video, 2000.

The Matrix Revisited, Warner Home Video, 2001.

Doom Nation, 2006.

First Person Shooter Sequence, 2006.

Master Monster Makers, 2006.

The Making of "Derailed," Weinstein Company, 2006.

Survival of the Fittest: The Making of "Shooter," Paramount Home Entertainment, 2007.

Our World, DreamWorks Home Entertainment, 2007.

Their War, DreamWorks Home Entertainment, 2007.

The Human Factor: Exacting Revenge of the Fallen, Paramount Home Video, 2009.

The Big Bang Theory: The Making of "G.I.Joe," Paramount Home Video, 2009.

OTHER SOURCES

Periodicals:
movieScope, September, 2007, pp. 42–45.
Variety, May 31, 2004, p. 5; August 9, 2004, p. 1.

DIER, Brett 1990–

PERSONAL

Born February 14,. 1990, in London, Ontario, Canada. *Education:* Studied acting with Adrian Hough at the Spotlight Academy; studied piano; studied tae kwon do (black belt); also studied for a lifeguard certificate. *Avocational Interests:* Breakdancing.

Addresses: *Agent*—Levine Okwu Erickson, 6363 Wilshire Blvd., Suite 300, Los Angeles, CA 90048. *Manager*—Red Talent Management, Box 3, 415 West Esplanade, North Vancouver, British Columbia V7M 1A6, Canada.

Career: Actor. Appeared in advertisements. Guitarist in a band.

Member: Union of British Columbia Performers/ Alliance of Canadian Cinema, Television and Radio Artists (ACTRA).

CREDITS

Television Appearances; Movies:
Bradley, *The Secrets of Comfort House* (also known as *Comfort House* and *Sombres Secrets*) Lifetime, 2006.
Kevin Janzen, *Seventeen & Missing* (also known as *Seventeen and Missing* and *Vivid Dreams*), Lifetime, 2006.
Matt Peterson, *Family in Hiding*, Lifetime, 2006.
Caden, *Every Second Counts* (also known as *Fast Time* and *Ride of Their Lives*), Hallmark Channel, 2008, Showcase Television, 2009.
Taz, *Phantom Racer* (also known as *Death Speed*), Syfy, 2009.
Jason Young, *Meteor Storm*, Syfy, 2010.
Marshall, *Made ... The Movie* (also known as *Made*), MTV, 2010.
Matt, *Goblin*, Syfy, 2010.

Television Appearances; Episodic:
Jake, "You Can't Always Get What You Want," *Kaya*, MTV, 2007.

Junior, "Junior Prank," *Aliens in America*, The CW, 2007.
Alternate Clark Kent, "Apocalypse," *Smallville* (also known as *Smallville Beginnings* and *Smallville: Superman the Early Years*), The CW, 2008.
Derek Edlund, "Skin and Bones," *Fear Itself*, NBC, 2008.
Richard, "Forest Grump," *The Troop*, Nickelodeon, 2009.
Dylan, "99 Problems," *Supernatural* (also known as *Sobrenatural*), The CW, 2010.
James May, "John May," *V*, ABC, CTV, and other channels, 2010.

Film Appearances:
Second protester, *Battle in Seattle*, Remstar Distribution/ Hyde Park International, 2007, Redwood Palms Pictures, 2008.
Breakdancer, *Diary of a Wimpy Kid*, Twentieth Century– Fox, 2010.
Marcus, *Dear Mr. Gacy*, 2010.

OTHER SOURCES

Periodicals:
Nanaimo News Bulletin, August 19, 2008.

Electronic:
Vancouver Observer, http://www.vancouverobserver. com, March 25, 2010.

DONAT, Richard 1941–

PERSONAL

Born June 1, 1941, in Kentville, Nova Scotia, Canada; nephew of Robert Donat (an actor); brother of Peter Donat (an actor). *Education:* Graduated from the National Theatre School, Canada, 1967; studied acting at the University of British Columbia.

Addresses: *Agent*—Fountainhead Talent, Inc., 131 Davenport Rd., Toronto, Ontario M5R 1H8, Canada.

Career: Actor and director. Involved in the organization of the Chester Summer Theatre, Chester, Nova Scotia, Canada.

Member: Alliance of Canadian Cinema, Television and Radio Artists (ACTRA), Screen Actors Guild, Canadian Actors' Equity Association (member of the Directors, Choreographers and Fight Directors Councillor Policy Advisor Group).

Awards, Honors: Dora Mavor Moore Award, outstanding performance by a male in a featured role, Toronto Alliance for the Performing Arts, 1984, for *In the Jungle of Cities;* Genie Award nomination, best performance by an actor in a supporting role, Academy of Canadian Cinema and Television, 1986, for *My American Cousin;* Montreal English Critics Circle Award (MECCA), best director, 2004, for *Wade in the Water;* Montreal English Critics Circle Award (MECCA), best director, 2004, and Robert Merritt Award nomination, outstanding direction, Theatre Nova Scotia, 2008, for different productions of *The Drawer Boy;* Robert Merritt Award, outstanding performance—supporting actor, 2007, for *Fool for Love;* life membership honors, Alliance of Canadian Cinema, Television and Radio Artists (ACTRA) Maritimes, 2007.

CREDITS

Television Appearances; Series:
Voice of Deej, *Ewoks* (animated; also known as *Star Wars: Ewoks*), ABC, 1985–86, then known as *The Ewoks and Droids Adventure Hour* (also known as *Ewoks & Droids Adventure Hour, Ewoks and Star Wars Droids Adventure Hour,* and *The Ewoks and Star Wars Droids Adventure Hour*), ABC, 1986, then known as *The All New Ewoks* (also known as *The All–New Ewoks*), ABC, 1986–87.
Dr. Allan Burnley, *Emily of New Moon,* CBC, 1998–2000.
Colonel Boyle, *Blackfly,* CanWest Global Television, 2001–2002.
Narrator, *The Sea Hunters* (documentary; also known as *Clive Cussler's "The Sea Hunters"*), National Geographic Channel, c. 2001–2002.
Narrator, *Nova* (documentary), PBS, beginning 2004.
Vincent "Vince" Teagues, *Haven,* Syfy, beginning 2010.

Some sources cite appearances in the program *Oceans of Mystery* (documentary), beginning c. 1998.

Television Appearances; Miniseries:
Constable Snow, *Life with Billy,* CBC, 1994.
MacDonald, *Trudeau,* CBC, 2002.
Patrick Collins, *Shattered City: The Halifax Explosion,* CBC, 2003.
Monseigneur Desranleau, *Trudeau II: Maverick in the Making* (also known as *Trudeau: The Early Years, Trudeau: Pierre–Elliott,* and *Trudeau II*), CBC, 2005.
First clerk (crewing office), *Sea Wolf* (also known as *The Sea Wolf* and *Der Seewolf*), multiple channels, 2009.
Moby Dick, c. 2010.

Television Appearances; Movies:
Sheriff Harmon, *Draw!* (also known as *Draw*), HBO, 1984.
Sam Hughes's War, CBC, 1984.

Vern Harrington, *The Suicide Murders,* CBC, 1985.
Hans Hooft, *The Little Kidnappers,* The Disney Channel, 1990.
Jim Curtis, *Deadly Betrayal: The Bruce Curtis Story* (also known as *The Bruce Curtis Story* and *Journey into Darkness: The Bruce Curtis Story*), CBC, 1991.
Shane, *The Secret,* CBS, 1992.
Selleck Silliman, *Mary Silliman's War* (also known as *The Way of Duty* and *L'appel du devoir*), Lifetime, 1994.
Jimmy Norris, *Net Worth,* CBC, 1995.
Robert Harris, *Dangerous Offender: The Marlene Moore Story,* CBC, 1996.
Rory MacLean, *Pit Pony,* 1997.
Sergeant Hulce, *Major Crime,* Lifetime, 1997.
Wilbur Bennett, *Promise the Moon,* CBC and Odyssey, 1997.
Justice of the peace, *Blue Moon,* CBS, 1999.
Father McGregor, *Our Daily Bread* (short film), CBC, 2000.
District attorney Bridges, *Passion and Prejudice,* USA Network, 2001.
Father Paul, *The Pilot's Wife* (also known as *La femme du pilote*), CBS, 2002.
Phillip, *Heart of a Stranger,* Lifetime, 2002.
Kmart executive, *Martha, Inc.: The Story of Martha Stewart* (also known as *Driven to Succeed* and *Martha Stewart—L'obcession du succes*), NBC, 2003.
Judge Walter, *Sleep Murder,* CTV, 2004.
Earl, *Suzanne's Diary for Nicholas* (also known as *James Patterson's "Suzanne's Diary for Nicholas"*), CBS, 2005.

Television Appearances; Specials:
Reuben Bright, "Cougar" (also known as "Cougar!"), *The ABC Weekend Special* (also known as *ABC Weekend Specials*), ABC, 1984.
Gil, "Calm at Sunset" (also known as "Calm at Sunset, Calm at Dawn"), *Hallmark Hall of Fame* (also known as *Hallmark Television Playhouse*), CBS, 1996.
(In archive footage) Major Wilcox, *Weird Sex and Snowshoes: A Trek through the Canadian Cinematic Psyche* (documentary), 2004.
Walter, "Candles on Bay Street," *Hallmark Hall of Fame* (also known as *Hallmark Television Playhouse*), CBS, 2006.

Appeared in other programs, including *The Shed Next Door,* CBC.

Television Appearances; Episodic:
Bartender Sam, "Manhunt: Part 1," *The Littlest Hobo,* CTV and syndicated, 1979.
Charlie, "Manhunt: Part 2," *The Littlest Hobo,* CTV and syndicated, 1979.

Joe Dortmunder, "The Angry Heart," *Little House on the Prairie* (also known as *L.H.O.T.P.* and *Little House: A New Beginning*), NBC, 1979.

"1911," *The Newcomers,* CBC, 1979.

Stan Geddis, "Euthanasia," *Nurse,* CBS, 1982.

Mac Devlin, "Trucker," *The Littlest Hobo,* CTV and syndicated, 1983.

Luke, "Seeing the Country," *Seeing Things,* CBC, 1985.

Dr. Betterman, "Heavy Sweat," *The Edison Twins,* CBC and The Disney Channel, 1986.

Waxnose, "Trouble Is My Business," *Philip Marlowe, Private Eye* (also known as *Marlowe* and *Philip Marlowe*), HBO, 1986.

Barry Cade, "Bull's Eye," *Seeing Things,* CBC, 1987.

Sheriff, "No One Gets out of Here Alive," *Wiseguy,* CBS, 1987.

Hugh Carver, "Eagles Fly Alone," *Danger Bay,* CBC and The Disney Channel, 1988.

Dr. Duchene, "Snap, Crackle, Pop!," *Side Effects,* CBC, 1995.

Cole Conacher, "The Greenhouse Effect/The Buzz," *PSI Factor: Chronicles of the Paranormal* (also known as *PSI Factor, Psi Factor,* and *Psi Factor: Chronicles of the Paranormal*), CanWest Global Television and syndicated, 1997.

Gene MacFarlane, "By Gosh or by Golly," *Wind at My Back,* CBC, 1997.

Gene MacFarlane, "Summer Dreams, Summer Nightmares," *Wind at My Back,* CBC, 1997.

"The Christmas Show," *Made in Canada* (also known as *The Industry*), CBC, 1999.

Gene MacFarlane, "A Girl in Trouble," *Wind at My Back,* CBC, 2000.

Judge, "Three Good Men Are Dead," *Trailer Park Boys,* Showcase and BBC America, 2007.

Dr. Robert Darwin, "Darwin's Darkest Hour," *Nova,* PBS, 2009.

Appeared in other programs, including *Adderly* (also known as *V. H. Adderly*), CBS; *Canada Confidential,* CBC; *For the Record,* CBC; *The Great Detective,* CBC and The Entertainment Channel; *Judge,* CBC; and *T. and T.* (also known as *Mister T* and *T. & T.*), The Family Channel and syndicated. Some sources cite appearances in other programs.

Television Appearances; Pilots:

Megashadow admiral, "I Worship His Shadow," *Lexx* (also known as *Lexx, Lexx: I Worship His Shadow, Lexx: The Dark Zone, Lexx: The Dark Zone Stories, Lexx: The Movies, Lexx: The Series, Tales from a Parallel Universe,* and *Tales from a Parallel Universe: I Worship His Shadow*), Showtime, The Movie Channel, Sci–Fi Channel, and syndicated, 1997.

Vincent "Vince" Teagues, "Welcome to Haven," *Haven,* Syfy, 2010.

Television Appearances; Other:

Appeared in *Nobody Wants to Know* and *Wildcat,* both CBC.

Film Appearances:

Police officer, *Death Weekend* (also known as *The House by the Lake* and *Fin de semaine infernale*), Cinepix, 1976, American International Pictures, 1977.

Ray, *Tomorrow Never Comes,* J. Arthur Rank/Cinepix, 1978.

Fire captain Harrison Risley, *City on Fire,* Astral Films/AVCO Embassy/J. Arthur Rank, 1979.

Fred, *Gas,* Paramount, 1981.

Loose Ends (also known as *Divine Light, Girl Bikers,* and *Screwball Academy*), c. 1983 (some sources cite c. 1986.

Senior police officer, *Martin's Day,* Metro–Goldwyn–Mayer/United Artists, 1984.

Sheriff Jarvis, *Samuel Lount,* Utopia Pictures, 1985.

Major Wilcox, *My American Cousin* (also known as *Mon cousin americain*), 1985, International Spectrafilm, 1986.

Lost!, c. 1986.

Micradyne man, *Deep Sea Conspiracy,* 1987.

Major Wilcox, *American Boyfriends* (also known as *California Dreamin', My American Boyfriend,* and *Mes copains americains*), CBS Films, 1989.

Eldorado, Alliance, 1995.

Les annees noires, National Film Board of Canada, 1995.

(In archive footage) Voice of Deej, *The Haunted Village* (animated; consists of edited episodes of the television series *Ewoks*), 1997, Lucasfilm, 2004.

(In archive footage) Voice of Deej, *Tales from Endor Woods* (animated; consists of edited episodes of the television series *Ewoks*), 1997, Lucasfilm, 2004.

Mr. Plaisted, *The Weight of Water* (also known as *Le poids de l'eau*), Buena Vista, 2000.

Karl Dean, *Phase IV,* FWP Productions/M.I.B., 2001.

Reverend Matherson, *Dragonwheel,* Mongrel Media, 2002.

Undertaker, *The Event,* THINKFilm, 2003.

Will, *A Summer Fling* (short film), Grips Don't Get Oscars Productions, 2004.

Cardinal Pietro Barbo, *The Conclave* (also known as *Conclave* and *Das Konklave*), c. 2006.

Gallagher, *Amelia* (also known as *Amelia Earhart*), Fox Searchlight, 2009.

Voice, *Like Father* (short film), 2010.

Film Work:

Development executive, *Lost!,* c. 1986.

Stage Appearances:

Brassett, *Charley's Aunt,* Neptune Theatre, Halifax, Nova Scotia, Canada, 1969.

Bystander, *Pygmalion,* Neptune Theatre, 1969.

The general, *The Police,* Studio Neptune, University of King's College, Halifax, 1969.

Igor Sullivan, *Cactus Flower,* Neptune Theatre, 1969.

Pierre, *The Boy Friend* (musical), Neptune Theatre, 1969.

Second plainclothes man, second mounted police officer, and second heavenly police officer, *Liliom,* Neptune Theatre, 1969.

Cuirette, *Hosanna,* Tarragon Theatre, Toronto, Ontario, Canada, and Bijou Theatre, New York City, both 1974.

Far as the Eye Can See, Theatre Passe Muraille, Toronto, and Tarragon Theatre, both 1977.

Worm, *In the Jungle of Cities* (also known as *Jungle of Cities*), Toronto Free Theatre, Toronto, 1983.

General Douglas MacArthur, *Thunder, Perfect Mind,* McLaughlin Planetarium, Toronto, 1985.

Jacob Mercer, *1949,* Neptune Theatre, 1991.

Peter, *Saints and Apostles,* Neptune Theatre, Studio Series, 1994.

Morgan, *The Glorious Twelfth* (also known as *The Glorious 12th*), Neptune Theatre, 1995.

The old man, *Fool for Love,* F4L Productions, The Space Studio, Halifax, 2006.

Narrator, *Swimmy, Frederick & Inch by Inch* (also known as *Leo Lionni's "Swimmy, Frederick & Inch by Inch"*), Mermaid Theatre of Nova Scotia, Windsor, Nova Scotia, 2007.

The Ark: The Theatre of Bertolt Brecht (workshops followed by a public reading; also known as *The Ark* and *The Ark 2008*), English Theatre Company, National Arts Centre, Dominion–Chalmers United Church, Ottawa, Ontario, 2008.

Mr. Fezziwig, Old Joe, and second gentleman, *A Christmas Carol,* English Theatre Company, National Arts Centre, NAC Theatre, Ottawa, 2009.

Chaplain, *Mother Courage and Her Children,* English Theatre Company, National Arts Centre, NAC Theatre, and Manitoba Theatre Centre, Winnipeg, Manitoba, Canada, both 2010.

Appeared in other productions, including an appearance in *The Drawer Boy,* Eastern Front Theatre, Dartmouth, Nova Scotia, Canada; and an appearance as a messenger, *Much Ado about Nothing.* Appeared in productions the Chester Summer Theatre, Chester, Nova Scotia, Canada; the Neptune Theatre Second Stage, Halifax, Nova Scotia, Canada; the Ship's Company, Parrsboro, Nova Scotia, Canada; and the Stratford Shakespearean Festival of Canada, Stratford, Ontario, Canada. Reader of writings by Stephen Leacock at the Atlantic Theatre Festival, Summer Laughter! Series, Wolfville, Nova Scotia, Canada, 2006, at the CentreStage Theatre, Kentville, Nova Scotia, Canada, 2009, and at the Chester Playhouse, Chester, Nova Scotia, Canada, 2010. Member of the acting ensemble for the Women in the Director's Chair (WIDC) program, Banff Centre, Banff, Alberta, Canada, 2003; and member of the acting company, English Theatre Company, National Arts Centre, Ottawa, Ontario, Canada.

Major Tours:
Cuirette, *Hosanna,* Canadian cities, c. 1974.

Stage Director:
The Elephant Man, Festival Antigonish, Antigonish, Nova Scotia, Canada, 1994.

Riot, Neptune Theatre, Halifax, Nova Scotia, 1998.

Consecrated Ground, Eastern Front Theatre, Dartmouth, Nova Scotia, 1999.

Rough Waters, Neptune Theatre, 2000.

The Drawer Boy, Stephenville Theatre Festival, Stephenville, Newfoundland, Canada, 2002, Centaur Theatre Company, Montreal, Quebec, Canada, 2004, and Atlantic Theatre Festival, Theatre, Wolfville, Nova Scotia, 2007.

Wade in the Water, Black Theatre Workshop, Centaur Theatre Company, 2004.

The God of Hell, Neptune Theatre, 2006.

Krapp's Last Tape, Pale Blur Productions/Vocalypse, BusStop Theatre, Halifax, 2007.

Let's Be Frank (musical play), Theatre Lac Brome, Knowlton, Quebec, 2008.

Le Code Noir, Black Theatre Workshop, Centre Segal Performing Arts (Segal Centre for Performing Arts), Montreal, 2009.

Director of other stage productions.

Radio Appearances; Series:
Also appeared as Big Ben Marsden, *Clean Sweep,* broadcast as part of *The Mystery Project,* CBC Radio One, 1997, 1997-2000, also broadcast as part of *Richardson's Roundup* (also known as *The Roundup*), CBC Radio One, 1990s-2000s.

Radio Appearances; Episodic:
"The Body Snatchers," *Nightfall,* CBC Radio, 1980, National Public Radio (NPR), 1981.

"Late Special," *Nightfall,* CBC Radio, c. 1981, National Public Radio (NPR), 1982.

"Angel of Death," *Nightfall,* CBC Radio, 1983.

Appeared in various radio productions.

RECORDINGS

Audiobooks:
(As the role of Cuirette) *Hosanna by Michel Tremblay,* translated by Bill Glassco and John Van Burek, CBC Audio, c. 2000.

WRITINGS

Writings for the Radio; Miniseries:

(With Douglas Rodger) *Wacousta* (based on a novel by John Richardson), broadcast as part of *Sunday Matinee* (also known as *CBC Sunday Matinee*), CBC Radio, 1991.

D'ORSAY, Brooke 1982–

PERSONAL

Born February 17, 1982, in Toronto, Ontario, Canada. *Education:* Attended the Cindy Tanas Actors Studio. *Avocational Interests:* Gymnastics.

Addresses: *Agent*—The Kohner Agency, 9300 Wilshire Blvd., Suite 555, Beverly Hills, CA 90212. *Manager*—H2F, 9000 Sunset Blvd., Suite 710, West Hollywood, CA 90069.

Career: Actress. Appeared in advertisements. Red 7 (production company), founder and principal. Participated in gymnastics competitions.

Awards, Honors: DVDX Award nomination, best supporting actress, DVD Exclusive awards, 2005, for *The Skulls III*; Gemini Award nomination (with others), best individual or ensemble performance in an animated program or series, Academy of Canadian Cinema and Television, 2008, for *6Teen*.

CREDITS

Television Appearances; Series:

Voice of Caitlin Cooke, *6Teen* (animated; also known as *The Mall*), Nickelodeon, 2004–2007, TeleToon, 2004–10, and Cartoon Network, 2008–10.
Heather Hanson, *Happy Hour,* Fox, 2006–2008.
Sasha, *Gary Unmarried* (also known as *Project Gary* and *Untitled Ed Yeager Project*), CBS, 2009–10.
Deb Dobkins, *Drop Dead Diva,* Lifetime, 2009—.

Television Appearances; Movies:

Caroline, *Everybody's Doing It,* MTV, 2002.
Cassandra, *Fortune's Sweet Kiss,* The Movie Network, 2002.
Eve Kindley, *Beautiful Girl,* ABC Family, 2003.
Paulina, *The Boy Who Cried Werewolf,* Nickelodeon, 2010.

Television Appearances; Episodic:

Ellen, "All in the Family," *Doc,* PAX, 2002.
Justine, "Lovers and Other Strangers," *Soul Food,* Showtime, 2002.
Heather Robbins, "Bullet Proof," *Wild Card* (also known as *Zoe Busiek: Wild Card*), Lifetime, 2003.
Felicity Fury, "Another Level," *Ace Lightning* (live action and animated), BBC, 2004.
Felicity Fury, "The Game's On," *Ace Lightning* (live action and animated), BBC, 2004.
Felicity Fury, "A Secret Life," *Ace Lightning* (live action and animated), BBC, 2004.
Felicity Fury, "Uninvited Guest," *Ace Lightning* (live action and animated), BBC, 2004.
Melissa Getemer, "Team," *Medical Investigation* (also known as *The Cure*), NBC, 2004.
Carol, "The Littlest Yarbo," *Corner Gas,* CTV, 2005.
Nancy, "Breaking Away," *Life on a Stick* (also known as *Related by Family*), Fox, 2005.
Voice of Claire, "All about Sharon," *Braceface* (animated; also known as *Sourire d'enfer*), TeleToon and other channels, 2005.
Voice of Claire, "Clean Slate," *Braceface* (animated; also known as *Sourire d'enfer*), TeleToon and other channels, 2005.
Christy, "The Dumpling Paradox," *The Big Bang Theory,* CBS, 2007.
Robin, "Young People Have Phlegm Too," *Two and a Half Men* (also known as *Dos hombres y medio, Dyo kai 1/2 andres, Mein cooler Onkel Charlie, Miehenpuolikkaat, Mon oncle Charlie, 2.5 cheloveka,* and *2 1/2 maen*), CBS, 2007.
April MacArthur, "Six Feet under the Sea," *Psych,* USA Network, 2009.
Margaret, "The Stinsons," *How I Met Your Mother* (also known as *H.I.M.Y.M*), CBS, 2009.

Television Appearances; Pilots:

Brenda Dellacasa, *My Life as a Movie* (also known as *My Life Is a Movie*), MTV, 2003.
Jenna Schwammie, *Then Comes Marriage,* The WB, 2004.
Voice of Caitlin Cooke, "Take This Job and Squeeze It," *6Teen* (animated; also known as *The Mall*), TeleToon and Nickelodeon, 2004.
Heather Hanson, *Happy Hour,* Fox, 2006.
Missy, *Wildlife* (also known as *Wild Life*), NBC, 2007.
Darcie, *Five Year Plan* (also known as *5 Year Plan*), ABC, 2008.
Angela Becker, *Single White Millionaire,* CBS, 2009.
Deb Dobkins, *Drop Dead Diva,* Lifetime, 2009.

Film Appearances:

Jennifer Kruz, *Why Can't I Be a Movie Star?* (also known as *Trailervision: The Movie*), 2001.
Girl, *Truths of Insanity* (short film), Jordan Entertainment, 2002.
Sandy, *19 Months,* 2002, THINKFilm, 2004.

Lisa, *Home Security* (short film), 2003.

Mother, *The Republic of Love,* Seville Pictures/Helkon SK, 2003.

Veronica Bell, *The Skulls III* (also known as *The Skulls 3*), Universal Studios Home Entertainment, 2003.

Clarissa, *Harold & Kumar Go to White Castle* (also known as *American High, Harold & Kumar, Harold & Kumar Get the Munchies,* and *Harold et Kumar chassent le burger*), New Line Cinema, 2004.

Brooke Mayo, *King's Ransom* (also known as *Untitled Anthony Anderson Project*), New Line Cinema, 2005.

Breanna, *It's a Boy Girl Thing* (also known as *He's the Girl, It's a Boy/Girl Thing,* and *Toi, c'est moi*), Icon Pictures, 2006.

Jessica, *Room 10* (short film), Moxie Pictures, 2006.

Film Work:

Stunt performer, *Why Can't I Be a Movie Star?* (also known as *Trailervision: The Movie*), 2001.

Internet Appearances:

As a member of the comedy troupe Trailervision, appeared in film trailer parodies posted on the Internet.

WRITINGS

Screenplays:

(With others) *Why Can't I Be a Movie Star?* (also known as *Trailervision: The Movie*), 2001.

Wrote screenplays.

Writings for the Internet:

As a member of the comedy troupe Trailervision, helped create film trailer parodies posted on the Internet.

OTHER SOURCES

Periodicals:

Toronto Sun, May 17, 2006, p. 14.

DYKSTRA, Ted 1961–

PERSONAL

Born January 1, 1961, in Chatham, Ontario, Canada; raised in St. Albert, Alberta, Canada; son of Theo C. and Truus (maiden name, Jagt) Dykstra; married Melanie Doane (a singer and songwriter); children: The-

odore (Theo), Roseanna (Rosie). *Education:* Graduated from the National Theatre School, Canada, 1984; studied classical piano. *Avocational Interests:* Playing tennis.

Addresses: *Agent*—Gary Goddard Agency, 10 St. Mary St., Suite 305, Toronto, Ontario M4Y 1P9, Canada.

Career: Actor, director, and composer. Soulpepper Theatre Company, founding member; Talking Fingers, founder (with Richard Greenblatt). Actorboy Records, founder (with Gary Sinise). Director of scene studies with students, National Theatre School, Canada. Affiliated with Dorian Productions and Prairie Ocean, Inc.

Member: Canadian Actors' Equity Association, Alliance of Canadian Cinema, Television and Radio Artists (ACTRA).

Awards, Honors: Dora Mavor Moore Award, outstanding performance by a male (musical), Toronto Alliance for the Performing Arts, 1989, for *Fire;* Dora Mavor Moore Award nomination, outstanding performance in a musical, 1995, for *Tommy;* Dora Mavor Moore Award, outstanding production, 1996, and Floyd S. Chalmers Canadian Play Award, 1997, both with Richard Greenblatt, for *2 Pianos, 4 Hands;* Dora Mavor Moore Award nomination, outstanding performance by a male in a principal role (play), 2003, for *A Chorus of Disapproval;* Gemini Award, best performance by an actor in a featured supporting role in a dramatic program or miniseries, Academy of Canadian Cinema and Television, 2004, for *Shattered City: The Halifax Explosion;* Dora Mavor Moore Award nominations, outstanding direction of a musical and outstanding production of a musical, both 2004, for *Tequila Vampire Matinee;* Dora Mavor Moore Award nominations, outstanding direction of a musical and outstanding production of a musical, both 2005, for *Aladdin— The Magical Family Musical;* Robert Merritt awards, outstanding direction and outstanding production, both Theatre Nova Scotia, 2006, for *The Diary of Anne Frank;* Dora Mavor Moore Award nominations, outstanding direction of a musical and outstanding production of a musical, both 2006, for *Snow White and the Group of Seven;* Dora Mavor Moore Award nominations, outstanding direction of a play and outstanding production of a play, both 2007, for *Leaving Home;* Dora Mavor Moore Award nomination, outstanding direction of a musical, 2007, for *Richard O'Brien's "The Rocky Horror Show";* Robert Merritt Award nominations, outstanding direction and outstanding production, 2007, for *A Few Good Men;* Dora Mavor Moore awards, outstanding performance by a male in a principal role (musical) and outstanding musical direction, both 2008, for *Fire;* Dora Mavor Moore Award nominations, outstanding direction of a musical and outstanding production of a musical, both 2008, for

Little Shop of Horrors; Robert Merritt Award nomination, outstanding production, 2008, for *The Miracle Worker;* Dora Mavor Moore Award nomination, outstanding production of a musical, 2009, for *Cinderella: The Sillylicious Family Musical;* Dora Mavor Moore Award nomination (with John Gray), outstanding original sound design/composition, 2010, for *Billy Bishop Goes to War.*

CREDITS

Stage Appearances:

Second bird, *Once upon a Clothesline,* c. 1971.

Junior, *Criminals in Love,* Factory Theatre, Toronto, Ontario, Canada, 1984.

Michael, *Peter Pan,* Shaw Festival, Niagara–on–the–Lake, Ontario, c. 1987.

Snobby Price, *Major Barbara,* Shaw Festival, c. 1987.

Jerry, *Once in a Lifetime,* Shaw Festival, c. 1988.

Seymour, *Little Shop of Horrors* (musical), Centaur Theatre Company, Montreal, Quebec, Canada, c. 1988.

Willy Moore, *Observe the Sons of Ulster Marching towards the Somme,* Centaur Theatre Company, c. 1988.

Cale Blackwell, *Fire* (play with music), Theatre Passe Muraille, Toronto, 1989.

Robert Sideway, *Our Country's Good,* Centaur Theatre Company, 1990, and Neptune Theatre, Halifax, Nova Scotia, Canada, c. 1990.

Dmitri Shostakovich, *Master Class,* Manitoba Theatre Centre, Mainstage, Winnipeg, Manitoba, Canada, c. 1990.

Wolfgang Amadeus Mozart (title role), *Amadeus,* Theatre Calgary, Calgary, Alberta, Canada, 1991.

Ariel, *The Tempest,* Stratford Shakespearean Festival of Canada, Festival Theatre, Stratford, Ontario, 1992.

Magnus, *World of Wonders,* Stratford Shakespearean Festival of Canada, Stratford, c. 1992.

Sloane, *Entertaining Mr. Sloane,* Stratford Shakespearean Festival of Canada, c. 1992.

Piano student, *So You Think You're Mozart?* (musical), Chamber Concerts Canada, Tarragon Theatre, Toronto, c. 1992–93.

Bottom, *A Midsummer's Night Dream,* Stratford Shakespearean Festival of Canada, Festival Theatre, 1993.

Pentheus, *The Bacchae,* Stratford Shakespearean Festival of Canada, c. 1993.

Title role, *Hamlet,* Theatre Calgary, c. 1994.

Ted, *2 Pianos, 4 Hands* (also known as *Two Pianos, Four Hands*), various venues, including workshops at the Tarragon Theatre, 1994, and productions at the Tarragon Theatre, 1996–97, Promenade Theatre, New York City, 1997–98, John F. Kennedy Center for the Performing Arts, Eisenhower Theater, Washington, DC, 1998, and other productions, including Elgin Theatre, Toronto, 2003.

Cousin Kevin, *Tommy* (rock opera), Elgin Theatre, 1995.

R. J., *Problem Child,* part of the play cycle *Suburban Motel,* Factory Theatre, 1998.

Mercutio, *Romeo & Juliet,* Soulpepper Theatre Company, du Maurier Theatre Centre, Toronto, c. 2000.

Hedwig, *Hedwig and the Angry Inch* (rock musical), Crow's Theatre, Bathurst Street Theatre, Toronto, 2001.

Daffyd Llewellyn, *A Chorus of Disapproval,* Soulpepper Theatre Company, Premiere Dance Theatre, Toronto, 2002.

Lockit, *The Beggar's Opera* (concert productions; also known as *John Gay's "The Beggar's Opera"*), Soulpepper Theatre Company, Toronto, 2002.

Bobchinsky, *The Government Inspector,* Soulpepper Theatre Company, Young Centre for the Performing Arts, Toronto, 2006.

Teach, *American Buffalo,* Soulpepper Theatre Company, Marilyn and Charles Baillie Theatre, Toronto, 2006.

Glenn Gould, *An Evening with Glenn Gould* (solo show), Luminato (Toronto Festival of Arts + Creativity), Young Centre for the Performing Arts and National Arts Centre Studio, Ottawa, Ontario, both 2007.

Performer of the poem *Howl, America & the Black Angel* (spoken word and music performance), The Art of Time Ensemble, Enwave Theatre at Harbourfront Centre, Toronto, 2007.

Cale Blackwell, *Fire* (play with music), The Canadian Stage Company (CanStage), St. Lawrence Centre for the Arts, Bluma Appel Theatre, Toronto, and Citadel Theatre, Edmonton, Alberta, Canada, both 2008.

Performer in spoken word sections, *Words & Music* (spoken word and music performance), The Art of Time Ensemble, Enwave Theatre at Harbourfront Centre, 2008.

The Kreutzer Sonata (solo show), commissioned, 2008, The Art of Time Ensemble, Enwave Theatre at Harbourfront Centre, 2009 and 2010, and The Art of Time Ensemble/Prairie Ocean, Inc., Summerworks Theatre Festival, Theatre Passe Muraille Mainspace, Toronto, 2010.

Judge and Caiaphas, *The Last Days of Judas Iscariot,* Birdland Theatre, Toronto, 2009.

Performer, *Paul Quarrington: A Life in Music, Words, and on Screen* (readings and music), BookShorts and Humber School of Creative & Performing Arts, International Festival of Authors, Harbourfront Centre, Toronto, 2009.

Songs & Celebration: An Evening of Songs from Jewish Composers (benefit concert), St. Lawrence Centre for the Arts, Toronto, 2009.

Performer, *Shakespeare: If Music Be ...* (music, dance, and theatre performances), The Art of Time Ensemble, Enwave Theatre at Harbourfront Centre, 2010.

Appeared in other productions, including *War and Peace.* Appeared in productions of St. Albert on Sturgeon Players; and in productions in Edmonton, Alberta, Canada, beginning 1976; productions of the Stratford Young Company, Shakespearean Festival of Canada, Stratford, Ontario, Canada, 1985–86; and productions with the Impromptu Splendor! troupe, The BUZZ Festival, Ontario, Canada, 2009. Some sources cite an appearance in *Odd Jobs.*

Major Tours:

Ted, *2 Pianos, 4 Hands* (also known as *Two Pianos, Four Hands*), different versions, Canadian and international cities, beginning c. 1994, Japanese cities, 2004.

Stage Director:

Science Fiction, Factory Theatre, Toronto, Ontario, Canada, 2000.

2 Pianos, 4 Hands (also known as *Two Pianos, Four Hands*), various productions, including productions in Australia and at the American Conservatory Theatre, Geary Theatre, San Francisco, CA, 2000.

Club Lafayette (musical), concert workshop productions, Soulpepper Theatre Company, Premiere Dance Theatre, Toronto, 2001.

The Beggar's Opera (concert productions; also known as *John Gay's "The Beggar's Opera"*), Soulpepper Theatre Company, Toronto, 2002.

Bully (also known as *BULLY*), The Theatre Centre, Toronto, 2002.

The Lowest Show on Earth (solo show; also known as *Scott Thompson's "Lowest Show on Earth"*), New Yorker Theatre, Toronto, 2002.

Tequila Vampire Matinee (musical; also known as *Tequila Vampire Matinee: The Musical*), Theatre Passe Muraille, Toronto, 2003.

A Funny Thing Happened on the Way to the Forum (musical), Ryerson University, Toronto, 2004.

The Dumb Waiter (produced as part of a double-bill with *The Zoo Story*), Soulpepper Theatre Company, Harbourfront Centre, Toronto, 2004, National Arts Centre Studio, Ottawa, Ontario, 2005.

Aladdin—The Magical Family Musical (pantomime production; also known as *Aladdin*), Elgin Theatre, Toronto, 2004 and 2006.

Fool for Love, Soulpepper Theatre Company, Harbourfront Centre, 2005.

Snow White and the Group of Seven (pantomime production), Elgin Theatre, 2005–2006.

A Few Good Men, Neptune Theatre, 2006.

The Diary of Anne Frank, Neptune Theatre, c. 2006.

To Kill a Mockingbird, Neptune Theatre, c. 2006.

Leaving Home, Soulpepper Theatre Company, Young Centre for the Performing Arts, Toronto, 2007.

Little Shop of Horrors (musical), The Canadian Stage Company (CanStage), St. Lawrence Centre for the Arts, Toronto, 2007.

Richard O'Brien's "The Rocky Horror Show" (musical; also known as *The Rocky Horror Show*), Manitoba Theatre Centre, Mainstage, Winnipeg, Manitoba, Canada, and The Canadian Stage Company (CanStage), St. Lawrence Centre for the Arts, Bluma Appel Theatre, Toronto, both 2007.

Under Milk Wood (also known as *Under Milk Wood, a Play for Voices*), various productions, including Luminato (Toronto Festival of Arts + Creativity), Young Centre for the Performing Arts, 2007, and Soulpepper Theatre Company, Young Centre for the Performing Arts, 2008.

Frost/Nixon, Playhouse Theatre, Vancouver, British Columbia, Canada, and The Canadian Stage Company (CanStage), St. Lawrence Centre for the Arts, Bluma Appel Theatre, both 2008.

Salt–Water Moon (also known as *Saltwater Moon*), Soulpepper Theatre Company, Young Centre for the Performing Arts, 2008.

The Miracle Worker, Neptune Theatre, c. 2008.

Cinderella: The Sillylicious Family Musical (pantomime production; also known as *Cinderella* and *The Pantos Cinderella*), Elgin Theatre, 2008–2009.

The Kreutzer Sonata (solo show), The Art of Time Ensemble, Enwave Theatre at Harbourfront Centre, Toronto, 2009.

Of the Fields, Lately, Soulpepper Theatre Company, Young Centre for the Performing Arts, 2009.

Tuesdays with Morrie, Harold Green Jewish Theatre Company, Winter Garden Theatre, Toronto, 2009.

Robin Hood—The EnvironMENTAL Family Musical (pantomime production; also known as *Robin Hood*), Elgin Theatre, 2009–10.

Billy Bishop Goes to War (musical), Soulpepper Theatre Company, Young Centre for the Performing Arts, 2009 and 2010, High Performance Rodeo (arts festival), Theatre Calgary, Calgary, Alberta, Canada, 2011, and Centre Segal Performing Arts (Segal Centre for Performing Arts), Montreal, Quebec, Canada, 2011.

Jitters, Soulpepper Theatre Company, Young Centre for the Performing Arts, 2010.

Talk, Harold Green Jewish Theatre Company, St. Lawrence Centre for the Arts, Jane Mallett Theatre, Toronto, 2010.

Stage Musical Director:

Our Town, Soulpepper Theatre Company, Young Centre for the Performing Toronto, Ontario, Canada, 2006 and 2007.

Fire (play with music), The Canadian Stage Company (CanStage), St. Lawrence Centre for the Arts, Bluma Appel Theatre, Toronto, and Citadel Theatre, Edmonton, Alberta, Canada, both 2008.

Stage Sound Designer:

Billy Bishop Goes to War (musical), Soulpepper Theatre Company, Young Centre for the Performing Arts,

Toronto, Ontario, Canada, 2009 and 2010, High Performance Rodeo (arts festival), Theatre Calgary, Calgary, Alberta, Canada, 2011, and Centre Segal Performing Arts (Segal Centre for Performing Arts), Montreal, Quebec, Canada, 2011.

Television Appearances; Series:
Dr. Seymour Allen, *Side Effects*, CBC, 1994–96.
Voice of Reg Roach, *RoboRoach* (animated; also known as *Roboroach* and *RoboBlatte*), TeleToon, Fox, and Jetix, 2002–2004.
Voice of muse, *Wonderfalls* (also known as *Maid of the Mist* and *Touched by a Crazy Person*), Fox, 2004.

Television Appearances; Miniseries:
Alan Ferrier, *Life with Billy,* CBC, 1994.
Francis Mackey, *Shattered City: The Halifax Explosion,* CBC, 2003.
Hank, *The Englishman's Boy,* CBC, 2008.

Television Appearances; Movies:
Amber Waves, ABC, 1980.
Mike, *The Cuckoo Bird*, CBC, 1985.
Gerald Arthur (some sources cite role as Gerald Arnold), *Final Notice*, USA Network, 1989.
Terry, *The Kissing Place*, USA Network, 1990.
Undercover officer, *Murder Most Likely* (also known as *The Judas Kiss*), TNT, 1999.

Television Appearances; Specials:
Johann Sebastian Bach, *Bach's Fight for Freedom,* part of the Composers' Specials, HBO, 1995.

Television Appearances; Episodic:
Carver, "Small Change," *The Littlest Hobo,* CTV and syndicated, 1985.
Jeffrey Tate, "The Eyes of Ra," *Seeing Things,* CBC, 1986.
Crown Davidson, "Beauties and Beasts," *Street Legal,* CBC, 1989.
Frank Tesh, "What the Doctor Ordered," *Katts and Dog* (also known as *Rin Tin Tin: K–9 Cop*), CTV and The Family Channel, 1991.
Joe Avery, "Officer Missing," *RoboCop: The Series* (also known as *RoboCop*), syndicated, 1994.
Joe Avery, "What Money Can't Buy," *RoboCop: The Series* (also known as *RoboCop*), syndicated, 1994.
Himself, *The Rosie O'Donnell Show,* syndicated, 1998.
Mr. Truman, "Phoenix Rising," *Missing* (also known as *1–800–Missing* and *Porte disparu*), Lifetime, 2005.
David Larson, "Blue–Eyed Blues," *Angela's Eyes* (also known as *Emily's Eyes*), Lifetime, 2006.

Television Appearances; Pilots:
Son, *Home Free!* (also known as *Home Free*), CBC, 1985.

Television Director; Specials:
Mordecai Richler: A Celebration, CBC, 2002.

Film Appearances:
First Hanlan man, *The Boy in Blue* (also known as *La race des champions*), Twentieth Century–Fox, 1986.
Graeme Gaines, *Giant Steps,* OB&D Films, 1992.
Don Froese, *Soft Deceit,* Chesler/Perlmutter Productions/Dark Line Productions/Le Monde Entertainment, 1994.
Clive, *Black Swan* (also known as *Murder in Hopeville*), Lions Gate Films/PorchLight Entertainment, 2002.
Jay, *Pavane* (short film), BookShorts, 2008.
Henk, *The Deaths of Chet Baker* (short film), 2009, IFC Films, 2010.

Radio Appearances:
Performer of the poem *Howl, America & the Black Angel* (spoken word and music performance), broadcast by CBC Radio 2, 2007.
Words & Music (spoken word and music performance), segments broadcast on *The Signal,* CBC Radio 2, 2008.

Appeared in various radio productions.

RECORDINGS

Songs:
Melanie Doane featuring Ted Dykstra, "Martha," track on Doane's album *A Thousand Nights,* Prairie Ocean, Inc., 2008.

WRITINGS

Writings for the Stage:
(With Richard Greenblatt) *2 Pianos, 4 Hands* (also known as *Two Pianos, Four Hands*), produced at various venues, including workshops at the Tarragon Theatre, Toronto, Ontario, Canada, 1994, versions at other various venues, productions in foreign languages at various venues, and productions in Canadian and international cities, beginning c. 1994, and productions at several venues, including the Tarragon Theatre, 1996–97, Promenade Theatre, New York City, 1997–98, John F. Kennedy Center for the Performing Arts, Eisenhower Theater, Washington, DC, 1998, British cities, 1998 and 1999, Citadel Theatre, Shoctor Theatre, Edmonton, Alberta, Canada, 2000, American Conservatory Theater, Geary Theater, San Francisco, CA, 2000, Elgin Theatre, Toronto, Ontario, Canada, 2003, Japanese cities, 2004, Center REPertory Company of Walnut Creek, Lesher

Center for the Arts, Margaret Lesher Theatre, Walnut Creek, CA, 2009, and Colony Theatre Company, Burbank, CA, 2009.

Author of libretto, *Swingstep* (musical with music by Charles Cozens and lyrics by Cozens and Steven Mayoff), produced at Ford Centre of Performing Arts (later known as Toronto Centre for the Arts), Toronto, 1999.

The Kreutzer Sonata (solo show; based on a novella by Leo Tolstoy), commissioned, 2008, produced at The Art of Time Ensemble, Enwave Theatre at Harbourfront Centre, Toronto, 2009 and 2010, The Art of Time Ensemble/Prairie Ocean, Inc., Summerworks Theatre Festival, Theatre Passe Muraille Mainspace, Toronto, 2010.

(With others) *Paul Quarrington: A Life in Music, Words, and on Screen* (readings and music), produced at BookShorts and Humber School of Creative & Performing Arts, International Festival of Authors, Harbourfront Centre, Toronto, 2009.

Helped create material for his performances with the Impromptu Splendor! troupe, The BUZZ Festival, Ontario, Canada, 2009.

Music for the Stage:

Dorian (rock musical; libretto by Steven Mayoff; also known as *The Picture of Dorian Gray*), Cameron House, Toronto, Ontario, Canada, 1989, produced as workshops and productions at the Tarragon Theatre Extra Space and St. Anne's, both Toronto, produced as workshops for the Blyth Festival, Blyth, Ontario, Canada, VideoCabaret, Toronto, and in New York City, c. 1998 (some sources cite c. 2000, some sources cite a production in 2002.

Club Lafayette (musical; with lyricist Mayoff and playwright Paula Wing; based on *Measure for Measure*, by William Shakespeare), concert workshop productions, Soulpepper Theatre Company, Premiere Dance Theatre, Toronto, 2001.

Composer, lyricist, and author of the book for *Evangeline* (musical; based on the poem by Henry Wadsworth Longfellow), workshop productions, Mirvish Productions, Canada; wrote music for Robert Priest's production *Knights of the Endless Day*.

Teleplays; Specials:

Mordecai Richler: A Celebration, CBC, 2002.

Screenplays:

Author of screenplays.

Albums; with Steven Mayoff:

Dorian (recording of rock musical), Dorian Productions, 2002.

Wrote songs with Mayoff.

OTHER SOURCES

Periodicals:

Maclean's, April 21, 2008, p. 76.
Toronto Star, March 8, 2008; March 22, 2008.

Electronic:

Playbill.com, http://www.playbill.com, December 9, 1997.

E–F

ELFMAN, Richard 1949–
(Richard Helfman, Aristide Sumatra, Mahatma Kane Sumatra)

PERSONAL

Born March 6, 1949, in Los Angeles, CA; son of Milton (a jazz trumpeter) and Clare Elfman (a writer; also known as Blossom Elfman); brother of Danny Elfman (a composer); married Marie–Pascale (an actress and production designer), 1969 (divorced, 1979); married Lauren (an editor and photographer), 2006; children: (first marriage) Bodhi Elfman (an actor), Louis Elfman (an actor and publisher).

Addresses: *Office*—c/o *Buzzine,* 5419 Hollywood Blvd., Suite C805, Hollywood, CA 90027.

Career: Director, producer, writer, composer, actor, musician, and special effects technician. Worked as a semiprofessional boxer, food and wine critic, and stage director. Grand Magic Circus (musical theatre company), Paris, member of company, 1970–72; Mystic Knights of the Oingo–Boingo (later known as Oingo Boingo), cofounder and percussionist, 1972–76; public speaker and participated in various events; *Buzzine,* Hollywood, CA, publisher and editor in chief; also affiliated with Buzzine Media Group.

Awards, Honors: Nomination for best film, Sitges–Catalonian International Film Festival, 1998, International Fantasy Film Award nomination, best film, Fantasporto, 1999, and nomination for best international film, Fant–Asia Film Festival, 1999, all for *Modern Vampires;* Los Angeles Drama Critics Circle Award, best smaller production, for *L'Histoire de Soldat.*

CREDITS

Film Director:
Forbidden Zone, F Z Distribution, 1982.
Shrunken Heads, Full Moon Entertainment, 1994.
(As Aristide Sumatra) *Streets of Rage,* 1994.
Modern Vampires (also known as *Revenant* and *Vamps*), Full Moon Entertainment, 1998.
Date or Disaster (short film), 2003.
28 Days to Vegas (documentary), Buzzine Media Group, 2008.
(As Mahatma Kane Sumatra) *30 Days to Vegas* (documentary), 2009.
Forbidden Zone 2: The Forbidden Galaxy, 11th Man Media, c. 2010.

Film Producer:
Forbidden Zone, F Z Distribution, 1982.
Coproducer, *Modern Vampires* (also known as *Revenant* and *Vamps*), Full Moon Entertainment, 1998.
Date or Disaster (short film), 2003.
28 Days to Vegas (documentary), Buzzine Media Group, 2008.
30 Days to Vegas (documentary), 2009.
Executive producer, *Forbidden Zone 2: The Forbidden Galaxy,* 11th Man Media, c. 2010.

Film Appearances:
(As Richard Helfman) A man from the Grand Magic Circue, *La vie facile* (also known as *The Easy Life*), Films 13, 1973.
Drumming demon, *I Never Promised You a Rose Garden,* New World, 1977.
Masseuse and prisoner, *Forbidden Zone,* F Z Distribution, 1982.
Preacher on bus, *Shrunken Heads,* Full Moon Entertainment, 1994.
(As Aristide Sumatra) Bongo dancer at dance club, *George of the Jungle* (also known as *Jungle George*), Buena Vista, 1997.

Police officer with doughnut, *Modern Vampires* (also known as *Revenant* and *Vamps*), Full Moon Entertainment, 1998.

Police officer with doughnut, *Date or Disaster* (short film), 2003.

(As Aristide Sumatra) Sheriff Patterson and Hewitt, *Scarecrow,* Anchor Bay Entertainment, 2003.

Himself, *Don't You Forget about Me* (documentary), Alliance Films, 2009, Phase 4 Films, 2010.

Carnival person, *Forbidden Zone 2: The Forbidden Galaxy,* 11th Man Media, c. 2010.

Television Director; Episodic:

"Charlotte's Revenge," *Bone Chillers,* ABC, 1996.

"Mr. Fitz and Dr. Hyde," *Bone Chillers,* ABC, 1996.

"Mummy Dearest," *Bone Chillers,* ABC, 1996.

"Teacher Creature," *Bone Chillers,* ABC, 1996.

Second unit director, "Art Intimidates Life," *Bone Chillers,* ABC, 1996.

Second unit director, "Back to School," *Bone Chillers,* ABC, 1996.

Television Special Effects Technician; Episodic:

"Art Intimidates Life," *Bone Chillers,* ABC, 1996.

"Back to School," *Bone Chillers,* ABC, 1996.

"Teacher Creature," *Bone Chillers,* ABC, 1996.

Television Appearances; Episodic:

(In archive footage) Himself, *Cinema mil,* Televisio de Catalunya, 2005.

Stage Work:

Producer and director of the production *L'Histoire de Soldat,* Los Angeles; involved with various productions.

RECORDINGS

Videos:

Director of "Private Life," *Oingo Boingo: Skeletons in the Closet,* A&M Records, 1989.

Himself, *A Look into "The Forbidden Zone"* (short documentary), Fantoma/F Z Distribution, 2004.

Director of the Oingo Boingo music video "Private Life," 1982.

WRITINGS

Screenplays:

(With others; and story) *Forbidden Zone,* F Z Distribution, 1982.

(With Mimi Lesseos; and story) *Streets of Rage,* 1994.

(With others) *Date or Disaster* (short film), 2003.

30 Days to Vegas (documentary), 2009.

(With Matthew Bright) *Forbidden Zone 2: The Forbidden Galaxy,* 11th Man Media, c. 2010.

Film Music:

Composer, *La vie facile* (also known as *The Easy Life*), Films 13, 1973.

Song "Pumpkin Pie Man," *The Cockettes* (documentary), Strand Releasing, 2002.

OTHER SOURCES

Periodicals:

Film Threat, February, 1994, p. 10.

Screem, October, 2008, pp. 19–21.

Electronic:

Buzzine, http://www.buzzine.com, June 18, 2010.

ELLISON, Chase 1993–

PERSONAL

Born September 22, 1993, in Reno, NV.

Addresses: *Agent*—Joseph Le, ABA Talent Agency, 9107 Wilshire Blvd., Suite 500, Beverly Hills, CA 90210. *Manager*—Daniel Spilo, Industry Entertainment, 955 South Carrillo Dr., 3rd Floor, Los Angeles, CA 90048.

Career: Actor. Worked as a model; appeared in advertisements.

Awards, Honors: Young Artist Award nomination, best performance in a feature film—supporting young actor, Young Artist Foundation, 2007, for *End of the Spear;* Young Artist Award nomination, best performance in a television movie, miniseries, or special—supporting young actor, 2008, for *You've Got a Friend;* Young Artist Award nomination, best performance in a feature film—supporting young actor, 2010, for *Fireflies in the Garden.*

CREDITS

Film Appearances:

Neil at the age of eight, *Mysterious Skin,* TLA Releasing/Tartan, 2005.

Toby Fisher, *Quake* (short film), American Film Institute, 2006.

Young Ethan Green, *The Mostly Unfabulous Social Life of Ethan Green* (also known as *Ethan Green*), Regent Releasing, 2006.

Young Steve Saint, *End of the Spear,* Every Tribe Entertainment/M Power Releasing/Rocky Mountain Pictures, 2006.

Kid Kostya, *Wristcutters: A Love Story* (also known as *Pizzeria Kamikaze*), Autonomous Films, 2007.

Young Christopher Rocket, *The Year of Getting to Know Us,* Inferno Distribution, 2007.

Christopher Lawrence, *Fireflies in the Garden,* Nu Metro Productions, 2008.

Zack Vuoso, *Nothing Is Private* (also known as *Towelhead*), Warner Independent Pictures, 2008.

Andy Nichol, *That's What I Am* (also known as *Big Ginger* and *Big Red*), World Wrestling Entertainment, 2010.

Randy, *Tooth Fairy,* Twentieth Century–Fox, 2010.

Television Appearances; Series:

Noah Newman, *The Young and the Restless* (also known as *Y&R, The Innocent Years, Atithasa niata, Les feux de l'amour, Schatten der Leidenschaft,* and *Tunteita ja tuoksuja*), CBS, 2005.

Television Appearances; Movies:

Ruben Tyman at the age of five, *The Perfect Wife,* Lifetime, 2001.

Christopher, *Santa, Jr.,* Hallmark Channel, 2002.

Blake Berg, *Scenes of the Crime,* Starz!, 2003.

Tommy Billings, *You've Got a Friend,* Hallmark Channel, 2007.

Hunter Sands, *The Boy Who Cried Werewolf,* Nickelodeon, 2010.

Television Appearances; Awards Presentations:

Nickelodeon "Kids' Choice Awards" (also known as *KCA, KCA 2010,* and *Kids' Choice Awards*), Nickelodeon, 2010.

Television Appearances; Episodic:

Ryan McClendon/Pierce, "Going Home," *Family Law,* CBS, 2000.

Jake, "The Invisible Man," *Providence,* NBC, 2001.

Little boy, "Surgery," *Malcolm in the Middle* (also known as *Fighting in Underpants*), Fox, 2001.

Young Simon, "V–Day," *7th Heaven* (also known as *Seventh Heaven* and *7th Heaven: Beginnings*), The WB, 2001.

Willie Stevens, "All Hallow's Eve," *Boomtown* (also known as *Metropolis*), NBC, 2002.

Willie Stevens, "The David McNorris Show," *Boomtown* (also known as *Metropolis*), NBC, 2002.

Justin Brinkmeyer, "Rush to Judgment," *The Division* (also known as *Heart of the City*), Lifetime, 2003.

Willie Stevens, "Storm Watch," *Boomtown* (also known as *Metropolis*), NBC, 2003.

Young Francis, "No Motorcycles," *Malcolm in the Middle* (also known as *Fighting in Underpants*), Fox, 2005.

Young George, "Hold My Hand," *Six Feet Under,* HBO, 2005.

Ben Castine, "Crossroads," *Saved,* TNT, 2006.

Danny Dunston, "Sleepover," *Rodney* (also known as *That's Just Rodney* and *That's My Rodney*), ABC, 2006.

Richie, "I Am Not the Fine Man You Take Me For," *Deadwood,* HBO, 2006.

Richie, "Tell Your God to Ready for Blood," *Deadwood,* HBO, 2006.

(Uncredited) Richie, "True Colors," *Deadwood,* HBO, 2006.

Television Appearances; Pilots:

Derek Matson, *Summer Camp,* Nickelodeon, 2010.

OTHER SOURCES

Electronic:

Chase Ellison, http://www.chaseellison.net, June 18, 2010.

ERNETA, GiGi
(Gigi Erneta, Petra Sanchez)

PERSONAL

Born in New York, NY. *Education:* Trained at Playhouse West and Second City Hollywood.

Addresses: *Agent*—Linda McAllister, Linda McAllister Talent, 100 Oak Lane, Waxahachie, TX 75167–8412.

Career: Actress, stunt performer, producer, and writer. Appeared in, voice artist for, and provided stunt work for advertisements. GiGi Erneta Films, principal.

Member: Screen Actors Guild, American Federation of Television and Radio Artists.

Awards, Honors: *Drama–Logue* Award (with others), best ensemble cast, c. 1998, for *Yuletidings!.*

CREDITS

Film Appearances:

Marla, *The Searcher,* 1996.

Model, *Secret Places,* Playboy Entertainment Group, 1996.

Nurse, *Bitterland,* Chehre Film Productions, 1997.

Female police officer, *Mistress of Seduction,* New City Releasing, 1998.

Third police officer, *Intimate Nights,* MRG Entertainment, 1998.

Shannon, *The Black Rose,* Dreamfactory, 2000.

Cristina, *The Price of the American Dream* (also known as *El precio del sueno americano*), Laguna Productions, 2001.

Detective Miceli, *Passion Crimes* (also known as *Every Woman Has a Secret*), After Dark Pictures/New City Releasing, 2001.

Henderson, *Raptor,* New Concorde, 2001.

Leah Andrews, *Firestorm Rising,* 2001.

Morgan Chase, *Reasonable Doubt* (also known as *The Baptist* and *Crime Scene*), American World Pictures, 2001.

Gale, *The Model Solution,* Indigo Entertainment, 2002.

Lisa Travanti, *Crossed,* Ground Zero Entertainment, 2002.

Lula, *The Chatroom* (also known as *Chat Room*), Artisan Entertainment/Megastar Pictures, 2002.

Officer Panameno, *Passage of the Four* (also known as *Screaming Night*), Blueridge Productions/New Castle Pictures, 2002.

Secretary, *Burning Desires,* Megastar Pictures, 2002.

Deputy Adams, *Cheerleader Massacre* (also known as *The Cheerleader Massacre*), Califilm, 2003.

(As Petra Sanchez) Girl on the telephone, *Lost Treasure,* DEJ Productions, 2003.

Hotel maid, *More Mercy* (also known as *Bad Bizness*), Artisan Entertainment, 2003.

Mrs. Pinta, *El Chupacabra,* York Entertainment, 2003.

Beautiful girl, *Quiet Kill* (also known as *Nightmare Boulevard*), I.Q. Entertainment, 2004.

Angel Delight, *Hercules in Hollywood,* EagleEye Pictures/Pepper Jay Productions/Talk of the Town Productions, 2005.

Mary, *I Feel Your Pain* (short film), Floppy King Productions, 2005.

Bimbo, *My Father's Eulogy* (short film), Tidal Pictures, 2007.

Danielle, *Deadly Obsession,* 2007.

Female detective, *The Insatiable,* THINKFilm, 2007.

Killa Zombies, Alcano Productions, 2007.

Lobby Lobster, 2007.

Dr. Welch, *The Name of God,* Exposition, 2008.

Jenny Mills, *Risen,* AdHoc Film Co–Op/Frame by Frame/Red Trac Productions, 2008.

Mrs. Jensen, *Hallettsville,* Westlake Entertainment Group, 2008.

Officer Panameno, *The Fresh Air Will Do You Good,* 3 O'Clock Productions/Indy Film Co–Op, 2008.

Detective O'Hara, *Vampire in Vegas,* Nu Image, 2009.

Sally, *Secret at Arrow Lake* (also known as *Mia's Father*), Palm Tree Productions/Ranch Studios, 2009.

Captain Judith Rainier, *Flag of My Father,* R–Squared Productions, 2010.

Mother, *Dusk,* Foggy Notions Unlimited, 2010.

Niki Karlin, *Endings,* Theoretical Entertainment, 2010.

Second deputy, *Code Enforcer,* Tom Foolery Productions, 2010.

Toni Nelson, *Fire from Below,* Screen Media Films, 2010.

Film Producer:

Crossed, Ground Zero Entertainment, 2002.

Executive producer, *The Fresh Air Will Do You Good,* 3 O'Clock Productions/Indy Film Co–Op, 2008.

Counterplay, c. 2008.

Film Stunt Performer:

The Searcher, 1996.

Bitterland, Chehre Film Productions, 1997.

(Uncredited) *Mistress of Seduction,* New City Releasing, 1998.

Firestorm Rising, 2001.

Reasonable Doubt (also known as *The Baptist* and *Crime Scene*), American World Pictures, 2001.

Thy Neighbor's Wife (also known as *Midnight Vendetta, Poison,* and *Sex Attraction*), New City Releasing, 2001.

Quiet Kill (also known as *Nightmare Boulevard*), I.Q. Entertainment, 2004.

Fire from Below, Screen Media Films, 2010.

Flag of My Father, R–Squared Productions, 2010.

Film Work; Other:

Script supervisor, *Age of Slavery* (documentary), Anderson Group, 2000.

Stand–in, *Thy Neighbor's Wife* (also known as *Midnight Vendetta, Poison,* and *Sex Attraction*), New City Releasing, 2001.

Stunt coordinator, *Crossed,* Ground Zero Entertainment, 2002.

Stunt driver, *Deadly Obsession,* 2007.

Television Appearances; Series:

Voice of Esperanza, *Maya & Miguel* (animated), PBS, beginning 2004.

Jane, *La ley del silencio,* Telemundo, 2005.

Television Appearances; Movies:

(Uncredited) Paramedic, *About Sarah,* CBS, 1998.

Second nurse, *Visions* (also known as *Blind Sight*), syndicated, 1998.

Photographer, *She's No Angel,* Lifetime, 2001.

Girl by the pool, *Project Viper,* Sci–Fi Channel, 2002.

Reba, *Camel Spiders,* Syfy, 2011.

Television Appearances; Specials:

Giselle LaVigne, *The Night Stalker,* 2002.

Television Appearances; Episodic:

Mabel Normand, "William Desmond Taylor," *E! Mysteries & Scandals* (also known as *Mysteries and Scandals* and *Mysteries & Scandals*), E! Entertainment Television, 1998.

Marjorie, "The Neighbors," *Hidden Hills,* NBC, 2003.

Alison, "Omissions," *Strong Medicine,* Lifetime, 2004.

Mrs. Goodman, "Nobody Puts Baby in a Corner," *Veronica Mars,* UPN, 2005.

Casey, "Getting Served," *Desire,* MyNetworkTV, 2006.

Casey, "A Star Is Born," *Desire,* MyNetworkTV, 2006.

Mrs. Dunn, "It's Different for Girls," *Friday Night Lights* (also known as *FNL* and *F.N.L.*), NBC, 2006.

Mrs. Goodman, "Happy Go Lucky," *Veronica Mars,* UPN, 2006.

As Gigi Erneta, appeared in "Bordello Murders," part of *Unsolved Mysteries.*

Television Work; Movies:

Grip, *The Wasp Woman* (also known as *Forbidden Beauty* and *Roger Corman Presents "The Wasp Woman"*), Showtime, 1995.

Stunt double, *Project Viper,* Sci–Fi Channel, 2002.

Stage Appearances:

Francesca, *Yuletidings!* (collection of one–acts), Road Theatre Company, Lankershim Arts Center, North Hollywood, CA, 1997.

Lupe Velez, *The Soap Also Rises* (improvisational soap opera), Second City Hollywood, Los Angeles, 2002.

Performed as Bonnie Chockful, *Improv Fight Club,* Second City Hollywood.

Internet Appearances; Series:

Alexandra Mireles, *Alamo Heights SA,* http://www.alamoheightssa.com, beginning 2006.

RECORDINGS

Video Games:

(As Gigi Erneta) Voice of Flame for English–language version, *Cy Girls* (originally known as *Cool Girl*), Konami Digital Entertainment America, 2004.

WRITINGS

Screenplays:

Crossed, Ground Zero Entertainment, 2002.

Counterplay, c. 2008.

Writings for the Stage:

(With others) *The Soap Also Rises* (improvisational soap opera), Second City Hollywood, Los Angeles, 2002.

With others, contributed to *Improv Fight Club,* Second City Hollywood.

OTHER SOURCES

Electronic:

GiGi Erneta, http://www.gigierneta.com, June 16, 2010.

FAST, Cheryl–Lee 1967–

PERSONAL

Born September 13, 1967, in Saskatchewan, Canada; raised in Saskatoon, Saskatchewan, Canada; married Milan Zivkovic, October 29, 2005; children: Alexia Fast (an actress and writer). *Education:* University of Calgary, bachelor of commerce degree.

Career: Producer. Fast Productions, Ltd., founder and president. Massey Productions/Massey Films, head of business and development; Global Television, intern. Participated in film festivals and panels. Writer and editor for an English newspaper, Nagoya, Japan.

Member: Academy of Canadian Cinema & Television, Canadian Film & Television Production Association, Women in Film.

Awards, Honors: Phillip Borsos Award for best new Canadian feature film (with others), Whistler Film Festival, 2004, for *The Papal Chase;* Leo Award nomination (with others), short drama: best short drama, Motion Picture Arts & Sciences Foundation of British Columbia, 2005, for *Just Smile & Nod;* Toronto ReelWorld Film Festival, outstanding feature film, 2006, and Canadian Filmmakers' Festival, best feature film, 2007, both for *The Zero Sum;* Gemini Award nomination (with others), best children's or youth fiction program or series, Academy of Canadian Cinema and Television, 2007, for *Spirit Bear: The Simon Jackson Story.*

CREDITS

Film Producer:

(And director) *The Wrappers* (short film), 2000.

The Red Bridge (short film), 2001, Atlantic Film Festival, 2002, Reel 2 Real International Film Festival for Youth, 2006.

(And executive producer) *The Papal Chase* (documentary), Film Transit, 2004.

Hide (short film; also known as *HIDE*), 2005.

The Zero Sum (also known as *Letters*), 2005, Kaleido-scope Entertainment, 2006.

Coproducer, *Birthdays and Other Traumas* (short film), 2006.

Executive producer, *Blood, Sweat & Gears* (documentary), 2006.

Swimming Lessons (short film), 2006.

Associate producer and development producer, *Iron Road,* Equinoxe Films, 2008, also broadcast as a miniseries, CBC, 2008.

Dream (short film), Hauka Films, 2008.

Love Bites, c. 2010.

Worked on other projects.

Film Work; Other:

Producer's intern, *Long Life, Happiness & Prosperity,* Odeon Films, 2002, version with English subtitles, Film Movement, 2004.

Production assistant, *The Burial Society,* Seville Pictures, 2002, Regent Releasing, 2004.

Television Producer; Series:

Producer of *The Triple Eight* (also known as *The Triple 8, The Triple Eight Happy Lucky Golden Dragon All–Nite Market,* and *The Triple Eight Happy Lucky Golden Dragon All–Nite Market Television Telecast*).

Television Producer; Miniseries:

Associate producer and development producer, *Iron Road,* CBC, 2008, also released as a feature film, Equinoxe Films, 2008.

Television Producer; Movies:

Spirit Bear: The Simon Jackson Story, CTV, 2005.

Executive producer, *Seventeen & Missing* (also known as *Seventeen and Missing* and *Vivid Dreams*), Lifetime, 2006.

Cries in the Dark, Lifetime, 2006.

A Decent Proposal, Lifetime, 2006.

Past Sins, Lifetime, 2006.

My Baby Is Missing (also known as *Stolen Innocence*), Lifetime, 2007.

NYC: Tornado Terror (also known as *New York City: Tornado Terror* and *New York Tornado*), Sci–Fi Channel, 2008.

Special Delivery, Lifetime Movie Network, 2008.

Television Producer; Short Movies:

Canadian Zombie, CBC, 2002.

Just Smile & Nod (also known as *Just Smile and Nod*), CBC, 2004.

Little Black Caddy, CBC, 2005.

Producer of *The Cure,* Bravo!Canada.

Stage Appearances:

Worked with a theatre troupe in Japan, c. 1980s.

WRITINGS

Screenplays:

The Wrappers (short film), 2000.

Teleplays; Pilots:

With Alexia Fast, wrote *Lily's Reality.*

Writings for the Stage:

Wrote material for a theatre troupe in Japan, c. 1980s.

OTHER SOURCES

Periodicals:

Province (Vancouver), July 30, 2006.

FRAKER, William 1923–2010

PERSONAL

Full name, William A. Fraker; born September 29, 1923, in Los Angeles, CA; died of cancer, May 31, 2010, in Los Angeles, CA. Cinematographer. Fraker was one of the most highly regarded cinematographers in American film for nearly forty years. After serving in the navy during World War II, he attended film school at the University of Southern California. He was a camera operator for the television series *The Adventures of Ozzie and Harriet* in 1961 and earned his first director of photography credit in the 1967 film *Games.* In 1968 he secured his reputation by working as cinematographer on two classic films, Roman Polanskis thriller *Rosemarys Baby* and the Steve McQueen crime drama *Bullitt.* Fraker was nominated for Academy Awards on five separate occasions: in 1978 for *Looking for Mr. Goodbar,* in 1979 for *Heaven Can Wait,* in 1980 for Stephen Spielbergs *1941,* in 1984 for *War Games,* and in 1986 for *Murphys Romance.* His other notable productions as cinematographer include *The Best Little Whorehouse in Texas, The Freshman, Honeymoon in Vegas,* and *Tombstone.* He also directed several films, including *Monte Walsh* and *The Legend of the Lone Ranger,* and such television shows as *Wiseguy* and *Walker, Texas Ranger.* Fraker taught courses at the University of Southern California late in life and received the American Society of Cinematographers Lifetime Achievement Award in 2000.

PERIODICALS

Guardian, June 10, 2010.
Independent, July 28, 2010.
Los Angeles Times, June 2, 2010.

FUQUA, Antoine 1966–

PERSONAL

Born January 19, 1966 (some sources cite May 30, 1965), in Pittsburgh, PA; father a food factory foreman; mother a medical technician; nephew of Harvey Fuqua (a composer, songwriter, and rock music artist); married Lela Rochon (an actress and model), April 9, 1999; children: Asia Rochon, Brando; (previous relationship) Zachary. *Education:* Attended West Virginia University (and, according to some sources, West Virginia State College).

Addresses: *Agent*—Scott Greenberg, Creative Artists Agency, 2000 Avenue of the Stars, Los Angeles, CA 90067.

Career: Director and producer. Worked as a production assistant in New York; Propaganda Films, director of music videos, film trailers, and commercials, including work for Armani fashions, Big Star Jeans, Miller Genuine Draft beer, Reebok athletic wear, Sprite soft drinks, Stanley tools, Toyota motor vehicles, and Wings for Men.

Member: Academy of Motion Picture Arts and Sciences.

Awards, Honors: Black Reel Award, best director of a theatrical film, 2002, for *Training Day;* Black Reel Award nomination, best director of a film, 2004, for *Tears of the Sun;* Black Reel Award nomination, best director, 2005, for *Lightning in a Bottle;* Young Generators Award, for "Gangsta's Paradise"; Sinclair Tenebaum Olesiuk and Emanual Award, for a film trailer for *Dangerous Minds.*

CREDITS

Film Director:
The Replacement Killers, Columbia, 1998.
Bait (also known as *Wild Chase*), Warner Bros., 2000.
Training Day, Warner Bros., 2001.
Tears of the Sun, Columbia, 2003.
Lightning in a Bottle (music documentary), Sony Pictures Classics, 2004.

King Arthur (also released as *King Arthur: Director's Cut*), Buena Vista, 2004.
The Call (short film), Movie Magic International, 2006.
Shooter, Paramount, 2007.
(And executive producer) *Brooklyn's Finest,* Overture Films, 2009.

Also directed the short film *Exit.*

Film Appearances:
(Uncredited) *Bait* (also known as *Wild Chase*), Warner Bros., 2000.

Television Executive Producer; Movies:
Bastards of the Party, HBO, 2005.

Television Director; Pilots:
Murder Book, Fox, 2005.
(And executive producer) *The Takedown,* CBS, 2006.
(And executive producer) *ICE,* NBC, 2009.

Television Appearances; Specials:
The 4th Annual Celebrity Weddings in Style, ABC, 2000.
Intimate Portrait: Lela Rochon, Lifetime, 2001.
AFI's 100 Years ... 100 Heroes & Villains (also known as *AFI's 100 Years, 100 Heroes & Villains: America's Greatest Screen Characters*), CBS, 2003.
The Making of "King Arthur," 2004.
Precinct Hollywood, AMC, 2005.

Television Appearances; Episodic:
"The Replacement Killers," *HBO First Look,* HBO, 1998.
Stracult2, 2001.
"Training Day: Crossing the Line," *HBO First Look,* HBO, 2001.
This Morning, ITV, 2004.
Up Close with Carrie Keagan, ABC, 2007.
Judge, "10 Cut to 8 & 8 Directors Compete," *On the Lot,* Fox, 2007.
Dias de cine, 2009.
Made in Hollywood, 2010.
The Mo'Nique Show, Black Entertainment Television, 2010.
Tavis Smiley, PBS, 2010.
Last Call with Carson Daly, NBC, 2010.

RECORDINGS

Video Appearances:
Chow Yun–Fat Goes Hollywood, Columbia TriStar Home Video, 2001.
Journey to Safety: Making "Tears of the Sun," Columbia TriStar Home Video, 2001.

Made Men: The "GoodFellas" Legacy, Warner Home Video, 2004.

King Arthur: A Roundtable Discussion (also known as *Cast and Filmmakers Roundtable*), Buena Vista Home Video, 2005.

Blood on the Land: The Making of a King, Buena Vista Home Video, 2005.

Survival of the Fittest: The Making of "Shooter," Paramount Home Entertainment, 2007.

Conflict and Chaos: Brooklyn's Finest, Anchor Bay Entertainment/Overture Films, 2010.

Video Director:

Inside Out IV (adult film), Playboy Video Enterprises, 1992.

Usher Live, Arista/BMG/LaFace, 1998.

From Toni with Love: The Video Collection, Arista, 2001.

Director of the music videos "Another Sad Love Song" by Toni Braxton, "Love's Taken Over" by Chante Moore, and "Saving Forever for You" by Shanice, 1993; "Ain't Nobody" by Jackie Graham, "In the Mood" by Ce Ce Peniston, "The Most Beautiful Girl in the World" by Prince, and "United Front" by Arrested Development, 1994; "For Your Love" by Stevie Wonder, "Freedom" by Queen Latifah, and "Gangsta's Paradise" by Coolio, 1995; "Bedtime" by Usher, 1998; "Blue Angels" by Pras, 1999; and "Citizen/Soldier" by 3 Doors Down, 2007.

OTHER SOURCES

Books:

Contemporary Black Biography, Volume 35, Gale, 2002.

Periodicals:

Black Talent News, December, 2001, pp. 14, 22.
Ebony, February, 2002, p. 120.
Jet, March 17, 2003, p. 58.

G

GABRIELLE, Josefina

PERSONAL

Education: Trained at Arts Educational School, London.

Career: Actress and dancer. National Ballet of Portugal, performed as dancer and soloist.

Awards, Honors: Laurence Olivier Theatre Award, best actress in a musical, Society of West End Theatre, c. 1999, Drama League Award nomination, outstanding actress in a musical, 2002, and Astaire Award nomination, best female dancer, Theatre Development Fund, all for *Oklahoma!*.

CREDITS

Stage Appearances:
Roxie Hart, *Chicago* (musical), Adelphi Theatre, London, 2000–2001, 2005.
Laurey Williams, *Oklahoma!* (musical), Lyceum Theatre, London, 2000, then George Gershwin Theatre, New York City, 2002–2003.
Alex, *The Witches of Eastwick,* Prince of Wales Theatre, London, 2001.

Appeared in *Carousel* (musical), Royal National Theatre, London; as Maggie, *A Chorus Line* (musical), Derby Playhouse, England; as Iris Kelly, *Fame* (musical); as Jenna, *The Goodbye Girl;* as Helena, *A Midsummer Night's Dream;* and as Dot and Marie, *Sunday in the Park with George,* Leicester Haymarket Theatre, Leicester, England.

Major Tours:
Toured as Cassie in *A Chorus Line,* British cities.

Television Appearances; Series:
Debbie Bellamy, a recurring role, *Heartbeat,* ITV, between 2001 and 2006.
Ofelia Ortiz, a recurring role, *Auf Wiedersehen, Pet,* BBC, 2004.

Television Appearances; Specials:
Laurey Williams, *Oklahoma!,* 1999.
The 56th Annual Tony Awards, 2002.

Television Appearances; Miniseries:
Multiple roles, *Ronni Ancona & Co.,* BBC, 2007.

Television Appearances; Episodic:
Receptionist, "New Opportunities, Second Chances, and Dominoes," *Sunburn,* BBC, 2000.
Veronica, "Killing Me Softly," *Heartbeat,* ITV, 2001.
The Rosie O'Donnell Show, syndicated, 2002.
Jacqueline Williamson, "Flying Home," *Born and Bred,* PBS, 2005.
Rachel, "Wedding," *Totally Frank,* 2005.
Marion Pilmer, "The Way I Am," *Doctors,* BBC, 2009.
Tango teacher, "Teacher," *Miranda,* 2009.

RECORDINGS

Videos:
Voice, *Divinity II: Ego Draconis* (video game), DTP Entertainment, 2009.

Albums:
Performed for the cast recordings of *Carousel, Fame, The Goodbye Girl,* and *Oklahoma!.*

GADE, Ariel 1997–

PERSONAL

Born May 1, 1997, in San Jose, CA.

Addresses: *Agent*—Abrams Artists Agency, 9200 Sunset Blvd., Suite 1130, Los Angeles, CA 90069.

Career: Actress.

Awards, Honors: Young Artist Award nomination, best performance in a television series (comedy or drama)—young actress age ten or younger, 2006, for *Invasion*.

CREDITS

Film Appearances:
Lula Dingman, *Envy,* DreamWorks, 2004.
Ceci, *Dark Water,* Buena Vista, 2005.
Herself, *"Dark Water": Extraordinary Ensemble* (short documentary), Buena Vista Home Entertainment, 2005.
Herself, *Beneath the Surface: The Making of "Dark Water"* (short documentary), Buena Vista Home Entertainment, 2005.
Molly, *AVPR: Aliens vs Predator—Requiem* (also known as *AVP: Aliens vs. Predator—Requiem, AVP: Requiem, Aliens Vs. Predator 2, AvP2,* and *AvPR*), Twentieth Century–Fox, 2007.
Herself, *"AVP–R": Preparing for War—Development and Production* (short documentary), Twentieth Century Fox Home Entertainment, 2008.
Ryann Hale, *Call of the Wild* (also known as *Call of the Wild 3D*), Vivendi Entertainment, 2009.
Amy Wheeler, *Some Guy Who Kills People,* 2010.

Television Appearances; Series:
Rose Varon, *Invasion,* ABC, 2005–2006.

Television Appearances; Miniseries:
M. Keely Payne, *Meteor,* NBC, 2009.

Television Appearances; Movies:
Kaitlin, *Then Came Jones,* 2003.

Television Appearances; Pilots:
Rose Varon, *Invasion,* ABC, 2005.

Television Appearances; Episodic:
Jewel Wheeler, "Seize the Day," *Strong Medicine,* Lifetime, 2003.
The Tonight Show with Jay Leno, NBC, 2005.
The View, ABC, 2005.
Last Call with Carson Daly, NBC, 2006, 2008.
Emma Perez, "Identity," *NCIS: Los Angeles,* CBS, 2009.

GAIMBALVO, Louis
   See **GIAMBALVO, Louis**

GARRIS, Mick 1951–

PERSONAL

Full name, Michael Alan Garris; born December 4, 1951, in Santa Monica, CA; married Cynthia (an actor and songwriter), c. 1983.

Addresses: *Agent*—Creative Artists Agency, 9830 Wilshire Blvd., Beverly Hills, CA 90212–1825.

Career: Director, producer, writer, editor, and actor. Avco Embassy Pictures, project coordinator in publicity, 1977–?; Universal Studios, publicist; Horsefeathers (a rock band), lead singer; *Fantasy Film Festival* (fifteen–minute weekly program), Channel Z (cable channel), Los Angeles, host; previously worked as a receptionist for Star Wars Corp., journalist, and fiction writer.

Awards, Honors: Edgar Allan Poe Award, best television episode, Mystery Writers of America, 1986, for *Amazing Stories;* Best Film Award nomination, Sitges Catalonian International Film Festival, 1988, International Fantasy Film Award nomination, best film, 1989, for *Critters 2: The Main Course;* Fantafestival Awards, best direction and best film, 1992, both for *Sleepwalkers;* Apex Award nomination, best original screenplay—fantasy/science fiction/horror, 1993, for *Hocus Pocus;* International Fantasy Film Award nomination, best film, 1998, for *Quicksilver Highway;* Hall of Fame, Phoenix International Horror and Sci–Fi Film Festival, 2006.

CREDITS

Film Work:
Producer, *Coming Soon,* MCA Home Video, 1982.
Director, *Critters 2: The Main Course,* New Line Cinema, 1988.
Director, *Sleepwalkers* (also known as *Sleepstalkers* and *Stephen King's "Sleepwalkers"*), Columbia, 1992.
Co–executive producer, *Hocus Pocus,* Buena Vista, 1993.
Director and producer, *Riding the Bullet* (also known as *Stephen King's "Riding the Bullet"*), Lions Gate, 2004.
Producer, *Ghost Cat,* Rice Girl Prod., 2010.

Film Appearances:
Young Herod's man, *The Quick and the Dead,* TriStar, 1995.
Second reporter, *The Stupids,* New Line Cinema, 1996.
Dr. Higgins, *Riding the Bullet* (also known as *Stephen King's "Riding the Bullet"*), Lions Gate Films, 2004.
Father Callahan, *Gotham Cafe,* Turtle Bay, 2005.

Brutal Massacre: A Comedy, Anchor Bay Entertainment, 2007.
Dead On: The Life and Cinema of George A. Romero, New Eye Films, 2008.
Trailers from Hell, Metaluna Prod., 2008.
Into the Dark: Exploring the Horror Film, Blaze Films, 2009.
Tales from the Script, First Run Features, 2009.
Nightmares in Red, White and Blue, Lox Digital, 2009.
Never Sleep Again: The Elm Street Legacy, 1428 Films, 2010.
The Psycho Legacy, 2010.
Brides of Horror, Pretty Scary Prod., 2010.

Television Work; Series:
Story editor, *Amazing Stories,* NBC, 1985–86.
Executive consultant and creator, *She–Wolf of London* (also known as *Love & Curses*), syndicated, 1990.
Supervising producer, *The Others,* NBC, 2000.
Executive producer, *Masters of Horror,* 2005–2007.

Television Work; Movies:
Director, *Psycho IV: The Beginning,* NBC, 1990.
Producer and director, *Quicksilver Highway,* Fox, 1997.
Producer and director, *Host* (also known as *Virtual Obsession*), ABC, 1998.
Director, *Beauty and Power,* 2001.
Director, *Lost in Oz,* 2002.
Executive producer, *Desperation* (also known as *Stephen King's "Desperation"*), 2006.

Television Director; Miniseries:
The Stand (also known as *Stephen King's "The Stand"*), ABC, 1994.
The Shining (also known as *Stephen King's "The Shining"*), ABC, 1997.
The Judge (also known as *Steve Martini's "The Judge"*), NBC, 2001.
Desperation (also known as *Stephen King's "Desperation"*), ABC, 2003.

Television Work; Specials:
Producer, *Fear on Film: Inside "The Fog,"* 1980.
Director and producer, *Making a Monster Movie: Inside "The Howling,"* 1981.
Story consultant, *The Making of "Indiana Jones and the Temple of Doom"* (documentary), 1984.
Director, *The Making of "The Goonies,"* 1985.
Director and producer, *Fuzzbucket,* ABC, 1986.
Co–executive producer, *Hocus Pocus,* 1993.
Codirector and coproducer, *Ghosts* (also known as *Michael Jackson's "Ghosts"*), 1997.

Television Work; Episodic:
Director, "Life on Death Row," *Amazing Stories,* NBC, 1986.

Director, "Killer Instinct," *Freddy's Nightmares* (also known as *Freddy's Nightmares: A Nightmare on Elm Street: The Series*), syndicated, 1988.
Director, "Whirlpool," *Tales from the Crypt* (also known as *HBO's "Tales from the Crypt"*), HBO and Fox, 1994.
Director, "The Smoking Section," *New York Undercover,* Fox, 1995.
Director, "Don't Dream It's Over," *The Others,* NBC, 2000.
Director, "Luciferous," *The Others,* NBC, 2000 producer, "Valerie on the Stairs," *Masters of Horror,* 2006.
Co–executive producer, "A Clean Escape," *Masters of Science Fiction,* 2007.
Co–executive producer, "The Awakening," *Masters of Science Fiction,* 2007.
Co–executive producer, "Jerry Was a Man," *Masters of Science Fiction,* 2007.
Co–executive producer, "The Discarded," *Masters of Science Fiction,* 2007.
Director, "Polly Wants a Crack at Her," *Happy Town,* ABC, 2010.
Executive producer, "Wes Craven," *Post Mortem with Mick Garris,* 2010.
Executive producer, "Robert Englund," *Post Mortem with Mick Garris,* 2010.
Executive producer, "Rick Baker," *Post Mortem with Mick Garris,* 2010.

Television Director; Pilots:
The Others, NBC, 2000.

Television Appearances; Miniseries:
Henry Dunbarton, *The Stand* (also known as *Stephen King's "The Stand"*), ABC, 1994.
A. A. Hartwell (episode 3), *The Shining* (also known as *Stephen King's "The Shining"*), ABC, 1997.

Television Appearances; Specials:
The Making of "The Stand," 1994.
Stephen King: Shining in the Dark, 1999.
Stephen King: Master of Macbre, The Learning Channel, 1999.
The 100 Scariest Movie Moments, Bravo, 2004.
Starz Inside: Fantastic Flesh, Starz!, 2008.

Television Appearances; Episodic:
Host, "Wes Craven," *Post Mortem with Mick Garris,* 2010.
Host, "Robert Englund," *Post Mortem with Mick Garris,* 2010.
Host, "Rick Baker," *Post Mortem with Mick Garris,* 2010.

RECORDINGS

Videos:

Shadows in the Dark: The Val Lewton Legacy, Warner Bros., 2005.

Shooting the Bullet, Lions Gate Films, 2005.

The Sweet Taste of Fear, Anchor Bay Entertainment, 2006.

Working with a Master: Lucky McKee, Anchor Bay Entertainment, 2006.

Imprinting: The Making of "Imprint," Anchor Bay Entertainment, 2006.

Sping Tingler: The Making of "Valerie on the Stairs," Anchor Bay Entertainment, 2007.

Pure in Heart: The Life and Legacy of Lon Chaney Jr., Universal Studios Home Video, 2010.

WRITINGS

Screenplays:

Coming Soon, MCA Home Video, 1982.

(With D. T. Twohy) *Critters 2: The Main Course,* New Line Cinema, 1988.

(With Frank Darabout, Jim Wheat, and Ken Wheat) *The Fly II,* Twentieth Century–Fox, 1989.

(With Neil Cuthbert) *Hocus Pocus,* Buena Vista, 1993.

Riding the Bullet (also known as *Stephen King's "Riding the Bullet"*), Lions Gate Films, 2004.

Film Stories:

The Fly II, Twentieth Century–Fox, 1989.

Hocus Pocus, Buena Vista, 1993.

Television Movies:

Quicksilver Highway, Fox, 1997.

Host (also known as *Virtual Obsession*), ABC, 1998.

Television Episodes:

(With Brad Bird) "The Main Attraction," *Amazing Stories,* NBC, 1985.

"The Amazing Falsworth," *Amazing Stories,* NBC, 1985.

"The Sitter," *Amazing Stories,* NBC, 1986.

"No Day at the Beach," *Amazing Stories,* NBC, 1986.

"The Greibble," *Amazing Stories,* NBC, 1986.

(Story only) "Life on Death Row," *Amazing Stories,* NBC, 1986.

(With Tom McLoughlin and Bob Gale; and story) "Go to the Head of the Class," *Amazing Stories,* NBC, 1986.

"Without Diana," *Amazing Stories,* NBC, 1987.

(With McLoughlin and Michael McDowell) "Such Interesting Neighbors," *Amazing Stories,* NBC, 1987.

"Don't Dream It's Over," *The Others,* NBC, 2000.

Television Series:

(With Tom McLoughlin) "She–Wolf of London," *She–Wolf of London* (also known as *Love & Curses*), syndicated, 1990.

Masters of Horror, 2005–2007.

Nightmares & Dreamscapes: From the Stories of Stephen King, TNT, 2005–2006.

Fear Itself, 2008–2009.

Television Specials:

Fuzzbucket, ABC, 1986.

(With others) *Ghosts* (also known as *Michael Jackson's "Ghosts"*), 1997.

Fiction:

Contributor, *Silver Scream,* Tor/Dark Harvest, 1988.

Contributor, *Hot Blood,* Pocket, 1989.

Contributor, *Hotter Blood,* Pocket, 1991.

Contributor, *Robert Bloch: Appreciation of the Master,* Tor, 1995.

Life in the Cinema (short stories and screenplay), Gauntlet, 2000.

Also contributed short stories, articles, and essays to *Midnight Graffiti, Photon, Famous Monsters of Filmland, Fangoria, Starlog, Cinefantastique,* and others.

ADAPTATIONS

Garris's story "*batteries not included" was adapted for film by Matthew Robbins, Brad Bird, Brent Maddock, and S. S. Wilson and released by Universal, 1987.

OTHER SOURCES

Books:

Contemporary Authors, Gale, 2002.

Periodicals:

Starlog, April, 1998.

GERASIMOVICH, Alexa 2002–

PERSONAL

Full name, Alexa Veronica Gerasimovich; born April 11, 2002, in New York, NY; sister of Ashley Gerasimovich (an actress and model) and Erin Gerasimovich (a model). *Education:* Studied dance.

Addresses: *Agent*—Mara Glauberg, Cunningham/Escott/Slevin & Doherty Talent Agency, 257 Park Ave. South, Suite 900, New York, NY 10010.

Career: Actress. Worked as a model; appeared in commercials and print advertisements; also appeared on the covers of magazines. Involved with charities.

Member: American Federation of Television and Radio Artists, Screen Actors Guild.

CREDITS

Film Appearances:
Erin McLoughlin, *World Trade Center* (also known as *September* and *Untitled Oliver Stone/September 11 Project*), Paramount, 2006.
Lucinda, *Bella* (also known as *Beauty*), 2006, Roadside Attractions, 2007.
Flower girl, *27 Dresses*, Twentieth Century–Fox, 2008.

Television Appearances; Series:
Natalie Snyder, *As the World Turns*, CBS, 2006.
Kathleen "Kathy" Mershon (also known as Kathy Martin and Kate Louise Martin), *All My Children* (also known as *All My Children: The Summer of Seduction* and *La force du destin*), ABC, beginning 2006.

Television Appearances; Pilots:
Young Karen Darling, *Dirty Sexy Money* (also known as *Sexy Money*), ABC, 2007.

GERTNER, Jordan 1973–
(Jordon Gertner)

PERSONAL

Born March 9, 1973, in Toronto, Ontario, Canada. *Education:* York University, graduated (with honors). *Avocational Interests:* Photography.

Addresses: *Office*—Replay Pictures, 3001 Second St., Santa Monica, CA 90405.

Career: Producer. Muse Productions, vice president and production executive, 19902; Replay Productions, Santa Monica, CA, principal. Sometimes credited as Jordon Gertner.

CREDITS

Film Executive Producer:
I Woke Up Early the Day I Died (also known as *I Awoke Early the Day I Died*), Cinequanon Pictures International, 1998.

Co–executive producer, *Modern Vampires* (also known as *Camps*), 1998.
Woundings (also known as *Brand New World*), 1998, UAV Entertainment, 2003.
Bully, Lions Gate Films/Amuse Pictures, 2001.
Jack and Jill vs. the World, Lantern Lane Entertainment, 2008.
The Killer inside Me, IFC Films, 2010.

Film Producer:
Coproducer, *Buffalo '66,* Lions Gate Films, 1998.
Kiss the Bride, 2002, Metro–Goldwyn–Mayer, 2004.
The Poker Club, Sony Pictures Home Entertainment, 2008.
As Good as Dead, VVS Films, 2010.

Film Associate Producer:
The Virgin Suicides (also known as *Sofia Coppola's "The Virgin Suicides"*), Paramount, 1999.

Television Appearances; Miniseries:
On Set, on Edge, 2007.

GIAMBALVO, Louis 1945–
(Louis Gaimbalvo, Louis Gambalvo)

PERSONAL

Born February 8, 1945, in Brooklyn, New York, NY.

Addresses: *Agent*—Judy Schoen & Associates, 606 North Larchmont Blvd., Suite 309, Los Angeles, CA 90004.

Career: Actor. Colonnades Theatre Lab (CTL), New York City, founding member.

CREDITS

Television Appearances; Series:
Al Capone, *The Gangster Chronicles* (also known as *The Gangster Chronicles: An American Story*), NBC, 1981, edited and released as the feature film *Gangster Wars*, CIC, 1981.
Rob Nelson, *Hill Street Blues*, NBC, 1981–87.
Lieutenant Earl Borden, *The Devlin Connection* (also known as *Devlin & Devlin* and *Devlin Connection*), NBC, 1982.
Gus, *Goodnight, Beantown*, CBS, 1983.
Robert Leone, *Oh Madeline*, ABC, 1983–84.

Phil Harbert, *Knots Landing* (also known as *California*), CBS, 1986.

Norman Keil, *Anything but Love,* ABC, 1989.

Television Appearances; Miniseries:

Clarence Anglin, *Alcatraz: The Whole Shocking Story* (also known as *Alcatraz, Alcatraz and Clarence Carnes,* and *Escape from Alcatraz*), NBC, 1980.

Paul Chiapparone, *On Wings of Eagles* (also known as *Teheran*), NBC, 1986.

Television Appearances; Movies:

Dutch, *Reward,* ABC, 1980.

Hank, *Escape,* CBS, 1980.

Vogel, *Fly Away Home* (also known as *Saigon 68*), ABC, 1981.

Eddy White, *Marian Rose White,* CBS, 1982.

George Kane, *Mae West,* ABC, 1982.

Glenn Landis, *The Ambush Murders,* CBS, 1982.

Goody DeSalvo, *The Ratings Game* (also known as *The Mogul*), The Movie Channel, 1984.

Dr. Santini, *Leap of Faith* (also known as *Question of Faith*), CBS, 1988.

Donny, *Crossing the Mob* (also known as *Philadelphia Gang* and *Philly Boy*), NBC, 1988.

Eddie, *Liberace,* ABC, 1988.

Charles Kerwin, *Till Death Us Do Part* (also known as *Married for Murder*), NBC, 1992.

Kobe, *Those Secrets,* ABC, 1992.

Lance Boil, *Mastergate,* Showtime, 1992.

Chief Hugh Halliday, *Donato and Daughter* (also known as *Dead to Rights* and *Under Threat*), CBS, 1993.

Detective Miflin, *Fade to Black,* USA Network, 1993.

Lou Panetta, *Moment of Truth: Murder or Memory?* (also known as *Murder or Memory?* and *Murder or Memory?: A Moment of Truth Movie*), NBC, 1994.

Joe Carangi, *Gia* (also known as *Top Model*), HBO, 1998.

Television Appearances; Specials:

Karl, "The Lost Child," *Hallmark Hall of Fame* (also known as *Hallmark Television Playhouse*), CBS, 2000.

Television Appearances; Episodic:

Delaney, "George and Emma," *Here's Boomer* (also known as *Here's Johnny*), NBC, 1980.

Gerald Serrano, "Agent Orange," *Barney Miller* (also known as *The Life and Times of Captain Barney Miller*), ABC, 1980.

Ernie Doyle, "Closeup News," *Jessica Novak* (also known as *Close–Up: Jessica Novak*), CBS, 1981.

Officer Colletta, "Cops," *The White Shadow,* CBS, 1981.

Sal, "Vendetta," *Chicago Story,* NBC, 1982.

"Examination Day," *Barney Miller* (also known as *The Life and Times of Captain Barney Miller*), ABC, 1982.

"Temporarily Disconnected," *9 to 5* (also known as *Nine to Five*), ABC, 1982.

Anthony Rizzo, "Baron von Munchausen," *St. Elsewhere,* NBC, 1983.

Lieutenant Davern, "As the Hart Turns," *Hart to Hart* (also known as *Hart & Hart, Detectivii Hart, Hart aber herzlich, Par i hjaerter, Par i hjerter,* and *Pour l'amour du risque*), ABC, 1983.

Carmine Amatullo, "I Never Danced for My Father," *Fame,* syndicated, 1984.

Eyeball Warner (a loan shark), "Yes, Virginia, There Is a Liberace," *Simon & Simon* (also known as *Pirate's Key*), CBS, 1984.

Jake Crowley, "Second Base Steele," *Remington Steele,* NBC, 1984.

Walter Milner, "Ace Meets the Champ/Why Justin Can't Read/Call Me a Doctor," *The Love Boat* (also known as *Love Boat*), ABC, 1984.

Carmine Amatullo, "Parent's Week," *Fame,* syndicated, 1985.

Jason Webb (brewery owner), "Trouble Brewing," *The A Team* (also known as *A Team, A–Team,* and *The A–Team*), NBC, 1985.

Dr. Templeton, "Dorothy and Ben," *Amazing Stories* (also known as *Steven Spielberg Presents "Amazing Stories"* and *Steven Spielberg's "Amazing Stories"*), NBC, 1986.

Haggerty, "The Wedding Ring," *Amazing Stories* (also known as *Steven Spielberg Presents "Amazing Stories"* and *Steven Spielberg's "Amazing Stories"*), NBC, 1986.

Nick Damion, "The Day the Music Died," *Hardcastle and McCormick,* ABC, 1986.

Raymond Livingston, "Profile in Silver/Button, Button," *The Twilight Zone* (also known as *The New Twilight Zone*), CBS, 1986.

Leo Mundy, "Siege," *Beauty and the Beast* (also known as *A Szepseg es a szoernyeteg, Die Schoene und das Biest, I pentamorfi kai to teras, La bella e la bestia, La bella y la bestia, La belle et la bete,* and *Skonheden og udyret*), CBS, 1987.

Phil Cooper, "Ordinary Heroes," *Life Goes On* (also known as *Glenbrook*), ABC, 1989.

Jerry Forchette, "Jerry Forchette," *Lifestories,* NBC, 1990.

Paul Massari, "The Price of Justice," *Equal Justice,* ABC, 1990.

Lieutenant Blaisdell, "The List of Yuri Lermentov," *Murder, She Wrote* (also known as *Arabesque*), CBS, 1991.

Vincent Iannello, "Denise and De Nuptials," *Civil Wars,* ABC, 1992.

Vincent Iannello, "Mob Psychology," *Civil Wars,* ABC, 1992.

Dominic Bucci, "Black Men Can Jump," *NYPD Blue* (also known as *New York Blues, New York Cops— NYPD Blue, New York Police, New York Police*

Blues, New York Police Department, N.Y.P.D, and *N.Y.P.D.*), ABC, 1994.

Dominic Bucci, "Rockin' Robin," *NYPD Blue* (also known as *New York Blues, New York Cops—NYPD Blue, New York Police, New York Police Blues, New York Police Department, N.Y.P.D,* and *N.Y.P. D.*), ABC, 1994.

Enzio Tataglia, "Wild Card," *The Adventures of Brisco County, Jr.* (also known as *Brisco County* and *Brisco County, Jr.*), Fox, 1994.

M. L., "The Squeaky Wheel," *Love & War* (also known as *New York cafe*), CBS, 1994.

Cosimo, "Non Sequitur," *Star Trek: Voyager* (also known as *Voyager*), UPN, 1995.

Don Luigi Vito, "Judgement Day," *Pointman,* syndicated, 1995.

Don Luigi Vito, "That's Amore," *Pointman,* syndicated, 1995.

Hank McCormick, "'Til Death Do Us Part," *University Hospital,* syndicated, 1995.

Marty Khulduff, "Conflict of Interest," *Courthouse,* CBS, 1995.

Raimondo Bonelli, "Shooting in Rome," *Murder, She Wrote* (also known as *Arabesque*), CBS, 1995.

Buddy Del Rosick, "The Man That Got Away," *Sisters,* NBC, 1996.

(Sometimes credited as Louis Gaimbalvo) Don Alfredo Angeletti, "The Grape Escape," *Mr. & Mrs. Smith,* CBS, 1996.

George, "The Life of Ryan," *Townies,* ABC, 1996.

Lou Spadaro, "Caroline and the Red Sauce," *Caroline in the City* (also known as *Caroline*), NBC, 1996.

Victor Canetti, "In the Line of Duty," *Hudson Street,* ABC, 1996.

Harold Jordan, "Happy Trails," *Ally McBeal* (also known as *Ally* and *Ally My Love*), Fox, 1998.

Sergeant Paul Cerutti, "Skel in a Cell," *Brooklyn South* (also known as *A esquadra de Brooklyn* and *Brooklyn Sud*), CBS, 1998.

David Hilliker (a security guard), "If I Should Fall from Grace," *ER* (also known as *Emergency Room* and *E.R.*), NBC, 2001.

Mr. Twinkles (a clown), "Things That Go Bump in the Night," *Providence,* NBC, 2002.

Roy Shaughnessy, "Only Schmucks Pay Income Tax," *NYPD Blue* (also known as *New York Blues, New York Cops—NYPD Blue, New York Police, New York Police Blues, New York Police Department, N.Y.P.D,* and *N.Y.P.D.*), ABC, 2003.

Judge Franzetti, "An Eye for an Eye," *Boston Legal* (also known as *Fleet Street, The Practice: Fleet Street,* and *The Untitled Practice*), ABC, 2004.

Ed Garrett, "The Red and the Blue," *Cold Case* (also known as *Anexihniastes ypothesis, Caso abierto, Cold case—affaires classees, Cold Case—Kein Opfer ist je vergessen, Doegloett aktak, Kalla spaar, Todistettavasti syyllinen,* and *Victimes du passe*), CBS, 2006.

Gary Robertson, "Win Today," *Without a Trace* (also known as *Vanished* and *W.A.T*), CBS, 2006.

Ken Billings, "Living Legend," *CSI: Crime Scene Investigation* (also known as *C.S.I., CSI, CSI: Las Vegas, CSI: Weekends,* and *Les experts*), CBS, 2006.

Dr. Squazzi, "Odor in the Court," *Ugly Betty* (also known as *Betty in the USA, Betty the Ugly, Alles Betty!, Betty en los Estados Unidos, Cimlapsztori, Fula Betty,* and *Ruma Betty*), ABC, 2008.

Lance Dietrich, "Hello, Henry," *My Own Worst Enemy,* NBC, 2008.

Mr. Lugano, "Richie Richer," *Raising the Bar* (also known as *Untitled Steven Bochco/TNT Project*), TNT, 2008.

Proctor and Agent Banks, "That Is Not My Son," *My Own Worst Enemy,* NBC, 2008.

John Terzian, "An Honest Mistake," *Grey's Anatomy* (also known as *Complications, Procedure, Surgeons, Under the Knife,* and *Grey's Anatomy—Die jungen Aerzte*), ABC, 2009.

"The Facts," *Dirty Sexy Money* (also known as *Sexy Money*), ABC, 2009.

(Sometimes uncredited) Ralph, *General Hospital* (also known as *Hopital central* and *Hospital general*), ABC, multiple episodes, 2009.

While credited as Louis Gaimbalvo, appeared as Prescott in *Sirens* (also known as *Lady Cops*), ABC and syndicated.

Television Appearances; Pilots:

George Wylie, *Dirty Work,* CBS, 1985.

Rudy Brodbeck, *The City,* ABC, 1986.

Reno, "Reno and Yolanda," *CBS Summer Playhouse,* CBS, 1987.

Norman Keil, "Fear of Flying," *Anything but Love,* ABC, 1989.

The Please Watch the Jon Lovitz Special (also known as *The Jon Lovitz Show* and *Please Watch the Jon Lovitz Show*), Fox, 1992.

Don Luigi Vito, *Pointman,* syndicated, 1994.

Film Appearances:

Al Capone, *Gangster Wars* (edited from television series *The Gangster Chronicles*), CIC, 1981.

Witness, *Airplane II: The Sequel* (also known as *Flying High II* and *Flying High II: The Sequel*), Paramount, 1982.

Freddie Muntz, *Deal of the Century,* Warner Bros., 1983.

Jerry Cooney, "Bishop of Battle" segment, *Nightmares,* Universal, 1983.

Sergeant Cabrillo, *Second Thoughts,* Universal/Associated Film Distribution, 1983.

Fabrizi, *Jagged Edge,* Columbia TriStar, 1985.

Major Carnagle, *Real Genius,* TriStar, 1985.

Army sergeant, *Kansas,* Metro–Goldwyn–Mayer/Cineplex Odeon/Trans World Entertainment, 1988.

Ed, *Bad Dreams,* Twentieth Century–Fox, 1988.

Gus Wheeler, *The Dead Pool* (also known as *Dirty Harry 5* and *Dirty Harry in The Dead Pool*), Warner Bros., 1988.

Gatlin, *See No Evil, Hear No Evil,* TriStar, 1989.

Vito, *Weekend at Bernie's* (also known as *Hot and Cold*), Twentieth Century–Fox, 1989.

Ray Andruitti, *The Bonfire of the Vanities,* Warner Bros., 1990.

Representative, *Hoffa* (also known as *Jimmy Hoffa*), Twentieth Century–Fox, 1992.

Al Sherwin, *Flashfire* (also known as *August Fires*), Trimark Pictures, 1993.

Lieutenant Cavanaugh, *Illegal in Blue* (also known as *Intimate Blue*), Orion, 1995.

Delicatessen man, *Always Say Goodbye* (also known as *Desperate Housewife: The Early Years* and *A Little Romance*), 1996, Indican Pictures, 2005.

Lonny Ward, *Gun Shy* (also known as *Gunshy*), Buena Vista, 2000.

Sonny Gordon, *Death to Smoochy* (also known as *Eliminate Smoochy, Smoochy,* and *Toetet Smoochy*), Warner Bros., 2002.

Pharmacist, *Duplex* (also known as *Our House* and *Der Appartement–Schreck*), Miramax, 2003.

George Taber, *Bottle Shock* (also known as *Wine Miracle*), Freestyle Releasing, 2008.

Some sources cite appearances in other films.

Stage Appearances:

Roberta, *Cracks,* Lucille Lortel Theatre, New York City, 1976.

(Sometimes credited as Louis Gambalvo) Zeno, boy, old woman of the sheets, and guitarist, *Old Man Joseph and His Family,* Colonnades Theatre Lab, New York City, 1977, and Brooklyn Academy of Music, Chelsea Theatre Center (also known as Westside Theatre Upstairs), New York City, 1978.

Archbishop, *Moliere in Spite of Himself,* Colonnades Theatre Lab, 1978.

Stage Work:

Coproducer, *Old Man Joseph and His Family,* Colonnades Theatre Lab, New York City, 1977, and Brooklyn Academy of Music, Chelsea Theatre Center (also known as Westside Theatre Upstairs), New York City, 1978.

GOLDENTHAL, Elliot 1954–

PERSONAL

Born May 2, 1954, in New York, NY; father, a house painter; mother, a seamstress; companion of Julie Taymor (a director and puppeteer), 1980—. *Education:* Manhattan School of Music, B.Mus. and M.Mus., music composition; studied with Aaron Copland and John Corigliano.

Addresses: *Agent*—The Gorfaine/Schwartz Agency, 4111 West Alameda Ave., Suite 509, Burbank, CA 91505.

Career: Composer and conductor.

Awards, Honors: Obie Award, citations—music, *Village Voice,* 1988, for *Juan Darien—A Carnival Mass;* ASCAP Award, top box office films, American Society of Composers, Authors, and Publishers, 1994, for *Demolition Man;* Academy Award nomination, best music—original score, Golden Globe Award nomination, best original score—motion picture, ASCAP Award, top box office films, 1995, all for *Interview with the Vampire;* Universe Reader's Choice Award, best score for a genre motion picture, *Sci–Fi Universe Magazine,* 1995, ASCAP Award, top box office films, Grammy Award nomination, National Academy of Recording Arts and Sciences, c. 1996, all for *Batman Forever;* Grammy Award nomination, c. 1996, for *Heat;* ASCAP Award, top box office films, Grammy Award nomination, c. 1997, both for *A Time to Kill;* Academy Award nomination, best music—original dramatic score, Golden Globe Award nomination, best original score—motion picture, Golden Satellite Award nomination, outstanding original score, International Press Academy, 1997, all for *Michael Collins;* ASCAP Award, top box office films, 1998, for *Batman and Robin;* Los Angeles Film Critics Association Award, best music, 1998, and Chicago Film Critics Association Award, best original score, 1999, both for *The Butcher Boy;* World Soundtrack Award nomination, best original song written for a film, 2002, for *Final Fantasy: The Spirits Within;* Academy Award, best achievement in music written for motion pictures—original scores, Golden Globe Award, best original score—motion picture, Academy Award nomination (with Julie Taymor), best achievement in music written for motion pictures—original song, Golden Satellite Award, best original score, World Soundtrack Awards, best original soundtrack of the year and soundtrack composer of the year, World Soundtrack Award nomination (with others), best original song written for a film, 2003, all for *Frida;* ASCAP Award, top box office films, 2004, for *S.W.A.T.;* Emmy Award nomination, outstanding music composition for a miniseries, movie or a special—dramatic underscore, 2004, for "Lar Lubovitch's 'Othello,'" *Great Performances: Dance in America;* Grammy Award nomination, best compilation soundtrack album for motion picture, television or other visual media, 2008, for *Across the Universe;* Satellite Award nomination, best original score, 2009, for *Public Enemies;* composition prize, New Music for Young Ensembles; Stephen Sondheim Award in Music Theatre; Arturo

Toscanini Award; and fellowship, New York Foundation for the Arts.

CREDITS

Film Work:
Orchestrator, *Alien 3,* Twentieth Century–Fox, 1992.
Orchestrator, *Interview with the Vampire* (also known as *Interview with the Vampire: The Vampire Chronicles*), Warner Bros., 1994.
Orchestrator, *Golden Gate,* TriStar, 1994.
Orchestrator, *Heat,* Warner Bros., 1995.
Orchestrator, *Batman Forever* (also known as *Forever*), Warner Bros., 1995.
Orchestrator and song arranger ("She Moved through the Fair"), *Michael Collins,* Warner Bros., 1996.
Orchestrator, *A Time to Kill,* Warner Bros., 1996.
Orchestrator, *Sphere,* Warner Bros., 1997.
Orchestrator, *Batman and Robin,* Warner Bros., 1997.
Orchestrator, *The Butcher Boy,* Warner Bros., 1998.
Music producer and orchestrator, *Titus,* Fox Searchlight Pictures, 1999.
Music coproducer and orchestrator, *In Dreams,* DreamWorks, 1999.
Music producer, orchestrator, and (uncredited) music arranger, *Final Fantasy: The Spirits Within* (also known as *Fainaru fantaji*), Columbia, 2001.
Orchestrator, *Frida,* Miramax, 2002.
Orchestrator, *The Good Thief,* Fox Searchlight Pictures, 2002.
Music producer and orchestrator, *S.W.A.T.,* Columbia, 2003.
Music producer, orchestrator, song producer, and additional off–camera musician, *Across the Universe,* Columbia, 2007.
Orchestrator and song performer ("Hanna Shoots Neil"), *Public Enemies,* Universal, 2009.

Film Appearances:
Himself, *The Making of "Titus,"* 2000.
Himself, *The Making of "Final Fantasy: The Spirits Within,"* 2001.
Voice of newsreel reporter, *Frida,* 2002.
Himself, *The Making of "Alien"* (documentary), Twentieth Century–Fox Home Entertainment, 2003.
Himself, *The Making of "Heat"* (documentary), Warner Home Video, 2005.

Television Appearances; Specials:
Copland's America, PBS, 2001.
The 60th Annual Golden Globe Awards, 2003.
The 75th Annual Academy Awards, ABC, 2003.
Lights! Action! Music!, WLIW, 2007.

RECORDINGS

Soundtrack Albums:
Song performer ("Sea of Heartbreak"), *The Butcher Boy,* Warner Bros., 1997.

WRITINGS

Film Scores:
Cocaine Cowboys, Media Home Entertainment, 1979.
Blank Generation, 1979.
Pet Sematary (also known as *Pet Cemetary* and *Stephen King's "Pet Sematary"*), Paramount, 1989.
Drugstore Cowboy, Avenue Pictures Productions, 1989.
Alien 3, Twentieth Century–Fox, 1992.
Fool's Fire, 1992.
Demolition Man, Warner Bros., 1993.
Interview with the Vampire (also known as *Interview with the Vampire: The Vampire Chronicles*), Warner Bros., 1994.
Golden Gate, TriStar, 1994.
Cobb, Warner Bros., 1994.
Heat, Warner Bros., 1995.
Batman Forever (also known as *Forever*), Warner Bros., 1995.
Voices (also known as *Voices from a Locked Room*), Voices Productions, 1995.
Michael Collins, Warner Bros., 1996.
A Time to Kill, Warner Bros., 1996.
Sphere, Warner Bros., 1997.
Batman and Robin, Warner Bros., 1997.
The Butcher Boy, Warner Bros., 1998.
In Dreams, DreamWorks, 1999.
Titus (also known as *Titus Andronicus*), Clear Blue Sky Productions, 1999.
The Making of "Titus," 2000.
Final Fantasy: The Spirits Within (also known as *Fainaru fantaji*), Columbia, 2001.
Frida, Miramax, 2002.
The Good Thief, Fox Searchlight Pictures, 2002.
S.W.A.T., Columbia, 2003.
The Making of "Heat" (documentary), Warner Home Video, 2005.
Across the Universe, Columbia, 2007.
Public Enemies, Universal, 2009.
The Tempest, Touchstone Pictures, 2010.

Film Stock Music:
(Uncredited) *300* (also known as *300: The IMAX Experience*), Warner Bros., 2006.

Film Songs:
"Hanna Shoots Neil," *Public Enemies,* Universal, 2009.

Television Scores; Series:
Behind the Scenes, PBS, 1992.

Television Logo Music; Series:
Behind the Scenes, PBS, 1992.

Television Scores; Movies:
"Criminal Justice," *HBO Showcase,* HBO, 1990.
Grand Isle (also known as *The Awakening*), TNT, 1992.

Roswell (also known as the *Roswell: The U.F.O. Cover–Up* and *Incident at Roswell*), Showtime, 1994.

Television Music Adaptor; Movies:
Grand Isle (also known as *The Awakening*), TNT, 1992.

Television Scores; Specials:
Fool's Fire, PBS, 1992.

Television Music; Episodic:
"Lar Lubovitch's 'Othello,'" *Great Performances: Dance in America* (also known as *Dance in America*), PBS, 2003.

Television Additional Music; Episodic:
"Por un beso," *Por un beso,* 2000.

Stage Scores:
The King Stag [and] *The Love of Three Oranges,* American Repertory Theatre, Cambridge, MA, 1984.
The Transposed Heads, Mitzi E. Newhouse Theatre, New York City, 1986.
The Taming of the Shrew, Triplex Theatre, New York City, 1988.
Juan Darien—A Carnival Mass, Music–Theatre Group, Theatre of St. Clement's Church, New York City, 1988, revised version produced at Vivian Beaumont Theatre, New York City, 1996.
Titus Andronicus, Theatre for a New Audience, Theatre of St. Clement's Church, 1994.
The Green Bird, La Jolla Playhouse, La Jolla, CA, then New Victory Theatre, New York City, 1996.
Othello (ballet), Metropolitan Opera Theatre, New York City, 1997.
Grendel (opera), Los Angeles Opera, 2006.

Also composed music for *Liberty's Taken.*

Other Compositions:
Composed *Fire Water Paper: A Vietnam Oratorio,* produced by Pacific Symphony Orchestra, Los Angeles, 1995, then Boston, then Carnegie Hall, New York City, then Kennedy Center, Washington, DC. Also composed *Shadow Play Scherzo,* Town Hall, New York City.

OTHER SOURCES

Books:
Contemporary Musicians, Vol. 49, Gale Group, 2005.

Periodicals:
Hollywood Reporter, January 26, 1995, p. S–12.
Opera News, May, 2006, p. 8.
People Weekly, December 1, 2003, p. 131.

Electronic:
Elliot Goldenthal Home Page, http://goldenthal. filmmusic.com, June 15, 2010.

GOLDFARB, Philip M. 1940–
    (Phil Goldfarb, Phillip Goldfarb)

PERSONAL

Born February 24, 1940, in Brooklyn, NY.

Addresses: *Agent*—Innovative Artists, 1505 10th St., Santa Monica, CA 90401.

Career: Producer, production manager, and assistant director.

Awards, Honors: Emmy Awards (with others), outstanding drama series, 1987, 1989, Emmy Award nomination (with others), outstanding drama series, 1988, Directors Guild of America Award (with others), outstanding directorial achievement in dramatic series—night, 1990, for *L.A. Law.*

CREDITS

Film Work:
(Uncredited) Production assistant, *Rachel, Rachel,* Warner Bros./Seven Arts, 1968.
(As Phil Goldfarb) Production manager, *Last Summer,* Allied Artists, 1969.
Production manager, *Diary of a Mad Housewife,* Universal, 1970.
Unit production manager, *I Never Sang for My Father,* Columbia, 1970.
(As Phillip Goldfarb) First assistant director, *Taking Off,* Universal, 1971.
Assistant director, *Journey through Rosebud,* GSF, 1972.
Production manager, *Irish Whiskey Rebellion,* GSF, 1972.
Production manager, *To Find a Man* (also known as *Sex and the Teenager*), Columbia, 1972.
Associate producer and (uncredited) production manager, *Taxi Driver,* Columbia, 1976.
(As Phil Goldfarb) Assistant director and production manager, *Thunder and Lightning,* Twentieth Century–Fox, 1977.
(As Phillip Goldfarb) Unit production manager, *Casey's Shadow,* Columbia, 1978.
(As Phillip Goldfarb) Coproducer and unit production manager, *Thank God It's Friday,* Columbia, 1978.
(As Phillip Goldfarb) Unit production manager, *Almost Summer,* Universal, 1978.

Unit production manager, *Ice Castles,* Columbia, 1978.

(As Phillip Goldfarb) Associate producer and unit production manager, *My Bodyguard* (also known as *Bodyguard*), Twentieth Century–Fox, 1980.

Unit production manager, *Nice Dreams* (also known as *Cheech & Chong's "Nice Dreams"*), Columbia, 1981.

(As Phillip Goldfarb) Production manager, *Taps,* Twentieth Century–Fox, 1981.

(As Phillip Goldfarb) Coproducer and unit production manager, *All the Right Moves,* Twentieth Century–Fox, 1982.

Executive producer and second unit director, *Truth or Consequences, N.M.,* Triumph Films, 1997.

Executive producer, *Flyboys,* Metro–Goldwyn–Mayer, 2006.

(As Phil Goldfarb) Unit production manager, *Captivity,* Lions Gate Films, 2007.

Television Work; Series:

Coordinating producer and unit production manager, *L.A. Law,* NBC, 1986–89.

Coordinating producer and unit production manager, *Hooperman,* ABC, 1987–89.

Producer and production manager, *C–16: FBI* (also known as *C–16*), ABC, 1997.

Producer and unit production manager, *Monk,* USA Network, 2002–2004.

Television Work; Movies:

(As Phillip Goldfarb) Unit production manager, *The Shadow Box,* ABC, 1980.

Producer, *Bailey's Mistake,* ABC, 2001.

Producer, *"L.A. Law": The Movie,* NBC, 2002.

Producer, *The Librarian: Quest for the Spear,* TNT, 2004.

Producer, *The Librarian: The Curse of the Judas Chalice* (also known as *The Librarian: Curse of the Judas Chalice*), TNT, 2008.

Television Work; Specials:

Producer, *Endgame: Ethics and Values in America,* PBS, 2002.

Television Work; Pilots:

Unit production manager, *L.A. Law,* NBC, 1986.

Coordinating producer, *Hooperman,* ABC, 1987.

Coordinating producer and unit production manager, *Doogie Howser, M.D.,* ABC, 1989.

Producer, *Michael Hayes,* CBS, 1997.

Producer and unit production manager, *Roswell* (also known as *Roswell High*), The WB, 1999.

Television Work; Episodic:

Stage manager, "Stubby Pringle's Christmas," *Hallmark Hall of Fame,* NBC, 1978.

Director, "Leave It to Geezer," *L.A. Law,* NBC, 1989.

Unit production manager, "Chapter One," *Murder One,* ABC, 1995.

Producer and unit production manager, "The Phantom Menace," *Popular,* The WB, 1999.

Producer, "The Two–Horse Job," *Leverage,* TNT, 2008.

Line producer, "The Bank Shot Job," *Leverage,* TNT, 2008.

Producer, "The Wedding Job," *Leverage,* TNT, 2009.

Line producer, "The Snow Job," *Leverage,* TNT, 2009.

GOULD, Harold 1923–2010

PERSONAL

Original name, Harold V. Goldstein; born December 10, 1923, in Schenectady, NY; died of prostate cancer, September 11, 2010, in Woodland Hills, CA. Actor. A longtime character actor, Gould was well known for playing suave, authoritative gentlemen on television and the stage. He taught drama courses at Cornell University, Randolph College, and the University of California, Riverside, from 1948 to 1960 then left education to pursue acting full time. In 1961 he landed his first television role in the series *Cains Hundred.* Appearances in *The Donna Reed Show, The Untouchables, Twilight Zone, The Jack Benny Program, The Virginian, I Dream of Jeannie, Hogans Heroes, Hawaii Five-O,* and many other popular television series in the 1960s led to a recurring role as Martin Morgenstern, first in *The Mary Tyler Moore Show* and later in its spin-off, *Rhoda.* He also acted in fourteen episodes of *The Golden Girls* as Miles Webber, the suitor of Betty Whites character, Rose. Later in his career Gould appeared in the series *Touched by an Angel* and *Nip/Tuck* and was a regular in made-for-television movies. He played supporting roles in a number of films, most notably *The Sting, Love and Death, Stuart Little, Freaky Friday,* and the Buddy Holly biopic *The Day the Music Died.* His stage credits include an Obie award-winning role as Dr. Eduard Huml in an off-Broadway production of *The Increased Difficulty of Concentration* and parts in the Broadway plays *Fools, Grown Ups, Artist Descending a Staircase,* and *Mixed Emotions.*

PERIODICALS

Guardian, September 20, 2010.
Los Angeles Times, September 14, 2010.
New York Times, September 13, 2010.
Washington Post, September 14, 2010.

H

HALL, Edd 1958–
(Ed Hall)

PERSONAL

Born December 7, 1958, in Boston, MA; raised in Corning, NY; son of Thelma Hall (a nurse); stepson of Bill Hall (a school administrator); married Liza Forster (a writer and talent coordinator; some sources state that the marriage ended); children: one daughter, two sons. *Education:* Studied radio and television at Syracuse University.

Addresses: *Agent*—Venture IAB, 3211 Cahuenga Blvd. West, Suite 104, Los Angeles, CA 90068; VOX, Inc., 5670 Wilshire Blvd., Suite 820, Los Angeles, CA 90036 (voice work).

Career: Actor and announcer. Performer and voice artist for various projects; appeared in advertisements and educational projects; also served as the master of ceremonies for galas. Worked as an instructor of voice acting. Worked as a professional clown, magician, and fire eater. Worked as a page for NBC, beginning 1979. Worked as a graphic designer and designed logos and animation; some sources cite other work in the entertainment industry.

Member: Screen Actors Guild, American Federation of Television and Radio Artists, Writers Guild of America, West, Academy of Television Arts and Sciences.

CREDITS

Television Appearances; Series:
Performer and voice artist, *Late Night with David Letterman,* NBC, c. 1982–92.

Announcer, *Max Headroom* (also known as *Max Headroom: 20 Minutes into the Future, Original Max Headroom,* and *The Original Max Talking Headroom Show*), Cinemax, 1986–87, ABC, 1987.

Announcer, *Michelob Presents "Sunday Night"* (also known as *Sunday Night*), syndicated, 1987–88, then known as *Michelob Presents "Night Music"* (also known as *Night Music*), syndicated, 1989–90.

Television announcer, *Married … with Children* (also known as *Married, Married with Children,* and *Not the Cosbys*), Fox, 1991–95.

Voiceovers, *The Edge,* Fox, 1992–93.

Announcer and performer, *The Tonight Show with Jay Leno* (also known as *Jay Leno* and *Jay Leno Show*), NBC, 1992–2004.

Announcer, *The Paula Poundstone Show,* ABC, 1993.

Cohost, *Friday Night Videos* (also known as *Friday Night*), NBC, 1994–2000.

(As Ed Hall) Radio announcer, *Katie Joplin* (also known as *You're on with Kate*), The WB, 1999.

Voice of Vito, *Animal Trax* (animated), VH1, beginning 2001.

Announcer, *Crosswords* (also known as *Let's Do Crosswords, Let's Play Crosswords,* and *Merv Griffin's "Crosswords"*), NBC, beginning 2007.

Television Appearances; Specials:
Announcer, "FDR: A One Man Show" (also known as "Chris Elliott's 'FDR: A One Man Show'"), *Cinemax Comedy Experiment,* Cinemax, 1986.

Announcer, *Cats, Cops and Stuff* (also known as *Paula Poundstone: Cats, Cops, and Stuff*), HBO, 1990.

Narrator, *A Day in the Life of Hollywood* (documentary), Showtime, 1992.

Announcer, *Christmas in Rockefeller Center,* NBC, 1998.

Announcer, *Diet Coke with Lemon Celebrates 40 Years of Laughter: At the Improv,* NBC, 2002.

Television Appearances; Episodic:

Tom Snyder impressionist, *Tomorrow* (also known as *Tomorrow Coast to Coast, The Tomorrow Show,* and *The Tomorrow Show with Tom Snyder*), NBC, 1980.

Ticket scalper, "Roy Scheider/Billy Ocean," *Saturday Night Live* (also known as *The Albert Brooks Show, The Best of Saturday Night Live, NBC's "Saturday Night," Saturday Night, Saturday Night Live '80, Saturday Night Live 15, Saturday Night Live 20, Saturday Night Live 25, SNL,* and *SNL 25*), NBC, 1985.

Tour guide, "The Goodbye Girl," *Married ... with Children* (also known as *Married, Married with Children,* and *Not the Cosbys*), Fox, 1992.

Himself, "Big Doings: Part 1," *Blossom,* NBC, 1993.

Johnny, "Executive Decision," *Murphy Brown,* CBS, 1996.

Johnny, "A One Night Stan," *Murphy Brown,* CBS, 1996.

Himself, *Oddville, MTV,* MTV, 1997.

Himself, *Pictionary,* syndicated, 1998.

Himself, *I've Got a Secret,* Oxygen, c. 2000.

Himself, *You Lie Like a Dog,* Animal Planet, c. 2000.

Himself, *RI:SE,* Channel 4, 2002.

Voice of television announcer, "A Very Possible Christmas," *Kim Possible* (animated; also known as *Disney's "Kim Possible"*), The Disney Channel, 2003.

Himself, *Brainiac: Science Abuse,* Sky Television, 2004.

Celebrity judge, "TV's Next Late Night Host," *Open Call,* TV Guide Network, 2005.

Himself, *Late Show with David Letterman* (also known as *The Late Show, Late Show Backstage,* and *Letterman*), CBS, 2006.

(In archive footage) Himself, *The Tonight Show with Jay Leno* (also known as *Jay Leno* and *Jay Leno Show*), NBC, 2009.

Television news reporter, *The Young and the Restless* (also known as *Y&R, The Innocent Years, Atithasa niata, Les feux de l'amour, Schatten der Leidenschaft,* and *Tunteita ja tuoksuja*), CBS, multiple episodes, 2009.

The Tonight Show announcer, *Late Show with David Letterman* (also known as *The Late Show, Late Show Backstage,* and *Letterman*), CBS, 2010.

Television Work; Series:

Production manager, *The David Letterman Show,* NBC, 1980.

Graphic design coordinator and visuals coordinator (sources also cite production assistant), *Late Night with David Letterman,* NBC, c. 1982–92.

Television Graphics Producer; Specials:

Late Night with David Letterman: 3rd Anniversary Special, NBC, 1985.

Late Night with David Letterman: 6th Anniversary Special, NBC, 1988.

Late Night with David Letterman: 7th Anniversary Special, NBC, 1989.

Television Work; Other; Specials:

Graphics researcher, "Action Family" (also known as "Chris Elliott's 'Action Family'"), *Cinemax Comedy Experiment,* Cinemax, 1987.

Film Appearances:

Himself, *Comic Book: The Movie,* Miramax, 2004.

Voice of Big Bad Wolf, *Geppetto's Secret* (animated), DVX Entertainment, 2005.

Dr. Sheldrake, *Lose with English,* Bright Blue Gorilla, 2011.

Stage Appearances:

Title role and Professor Marvel, *The Wizard of Oz* (musical), Cabrillo Music Theatre, Thousand Oaks Civic Arts Plaza, Fred Kavli Theatre, Thousand Oaks, CA, 2005, and Starlight Theatre, San Diego, CA, 2006.

Ebenezer Scrooge, *A Christmas Carol,* Thousand Oaks Repertory Company, Thousand Oaks Civic Arts Plaza, Thousand Oaks, CA, 2007, 2008, 2009.

Radio Appearances:

Host of *Country Giants,* United Stations Radio Networks (syndicated); and of *Last Night on Tonight with Jay Leno,* Westwood One (syndicated). Worked as a radio announcer, beginning c. 1972; also worked as a disc jockey.

Internet Appearances:

Appeared as the second victim in the short video clip *Out of the Bloo,* posted on *Funny or Die,* http://www.funnyordie.com.

Internet Work:

Producer of the short video clip *Out of the Bloo,* posted on *Funny or Die,* http://www.funnyordie.com.

WRITINGS

Teleplays; Episodic:

(With others) Comedy bits, *The David Letterman Show,* NBC, 1980.

(With others) Comedy bits, *Late Night with David Letterman,* NBC, c. 1982–92.

"The One Where Chris and Larry Switch Lives" (also known as "Chris and Larry Switch Lives"), *Get a Life,* Fox, 1991.

OTHER SOURCES

Periodicals:
People Weekly, March 23, 1992; July 6, 1998.
Ventura County Star, December 17, 2007.

Electronic:
... And Me, I'm Edd Hall, http://www.eddhall.com, February 24, 2010.

HASKELL, Peter 1934–2010

PERSONAL

Full name, Peter Abraham Haskell; born October 15, 1934, in Boston, MA; died of a heart attack, April 12, 2010, in Northridge, CA. Actor. Best known for his role in the 1970s series *Brackens World,* Haskell was a prolific actor in stage, television, and film productions. He began his career while attending Harvard University and played roles in numerous stage productions in the 1960s, including the off-Broadway drama *The Love Nest.* In 1964 he debuted on television, acting in the western series *Death Valley Days.* He appeared in a number of science fiction and western series throughout the decade, including *The Outer Limits, The Man from U.N.C.L.E., Rawhide,* and *The Iron Horse.* A recurring part in the classic series *Lassie* in 1968 preceded Haskells role as writer/producer Kevin Grant in *Brackens World,* a series centered on the behind-the-scenes drama of the film industry. In 1976 and 1977 he acted in the television miniseries *Rich Man, Poor Man—Book II* followed by roles in the series *The Love Boat; The A-Team; MacGyver; Murder, She Wrote; Matlock; Frasier;* and *ER,* among others. In the 1990s Haskell performed in the horror movies *Childs Play 2* and *Childs Play 3.*

PERIODICALS

Los Angeles Times, April 15, 2010.

HAUER, Rutger 1944–

PERSONAL

Full name, Rutger Oelsen Hauer; born January 23, 1944, in Breukelen, Utrecht, Netherlands; son of Arend (an actor and operator of an acting school) and Teunke (an actress and operator of an acting school) Hauer; married Heidi Merz (divorced); married Ineke ten Kate (a painter and sculptress), November 22, 1985; children: (first marriage) Aysha (an actress). *Education:* Attended University of Amsterdam, 1967. *Avocational Interests:* Environmental causes.

Addresses: *Agent*—Steve Glick, Glick Agency, 1250 Sixth St., Suite 100, Santa Monica, CA 90401; Steve Kenis, Steve Kenis and Co., 72 Dean St., London W1D 3SG, England. *Manager*—Joan Hyler, Hyler Management, 25 Sea Colony Dr., Santa Monica, CA 90405.

Career: Actor and producer. Noorder Compagnie (Frisian theatre group), member of company, 1967–73; Rutger Hauer Film Factory (also known as Rotterdam Film Factory), Rotterdam, Netherlands, cofounder, 2006, and teacher of master classes in filmmaking; appeared in commercials, including ads for Guinness products, 1987–94; narrator of "Walks with Giants" ad campaign, 2009. Antroposofisch Centrum, Basel, Switzerland, worked as a stagehand, gardener, and heating engineer; also worked as a merchant seaman, scene decorator, car washer, carpenter, and welder. Rutger Hauer Starfish Foundation (for AIDS research), founder. *Military service:* Served in the Dutch Army.

Member: Screen Actors Guild.

Awards, Honors: Golden Calf Award, best actor, Nederlands Film Festival, 1981; Saturn Award nomination, best supporting actor, Academy of Science Fiction, Fantasy, and Horror Films, 1983, for *Blade Runner;* Golden Globe Award, best supporting actor in a television miniseries or movie, 1988, for *Escape from Sobibor;* Golden Space Needle Award, best actor, Seattle International Film Festival, 1989, and Sant Jordi Award nomination, best foreign actor, 1990, both for *La leggenda del Santo Bevitore;* Golden Globe Award nomination, best actor in a television miniseries or movie, 1995, for *Fatherland;* Audience Award, Rembrandt Awards, 1997; Best Short Film Award (with Erik Lieshout), Paris Film Festival, 2001, for *The Room;* Career Achievement Awards, Montecatini Filmvideo/International Short Film Festival, 2004, and Sarasota Film Festival and Malaga Film Festival, both 2005; Dutch Culture Award, Golden Calf Awards, 2008.

CREDITS

Film Appearances:
Repelsteeltje (also known as *Rumplestiltskin*), 1973.
Eric Vonk, *Turkish Delight* (also known as *Eric and Olga* and *Turks Fruit*), Nederland, 1973.
Rik Van de Loo, *Pusteblume* (also known as *Hard to Remember*), Cinecenta, 1974.
Hugo, *Keetje Tippel* (also known as *Cathy Tippel* and *Katie Tippel*), Tuschinski Film Distribution, 1975.

Blaine Van Nierkirk, *The Wilby Conspiracy,* United Artists, 1975.

Cris, *Das amulett des todes* (also known as *Cold Blood*), 1975.

Pierre, *Het jaar van de kreeft* (also known as *The Year of the Cancer*), 1975.

La donneuse, 1975.

Duclari, *Max Havelaar* (also known as *Max Havelaar of de koffieveiliingen der Nederlandsche handelsmaatschappij*), Netherlands Fox Film, 1976.

Johan Nagel, *Mysteries* (also known as *Evil Mysteries* and *Knut Hamsun's "Mysteries"*), Cine–Vog, 1978.

August Schultz, *Pastorale 1943,* 1978.

Adriaan, *A Woman between Dog and Wolf* (also known as *Een vrouw tussen hond en wolf*), Gaumont International, 1979.

Erik Lanshof, *Soldier of Orange* (also known as *Soldaat van Oranje*), International Picture Show, 1979.

Gerrit Witkamp, *Spetters,* Embassy, 1980.

Etienne De Balsan, *Chanel solitaire,* United Film Distribution, 1981.

Reinhardt Heymar Wulfgar/Eric, *Nighthawks,* Universal, 1981.

Roy Batty, *Blade Runner* (also released as *Blade Runner: The Final Cut*), Warner Bros., 1982.

Claude Maillot Van Horn, *Eureka,* United Artists, 1983.

John Tanner, *The Osterman Weekend* (also known as *Mission CIA*), Twentieth Century–Fox, 1983.

Brigadier Rinus de Gier, *Grijpstra & de Gier,* Verenigade Nederland, 1983.

(In archive footage) Wulfgar, *Terror in the Aisles* (also known as *Time for Terror*), Universal, 1984.

Jim Malden, *A Breed Apart,* Orion, 1984.

Martin, *Flesh + Blood* (also known as *The Rose and the Sword*), Orion, 1985.

Captain Etienne Navarre, *Ladyhawke,* Warner Bros., 1985.

John Ryder, *The Hitcher,* TriStar, 1986.

Nick Randall, *Wanted: Dead or Alive,* New World, 1986.

Andreas Kartak, *La leggenda del Santo Bevitore* (also known as *The Legend of the Holy Drinker*), 1988.

John Knott, *In una notte di chiaro di luna* (also known as *As Long As It's Love, Clair, Crystal or Ash, Fire or Wind, as Long as It's Love,* and *On a Moonlight Night*), 1989.

The Brain, *Bloodhounds of Broadway,* Columbia, 1989.

Nick Parker, *Blind Fury,* TriStar, 1989.

Sallow, *The Blood of Heroes* (also known as *The Salute of the Jugger*), New Line Cinema, 1990.

Harley Stone, *Split Second,* InterStar Releasing, 1992.

Lothos, *Buffy the Vampire Slayer,* Twentieth Century–Fox, 1992.

Tom Burton, *Beyond Justice* (also known as *Desert Law*), Vidmark, 1992.

Mystic monk, *Nostradamus,* Orion Classics, 1994.

Thomas Burns, *Surviving the Game,* New Line Cinema, 1994.

Reuben Bean, *The Beans of Egypt, Maine* (also known as *Forbidden Choices*), IRS Releasing, 1994.

Armond Crille, *Precious Find,* 1996.

Title role, *Omega Doom,* 1996.

Chaplain, *Mariette in Ecstasy,* 1996.

Leo, *Blast,* 1996.

Curtiz, *Knockin' on Heaven's Door,* Myriad Pictures, 1997.

Dr. Marlowe, *Bleeders* (also known as *The Descendant* and *Hemoglobin*), 1997.

Count Albrecht, the Squire, *Simon Magus,* Fireworks Pictures, 1999.

David Marx (The Coroner), *New World Disorder,* York Entertainment, 1999.

Gene Reardon, *Partners in Crime,* Artisan Entertainment, 2000.

Himself, *Road to Sundance,* 2000.

Dr. Sam Dennis Charney, *Wilder* (also known as *Slow Burn*), Bedford Entertainment, 2000.

Keith Miller, *Lying in Wait,* Itasca Pictures, 2000.

Harry, *The Room* (short film), 2001.

Mr. Ezekial, *Flying Virus* (also known as *Killer Buzz*), American Cinema International, 2001.

Voice of Arthur Flegenheimer/Dutch Schultz, *The Last Words of Dutch Schultz,* 2001.

Cardinale Marcinkus, *The Bankers of God: The Calvi Affair* (also known as *The God's Bankers* and *I banchieri di Dio*), 2002.

President Nelson, *Scorcher* (also known as *Deep Core 2002*), Cinetel Films, 2002.

Grekkor, *Warrior Angels* (also known as *Crusade of Vengeance*), 2002.

Keeler, *Confessions of a Dangerous Mind* (also known as *Confession*), Miramax, 2002.

(Uncredited) Dracula III, *Dracula II: Ascension,* Buena Vista Home Video, 2003.

Gallo, *In the Shadow of the Cobra,* Showcase Entertainment, 2003.

Van Beuningen, *Tempesta,* Lightning Home Entertainment, 2004.

Sebastian, *Never Enough* (also known as *Camera ascunsa*), Romania Film, 2004.

(Uncredited; in archive footage) Floris van Rozemond, *Floris,* Independent Films, 2004.

Cardinal Roark, *Sin City* (also known as *Frank Miller's "Sin City"*), Dimension Films, 2005.

Earle, *Batman Begins* (also known as *Batman Begins: The IMAX Experience*), Warner Bros., 2005.

Mysterious man, *Zerkalnie voyni: Otrazhenie pervoye* (also known as *Mirror Wars: Reflection One*), Seven Arts Pictures, 2005.

Sanford Pollard, *Mentor,* MTI Home Video, 2006.

General Frank Lewis, *The Hunt for Eagle One,* Sony Pictures Home Entertainment, 2006.

General Frank Lewis, *The Hunt for Eagle One: Crash Point,* Sony Pictures Home Entertainment, 2006.

Detective John Criton, *Dead Tone* (also known as *7eventy 5ive*), Codeblack Entertainment, 2007.

Maxwell McAllister, *Moving McAllister,* First Independent Pictures, 2007.

Psychiatrist, *Sweet Betty* (short film), Rotterdam Film Factory, 2007.

Rudi van der Merwe, *Goal II: Living the Dream,* Arenas Entertainment/Peace Arch Releasing, 2008.

Victor Spoon, *Spoon,* Distant Horizon, 2008.

Dr. Richard Nagel, *Magic Flute Diaries,* Sullivan Entertainment, 2008.

The Rhapsody (short film), 2008.

Old Frank, *Bride Flight,* A–Film Distribution, 2008, Music Box Films, 2010.

The Letters, 2009.

Dazzle (also known as *Oogverblindend*), Filmfreak Distributie, 2009.

Federico Barbarossa, *Barbarossa,* 01 Distribuzione, 2009.

Insley, *Happiness Runs,* Strand Releasing, 2010.

Mr. Hunt, *The 5th Execution,* 2010.

Jean–Luc, *Life's a Beach* (also known as *Jungle Juice*), Bronx Born Films/Miracle Entertainment, 2010.

Diego, *Tonight at Noon,* Unison Films, 2010.

Peter Bruegel, *The Mill and the Cross,* Silesia Film, 2010.

Documentary Film Appearances:

Furious, 1989.

Heroic, 1989.

Prosit, Ermanno!, 1989.

Submitting, 1989.

Kill the Camera, 1992.

The Revenge of the Dead Indians, 1993.

De Bevrijders Herdacht, 1995.

Blond, Blue Eyes, RNtv, 2006.

Narrator, *Buddha's Medicine,* 2008.

Narrator, *Club Mama Gemuetlich,* 2009.

Film Producer:

Coproducer, *Mysteries,* Cine–Vog, 1978.

Who Are They? (documentary), 1987.

Prosit, Ermanno! (documentary), 1989.

Submitting (documentary), 1989.

Coproducer, *Kill the Camera* (documentary), 1992.

Dazzle (also known as *Oogverblindend*), Filmfreak Distributie, 2009.

Film Director:

The Room (short film), 2001.

Television Appearances; Miniseries:

Erik Lanshof, *Soldaat ven Oranje,* 1977.

Albert Speer, *Inside the Third Reich,* ABC, 1982.

Tom Burton, *Maketub: The Law of the Desert* (also known as *Il principe del deserto*), 1991.

Bog, "Eating Pattern," *Lexx: The Dark Zone Stories* (also known as *Lexx: The Dark Zone, Lexx: The Movies,* and *Tales from a Parallel Universe*), The Movie Channel, 1997.

Lord Vortigern, *Merlin,* NBC, 1998.

Huntsman, *The 10th Kingdom,* NBC, 2001.

Kurt Barlow, *Salem's Lot* (also known as *Stephen King's "Salem's Lot"*), TNT, 2004.

Presenter, *Shock Treatment,* 2004.

Television Appearances; Movies:

Ryder, *Es begann bei Tiffany,* 1979.

Lieutenant Alexander "Sasha" Pechersky, *Escape from Sobibor,* CBS, 1987.

Frank Warren, *Deadlock* (also known as *Wedlock*), HBO, 1991.

Ben Jordan, *Past Midnight,* USA Network, 1991.

Kid Satin, *T.V.,* 1992.

Ben Corbett, *Arctic Blue,* HBO, 1993.

Jake Shell, *Blind Side,* NBC, 1993.

Morgan Norvell, *Voyage* (also known as *Cruise of Fear*), USA Network, 1993.

SS–Sturmbannfuehrer Xavier March, *Fatherland,* HBO, 1994.

Fred Noonan, *Amelia Earhart: The Final Flight,* TNT, 1994.

Doctor Lem, *Blood of the Innocent* (also known as *AK–47: The Death Machine*), Showtime, 1994.

A. T., *Crossworlds,* HBO, 1996.

Dr. Rue Wakeman, *Mr. Stitch,* Sci–Fi Channel, 1996.

John Thornton, *The Call of the Wild: Dog of the Yukon* (also known as *Jack London's "The Call of the Wild"* and *Jack London's "The Call of the Wild: Dog of the Yukon"*), The Family Channel, 1997.

Captain Britanov, *Hostile Waters,* HBO, 1997.

Patrick Collins, *The Ruby Ring,* Showtime, 1997.

John Anderson Wade, *Deathline* (also known as *Armageddon, Redline,* and *The Syndicate*), HBO, 1997.

William H. Palmer, *Bone Daddy* (also known as *Palmer's Bones*), HBO, 1998.

Captain John "Doc" Holiday, *Tactical Assault,* HBO, 1998.

Copilot, *Turbulence 3: Heavy Metal,* Cinemax, 2001.

Bishop August Schmidt, *The Poseidon Adventure,* NBC, 2005.

Cyrnan, *Minotaur,* Sci–Fi Channel, 2006.

Peter Rossen, *Starting Over,* 2007.

Television Appearances; Specials:

De Geheime Vier (play), c. 1956, 1957.

De Valvert and Gascon cadet, *Cyrano de Bergerac* (play), 1975.

Dunois, *Heilige Jeanne* (play), KRO and RKK, 1978.

Emil, "Indian Poker," *The Edge,* HBO, 1989.

The Revenge of the Dead Indians, 1993.

The Making of "Blade Runner," 1997.

De Ridder en de Fakir, 1999.

In Search of the Muse, 2000.

On the Edge of Blade Runner, Channel 4, 2000.

(In archive footage) *Soldaat van Oranje revisited,* 2002.

Television Appearances; Pilots:

William Hamilton, *The Prince of Motor City,* ABC, 2008.

Television Appearances; Series:

Floris van Rozemund (title role; character's name is sometimes spelled "Rosemond" or "Rozemond"), *Floris,* 1969.

Title role, *Floris von Rosemund,* 1975.

Television Appearances; Episodic:

(Television debut) *Asmodee,* 1956.

Pieter van Pearsen, "Sitting Ducks," *The Pathfinders,* 1972.

"Taxi, Meneer?," *Waaldrecht,* 1973.

John van der Velde, *Duel in de diepte,* four episodes, 1979.

The Late Show (also known as *The Late Show Starring Joan Rivers*), 1987.

Wogan, 1990.

The Tonight Show with Jay Leno, NBC, 1992.

Showbiz Today, 1994.

"Rutger Hauer," *Willemsen–Das Fernsehgespraech,* 1994.

Amazing Animals, Animal Planet, 1998.

The Roseanne Show, 2000.

"Science Fiction," *Film Genre,* 2002.

Anthony Geiger, "Phase One," *Alias,* ABC, 2003.

Morgan Edge, "Exile," *Smallville* (also known as *Smallville Beginnings*), The WB, 2003.

Morgan Edge, "Phoenix," *Smallville* (also known as *Smallville Beginnings*), The WB, 2003.

Banzai (quiz show), 2003.

V Graham Norton, Channel 4, 2003.

De wereld draait door, 2007.

(In archive footage) *Allemaal film,* 2007.

(In archive footage) Erik Vonk, *RTL Boulevard,* 2007.

(In archive footage) Roy Batty, *Pagina 2,* 2007.

Pauw & Witteman, 2008.

(In archive footage) Roy Batty, *Banda sonora,* 2009.

Television Appearances; Awards Presentations:

The 49th Annual Golden Globe Awards, TBS, 1992.

My VH1 Music Awards, VH1, 2000.

Television Work; Movies:

Co–executive producer, *Arctic Blue,* HBO, 1993.

Executive producer, *Mr. Stitch,* Sci–Fi Channel, 1996.

Stage Appearances:

Eurysakes, *Ajax,* 1955.

Jerry, *Zoo Story,* 1961.

Second watchman, *Antonius and Cleopatra,* Nederlandse Comedie, 1963.

Choir boy, *Antigone,* Noorder Compagnie, 1967.

Fire brigade commander, *De Kale Zangeres,* Noorder Compagnie, 1967.

Grandson, *Karel,* Noorder Compagnie, 1968.

Orlando, Gloucester, and Petrucchio, *Shakespeare–Fragmenten,* Noorder Compagnie, 1968.

Worker, *Dubbelhartige Onthullingen,* Noorder Compagnie, 1968.

First man, *De Man der Herrinnering,* Noorder Compagnie, 1969.

Milkman, *De Minaar,* Noorder Compagnie, 1969.

Simeon, *Joseph in Dothan,* Noorder Compagnie, 1969.

Georges, *De Ontvoering,* Noorder Compagnie, 1969.

Nat Bartlett, *Waar Het Kruis bij Staat,* Noorder Compagnie, 1969.

Joe, *Traan,* Noorder Compagnie, 1969.

Tony Wendice, *U Spreekt Met uw Moordenaar* (Dutch production of *Dial "M" for Murder*), Noorder Compagnie, 1970.

Lennie, *Van Muizen en Mensen* (Dutch production of *Of Mice and Men*), Noorder Compagnie, 1970.

Choir boy, *Biedermann en de Brandstichters,* Noorder Compagnie, 1971.

Uwe Sievers, *De Fysici,* Noorder Compagnie, 1971.

Tittanane, *Kaball in Chioggia,* Noorder Compagnie, 1972.

Bill Starbuck, *De Regenmaker* (Dutch production of *The Rainmaker*), Noorder Compagnie, 1972.

Max, *Suiker,* Noorder Compagnie, 1972.

Appeared as Stanley Kowalski, *Tramlijn Begeerte* (Dutch production of *A Streetcar Named Desire*); also appeared in a Dutch production of *Hair.*

Stage Director:

(And costume designer) *Van Muizen en Mensen* (Dutch production of *Of Mice and Men*), Noorder Compagnie, 1970.

De Dienstlift, Noorder Compagnie, 1972.

'T Groene Hart, Noorder Compagnie, 1973.

RECORDINGS

Videos:

(From archive footage) Voice of Secret Agent Prisoner, *Rambo III,* 1989.

De ridder en de fakir, 2002.

Hitcher—How Do These Movies Get Made?, Kinowelt Home Entertainment, 2003.

Alpha to Omega: Exposing "The Osterman Weekend," Anchor Bay Entertainment, 2004.

Dracula III: Legacy, Dimension Home Video, 2005.

(And director) Himself, *Starfish Tango,* Rutger Hauer Starfish Association, 2006.

Dangerous Days: Making Blade Runner (also known as *Dangerous Days*), Warner Home Video, 2007.

Fashion Forward: Wardrobe and Styling, Warner Home Video, 2007.

Deck–a–Rep: The True Nature of Rick Deckard, Warner Home Video, 2007.

(In archive footage) Roy Batty, *Blade Runner: Deleted and Alternate Scenes,* Warner Home Video, 2007.

Char.ac.ter: The Interviews, Americana Entertainment, 2010.

Appeared in the music video "On a Night like This" by Kylie Minogue, 2000.

WRITINGS

Books:
(With Patrick Quinlan) *All Those Moments: Stories of Heroes, Villains, Replicants, and Blade Runners* (autobiography), HarperEntertainment, 2007.

Stage Plays:
(Translator) *Van Muizen en Mensen* (Dutch production of *Of Mice and Men*), Noorder Compagnie, 1970.

OTHER SOURCES

Books:
Hauer, Rutger, and Patrick Quinlan, *All Those Moments: Stories of Heroes, Villains, Replicants, and Blade Runners,* HarperEntertainment, 2007.

Periodicals:
Playboy, June, 2005, p. 54.
Premiere, June, 2005, p. 34.
Variety, June 15, 2009, p. 7.

Electronic:
Rutger Hauer Official Site, http://www.rutgerhauer.org, June 28, 2010.

━━━━━━━━━━

HELFMAN, Richard
    See ELFMAN, Richard

━━━━━━━━━━

HOBBS, Chelsea 1984(?)–

PERSONAL

Full name, Chelsea Raelle Hobbs; born February 18, 1984 (some sources cite 1985), in Vancouver, British Columbia, Canada. *Education:* Studied acting.

Addresses: *Agent*—Abrams Artists Agency, 9200 Sunset Blvd., Suite 1130, Los Angeles, CA 90069.

Career: Actress. Appeared in advertisements.

Awards, Honors: Leo Award nomination, feature length drama: best lead performance—female, Motion Picture Arts & Sciences Foundation of British Columbia, 2003, for *Snow Queen;* named a face to watch, *Teen* magazine, 2005.

CREDITS

Television Appearances; Series:
Chelsea Wright, *No Adults Aloud* (improvisational series), [Canada], beginning c. 1994.
Meredith Weller, *Pasadena,* Fox, 2001–2002.
Nell Kilvert and Emma, *Beach Girls,* Lifetime, 2005.
Emily Kmetko, *Make It or Break It* (also known as *Perfect 10*), ABC Family, 2009—.

Television Appearances; Movies:
Young Laura, *Sweet Dreams,* NBC, 1996.
New gymnast, *Perfect Body,* NBC, 1997.
Megan McKinley, *Miracle on the 17th Green,* CBS, 1999.
Gerda, *Snow Queen* (also known as *The Snow Queen* and *La reine des neiges*), Hallmark Channel, 2002.
Sara Gradwell, *More Sex and the Single Mom* (also known as *More Sex & the Single Mom*), Lifetime, 2005.
Shanna, *The Party Never Stops: Diary of a Binge Drinker,* Lifetime, 2007.
Jane McCoy, *Confessions of a Go–Go Girl* (also known as *True Confessions of a Go–Go Dancer*), Lifetime, 2008.

Television Appearances; Episodic:
Amy, "The Brink," *Seven Days* (also known as *7 Days* and *Seven Days: The Series*), UPN, 2001.
Fourteen–year–old girl, "Do You See What I See?," *Mysterious Ways* (also known as *One Clear Moment, Anexegeta phainomena, Les chemins de l'etrange, Mysterious ways—les chemins de l'etrange, Rajatapaus,* and *Senderos misteriosos*), PAX, 2001.
Madison, "The Tux," *The Sausage Factory* (also known as *MTV's "Now What?," Much Ado about Whatever, Now What?,* and *Special Ed*), MTV and The Comedy Network, 2002.
Herself, *MDN,* Spike TV, 2004.
Brooke, "Lassoed," *The L Word* (also known as *Earthlings, L.,* and *L Word*), Showtime, 2007.
Brooke, "Layup," *The L Word* (also known as *Earthlings, L.,* and *L Word*), Showtime, 2007.
Brooke, "Livin' La Vida Loca," *The L Word* (also known as *Earthlings, L.,* and *L Word*), Showtime, 2007.
Betty Sue Baker (1953), "Pin Up Girl," *Cold Case* (also known as *Anexihniastes ypothesis, Caso abierto, Cold case—affaires classees, Cold Case—Kein*

Opfer ist je vergessen, Doegloett aktak, Kalla spaar, Todistettavasti syyllinen, and *Victimes du passe*), CBS, 2008.

Herself, *It's On with Alexa Chung,* MTV, 2009.

Courtney Haywood, "Spring Breakdown," *CSI: Miami* (also known as *CSI Miami* and *CSI: Weekends*), CBS, 2010.

Television Appearances; Pilots:

Sara Johnson, *Save the Last Dance,* Fox, 2002.

Emily Kmetko, *Make It or Break It* (also known as *Perfect 10*), ABC Family, 2009.

Film Appearances:

Suzy Cooper, *Christina's House,* 1999.

Caroline, *Lords of Dogtown* (also known as *American Knights* and *Dogtown Boys*), TriStar/Sony Pictures Entertainment, 2005.

Jenny Ackers, *The Unknown* (also known as *Clawed: The Legend of Sasquatch, The Legend of Echo Mountain,* and *Project Bigfoot*), First Look International, 2005.

Stage Appearances:

Appeared in stage productions.

WRITINGS

Teleplays; with Others; Episodic:

No Adults Aloud (improvisational series), beginning c. 1994.

Writings for the Internet:

Author of the blog *Through My Eyes,* posted on http://chelseahobbs.blogspot.com.

OTHER SOURCES

Periodicals:

Teen, July, 2005.

Electronic:

Chelsea Raelle Hobbs.com: The Official Site, http://www.chelsearaellehobbs.com, February 23, 2010.

HOLMES, Ashton 1978–

PERSONAL

Born February 17, 1978, in Albany, NY. *Education:* Studied acting.

Addresses: *Agent*—International Creative Management, 10250 Constellation Blvd., 9th Floor, Los Angeles, CA 90067. *Manager*—Jeff Morrone Management, 9350 Wilshire Blvd., Suite 224, Beverly Hills, CA 90212.

Career: Actor. Appeared in advertisements.

CREDITS

Television Appearances; Series:

Greg Johnson, *One Life to Live* (also known as *Between Heaven and Hell, OLTL,* and *One Life to Live: The Summer of Seduction*), ABC, c. 2002–2004.

Narrator, *Timeless* (documentary), ESPN, beginning 2005.

Scott Little, *Boston Legal* (also known as *Fleet Street, The Practice: Fleet Street,* and *The Untitled Practice*), ABC, 2006.

Television Appearances; Miniseries:

Private first class Sidney "Sid" Phillips, *The Pacific* (also known as *Untitled World War II Pacific Theater Project*), HBO, 2010.

Television Appearances; Episodic:

Davis Harrington, "Soulless," *Law & Order: Special Victims Unit* (also known as *Law & Order's Sex Crimes, Law & Order: SVU,* and *Special Victims Unit*), NBC, 2003.

Sean Morgan/Bobby Gordon, "Maternal Instincts," *Cold Case* (also known as *Anexihniastes ypothesis, Caso abierto, Cold case—affaires classees, Cold Case—Kein Opfer ist je vergessen, Doegloett aktak, Kalla spaar, Todistettavasti syyllinen,* and *Victimes du passe*), CBS, 2004.

Himself, "A History of Violence," *HBO First Look,* HBO, 2005.

Kirk Jensen, "Voices," *Ghost Whisperer,* CBS, 2005.

Himself, *Comme au cinema* (also known as *Comme au cinema: le magazine* and *Comme au cinema: l'emission*), 2005.

Emerson Laidlaw, "Scan Man," *Numb3rs* (also known as *Numbers* and *Num3ers*), CBS, 2008.

Hank, "Rock Star," *Law & Order: Criminal Intent* (also known as *Law & Order: CI*), NBC, 2009.

Sam Trent, "Better Off Dead," *CSI: Crime Scene Investigation* (also known as *C.S.I., CSI, CSI: Las Vegas, CSI: Weekends,* and *Les experts*), CBS, 2009.

Scott, "Both Sides Now," *House M.D.* (also known as *Doctor House, Dr House, Dr. House, Dr. [H]ouse, Dr. House—Medical Division, Dr. House: Medical Division,* and *House*), Fox, 2009.

Television Appearances; Pilots:

Thom, "2.0," *Nikita,* The CW, 2010.

Film Appearances:

Zach Alder, *Raising Hell,* Sub Rosa Studios, 2003.

Rice, *A Million Miles to Sunshine* (short film), 2004.

Jack Stall, *A History of Violence,* New Line Cinema, 2005.

Tommy, *Peaceful Warrior,* DEJ Productions/Lions Gate Films/Universal, 2006.

Guy, *Wind Chill,* TriStar, 2007.

Sean, *Normal Adolescent Behavior* (also known as *Fucking Teens, Havoc 2: Normal Adolescent Behavior, Normal Adolescent Behavior—A story of a teenager, A Story of a Teenager,* and *Ultimatum*), New Line Cinema, 2007.

Rob Henley, *What We Do Is Secret,* Peach Arch Entertainment Group, 2007, Vitagraph Films, 2008.

James Wetherhold, *Smart People,* Miramax, 2008.

Adrien, *The Divide* (also known as *The Fallout*), Instinctive Film/Parlay Media/Julijette, Inc., 2011.

Stage Appearances:

Appeared in stage productions.

Internet Appearances:

Appeared in footage posted on the Internet.

RECORDINGS

Videos; Documentaries; as Himself:

Acts of Violence (also known as *Acts of violence*), Warner Home Video, 2006.

Too Commercial for Cannes (short documentary), New Line Home Video, 2006.

A Frozen Set: The Making of "Wind Chill" (short documentary), Sony Pictures Home Entertainment, 2007.

HOLMES, Jessica 1973–

PERSONAL

Born August 29, 1973, in Ottawa, Ontario, Canada; daughter of Randy Holmes (a computer programmer and network manager) and Laura Cain (a counselor at a crisis center); married Scott Yaphe (an actor and Reiki master), 2003; children: Alexa Lola, Jordan (Jordy). *Education:* Ryerson Polytechnic University, B.A.; studied with The Second City; graduated from Canterbury High School; studied music and dance.

Addresses: *Agent*—Parent Management, Inc., 530 Queen St. East, Toronto, Ontario M5A 1V2, Canada.

Career: Actress, comedienne, and writer. Comedienne at various venues and opening artist for artists; also a public speaker. Affiliated with Lady Lola (production company). Canadian Broadcasting Corporation (CBC), data entry clerk. Worked at a religious mission in Venezuela; involved in galas and fund–raisers as well as charity work, including involvement with the organizations Friends of Honduran Children and World Society for the Protection of Animals.

Awards, Honors: Canadian Improv Games championship with the Canterbury High School improvisational performance team; named funniest girl, Canterbury High School; Tim Sims Encouragement Award nomination, The Ontario Arts Foundation, 1999; Canadian Comedy Award nomination, 2000, for *The Best of the Very Last;* Canadian Comedy Award nomination, television—pretty funny female performance, 2001, for *The Itch;* WorldFest Houston Platinum Award, television and cable production—TV special—comedy, 2001, Gemini Award nomination, best individual performance in a comedy program or series, Academy of Canadian Cinema and Television, 2001, and Canadian Comedy Award nomination, television—pretty funny writing—special or episode, 2002, all for "Holmes Alone," *Comedy Now!;* Canadian Comedy Award nominations, television—pretty funny female performance, 2004 and 2005, and Gemini Award nominations, best ensemble performance in a comedy program or series, both with others, 2006 and 2007, all for *Royal Canadian Air Farce.*

CREDITS

Television Appearances; Series:

Title role, *Little Big Kid,* YTV, beginning 1999.

Various characters, *The Itch,* The Comedy Network, 2000–2001.

Various characters, *Sonic Temple,* CTV, beginning 2001.

Various characters, *The Endless Grind,* The Comedy Network, 2001–2002.

Host and various characters, *The Holmes Show,* CTV, 2002–2003.

Various characters, *Royal Canadian Air Farce* (also known as *Air Farce, Air Farce Live,* and *Air Farce: Final Flight*), CBC, 2003–2008.

Voice of bride, *Gruesomestein's Monsters* (series of animated shorts), YTV, 2005.

Television Appearances; Movies:

Phylis French, *Lives of Girls & Women* (also known as *Lives of Girls and Women*), CBC, 1994.

Television Appearances; Specials:

Leanne, *Burnt Toast* (short operatic films), c. 2005.

Canadian Comedy Awards: Weekend Wrap–Up, 2006.

Television Appearances; Awards Presentations:
Nominee, *Cream of Comedy* (also known as *The Fourth Annual Tim Sims Award* and *The Tim Sims Award*), The Comedy Network, 1999.
The 2000 Canadian Comedy Awards (also known as *The CCAs*), The Comedy Network, 2000.
The ... Annual Canadian Comedy Awards, The Comedy Network, 2001, 2005, 2006.

Television Appearances; Episodic:
Canada A.M. (also known as *Canada AM, Canada AM Weekend,* and *Canada A.M. Weekend*), CTV, 2000.
Eleanor of Aquitaine, "Truth or Prayer, the Crusade Tour," *History Bites,* History Television, c. 2000.
Various characters, "Goodbye Tudor Rose," *History Bites,* History Television, c. 2000.
"Holmes Alone," *Comedy Now!* (also known as *Comedy Now*), CTV, 2001.
Herself, *Open Mike with Mike Bullard* (also known as *The Mike Bullard Show* and *Open Mike*), Global TV, 2002.
Royal Canadian Air Farce (also known as *Air Farce, Air Farce Live,* and *Air Farce: Final Flight*), CBC, various episodes, c. 2002–2003.
Receptionist, "Smoke Gets in Your Eyes," *Doc,* PAX, 2003.
Herself, "Why Are Canadians So Funny?," *Global Late Night,* Global TV, 2004.
Rosie, "Die, Die, Who Am I?," *Wild Card* (also known as *Zoe Busiek: Wild Card*), Lifetime, 2004.
"Becoming My Mother," *CBC Winnipeg Comedy Festival* (also known as *Winnipeg Comedy Festival*), CBC, 2004.
Special agent Elizabeth First, "Richard III" segment, *The Shakespeare Comedy Show,* The Comedy Network, 2006.
Voice of scab fairy, "The Scab Fairy," *Grossology* (animated; also known as *Glurp Attack*), YTV and Discovery Kids, 2006.
Zoe, "Everything in Its Right Place," *Da Kink in My Hair,* Global TV, 2009.

Appeared in other programs, including *Laughing Matters.*

Television Appearances; Pilots:
Host and various characters, *The Holmes Show,* CTV, 2002.
Jasmine, *XPM,* CBC, 2004.

Film Appearances:
Dina, *Welcome to Mooseport* (also known as *Mooseport* and *Willkommen in Mooseport*), Twentieth Century–Fox, 2004.
Kim Vegas, *Citizen Duane,* THINKFilm, 2006.

Stage Appearances:
Laugh Lines (fund–raising benefit), Yuk Yuk's, Toronto, Ontario, Canada, 2003.

Fun with Friends Gala Benefit (fund–raiser), Showplace Performance Centre, Peterborough, Ontario, 2008.
Eyuba (queen of the forest), *Robin Hood—The Environ-MENTAL Family Musical* (pantomime production; also known as *Robin Hood*), Elgin Theatre, Toronto, 2009–10.

Performed in the solo show *Jessie's Girls.* Performed comedy at various venues, including the Toronto Laugh Resort and the ALTdot COMedy Lounge at the Rivoli, both Toronto, Ontario, Canada. Competitor at the Comedy Night in Canada, Just for Laughs Festival (Juste pour rire), Montreal, Quebec, Canada; and competitor at international improv championships; also competed with her high school improvisational performance team.

Major Tours:
Various characters, *The Best of the Very Last* (sketch show), The Second City, c. 2000.

Appeared in The Second City touring productions, including *If It's Tuesday, It Must Be Belleville* and *The Puck Stops Here.*

RECORDINGS

Comedy Albums:
25 Laughs to the Gallon, Lady Lola, c. 2006, Maple, 2008.

Videos:
Herself, *The Third Annual Canadian Comedy Awards,* Higher Ground Productions, 2002.

WRITINGS

Teleplays; with Others; Episodic:
The Itch, The Comedy Network, 2000–2001.
"Holmes Alone," *Comedy Now!* (also known as *Comedy Now*), CTV, 2001.
The Holmes Show, CTV, 2002–2003.
Royal Canadian Air Farce (also known as *Air Farce, Air Farce Live,* and *Air Farce: Final Flight*), CBC, 2003–2008.
"Becoming My Mother," *CBC Winnipeg Comedy Festival* (also known as *Winnipeg Comedy Festival*), CBC, 2004.

Teleplays; with Others; Pilots:
The Holmes Show, CTV, 2002.

Writings for the Stage; with Others:
The Best of the Very Last (sketch show), The Second City, c. 2000.

Laugh Lines (fundraising benefit), Yuk Yuk's, Toronto, Ontario, Canada, 2003.

Fun with Friends Gala Benefit (fundraiser), Showplace Performance Centre, Peterborough, Ontario, 2008.

Cowrote The Second City touring productions, including *If It's Tuesday, It Must Be Belleville* and *The Puck Stops Here*. Involved with the solo show *Jessie's Girls*. Created comedic material for performance at various venues, including the Toronto Laugh Resort and the ALTdot COMedy Lounge at the Rivoli, both Toronto, Ontario, Canada. Contributor to the Comedy Night in Canada, Just for Laughs Festival (Juste pour rire), Montreal, Quebec, Canada; and to international improv championships as well as her high school improvisational performance team.

Comedy Albums:

25 Laughs to the Gallon, Lady Lola, c. 2006, Maple, 2008.

Writings for Videos; with Others:

The Third Annual Canadian Comedy Awards, Higher Ground Productions, 2002.

OTHER SOURCES

Periodicals:

Toronto Sun, September 24, 2002; October 27, 2004, p. 66.

Electronic:

Jessica Holmes, http://www.jessicaholmes.com, July 29, 2010.

HOWARD, Rance 1928–

PERSONAL

Full name, Harold Rance Beckenholdt; born November 17, 1928, in OK; son of Engel Beckenholdt and Ethel Cleo Tomli; married Jean Speegle, 1949 (died September 2, 2000); married Judy O'Sullivan, June 29, 2001; children: (first marriage) Ron (an actor, producer, director, and writer), Clint (an actor).

Addresses: *Agent*—Kazarian, Spencer, Ruskin, and Associates, 11969 Ventura Blvd., 3rd Floor, Box 7409, Studio City, CA 91604.

Career: Actor, writer, and producer. Appeared in a touring children's theater as a child; The Hilltop Theatre (a repertory company), Baltimore, MD, resident director;

directed stage productions in Los Angeles, CA. Appeared in television commercials, including Disneyland, 2003, and Disneyland.

Awards, Honors: Emmy Award nomination (with others), outstanding children's performance, 1982, for *Through the Magic Pyramid;* Lifetime Achievement Award, Ashville Film Festival, 2004.

CREDITS

Film Appearances:

Prewitt, *Frontier Woman,* 1955.

(Uncredited) Oscar Jackson, *The Music Man* (also known as *Meredith Wilson's "The Music Man"*), Warner Bros., 1962.

(Uncredited) Camp counselor, *The Courtship of Eddie's Father,* 1963.

Deputy, *Village of the Giants,* Embassy, 1965.

Reggie, *The Desert Raven,* 1965.

Harry, *An Eye for an Eye* (also known as *Talion*), Embassy, 1966.

Tater Coughlin, *Gentle Giant,* Paramount, 1967.

(Uncredited) Sheriff, *Cool Hand Luke,* Warner Bros., 1967.

Deed of Daring–Do, 1969.

Cowboy, *Old Paint,* 1969.

(Uncredited) Cleve, *The Wild Country* (also known as *The Newcomers*), 1971.

Bloody Trail (also known as *Montego* and *White Justice*), 1972.

Salty, 1973.

Roy Luther, *Where the Lilies Bloom,* United Artists, 1974.

Irate farmer at council meeting, *Chinatown,* Paramount, 1974.

Deputy Clerk, *Eat My Dust,* New World, 1976.

Wagonmaster, *Un autre homme, une autre chance* (also known as *Another Man, Another Chance* and *Another Man, Another Woman*), 1977.

Howard Blacker, *The Legend of Frank Woods,* 1977.

Ned Slinker, private detective, *Grand Theft Auto,* New World Pictures, 1977.

Lou's sidekick, *Mr. No Legs* (also known as *The Amazing Mr. No Legs*), 1979.

Technician, *Forever and Beyond,* 1981.

Football coach, *Smokey Bites the Dust,* 1981.

First person, *Airplane II: The Sequel,* Paramount, 1982.

Joseph Chesley, *Love Letters* (also known as *My Love Letters* and *Passion Play*), New World, 1983.

McCullough, *Splash,* Buena Vista, 1984.

Minister, *The Lonely Guy,* Universal, 1984.

Mr. Spencer, *Creator* (also known as *The Big Picture*), Universal, 1985.

Detective, *Cocoon,* Twentieth Century–Fox, 1985.

Mayor Zwart, *Gung Ho* (also known as *Working Class Man*), Paramount, 1986.

Supermarket customer, *Innerspace,* Warner Bros., 1987.

Robert Morrison, *B.O.R.N.* (also known as *Merchants of Death*), Movie Outfit, 1988.

Vern, *Trust Me,* Cinecom, 1989.

Tucker's Father, *Listen to Me,* Columbia, 1989.

Chuck Feeney, *Limit Up,* MCEG, 1989.

Glen Logan, *Dark Before Dawn,* 1989.

Detective, *The 'Burbs,* Universal, 1989.

Dean at college, *Parenthood,* Universal, 1989.

Detective Sturgis, *Wishman,* Monarch Home Video, 1991.

Ninja negotiator, *9 1/2 Ninjas!,* Republic, 1991.

Tomlin, *Far and Away,* Universal, 1992.

Mr. Devreux, *Universal Soldier,* TriStar, 1992.

Priest, *Snapdragon,* 1992.

Elderly man, *I Don't Buy Kisses Anymore,* Skouras, 1992.

Rance, *Forced to Kill,* PM Home Video, 1993.

Sheriff Parker, *Ticks* (also known as *Infested*), Republic, 1993.

Reverend Paxton, *Ed and His Dead Mother* (also known as *Motherhood* and *Bon Appetit, Mama*), 1993.

Bald caddy, *Fearless,* Warner Bros., 1993.

Farmer, *Savate* (also known as *The Fighter*), A–Pix Entertainment, 1994.

Employee, *Children of the Corn III* (also known as *Children of the Corn III: Urban Harvest*), Dimension, 1994.

Todd Brandell, *Bigfoot: The Unforgettable Encounter,* Republic, 1994.

Alicia's doctor, *The Paper,* Universal, 1994.

Old gentleman, *The Cowboy Way,* Universal, 1994.

Stunt pilot Chuck, *Terminal Velocity,* Buena Vista, 1994.

Old Man McCoy, *Ed Wood,* Buena Vista, 1994.

Priest, *Little Giants,* Warner Bros., 1994.

Rance, *Forced to Kill,* 1994.

Dr. Burns, *Malevolence,* 1995.

Eddie Calhoun—employer, *Children of the Corn III: Urban Harvest,* 1995.

Reverend, *Apollo 13* (also known as *Apollo 13: The IMAX Experience*), Universal, 1995.

Judge Bloom, *Where the Truth Lies,* Paramount, 1996.

Mr. Johnson, *Tiger Heart,* PM Entertainment, 1996.

Mayor Davies, *Busted,* 1996.

Mr. Robbins, *Sgt. Bilko* (also known as *Sergeant Bilko*), Universal, 1996.

Chaplain, *Independence Day* (also known as *ID4*), Twentieth Century–Fox, 1996.

Texan investor, *Mars Attacks!,* Warner Bros., 1996.

Ralph Hargrove, *Ghosts of Mississippi* (also known as *Ghosts of the Past*), Sony, 1996.

Hank, *The Night Caller,* Live Entertainment, 1997.

Hote, *Land of the Free,* PM Entertainment, 1997.

Farmer, *Traveller,* October Films, 1997.

Reverend, *Money Talks* (also known as *Runaway*), New Line Cinema, 1997.

Dr. Brown, *The Lay of the Land* (also known as *The Student Affair*), Northern Arts Entertainment, 1997.

Mr. Houghton, *Sparkle and Chain,* 1997.

Mr. Lowry, *Psycho,* Universal, 1998.

Husband, *Small Soldiers,* DreamWorks, 1998.

Reverend Hatley, *Chairman of the Board,* Trimark Pictures, 1998.

Hank, *The Night Caller,* 1998.

Arliss, *Abilene* (also known as *Shadows of the Past*), 1999.

Ely the tractor driver, *Happy, Texas,* Miramax, 1999.

Earl, *Love & Sex,* Lions Gate Films, 2000.

Elderly timekeeper, *How the Grinch Stole Christmas* (also known as *The Grinch* and *Dr. Seuss' "How the Grinch Stole Christmas"*), MCA/Universal, 2000.

Mr. Houghton, *Sparkle and Charm,* Independent, 2000.

Old man, *Ping!,* Initial Entertainment Group, 2000.

Floyd Fryed, *A Crack in the Floor,* Norris Johnson, 2000.

Grandpa Morton, *Artie* (also known as *Big Wind on Campus*), 2000.

Bomb squad cop, *Joe Dirt* (also known as *The Adventures of Joe Dirt*), Columbia, 2001.

Feed the Earth spokesman, *Rat Race,* Paramount, 2001.

White–haired patient, *A Beautiful Mind,* Universal, 2001.

Geezer, *D–Tox* (also known as *Eye See You* and *Im Auge der angst*), MCA/Universal, 2002.

(Uncredited) Man in street, *Spider–Man,* Columbia, 2002.

Doc Fisher, *Legend of the Phantom Rider,* 2002.

Jumping for Joy, Visiplex, 2002.

Priest, *Back by Midnight,* 2002.

Uncle Solomon, *Leaving the Land,* 2002.

Old man, *The Long Ride Home,* Lion Gate Films, 2003.

Telegraph operator, *The Missing,* Columbia, 2003.

Circuit court judge, *Death and Texas,* 2003.

Himself, *"Toolbox Murders": As It Was* (documentary), 2003.

Zeke, *Killing Cupid* (also known as *Warrior or Assassin*), 2004.

Gaffer, *I Am Stamos* (short film), Red Navel Filmworks, 2004.

Circuit court judge, *Death and Texas,* 2004.

Chas Rooker, *Toolbox Murders,* Lions Gate Films, 2004.

Governor Smith, *The Alamo,* Buena Vista, 2004.

Lance Summers, *Eulogy,* Lions Gate Films, 2004.

Cash, *Ghost Rock* (also known as *The Reckoning*), Lions Gate Films, 2004.

Announcer Al Fazin, *Cinderella Man,* Universal, 2005.

Dr. Babcock, *Miracle at Sage Creek* (also known as *Christmas Miracle at Sage Creek*), American World Pictures, 2005.

James Kennedy, *Aimee Semple McPherson* (also known as *Sister Aimee: The Aimee Semple McPherson Story*), Maverick Entertainment Group, 2006.

Zippy, *Be My Baby,* Marvista Entertainment, 2006.

Harris Zeff, *Sasquatch Mountain,* WE Productions, 2006.

Narrator, *Harrison Bergeron* (short film), Crashwave Entertainment, 2006.

Dog bite man, *Georgia Rule,* Universal, 2007.

Sheriff Tom Parker, *Ghost Town: The Movie* (also known as *Dean Teaster's "Ghost Town"*), Lions Gate Films Home Entertainment, 2007.

Preacher, *Walk Hard: The Dewey Cox Story* (also known as *Walk Hard* and *Walk Hard: American Cox, the Unbearably Long, Self–Indulgent Director's Cut*), 2007.

Ranger Howard, *Grizzly Park*, American World Pictures, 2008.

Older man, *Drillbit Taylor* (also known as *Drillbit Taylor: Budget Bodyguard*), Paramount, 2008.

(Uncredited) Old man, *Keith*, Image Entertainment, 2008.

Dr. Maleosis, *Audie & the Wolf*, 2008.

Ollie, *Frost/Nixon*, Universal, 2008.

Mervin, *Play the Game*, Slowhand Cinema Releasing, 2008.

Himself, *Behind the Scenes of "Ghost Town: The Movie"* (documentary), Lions Gate Films Home Entertainment, 2008.

Cardinal Beck, *Angels & Demons*, Columbia, 2009.

Deli owner, *Within*, Bigfoot Entertainment, 2009.

Walker Bill, *Boppin' at the Glue Factory* (also known as *Junkie Nurse*), 2009.

Andrew Jackson Bennett, *Easy Rider: The Ride Back*, 2009.

Wedding preacher, *Shadowheart*, Anchor Bay Entertainment, 2009.

Old man, *Play Dead*, 2009.

Ira, *Provinces of the Night*, 2010.

Bistro Gardens diner, *Valentine's Day*, New Line Cinema, 2010.

Judge Danielson, *The Trial*, Twentieth Century–Fox Home Entertainment, 2010.

Harry, *Once Fallen*, 2010.

Dr. Tolley, *The Genesis Code*, America Saga Releasing, 2010.

Henry Barrow, *The Story of Bonnie and Clyde*, 2010.

Film Work:

Associate producer, *Grand Theft Auto*, 1977.

Stunts, *Terminal Velocity*, 1994.

Also worked as dialogue supervisor, *Salty.*

Television Appearances; Series:

Henry Broomhauer, *Gentle Ben*, 1967.

Henry Clovis, *Days of Our Lives* (also known as *DOOL* and *Days*), 1985.

Charly Girabaldi, *Driving Me Crazy*, 2000.

Television Appearances; Miniseries:

Lieutenant Nelson, *The Executioner's Song*, NBC, 1982.

Doc Wilson, *The Thorn Birds*, ABC, 1983.

Ralph Lee, *A Death in California* (also known as *Psychopath*), ABC, 1985.

Wilk, *The Long Hot Summer*, NBC, 1985.

Frank Hill, *Switched at Birth*, NBC, 1991.

Television Appearances; Movies:

Sheriff Bill Smith, *The Red Pony*, NBC, 1973.

Aaron, *Locusts*, ABC, 1974.

Pap Finn, *Huckleberry Finn*, ABC, 1975.

Mr. Bremmercamp, *Cotton Candy* (also known as *Ron Howard's "Cotton Candy"*), NBC, 1978.

Mr. Murray, *Flatbed Annie & Sweetiepie: Lady Truckers* (also known as *Flatbed Annie* and *Girls of the Road*), CBS, 1979.

Harry the bartender, *The Kid from Left Field*, NBC, 1979.

Second pilot, *Skyward* (also known as *Ron Howard's "Skyward"*), NBC, 1980.

Captain, *Scout's Honor*, NBC, 1980.

Dr. Jewell, *The Miracle of Kathy Miller*, CBS, 1981.

Coach Ramsdell, *The Kid with the Broken Halo*, NBC, 1982.

Still photographer, *Rita Hayworth: The Love Goddess*, CBS, 1983.

Harry the bartender, *The Kid with the 200 I.Q.*, NBC, 1983.

Policeman, *The Fantastic World of D. C. Collins*, NBC, 1984.

Hank, *Finder of Lost Loves*, 1984.

Mr. Bell, *Scandal Sheet* (also known as *The Devil's Bed*), ABC, 1985.

Fireman Goodwin, *Playing with Fire*, NBC, 1985.

Preacher, *Return to Mayberry*, NBC, 1986.

Dr. Jennings, *A Smoky Mountain Christmas*, ABC, 1986.

Bernie, *Lucy & Desi: Before the Laughter*, CBS, 1991.

Polygraph man, *Boris and Natasha*, Showtime, 1992.

Third minute man, *Runaway Daughters*, Showtime, 1994.

The janitor, *Problem Child 3* (also known as *Problem Child 3: Junior in Love*), NBC, 1995.

Stan Benson, *The Colony*, USA Network, 1995.

Arnold Tooney, Jr., *The Second Civil War* (also known as *Second Impact*), HBO, 1997.

Jarvis Bean, *Murder, She Wrote: South by Southwest*, CBS, 1997.

Max, *The Sender*, HBO, 1997.

Blind man, *Holiday in Your Heart*, ABC, 1997.

Hotel manager, *Land of the Free*, HBO, 1998.

Old Man Dickens, *Skip Tracer*, 2008.

Television Appearances; Specials:

Myron Farrady, "The Skating Rink," *ABC Afterschool Special*, ABC, 1975.

The New Daughters of Joshua Cabe, 1976.

Counterattack: Crime in America, ABC, 1982.

Mr. Sellers, "The Drug Knot," *CBS Schoolbreak Special*, CBS, 1986.

Vern Logan, *The Letters from Moab*, Showtime, 1991.

1998 MTV Movie Awards, MTV, 1998.

Ron Howard: Hollywood's Favorite Son, Arts and Entertainment, 1999.

Andy of Mayberry: The E! True Hollywood Story, E! Entertainment Television, 2000.

Inside TV Land: "The Andy Griffith Show," TV Land, 2000.

The Clint Howard Variety Show, 2002.

The 2nd Annual TV Land Awards, TV Land, 2004.

Presenter, *Moving Image Salutes Ron Howard,* Bravo, 2006.

Voice of Rudolph, *Elf Sparkle and the Special Red Dress* (animated), 2010.

Television Appearances; Pilots:

Deputy, *State Fair,* CBS, 1976.

Charly Girabaldi, *Driving Me Crazy,* 2000.

Also appeared as customer II, "What's in a Name?," *That Girl.*

Television Appearances; Episodic:

"Paper Foxhole," *Kraft Television Theatre* (also known as *Kraft Mystery Theatre* and *Kraft Theatre*), 1956.

"Most Blessed Woman," *Kraft Television Theatre* (also known as *Kraft Mystery Theatre* and *Kraft Theatre*), 1957.

"Sheriff's Man," *Kraft Television Theatre* (also known as *Kraft Mystery Theatre* and *Kraft Theatre*), 1957.

Corporal, "Hit and Run," *How to Marry a Millionaire,* 1958.

Court clerk, "The Cast of the Sardonic Sergeant," *Perry Mason,* CBS, 1958.

Fletcher, "Promised Land," *Bat Masterson,* 1959.

"Danny Meets Andy Griffith," *Make Room for Daddy* (also known as *The Danny Thomas Show*), 1960.

Bus driver, "Cousin Virgil," *The Andy Griffith Show* (also known as *Andy of Mayberry*), CBS, 1962.

Governor's chauffeur, "Barney and the Governor," *The Andy Griffith Show* (also known as *Andy of Mayberry*), CBS, 1963.

Wilkerson, "The Bridge at Chalons," *Combat!,* 1963.

Treasury agent, "A Black Day for Mayberry," *The Andy Griffith Show* (also known as *Andy of Mayberry*), CBS, 1963.

"Come a–Runnin'," *Vacation Playhouse,* 1963.

Party guest, "The Rumor," *The Andy Griffith Show* (also known as *Andy of Mayberry*), CBS, 1964.

Luka, "Ride a Cock–Horse to Laramie Cross," *The Virginian* (also known as *The Men from Shiloh*), 1966.

"The Intruders," *The Monroes,* 1966.

"Killer Cougar," *The Monroes,* 1967.

"Teaching the Tiger to Purr," *The Monroes,* 1967.

"Two Worlds," *Here Come the Brides,* 1970.

Mr. Mueller, "That Undiscovered Country ...," *Then Came Bronson,* 1970.

Judge Franklin, "Jenny," *Gunsmoke* (also known as *Marshal Dillon*), 1970.

Sam, "A Time to Die," *Bonanza* (also known as *Ponderosa* and *Ride the Wind*), NBC, 1970.

Cameraman, "The Boy Who Predicted Earthquakes," *Night Gallery* (also known as *Rod Serling's "Night Gallery"*), NBC, 1971.

Bogardus, "Shanklin," *Bonanza* (also known as *Ponderosa* and *Ride the Wind*), NBC, 1972.

Sheriff Byrd, "The Hoots," *Kung Fu,* ABC, 1973.

Dr. McIvers, "The Thanksgiving Story," *The Waltons,* CBS, 1973.

Ranger, "Desperate Journey," *The F.B.I.,* 1973.

Dr. McIvers, "The Birthday," *The Waltons,* CBS, 1974.

Frank Benton, "In Performance of Duty," *Gunsmoke* (also known as *Marshal Dillon*), 1974.

Dr. McIvers, "The Venture," *The Waltons,* CBS, 1975.

Truck driver, "Nightmare," *The Rookies,* 1975.

Dr. McIvers, "The Competition," *The Waltons,* CBS, 1975.

Collins, "The Deadly Missiles Caper," *Switch,* 1975.

Announcer, "Dance Contest," *Happy Days,* 1976.

Simpson, "Quarantine," *Little House on the Prairie,* NBC, 1977.

Farnes, "The Magnificent Warriors," *Battlestar Galactica,* ABC, 1978.

Ben Wilson, "Spunkless Spinky," *Happy Days,* 1978.

Doctor, "Who's Papa?," *Laverne & Shirley* (also known as *Laverne & Shirley & Company, Laverne & Shirley & Friends,* and *Laverne DeFazio & Shirley Feeney*), 1979.

Mr. Burkhart, "Here Comes the Bride, Again," *Happy Days,* 1979.

"House Cleaners," *Enos,* 1981.

Guard, "Mork Meets Robin Williams," *Mork & Mindy,* 1981.

Gifford, "The Voice: Part 2," *Dynasty,* 1984.

Hank, "Maxwell Ltd: Finder of Lost Loves," *Finder of Lost Loves,* 1984.

Fillmore, "Death Casts a Spell," *Murder, She Wrote,* CBS, 1984.

"Deeds and Misdeeds," *Dallas,* CBS, 1985.

"Smokey Mountain Requiem," *Wiseguy,* CBS, 1988.

Fireman, "Heat Wave," *Baywatch,* NBC, 1989.

Colonel, "Luthor Unleashed," *The Adventures of Superboy* (also known as *Superboy*), 1989.

Richard Walton, "The King of Jazz," *B. L. Stryker,* ABC, 1989.

Mr. Williams, "The Price of Justice," *Equal Justice,* 1990.

Lamar, "Heart of a Champion—July 23, 1995," *Quantum Leap,* NBC, 1991.

Joe, "The Lost Treasure of Tower 12," *Baywatch,* 1992.

Blind man, "The Glasses," *Seinfeld,* NBC, 1993.

Pa Keller, "Dottie's Back," *A League of Their Own,* CBS, 1993.

Herman Van Dam, "Christmas of the Van Damned," *Coach,* ABC, 1993.

Garbage truck driver, "Murder with Mirrors," *Diagnosis Murder* (also known as *Dr. Mark Sloan*), CBS, 1994.

Des, "Surprise Party," *Tales from the Crypt,* HBO, 1994.

Jeff Foster, "Parentnapping," *Land's End,* 1995.

Farmer, "The Bottle Deposit," *Seinfeld,* NBC, 1996.

Funeral director, "The Sandwich," *Ink,* CBS, 1996.

Edwin, "Enemies," *Married ... with Children* (also known as *Married with Children*), Fox, 1996.

David Sheridan, "Severed Dreams," *Babylon 5* (also known as *B5*), syndicated, 1996.

Motel manager, "Full Metal Betsy," *Melrose Place,* Fox, 1996.

David Sheridan, "Interludes and Examinations," *Babylon 5* (also known as *B5*), syndicated, 1996.

David Sheridan, "Rising Star," *Babylon 5* (also known as *B5*), 1997.

"Hot Winds," *Baywatch Nights* (also known as *Baywatch Hawaii*), 1997.

Reverend, "How to Marry a Moron," *Married ... with Children* (also known as *Married with Children*), Fox, 1997.

Jarvis Bean, "South by Southwest," *Murder, She Wrote,* CBS, 1997.

"The Viewing," *Beyond Belief: Fact or Fiction* (also known as *Beyond Belief*), 1997.

Mr. Filmore, "Putting Two 'n Two Together," *Two of a Kind,* ABC, 1998.

Mr. Filmore, "Peeping Twins," *Two of a Kind,* ABC, 1998.

Mr. Bell, "Bakersfield Blues," *Clueless,* UPN, 1998.

Mr. Bell, "Back from Bakersfield," *Clueless,* UPN, 1998.

Blind flower guy, "When Nina Met Elliott," *Just Shoot Me!,* NBC, 1999.

Old man in park, "Help," *7th Heaven,* The WB, 2000.

Foreman, "Black Widow," *The Huntress,* USA Network, 2001.

Marcus Rosco, "Carpe Noctem," *Angel* (also known as *Angel: The Series*), The WB, 2001.

Mr. Bailey, "Tuesday Comes Over," *That 80's Show,* Fox, 2002.

Dean Faraday, "Witness for the Prostitution," *Son of the Beach,* FX Network, 2002.

Buddie, "Factory Girls," *Cold Case,* CBS, 2004.

Murphy, "Sweeps," *That's So Raven* (also known as *That's So Raven!*), The Disney Channel, 2004.

Dirk Abrams, "Lost Boys," *The Ghost Whisperer,* CBS, 2005.

"Child Stars II: Growing up in Hollywood," *Biography,* Arts and Entertainment, 2005.

Henry, "The Crying Game," *Twenty Good Years,* Australian Broadcasting Corporation, 2006.

Samuel Cooper, "Fare Game," *CSI: NY* (also known as *CSI: New York*), CBS, 2006.

Joe Metz, "Moral Waiver," *Lie to Me,* Fox, 2009.

Dr. Oliver Kostin, "A Long, Strange Trip," *ER,* NBC, 2009.

Also appeared in "Red China Rescue," *Flight.*

Television Producer; Movies:
Cotton Candy (also known as *Ron Howard's "Cotton Candy"*), NBC, 1978.

Through the Magic Pyramid (also known as *Tut and Tuttle*), NBC, 1981.

Stage Plays:
Appeared in *Mister Roberts.*

WRITINGS

Screenplays:
(With others) *Grand Theft Auto,* 1977.

Television Movies:
Through the Magic Pyramid (also known as *Tut and Tuttle*), NBC, 1981.

Television Episodes:
"Indianrockolis 500," *The Flintstones* (animated), 1964.

"Fred's Second Car," *The Flintstones* (animated), 1965.

(With Hoke Howell), "The Commitment," *The Rookies,* 1972.

Also wrote episodes of *Partridge Family: 2200 A.D.* (also known as *The Partridge Family in Outer Space*), CBS.

Television Episode Stories:
"The Ball Game," *The Andy Griffith Show* (also known as *Andy of Mayberry*), CBS, 1966.

HUGGINS, Erica

PERSONAL

Raised in Ann Arbor, MI, and southern California. *Education:* Hampshire College, B.A.

Addresses: *Office*—Imagine Entertainment, 9465 Wilshire Blvd., 7th Floor, Beverly Hills, CA 90212.

Career: Producer, film editor, and executive. Interscope Communications, Los Angeles, producer, beginning 1994; Radar Pictures, Los Angeles, producer; Imagine Entertainment, Beverly Hills, CA, executive vice president for motion pictures.

CREDITS

Film Producer:
Boys, Buena Vista, 1996.
Gridlock'd, Gramercy, 1997.
Evil Alien Conquerors, RCV Film Distribution, 2002.

How to Deal, New Line Cinema, 2003.
Son of the Mask (also known as *Mask 2*), New Line Cinema, 2005.

Film Executive Producer:
What Dreams May Come, PolyGram Filmed Entertainment, 1998.
Teaching Mrs. Tingle (also known as *Killing Mrs. Tingle*), Dimension Films, 1999.
Le Divorce, Fox Searchlight, 2003.
Flightplan, Buena Vista, 2005.

Film Editor:
Assistant film editor, *Big Girls Don't Cry ... They Get Even* (also known as *Stepkids*), New Line Cinema, 1991.
Additional film editor, *Freddy's Dead: The Final Nightmare,* New Line Cinema, 1991.
The Gun in Betty Lou's Handbag, Buena Vista, 1992.
Ghost in the Machine (also known as *Deadly Terror*), Twentieth Century–Fox, 1993.
Serial Mom, Savoy Pictures, 1994.

Film Appearances:
Patron of Musso and Frank's, *Greenberg,* Focus Features, 2010.

Television Executive Producer; Specials:
The WIN Awards, PAX, 2005.

Television Appearances; Episodic:
"Son of the Mask," *HBO First Look,* HBO, 2005.

RECORDINGS

Videos:
Paw Prints and Baby Steps: On the Set of "Son of the Mask," New Line Home Video, 2005.
Creating "Son of the Mask:" Digital Diapers and Dog Bytes, New Line Home Video, 2005.

HYNES, Jessica 1972–
(Jessica Stevenson)

PERSONAL

Original name, Jessica Stevenson; changed stage name to Jessica Hynes; born November 15, 1972, in London, England; father, a carpenter; mother, a special needs teacher; married Adam Hynes, 2002; children: one son, two daughters. *Education:* Trained with the National Youth Theatre, London.

Addresses: *Agent*—Ruth Young, United Agents, 12–26 Lexington St., London W1F 0LE, England; (writing) Abby Singer, Casarotto Ramsay and Associates, Ltd., Waverley House, 7–12 Noel St., London W1F 8GQ, England.

Career: Actress, comedienne, and writer. Provided voice work for advertisements. Involved with charities.

Awards, Honors: British Comedy Award, best female comedy newcomer, 1999, for *Spaced* and *The Royle Family;* British Comedy Award, best television comedy actress, 2001, Television Award nomination (with others), situation comedy award, British Academy of Film and Television Arts, 2002, *Spaced* designated as one of the top comedies on the television program *The Ultimate Sitcom,* Channel 4, 2006, and *Spaced* named one of the best shows of the noughties by the periodical the *Guardian,* 2009, all for *Spaced;* Television Award nomination, best actress, British Academy of Film and Television Arts, and Royal Television Society Award nomination, best actor—female, both 2003, for *Tomorrow La Scala!;* Laurence Olivier Award nomination, best supporting performance in a supporting role, Society of West End Theatre, 2003, for *The Night Heron;* Drama Desk Award and Outer Critics Circle Award, both outstanding ensemble performance, and *Theatre World Award,* special award for the ensemble, all with others, and Antoinette Perry Award nomination, best featured actress in a play, all 2009, for *The Norman Conquests* trilogy (*The Norman Conquests: Living Together, The Norman Conquests: Round and Round the Garden,* and *The Norman Conquests: Table Manners*).

CREDITS

Television Appearances; as Jessica Stevenson; Series:
Jackie South, *Crown Prosecutor,* BBC, 1995.
Various characters, *Six Pairs of Pants,* Channel 4, 1995.
Nurse McFadden and Martha, *Asylum,* The Paramount Channel, 1996.
Various characters, *Mash and Peas,* The Paramount Channel and Channel 4, 1996–97.
Alice Timpson, *Staying Alive* (also known as *Angels 2000*), London Weekend Television, c. 1996–97.
Various characters, *Armstrong and Miller* (also known as *The Armstrong and Miller Show*), Paramount Comedy Channel, 1997, Comedy Central, 1997–98.
Alice, *Merry–Go–Round* (also known as *Alexei Sayle's "Merry–Go–Round"* and *Alexei Show*), BBC2, 1998.
Various characters, *Unnatural Acts,* 1998.
Cheryl Carroll, *The Royle Family,* BBC and BBC America, 1998–2000.
Daisy Steiner, *Spaced,* Channel 4, 1999–2001.

Holly Vance, *Bob & Rose,* ITV, 2001.

Rebecca "Bex" Atwell, *According to Bex* (also known as *Everything I Know about Men* and *The World according to Bex*), BBC, 2005.

Narrator, *British Film Forever* (documentary), BBC2, 2007.

Television Appearances; as Jessica Stevenson; Miniseries:

Maggie, *Tears before Bedtime,* BBC, 1995.

Woman with Black Death victim, *The Nearly Complete and Utter History of Everything,* BBC, 2000.

Television Appearances; as Jessica Stevenson; Movies:

Victoria, *Tomorrow La Scala!* (also known as *Sweeney*), BBC2, 2002.

Aimee Griffith, *Marple: The Moving Finger* (also known as "The Moving Finger," *Agatha Christie "Marple,"* "The Moving Finger," *Agatha Christie's "Marple,"* "The Moving Finger," *Marple,* "The Moving Finger," *Miss Marple,* "The Moving Finger," *Miss Marple, Series II, Agatha Christie—Marple: The Moving Finger,* and *Miss Marple: The Moving Finger*), ITV, 2006, broadcast as part of *Mystery!,* PBS, 2006.

WPC (woman police constable) Broughton, *Pinochet in Suburbia* (also known as *Pinochet's Last Stand*), BBC2 and HBO, 2006.

Television Appearances; as Jessica Hynes; Movies:

Beverley, *Learners,* BBC, 2007.

Television Appearances; as Jessica Stevenson; Specials:

(Uncredited) *Harry Enfield and His Yule Log Chums* (special related to *Harry Enfield and Chums;* also known as *Harry Enfield and His Yule Loggy Chums* and *Harry Enfield's Christmas Chums*), BBC, 1997.

The good fairy, "Dick Whittington," *ITV Pantomime* (also known as *ITV Pantomime: Dick Whittington*), ITV, 2002.

Herself, *Generation Jedi,* BBC3, 2005.

Herself, *"Star Wars": Feel the Force,* Sky Television, 2005.

Presenter, *Comic Aid,* BBC, 2005.

Cheryl Carroll, *The Queen of Sheba* (special related to *The Royle Family*), BBC and BBC America, 2006.

Herself, *The 50 Greatest Comedy Films,* Channel 4, 2006.

Herself and Mrs. Peacock, *The Secret Policeman's Ball: The Ball in the Hall* (benefit; also known as *The Secret Policeman's Ball* and *The Secret Policeman's Ball 2006*), Channel 4, 2006.

Herself, *The Ultimate Sitcom,* Channel 4, 2006.

Herself and Daisy Steiner, *The World's Greatest Comedy Characters,* Channel 4, 2007.

Television Appearances; as Jessica Hynes; Specials:

(Uncredited; in archive footage) Cheryl Carroll, *50 Greatest Comedy Catchphrases* (also known as *Greatest Comedy Catchphrases*), Channel 4, 2008.

(Uncredited; in archive footage) Joan Redfern, *Verity Lambert: Drama Queen* (documentary), BBC4, 2008.

Cheryl Carroll, *The Golden Eggcup* (special related to *The Royle Family;* also known as *The Golden Egg Cup*), BBC and BBC America, 2009.

Narrator, *Watching the Dead* (documentary), BBC4, 2009.

Television Appearances; Awards Presentations:

(As Jessica Stevenson) *The British Comedy Awards 2001,* ITV, 2001.

(As Jessica Stevenson) *The Evening Standard British Film Awards,* ITV3, 2005.

(As Jessica Hynes) *The 63rd Annual Tony Awards,* CBS, 2009.

Television Appearances; as Jessica Stevenson; Episodic:

Charlotte Parker, *The House of Eliott,* BBC, 1994.

Judith Lessiter, "The Killings at Badger's Drift," *Midsomer Murders,* ITV, BBC, and Arts and Entertainment, 1997.

Sarah, "The Estate Agent," *People Like Us,* BBC, 1999.

Herself, *Comedy Cafe,* ITV, 1999.

Felia Siderova, "Drop Dead," *Randall & Hopkirk (Deceased)* (also known as *Randall & Hopkirk*), BBC, 2000.

Felia Siderova, "Mental Apparition Disorder," *Randall & Hopkirk (Deceased)* (also known as *Randall & Hopkirk*), BBC, 2000.

Eva, "Hello Sun," *Black Books,* Channel 4, BBC America, and Comedy Central, 2002.

Herself, *Room 101,* BBC, 2002.

Herself, *Friday Night with Jonathan Ross,* BBC, 2004.

Herself, *Richard & Judy,* Channel 4, 2005, 2008.

Herself, "Domesticity," *QI* (also known as *QI XL* and *Quite Interesting*), BBC, 2006.

Special guest, "Does True Love Exist?," *Got Issues* (also known as *Russell Brand's "Got Issues"*), E4, 2006.

Herself, *The Charlotte Church Show,* Channel 4, 2006.

Herself, *8 out of 10 Cats,* Channel 4 and E4, 2006.

Herself, *GMTV* (also known as *GMTV Today*), ITV, 2006.

Herself, "Lucas and Walliams' Perfect Night In," *Perfect Night In,* Channel 4, 2007.

Television Appearances; as Jessica Hynes; Episodic:

Herself, "Alter Ego," *Doctor Who Confidential* (also known as *Doctor Who Confidential: Cut Down*), BBC, 2007.

Joan Redfern, "The Family of Blood," *Doctor Who* (also known as *Dr. Who*), BBC, 2007.

Joan Redfern, "Human Nature," *Doctor Who* (also known as *Dr. Who*), BBC and Sci–Fi Channel, 2007.

Guest panelist, *The Wright Stuff*, Channel 5, 2007.

Herself, *Breakfast* (also known as *BBC Breakfast*), BBC, 2007.

Herself, *GMTV Today* (also known as *GMTV*), ITV, 2007.

Herself, *Never Mind the Buzzcocks*, BBC, 2007.

Herself, *Saturday Kitchen*, BBC, 2007.

Herself, *Strictly Come Dancing: It Takes Two*, BBC2, 2007.

(In archive footage) Herself, "Never Mind the Buzzcocks: A Moving Tribute," *Never Mind the Buzzcocks*, BBC, 2008.

Herself, *The F Word* (also known as *Gordon Ramsay's "F Word"*), Channel 4 and BBC America, 2008.

Herself, *Richard & Judy's New Position* (also known as *Richard & Judy*), Watch, 2008.

Herself, *The Soup*, E! Entertainment Television, 2008.

Herself, *Loose Women*, ITV, 2008, 2009.

Verity Newman, "The End of Time: Part Two," *Doctor Who* (also known as *Dr. Who*), BBC and Syfy, 2010.

Appeared in other programs.

Television Appearances; Pilots:

(As Jessica Stevenson) Voice of Janine (the wife), "Knife & Wife" (animated), *Comedy Lab*, Channel 4, 2001.

(As Jessica Hynes) Sarah and Ellie, *Lizzie and Sarah*, BBC2, 2010.

Television Work; as Jessica Hynes; Pilots:

(With Simon Pegg and Edgar Wright) Creator, *Spaced*, Fox, 2008.

Script consultant, *Phoo Action*, BBC3, 2008.

Associate producer, *Lizzie and Sarah*, BBC2, 2010.

Film Appearances; as Jessica Stevenson:

First midwife, *The Baby of Macon* (also known as *Das Wunder von Macon*), Channel Four Films, 1993.

Helga, *Swing Kids*, Buena Vista, 1993.

Libby, *Born Romantic*, United Artists, 2001.

Paramedic, *Pure*, 2002, Indican Pictures, 2005.

Magda, *Bridget Jones: The Edge of Reason* (also known as *Bridget Jones's Diary 2*, *Bridget Jones 2*, *Bridget Jones—Am Rande des Wahnsinns*, *Bridget Jones: L'age de raison*, and *Bridget Jones—L'age 2 raison*), Universal, 2004.

Yvonne, *Shaun of the Dead* (also known as *Tea–Time of the Dead*, *Zombies Party*, *Ein Zombie kommt selten allein*, *L'alba dei morti dementi*, *Muertos de risa*, *Shaun dei morti*, *Shaun et les zombies*, *Shaun of the Dead—Ein Zombie kommt selten allein*, and *Todo mundo quase morto*), Focus Features, 2004.

Miranda, *Four Last Songs* (also known as *Mallorca's Song*), Capitol Films, 2006.

Sam, *Confetti*, Fox Searchlight, 2006.

Linda, *Magicians*, Universal, 2007.

Mafalda Hopkirk, *Harry Potter and the Order of the Phoenix* (IMAX version known as *Harry Potter and the Order of the Phoenix: The IMAX Experience*; also known as *Order of the Phoenix*, *The Order of the Phoenix*, *Tip Top*, *Hari Poter i Red Feniksa*, *Harry Potter e a Ordem da Fenix*, *Harry Potter e l'ordine della Fenice*, *Harry Potter en de orde van de feniks*, *Harry Potter es a Foenix Rendje*, *Harry Potter et l'ordre du phenix*, *Harry Potter i l'orde del Fenix*, *Harry Potter ja feeniksin kilta*, *Harry Potter och fenixorden*, *Harry Potter og foniksordenen*, *Harry Potter und der Orden des Phoenix*, and *Harry Potter y la orden del Fenix*), Warner Bros., 2007.

Mary Proudfoot, *Son of Rambow* (also known as *Der Sohn von Rambow*, *Le fils de Rambow*, and *Son of Rambo—Ein garantiert unwiderstehlicher Actionheld*), Paramount Vantage, 2008.

Film Appearances; as Jessica Hynes:

Cath, *Faintheart*, Vertigo Films, 2008.

Lucky, *Burke and Hare*, Entertainment Film Distributors, 2010.

Stage Appearances; as Jessica Stevenson:

Fifty–year–old person, *Lip*, c. 1980.

Mrs. Blitzstein, *Blitz!* (musical), National Youth Theatre, Playhouse Theatre, London, 1990.

Grandma Tzietl, *Fiddler on the Roof* (musical), West Yorkshire Playhouse, Leeds, England, 1992.

Rosie, *The Plough and the Stars*, West Yorkshire Playhouse, 1993.

Edith, *Blithe Spirit*, York Theatre Royal, York, England, 1995.

Bolla, *The Night Heron*, Royal Court Theatre, Jerwood Theatre Downstairs, London, 2002.

Herself and Mrs. Peacock, *The Secret Policeman's Ball: The Ball in the Hall* (benefit; also known as *The Secret Policeman's Ball* and *The Secret Policeman's Ball 2006*), Royal Albert Hall, London, 2006.

Appeared in other productions, including an appearance as Sylvie, *Brighton Rock*. Appeared in productions at the Crucible Theatre, Sheffield, England. Performed with Katy Carmichael in the comedy act The Liz Hurleys.

Stage Appearances; as Jessica Hynes:

Jacqueline, *Elephant Hotel*, produced as part of *The 24 Hour Plays* (also known as *The 24 Hour Plays Celebrity Gala*), Old Vic Theatre, London, 2008.

Annie, *The Norman Conquests: Living Together*, Old Vic Theatre, 2008, and Circle in the Square, New York City, 2009.

Annie, *The Norman Conquests: Round and Round the Garden,* Old Vic Theatre, 2008, and Circle in the Square, 2009.

Annie, *The Norman Conquests: Table Manners,* Old Vic Theatre, 2008, and Circle in the Square, 2009.

Huggies Little Bundle of Laughs (benefit), Leicester Square Theatre, London, 2010.

Radio Appearances:

(As Jessica Stevenson; with others) Narrator, *Giles Wemmbley Hogg Goes Off* (also known as *Giles Wemmbley Hogg Goes Off Series 3*), BBC Radio 4, beginning c. 2005.

(With Julia Davis) Presenter, *June Loves Janet,* Resonance Radio, beginning c. 2006, later known as *Peppatits,* Resonance Radio, beginning c. 2008.

Herself, *The Leonard Lopate Show* (episodic), WNYC, 2009.

Involved in productions for BBC Radio 4.

Internet Appearances:

Herself in a podcast interview, posted on *Pop Candy,* part of the *USA Today* Internet site, http://content.usatoday.com, c. 2008.

RECORDINGS

Videos; as Herself; as Jessica Stevenson; Documentaries:

And as Daisy Steiner, *Skip to the End,* Channel 4 Video, 2004.

Lucy's Cam (short documentary), Universal, 2004.

The Making of "Son of Rambow" (short documentary; also known as *Boys Will Be Boys: The Making of "Son of Rambow"*), Paramount Home Entertainment, 2008.

Appeared in corporate videos.

Videos; as Herself; as Jessica Hynes; Short Documentaries:

Behind the Tricks: Making "Magicians," Universal Studios Home Video, 2007.

WRITINGS

Teleplays; Movies:

Learners (based on an idea by Francesca Joseph), BBC, 2007.

Teleplays; with Others; as Jessica Stevenson; Episodic:

Six Pairs of Pants, Channel 4, 1995.

Asylum, The Paramount Channel, 1996.

(With Simon Pegg) *Spaced,* Channel 4, 1999–2001.

Teleplays; as Jessica Hynes; Pilots:

(With Julia Davis) *Lizzie and Sarah,* BBC2, 2010.

Screenplays; as Jessica Hynes:

(With others) *Faintheart,* Vertigo Films, 2008.

Author of other screenplays, including *Double Au Pair,* New Line Cinema; and *Suffrage!!!,* BBC Films. With Katy Carmichael, wrote the short film *Ruby's Room.*

Writings for the Stage:

(With others) *Huggies Little Bundle of Laughs* (benefit), Leicester Square Theatre, London, 2010.

With Katy Carmichael, created material for the comedy act The Liz Hurleys.

Writings for the Radio:

(With Julia Davis) *June Loves Janet,* Resonance Radio, beginning c. 2006, later known as *Peppatits,* Resonance Radio, beginning c. 2008.

Writings for Children:

Author of the children's book *Ants in the Marmalade.*

Nonfiction:

Author of writings posted on the Internet.

OTHER SOURCES

Periodicals:

Evening Standard (London), September 27, 1999, p. 29.

Guardian (London), January 1, 2005; May 25, 2007.

Independent: Extra (London), November 6, 2007, pp. 14–15.

New Review [The Independent on Sunday] (London), April 6, 2008, pp. 24–25.

sleazenation, April, 2000.

Sunday Times (London), January 31, 2009.

I

INNIS, Chris 1966–
(Christina Jean Innis)

PERSONAL

Born March 20, 1966, in San Diego, CA; daughter of Donald Alwyn Sr. (an architect) and Virginia Inez Calais (maiden name, Maples) Innis. *Education:* University of California Berkeley, B.A., film, 1988; California Institute of the Arts, M.F.A., 1991. *Politics:* Democrat. *Avocational Interests:* Writing, skiing, sailing.

Career: Voice actress, editor, producer, and director. Karaoke Videos/Pioneer Electronics, Los Angeles, CA, director and producer, 1990. Previously worked at United Artists, Mann's, and Landmark theaters as a cashier and in concessions.

Awards, Honors: Boston Society of Film Critics Award (with Bob Murawski), best film editing, Satellite Award (with Murawski), best film editing, International Press Academy, Sierra Award (with Murawski), best film editing, Las Vegas Film Critics Society, 2009, Academy Award (with Murawski), best achievement in editing, Film Award (with Murawski), best editing, Critics Choice Award (with Murawski), best editing, Broadcast Film Critics Association, Eddie Award (with Murawski), best edited feature film—dramatic, American Cinema Editors, Online Film Critics Society Award (with Murawski), best editing, 2010, all for *The Hurt Locker.*

CREDITS

Film Work:
Assistant editor, *West Is West,* Milestone Film & Video, 1987.
Apprentice editor, *The Wash,* Skouras Pictures, 1988.

Creative consultant and production sound, *Rumba* (short film), 1990.
Director, producer, editor, and sound editor, *Love Pig* (short film), 1990.
Apprentice editor, *JFK,* Warner Bros., 1991.
Apprentice editor, *Indecent Proposal,* Paramount, 1993.
First assistant editor, *Dead Beat,* Live Entertainment, 1994.
First assistant editor, *The Quick and the Dead* (also known as *Quick & Dead*), TriStar, 1995.
Assistant editor, *I Shot a Man in Vegas,* Arrow Entertainment, 1995.
Assistant editor, *White Man's Burden,* Savoy Pictures, 1995.
Associate editor, *G.I. Jane,* Buena Vista, 1997.
Director, producer, editor, and sound editor, *Vermin,* 1998.
Editor, *The Boy with the X–Ray Eyes* (also known as *X–Ray Boy* and *X–treme Teens*), Amazing Fantasy Entertainment, 1999.
Music editor, *The Gift,* Paramount Classics, 2000.
Music editor: temp music, *Spider–Man,* Columbia, 2002.
Assistant editor: New York, *Spider–Man 3* (also known as *Spider–Man 3: The IMAX Experience*), Columbia, 2007.
Editor, *The Hurt Locker* (also known as *The Hurt Locker*), Summit Entertainment, 2008.
Editor and translator, *Pieces of Juan (Piquer Simon)* (documentary; also known as *Pieces of Juan: Interview with Director Juan Piquer Simon*), Grindhouse Releasing, 2008.
Associate producer, *Gone with the Pope,* Grindhouse Releasing, 2010.
Editor, *Black Tulip,* 2010.

Also worked as editor, *Cannibal Holocaust Theatrical Re–Release World Premiere* (short documentary), Grindhouse Releasing; associate producer, *Cannibal Holocaust,* Grindhouse Releasing; director, *Bullet;* director, *He Asked Me To Ask You Not to Surprise Him* (short film); coproducer, *Cat in the Brain,* Grindhouse Releasing; coproducer, *Pieces,* Grindhouse Releasing.

Film Additional Voices:
Octopus, Lions Gate Films Home Entertainment, 2000.
(Uncredited) *Spiders,* Nu Image Films, 2000.
Octopus 2: River of Fear, Nu Image Films, 2001.
Don't Let Go, Jimmy Ray Productions, 2002.

Film Automated Dialogue Replacement (ADR) Voice:
Crocodile, Nu Image Films, 2000.
(Uncredited) *Cold Heart,* 2001.
Don't Let Go, Jimmy Ray Productions, 2002.

Film Appearances:
Drugged–out Rumbaee, *Rumba* (short film), 1990.
Waitress, *Vermin,* 1998.

Television Work; Series:
Production assistant, *Beach Boys: Endless Summer,* syndicated, 1988.
Production coordinator, *America's Funniest Home Videos* (also known as *A.F.V., AFHV, America's Funniest,* and *America's Funniest Videos*), ABC, 1990.
Associate editor and editor, *American Gothic,* CBS, 1995–96.

Television Work; Pilots:
Associate editor, *American Gothic,* CBS, 1995.

Television Work; Movies:
Assistant editor and assistant sound editor, *Jake Spanner, Private Eye,* USA Network, 1989.

RECORDINGS

Music Videos:
Edited "We Be Clubbin'" by Ice Cube, "Shut 'Em Down" by ONYX, and "Industrial Is Dead" by Fine; produced "Mr. Blue Veins" by Carnival Art; assistant director on "Satan Lend Me A Dollar" by Hill of Beans. Also worked on karaoke videos, including directing "Chains of Love" by Erasure; directing and producing "Say Goodbye to Hollywood" by Billy Joel, "Kiss" by Prince, and "Nick of Time" by Bonnie Raitt; and producing "Draw the Line" by Aerosmith,"Let's Go Crazy" by Prince, "Boogie Woogie Bugle Boy" by Andrews Sisters, "Knock on Wood" by Eddie Floyd, "Centerfold" by J. Geils Band, "I Think We're Alone Now" by Tiffany, and "All My Life" by Linda Rondstadt.

WRITINGS

Screenplays:
Love Pig, 1990.
Vermin, 1998.

IZZARD, Eddie 1962–

PERSONAL

Full name, Edward John Izzard; born February 7, 1962, in Aden, Yemen; raised in England; son of John (a British oil company accountant; some sources cite given name as Harold) and Dorothy Ella (a nurse and midwife) Izzard. *Education:* Attended University of Sheffield, 1980s. *Politics:* Labour.

Addresses: *Agent*—Carol Goll, International Creative Management, 10250 Constellation Way, 9th Floor, Los Angeles, CA 90067; (film animation work) Nicola Van Gelder, Conway Van Gelder Ltd., 18–21 Jermyn St., 3rd Floor, London SW1Y 6HP, England. *Manager*—The Collective, 8383 Wilshire Blvd., Suite 1050, Beverly Hills, CA 90211; Caroline Chignell, PBJ Management, 7 Soho St., London W1D 3DQ, England. *Publicist*—Ina Treciokas, Slate Public Relations, 8322 Beverly Blvd., Suite 201, Los Angeles, CA 90048.

Career: Actor, comedian, producer, and writer. Ella Communications, partner; worked as a street performer in London; began comedy career at Comedy Store, London, 1987; participant in numerous live awards presentations; appeared in commercials for Gift Aid and other charities.

Awards, Honors: Nomination for Perrier Award, 1991; Laurence Olivier Theatre Award nomination, outstanding achievement, Society of West End Theatre, and British Comedy Award, both 1993, for *Eddie Izzard: Live at the Ambassadors;* British Comedy Award, 1996, for *Eddie Izzard: Definite Article;* Special *Theatre World* Award, 1998, for stage show *Eddie Izzard: Dress to Kill;* Emmy Awards, outstanding individual performance in a variety or music program and outstanding writing for a variety, music, or comedy program, and Emmy Award nomination (with others), outstanding variety, music or comedy special, all 2000, for television special *Eddie Izzard: Dress to Kill;* Antoinette Perry Award nomination, Outer Critics Circle Award, Drama Desk Award, all best actor in a play, and Drama League Award, distinguished performance, all 2003, for *A Day in the Death of Joe Egg;* honorary doctorate, University of Sheffield, 2006; Teen Choice Award nomination (with others), choice movie chemistry, 2007, for *Ocean's Thirteen;* Satellite Award nomination, best actor in a drama series, International Press Academy, 2007, and Astra Award nomination, favorite international personality or actor, Australian Subscription Television and Radio Association, 2008, both for *The Riches.*

CREDITS

Film Appearances:
Hanging Around, 1996.

Vladimir, *The Secret Agent* (also known as *Joseph Conrad's "The Secret Agent"*), Fox Searchlight, 1996.

Bailey, *The Avengers*, Warner Bros., 1996.

Jerry Devine, *Velvet Goldmine*, Miramax, 1998.

Tony Pompadour, *Mystery Men*, Universal, 1999.

Troy Cabrera, *Circus*, Sony Pictures Entertainment, 1999.

Detective Peter Hume, *The Criminal*, Paramount, 1999.

Gustav von Wangenheim, *Shadow of the Vampire* (also known as *Burned to Light*), Lions Gate Films, 2000.

Charlie Chaplin, *The Cat's Meow*, 2001.

Tony Parker, *All the Queen's Men*, Strand Releasing, 2001.

Tiny Diamonds, *Rage*, 2001.

Lussurioso, *The Revenger's Tragedy*, 2002.

Baron Werner Amadeus von Luckner/Prosit, *Renegade* (also known as *Blueberry*), Columbia TriStar Home Entertainment, 2003.

Voice of It, *Five Children and It*, Capitol Films, 2004.

Roman Nagel, *Ocean's Twelve*, Warner Bros., 2004.

Gene Vincent, *Romance & Cigarettes*, Metro–Goldwyn–Mayer, 2005.

The Aristocrats (documentary; also known as *The @r!$t*(r@t$)*), THINKFilm, 2005.

I Told You I Was Ill: The Life and Legacy of Spike Milligan (documentary; also known as *The Life and Legacy of Spike Milligan*), ABC Content Sales, 2005.

Voice of Nigel, *The Wild* (animated), Walt Disney, 2006.

Professor Bedlam and Barry, *My Super Ex–Girlfriend*, Twentieth Century–Fox, 2006.

Diva 51 (documentary), THINKFilm, 2006.

Roman Nagel, *Ocean's Thirteen*, Warner Bros., 2007.

Mr. Kite, *Across the Universe*, Columbia, 2007.

Voice of Reepicheep, *The Chronicles of Narnia: Prince Caspian* (animated; also known as *Prince Caspian*), Walt Disney, 2008.

Voice of Dr. Schadenfreude, *Igor* (animated); Metro–Goldwyn–Mayer, 2008.

General Erich Fellgiebel, *Valkyrie* (also known as *Walkuere*), United Artists, 2008.

Believe: The Eddie Izzard Story (documentary), Salient Media, 2009.

Garrett, *Every Day*, Eagle Films, 2010.

Himself, *Huge*, Toff Media/Matador Pictures/Cinema Three/Fortuitous Films, 2010.

Television Appearances; Series:

Wayne Malloy, *The Riches*, FX Network, 2007–2008.

Doug Rich, *The Riches*, FX Network, 2008.

Television Appearances; Miniseries:

Channel Izzard, Channel 4, 1997.

30 Years of Billy Connolly, 1998.

Ralph Outen, *40*, BBC, 2002.

Presenter, *Mongrel Nation*, The Discovery Channel, 2003.

Nick Malone, *Kitchen*, Channel 5, 2007.

Torrence, *The Day of the Triffids*, BBC, 2009.

Monty Python: Almost the Truth—The Lawyers Cut, Independent Film Channel, 2009.

Eddie Izzard: Marathon Man, BBC, 2010.

Television Appearances; Specials:

Host, *It's the Monty Python Story* (also known as *Life of Python*), 1993.

It's Just a Ride, 1994.

Socrates, *Aristophanes: The Gods Are Laughing*, Channel 4, 1995.

The Big Snog (broadcast of live benefit performance), Channel 4, 1995.

Je suis a Stand–up: Eddie Izzard Abroad, 1996.

Lust for Glorious, 1997.

Comic Relief VIII, HBO, 1998.

Monty Python imposter, *Monty Python's Flying Circus: Live at Aspen* (also known as *US Comedy Arts Festival Tribute to Monty Python*), 1998.

Eddie Izzard: Dress to Kill (broadcast of live stage show), HBO, 1998.

Fairy, *Pythonland*, BBC, 1999.

Host, *Python Night: 30 Years of Monty Python*, BBC, 1999.

Here, There and Everywhere: A Concert for Linda, 1999.

Presenter, *Life of Python*, Arts and Entertainment, 2000.

We Know Where You Live (also known as *Amnesty International's We Know Where You Live Live!*), Channel 4, 2001.

Bri, *A Day in the Death of Joe Egg* (broadcast of stage performance), BBC, 2002.

Spike Milligan: I Told You I Was Ill—A Live Tribute (broadcast of live stage show), BBC, 2002.

Best Ever Bond, ITV1, 2002.

Billy Connolly: A BAFTA Tribute, BBC, 2002.

RIP 2002, 2002.

(In archive footage) *Comedy Central Presents: 100 Greatest Stand–ups of All Time*, Comedy Central, 2004.

Comic Aid, BBC, 2005.

(In archive footage) *The Comedians' Comedian*, Channel 4, 2005.

The Secret Policeman's Ball, Channel 4, 2006.

The Secret Policeman's Ball: The Ball in the Hall, Channel 4, 2006.

Presenter, *AFI Life Achievement Award: A Tribute to Sean Connery*, USA Network, 2006.

100 Greatest Stand–ups, Channel 4, 2007.

The World's Greatest Comedy Characters, Channel 4, 2007.

50 Greatest Comedy Catchphrases, Channel 4, 2008.

ITV Premiere Special: The Chronicles of Narnia–Prince Caspian, ITV, 2008.

The Chronicles of Narnia: Prince Caspian T4 Movie Special, T4, 2008.

U.S. Election Night, 2008.

Morecambe and Wise: The Show What Paul Merton Did, BBC, 2009.
Sport Relief, BBC, 2010.

Television Appearances; Movies:
Rich, *Open Fire,* 1994.
Voice, *Inspector Derrick,* 1997.

Television Appearances; Pilots:
Himself, *QI,* BBC, 2006.
Wayne Malloy, *The Riches,* FX Network, 2007.

Television Appearances; Episodic:
Guest captain, *Have I Got News for You,* BBC, multiple appearances, between 1994 and 1996.
Whose Line Is It Anyway?, Channel 4, 1995.
Evans, "Confession," *Tales from the Crypt,* HBO, 1996.
Premiere episode, *Where's Elvis This Week?,* BBC, 1996.
The End of the Year Show, BBC1, 1996, 1997.
Narrator, "David Bowie," *VH1 Legends,* VH1, 1996.
Shooting Stars, BBC, 1997.
"The Goons," *Heroes of Comedy,* 1997.
Narrator, "David Bowie," *Behind the Music* (also known as *VH1's Behind the Music*), VH1, 1997.
Voice of Easter Island head, "Easter Island," *Rex the Runt* (animated), 1998.
Voice of melting blob man, "Adventures on Telly 3," *Rex the Runt* (animated), 1998.
Question Time, BBC, 1998, 2005.
The Priory, Channel 4, 1999.
Full Mountie, 2000.
Comedian, *Best of British,* 2000.
Stop! Kong Fu!, 2001.
RI:SE, Channel 4, 2002.
Channel 4 News, Channel 4, 2002.
Newsnight, Cable News Network, 2002.
Top Gear, BBC, 2004.
Sen kvaell med Luuk, 2004.
29 Minutes of Fame, 2005.
Dokument: Humor, SVT, 2005.
Foerst & sist, 2005.
"Monty Python's Spamalot," *The South Bank Show,* Channel 4, 2006.
(In archive footage) *The Comedy Map of Britain,* BBC, 2007.
American Idol (also known as *American Idol: The Search for a Superstar* and *Idol*), Fox, 2008.
Voices of Nigel Baker–Butcher and Queen Elizabeth, "To Surveil, with Love," *The Simpsons* (animated), Fox, 2010.
(In archive footage) *Breakfast,* BBC, 2010.

Also appeared in an episode of *Comedy Store,* Channel 5.

Television Talk Show Guest Appearances; Episodic:
Clive Anderson Talks Back, 1993, 1995.
Ruby, BBC, 1997, 1999.
The Roseanne Show, syndicated, 1998.
Clive Anderson All Talk, BBC1, 1998.
TFI Friday, Channel 4, 1998, 1999.
The Tonight Show with Jay Leno, NBC, multiple appearances, between 1998 and 2007.
"Eccentricity," *Dennis Miller Live,* HBO, 1999.
Parkinson, BBC, 1999, 2003, 2004.
Stand Up with Alan Davies, 2000.
The Daily Show with Jon Stewart (also known as *The Daily Show* and *The Daily Show with Jon Stewart Global Edition*), Comedy Central, 2000, 2003, 2007.
The Frank Skinner Show, ITV, 2001.
Des O'Connor Tonight, ITV, 2001.
Friday Night with Jonathan Ross, BBC America, multiple appearances, between 2002 and 2009.
The Late Late Show with Craig Kilborn (also known as *The Late Late Show*), CBS, 2002, 2004.
Dinner for Five, Independent Film Channel, 2003.
The Sharon Osbourne Show (also known as *Sharon*), syndicated, 2003.
Charlie Rose (also known as *The Charlie Rose Show*), PBS, 2003.
Rove Live, Ten Network, 2003.
Late Night with Conan O'Brien, NBC, multiple appearances, between 2003 and 2008.
Real Time with Bill Maher (also known as *Real Time with Bill Maher: Electile Dysfunction '08*), HBO, 2004.
The Late Late Show, CBS, 2004.
Richard and Judy, Channel 4, 2004, 2006.
Breakfast, BBC, 2005.
The Late Late Show with Craig Ferguson, CBS, multiple appearances, beginning 2005.
The Henry Rollins Show, Independent Film Channel, 2006.
Last Call with Carson Daly, NBC, 2006, 2008.
Ellen: The Ellen DeGeneres Show, syndicated, 2007.
The View, ABC, 2008.
Up Close with Carrie Keagan, ABC, 2008.
The Graham Norton Show, BBC America, 2008.
Richard & Judy's New Position, 2008.
The Paul O'Grady Show, ITV, 2009.
The Tonight Show with Conan O'Brien, NBC, 2009.
Late Night with Jimmy Fallon, NBC, 2009, 2010.
In the House with Peter Bart & Peter Guber (also known as *In the House*), NBC, 2010.
The Green Room with Paul Provenza, Showtime, 2010.

Also made appearances on *Open Mike with Mike Bullard* and *The Wayne Brady Show,* syndicated.

Television Appearances; Awards Presentations:
Presenter, *The British Comedy Awards,* ITV, 2002, 2004.
The 57th Annual Tony Awards, CBS, 2003.

Presenter, *Tribeca Film Festival Awards,* 2004.
Presenter, *The 61st Annual Tony Awards,* CBS, 2007.
13th Annual Critics' Choice Awards, VH1, 2008.
Host, *25th Film Independent Spirit Awards,* Independent Film Channel, 2010.

Television Appearances; Other:
It's Just a Ride, 1994.
Mondo Rosso, 1995.
Street–Porters Men, 1995.

Television Executive Producer; Series:
The Riches, FX Network, 2007–2008.

Television Executive Producer; Specials:
Eddie Izzard: Dress to Kill (broadcast of live stage show), HBO, 1999.

Television Executive Producer; Pilots:
The Riches, FX Network, 2007.

Stage Appearances:
Del, *The Cryptogram,* Ambassadors Theatre, London, 1994.
900 Oneonta, Lyric Hammersmith Theatre, then Old Vic Theatre, and Ambassadors Theatre, all London, 1994.
The Equality Show (benefit), Royal Albert Hall, London, 1995.
The Big Snog (benefit), Astoria Theatre, London, 1995.
Improv MD, Royal Court Theatre, London, 1995, revived as *One Word Improv,* Albery Theatre, London, 1997.
Title role, *Edward II,* Leicester Haymarket Theatre, Leicester, England, 1995.
Lenny Bruce (title role), *Lenny,* Queens Theatre, London, 1999.
Bri, *A Day in the Death of Joe Egg,* Ambassadors Theatre, then Comedy Theatre, London, 2001–2002, later Roundabout Theatre Company, American Airlines Theatre, New York City, 2003.
Spike Milligan: I Told You I Was Ill—A Live Tribute, Guildhall Theatre, London, 2002.
Gutted, Piccadilly Theatre, London, 2003.
Dalton Trumbo (title role; with others appearing on alternating nights), *Trumbo,* Westside Theatre, New York City, 2003.
Eddie Izzard, Union Square Theatre, New York City, 2008.
Jack Lawson, *Race,* Ethel Barrymore Theatre, New York City, 2010.

Also appeared in West End productions of *The Death of Everything, Geoffrey of Kent, Give Me Some Soap Mister, Jack and His Bench, Henry IX,* and *The Two Losers;* in *Let Go of My Head, Go!,* Royal Shakespeare Company, Stratford–upon–Avon, England; and in other productions such as *Bad Day at the Kangaroo Court, Good God Give Me Gravy, Sod Off,* and *That's My Lung.*

Solo Stage Shows:
Eddie Izzard: Live at the Ambassadors (also known as *Live at the Ambassadors*), Ambassadors Theatre, London, 1993.
Eddie Izzard: Unrepeatable (also known as *Unrepeatable*), Albery Theatre, London, 1994.
Eddie Izzard: Definite Article (also known as *Definite Article*), Shaftesbury Theatre, London (also presented in New York City), 1996.
The Campaign to Free Danny McNamee (benefit), Clapham Grand Theatre, London, 1996.
Eddie Izzard: Glorious (also known as *Glorious*), Theatre at Union Chapel, London, then Performance Space 122, New York City, 1997.
The Dirty Three and a Half Dozen/What's Up Dockers (benefit), Palladium, London, 1997.
Here, There, and Everywhere (benefit), Royal Albert Hall, London, 1999.
Eddie Izzard: Live from Wembly, 2009.

Major Tours:
Rock the Vote (benefit), British cities, 1996.
Eddie Izzard: Dress to Kill (solo show; also known as *Dress to Kill*), North American cities, beginning 1998.
Eddie Izzard: Circle (solo show; also known as *Circle*), international cities, 2000.
Eddie Izzard: Sexie (solo show; also known as *Sexie*), international cities, 2003.
Eddie Izzard: Stripped (solo show; also known as *Stripped*), 2008, then North American cities, 2010.

Radio Appearances; Episodic:
Talking Comedy, 1995.
Evening Session, BBC1, 1997.

Appeared in presentations of *Everything You Wanted to Know about Busking,* BBC2; and *Turns of the Century,* BBC3.

Radio Appearances; Other:
Missed Demeanours (miniseries), BBC4, 1995.
The Improv Musical (special), BBC2, 1998.

Also appeared in *The Smith Lectures* (miniseries), BBC2.

Internet Appearances; Episodic:
Kevin Pollak's Chat Show, 2009.

RECORDINGS

Video Appearances; Recordings of Solo Stage Shows:
Eddie Izzard: Live at the Ambassadors (also known as *Live at the Ambassadors*), 1993.

Eddie Izzard: Unrepeatable (also known as *Unrepeatable*), 1994.
Eddie Izzard: Definite Article (also known as *Definite Article*), 1996.
Eddie Izzard: Glorious (also known as *Glorious*), 1997.
Eddie Izzard: Dress to Kill (also known as *Dress to Kill*), 1999.
Eddie Izzard: Circle (also known as *Circle*), 2002.
Eddie Izzard: Sexie (also known as *Sexie*), 2003.
Eddie Izzard: Live from Wembly, Salient Media, 2009.
Eddie Izzard: Stripped, Universal, 2009.

Video Appearances Other:
Totally Bill Hicks, 1994.
Unbroadcastable "Have I Got News For You," 1995.
The Unseen Frank Skinner TV Show, 1997.
(In archive footage) *The Very Best of "Have I Got News for You,"* 2002.
Billy Connolly: Erect for 30 Years, 2003.
The Making of "My Super Ex–Girlfriend," 2006.
The Cast of "My Super Ex–Girlfriend," 2006.

Video Executive Producer:
Eddie Izzard: Live at the Ambassadors (also known as *Live at the Ambassadors*), 1993.
Eddie Izzard: Unrepeatable (also known as *Unrepeatable*), 1994.
Eddie Izzard: Definite Article (also known as *Definite Article*), 1996.
Eddie Izzard: Glorious (also known as *Glorious*), 1997.
Eddie Izzard: Dress to Kill (also known as *Dress to Kill*), 1999.
Eddie Izzard: Circle (also known as *Circle*), 2002.
Eddi Izzard: Sexie (also known as *Sexie*), 2003.
Eddie Izzard: Live from Wembly, Salient Media, 2009.
Eddie Izzard: Stripped, Universal, 2009.

WRITINGS

Stage Shows:
Eddie Izzard: Live at the Ambassadors (also known as *Live at the Ambassadors*), Ambassadors Theatre, London, 1993.
Eddie Izzard: Unrepeatable (also known as *Unrepeatable*), Albery Theatre, London, 1994.
Improv MD, Royal Court Theatre, London, 1995, revived as *One Word Improv,* Albery Theatre, 1997.
Eddie Izzard: Definite Article (also known as *Definite Article; also presented in New York City*), London, 1996.
Eddie Izzard: Glorious (also known as *Glorious*), West End, then Performance Space 122, New York City, 1997.
Eddie Izzard: Dress to Kill (also known as *Dress to Kill*), North American cities, beginning 1998.

Eddie Izzard: Circle (also known as *Circle*), international cities, 2000.
Eddie Izzard: Sexie (also known as *Sexie*), international cities, 2003.
Eddie Izzard: Stripped (also known as *Stripped*), 2008, then North American cities, 2010.
Eddie Izzard: Live from Wembly, 2009.

Television Miniseries:
(With others) *Mongrel Nation,* The Discovery Channel, 2003.

Television Pilots:
Cows, Channel 4, 1996.

Books:
(With David Quantick) *Dress to Kill,* photographs by Steve Double, Virgin Books, 1998.

ADAPTATIONS

The television series *The Riches,* broadcast by FX Network in 2007 and 2008, was based on a story by Izzard.

OTHER SOURCES

Periodicals:
Artforum, September, 1998, p. 150.
Daily Mail (London), July 15, 2003, p. 23.
Entertainment Weekly, June 26, 1998, p. 24.
Evening Standard (London), December 18, 2003, p. 80.
Independent (London), November 22, 2008, pp. 46–47.
Independent Arts & Books, December 4, 2009, pp. 4–7.
Los Angeles Times, September 6, 1998, p. 6.
New Statesman, December 10, 2001, p. 8.
Newsweek, March 20, 2000, p. 66; April 28, 2008, p. 63.
New York Times, March 16, 2008, pp. AR1, AR28.
Playboy, December, 2004, p. 30.
Premiere, July, 2006, p. 22.
Sunday Times (London), November 30, 2008; February 8, 2009.
Time Out New York, March 20, 2003, p. 167.
Times (London), February 22, 2008.
USA Today, March 3, 2010, p. 3D.
Variety, March 30, 1998, p. 171.
Washington Post, October 27, 2003, pp. C1, C4.

Electronic:
Eddie Izzard Official Site, http://www.eddieizzard.com, July 12, 2010.

J

JACKSON, Joshua 1978–
(Josh Jackson)

PERSONAL

Full name, Joshua Carter Jackson; born June 11, 1978, in Vancouver, British Columbia, Canada; citizenship: Canadian and U.S.; son of John (an advertising executive) and Fiona (a casting director, life coach, and writer) Jackson. *Education:* Attended high school in Vancouver, British Columbia, Canada. *Avocational Interests:* Playing the harmonica.

Addresses: *Agent*—Creative artists Agency, 2000 Avenue of the Stars, Los Angeles, CA 90056; Abi Harris, Ken McReddie Associates Ltd., 11 Connaught Pl., London W2 2ET, England. *Publicist*—Baker, Winokur, Ryder, 5700 Wilshire Blvd., Suite 550, Los Angeles, CA 90036.

Career: Actor, director, and producer. Performed as a child with San Francisco Boys Chorus; appeared in commercials, including work for Keebler's snack foods, also as a child.

Awards, Honors: Young Artist Award nomination (with others), outstanding young ensemble in a motion picture, 1993, for *The Mighty Ducks*; Teen Choice Awards, 1999, 2000, and 2001, and Teen Choice Award nominations, 2002, 2003, all choice actor in a television drama, for *Dawson's Creek*; Young Hollywood Award, male superstar of tomorrow, *Movieline*, 2000; Teen Choice Award nomination, choice liar in a film, 2000, for *The Skulls*; Satellite Award nomination, best actor in a motion picture drama, International Press Academy, and Jury Award, best actor, Fort Lauderdale International Film Festival, both 2005, for *Aurora Borealis*; Hollywood Film Award (with others), ensemble of the year, Hollywood Film Festival, 2006, and Screen Actors Guild Award nomination, outstanding cast in a motion picture, 2007, both for *Bobby*; Genie Award, best actor, Academy of Canadian Cinema and Television, 2009, for *One Week*; Teen Choice Award nomination, choice actor in a television drama, 2009, for *Fringe*.

CREDITS

Film Appearances:
(Uncredited) Infant, *The Changeling*, 1980.
Tom at age eleven, *Crooked Hearts*, Metro–Goldwyn–Mayer, 1991.
Charlie Conway, *The Mighty Ducks* (also known as *Champions* and *The Mighty Ducks Are the Champions*), Buena Vista, 1992.
Billy, *Digger*, 1993, Paramount Home Video, 1995.
Charlie Conway, *D2: The Mighty Ducks* (also known as *The Mighty Ducks 2*), Buena Vista, 1994.
Mark Baker, *Andre* (also known as *Andre the Seal*), Paramount, 1994.
Joshua Black, *Magic in the Water* (also known as *Magic Dinosaur*), TriStar, 1995.
Charlie Conway, *D3: The Mighty Ducks*, Buena Vista, 1996.
(As Josh Jackson) First film class guy, *Scream 2* (also known as *Scream Again*, *Scream Louder*, and *Scream: The Sequel*), Dimension Films, 1997.
Joey, *Apt Pupil* (also known as *Golden Boy*), TriStar, 1998.
Damon Brooks, *Urban Legend* (also known as *Mixed Culture* and *Rule*), TriStar, 1998.
Blaine Tuttle, *Cruel Intentions* (also known as *Cruel Inventions*, *Seduction Games*, and *Sexual Provocation*), Columbia, 1998.
The Battery, 1998.
Beau Edson, *Gossip*, Warner Bros., 2000.
Lucas "Luke" McNamara, *The Skulls*, Universal, 2000.
Paul Gold, *The Safety of Objects*, IFC Films, 2001.

(Uncredited) Himself, *Ocean's Eleven* (also known as *11* and *O11*), Warner Bros., 2001.

John, *I Love Your Work,* 2003, THINKFilm, 2005.

Jake, *Cursed* (also known as *Wes Craven's "Cursed"*), Miramax/Dimension Films, 2005.

Voice of Trenton's pride, *Racing Stripes,* Warner Bros., 2005.

Behind the Fangs: The Making of "Cursed," Dimension Home Video, 2005.

Chris McKinley, *Americano,* Spirit Lake Pictures, 2006.

Duncan Shorter, *Aurora Borealis,* Regent Releasing, 2006.

Wade Buckley, *Bobby,* Metro–Goldwyn–Mayer, 2006.

(In archive footage) *Going to Pieces: The Rise and Fall of the Slasher Film,* THINKFilm, 2007.

Randall, *Battle in Seattle,* Redwood Palms Pictures, 2008.

Benjamin Shaw, *Shutter,* Twentieth Century–Fox, 2008.

GasHole (documentary), Film Racket, 2008.

Ben, *One Week,* 2008, IFC Films, 2010.

Tarp, *The Man from the Moon* (short film), 2010.

Film Executive Producer:
One Week, 2008, IFC Films, 2010.

Television Appearances; Series:
Pacey Witter, *Dawson's Creek,* The WB, 1998–2003.

Peter Bishop, *Fringe,* Fox, 2008—.

Television Appearances; Movies:
(As Josh Jackson) Young Mac, *Payoff,* Showtime, 1991.

(As Josh Jackson) John Prince, Jr., *Robin of Locksley,* Showtime, 1996.

Ronnie Monroe, *Ronnie & Julie,* Showtime, 1997.

Sammy, *On the Edge of Innocence,* NBC, 1997.

Matt Galloway, *The Laramie Project,* HBO, 2002.

Earl Crest, *Lone Star State of Mind* (also known as *Cowboys and Idiots* and *Road to Hell*), Starz!, 2002.

Jeremy Taylor, *Shadows in the Sun* (also known as *The Shadow Dancer*), ABC Family, 2005.

Television Appearances; Pilots:
Pacey Witter, *Dawson's Creek,* The WB, 1998.

Mark Clayton, *Capitol Law,* CBS, 2006.

Peter Bishop, *Fringe,* Fox, 2008.

Television Appearances; Specials:
Dawson's Creek: Behind the Scenes, E! Entertainment Television, 1998.

Host, *Seventeen: Faces for Fall,* The WB, 1998.

(In archive footage) Pacey Witter, *Songs from Dawson's Creek,* 1999.

Teen People's 21 Hottest Stars under 21 (also known as *The 21 Hottest Stars under 21*), ABC, 1999.

Kids of Dawson's Creek: The E! True Hollywood Story, E! Entertainment Television, 2005.

Speechless, 2008.

Canada for Haiti, 2010.

Television Appearances; Episodic:
Matt Mazzilli "Breaking Up Is Hard to Do," *Champs,* ABC, 1996.

Matt Mazzilli "For Art's Sake," *Champs,* ABC, 1996.

Devon Taylor, "Music of the Spheres," *The Outer Limits* (also known as *The New Outer Limits*), Showtime, 1997.

Vibe, 1998.

(As Josh Jackson) Joey, "Family Is Family," *Any Day Now,* Lifetime, 1999.

Host, *Saturday Night Live* (also known as *SNL*), NBC, 2000.

Voice of Jesse Grass, "Lisa the Tree Hugger," *The Simpsons* (animated), Fox, 2000.

(Uncredited) Angry high school student, "Tru Love," *Law & Order: Criminal Intent* (also known as *Law & Order: CI*), NBC, 2006.

"Bobby," *History in Focus,* 2006.

Entertainment Tonight (also known as *E.T.* and *This Week in Entertainment*), syndicated, 2008.

Xpose, TV3, 2008.

Entertainment Tonight Canada (also known as *ET Canada*), 2009.

The Hour (also known as *CBC News: The Hour*), CBC, 2009.

Television Talk Show Guest Appearances; Episodic:
The Rosie O'Donnell Show, syndicated, 1999, 2000.

TFI Friday, Channel 4, 2000.

The Daily Show with Jon Stewart (also known as *The Daily Show* and *The Daily Show with Jon Stewart Global Edition*), Comedy Central, 2000, 2003.

Late Night with Conan O'Brien, NBC, 2000, 2003.

The Big Breakfast, Channel 4, 2001.

Late Show with David Letterman, CBS, 2001.

Revealed with Jules Asner, E! Entertainment Television, 2002.

V Graham Norton, Channel 4, 2003.

GMTV, ITV, 2005.

Tubridy Tonight, 2007.

The Bonnie Hunt Show, NBC, 2008.

Jimmy Kimmel Live!, ABC, 2008, 2009.

The Late Late Show with Craig Ferguson, CBS, 2009.

Live with Regis and Kelly, syndicated, 2009.

The Graham Norton Show, BBC America, 2010.

Television Appearances; Awards Presentations:
The 51st Annual Primetime Emmy Awards, Fox, 1999.

Presenter, *The WB Radio Music Awards,* The WB, 1999.

Presenter, *MTV Europe Music Awards,* MTV, 2001.

Presenter, *The Teen Choice Awards,* Fox, 2002.

Television Director; Episodic:
"Lovelines" (also known as "The Eddie"), *Dawson's Creek,* The WB, 2003.

Stage Appearances:
Charlie, *Charlie and the Chocolate Factory,* Seattle Children's Theatre, Seattle, WA, c. 1988.
A Life in the Theatre, Apollo Theatre, London, 2005.

Internet Appearances; Videos:
Project Phin: Clean My Ride, Flex My Fuel, YouTube, 2007.

RECORDINGS

Videos:
Spotlight on Location: The Skulls, 2000.
Making of "Shadows in the Sun," Walt Disney, 2006.
Peter Bishop, *Behind the Real Science of "Fringe Season 1,"* Warner Bros. Home Video, 2009.
Peter Bishop, *Evolution: The Genesis of "Fringe Season 1,"* Warner Bros. Home Video, 2009.
Peter Bishop, *Fringe Season 1 Visual Effects,* Warner Bros. Home Video, 2009.

Appeared in the music video "Every You, Every Me" by Placebo, 1999.

OTHER SOURCES

Periodicals:
Entertainment Weekly, September 2, 2005, p. 33.
Evening Standard (London), March 11, 2005, p. 12.
Maclean's, April 20, 1998, p. 49; June 9, 2003, p. 64.
Movieline, November, 2000, pp. 76–77, 101; November, 2002, p. 22.
People Weekly, September 21, 2009, p. 156.
Starlog, April, 2009, pp. 16–19.
Teen, February, 1999, p. 44.
TV Guide, March 7, 1998, pp. 18–25; April 22, 2000, pp. 46–48, 59.

JILLETTE, Penn 1955–

PERSONAL

Full name, Penn Fraser Jillette; born March 5, 1955, in Greenfield, MA; son of Sam (a Canadian antique coin dealer) and Velda Jillette; citizenship: U.S. and Canadian; married Emily Zolten (a television producer), November 23, 2004; children: Moxie CrimeFighter (daughter), Zolten Penn (son). *Education:* Attended Ringling Brothers Clown College, 1974. *Politics:* Libertarian. *Religion:* Atheist.

Addresses: *Office*—Buggs and Rudy A Discount Corporation, 3555 West Reno Ave., Suite L, Las Vegas, NV 89118. *Agent*—Agency for the Performing Arts, 405 South Beverly Dr., Beverly Hills, CA 90212; (voice work and commercials) Tim Curtis, WME Entertainment, 9601 Wilshire Blvd., 3rd Floor, Beverly Hills, CA 90210. *Manager*—Peter Adam Golden, Golden Entertainment West, 10921 Wilshire Blvd., Los Angeles, CA 90024.

Career: Actor, producer, writer, composer, executive, magician, and comedian. Worked as musician (upright bass), camera operator, sound recordist, and consultant; also trained in various circus skills, including fire eating. Asparagus Valley Cultural Society (comedy team), founder (with Robert Teller and Wier Chrisemer); Penn & Teller (comedy–magic team), founder and partner, 1981—; Buggs and Rudy A Discount Corporation, partner; Star Price Productions, Las Vegas, partner. Performer with Penn & Teller at hotels and casinos in Las Vegas, NV, beginning 1981; Comedy Central, former cable network announcer; appeared in television commercials for Powerstreet online trading, 1999, Pizza Hut restaurants, 2001, HP Media Center, 2002, and other products. Cato Institute, H. L. Mencken Research Fellow.

Awards, Honors: Emmy Award nomination (with others), outstanding music and lyrics, 1999, for the song "Freedom Dot Com," *Sin City Spectacular;* Writers Guild Award, 2004, and Writers Guild Award nominations, 2005, 2006, 2007, all outstanding television comedy or variety series, and Emmy Award nominations, outstanding writing for nonfiction programming, 2004, 2005, 2006, 2007, 2009, and outstanding reality program, 2004, 2005, 2006, 2007, all (with others) for *Penn & Teller: Bullshit!*.

CREDITS

Television Appearances; Series:
Voice of Flea, *The Moxy & Flea Show* (animated; also known as *The Moxy Show*), Cartoon Network, 1994–95.
Cohost, *Sin City Spectacular* (also known as *Penn & Teller's Sin City Spectacular*), FX Network, 1998–99.
(With Penn & Teller) Recurring appearances, *Hollywood Squares* (also known as *H2* and *H2: Hollywood Squares*), syndicated, 1998–2004.
Penn & Teller: Bullshit! (also known as *Penn & Teller: BS!*), Showtime, 2003–10.
Host, *Identity,* NBC, 2006–2007.
Contestant, *Dancing with the Stars* (also known as *D.W.T.S.*), ABC, 2008–2009.

Television Appearances; Specials:
Penn & Teller Go Public (broadcast of stage performance), PBS, 1985.

Penn & Teller's Invisible Thread (also known as *Invisible Thread*), Showtime, 1987.

The Search for Houdini, syndicated, 1987.

Comic Relief II, HBO, 1988.

Ron Reagan Is the President's Son, Cinemax, 1988.

(With Penn & Teller) *Free to Be ... a Family,* ABC, 1988.

Negligee and Underpants Party (also known as *Howard Stern's Negligee and Underpants Party*), 1988.

(With Penn & Teller) *Comic Relief III,* HBO, 1989.

Host, *Showtime Comedy Club All–Stars III,* Showtime, 1989.

Woodstock: Return to the Planet of the '60s, CBS, 1989.

Exploring Psychic Powers ... Live, syndicated, 1989.

Penn & Teller: Don't Try This At Home! (also known as *Don't Try This at Home!*), NBC, 1990.

Camera retriever, *The Magic of David Copperfield XII: The Niagara Falls Challenge,* CBS, 1990.

Memory & Imagination: New Pathways to the Library of Congress, PBS, 1990.

Martin Mull: Talent Takes a Holiday, Showtime, c. 1991.

Host, "This Is MST3K," *Mystery Science Theatre 3000,* Comedy Central, 1992.

Indecision '92: The Republican National Convention, Comedy Central, 1992.

10th Annual Montreal Comedy Festival, Showtime, c. 1992.

Host, *Fox New Year's Eve Live,* Fox, 1992.

Harley–Davidson's 90th Birthday Blast, Showtime, 1993.

Fox New Year's Eve Live, Fox, 1993.

Host, *Discover Magazine's 5th Annual Technology Awards,* The Disney Channel, 1994.

Narrator, *Hal Roach: Hollywood's King of Laughter,* The Disney Channel, 1994.

Aspen Comedy Festival, Comedy Central, 1994.

"Houdini: The Great Escape," *Biography,* Arts and Entertainment, 1994.

New Year's Eve '94, Fox, 1994.

New Year's Eve in Vegas, Fox, 1995.

The World' Greatest Magic II, NBC, 1995.

Penn, *Phobophilia: The Love of Fear* (also known as *Penn & Teller's Phobophilia: The Love of Fear*), 1995.

It's a Wonderful Cyberlife: A Holiday Buying Guide, The Discovery Channel, 1996.

Caesars Palace 30th Anniversary Celebration, 1996.

The World's Wildest Magic, NBC, 1997.

Penn & Teller's Home Invasion Magic (also known as *Home Invasion*), ABC, 1997.

Announcer, *Pulp Comics: Jim Breuer,* 1997.

The Secret World of Magicians and Mentalists, The Learning Channel, c. 1997.

NFL All–Star Comedy Blitz, CBS, 1999.

The Unpleasant World of Penn and Teller, Comedy Central, 2000.

The Master of Deception, The Discovery Channel, 2000.

The Great American History Quiz: 50 States, History Channel, 2001.

The Great American History Quiz: America at War, History Channel, 2001.

Las Vegas Live!, Bravo, 2004.

Super Secret Movie Rules: Slashers (also known as *SSMR: Slashers*), VH1, 2004.

E! 101 Most Awesome Moments in Entertainment, E! Entertainment Television, 2004.

(In archive footage) *101 Most Unforgettable SNL Moments,* E! Entertainment Television, 2004.

Penn & Teller: Off the Deep End, NBC, 2005.

50 Hottest Vegas Moments, E! Entertainment Television, 2005.

AFI's 100 Years ... 100 Movie Quotes: America's Greatest Quips, Comebacks, and Catchphrases, CBS, 2005.

Hollywood's Master Storytellers: The Aristocrats, 2006.

Generation Boom, TV Land, 2006.

"Steve Martin," *Biography,* Arts and Entertainment, 2006.

100 Greatest Funny Moments, Channel 4, 2006.

Ghost of Christmas Present, *Larry the Cable Guy's Christmas Spectacular,* VH1, 2007.

Mr. Warmth: The Don Rickles Project, HBO, 2007.

Cheech & Chong: Roasted, TBS, 2008.

History of the Joke, History Channel, 2008.

(With Penn & Teller) Voice, *Futurama: Into the Wild Green Yonder* (animated), Comedy Central, 2009.

Television Appearances; Movies:

The director, *Hayley Wagner, Star,* Showtime, 1999.

Television Appearances; Miniseries:

Behind the Scenes, PBS, 1992.

The Unpleasant World of Penn & Teller, Channel 4, 1994.

Great Drives, 1996.

Magic and Mystery Tour (also known as *Penn & Teller's Magic and Mystery Toru*), The Learning Channel, 2002.

I Love the '70s, VH1, 2003.

Magic, 2004.

My Coolest Years, VH1, 2004.

The 100 Most Memorable TV Moments, TV Land, 2004.

The 100 Most Unexpected TV Moments, TV Land, 2005.

(In archive footage) *The Story of Light Entertainment,* BBC2, 2006.

Great American Road Trip, 2009.

Television Appearances; Pilots:

Orwell Kravitz, *VR.5,* Fox, 1995.

Drell, *Sabrina, the Teenage Witch,* ABC, 1996.

Television Appearances; Episodic:

Jimmy Borges, "The Prodigal Son," *Miami Vice,* NBC, 1985.

Saturday Night Live (also known as *SNL*), NBC, multiple appearances, 1985, 1986.

The Original Max Talking Headroom Show, Cinemax, 1987.

The Word, 1993.

Darrin Romick, "Illusions of Grandeur," *Lois & Clark: The New Adventures of Superman,* ABC, 1994.

Archibald Fenn, "Drew Meets Lawyers," *The Drew Carey Show,* ABC, 1995.

Himself, "$20.01," *Space Ghost Coast to Coast* (also known as *SGC2C*), Cartoon Network, 1996.

Drell, "Terrible Things," *Sabrina, The Teenage Witch* (also known as *Sabrina* and *Sabrina Goes to College*), ABC, 1996.

Drell, "Jenny's Non–Dream," *Sabrina, The Teenage Witch* (also known as *Sabrina* and *Sabrina Goes to College*), ABC, 1997.

Drell, "First Kiss," *Sabrina, The Teenage Witch* (also known as *Sabrina* and *Sabrina Goes to College*), ABC, 1997.

Archibald Fenn, "See Drew Run," *The Drew Carey Show,* ABC, 1997.

Encyclopedia salesman, "The One with the 'Cuffs," *Friends,* NBC, 1997.

Himself, "The Gary Cahuenga Episode," *Muppets Tonight!,* ABC, 1997.

Ed's Night Party (also known as *Ed the Sock*), 1997.

Rebo, "Day of the Dead," *Babylon 5* (also known as *B5*), syndicated, 1998.

(Uncredited) Vincent, "The Cat's Out of the Bag," *Dharma & Greg,* ABC, 1998.

Himself, "Knee Deep," *Home Improvement,* ABC, 1999.

Himself, "Val the Hard Way," *V.I.P.,* syndicated, 1999.

Voice, "Hello Gutter, Hello Fadder," *The Simpsons* (animated), Fox, 1999.

Voice of Pluto Devil, *Mickey Mouse Works* (animated; also known as *Mouseworks*), ABC, 1999, 2000.

Famous Homes & Hideaways, syndicated, 2000.

Terry, "The Proposal: Part 2," *Just Shoot Me!,* NBC, 2001.

"Penn and Teller," *Bravo Profiles,* Bravo, 2001.

Voice of Pluto Devil, "Pluto Saves the Day," *House of Mouse* (animated), ABC, 2001.

Voice of Pluto Devil, "Pluto vs. Figaro," *House of Mouse* (animated), ABC, 2002.

"Celebrity Special," *Fear Factor,* NBC, 2002.

(With Penn & Teller) *Just for Laughs* (also known as *Ed Byrne's "Just for Laughs," Just for Laughs Comedy Festival,* and *Just for Laughs Montreal Comedy Festival*), 2002.

Pyramid (also known as *The $100,000 Pyramid*), syndicated, 2003.

"Luck Be a Lady," *Las Vegas,* NBC, 2003.

"Las Vegas: Live Reveal," *Trading Spaces,* The Learning Channel, 2003.

Himself, "Magic Jordan," *The Bernie Mac Show,* Fox, 2003.

Clem Valesco, "Porn to Write," *Girlfriends,* UPN, 2004.

Himself, "In the Room," *The West Wing* (also known as *The White House*), NBC, 2004.

The Smoking Gun, 2004.

"Keith Lockhart's 10th Anniversary Special," *Evening at Pops,* PBS, 2004.

Contestant, *Celebrity Poker Showdown,* Bravo, 2004.

(With Penn & Teller) *Inside Dish with Rachael Ray,* Food Network, 2005.

Narrator, "Millionaire Condo Heist," *Impossible Heists,* TruTV, 2005.

"Last Vegas," *Listen Up,* CBS, 2005.

Tucker (also known as *The Situation with Tucker Carlson*), 2005.

(With Penn & Teller) "C4 Crate," *Criss Angel Mindfreak,* Arts and Entertainment, 2005.

Dirty Tricks, 2005.

"Turn a Poker Dud into a Five Card Stud: Ed M," *Queer Eye* (also known as *Queer Eye for the Straight Guy*), 2006.

"Top 10 TV Weddings," *TV Land's Top Ten,* TV Land, 2006.

"Top Ten Musical Moments," *TV Land's Top Ten,* TV Land, 2006.

Voice of Magic Marty, "Halloween/Squeeze's Magic Show," *Handy Manny* (animated), The Disney Channel, 2007.

(In archive footage) "Top Kitchens," *Trading Spaces,* The Learning Channel, 2007.

(Uncredited; in archive footage) *Have I Got News for You,* BBC, 2007.

Last Comic Standing (also known as *Last Comic Standing: The Search for the Funniest Person in America*), NBC, 2008.

"Wet and Wild," *Battleground Earth: Ludacris vs. Tommy Lee,* 2008.

Himself, "Magic Show," *Numb3rs* (also known as *Num3ers*), CBS, 2008.

Entertainment Tonight (also known as *E.T.* and *This Week in Entertainment*), syndicated, 2008.

The Insider, syndicated, 2008.

(In archive footage) *The O'Reilly Factor,* Fox News Channel, 2008.

Access Hollywood, syndicated, 2008, 2009.

"Penn & Teller," *Top Chef,* Bravo, 2009.

Voice for an episode of *Glenn Martin, DDS,* Nickelodeon; voice of Frank Grimes, *Nightmare Ned,* ABC; himself, "Las Vegas: Teller in Wonderland," *While You Were Out,* The Learning Channel; also appeared in episodes of *Alan King: Inside the Comedy Mind,* Comedy Central; *America's Got Talent,* NBC; *Desperate Landscapes,* DIY Network; *Don't Forget the Lyrics,* Fox; *Future Quest,* PBS; *The Pet Shop,* Animal Planet; *True Beauty,* ABC; and *Where in the World Is Carmen Sandiego?,* PBS.

Television Talk Show Guest Appearances; Episodic:
Late Night with David Letterman, NBC, 1989.

The Howard Stern Show (also known as *The Howard Stern Summer Show*), 1990.

(With Penn & Teller) *The Howard Stern Interview,* 1993.

The Tonight Show with Jay Leno, NBC, 1995, 1998, 2004, 2008.

Late Night with Conan O'Brien, NBC, 1997, 2000, 2003.

The Daily Show with Jon Stewart (also known as *The Daily Show* and *The Daily Show with Jon Stewart Global Edition*), Comedy Central, 1998, 2000.

The Late Late Show with Craig Kilborn (also known as *The Late Late Show*), CBS, 2004.

The View, ABC, 2004, 2005, 2006.

Last Call with Carson Daly, NBC, multiple appearances, between 2004 and 2010.

Real Time with Bill Maher (also known as *Real Time with Bill Maher: Electile Dysfunction '08*), HBO, 2006.

The Colbert Report, Comedy Central, 2006.

The Big Idea with Donny Deutsch, CNBC, 2007.

Late Show with David Letterman (also known as *The Late Show* and *Letterman*), CBS, 2007, 2008.

Jimmy Kimmel Live!, ABC, 2008.

"Lance's Birthday," *Free Radio,* VH1, 2008.

"Penn Jillette and Wife," *Howard Stern on Demand* (also known as *Howard TV on Demand*), 2008.

The Oprah Winfrey Show (also known as *Oprah*), syndicated, 2008.

Larry King Live, Cable News Network, multiple appearances, between 2008 and 2010.

Talkshow with Spike Feresten, Fox, 2009.

Glenn Beck, Fox News Channel, 2009.

Late Night with Jimmy Fallon, NBC, 2009.

Holly's World, E! Entertainment Television, 2009.

Also guest on *The Green Room with Paul Provenza,* Showtime.

Television Appearances; Awards Presentations:

1988 MTV Video Music Awards, MTV, 1988.

(With Penn & Teller) Presenter, *The 45th Annual Tony Awards,* CBS, 1991.

Discover Magazine's Technology Awards, 1992.

Presenter, *12th Annual American Comedy Awards,* Fox, 1998.

The World of Magic Awards, PAX, 2000.

Presenter, *The ... Annual Academy of Country Music Awards,* CBS, 2003, 2004.

Spike TV VGA Video Game Awards, Spike TV, 2003.

Presenter, *The ... Primetime Creative Arts Emmy Awards,* E! Entertainment Television, 2004, 2009.

Host, *Primetime Creative Arts Emmy Awards,* E! Entertainment Television, 2006.

Presenter, *2007 World Magic Awards,* MyNetwork, 2007.

Television Work; Series:

Co–executive producer, *Penn & Teller's Sin City Spectacular* (also known as *Sin City Spectacular*), FX Network, 1998.

Co–executive producer, *Penn & Teller: Bullshit!* (also known as *Penn & Teller: BS!*), Showtime, 2003–2006.

Executive producer, *Penn & Teller: Bullshit!* (also known as *Penn & Teller: BS!*), Showtime, 2007–2009.

Television Work; Specials:

Creator, *Penn & Teller Go Public* (broadcast of stage performance), PBS, 1985.

Executive producer, *Phobophilia: The Love of Fear* (also known as *Penn & Teller's Phobophilia: The Love of Fear*), 1995.

Creator and co–executive producer, *Penn & Teller's Home Invasion Magic* (also known as *Home Invasion*), ABC, 1997.

Executive producer, *Penn & Teller: Off the Deep End,* NBC, 2005.

Film Appearances:

Security guard in U.S. version, *Savage Island,* Empire Pictures, 1985.

Norman, *Off Beat,* Buena Vista, 1986.

Bone, *My Chauffeur* (also known as *My Chauffeur: Licensed to Love*), Crown, 1986.

Big Stoop, *Tough Guys Don't Dance,* Cannon, 1987.

Voice of the Chief of the Deformed, *Light Years* (also known as *Gandahar*), Miramax, 1988.

Penn & Teller Get Killed (also known as *Dead Funny*), Warner Bros., 1989.

Half Japanese: The Band Who Would Be King, Tara Releasing, 1993.

First of the Luthers, *Car 54, Where Are You?,* 1994.

Hal, *Hackers* (also known as *Cybernet*), Metro–Goldwyn–Mayer, 1995.

Voice of television announcer, *Toy Story* (animated; also known as *Toy Story in 3–D*), Buena Vista, 1995.

Radio disc jockey, *Burnzy's Last Call,* 1995.

Nothing Sacred, 1997.

Fred, *Life Sold Separately,* 1997.

Lou Reed: Rock and Roll Heart (documentary), Fox Lorber, 1997.

Kid Nerd, 1997.

Barker at Bazooko Circus, *Fear and Loathing in Las Vegas,* Universal, 1998.

Host, "The Sorcerer's Apprentice," *Fantasia/2000,* Buena Vista, 1999.

Albert, *Fear of Fiction,* Pow Wow, 2000.

Michael Moore Hates America (documentary), Allumination Filmworks, 2004.

Goodnight, We Love You, Mansfield Avenue Productions, 2004.

(With Penn & Teller) *The Aristocrats* (documentary; also known as *The @r!$t*(r@t$*), THINKFilm, 2005.

Magic: The Science of Illusion (short film), 2005.

Caller, *Phone Sex* (documentary), Dikenga Films, 2006.

Brother Theodore (also known as *To My Great Chagrin*), Spontaneous Productions, 2007.

Voice, *American Carny: True Tales from the Circus Sideshow*, Cinema Epoch, 2008.

Flow: For Love of Water (documentary), Oscilloscope Pictures, 2008.

Dead On: The Life and Cinema of George A. Romero, New Eye Films, 2008.

Voice of Dave, *The Growth* (short film), Ghost Works, 2009.

Film Work:

Musician with the group Bongos, Bass, and Bob, *Oral Hygiene*, Expanded Entertainment, 1991.

Executive producer, *The Aristocrats* (documentary; also known as *The @r!$t*(r@t$)*), THINKFilm, 2005.

Stage Appearances:

Penn & Teller Go Public, produced off Broadway, then on Broadway, beginning 1985.

Penn & Teller, Ritz Theatre, New York City, 1987–88.

Penn & Teller: The Refrigerator Tour, Eugene O'Neill Theatre, New York City, 1991.

Penn & Teller Rot in Hell, John Houseman Theatre, New York City, 1991–92.

Penn & Teller, Wilshire Theatre, Beverly Hills, CA, 1998.

Narrator, *The Rocky Horror Show* (musical), Circle in the Square, New York City, 2001.

The Exonerated, Bleecker Street Theatre, New York City, between 2002 and 2004.

Internet Appearances; Series:

Presenter, *Penn Says*, 2008.

Radio Appearances; Series:

Host of a live broadcast from Las Vegas, NC, on Free FM Radio, 2006.

RECORDINGS

Videos:

Penn & Teller's Cruel Tricks for Dear Friends (also known as *Cruel Tricks for Dear Friends*), 1987.

Host, *The Eyes Scream: A History of the Residents*, 1991.

The Best of Ed's Night Party, 1996.

"It's Tricky," *Run–DMC: Together Forever—Greatest Hits 1983–2000*, 2000.

Multiple voices, *Mucha Lucha! The Return of El Malefico* (animated), Warner Bros., 2005.

Appeared in the music videos "It's Tricky" by Run DMC, 1986, and "Waking Up in Vegas" by Katy Perry.

Video Games:

Penn & Teller's Smoke and Mirrors, 1995.

Voice of Leroy Paine, *Steven Spielberg's Director's Chair*, 1996.

Voice of Drell, *Sabrina, the Teenage Witch: Spellbound*, 1998.

Audio Books:

Reader, *The Golden Rule of Schmoozing: The Authentic Practice of Treating Others Well by Aye Jaye*, Listen & Live Audio, 1998.

Albums:

Lead vocalist for the song "The Horse You Rode In On," included in the album *Easy Listening … by Pigface*, 2003.

WRITINGS

Television Series:

The Moxy Show (animated), Cartoon Network, 1994–95.

(And song lyricist) *Penn & Teller's Sin City Spectacular* (also known as *Sin City Spectacular*), FX Network, 1998–99.

Penn & Teller: Bullshit! (also known as *Penn & Teller: BS!*), Showtime, 2003–10.

Television Specials:

Penn & Teller Go Public, PBS, 1985.

Penn & Teller's Invisible Thread (also known as *Invisible Friend*; also based on story by Jillette), Showtime, 1987.

Ron Reagan Is the President's Son, Cinemax, 1988.

(And song lyricist, "Lift Off for Love") *Penn & Teller: Don't Try This at Home!* (also known as *Don't Try This at Home!*), NBC, 1990.

Phobophilia: The Love of Fear (also known as *Penn & Teller: Phobophilia: The Love of Fear*), 1995.

Penn & Teller's Home Invasion Magic (also known as *Home Invasion*), ABC, 1997.

The Unpleasant World of Penn & Teller, Comedy Central, 2000.

Penn & Teller: Off the Deep End, NBC, 2005.

Television Miniseries:

Behind the Scenes, PBS, 1992.

The Unpleasant World of Penn & Teller, Channel 4, 1994.

Screenplays:

Penn & Teller Get Killed (also known as *Dead Funny*), Warner Bros., 1989.

Stage Shows:

Penn & Teller, Ritz Theatre, New York City, 1987–88.

Songwriter, *Penn & Teller: The Refrigerator Tour,* Eugene O'Neill Theatre, New York City, 1991.

Videos:

Author of script and composer of musical score, *Penn & Teller's Cruel Tricks for Dear Friends* (also known as *Cruel Tricks for Dear Friends*), 1987.

Scriptwriter, *Penn & Teller's Smoke and Mirrors* (video game), 1995.

Books:

(With Robert Teller) *Penn & Teller's Cruel Tricks for Dear Friends,* Villard Books, 1989.

(With Teller) *Penn & Teller's How to Play with Your Food,* Villard Books, 1992.

(With Teller) *Penn & Teller's How to Play in Traffic,* Boulevard Books, 1997.

Sock (novel), St. Martin's Press, 2004.

How to Cheat Your Friends at Poker/The History of Playing Cards in America, St. Martin's Press, 2005.

(With Teller) Author of foreword to the book *The Golden Rule of Schmoozing: The Authentic Practice of Treating Others Well,* by Aye Jaye, Sourcebooks, 1998.

Other:

Former author of a monthly column for *PC/Computing.* Contributor to magazines, including *Playboy.*

OTHER SOURCES

Periodicals:

Entertainment Weekly, November 21, 1997, p. 122.

FHM, February, 2005, p. 93.

Playboy, July, 2006, pp. 92–94.

Reason, April, 1994, p. 35.

TV Guide, February 8, 2003, p. 8; March 17, 2008, p. 35.

JONES, Evan

(Dean Bukowsky)

PERSONAL

Raised in College Station, TX. *Education:* Attended University of California, Santa Barbara.

Addresses: *Agent*—Dan Baron, Agency for the Performing Arts, 405 South Beverly Dr., Beverly Hills, CA 90212; Carol Goll, International Creative Management, 10250 Constellation Way, 9th Floor, Los Angeles, CA 90067. *Manager*—Curtis Talent Management, 9607 Arby Dr., Beverly Hills, CA 90210.

Career: Actor. Appeared in commercials, including an ad for Post Raisin Bran Crunch breakfast cereal, 1999.

CREDITS

Film Appearances:

(As Dean Bukowsky) Paul, *The Distraction,* Allied Entertainment Group/The Asylum, 1999.

Stoner roommate, *Going Greek,* Miramax, 2001.

Cheddar Bob, *8 Mile,* Universal, 2002.

First thug, *Carnival Sun* (short film), 2003.

Fryman, *Mr. 3000,* Buena Vista, 2004.

Troy Haines, *The Last Shot,* Buena Vista, 2004.

Dave Fowler, *Jarhead,* Universal, 2005.

Moe Iba, *Glory Road,* Buena Vista, 2006.

Pilot, *Rescue Dawn,* Metro–Goldwyn–Mayer, 2006.

Jason Keyes, *Lucky You,* Warner Bros., 2007.

Trot Mitchell, *Gordon Glass,* Big Easy Productions, 2007.

Timmy "Mac" McClanahan, *Touching Home,* 2008, CFI Releasing, 2010.

Roger "Hound Dog" Davis, *The Express* (also known as *The Express: The Ernie Davis Story*), Universal, 2008.

Doc, *Pants on Fire,* Red Deer Pictures, 2008.

Martz, *The Book of Eli* (also known as *The Walker*), Warner Bros., 2010.

Joe Davis, *The Dry Land,* Maya Releasing, 2010.

Izzy "The Ice" Dasselway, *Trivial Pursuits,* 3,4 Women Productions, 2010.

Television Appearances; Series:

Ikey, *October Road,* ABC, 2007–2008.

Television Appearances; Movies:

District Attorney Lotchen, *On the Line,* ABC, 1998.

Eddie, *Wishcraft,* HBO, 2002.

Ruby, *The Book of Ruth,* CBS, 2004.

Mike, *Healing Hands,* Hallmark Channel, 2010.

Television Appearances; Episodic:

Billy, "Heat of the Moment," *Pacific Blue,* USA Network, 1998.

First R.A., "Drawing the Line: Part 1," *Felicity,* The WB, 1998.

Teenager, "The Principal," *Walker, Texas Ranger,* CBS, 1999.

Munro, "Thieves among Thieves," *Martial Law,* CBS, 1999.

Buddy, "Lady Evil," *G vs E* (also known as *Good vs. Evil*), USA Network, 1999.

Ethan, "Eyes," *The Others,* NBC, 2000.

Johnny Pope, "War Surplus," *Beyond Belief: Fact or Fiction* (also known as *Beyond Belief*), Fox, 2000.

Ronnie, "Pot Scrubbers," *The District,* CBS, 2000.

Todd, "The Longer You Stay," *ER,* NBC, 2001.

David "Ikey" Eichorn, "Blowing Free: Parts 1 & 2," *Going to California,* Showtime, 2001.

David "Ikey" Eichorn, "The Big Padoodle," *Going to California,* Showtime, 2001.

David "Ikey" Eichorn, "Our Sunshine State of Affairs," *Going to California,* Showtime, 2001.

Malcolm Dempsy, "Feeding Frenzy," *The Guardian* (also known as *Ochita bengoshi Nick Fallin*), CBS, 2001.

Bob Morrisey, "Drive, He Said," *Joan of Arcadia,* CBS, 2003.

Bill, "Last Resort," *House, M.D.* (also known as *Dr. House* and *House*), Fox, 2008.

Hallsy, "Venice Kings," *Dark Blue,* TNT, 2009.

Junior Mosley, "Blacklist (Featuring Grave Digger)," *CSI: NY,* CBS, 2009.

Television Appearances; Pilots:

Ikey, *October Road,* ABC, 2007.

Television Work; Series:

Additional voices, *Dragon Ball Z* (animated; also known as *DBZ*), Cartoon Network, 1999.

RECORDINGS

Videos:

Jarhead Diaries, Universal Studios Home Video, 2006.

K

KAPOOR, Shekhar
See **KAPUR, Shekhar**

KAPUR, Shekhar 1945(?)–
(Shekhar Kapoor)

PERSONAL

Born December 6, 1945 (some sources cite 1951 or 1954), in Bombay (now Mumbai), India (some sources cite birthplace as Lahore, India, now Pakistan); immigrated to England, 1970; nephew of Vijay Anand (an actor, writer, director, and producer); married Suchitra Krishnamurti (an actress and singer), 1996 (divorced, 2007). *Education:* Institute of Chartered Accountants in England and Wales, Chartered Accountant, 1970s; studied economics in New Delhi, India; studied film in London. *Religion:* Hindu.

Addresses: *Agent*—Creative Artists Agency, 2000 Avenue of the Stars, Los Angeles, CA 90067; (commercials) Alturas Films, 1617 Broadway Ave., 2nd Floor, Santa Monica, CA 90404.

Career: Producer, director, and actor. Cofounder of Virgin Comics and Virgin Animation, 2006. Worked as a model. Burmah Oil, London, corporate planner for seven years; also worked as a chartered accountant, 1980s. Speaker on behalf of Confederation of Indian Industry.

Awards, Honors: India Film Critics Award, 1982, and Filmfare Award, 1983, both best film, for *Masoom;* India Film Critics Award, best film, 1994, and Filmfare Awards, best film, 1995, and best director, 1997, all for *Bandit Queen;* National Board of Review Award, best director, 1998, Atlantic Film Festival Award, best international feature film or vide, 1998, Golden Globe Award nomination, best director of a film, and Golden Satellite Award nomination, best director of a motion picture, International Press Academy, Alexander Korda Award (with others), outstanding British film, and nomination for David Lean Award for Direction, both British Academy of Film and Television Arts, Australian Film Institute Award nomination (with others), best foreign film, and Silver Guild Film Award, best foreign film, Guild of German Art House Cinemas, all 1999, and Bodil Award nomination, best non–American film, 2000, all for *Elizabeth;* Special Filmfare Award, 1999; Special Award, outstanding Indian achievement in world Cinema, International Indian Film Academy, 2000; David di Donatello Award nomination, best European Union film, 2008, for *Elizabeth: The Golden Age.*

CREDITS

Film Director:
Masoom (also known as *Innocent*), Krsna Film Unit, 1983.
(Uncredited) Codirector, *Joshilay,* 1985.
Mr. India, 1987.
Bandit Queen (also known as *Phoolan Devi*), Arrow Films, 1994.
(Uncredited) Codirector, *Dushmani,* 1996.
Elizabeth (also known as *Elizabeth: The Virgin Queen*), Gramercy, 1998.
Long Way to Freedom (also known as *Long Walk to Freedom*), PolyGram Filmed Entertainment, 2001.
Codirector, *Yaadein* (also known as *Cherished Memories*), Mukta Arts, 2001.
The Four Feathers, Miramax/Paramount, 2002.
Elizabeth: The Golden Age, Universal, 2007.
Segment director, *New York, I Love You,* Vivendi Entertainment, 2009.
Passage (short film), Curious Pictures/Primary Productions/Swarovski Entertainment, 2009.

Also directed commercials.

Film Executive Producer:

Dil Se ... (also known as *From the Heart*), Eros International, 1998.
The Guru, Universal, 2003.

Film Appearances:

Ishq Ishq Ishq (also known as *Love, Love, Love*), 1974.
Jaan Hazir Hai, 1975.
Pal Do Pal ka Saath, 1978.
Toote Khilone, 1978.
Jeena Yahan (also known as *Living Here*), 1981.
Raj A. Kumar, *Bindiya Chamkegi,* 1984.
(As Shekhar Kapoor) Jimmy, *Falak (The Sky),* 1988.
Gawahi, 1989.
Nikhil, *Drishti* (also known as *Vision*), Udbhav, 1990.
Antique dealer/moneylender, *Nazar* (also known as *Eye and The Gaze*), 1991.
(As Kapoor) Dev, *Saatwan Aasman,* 1992.
Man who stabs bishop, *Elizabeth* (also known as *Elizabeth: The Virgin Queen*), Gramercy, 1998.
Bollywood Remixed—Das indische kino erobert den westen (documentary), Nanook Film Wien, 2004.
There Is No Direction (short documentary), Temps Noir/ Muse Films/Central Films, 2005.

Television Appearances; Specials:

The 100 Greatest Movie Stars, Channel 4, 2003.

Television Appearances; Episodic:

"Spotlights & Saris: Making Bombay Dreams," *Omnibus,* BBC, 2002.
"Cate Blanchett," *Bravo Profiles,* Bravo, 2002.
"Shekhar Kapur," *HARDtalk Extra,* BBC, 2006.
Cartelera, 2007.

Appeared in "Rendezvous with Shekhar Kapur and Suchitra," *Rendezvous with Simi Garewal.*

Television Appearances; Series:

Host of the British series *On the Other Hand,* Channel 4.

Also appeared in *Kehta Hai Joker,* c. 1999.

Television Director; Episodic:

Directed an episode of *Tahqiqat.*

Stage Work:

Associate producer, *Bombay Dreams* (musical), Really Useful Theatre Company, Apollo Victoria Theatre, London, 2002, then Broadway Theatre, New York City, 2004–2005.

WRITINGS

Print Materials:

Contributor to magazines, including *Independent* (London).

OTHER SOURCES

Periodicals:

Movieline, December, 1999, p. 18.
New Republic, July 10, 1995, p. 24.
New York Times, November 13, 1998, p. E14.
San Jose Mercury News, November 26, 2008.
Time, August 14, 1995, p. 67; March 14, 2005.
Time International, November 2, 1998, p. 71.
Village Voice, November 10, 1998, p. 126.

KAY, Lesli 1965–
    (Lesli Kay Pushkin, Lesli Kay Sterling, Leslie Kay Sterling)

PERSONAL

Original name, Lesli Kay Pushkin; born June 13, 1965, in Charleston, WV; married Mark Sterling, 1992 (divorced, 1999); married Keith Coulouris (an actor), December 25, 2003; children: (second marriage) Jackson William, Alec Jude.

Addresses: *Agent*—Tom Markley, Metropolitan Talent Agency, 204 North Rossmore Ave., Los Angeles, CA 90004; (commercials and voice work) Marcia Hurwitz, Innovative Artists Talent and Literary Agency, 1505 10th St., Santa Monica, CA 90401.

Career: Actress.

Awards, Honors: *Soap Opera Digest* Award nomination, favorite scene stealer, 2000, and Daytime Emmy Award, outstanding supporting actress in a drama series, 2001, both for *As the World Turns;* Daytime Emmy Award nomination, outstanding supporting actress in a drama series, 2007, for *The Bold and the Beautiful.*

CREDITS

Television Appearances; Series:

Molly Conlan, *As the World Turns,* CBS, 2002–10.
Lois Cerullo, *General Hospital,* ABC, 2004–2005.

Felicia Forrester, *The Bold and the Beautiful* (also known as *Belleza y poder*), CBS, 2005–2009.

Felicia Forrester, a recurring role, *The Young and the Restless* (also known as *Y&R*), CBS, 2008.

Television Appearances; Episodic:

(As Lesli Kay Pushkin) Colleen, "All that Glitters," *Hunter,* NBC, 1991.

(As Leslie Kay Sterling) Frenchie's secretary, "French Twist," *Counterstrike,* USA Network, 1993.

(As Lesli Kay Sterling) Tina, "You Really Got a Hold on Me," *Nowhere Man,* UPN, 1995.

(As Lesli Kay Sterling) Samantha, "The Gardener," *Hot Line,* 1996.

Agent Robin Foster, "Mission Improbable," *High Tide,* syndicated, 1996.

(As Lesli Kay Sterling) Sophie, "The Love Doctor," *The Big Easy,* USA Network, 1996.

(As Lesli Kay Sterling) Nurse, "Driving Ms. Money," *The Big Easy,* USA Network, 1997.

"Table Service," *Women: Stories of Passion,* Showtime, 1997.

Amanda Taylor, "Maritime," *Law & Order,* NBC, 2003.

The View, ABC, 2003.

SoapTalk, SoapNet, 2003, 2005, 2006.

Tanya Danville, "Zoo York," *CSI: NY,* CBS, 2005.

Dancing with the Stars (also known as *D.W.T.S.*), ABC, 2006.

Suzanne Zale/Celeste Barrington, "Stage Fright," *Ghost Whisperer,* CBS, 2009.

Massage complainant, "Happy Ending," *Raising the Bar,* TNT, 2009.

Film Appearances:

Shannon Douglas, *Forbidden Games,* PM Entertainment Group, 1995.

(As Lesli Kay Sterling) Julie Sharp, *Deadly Charades,* Mystique Films, 1996.

Jana, *Cyberella: Forbidden Passions,* Kushner–Locke/Twilight Movies, 1996.

(As Leslie Kay Sterling) Sheriff Sarah Parker, *Petticoat Planet,* Cult Video, 1996.

Miranda, *Guarded Secrets,* Mystique Films, 1997.

Vanessa, *Carpool Guy,* L.A. Ideas, 2005.

Gretchen, *Shadow People,* Radius 60 Studios, 2007.

Ginger, *Anna Nicole* (also known as *The Anna Nicole Smith Story*), 2007, Nasser Entertainment Group, 2009.

Carrie, *My New SweetHeart* (short film), Skippy Skippy Productions, 2009.

KEITH, Larry 1931–2010
(Lawrence Keith)

PERSONAL

Original name, Lawrence Jay Korn; born March 4, 1931, in Brooklyn, NY; died of cancer, July 17, 2010, in New York City, NY. Actor. A prolific stage actor, Keith was also an original cast member of the popular soap opera *All My Children,* for which he earned two Daytime Emmy Award nominations. Keith was trained in music at Brooklyn College in the early 1950s, and he performed in army musicals and dramatic productions while serving in Korea. After his Broadway debut in the original 1956 production of the musical *My Fair Lady,* he played roles in *High Spirits, I Had a Ball, The Best Laid Plans,* and *Gigi* during the 1960s and 1970s. In 1967 Keith appeared in the soap opera *Another World,* which led to a regular role as Nick Davis on *All My Children* from 1970 to 1978 and several guest performances on the show in the 1990s. His other notable television credits include supporting parts in *Law and Order* and *Damages.* In 1992 Keith was a founding member of the off-Broadway repertory group the Actors Company Theater. He returned to Broadway in 1997, playing roles in *Titanic, Cabaret,* and *Caroline, or Change* during the subsequent years.

PERIODICALS

Boston Globe, July 25, 2010.
Los Angeles Times, July 21, 2010.

KELL, Ayla 1990–

PERSONAL

Born October 7, 1990. *Education:* Studied at the Los Angeles Ballet Academy.

Addresses: *Agent*—The Savage Agency, 6212 Banner Ave., Los Angeles, CA 90038. *Manager*—Evolution Entertainment, 901 North Highland Ave., Los Angeles, CA 90038.

Career: Actress. Dancer; competitor in the Youth America Grand Prix (dance competition); also a dancer at various international venues.

Awards, Honors: Finalist in the Youth America Grand Prix, 2007.

CREDITS

Television Appearances; Series:
Payson Keeler, *Make It or Break It* (also known as *Perfect 10*), ABC Family, 2009—.

Television Appearances; Movies:
Barbara as a child, *Get to the Heart: The Barbara Mandrell Story,* CBS, 1997.

Television Appearances; Episodic:

Kylie, "Dewey's Special Class," *Malcolm in the Middle* (also known as *Fighting in Underpants*), Fox, 2004.

Chelsea, "Lude Awakening," *Weeds,* Showtime, 2005.

Young Mia, "One and Only," *Without a Trace* (also known as *Vanished* and *W.A.T*), CBS, 2007.

Chelsea March, "And How Does That Make You Kill?," *CSI: Miami* (also known as *CSI Miami* and *CSI: Weekends*), CBS, 2008.

Jade, "Cool Guys Don't Wear Periwinkle," *Just Jordan* (also known as *Untitled Lil' JJ Project*), Nickelodeon, 2008.

Television Appearances; Pilots:

Payson Keeler, *Make It or Break It* (also known as *Perfect 10*), ABC Family, 2009.

Film Appearances:

Maddie Lane, *The Omega Code* (also known as *The Code, Code: 0000,* and *Omega Code*), Providence Entertainment, 1999.

Cute girl and cheerleader, *Rebound* (also known as *Rage Control* and *Untitled ML Project*), Twentieth Century–Fox, 2005.

First Mary, *What Just Happened* (also known as *Inside Hollywood, Trouble in Hollywood,* and *What Just Happened?*), 2929 Productions, c. 2007, Magnolia Pictures, 2008.

Stage Appearances:

Trouble (a little boy), *Madama Butterfly* (opera; also known as *Madame Butterfly*), Los Angeles Opera, Los Angeles, c. 1994.

Greta, *The Nutcracker* (ballet), American Ballet Theatre, Kodak Theatre, Hollywood, CA, 2001.

KEYMAH, T'Keyah Crystal 1962–
(T'Keyah Keymah, Crystal Walker)

PERSONAL

Name is pronounced "Ta–Kee–ah Kristle Kee–Mah"; original name, Crystal Walker; born October 13, 1962, in Chicago, IL. *Education:* Florida A&M University, B.A., 1984; trained in ballet, jazz, and West African dance. *Avocational Interests:* Travel, gardening, writing, physical fitness, meditation.

Addresses: *Office*—T'Keyah Keymah, Inc., 10061 Riverside Dr., Suite 714, Toluca Lake, CA 91602.

Career: Actress, voice performer, producer, director, dancer and choreographer, and writer. Also works as stunt double, sometimes credited as Crystal Walker.

Performed as a high school student with Mary Wong Comedy Group; Call to Action Touring Company, performer, 1989; former member of Wavelength, Chocolate Chips, Light Opera Works, and Najwa (West African) Dance Corps; In Black World, Los Angeles, principal and producer; T'Keyah Keymah, Inc., Toluca Lake, CA, owner; teacher of theatre, dance, and pantomime; director, choreographer, and producer of Christian mime shows, Upward Bound stage and dance shows, and work for Majique Movement Dance Theatre. Chicago Public Schools, worked as substitute teacher, 1984–89; established T'Keyah Keymah Theatre Scholarship at Florida A&M University, 1990; Keymah Cultural Fund, member. Civic and environmental activist; volunteer with Citizens Committee for the Juvenile Court, 1986–87, Institute for Black Parenting, beginning 1991, prison outreach program of National Association of Brothers and Sisters In and Out, 1996, and with Rainbow/Push Coalition and Color Me Bright Youth Foundation; Women in the Arts, panelist, 1991; My Good Friend, celebrity partner, 1993, honorary board member, beginning 1994; Recycling Black Dollars, life member; also affiliated with Illinois Visually Handicapped Institute and Chicago Urban League.

Member: Screen Actors Guild, American Federation of Television and Radio Artists, Actors' Equity Association, Directors Guild of America, American Women in Radio and Television, National Association for the Advancement of Colored People, National Council of Negro Women (life member; volunteer), Florida A&M University Alumni Association, Delta Sigma Theta (life member).

Awards, Honors: Chosen Miss Black Illinois, 1985; Amazing Love Award, Institute for Black Parenting, 1993; Image Award nomination, best actress in a play, National Association for the Advancement of Colored People, c. 1994, for *The Five Heartbeats Live;* Image Awards, best actress in a play and best play, 1994, and Audelco Award nomination, best solo performance, Audience Development Committee, 1998, all for *Some of My Best Friends: A Collection of Characters Speaking in Verse and Prose;* Silver Award (with Bobby Mardis), best low–budget feature film, Worldfest Houston, 1995, and Outstanding Achievement Award, Saguaro Film Festival II, 1996, both for *One Last Time;* award nomination, Temecula Valley International Film Festival, and honorable mentions, Cinequest San Jose, Worldfest Charleston, and Hermosa Beach Film Festival, all 1997, for *Circle of Pain;* Image Award nominations, outstanding supporting actress in a comedy series, 1998 and 1999, for *Cosby;* National Black Theatre Festival Award, 1999; RPI Vision Award, Retinitis Pigmentosa International, 1999; World Village Award for Art and Music, 2000; Millennium Award and special President's Award, both Florida A&M University, 2001; Act–So Award for sponsorship and outstanding support, Beverly Hills–Hollywood chapter, National Association for the Advancement of Colored People, 2004.

CREDITS

Television Appearances; Series:
Member of ensemble, *In Living Color,* Fox, 1990–94.
Scotti Decker, a recurring role, *On Our Own,* ABC, 1995.
Denise Everett, *The Show,* Fox, 1996.
Voices of Mrs. LaSalle, Shavonne, and other characters, *Waynehead* (animated), The WB, 1996–97.
Erica Lucas, *Cosby,* CBS, 1996–2000.
Tonya Baxter, *That's So Raven!,* The Disney Channel, 2003–2006.

Also former guest anchor of *Channel One News.*

Television Appearances; Specials:
(As Crystal Walker) Contestant, *Miss Black America Pageant,* 1985.
Fox Live at the Taste: The Fireworks!, 1993.
Roc—Live, HBO, 1993.
Voice, *Cool Like That* (animated), 1993.
Voices of Charlene, Jaquita, and Aunt Hilda, *A Cool Like That Christmas,* Fox, 1993.
Comic Relief: Baseball Relief '93, 1993.
(In archive footage) *Mo' Funny: Black Comedy in America,* 1993.
Presenter, *Soul Train's 25th Anniversary,* 1995.
Counselor, Circle of Pain, 1996.
Host, *The Orange Bowl Parade,* CBS, 1997.
Host, *69th Annual Bud Billiken Back–to–School Parade,* 1998.
Host, *Aloha Parade,* 1998.
Host from Hawaii, *The All–American Thanksgiving Parade,* CBS, 1998.
Voices of robber girl and Gerda's grandmother, *The Snow Queen: An Animated Special from the "Happily Ever After: Fairy Tales for Every Child" Series,* HBO, 2000.
Missy May Banks, *The Gilded Six Bits,* Showtime, 2001.
Comedy Gold, CBC, 2005.

Television Talk Show Guest Appearances; Episodic:
A.M. Los Angeles, 1991.
Live with Regis and Kelly, syndicated, 1991.
Herself, *The Home Show,* 1991.
KTLA Morning News (also known as *KTLA Morning Show*), KTLA, 1997.
Crook & Chase, 1997.
Fox after Breakfast, 1997.
The Keenen Ivory Wayans Show, 1997, 1998.
CBS This Morning, CBS, 1998.
The O'Reilly Factor, 1998.
Politically Incorrect (also known as *P.I.*), 1999.
Happy Hour, 1999.

Television Appearances; Episodic:
Paula, "A Song for the Soul—April 7, 1963," *Quantum Leap,* NBC, 1992.
Darrelle, "Ebony and Ivory," *Roc,* Fox, 1992.
Guest host, *Soul Train,* 1993, 1997.
Sara Jones, "Good News/Bad News," *The John Larroquette Show* (also known as *Larroquette*), NBC, 1994.
Grace Caldwell, "Born in the USA," *The Commish,* ABC, 1994.
Sara Jones, "The Wedding," *The John Larroquette Show* (also known as *Larroquette*), NBC, 1995.
Voice of singer, "Inherit the Wheeze," *Pinky and the Brain* (animated), The WB, 1998.
Voice of old woman, "Babel," *Batman Beyond* (animated; also known as *Batman of the Future*), The WB, 2000.
(As T'Keyah Keymah) Voice of Monica (some sources cite Makeba), "Untouchable," *Batman Beyond* (animated; also known as *Batman of the Future*), The WB, 2000.
Voice of dispatch operator, "Countdown," *Batman Beyond* (animated; also known as *Batman of the Future*), The WB, 2001.
Voice of first teen girl, "Power Play," *Static Shock* (animated), The WB, 2002.
Voice of Allie Langford/Nails, "Hard as Nails," *Static Shock* (animated), The WB, 2003.
Realtor, "Moving On Out," *My Wife and Kids,* ABC, 2004.
Voice of Bumblebee, "Wavelength," *Teen Titans* (animated), Cartoon Network, 2004.
Voice of Bumblebee, "Titans East: Parts 1 & 2," *Teen Titans* (animated), Cartoon Network, 2005.
Voices of Bumblebee, old lady, young boy, and computer geek, "For Real," *Teen Titans* (animated), Cartoon Network, 2005.
Voice of Trixie's mom, "Professor Rotwood's Thesis," *American Dragon: Jake Long* (animated), The Disney Channel, 2005.
Voice of Marsha Brubert, "Half Baked," *American Dragon: Jake Long* (animated), The Disney Channel, 2006.
Voice of Mrs. Carter, "Hairy Christmas," *American Dragon: Jake Long* (animated), The Disney Channel, 2006.
Herself, "You Sold My Truck, Now I Am Out of Luck," *Jury Duty,* 2007.
Herself, "Was Charged Double for Stereo Trouble," *Jury Duty,* 2007.
Herself, "My Roommate Walked, Now He's All Talk," *Jury Duty,* 2007.
Celebrity Family Feud, NBC, 2008.

Television Appearances; Awards Presentations:
Presenter, *Soul Train Comedy Awards,* 1993.
Presenter, *The 8th Annual Soul Train Music Awards,* 1994.

Presenter, *3rd Annual Soul Train Lady of Soul Awards,* 1997.
Host, *NAACP ACT–SO Awards,* 1998.
Presenter, *The 30th NAACP Image Awards,* Fox, 1999.
The ... Annual Prism Awards, syndicated, 2001, FX Network, 2006.

Television Appearances; Other:
Gina, *One Last Time* (movie), Showtime, 1995.
Erica Lucas, *Cosby* (pilot), CBS, 1996.

Television Director; Episodic:
"Double Vision," *That's So Raven!,* The Disney Channel, 2004.

Television Work; Other:
Co–executive producer, *One Last Time* (movie), Showtime, 1995.
Coproducer, *Circle of Pain* (special), 1996.

Stage Appearances:
A Christmas Carol, Goodman Theatre, Chicago, IL, 1987–89.
Playboy of the West Indies, International Theatre Festival, 1988.
Melissa Gardner, *Love Letters,* Canon Theatre, Los Angeles, 1991.
Tonya, *The Five Heartbeats Live* (also known as *5 Heartbeats: The Musical*), Theatre at West Angeles Art Center, Los Angeles, 1994.
Beneatha, *A Raisin in the Sun,* Goodman Theatre, 2000.

Appeared in *Black to My Roots,* Stage Aurora, Jacksonville, FL; as Keentsing, *Homeland,* Civic Opera House, Chicago, IL; Valli and member of ensemble, *Land of Smiles,* Light Opera Works, Evanston, IL; Eunice Evers, *Miss Ever's Boys,* Stage Aurora, Aurora, IL; in *Moon on a Rainbow Shawl;* Berniece, *The Piano Lesson,* Virginia Stage Company, Norfolk, VA; and Ivy, *Playboy of the West Indies,* Court Theatre.

Major Tours:
Some of My Best Friends: A Collection of Characters Speaking in Verse and Prose (solo show), Call to Action Touring Company, U.S. cities, beginning 1991.
T'Keyah Live! ... Mostly: A Variety Show (solo show), U.S. cities, 2001.

Also performed as Lou Bessie, *The Old Settler,* Shelykova, Russia, then at Napokrovki Theatre, Moscow, Russia.

Stage Work:
Producer and director, *Some of My Best Friends: A Collection of Characters Speaking in Verse and Prose*

(solo tour), Call to Action Touring Company, U.S. cities, beginning 1991.
Producer and director, *T'Keyah Live! ... Mostly: A Variety Show* (solo tour), U.S. cities, 2001.

Producer of *Creative Instructions from My Crummy Life;* director of the solo show *S.I.S.T.E.R. (Sharing Intimate Secrets)* for performer Keisha Nicole; producer and director of in *An Evening with Ntozake Shange,* Theatre at Florida A&M University; producer, director, and choreographer, *The Cool Crystal & Carneil Comedy Half Hour.*

Film Appearances:
(Uncredited) Secretary, *Big Shots,* 1987.
(Uncredited) School nurse, *Tales from the Hood,* Savoy Pictures, 1995.
Raynelle, *Jackie Brown,* Miramax, 1997.
(Uncredited) Voice of Aoogah, *Tweety's High Flying Adventure* (animated), Warner Bros., 2000.
Tonya, *The Creature of the Sunny Side Up Trailer Park,* 2004, M.I.B., 2006.

RECORDINGS

Videos:
Tonya (some sources spell the name "Tanya"), *That's So Raven: Supernaturally Stylish,* Walt Disney Home Entertainment, 2005.
(As T'Keyah Keymah) Voice of Bumblebee, *Teen Titans* (video game), THQ, 2005.
Director, *That's So Raven: Raven's House Party,* Buena Vista Home Entertainment, 2005.

WRITINGS

Television Movies:
One Last Time, Showtime, 1995.

Television Specials:
Circle of Pain, 1996.

Television Episodes:
"Black World" segment, "A Date with Grave Jones," *In Living Color,* Fox, 1990.

Stage Shows:
Some of My Best Friends: A Collection of Characters Speaking in Verse and Prose (solo show), Call to Action Touring Company, tour of U.S. cities, beginning 1991.

Also coauthor of the solo show *S.I.S.T.E.R. (Sharing Intimate Secrets)* for performer Keisha Nicole.

Books:
Natural Woman/Natural Hair: A Hair Journey, 2002.

OTHER SOURCES

Books:
George, Nelson, *In Living Color: The Authorized Companion to the Fox TV Series,* Warner Books, 1991.
Hill, George, and Spencer Moon, *Blacks in Hollywood: Five Favorable Years in Film and Television,* Daystar Publishing, 1992.
Who's Who Among African Americans, 16th edition, Gale, 2003.

Periodicals:
Chicago Defender, September, 1991, p. 22.
Chicago Sun–Times, March 16, 2003.
Ebony Man, October, 1991, p. 41.
Washington Post, May, 1991, p. G1.

Electronic:
T'Keyah Crystal Keymah Official Site, http://www.tkeyah.com, July 9, 2010.

KRISTOFFERSON, Kris 1936–
(Kris Carson)

PERSONAL

Born June 22, 1936, in Brownsville, TX; son of Henry C. (an Air Force career officer) and Mary Ann (maiden name, Ashbrook) Kristofferson; married Fran Beer, February 11, 1961 (divorced, August 15, 1973); married Rita Coolidge (a singer and composer), August 17, 1973 (divorced, c. 1980); married Lisa Meyers, February 19, 1983; children: (first marriage) Tracy, Kris; (second marriage) Casey; (third marriage) Jesse Turner, Jody Ray, Johnny, Kelly Marie, Blake Cameron. *Education:* Pomona College, B.A., 1958; attended Oxford University, 1960.

Addresses: *Agent*—International Creative Management, 10250 Constellation Way, 9th Floor, Los Angeles, CA 90067.

Career: Actor, composer, singer, recording artist, and songwriter. Performed as a folksinger in England, as Kris Carson, early 1960s; performed at various clubs and folk festivals, and on concert tours, including Newport Folk Festival, Newport, RI, 1969, and *Welcome Home,* Washington, DC, 1987; toured with Johnny Cash, Way-

lon Jennings, and Willie Nelson as a member of the country band, the Highwaymen; Jody Ray Publishing (music publisher), principal. Formerly worked as a commercial helicopter pilot in Nashville, TN, 1965–59, and as a bartender, janitor, forest firefighter, and boxer. *Military service:* U.S. Army, 1960–65; served in Germany; became captain.

Awards, Honors: Winner of collegiate short story contest, *Atlantic Monthly,* 1958; Rhodes scholar, Oxford University, 1960; Song of the Year Award, Country Music Association, 1970, for "Sunday Mornin' Comin' Down"; Grammy Award, best song, National Academy of Recording Arts and Sciences, and Best Song Award, The Nashville Network/*Music City News,* both 1971, for "Help Me Make It through the Night"; Grammy Award nomination, best song, 1971, for "Me and Bobby McGee"; Grammy Award nomination, country song of the year, 1971, for "For the Good Times"; Best Songwriter Awards, The Nashville Network/*Music City News,* 1971 and 1972; Best Song Award, The Nashville Network/*Music City News,* 1972, and Grammy Award nominations, country song of the year and best male country vocalist, both 1973, all for "Why Me?"; Grammy Award (with Rita Coolidge), best vocal performance by a duo, 1973, for "From the Bottle to the Bottom"; Grammy Award nomination (with Coolidge), best vocal performance by a duo, 1974, for "Loving Arms"; honorary doctorate, Pomona College, 1974; Film Award nomination, most promising newcomer to leading film roles, British Academy of Film and Television Arts, 1974, for *Pat Garrett and Billy the Kid;* Grammy Award (with Coolidge), best vocal performance by a duo, 1975, for "Lover Please"; Golden Globe Award, best actor in a film musical or comedy, 1977, for *A Star Is Born;* Academy Award nomination, best original song score, 1984, for *Songwriter;* Grammy Award nomination, best country group with vocal, 1985, and American Music Awards, favorite country video single and best country video duo or group, 1986, all (with others) for "Highwayman"; inducted into Songwriters Hall of Fame, 1985; Bronze Wrangler Award (with others), Western Heritage Awards, 1987, for *Stagecoach;* Roger Miller Memorial Award, Country Songwriters Awards, *Music City News,* 1995; Blockbuster Entertainment Award, favorite supporting actor in a horror film, 1999, for *Blade;* Bronze Wrangler Award (with others), best television feature film, 1999, for *Two for Texas;* named veteran of the year, American Veteran Awards, 2002; Golden Boot Award, 2003; inducted into Country Music Hall of Fame, 2004; Johnny Mercer Award, Songwriters Hall of Fame, 2006; inducted into Texas Film Hall of Fame, 2006; Johnny Cash Visionary Award, Country Music Television network, 2007.

CREDITS

Film Appearances:
(Film debut) Minstrel Wrangler, *The Last Movie,* Universal, 1971.

Title role, *Cisco Pike,* Columbia, 1971.

Billy the Kid, *Pat Garrett and Billy the Kid,* Metro–Goldwyn–Mayer, 1973.

Elmo Cole, *Blume in Love,* Warner Bros., 1973.

Vocalist, *Gospel Road* (also known as *Gospel Road: A Story of Jesus*), Twentieth Century–Fox, 1973.

Paco, *Bring Me the Head of Alfredo Garcia,* United Artists, 1974.

David, *Alice Doesn't Live Here Anymore,* Warner Bros., 1975.

John Norman Howard, *A Star Is Born,* Warner Bros., 1976.

Aaron Arnold, *Vigilante Force,* United Artists, 1976.

Jim Cameron, *The Sailor Who Fell from Grace with the Sea,* Avco Embassy, 1976.

Marvin "Shake" Tiller, *Semi–Tough,* United Artists, 1977.

Martin "Rubber Duck" Penwald, *Convoy,* United Artists, 1978.

James Averill, *Heaven's Gate* (also known as *Michael Cimino's "Heaven's Gate"*), United Artists, 1980.

Hubbell "Hub" Smith, *Rollover,* Warner Bros., 1981.

(Uncredited) Himself, *The Last Horror Film* (also known as *Fanatical Extreme*), 1982.

Blackie Buck, *Songwriter,* TriStar, 1984.

Bob/Bobby Logan, *Flashpoint,* TriStar, 1984.

John "Hawk" Hawkins, *Trouble in Mind,* Island Alive, 1986.

Mace Montana, *Big Top Pee–Wee,* Paramount, 1988.

Lieutenant Jack Robbins, *Welcome Home,* Columbia, 1989.

Bill Smith, *Millennium,* Twentieth Century–Fox, 1989.

Tom Holte, *Sandino,* 1990.

Stan Wozniak, *Night of the Cyclone* (also known as *Perfume of the Cyclone*), Republic Home Video, 1990.

Jack Saunders, *Original Intent,* Paramount, 1992.

Gabriel, *Knights,* Paramount, 1993.

Joe Garvey, *No Place to Hide,* Cannon, 1993.

Tom, *Cheatin' Hearts* (also known as *Paper Hearts*), Trimark Pictures, 1993.

Preacher, *Pharaoh's Army,* Orion Home Entertainment, 1995.

Sheriff Charlie Wade, *Lone Star,* Sony Pictures Classics, 1996.

Orin Hanner, Sr., *Fire Down Below,* Warner Bros., 1997.

Bill Willis, *A Soldier's Daughter Never Cries,* October Films, 1998.

Voice of Doc, *The Land before Time VI: The Secret of Saurus Rock* (animated), Universal Home Video, 1998.

Cody, *Girls' Night,* Granada Films, 1998.

Abraham Whistler, *Blade,* New Line Cinema, 1998.

John Burnett, *Dance with Me,* Columbia, 1998.

Eddie, *The Joyriders,* Trident Releasing, 1999.

Bronson, *Payback,* Paramount, 1999.

Rudolph Meyer, *Molokai: The Story of Father Damien* (also known as *Father Damien*), Vine International Pictures, 1999.

Smilin' Jack Johannson, *Limbo,* Screen Gems, 1999.

Comanche, 2000.

Older Billy Coleman, *Where the Red Fern Grows,* Doty–Dayton Releasing, 2000.

Karubi, *Planet of the Apes,* Twentieth Century–Fox, 2001.

Bud, *Chelsea Walls* (also known as *Chelsea Hotel*), Lions Gate Films, 2001.

Shuck, *Wooly Boys,* PFG Entertainment, 2001.

Doctor "Doc" John Mitchell, *D–Tox* (also known as *Eye See You*), Universal, 2002.

Abraham Whistler, *Blade II,* New Line Cinema, 2002.

Wes Benteen, *Silver City,* Newmarket Films, 2004.

Abraham Whistler, *Blade: Trinity,* New Line Cinema, 2004.

Hank Williams, *Forever Is a Long, Long Time,* Verve Music Group, 2004.

Dr. Thomas Becker, *The Jacket,* Warner Bros., 2005.

L. R. Nasher, *The Wendell Baker Story,* THINKFilm, 2005.

Pop Crane, *Dreamer: Inspired by a True Story,* DreamWorks, 2005.

Himself, *The Life and Hard Times of Guy Terrifico,* THINKFilm, 2005.

Rudy Martin, *Fast Food Nation,* Fox Searchlight, 2006.

Howard Davis, *Room 10* (short film), Moxie Pictures, 2006.

Quebec Bill Bonhomme, *Disappearances,* Truly Indie, 2007.

Ray, *Crossing the Heart,* Without a Box, 2007.

Narrator, *I'm Not There,* Weinstein Company, 2007.

Raymond, *Jump Out Boys* (also known as *Lords of the Street*), Peach Arch Entertainment Group, 2008.

Voice of Talon, *Snow Buddies,* Walt Disney Studios Home Entertainment, 2008.

Shepherd Graves, *The Last Rites of Ransom Pride,* Screen Media Ventures, 2009.

Randall, *Powder Blue,* Speakeasy Releasing, 2009.

Ferlin Smith, *For Sale by Owner,* Monarch Home Video, 2009.

Ken Murphy, *He's Just Not That into You,* New Line Cinema, 2009.

E. F. Bloodworth, *Bloodworth* (also known as *Provinces of Night*), Dax Productions/Buffalo Bulldog Films, 2010.

Old Yohan, *Yohan—Barnevandrer,* 2010.

Film Appearances; Documentaries:

Message to Love: The Isle of Wight Festival (also known as *Message of Love: The Isle of Wight Festival, the Movie*), Strand Releasing, 1997.

(In archive footage) *The Righteous Babes,* 1998.

The Ballad of Ramblin' Jack, Lot 47, 2000.

Immaculate Funk, FBN Motion Pictures, 2000.

Easy Riders, Raging Bulls: How the Sex, Drugs and Rock 'n' Roll Generation Saved Hollywood, 2003.

(Uncredited; in archive footage) *Go West, Young Man!,* Filmmuseum Distributie, 2003.

Pre–Madonna, Genuine Human Productions, 2004.

Be Here to Love Me: A Film about Townes Van Zandt, Palm Pictures, 2005.

Passion & Poetry: The Ballad of Sam Peckinpah, 2005.

Narrator, *Brats: Our Journey Home,* Brats without Borders, 2006.

Narrator, *Sacred Tibet: The Path to Mount Kailash,* 2006.

(English version) Voice of Billy the Kid, *Requiem for Billy the Kid* (original version filmed, 2006, Park Circus, 2009.

Leonard Cohen: Live at the Isle of Wight 1970, Columbia Music Video, 2009.

Film Work; Song Performer:

"Help Me Make It through the Night," *Fat City,* 1972.

"For the Good Times," *Breakfast on Pluto,* Sony Pictures Classics, 2005.

"They Ain't Got 'em All," *Lucky You,* Warner Bros., 2007.

Kristofferson's recorded song performances have also been included in many other films.

Television Appearances; Movies:

Ben Cole, *The Lost Honor of Kathryn Beck* (also known as *Act of Passion*), CBS, 1984.

Jesse James, *The Last Days of Frank and Jesse James,* ABC, 1986.

Bill Williams (Ringo/Ringo Kid), *Stagecoach,* CBS, 1986.

Noble Adams, *The Tracker* (also known as *Dead or Alive*), HBO, 1988.

Captain Rip Metcalf, *Pair of Aces,* CBS, 1990.

Captain Rip Metcalf, *Another Pair of Aces: Three of a Kind,* CBS, 1991.

Jericho Adams, *Miracle in the Wilderness,* TNT, 1991.

Jefferson Jones, *Christmas in Connecticut,* TNT, 1992.

Stan Mather, *Trouble Shooters: Trapped Beneath the Earth* (also known as *Trapped*), NBC, 1993.

Destiny, *Sodbusters,* Showtime, 1994.

Abraham Lincoln, *Tad,* The Family Channel, 1995.

Captain Jack Guthrie, *Inflammable,* CBS, 1995.

Himself, *Big Dreams & Broken Hearts: The Dottie West Story* (also known as *Paper Mansions: The Dottie West Story*), CBS, 1995.

Davis, *Brothers' Destiny* (also known as *Long Road Home* and *The Road Home*), 1996.

Owen Whistler, *Blue Rodeo,* CBS, 1996.

Jesse Ray Torrance, *Outlaw Justice* (also known as *The Long Kill*), CBS, 1998.

Hugh Allison, *Two for Texas,* TNT, 1998.

Chuck Whortle, *14 Hours,* TNT, 2005.

Television Appearances; Miniseries:

Abner Lait, *Freedom Road,* NBC, 1979.

Captain Curtis "Curt" Maddox, *Blood and Orchids,* CBS, 1986.

Devin Milford, *Amerika,* ABC, 1987.

Coming and Going, PBS, 1994.

Host and narrator, *Adventures of the Old West,* The Disney Channel, 1995.

Narrator, *America's Music: The Roots of Country,* TBS, 1996.

Steve Day, *Tom Clancy's "NetForce"* (also known as *NetForce*), ABC, 1999.

Lou Smit, *Perfect Murder, Perfect Town: JonBenet and the City of Boulder,* CBS, 2000.

Narrator, *American Roots Music,* PBS, 2001.

Matthew Bok, *Lives of the Saints,* CTV, 2004.

Television Appearances; Specials:

Listening to You: The Who at the Isle of Wight, 1970.

The Real George Carlin (also known as *Monsanto Night Presents the Real George Carlin*), 1973.

I Believe in Music, NBC, 1973.

Marlo Thomas and Friends in Free to Be ... You and Me (also known as *Free to Be ... You & Me*), ABC, 1974.

Barbra: With One More Look at You (also known as *The Making of "A Star Is Born"*), 1976.

A Salute to American Imagination, 1978.

A Gift of Song: The Music for UNICEF Special (also known as *A Gift of Song: The Music for UNICEF Concert*), 1979.

Host, *The Unbroken Circle: A Tribute to Mother Maybelle Carter,* 1979.

Johnny Cash: The First 25 Years, CBS, 1980.

Country Comes Home, CBS, 1981.

A Special Anne Murray Christmas, CBS, 1981.

(Uncredited; audience member) *On Location: The Comedy Store's 11th Anniversary Show,* 1983.

Master of ceremonies, *Sunday Night Live,* 1984.

Glen Campbell and Friends: The Silver Anniversary, HBO, 1984.

Johnny Cash: Christmas on the Road, CBS, 1984.

The 10th Anniversary Johnny Cash Christmas Special, CBS, 1985.

Joan Rivers and Friends Salute Heidi Abromowitz, 1985.

The Door Is Always Open, syndicated, 1985.

The Winning Hand, 1985.

Texas 150: A Celebration Special, ABC, 1986.

The Best of Farm Aid: An American Event, HBO, 1986.

The Academy of Country Music's 20th Anniversary Reunion, NBC, 1986.

I Am What I Am, 1987.

Farm Aid '87, 1987.

A Tribute to Ricky Nelson, syndicated, 1987.

Welcome Home, HBO, 1987.

Kenny Rogers Classic Weekend, ABC, 1988.

A Country Music Celebration: The 30th Anniversary of the Country Music Association, CBS, 1988.

An All–Star Celebration: The '88 Vote, ABC, 1988.

Host, *Buddy Holly and the Crickets—A Tribute,* PBS, 1988.

Judy Collins: Going Home, The Disney Channel, 1989.

Grammy Living Legends, CBS, 1989.

Texas and Tennessee ... A Musical Affair, The Nashville Network, 1990.

In the Hank Williams Tradition, PBS, 1990.

Farm Aid IV, The Nashville Network, 1990.

Highwaymen Live!, The Disney Channel, 1991.

Texas, Our Texas Inaugural Gala, 1991.

(Uncredited) *Here's Looking at You,* Warner Bros., 1991.

Martin Luther King, Jr., National Holiday Parade, TBS, 1992.

The Highwaymen, The Nashville Network, 1992.

Farm Aid V, The Nashville Network, 1992.

Host, *In Country: Songs of the Vietnam War,* PBS, 1992.

Sam Peckinpah: Man of Iron (also known as *Sam Peckinpah: A Retrospective*), Arts and Entertainment, 1992.

Willie Nelson, the Big Six–O: An All–Star Birthday Celebration (also known as *Willie Nelson: The Big Six–O*), CBS, 1993.

Farm Aid VI, The Nashville Network, 1993.

Host, "The Bob Dylan 30th Anniversary Celebration" (also known as "The Bob Dylan 30th Anniversary Concert Celebration"), *In the Spotlight,* PBS, 1993.

Kris Kristofferson: His Life and Work, 1993.

Willie Nelson: My Life, Arts and Entertainment, 1994.

Elvis Aron Presley: The Tribute, pay per view, 1994.

American Music Shop, The Nashville Network, 1994.

Host and narrator, "The Songs of Six Families," *Great Performances,* PBS, 1994.

Kris Kristofferson: Songwriter, The Disney Channel, 1995.

Dolly Parton: Treasures, CBS, 1996.

The Kennedy Center Honors: A Celebration of the Performing Arts, CBS, 1996, 1998.

"Songwriters Special Featuring Kris Kristofferson," *Austin City Limits,* 1997.

The 25th American Film Institute Life Achievement Award: A Salute to Martin Scorsese, CBS, 1997.

Big Guns Talk: The Story of the Western, TNT, 1997.

The Life and Times of Willie Nelson, The Nashville Network, 1997.

(In archive footage) *Dolly Parton: She Ain't No Dumb Blonde,* 1997.

CMA 40th: A Celebration, CBS, 1998.

Roger Miller Remembered, The Nashville Network, 1998.

An All–Star Tribute to Johnny Cash, TNT, 1999.

Kris Kristofferson, Arts and Entertainment, 1999.

The Kennedy Center Mark Twain Prize Celebrating the Humor of Richard Pryor, Comedy Central, 1999.

AFI Life Achievement Award: A Tribute to Barbra Streisand (also known as *29th American Film Institute Life Achievement Award: A Salute to Barbra Streisand*), Fox, 2001.

Narrator, *John Ford Goes to War,* Starz!, 2002.

Willie Nelson & Friends: Live and Kickin', USA Network, 2003.

Get Up, Stand Up, 2003.

Final Cut: The Making and Unmaking of Heaven's Gate (documentary; also known as *Final Cut: The Making of "Heaven's Gate" and the Unmaking of a Studio*), Trio, 2004.

Z Channel: A Magnificent Obsession, Independent Film Channel, 2004.

Narrator, *Sam Peckinpah's West: Legacy of a Hollywood Renegade,* Starz!, 2004.

Ronnie Hawkins "Still Alive and Kickin'," CTV, 2004.

I Walk the Line: A Night for Johnny Cash, CBS, 2005.

Celebrating the Man in Black: The Making of "Walk the Line," 2005.

Narrator, *CMT: 20 Greatest Country Bands,* Country Music Television, 2005.

Ricky Nelson Sings, 2005.

Trudell, PBS, 2005.

CMT: The Greatest—40 Greatest Albums, Country Music Television, 2006.

CMA Red Carpet, Country Music Television, 2006, 2007.

"Jerry Lee Lewis: Last Man Standing Live," *Great Performances,* PBS, 2007.

Johnny Cash's America, Arts and Entertainment, 2008.

(Uncredited; in archive footage) William H. Bonney, *How the West Was Lost,* BBC, 2008.

Handy Manny's Motorcycle Adventure, The Disney Channel, 2009.

Voice, *For Love of Liberty: The Story of America's Black Patriots,* 2010.

Merle Haggard: Learning to Live with Myself, PBS, 2010.

Television Appearances; Episodic:

Disco 2, 1970.

The Johnny Cash Show, ABC, 1970.

Rollin' on the River (also known as *Rollin'*), syndicated, 1971.

"Kris Kristofferson," *Boboquivari,* 1971.

Flip (also known as *The Flip Wilson Show*), 1972.

"Celebrity Roast: Ronald Reagan," *The Dean Martin Comedy Show* (also known as *The Dean Martin Show*), 1973.

The Sonny and Cher Comedy Hour, 1973.

Dean Martin Presents Music Country, U.S.A., NBC, 1973.

Host, *Saturday Night Live* (also known as *SNL*), NBC, 1976.

The Muppet Show, 1978.

"Jerry Lee Lewis," *Salute!,* 1983.

Hee Haw, 1985.

Pero esto que es?, 1990.

Himself, "Arthur's Crises" (also known as "Artie's Crisis"), *The Larry Sanders Show,* HBO, 1994.

(With the Highwaymen) "Out of Country," *Lost in Music,* 1995.

Narrator, "Janis Joplin," *VH1 Legends,* VH1, 1995.

(In archive footage) Gabriel, "Viki Williamson Night," *Joe Bob's Drive–in Theatre,* 1995.

Narrator, "Curtis Mayfield," *VH1 Legends,* VH1, 1996.

The Heaven and Earth Show, BBC, 2004.

"Johnny Cash vs. Music Row," *Controversy,* 2004.

"Thirty Odd Foot of Grunts Featuring Russell Crowe and Kris Kristofferson," *Soundstage,* PBS, 2004.

CMT Insider, Country Music Television, (in archive footage) 2006, and 2009.

Nyhetsmorgon, 2008.

(In archive footage) *Entertainment Tonight* (also known as *E.T.* and *This Week in Entertainment*), syndicated, 2008.

Crook & Chase, The Nashville Network, 2009.

Also appeared in episodes of *Country Music Spotlight,* The Family Channel; *Super Dave,* Showtime; and *The Texas Connection,* The Nashville Network.

Television Talk Show Guest Appearances; Episodic:

The David Frost Show, 1971.

The Tonight Show Starring Johnny Carson, NBC, 1973, 1978.

Donahue (also known as *The Phil Donahue Show*), 1978.

The Rosie O'Donnell Show, syndicated, 1998.

Late Night with Conan O'Brien, NBC, 1998, 2006.

The Howard Stern Radio Show, 1999.

Enough Rope with Andrew Denton, Australian Broadcasting Corporation, 2005.

The Tonight Show with Jay Leno, NBC, 2006.

The Oprah Winfrey Show (also known as *Oprah*), syndicated, 2006.

Breakfast, 2008.

Spectacle: Elvis Costello With ..., 2008.

The Colbert Report, Comedy Central, 2009.

Tavis Smiley, PBS, 2009.

Also guest for episodes of *Late Night with David Letterman,* NBC.

Television Appearances; Awards Presentations:

The ... Annual Grammy Awards, 1972, 1975, 1979, 1980, CBS, 1987.

Presenter, *The 51st Annual Academy Awards,* 1979.

The ... Annual Country Music Association Awards, CBS, 1984, 1985, 1991, 1993, 2003, ABC, 2007.

Host, *The ... Annual Country Music Association Awards,* CBS, 1985, 1986.

The American Music Awards, ABC, 1986.

The ... Annual Academy of Country Music Awards, NBC, 1988, 1991, 1992, 1996, 1998.

The 21st Annual NAACP Image Awards, NBC, 1989.

Presenter, *The ... Annual Grammy Awards,* CBS, 1990, 1995.

Music City News Country Songwriters Awards, The Nashville Network, 1995.

Presenter, *The ... Annual Country Music Association Awards,* CBS, 1998, CBS, 2005, ABC, 2006, ABC, 2009.

CMT Music Awards, Country Music Television, 2007.

Television Appearances; Other:

Narrator, *Dead Man's Gun* (pilot), Showtime, 1997.

Narrator, *Dead Man's Gun* (series), Showtime, 1997–99.

Izzy Patterson, *The Break* (pilot), Fox, 2003.

RECORDINGS

Albums:

Kristofferson, Monument, 1970.

Me & Bobby McGee, Monument, 1971.

The Silver–Tongued Devil and I, Monument, 1971.

Jesus Was a Capricorn, Monument, 1972.

Border Lord, One Way, 1972.

Full Moon, A&M, 1973.

(With Rita Coolidge) *Breakaway,* Monument/Sony, 1974.

Spooky Lady's Sideshow, One Way, 1974.

Who's to Bless and Who's to Blame, One Way, 1975.

Third World Warrior, Mercury, 1976.

Surreal Thing, One Way, 1976.

The Songs of Kristofferson, Monument, 1977.

A Star Is Born, Monument, 1977.

(With Coolidge) *Natural Act,* A&M, 1978.

Easter Island, Columbia, 1978.

Big Sur Festival, 1978.

Shake Hands with the Devil, Columbia, 1979.

(With Willie Nelson) *A Tribute to Willie and Kris,* Columbia, 1981.

To the Bone, Columbia, 1981.

Winning Hand, Monument, 1983.

(With Nelson) *Music from Songwriter,* Columbia, 1984.

My Songs, CBS, 1984.

(With the Highwaymen) *Highwaymen,* Columbia, 1985.

Repossessed, Mercury, 1987.

(Contributor) Randy Travis, *Heroes & Friends,* Warner, 1990.

(With the Highwaymen) *Highwayman 2,* Columbia, 1990.

(With the Borderlords) *Third World Warrior,* Mercury, 1990.

The Best of Kris Kristofferson, Sony, 1991.

Singer, Songwriter, Monument, 1991.

(Contributor) *Live at the Philharmonic,* Monument, 1992.

(With the Highwaymen) *The Road Goes on Forever,* Liberty, 1995.

The Austin Sessions, Atlantic, 1999.

Broken Freedom Song: Live from San Francisco, Oh Boy, 2003.

This Old Road, New West, 2006.

Closer to the Bone, New West, 2009.

Also recorded (with Rita Coolidge) *Full Moon.* Several of Kristofferson's albums have been reprinted.

Videos:

A Celebration, DID Productions, 1981.

Johnny Cash: Half Mile a Day, Image Entertainment, 2000.

Second Chances: The Making of "Alice Doesn't Live Here Anymore," Warner Home Video, 2004.

Nightstalkers, Daywalkers, and Familiars: Inside the World of "Blade Trinity," New Line Cinema, 2005.

The Jacket: Project History and Deleted Scenes, Warner Independent Pictures, 2005.

Tootsie's Orchid Lounge: Where the Music Began, 2005.

Voice of Ned White, *Gun* (video game), Activision, 2005.

Folsom, Cash & the Comeback, Twentieth Century–Fox Home Entertainment, 2006.

Ring of Fire: The Passion of Johnny & June, Twentieth Century–Fox Home Entertainment, 2006.

The Manufacturing of "Fast Food Nation," Twentieth Century–Fox Home Entertainment, 2007.

(Uncredited; in archive footage) *A Company of Players,* Buena Vista Home Entertainment, 2008.

Sun Records and the Johnny Cash Sound, Fox Home Video, 2008.

Narrator, *Elvis: Return to Tupelo,* Solid Entertainment/ Michael Rose Productions, 2008.

Wisdom, Late Night and Weekends, 2008.

Appeared in the music video "This Is to Mother You" by Sinead O'Connor, 1997.

WRITINGS

Film Music Composer:

Clay Pigeon (also known as *Trip to Kill*), 1971.

The Last Movie, Universal, 1971.

Theme music, "Sea Dream Theme," *The Sailor Who Fell from Grace with the Sea,* Avco Embassy, 1976.

(And songwriter) *Songwriter,* TriStar, 1984.

Walking after Midnight, 1988.

Songwriter, *Cheatin' Hearts* (also known as *Paper Hearts*), Trimark Pictures, 1993.

Passion & Poetry: The Ballad of Sam Peckinpah (documentary), El Dorado Productions/Manic Entertainment, 2005.

Kristofferson's songs have appeared in numerous other films.

Television Music; Specials:

Just Friends, 1970.

Sam Peckinpah: Man of Iron (also known as *Sam Peckinpah: A Retrospective*), Arts and Entertainment, 1992.

Songwriter:

Among Kristofferson's best known songs are "Vietnam Blues," Buckhorn Music, 1965; "For the Good Times," Buckhorn Music, 1968; (with Fred L. Foster) "Me and Bobby McGee," Combine Music, 1969; "Sunday Mornin' Comin' Down," Combine Music, 1969; "Help Me Make It through the Night," Combine Music, 1970; "Loving Her Was Easier (than Anything I'll Ever Do Again)," Combine Music, 1970; (with Shel Silverstein) "Once More with Feeling," Combine Music, 1970; (with Silverstein) "The Taker," Evil Eye Music, 1970; "Please Don't Tell Me How the Story Ends," Combine Music, 1971; "I'd Rather Be Sorry," Buckhorn Music, 1971; "Why Me?," Resaca Music, 1972; "Jody and the Kid" and "When I Loved Her"; and (with Rita Coolidge) "From the Bottle to the Bottom," "Lover Please," and "Loving Arms."

ADAPTATIONS

Kristofferson's songs were featured in the stage musical *Ring of Fire,* presented at the Ethel Barrymore Theatre in New York City in the spring of 2006.

OTHER SOURCES

Books:

Contemporary Musicians, Volume 4, Gale Research, 1990.

Kalet, Beth, *Kris Kristofferson,* Quick Fox, 1979.

Periodicals:

AARP, March, 2010, p. 22.

Billboard, April 20, 1996, p. 50; May 29, 2004, p. 60.

Entertainment Weekly, September 25, 1998, p. 68.

Esquire, March, 2006, p. 84.

Evening Standard (London), April 3, 2008, p. 40.

Guardian (London), March 4, 2008.

Interview, September, 1998, p. 124.

People Weekly, September 21, 1998, p. 103.

Sunday Times (London), March 23, 2008.

Texas Monthly, March, 1997, p. 126.

TV Guide, January 24, 2004, p. 16; April 16, 2007, p. 48.

Variety, January 9, 2006, p. S38.

Washington Post, March 30, 2006, pp. C1, C9.

L

LANG, Perry 1959–

PERSONAL

Born December 24, 1959, in Palo Alto, CA; married Sage Parker (an actress), June 15, 1996; children: two.

Addresses: *Agent*—Jack Leighton, Agency for the Performing Arts, 405 South Beverly Dr., Beverly Hills, CA 90212. *Manager*—Stephen Marks, Evolution Entertainment, 901 North Highland Ave., Los Angeles, CA 90038.

Career: Director, actor, and writer.

Awards, Honors: Critics Award nomination, Deauville Film Festival, 1990, for *Little Vegas*.

CREDITS

Television Director; Series:
Everwood, The WB, multiple episodes, 2004–2006.

Television Director; Episodic:
"Don't Ask, Don't Tell," *ER*, NBC, 1996.
"Burnin' Love," *NYPD Blue* (also known as *N.Y.P.D.*), ABC, 1996.
"Girl Talk," *NYPD Blue* (also known as *N.Y.P.D.*), ABC, 1996.
"Monster," *Millennium*, Fox, 1997.
"The Last Wave," *Dark Skies*, NBC, 1997.
"The Warren Omission," *Dark Skies*, NBC, 1997.
"Shades of Gray," *Dark Skies*, NBC, 1997.
"Bloodlines," *Dark Skies*, NBC, 1997.
"What a Dump!," *NYPD Blue* (also known as *N.Y.P.D.*), ABC, 1997.

"Most Wanted," *Nash Bridges*, CBS, 1997.
"Mystery Dance," *Nash Bridges*, CBS, 1998.
"If: Parts 1 & 2," *Cracker* (also known as *Cracker: Mind over Murder* and *Cracker: The Complete Series*), ABC, 1998.
"I Don't Wanna Dye," *NYPD Blue* (also known as *N.Y.P.D.*), ABC, 1998.
"The Working Man's Friend," *Arli$$*, HBO, 1998.
"What Would I Do without Wu?," *Arli$$*, HBO, 1998.
"Dreams," *Fantasy Island*, ABC, 1998.
"Heroes," *Fantasy Island*, ABC, 1999.
"Friends," *Vengeance Unlimited* (also known as *Mr. Chapel*), ABC, 1999.
"Under Siege," *Popular*, The WB, 1999.
"The Trial of Emory Dick," *Popular*, The WB, 2000.
"All about Adam," *Popular*, The WB, 2000.
"Like Father, Like Monk," *Secret Agent Man*, UPN, 2000.
"Sight Unseen," *Charmed*, The WB, 2000.
"Kiss and Tell," *Young Americans*, The WB, 2000.
"The Longest Day," *Dawson's Creek*, The WB, 2000.
"Kiss Kiss Bang Bang," *Dawson's Creek*, The WB, 2000.
"Use Your Disillusion," *Dawson's Creek*, The WB, 2001.
"Emily in Wonderland," *Gilmore Girls* (also known as *Gilmore Girls: Beginnings*), The WB, 2001.
"Time Will Tell," *Alias*, ABC, 2001.
"Salvation," *Alias*, ABC, 2002.
"Endgame," *Alias*, ABC, 2002.
"Shades of Guilt," *The Twilight Zone*, UPN, 2002.
"The Stepford Cheerleaders," *The Chronicle* (also known as *News from the Edge*), Sci–Fi Channel, 2002.
"The Fighting Fridas," *American Family*, 2002.
"The Devil Made Me Do It," *Glory Days*, The WB, 2002.
"No Guts, No Glory," *Glory Days*, The WB, 2002.
Breaking News, Bravo, 2002.
"Antarctica," *Veritas: The Quest*, ABC, 2003.
"That Was Then" (also known as "Before and After"), *Dawson's Creek*, The WB, 2003.
Tarzan, The WB, 2003.

"Natural Borne Killers," *Threat Matrix*, ABC, 2003.

"Year of the Tiger," *Las Vegas*, NBC, 2003.

"Flirtin' with Disaster," *10–8: Officers on Duty* (also known as *10–8*), ABC, 2004.

"What Is and What Should Never Be," *One Tree Hill*, The WB, 2004.

"Sucker Punch," *North Shore*, Fox, 2004.

"Running Scared," *Jack & Bobby*, The WB, 2005.

"Into the Woods," *Jack & Bobby*, The WB, 2005.

"Under the Influence," *Jack & Bobby*, The WB, 2005.

"Delta Does Detroit," *E–Ring*, NBC, 2005.

"Acceptance," *The Book of Daniel*, NBC, 2006.

"Sweet Child o' Mine," *Medium*, NBC, 2006.

"What about Denial …," *What about Brian*, ABC, 2006.

"Mulligan," *Hidden Palms*, The CW, 2007.

"Second Chances," *Hidden Palms*, The CW, 2007.

"After Birth," *Army Wives*, Lifetime, 2007.

"Truth and Consequences," *Army Wives*, Lifetime, 2007.

"Black & White and Read All Over," *Greek*, ABC Family, 2007.

"Grasshopper," *Weeds*, Showtime, 2007.

"Awakenings," *Side Order of Life*, Lifetime, 2007.

"Patience," *Eli Stone*, ABC, 2008.

"The Path," *Eli Stone*, ABC, 2008.

"Happy Birthday, Nate," *Eli Stone*, ABC, 2008.

"Breach," *NCIS: Los Angeles*, CBS, 2010.

Also directed episodes of *Family Law*, CBS; *Hyperion Bay*, The WB; and *Moloney*, CBS.

Television Appearances; Movies:

Billy, *Zuma Beach*, NBC, 1978.

Billy Robbins, *The Death of Ocean View Park*, ABC, 1979.

Revealing Evidence: Stalking the Honolulu Strangler, NBC, 1990.

Earl McNally, *Betrayed by Love*, ABC, 1994.

Captain, *Dead Weekend*, Showtime, 1995.

Television Appearances; Episodic:

Buddy Bonkers, "Say Goodbye to Buddy Bonkers," *The Fitzpatricks*, 1977.

"The Apple Tree, the Singing, and the Gold," *James at 16* (originally known as *James at 15*), 1977.

Brian, "The Most Likely to Succeed," *What Really Happened to the Class of '65?*, 1978.

Al, "A Chance to Live," *Police Story*, 1978.

Roberts, "The Challenges," *Flying High*, 1979.

Willie Johnson, "The Innocent," *How the West Was Won*, ABC, 1979.

Sandler, "Hey, Look Me Over," *M*A*S*H*, CBS, 1982.

Bobby, "The Children's' Song," *The Equalizer*, CBS, 1985.

Skip Mueller, "Trust Fund Pirates," *Miami Vice*, 1986.

Sandy, "My Own Place," *Tales from the Darkside*, Showtime, 1987.

Eddie, "Holly's House," *Monsters*, syndicated, 1988.

Lieutenant Commander Frederick Emmanuel, "Crossing the Great Water," *China Beach*, ABC, 1989.

Phil Partridge, "A Partridge in a Pair's Tree," *Civil Wars*, ABC, 1992.

Martin Swope, *The Commish*, ABC, c. 1994.

(Uncredited) Bartender, "Girl Talk," *NYPD Blue* (also known as *N.Y.P.D.*), ABC, 1996.

Television director, "All about Adam," *Popular*, 2000.

"The Devil Made Me Do It," *Glory Days*, The WB, 2002.

Also appeared as Kenner in an episode of *Fantasy Island*, ABC; and as Justin Previn in an episode of *Nash Bridges*, CBS.

Television Appearances; Other:

Hewitt Calder, "Hewitt's Just Different" (special), *ABC Afterschool Special*, ABC, 1977.

Woodward, *A Rumor of War* (miniseries), CBS, 1980.

John "Frenchy" Nuckles, *Bay City Blues* (series), NBC, 1983.

Wes "Hotshot" Williams, *The Bakery* (pilot), CBS, 1990.

Film Appearances:

Terry Davis, *Teen Lust* (also known as *The Girls Next Door* and *Mom Never Told Me*), Columbia, 1978.

The Great Ride, 1978.

Tall kid, *Big Wednesday* (also known as *Summer of Innocence*), Warner Bros., 1978.

Dennis DeSoto, *1941*, Universal, 1979.

Private Kaiser, *The Big Red One* (also known as *The Big Red One—The Reconstruction*), United Artists, 1980.

Paul Gordon, *The Hearse*, Crown International, 1980.

Officer Jim Kelly, *Alligator*, BLC, 1980.

Elrod, *Cattle Annie and Little Britches*, Universal, 1981.

Charles Golphin, *Body and Soul*, Citadel Films, 1981.

Frank English, *Tag: The Assassination Game* (also known as *Everybody Gets It in the End*), New World, 1982.

Rob O'Hara, *O'Hara's Wife*, PSO International, 1982.

Adam, *Spring Break*, Columbia, 1983.

Andy, *Sahara*, Metro–Goldwyn–Mayer, 1983.

Tim Johnson, *Flyers*, 1983.

Jeff, *Jocks* (also known as *Physical Lesson* and *Road Trip*), Crown International, 1987.

Fred McMullin, *Eight Men Out*, Orion, 1988.

Sam Grimm, *Mortuary Academy*, Taurus Entertainment, 1988.

Denny, *Jailbird Rock* (also known as *Can't Shake the Beat* and *Prison Dancer*), Continental Distributing, 1988.

Jacob's assailant, *Jacob's Ladder* (also known as *Dante's Inferno*), TriStar, 1990.

Steve, *Little Vegas* (also known as *Little Vegas: A Desert Story*), IRS Media, 1990.

Ralph Boshi, *Dead On: Relentless II* (also known as *Dead On* and *Relentless II: Dead On*), 1991.

Travis, *Jennifer Eight* (also known as *Jennifer 8*), Paramount, 1992.

Lyle, *Men of War* (also known as *A Safe Place, Professional Killers,* and *Soldiers of Fortune*), Dimension Films, 1994.

Greg, *Sunshine State,* Sony Pictures Classics, 2002.

Frank Borzage, Director (short documentary), Rhetorically Confuzzeled Entertainment, 2009.

Film Director:

Little Vegas (also known as *Little Vegas: A Desert Story*), IRS Media, 1990.

Men of War (also known as *A Safe Place, Soldiers of Fortune,* and *Hombres de acero*), Dimension Films, 1994.

Stage Appearances:

Sebastian, *Twelfth Night, or What You Will,* New York Shakespeare Festival, Delacorte Theatre, Public Theatre, New York City, 1986.

RECORDINGS

Videos:

(In archive footage) *The Making of "1941,"* 1996.

The Real Glory: Reconstructing "The Big Red One," Warner Home Video, 2005.

WRITINGS

Television Episodes:

(With Ted Gershuny) "My Own Place," *Tales from the Darkside,* Showtime, 1987.

Screenplays:

Little Vegas (also known as *Little Vegas: A Desert Story*), IRS Media, 1990.

LARROQUETTE, John 1947–

PERSONAL

Full name, John Bernard Larroquette; born November 25, 1947, in New Orleans, LA; son of John Edgar (in U.S. Navy) and Berthalla (or, according to some sources, Bertha) Oramous (a department store clerk; maiden name, Helmstetter) Larroquette; married Bertie Good, September 22, 1969 (divorced); married Elizabeth Ann Cookson (an actress), July 4, 1975; children: (second marriage) Lisa Katherina, Jonathan Preston,

Benjamin Lawrence. *Education:* Attended high school in New Orleans, LA. *Avocational Interests:* Collecting first-edition books and other antique collectibles.

Addresses: *Agent*—International Creative Management, 10250 Constellation Way, 9th Floor, Los Angeles, CA 90067; (animation voice work) Danis Panaro Nist, 9201 West Olympic Blvd., Beverly Hills, CA 90212. *Manager*—Brillstein Entertainment Partners, 9150 Wilshire Blvd., Suite 350, Beverly Hills, CA 90212. *Publicist*—WKT Public Relations, 335 North Maple Dr., Suite 351, Beverly Hills, CA 90210.

Career: Actor, producer, and director. Appeared in commercials for Holiday Inn motel chain; National Broadcasting Co., appeared in the public service announcement campaign *The More You Know.* Worked as a radio disc jockey in New Orleans, LA, Memphis, TN, Houston, TX, and Cincinnati, OH, between 1966 and 1973; bartender in Colorado, 1973; Decca Records, promotion director, 1973–74. *Military service:* U.S. Naval Reserve, active duty, 1965–66.

Awards, Honors: DramaLogue Award, 1984, for *Endgame;* Emmy Awards, outstanding supporting actor in a comedy series, 1985, 1986, 1987, and 1988, Golden Globe Award nomination, best supporting actor in a television series, miniseries, or movie, 1988, and American Comedy Award nomination, funniest supporting male in a television series, 1990, all for *Night Court;* Emmy Award nomination, outstanding lead actor in a comedy series, 1994, for *The John Larroquette Show;* Emmy Award, outstanding guest actor in a drama series, Q Award, best recurring player, Viewers for Quality Television, 1998, and Emmy Award nomination, outstanding guest actor in a drama series, 2002, all for *The Practice;* Screen Actors Guild Award nominations (with others), outstanding ensemble in a drama series, 2008, 2009, both for *Boston Legal.*

CREDITS

Television Appearances; Series:

Dr. Paul Herman, *Doctors' Hospital,* NBC, 1975–76.

Lieutenant Bob Anderson, *Black Sheep Squadron* (also known as *Baa Baa Black Sheep*), NBC, 1976–78.

Assistant District Attorney Daniel "Dan" Reinhold Fielding, *Night Court,* NBC, 1984–92.

John Hemingway, *The John Larroquette Show* (also known as *Larroquette*), NBC, 1993–96.

Joey Heric, a recurring role, *The Practice,* ABC, between 1997 and 2002.

Royal Payne, *Payne,* CBS, 1999.

Host and narrator, *The Incurable Collector,* syndicated, 2001.

Peter Brennan, *Happy Family,* NBC, 2003–2004.

Carl Sack, *Boston Legal,* ABC, 2007–2008.

Television Appearances; Movies:

Leading man, *Stunts Unlimited,* ABC, 1980.

Army officer, *The Last Ninja,* ABC, 1983.

Douglas Forbes, *Convicted,* ABC, 1986.

Gus, *Hot Paint,* CBS, 1988.

Brock "Bo" Arner, *One Special Victory* (also known as *Another Side of Winning* and *Good Enough to Win*), NBC, 1991.

Michael Lane, *The Defenders: Payback,* Showtime, 1997.

Walter, *Walter and Henry,* Showtime, 2001.

Gavin Corbett, *Till Dad Do Us Part,* Fox Family, 2001.

Patrick Korda, *Recipe for Disaster,* PAX, 2002.

Jack Landry, *Wedding Daze,* Hallmark Channel, 2004.

Mike McBride, *McBride: The Chameleon Murder,* Hallmark Channel, 2005.

Mike McBride, *McBride: Murder Past Midnight,* Hallmark Channel, 2005.

Mike McBride, *McBride: It's Murder, Madam,* Hallmark Channel, 2005.

Mike McBride, *McBride: The Doctor Is Out … Really Out,* Hallmark Channel, 2005.

Mike McBride, *McBride: Tune In for Murder,* Hallmark Channel, 2005.

Mike McBride, *McBride: Anybody Here Murder Marty?,* Hallmark Channel, 2005.

Mike McBride, *McBride: Requiem,* Hallmark Channel, 2006.

Mike McBride, *McBride: Murder at the Mission,* Hallmark Channel, 2006.

Mike McBride, *McBride: Fallen Idol,* Hallmark Channel, 2006.

Mike McBride, *McBride: Semper Fi,* Hallmark Channel, 2007.

Mike McBride, *McBride: Dogged,* Hallmark Channel, 2007.

Television Appearances; Miniseries:

Arthur Williams, *Bare Essence,* CBS, 1982.

Tony Lewis, *The 10th Kingdom,* NBC, 2000.

Bud McGrath, *The Storm,* NBC, 2009.

Television Appearances; Specials:

(Uncredited) Rocky the cigarette girl, *The Rodney Dangerfield Show: It's Not Easy Bein' Me,* 1982.

Hello Sucker! (also known as *Harry Anderson's "Hello Sucker!"*), Showtime, 1986.

Skip Distance, "The Rec Room," *American Film Institute Comedy Special* (also known as *NBC Presents the AFI Comedy Special*), NBC, 1987.

Host, "The 11th Annual Young Comedians Show," *On Location,* HBO, 1987.

Secrets Men Never Share, NBC, 1988.

Host, *Jackie Gleason: The Great One* (also known as *How Sweet It Is: A Wake for Jackie Gleason*), CBS, 1988.

Host, *Fifty Years of Television: A Golden Celebration,* CBS, 1989.

Comic Relief III, HBO, 1989.

Night of 100 Stars III, NBC, 1990.

Comic Relief IV, HBO, 1991.

Comic Relief VI, HBO, 1994.

The Tony Bennett Special: Here's to the Ladies: A Concert of Hope (also known as *Tony Bennett: Here's to the Ladies, a Concert of Hope*), CBS, 1995.

Star Trek: 30 Years and Beyond, UPN, 1996.

Host, *Lost in Space Forever,* 1998.

The Making of "Kill Your Darlings," 2006.

Television Appearances; Pilots:

Second Lieutenant Bob Anderson, *Baa Baa, Black Sheep* (also known as *Flying Misfits*), 1976.

Lieutenant Jackson MacCalvey, *The 416th,* CBS, 1979.

John Hemingway, *The John Larroquette Show* (also known as *Larroquette*), NBC, 1993.

Dr. Fred Biskin, *The Heart Department,* CBS, 2001.

Brandon Corsair, *Corsairs,* 2002.

Peter Bloom, *Happy Family,* NBC, 2003.

Martin Gold, *Pleading Guilty,* Fox, 2010.

Television Appearances; Episodic:

Murray Steinberg, "Steinberg and Son," *Sanford and Son,* 1975.

Bellboy, "The Adventure of the Pharaoh's Curse," *Ellery Queen,* 1975.

Sailor, "How Cruel the Frost, How Bright the Stars," *Kojak,* CBS, 1975.

Sailor, "Winner Takes Nothing," *Kojak,* CBS, 1975.

"Joseph in Egypt," *Greatest Heroes of the Bible,* 1978.

A cop, "Jack Moves Out," *Three's Company,* ABC, 1979.

Valery, "The Inventor/On the Other Side," *Fantasy Island,* ABC, 1979.

Baba Hope, "Alienation," *Mork & Mindy,* 1981.

"Dick Doesn't Live Here Anymore," *9 to 5* (also known as *Nine to Five*), ABC, 1982.

"Lover Come Back," *Cassie & Co.,* 1982.

Phillip Colton, "Hit and Run," *Dallas,* 1982.

Phillip Colton, "The Ewing Touch," *Dallas,* 1982.

Nathan Fitts, "Breath of Steele," *Remington Steele,* NBC, 1984.

Guest host, *Saturday Night Live* (also known as *SNL*), NBC, 1987, 1988.

Himself, *Madman of the People,* NBC, 1994.

Grayson Delamorte, "Health Hath No Fury," *Dave's World,* CBS, 1995.

Lionel Tribbey, "And It's Surely to Their Credit," *The West Wing* (also known as *The White House*), NBC, 2000.

Chef Gerard, "Dinner Date with Death," *Kitchen Confidential,* Fox, 2005.

Benjamin Lockwood, "Joey and the Spanking," *Joey,* NBC, 2005.

Benjamin Lockwood, "Joey and the ESL," *Joey,* NBC, 2005.

Gabriel Wozniak, "Son of Coma Guy," *House M.D.* (also known as *Dr. House* and *House*), Fox, 2006.

(Uncredited) Himself, "S.O.B.s," *Arrested Development,* Fox, 2006.

(In archive footage) Assistant District Attorney Dan Fielding, *La tele de tu vida,* 2007.

Voice of Mirror Master, "A Mirror Darkly," *The Batman,* The CW, 2007.

Voice of Mirror Master, "Lost Heroes: Part One," *The Batman,* The CW, 2008.

Roan Montgomery, "Chuck versus the Seduction," *Chuck,* NBC, 2008.

(In archive footage) Carl Sack, *The O'Reilly Factor,* Fox News Channel, 2008.

Randall Carver, "Anchor," *Law & Order: Special Victims Unit* (also known as *Law & Order: SVU* and *Special Victims Unit*), NBC, 2009.

Voice of Uncle Bob Webber, "The Lake Nose Monster," *Phineas and Ferb* (animated), The Disney Channel, 2009.

Voice of Uncle Bob Webber, "Just Passing Through/Candace's Big Day," *Phineas and Ferb* (animated), The Disney Channel, 2010.

Frank Beckerson, "Galentine's Day," *Parks and Recreation* (also known as *Parks and Rec*), NBC, 2010.

Donovan, "In the Red," *White Collar,* USA Network, 2010.

Chief Ted Carver, "Hide Sight," *CSI: NY,* CBS, 2010.

Chief Ted Carver, "Scared Stiff," *CSI: NY,* CBS, 2010.

Chief Ted Carver, "Justified," *CSI: NY,* CBS, 2010.

Roan Montgomery, "Chuck versus the Seduction Impossible," *Chuck,* NBC, 2011.

Also appeared as drunken man, *The Sonny and Cher Show.*

Television Appearances; Awards Presentations:

The ... Annual Emmy Awards, Fox, 1987, 1988, 1989.

Host, *The 9th Annual ACE Awards,* HBO, 1988.

The 47th Annual Golden Globe Awards, TBS, 1990.

Presenter, *The ... Annual Primetime Emmy Awards,* ABC, 1993, 1994.

Presenter, *The 8th Annual American Comedy Awards,* ABC, 1994.

Host, *The 11th Annual Soap Opera Awards,* NBC, 1995.

Host, *The 52nd Annual Golden Globe Awards,* TBS, 1995.

Presenter, *The Second Annual Screen Actors Guild Awards,* NBC, 1996.

Presenter, *The 50th Emmy Awards,* NBC, 1998.

Television Talk Show Guest Appearances; Episodic:

The Tonight Show Starring Johnny Carson, NBC, 1985, 1986, 1991.

The Barbour Report, ABC, 1986.

The Tonight Show with Jay Leno, NBC, 1992, 1993, 2003, 2007.

Late Night with Conan O'Brien, NBC, 1997.

The Daily Show with Jon Stewart (also known as *The Daily Show* and *A Daily Show with Jon Stewart Global Edition*), Comedy Central, 1999.

Last Call with Carson Daly, NBC, 2004.

The Late Late Show with Craig Kilborn (also known as *The Late Late Show*), CBS, 2004.

The Late Late Show with Craig Ferguson, CBS, multiple episodes, between 2005 and 2009.

Nyhetsmorgon, 2006.

The View, ABC, 2008.

Live with Regis and Kelly, syndicated, 2008.

Television Executive Producer; Series:

The John Larroquette Show (also known as *Larroquette*), NBC, 1993–96.

Payne, CBS, 1999.

Television Executive Producer; Movies:

One Special Victory (also known as *Another Side of Winning* and *Good Enough to Win*), NBC, 1991.

Television Director; Movies:

McBride: The Doctor Is Out ... Really Out, Hallmark Channel, 2005.

McBride: Murder at the Mission, Hallmark Channel, 2006.

McBride: Fallen Idol, Hallmark Channel, 2006.

McBride: Semper Fi, Hallmark Channel, 2007.

McBride: Dogged, Hallmark Channel, 2007.

Television Director; Episodic:

"Leon, We Hardly Knew Ye," *Night Court,* NBC, 1986.

"New Year's Leave," *Night Court,* NBC, 1986.

Film Appearances:

(Uncredited) Army soldier in war games, *Follow Me, Boys!,* 1966.

Narrator, *The Texas Chainsaw Massacre* (also known as *The Devil of Punishment* and *Stalking Leatherface*), Bryanston, 1974.

Television talk show host, *Heart Beat,* Warner Bros., 1979.

X–ray technician, *Altered States,* Warner Bros., 1980.

Captain Stillman, *Stripes,* Columbia, 1981.

Claude, *Green Ice,* ITC, 1981.

Bronte Judson, *Cat People,* Universal, 1982.

Klansman, "Back There," *Twilight Zone: The Movie,* Warner Bros., 1983.

Bob X. Cursion, *Hysterical,* Embassy, 1983.

Maltz, *Star Trek III: The Search for Spock,* Paramount, 1984.

Lieutenant Felix Foxglove, *Meatballs Part II* (also known as *Space Kid*), TriStar, 1984.

Billy Ace, *Choose Me,* Island Alive, 1984.

Don Moore, *Summer Rental,* Paramount, 1985.

David Bedford, *Blind Date* (also known as *Blake Edwards' "Blind Date"*), TriStar, 1987.

Wills, *Second Sight,* Warner Bros., 1989.

Mark Bannister, *Madhouse,* Orion, 1990.

Dr. Albert Quince, *Tune In Tomorrow* (also known as *Aunt Julia and the Scriptwriter*), Cinecom, 1990.

(In director's cut only) Jerry Johnson, *JFK: The Director's Cut,* Warner Bros., 1991.

Lawrence Van Dough, *Richie Rich,* Warner Bros., 1995.

(Uncredited) Slasher, *Tales from the Crypt Presents: Demon Knight* (also known as *Tales from the Crypt: Demon Knight*), Universal, 1995.

Maury Manning, *Isn't She Great,* Universal, 1999.

Narrator, *The Texas Chainsaw Massacre* (also known as *Texas Chainsaw*), New Line Cinema, 2003.

Mayor Harold Herman, *Beethoven's 5th* (also known as *Beethoven's 5th: Big Paw*), Universal, 2003.

Commentator, *Homeless in America* (short documentary), Wiseau–Films, 2004.

Dr. Bangley, *Kill Your Darlings,* 2006, Peace Arch Releasing, 2008.

(Uncredited) Narrator, *The Texas Chainsaw Massacre: The Beginning* (also known as *Texas Chainsaw: Beginning*), New Line Cinema, 2006.

Vaughn Smallhouse, *Southland Tales,* Destination Films/Samuel Goldwyn, 2007.

The interviewer, *The Rapture of the Athlete Assumed into Heaven,* Parallax Group, 2007.

Voice of Tomar Re, *Green Lantern: First Flight* (animated), Warner Home Video, 2009.

Commander Jenkins, *Sudden Death!* (short film), 2010.

Stage Appearances:

Endgame, Los Angeles, 1984.

Happy Jack, Los Angeles, 1989.

Casimir, *Aristocrats,* Center Theatre Group, Mark Taper Forum, Los Angeles, 1989–90.

Night of 100 Stars III, Radio City Music Hall, New York City, 1990.

Oscar, *Oscar and Felix: A New Look at the Odd Couple,* Geffen Playhouse, Westwood, CA, 2002.

Oliver Parker!, StageFARM, Cherry Lane Theatre, New York City, 2010.

Also appeared as Reverend Hale, *The Crucible,* and in *Enter Laughing,* both Colony Company Theatre, Los Angeles.

RECORDINGS

Videos:

The 10th Kingdom: The Making of an Epic, 2000.

It's a Dog's Life: Behind the Scenes and Cast Interviews "Beethoven's 5th," Universal Studios Home Video, 2003.

Stars and Stripes 1, Columbia TriStar Home Video, 2004.

Stars and Stripes 2, Columbia TriStar Home Video, 2004.

Behind the Story: Green Lantern—First Fight, Warner Bros., 2009.

OTHER SOURCES

Books:

Contemporary Newsmakers, 1986, Issue Cumulation, Gale, 1987.

Periodicals:

Bibliography, August, 1998, pp. 28–33.

Entertainment Weekly, September 28, 2007, p. 97.

Playboy, April, 1990, pp. 104–05, 164–66.

LEE–POTTS, Andrew
    See POTTS, Andrew Lee

LEHMAN, Kristin 1972–
    (Kristen Lehman)

PERSONAL

Born May 3, 1972, in Toronto, Ontario, Canada. *Education:* Studied at Gastown Actor's Studio, (Canadian) Royal Academy of Dance, and Canadian Dance World Studio.

Addresses: *Agent*—Joe Vance, Domain, 9229 Sunset Blvd., Suite 710, Los Angeles, CA 90069. *Manager*—Perry Zimel, Oscars Abrams Zimel and Associates, 438 Queen St. E., Toronto, Ontario M5A 1T4, Canada.

Career: Actress. Harbour Dance Center, studio member; Port Moody Players, dance choreographer.

Awards, Honors: Gemini Award nomination, best guest actress in a dramatic series, Academy of Canadian Cinema and Television, 2002, for *Andromeda.*

CREDITS

Television Appearances; Series:

Jordan McGuire, a recurring role, *Kung Fu: The Legend Continues,* syndicated, 1996.

Kristin Adams, *Poltergeist: The Legacy,* Showtime, 1998–99.

Dr. Sidney MacMillan, *Strange World,* Sci–Fi Channel, 2002.

Dr. Lily Reddicker, *Judging Amy,* CBS, 2002–2003.

Lee May Bristol, *Century City,* CBS, 2004.

Miami/Ellen, *Tilt,* ESPN, 2005.

Francesca, *G–Spot,* The Movie Network, 2005.

Detective Danielle Carter, *Killer Instinct,* Fox, 2005–2006.

Corinna Wiles, *Drive,* Fox, 2007.

Host of the series *Come On In,* Simon Fraser University.

Television Appearances; Movies:

Chana, *Toe Tags,* 1996.

Tina, *Ed McBain's 87th Precinct: Ice,* NBC, 1996.

Shannon Blackwell, *Verdict in Blood,* CTV, 2001.

Angela, *Rapid Fire,* USA Network, 2005.

Debra, *Burnt Toast,* 2005.

Marina, *Playing House,* CTV, 2006.

Television Appearances; Miniseries:

Ann Foster, *The Gathering,* Lifetime, 2007.

Television Appearances; Pilots:

Katiya, "F/X: The Illusion" (premiere episode), *F/X: The Series,* syndicated, 1996.

Dr. Sidney MacMillan, *Strange World,* 1999.

Lee May, *Century City,* CBS, 2004.

Susan Keever, *Damages,* Fox, 2006.

Caroline Garrison, *Backyards & Bullets* (also known as *The Watch*), NBC, 2007.

Gwen Eaton, *The Killing,* AMC, 2010.

Television Appearances; Episodic:

Cynthia, "Off Broadway: Parts 1 & 2," *The Commish,* ABC, 1995.

Urs, "The Black Buddha: Part 2," *Forever Knight,* USA Network and syndicated, 1995.

Urs, "Hearts of Darkness," *Forever Knight,* USA Network and syndicated, 1995.

Urs, "Trophy Girl," *Forever Knight,* USA Network and syndicated, 1995.

Janet Marshall, "Falling Star," *The Outer Limits* (also known as *The New Outer Limits*), Showtime, 1996.

Rhonda, "Flashback," *Due South* (also known as *Direction: Sud*), CBS, 1996.

Urs, "Ashes to Ashes," *Forever Knight,* USA Network and syndicated, 1996.

Alexa Lundqist, "Art of Death," *Once a Thief* (also known as *John Woo's "Once a Thief"*), CTV, 1997.

Cynthia Clarkson, "Resurrection," *Earth: Final Conflict* (also known as *EFC* and *Gene Roddenberry's "Earth: Final Conflict"*), syndicated, 1997.

Jackie Kinley/Julie Bright, "The Undead, Stalker Moon," *PSI Factor: Chronicles of the Paranormal,* syndicated, 1997.

Katya Rubinov, "Dead Man's Switch," *The Outer Limits* (also known as *The New Outer Limits*), Showtime, 1997.

Esther Nairn/Invisigoth, "Kill Switch," *The X–Files,* Fox, 1998.

Larissa, "Stasis," *The Outer Limits* (also known as *The New Outer Limits*), Showtime, 2000.

Miss Eastwood, "Go P.D.A.," *Go Fish,* NBC, 2001.

Miss Eastwood, "Blackout," *Go Fish,* NBC, 2001.

Miss Eastwood, "The Break–up," *Go Fish,* NBC, 2001.

Miss Eastwood, "Senioritis," *Go Fish,* NBC, 2001.

Avery Swanson, "Blackout," *Felicity,* The WB, 2001.

Avery Swanson, "The Break–Up Kit," *Felicity,* The WB, 2001.

Avery Swanson, "Girlfight," *Felicity,* The WB, 2001.

Avery Swanson, "Senioritis," *Felicity,* The WB, 2001.

Lorelle Palmer, "Time to Time," *The Outer Limits* (also known as *The New Outer Limits*), Showtime, 2001.

Becca Niles, "Dead Man's Eyes," *The Twilight Zone,* UPN, 2002.

Diane Robertson, "Manhunt," *UC: Undercover,* NBC, 2002.

Molly Noguchi, "Lava and Rockets," *Andromeda* (also known as *Gene Roddenberry's "Andromeda"*), Sci–Fi Channel, 2002.

Molly Noguchi, "Waking the Tyrant's Device," *Andromeda* (also known as *Gene Roddenberry's "Andromeda"*), Sci–Fi Channel, 2003.

Serena Quinn, "Going for the Juggler," *Kevin Hill,* UPN, 2004.

Honeypot, "Buttons on a Hot Tin Roof," *Puppets Who Kill,* Comedy Central, 2005.

Jane Phillips, "Rendezvous," *Prison Break,* Fox, 2006.

Jane Phillips, "Bolshoi Booze," *Prison Break,* Fox, 2006.

District Attorney Allyson Russo, "Run," *Human Target,* Fox, 2010.

Film Appearances:

Florence, *Alaska,* Columbia, 1996.

Kathleen Strauss, *Bleeders* (also known as *The Descendant* and *Hemoglobin*), A–Pix Entertainment, 1997.

Scope/steps woman, *Bliss* (also known as *Hard Technique*), Sony Pictures Entertainment, 1997.

Keiran, *Dog Park,* New Line Cinema, 1999.

Sarah Billings, *Dinner at Fred's,* Imperial Entertainment/PM Entertainment Group, 1999.

Francesca Chidduck, *The Way of the Gun,* Artisan Entertainment, 2000.

Shirah (in director's cut only), *The Chronicles of Riddick* (also known as *The Chronicles of Riddick: The Director's Cut*), Universal, 2004.

(As Kristen Lehman) Rachel, *Lie with Me,* THINKFilm, 2005.

Cindy Breckinridge, *The Sentinel,* Twentieth Century–Fox, 2006.

Stage Appearances:

Appeared as Sarah, *A Celebration;* as Ellie, *Leader of the Pack: The Ellie Greenwich Story;* as Cosette, *Les*

Miserables; as Jennifer Todd, *Shrunken Heads;* as Doris, *We Three, You and I;* and in *A Midsummer Night's Dream.*

RECORDINGS

Videos:
Voice of Shirah, *The Chronicles of Riddick: Escape from Butcher Bay* (video game), Vivendi Universal Games, 2004.

LEMKIN, Jonathan

PERSONAL

Raised in Ohio; son of a toy designer and an educator; married Kiersten Warren (an actress; divorced, 2005); children: Misti Traya. *Education:* Harvard University, graduated (magna cum laude); attended O'Neill National Theatre Institute at Eugene O'Neill Theatre Center, Waterford, CT, and American Filmmaking Institute, Los Angeles.

Addresses: *Agent*—WME Entertainment, 9601 Wilshire Blvd., 3rd Floor, Beverly Hills, Ca 90210.

Career: Writer, story editor, producer, and director.

Awards, Honors: Saturn Award nomination (with Tony Gilroy), best writer, Academy of Science Fiction, Fantasy, and Horror Films, 1998, for *The Devil's Advocate.*

CREDITS

Television Work; Movies:
Coproducer, *Exile,* NBC, 1990.

Television Work; Series:
Story editor, *21 Jump Street,* Fox, 1987–88.

Television Work; Episodic:
Story editor, "A Case of Klapp," *Hill Street Blues,* NBC, 1986.
Director, "Whattya Wanna Do Tonight?," *Glory Days,* Fox, 1990.

Film Appearances:
Tales from the Script (documentary), First Run Features, 2009.

RECORDINGS

Videos:
Survival of the Fittest: The Making of "Shooter," Paramount Home Entertainment, 2007.
More Tales from the Script, First Run Features, 2010.

WRITINGS

Screenplays:
The Devil's Advocate (also known as *Diabolos*), Warner Bros., 1997.
Red Planet, Warner Bros., 2000.
Shooter, Paramount, 2007.

Television Series:
21 Jump Street, Fox, between 1987–88.

Television Movies:
Exile, NBC, 1990.

Television Episodes:
"Meeting Mr. Pony" (also based on a story by Lemkin), *Beverly Hills, 90210* (also known as *Class of Beverly Hills*), Fox, 1992.

Other credits include *Moonlighting.*

ADAPTATIONS

The screenplay for *Lethal Weapon 4* (also known as *Lethal 4*), released by Warner Bros. in 1998, was based on a story by Lemkin. Some episodes of the television series *Hill Street Blues* were also based on stories by Lemkin.

LEONARD, Joshua 1975–
(Josh Leonard)

PERSONAL

Full name, Joshua Granville Leonard; born June 17, 1975, in Houston, TX; son of Robert (a professor of theatre and operator of a children's theatre) and Joann (an operator of a children's theatre) Leonard. *Education:* Attended Pennsylvania State University.

Addresses: *Agent*—Veronica Gabriel, United Talent Agency, 9560 Wilshire Blvd., Suite 500, Beverly Hills,

CA 90212. *Manager*—Laina Cohn, Laina Cohn Management, 15066 Sutton St., Sherman Oaks, CA 91403. *Publicist*—Much and House Public Relations, 8075 West Third St., Suite 500, Los Angeles, CA 90048.

Career: Actor, director, and writer. Worked as a camera operator and videographer; *Black Book,* former photographer; worked as a teacher in Puebla, Mexico, with an international youth service organization; also worked as a band promoter, gardener, and caretaker.

Awards, Honors: Blockbuster Entertainment Award nomination, Internet poll, favorite newcomer, 2000, for *The Blair Witch Project;* Jury Award, best live–action film under fifteen minutes, Palm Springs International ShortFest, 2005, for *The Youth in Us;* Gijon International Film Festival Award (with Mark Duplass), best actor, 2009, for *Humpday.*

CREDITS

Film Appearances:
Joshua "Josh" Leonard, *The Blair Witch Project,* Artisan Entertainment, 1999.
Staley, *The Blur of Insanity,* Blur Productions, 1999.
Adam, *In the Weeds,* Miramax, 2000.
(In archive footage) *Book of Shadows: Blair Witch 2* (also known as *Book of Shadows: Blair Witch Project 2, BWP2,* and *BW2*), Artisan Entertainment, 2000.
Timothy Douglas Isert, *Men of Honor* (also known as *The Diver*), Twentieth Century–Fox, 2000.
Jay, *Mission,* 2001.
Danny Graham, *Cubbyhouse* (also known as *The Cubby House* and *Hellion: The Devil's Playground*), Spartan Home Entertainment, 2001.
Ghost, *Dregs of Society,* 2001.
(As Josh Leonard) Punchy, *Deuces Wild,* Metro–Goldwyn–Mayer, 2002.
Bill Buehl, *Two Days,* American World Pictures, 2003.
Nick, *Larceny,* Empire Pictures, 2004.
Rick Becker, *Scorched,* Twentieth Century–Fox Home Entertainment, 2004.
Clark Stevens, *Madhouse* (also known as *Mad Cannibal*), Lions Gate Films, 2004.
Malcolm, *A Year and a Day,* Minetta Lane Productions, 2005.
Justin Forrester, *The Shaggy Dog,* Buena Vista, 2006.
Ainsley, *Hatcher,* Anchor Bay Entertainment, 2007.
First partygoer, *The Death and Life of Bobby Z* (also known as *Bobby Z* and *Let's Kill Bobby Z*), Sony Pictures Home Entertainment, 2007.
Tattoo artist, *The Strand,* Gearhead Pictures, 2007.
Darryl, *Simple Things* (also known as *Country Remedy*), Universal Studios Home Video, 2008.
Isaac's dad, *Quid Pro Quo,* Magnolia Pictures, 2008.

Ian, *Expecting Love* (also known as *Mala wielka milosc*), CrossCut Films, 2008.
Michael, *20 Years After,* MTI Home Video, 2008.
Bellhop, *Prom Night* (also known as *TV Dinner*), Screen Gems, 2008.
Pothead, *Dead in Love,* Wild Range Productions, 2009.
Andrew, *Humpday,* Magnolia Pictures, 2009.
Dinner party gust, *The Freebie,* Phase 4 Films, 2010.
J. T. Franks, *Bitter Feast,* Dark Sky Films, 2010.
Wyatt, *Bold Native,* Open Road Films, 2010.
Lonnie, *The Lie,* Perception Media, 2010.

Film Director:
The Youth in Us (short film), Apollo Cinema, 2005.
Codirector, *Beautiful Losers,* Sidetrack Films, 2008.
The Lie, Perception Media, 2010.

Television Appearances; Series:
Ian, *Expecting Love,* 2009.

Television Appearances; Movies:
Jason, *Sacrifice,* HBO, 2000.
Todd, *Things Behind the Sun,* Showtime, 2001.
Mark Biello, *Live from Baghdad,* HBO, 2002.
Robby Love, *Shooting Livien,* Showtime, 2005.

Television Appearances; Specials:
Presenter, *MTV Video Music Awards,* MTV, 1999.
The Curse of the Blair Witch, Sci–Fi Channel, 1999.
Presenter, *The 1999 MTV Video Music Awards,* MTV, 1999.
The Burkittsville 7, Sci–Fi Channel, 2000.
(As Josh Leonard) *The Perfect Scary Movie,* Channel 4, 2005.

Television Appearances; Pilots:
Taxi driver, *Destiny,* CBS, 2001.

Television Appearances; Episodic:
"The Making of 'Men of Honor,'" *HBO First Look,* HBO, 2000.
Andy, "Gettysburg," *The Outer Limits* (also known as *The New Outer Limits*), Showtime, 2000.
Todd Garvin, "Divorce, Detective Style," *NYPD Blue* (also known as *N.Y.P.D.*), ABC, 2004.
Matt Paulson, "A Man a Mile," *CSI: NY,* CBS, 2004.
Jim Markham, "Blood in the Water," *CSI: Miami,* CBS, 2005.
Jim Markham, "48 Hours to Life," *CSI: Miami,* CBS, 2005.
Jim Markham, "Shattered," *CSI: Miami,* CBS, 2005.
Roy Mitchell, "Guns and Roses," *Numb3rs* (also known as *Num3ers*), CBS, 2006.
Nate Gibbons, "The Headless Witch in the Woods," *Bones,* Fox, 2006.

Pierce, "The Rita Flower or the Indelible Stench," *Hung,* HBO, 2009.

Pierce, "Thith Ith a Prothetic or You Cum Just Right," *Hung,* HBO, 2009.

Pierce, "This Is America or Fifty Bucks," *Hung,* HBO, 2009.

Up Close with Carrie Keagan, ABC, 2009.

Ricky, "The Truth Hurts," *United States of Tara,* Showtime, 2010.

Stage Appearances:
Life with Father, c. 1981.

RECORDINGS

Videos:
Joshua "Josh" Leonard, *Sticks and Stones: Investigating the Blair Witch* (also known as *An Exploration of the Blair Witch Legend*), 1999.

Humpday: Behind the Scenes, Magnolia Home Entertainment, 2009.

Video Games:
Voices of Coyne and Two Tongue, *The Chronicles of Riddick: Escape from Butcher Bay,* Vivendi Universal Games, 2004.

Voice of Tyler, *Fight Club,* Vivendi Universal Games, 2004.

WRITINGS

Screenplays:
The Lie, Perception Media, 2010.

ADAPTATIONS

The 2005 short film *The Youth in Us* was based on a story by Leonard.

OTHER SOURCES

Periodicals:
People Weekly, August 23, 1999.

LISARAYE, 1966–
   (Lisa Ray McCoy, LisaRaye McCoy, Lisaraye McCoy, Lisa Raye)

PERSONAL

Full name, LisaRaye McCoy–Misick; original name, LisaRaye McCoy; born September 23, 1966, in Chicago, IL; father a hotel manager; mother a hotel manager and model; half–sister of Da Brat (a rap recording artist); according to some sources, married Tony Martin (marriage ended); married Michael E. Misick (former chief minister of Turks and Caicos), April 8, 2006 (separated, 2008); children: (previous relationship) Kaienia. *Education:* Attended Eastern Illinois University.

Addresses: *Manager*—Releve Entertainment, 8200 Wilshire Blvd., Suite 200, Los Angeles, CA 90048.

Career: Actress. Worked as a model; appeared in a commercial for Coors Light beer, 1999.

Awards, Honors: Image Award nomination, outstanding supporting actress in a comedy series, National Association for the Advancement of Colored People, 2007, for *All of Us.*

CREDITS

Film Appearances:
(As Lisa Ray McCoy) *Reasons,* 1996.

(As Lisa Raye) Diamond, *The Players Club,* New Line Cinema, 1998.

(As Lisaraye) Lisa, *The Wood,* Paramount, 1999.

The Cheapest Movie Ever Made, 2000.

Date from Hell (short film), 2001.

Lisa, *All About You,* Urbanworks, 2001.

Belinda/Star, *Go for Broke,* Artisan Entertainment, 2002.

Frances Shepard, *Civil Brand,* Lions Gate Films, 2003.

Marie Toursaant, *Love Chronicles,* Melee Entertainment, 2003.

Maria, *Gang of Roses,* DEJ Productions, 2003.

(As Lisaraye McCoy) Rochelle, *Beauty Shop,* Metro–Goldwyn–Mayer, 2005.

Envy, Fatboy Films, 2005.

Kiki, *Contradictions of the Heart,* Bennett Five Entertainment/Donlyn Productions, 2009.

Video Girl, Dan Garcia Productions/Datari Turner Productions/Most Wanted Films, 2010.

Television Appearances; Series:
Host, *Source: All Access,* syndicated, 2000.

Neesee James, *All of Us,* UPN, 2003–2007.

Herself, *Diamond Life,* 2005.

LisaRaye: The Real McCoy, 2010.

Television Appearances; Movies:
Victoria, *Rhapsody,* Black Entertainment Television, 2000.

(As LisaRaye McCoy) Voice of choreographer, *The Proud Family Movie* (animated), The Disney Channel, 2005.

Television Appearances; Specials:
(As Lisa Raye) Host, *Acapulco Black Film Festival,* Black Starz!, 2000.
All Shades of Fine: 25 Hottest Women of the Past 25 Years, Black Entertainment Television, 2005.
11–04–08: The Day of Change, Starz!, 2009.
(As LisaRaye McCoy) *An Evening of Stars: Tribute to Patti LaBelle,* 2009.
Top 12 Moments of the BET Awards, Black Entertainment Television, 2009.
Way Black When, TV One, 2010.

Television Appearances; Pilots:
Neesee James, *All of Us,* UPN, 2003.
Keisha, *Single Ladies,* VH1, 2010.

Television Appearances; Episodic:
(As Lisa Raye) Delivery woman, "Saint Marion," *In the House,* UPN, 1997.
(As Lisa Raye) Delivery woman, "Abstinence Makes the Heart Grow Fonder," *In the House,* UPN, 1997.
(As Lisa Raye) "An Affair to Forget," *The Parent 'Hood,* The WB, 1998.
"Video Girls," *Teen Summit,* Black Entertainment Television, 2002.
"Mali Finn Casts 9 New Actors," *The It Factor: Los Angeles,* Bravo, 2003.
The Sharon Osbourne Show (also known as *Sharon*), syndicated, 2004.
"Three 'R's to Protecting Stars," *Faking It,* 2004.
Big Time (also known as *Steve Harvey's Big Time* and *Steve Harvey's Big Time Challenge*), The WB, 2005.
106 & Park Top 10 Live (also known as *106 & Park*), Black Entertainment Television, 2005.
"Meals in Minutes," *Turn Up the Heat with G. Garvin,* TV One, 2005.
Hollywood Trials, 2008.
Entertainment Tonight (also known as *E.T.* and *This Week in Entertainment*), syndicated, 2008.
The Wendy Williams Show, 2010.
The Brian McKnight Show, 2010.

Appeared as a judge, *Coming to the Stage,* Black Entertainment Television.

Television Appearances; Awards Presentations:
The 1999 Source Hip–Hop Music Awards, UPN, 1999.
2003 Vibe Awards: Beats, Style, Flavor, UPN, 2003.
BET Comedy Awards, Black Entertainment Television, 2003, 2004.
(As LisaRaye) *The Second Annual Vibe Awards,* UPN, 2004.
BET Awards, Black Entertainment Television, 2005.
Host, *... Annual Trumpet Awards,* TV One, 2006, 2010.
Presenter, *38th NAACP Image Awards,* Fox, 2007.
The 6th Annual TV Land Awards, TV Land, 2008.

RECORDINGS

Videos:
(In archive footage) Diane "Diamond" Armstrong, *Ultimate Fights from the Movies,* Flixmix, 2002.

Appeared in the music videos "Never Be the Same" by Ghost Face Killah, 2002, "Number One Spot" by Ludacris, and "Toss It Up" by 2pac.

OTHER SOURCES

Books:
Contemporary Black Biography, Volume 27, Gale, 2001.

Periodicals:
Black Men, October, 2000, p. 43; December, 2001, pp. 26–35.
Jet, August 9, 1999, p. 38.
Just for Black Men, January, 1999, pp. 32–35; September, 1999, pp. 38–40.

LOGAN, Paul 1973–
(Paul Stone)

PERSONAL

Born October 15, 1973, in NJ; raised in Valley Cottage, NY. *Education:* Purchase College State University of New York, B.A., biochemistry; attended the Los Angeles College of Chiropractic; studied acting with Brian Reise and others; also studied martial arts.

Addresses: *Agent*—Gar Lester Agency, 4130 Cahuenga Blvd., Suite 108, Universal City, CA 91602.

Career: Actor.

Member: Screen Actors Guild, American Federation of Television and Radio Artists.

Awards, Honors: Black belt in Okinawa goju–ryu karate.

CREDITS

Film Appearances:
Greko, *Blazing Force,* Wildcat Entertainment/Maxim Media International, 1996.

(Uncredited) Terrorist, *American Tigers,* Gun for Hire Films, 1996.

Nicky, *Killers* (also known as *Killer Instinct*), The Asylum, 1997.

Doc Austin, *L.E.T.H.A.L. Ladies: Return to Savage Beach* (also known as *Return to Savage Beach*), Malibu Bay Films, 1998.

Tom, *Club Wild Side,* Mystique Films, 1998.

Joe, *Stripper Wives,* 1999.

(As Paul Stone) Carl, *Night Calls: The Movie, Part 2* (also known as *Lilo*), Cameo Films/Playboy Home Video, 2000.

Jack Howard, *The Seduction of Maxine* (also known as *The Stalker*), 2000.

James, *Passion's Peak* (also known as *Passions Extremes*), Indigo Entertainment, 2000.

Rick, *House of Love,* Indigo Entertainment, 2000.

Son, *The Independent* (also known as *King of B–Movies*), Arrow Entertainment/New City Releasing, 2000.

Kevin, *Savage Season,* 2001.

Sam Slater, *The Ultimate Game,* Amsell Entertainment/Melrose Films, 2001.

The Diamone, *Radius* (short film), K2 Films/Southwest Films, 2004.

Jesse, *The Eliminator* (also known as *Varley's Game*), Artist View Entertainment, 2004.

Dracula, *Way of the Vampire* (also known as *Bram Stoker's "Way of the Vampire," Van Helsing's "Way of the Vampire," Van Helsing vs. Dracula,* and *Way of the Vampire*), The Asylum, 2005.

Frix, *The Vault,* Tritan Northstar Entertainment, 2005.

Josef, *Crash Landing,* Cinetel Films, 2005.

SWAT team leader, *Freezerburn,* The Brookturn Co., 2005.

Tom, *Crippled Creek,* 2005.

Cannibal Taboo, Cravitas Ventures, 2006.

Jake Adams, *Fall Guy: The John Stewart Story* (also known as *High Octane*), InterDimensional Films/York Entertainment, 2007.

Pete, *White Air,* PorchLight Entertainment/Family Room Entertainment, 2007.

Mack, *The Last Bad Neighborhood,* NCK Films, 2008.

Mercenary, *Lost in the Woods,* 2008, New Horizons Home Video, 2009.

Alien king, *Aliens on Crack,* 2009.

Milo, *Vampire in Vegas,* Nu Image Films, 2009.

TR–4, *The Terminators,* The Asylum, 2009.

Damian, *Ballistica,* 2010.

Tom, *#1 Cheerleader Camp,* The Asylum, 2010.

Some sources cite appearances in other films.

Film Work:

Associate producer, *The Eliminator* (also known as *Varley's Game*), Artist View Entertainment, 2004.

Stunt performer, *Titanic II,* The Asylum Home Entertainment, 2010.

Television Appearances; Series:

Glen Reiber, *Days of Our Lives* (also known as *Cruise of Deception: Days of Our Lives, Days, DOOL, Tropical Temptation, Tropical Temptation: Days of Our Lives, Des jours et des vies, Horton–sagaen, I gode og onde dager, Los dias de nuestras vidas, Meres agapis, Paeivien viemaeae, Vaara baesta aar, Zeit der Sehnsucht,* and *Zile din viata noastra*), NBC, 2001–2002.

Television Appearances; Movies:

Drake, *The Curse of the Komodo,* Sci–Fi Channel, 2003.

Major Frank, *Komodo vs. Cobra* (also known as *Island of Beasts, Komodo versus Cobra, Komodo vs. King Cobra, KVC,* and *KVC: Komodo vs. Cobra*), 2005.

Saunders, *A.I. Assault* (also known as *Shockwave*), Sci–Fi Channel, 2006.

Major Boyd Grayson, *MegaFault,* Syfy, 2009.

Jason Fitch, *Mega Piranha* (also known as *Megapiranha*), Syfy, 2010.

Television Appearances; Episodic:

Jake, "Through an Open Window," *Erotic Confessions,* HBO, 1997.

Eric Sommers, "Fangs," *L.A. Heat* (also known as *Los Angeles Heat*), TNT, 1999.

Third dancer, "The Fool Monty," *Malcolm & Eddie,* UPN, 1999.

Brian, "A Most Dangerous Desire," *Thrills,* Cinemax, 2001.

Woody, "Carpe Noctem," *Angel* (also known as *Angel: The Series, Angel—Jaeger der Finsternis,* and *Skoteinos angelos*), The WB, 2001.

The soap actor, "The One Where Rachel Goes Back to Work," *Friends* (also known as *Across the Hall, Friends Like Us, Insomnia Cafe,* and *Six of One*), NBC, 2003.

Eli, "Five," *Smith* (also known as *Dossier Smith*), CBS, 2007.

Television Stunt Work; Movies:

Stunt coordinator, *MegaFault,* Syfy, 2009.

Stunt driver, *Mega Piranha* (also known as *Megapiranha*), Syfy, 2010.

Stage Appearances:

Appeared in stage productions, including appearances as Michael, *Key Exchange,* as Richard, *The Lion in Winter,* and as Danny, *Sexual Perversity in Chicago,* all Kaplan Theatre.

RECORDINGS

Videos:

Playboy: Freshman Class, Playboy Entertainment Group, 1998.

OTHER SOURCES

Electronic:
Paul Logan, http://www.paullogan.net, March 23, 2010.

LUNER, Jamie 1971–

PERSONAL

Full name, Jamie Michelle Luner; born May 12, 1971, in Palo Alto, CA; daughter of Stuart (a clothing sales representative) and Susan (an actress and manager) Luner. *Education:* Attended culinary school in Los Angeles. *Avocational Interests:* Cooking.

Addresses: *Agent*—Fortitude, 8619 Washington Blvd., Culver City, CA 90232. *Manager*—Martin Berneman, Precision Entertainment, 5820 Wilshire Blvd., Suite 200, Los Angeles, CA 90036.

Career: Actress. Appeared in numerous commercials, beginning as a young child. Drai's (French restaurant), worked as a chef, c. 1991.

Awards, Honors: Winner, competition for single monologues, Los Angeles Shakespeare Festival, 1986; Young Artist Award nomination (with others), best young ensemble in a television comedy, drama series, or special, 1989, for *Just the Ten of Us.*

CREDITS

Television Appearances; Series:
Cindy Lubbock, *Just the Ten of Us,* ABC, 1988–90.
Peyton Richards Massick, *Savannah,* The WB, 1996–97.
Lexi Sterling, *Melrose Place,* Fox, 1997–99.
Rachel Burke, *Profiler,* NBC, 1999–2000.
Senior Deputy Ryan Layne, a recurring role, *10–8: Officers on Duty* (also known as *10–8*), ABC, 2003–2004.
Liza Colby, *All My Children* (also known as *AMC*), ABC, 2009–10.

Television Appearances; Movies:
Diana Moffitt, *Moment of Truth: Why My Daughter?,* NBC, 1993.
Sabrina Masterson, *Confessions of a Sorority Girl* (also known as *Confessions of Sorority Girls*), Showtime, 1994.
Donna, *Moment of Truth: Cradle of Conspiracy* (also known as *Cradle of Conspiracy*), NBC, 1994.
Naomi Cohen, *Sacrifice,* HBO, 2000.

Dr, Savannah Bailey, *Threshold,* Sci–Fi Channel, 2003.
Diana Scott, *Blind Injustice,* Lifetime, 2005.
Sara Hansen, *Stranger in My Bed,* Lifetime, 2005.
Beth James (some sources cite role as Maggie), *The Suspect,* Lifetime, 2006.
Marianne Danforth/Annie Grayson, *The Perfect Marriage,* Lifetime, 2006.
Linda, *Nuclear Hurricane* (also known as *Atomic Hurricane*), 2007.
Kate Jansen, *Heat Wave,* 2009.
Sandra, *Trust,* Lifetime, 2009.

Television Appearances; Episodic:
Sheena Berkowitz, "Some Enchanted Evening," *Growing Pains,* ABC, 1987.
Cindy Lubbock, "How the West Was Won: Parts 1 & 2," *Growing Pains,* ABC, 1988.
Kara Daye, "Happy Halloween: Parts 1 & 2," *Growing Pains,* ABC, 1991.
Gerri, "Frat Chance," *Married ... with Children,* Fox, 1992.
(Uncredited) Tiffany Beamon, "Crumbling Systems," *Reasonable Doubts,* NBC, 1993.
Kimmy Marlowe, "The Last Laugh: Part 1," *Diagnosis Murder* (also known as *Dr. Mark Sloan*), CBS, 1994.
The Rosie O'Donnell Show, syndicated, 1997.
The Daily Show with Jon Stewart (also known as *The Daily Show* and *The Daily Show with Jon Stewart Global Edition*), Comedy Central, 1997.
The Martin Short Show, syndicated, 1999.
Rachel Burke, "Spin Doctor," *The Pretender,* NBC, 2000.
Jenny, "Drew and Kate Become Friends," *The Drew Carey Show,* ABC, 2000.
The Tonight Show with Jay Leno, NBC, 2000.
Dr. Candace Maguire, "Mind Reacher," *The Outer Limits* (also known as *The New Outer Limits*), Showtime, 2001.
Samantha Richardson, "Plus One," *That's Life,* CBS, 2001.
Samantha Richardson, "Idiots," *That's Life,* CBS, 2001.
Samantha Richardson, "Sex in the Suburbs," *That's Life,* CBS, 2001.
Nikki Olson, "Breathless," *CSI: Miami,* CBS, 2002.
Amanda Reed/Lieutenant Commander Hamilton Voss, "Dead Man Talking," *NCIS: Naval Criminal Investigative Service* (also known as *Navy NCIS: Naval Criminal Investigative Service* and *NCIS*), CBS, 2004.
Jodi, "Three's Company," *The War at Home,* Fox, 2006.
Elizabeth Rodriguez, "Lying Down with Dogs," *CSI: Crime Scene Investigation* (also known as *C.S.I.* and *CSI: Las Vegas*), CBS, 2007.

Television Appearances; Specials:
The 14th Annual Circus of the Stars, CBS, 1989.
Cohost, *The 24th International Emmy Awards,* 1996.
Beverly Hills High, E! Entertainment Television, 1997.

The Mod Squad: The E! True Hollywood Story, E! Entertainment Television, 2000.
Melrose Place: The E! True Hollywood Story, E! Entertainment Television, 2003.
101 Sexiest Celebrity Bodies, E! Entertainment Television, 2005.
The ... Annual Daytime Emmy Awards, The CW, 2009, 2010.

Television Appearances; Pilots:
Jennifer Grayson, *The Force,* The WB, 1999.

Film Appearances:
Mindy, *Tryst,* Suma, 1994.
Lootie, *The St. Tammany Miracle* (also known as *Heavenly Hoops*), Heartland Films, 1994.
Model, *Friends & Lovers* (also known as *Love and Testosterone*), Lions Gate Films, 1999.
Eldoran's girlfriend, *Warrior,* Imageworks, 2002.

Stage Appearances:
Susan, *Black & Bluestein,* Santa Monica Playhouse, Santa Monica, CA, 2007.
Apassionata von Climax, *L'il Abner* (musical), Freud Playhouse, Los Angeles, 2008.

Appeared in *Rise Up* and *White Woman,* both Young Playwrights Festival, Los Angeles.

OTHER SOURCES

Periodicals:
Entertainment Weekly, March 8, 1996, p. 51.
People Weekly, April 29, 1996, pp. 75–76.
Soap Opera Digest, April 13, 2009, p. 21; June 16, 2009, pp. 45–49.
TV Guide, April 13, 2009, p. 61.

M

MARINO, Ken 1968–

PERSONAL

Full name, Kenneth Joseph Marino; born December 19, 1968, in West Islip, NY; married Erica Oyama (an actress), 2005; children: one. *Education:* New York University, B.F.A.; also trained at Lee Strasberg Institute.

Addresses: *Agent*—David Boxerbaum, Agency for the Performing Arts, 405 South Beverly Dr., Beverly Hills, CA 90212. *Manager*—David Gardner, Principato/Young Management, 9465 Wilshire Blvd., Suite 880, Beverly Hills, CA 90212.

Career: Actor, writer, and producer. The State (comedy group; also known as The New Group and The State: Full–Frontal Comedy), cofounder and performer, beginning 1988.

CREDITS

Television Appearances; Series:
Member of ensemble, *You Wrote It, You Watch It,* MTV, 1992–94.
Member of ensemble, *The State,* MTV, 1993–95.
Steve, *Men Behaving Badly* (also known as *It's a Man's World*), NBC, 1997.
Professor David Wilder, a recurring role, *Dawson's Creek,* The WB, 2001–2002.
Andy, *Leap of Faith,* NBC, 2002.
Vinnie Van Lowe, a recurring role, *Veronica Mars,* UPN, 2005–2006, then The CW, 2006–2007.
Tony, *Reaper,* The CW, 2008–2009.
Ron Donald, *Party Down,* Starz!, 2009–10.

Television Appearances; Pilots:
Housebroken, The WB, 1997.
Smog, UPN, 1999.

Michael, *Welcome to the Jungle Gym,* CBS, 2006.
Out of Bounds, Comedy Central, 2007.
Greg Embry, *Outnumbered,* Fox, 2008.

Television Appearances; Movies:
Mark Lucas, *Falling in Love with the Girl Next Door,* Hallmark Channel, 2006.

Television Appearances; Episodic:
Bob Cabot, "Gobble, Gobble, Aggch!," *Boston Common,* NBC, 1996.
Big tipper, "The Deepest Cut," *The Single Guy,* NBC, 1996.
Dan Fuchs, "Bye Bye Love," *Spin City,* ABC, 1997.
Mike, "Viva Las Gordy," *Holding the Baby,* Fox, 1998.
Ben, "The Ultimatum," *Conrad Bloom,* NBC, 1998.
Voice of Tiphys, "Hercules and the Argonauts," *Hercules* (animated; also known as *Disney's "Hercules"*), ABC, 1998.
Kevin Michaels, "End Games," *The Practice,* ABC, 1999.
Todd West, "Truth and Consequences," *Nash Bridges,* CBS, 1999.
Sammy Coke Bottles, *Falcone,* CBS, 2000.
Wilson, "Expecting," *Angel* (also known as *Angel: The Series*), The WB, 2000.
Wayne, "Veronica Sets Josh Up," *Veronica's Closet,* NBC, 2000.
Mark, "Three's a Crowd, Six Is a Freak Show," *Will & Grace,* NBC, 2000.
Miles Lawton, "There's No Place Like Homo," *First Years,* NBC, 2001.
Bob Pratt (some sources cite Bob Price), "Fidelity," *Haunted,* UPN, 2002.
Reuben, "The Anniversary," *Do Over,* The WB, 2002.
Miles, "Sympathy for the Demon," *Charmed,* The WB, 2002.
Miles, "A Witch in Time," *Charmed,* The WB, 2002.
Frank, "Fireworks," *Reno 911!,* Comedy Central, 2003.
Anton McCarren, "Jokers and Fools," *Las Vegas,* NBC, 2003.

Kelly, "Coupling," *Rock Me, Baby,* UPN, 2003.

Kelly, "I Love You, You Don't Love Me," *Rock Me, Baby,* UPN, 2004.

Kelly, "Go, Otis! It's Your Birthday!," *Rock Me, Baby,* UPN, 2004.

Dr. Brad Turner, "The Hospital," *What I Like about You,* The WB, 2004.

Dr. Brad Turner, "The Interview," *What I Like about You,* The WB, 2004.

Dr. Brad Turner, "Rollin' in It," *What I Like about You,* The WB, 2004.

Lester Highsmith, "Mr. Monk Takes His Medicine," *Monk,* USA Network, 2004.

Detective Gerard Donnelly, "The 3–H Club," *NYPD Blue* (also known as *N.Y.P.D.*), ABC, 2004.

Peter, "Sex, Lies, and Sonograms," *Inconceivable,* NBC, 2005.

Mr. Fabrizio, "Paper Route," *Stella,* Comedy Central, 2005.

(In archive footage) Miles, "Charmageddon," *Charmed,* The WB, 2005.

Rookie Jared Reese, "Cop School," *Reno 911!,* Comedy Central, 2005.

Brad Acles, "17 Seconds," *Grey's Anatomy,* ABC, 2006.

First patient, "Joan of Arf," *The Sarah Silverman Program,* Comedy Central, 2007.

McGee, *The Black Donnellys,* NBC, 2007.

Alan Farris, "You May Now Kill the Bride," *CSI: Miami,* CBS, 2008.

Sergeant Andrew Blake, "Junior Runs for Office," *Reno 911!,* Comedy Central, 2008.

Mike Connor, "Possibility," *United States of Tara,* Showtime, 2009.

Camp leader/counselor, "Take Me Home, Cyprus Rhodes," *Greek,* ABC Family, 2009.

Shep, "It Takes a Village Idiot," *In the Motherhood,* ABC, 2009.

Shep, "Practice What You Preach," *In the Motherhood,* ABC, 2009.

Shep, "Shepfather," *In the Motherhood,* ABC, 2009 Larsen, "The Way We Were," *Private Practice,* ABC, 2009.

David Wilder, "So Here's the Thing …," *Californication,* Showtime, 2009.

Television Appearances; Other:

The State's 43rd Annual Halloween Special, CBS, 1995.
Younger news guy, *Kilroy,* 1999.

Television Work; Series:

Producer, *You Wrote It, You Watch It,* MTV, 1992–94.
Creator, *The State,* MTV, 1993–95.
Executive producer, *Off Limits,* 2001.

Television Work; Pilots:

Executive producer, *Out of Bounds,* Comedy Central, 2007.

Television Work; Specials:

Creator, *The State's 43rd Annual Halloween Special,* CBS, 1995.

Television Director; Episodic:

"Constance Carmell Wedding," *Party Down,* Starz!, 2010.

Film Appearances:

Sequencing technician, *Gattaca,* Columbia, 1997.

Mike Parker, *Love Happens,* Curb Entertainment, 1999.

Antonio Torello, *Carlo's Wake,* Four Starz Productions, 1999.

Rockin' Roller Coaster, 1999.

Officer Russotelli, *101 Ways (The Things a Girl Will Do to Keep Her Volvo),* 2000.

Victor Kulak, *Wet Hot American Summer,* USA Films, 2001.

Jeff, *Tortilla Soup,* Samuel Goldwyn Company, 2001.

Rick Raglow, *Joe Somebody,* Twentieth Century–Fox, 2001.

Voice of Raccoon Jerry, *Hoodwinked!* (animated; also known as *Little Red*), Weinstein Company, 2005.

Jack Mechanic, *The Baxter,* Lions Gate Films, 2005.

Dr. Neil Gardner, *Love for Rent* (also known as *Amor en alquiler*), MiamiLA Entertainment, 2005.

Ben, *Duncan Removed* (short film), American Film Institute, 2006.

Frankie Lozo, *Diggers,* Alliance Atlantis Communications, 2006, Magnolia Pictures, 2007.

Dr. Glenn Richie and cartoon voices, *The Ten,* THINK-Film, 2007.

Deaf tattoo artist, *Reno 911! Miami* (also known as *Reno 911! Miami: The Movie*), Twentieth Century–Fox, 2007.

Jim Stansel, *Role Models,* Universal, 2008.

Party host, *The Antagonist* (short film), Onomatope Productions, 2009.

Roger, *Jeffie Was Here,* Blue Yonder Films, 2010.

Film Producer and Director:

Diggers, Alliance Atlantis Communications, 2006, Magnolia Pictures, 2007.

The Ten, THINKFilm, 2007.

Internet Appearances; Series:

Dr. Glenn Richie, *Children's Hospital,* TheWB.com, 2008–10.

Internet Appearances; Pilots:

Dr. Glenn Richie, *Children's Hospital,* TheWB.com, 2008.

Internet Appearances; Episodic:

Career counselor, "The Bank," *Wainy Days,* Wainydays.com, 2007.

Gordon, "The Pact," *Wainy Days,* Wainydays.com, 2007.

Internet Director; Episodic:
"Happy Endings," *Wainy Days,* Wainydays.com, 2007.
"Wainy Nights," *Wainy Days,* Wainydays.com, 2007.

Internet Director; Pilots:
Children's Hospital, TheWB.com, 2008.

Stage Appearances:
Valley of the Dolls, Circle in the Square Downtown, New York City, 1996.

Major Tours:
Toured U.S. cities in *A Few Good Men* and *Molt.*

WRITINGS

Television Series:
You Wrote It, You Watch It, MTV, between 1992–94.
The State, MTV, 1993–95.
Party Down, Starz!, 2009–10.

Television Pilots:
Out of Bounds, Comedy Central, 2007.

Television Specials:
The State's 43rd Annual Halloween Special, CBS, 1995.

Screenplays:
Diggers, Alliance Atlantis Communications, 2006, Magnolia Pictures, 2007.
(And lyricist, "Who Am I (and Where Do I Go from Here?)" and "Written in Stone") *The Ten,* THINKFilm, 2007.
(And songwriter) *Role Models,* Universal, 2008.

Internet Episodes:
"Wainy Nights," *Wainy Days,* Wainydays.com, 2007.

MARTIN, J. V. 1955–

PERSONAL

Full name, James Vincent Martin III; born June 15, 1955, in Orlando, FL; married Sara (a producer), September 14, 1991.

Addresses: *Agent*—CESD Talent Agency, 10635 Santa Monica Blvd., Suite 130, Los Angeles, CA 90025; Voice Talent Productions, 17 Marblestone Lane, Centereach, NY 11720.

Career: Voice artist, producer, director, and writer. Provided the voice of William Bradford for the animated promotional spots *Crescent Hollow,* SOAPnet. As a voice artist, narrator for several television and film projects. Narrator of promotional films, industrial films, fund–raising films, instructional films, interactive exhibits, museum exhibits, video tributes, and videos for the tourism industry. Announcer for a number of events, including benefits and awards presentations. Provided announcing work and voice work for advertisements. Participated in workshops teaching voice work.

Member: American Federation of Television and Radio Artists.

CREDITS

Television Appearances; Documentary Series:
Disclaimer announcer, *In Search of ...* (also known as *In Search of*), Sci–Fi Channel, 2002.
Narrator, *More Than Human,* The Discovery Channel, 2003.
Narrator, *The System,* Court TV, beginning 2003.
Narrator, *Massive Nature,* BBC and Animal Planet, 2004.
Series announcer, *Second Verdict,* PAX, 2004.
Narrator, *Trace Evidence: The Case Files of Dr. Henry Lee,* Court TV (later known as truTV), beginning 2004.
Series narrator, *Cheating Death,* Discovery Health, beginning 2004.
Narrator, *Unsolved History,* The Discovery Channel, 2004–2005.
Series narrator, *Science of the Bible,* National Geographic Channel, c. 2005–2006.
Narrator, *Chefography* (also known as *Chef–O–Graphy*), Food Network, beginning 2006.
Series narrator, *Anything to Win,* Game Show Network, beginning 2006.
Series narrator, *Las Vegas Law,* Court TV, beginning 2006.
Narrator, *Planet's Best,* Travel Channel, beginning c. 2006.
Series narrator, *Pinks: All Out,* Speed, beginning c. 2006.
Series narrator, *Mega Disasters,* History Channel, 2006–2008.
Narrator, *Kitchen Nightmares* (also known as *Kitchen Nightmares USA* and *Ramsay's "Kitchen Nightmares"*), Fox, beginning 2007.

Series narrator, *Could You Survive?*, Discovery Health, 2008.

Narrator, *Call 911*, truTV, beginning 2008.

Narrator, *Time Warp*, The Discovery Channel, beginning 2008.

Series narrator, *Raging Nature*, The Discovery Channel, beginning 2008.

Series narrator, *Egypt Unwrapped*, National Geographic Channel, c. 2008–2009.

Narrator, *Monsters Resurrected* (also known as *Mega Beasts*), The Discovery Channel, beginning 2009.

Appeared in other programs, including serving as the series narrator for *Inside*, Court TV.

Television Appearances; Narrator of Documentary Specials:

Cold Clues: Guilty Conscience, Court TV, 2002.

Cold Clues: Without a Trace, Court TV, 2002.

ViCAP: On the Trail of Violence, The Discovery Channel, 2002.

Anatomy of a Shark Bite, The Discovery Channel, 2003.

Donut Crazy!, Travel Channel, 2003.

Inside Demolition Derbies, Travel Channel, 2003.

Soviet UFO Secrets Revealed, History Channel, 2003.

Truck and Tractor Pulls, Travel Channel, 2003.

Anatomy of a Bear Bite, The Discovery Channel, 2004.

Anatomy of a Snake Bite, The Discovery Channel, 2004.

Anatomy of a Tiger Bite, The Discovery Channel, 2004.

Dive to Bermuda Triangle, The Discovery Channel and BBC, 2004.

The Dolphin Murders, The Discovery Channel and BBC, 2004.

Rage against the Machines, Sci–Fi Channel, 2004.

Tiger Shark Attack: Beyond Fear, The Discovery Channel, 2004.

The True Story of Hidalgo, History Channel, 2004.

Beyond the Bible: The Crucifixion, National Geographic Channel, 2005.

Killer Jellyfish, The Discovery Channel, 2005.

Shark Attack: Predator in the Panhandle, The Discovery Channel, 2005.

Sharkbite! Surviving Great Whites, The Discovery Channel and BBC, 2005.

Presidential Prophecies, History Channel, 2005.

The Chief, Court TV, 2006.

JonBenet: Anatomy of a Cold Case, Court TV, 2006.

National Geographic: Hitler and the Occult (also known as *Hitler and the Occult*), National Geographic Channel, 2006.

New York's Secret War, Court TV, 2006.

Secrets of the Freemasons, National Geographic Channel, 2006.

Giant Squid: Caught on Camera (also known as *Big Science: Giant Squid: Caught on Camera*), The Discovery Channel, c. 2006.

Accidental Survival: Freefalls (also known as *Accidental Survival: Free Falls*), National Geographic Channel, 2007.

Cain and Abel: Brothers at War, National Geographic Channel, 2007.

Decoding Bible Relics, National Geographic Channel, 2007.

The Long March: China's Flickering Star (also known as *The Long March*), History Channel, 2007.

Fit to Live, Discovery Health, 2008.

Squid Invasion, The Discovery Channel, 2008.

Super City: New York, History Channel, 2008.

Tokyo: Living Small in the Big City, National Geographic Channel, 2008.

The Wild Yak Patrol, Animal Planet, c. 2008.

Great Escape: The Final Secrets, National Geographic Channel, 2009.

JFK: The Ruby Connection, The Discovery Channel, 2009.

Megalab Antarctica (also known as *Mega Lab Antarctica*), Science Channel, 2009.

Nostradamus Decoded, The Discovery Channel, 2009.

The Race to Bury Tut, National Geographic Channel, 2009.

Tomb of 1,000 Roman Skeletons, National Geographic Channel, 2009.

Narrator of other programs, including *America's Favorite Boardwalks*, *America's Favorite Campgrounds*, and *Extreme Truck Racing*, all Travel Channel.

Television Appearances; Specials:

Radio talk show host, *Criss Angel Mindfreak*, ABC Family, 2002.

Television Appearances; Awards Presentations:

Participated in awards presentations, including *The X Prize*, Science Channel.

Television Appearances; Narrator for Documentary Episodes:

"Jesus' Arrest," *Mysteries of the Bible*, National Geographic Channel, 2004.

"The Day after Roswell," *UFO Files*, History Channel, 2005.

"Places to Watch Sports," *World's Best*, Travel Channel, c. 2005.

"The Dead Sea Scrolls," *Mysteries of the Bible*, National Geographic Channel, 2006.

"Hell: The Devil's Domain," *History Alive*, History Channel, 2006.

"The Iceberg That Sank the Titanic," *The Natural World*, The Discovery Channel, 2006.

"Incredible Hotels: Dubai," *MegaStructures*, National Geographic Channel and other channels, 2007.

"Incredible Islands: Dubai," *MegaStructures*, National Geographic Channel and other channels, 2007.

"The Missing Years," *National Geographic Explorer,* National Geographic Channel and other channels, 2007.

"Secrets of the Shroud," *Is It Real?,* National Geographic Channel, 2007.

"Death of a Star," *Naked Science* (also known as *Superscience*), National Geographic Channel, 2009.

"A Gallon of Gas," *Man–Made* (also known as *Man Made*), National Geographic Channel, 2009.

"How the West Was Made," *Naked Science* (also known as *Superscience*), National Geographic Channel, 2009.

"Incinerator Earth," *Naked Science* (also known as *Superscience*), National Geographic Channel, 2009.

Narrator for other programs, including "Woodward Classic: Cruisin' Motor City," *Kings of the Road,* Travel Channel.

Television Appearances; Episodic:

Announcer in "Keyshop" promotional skit, "Tim Meadows," *Talkshow with Spike Feresten,* Fox, 2007.

Narrator of *Dog Whisperer with Cesar Millan* parody, *The Soup* (also known as *Talk Soup*), E! Entertainment Television, c. 2007.

Television Appearances; Pilots:

Narrator, *Monster Tracker,* The Discovery Channel, 2009.

Television Producer; Documentary Series:

Associate producer, *VH1 Legends* (also known as *Legends*), VH1, beginning 1996.

Coproducer, *Wild Rescues,* Animal Planet, beginning 1997.

Sworn to Secrecy: Secrets of War (also known as *Secrets of War*), History Channel, beginning 1998.

Coproducer, *Caught on Film,* History Channel, 2002.

Television Producer; Series:

Wild & Crazy Kids, Nickelodeon and YTV, 1990–92.

Television Work; Movies:

Second second assistant director: second unit, *Prey of the Chameleon,* Showtime, 1992.

Television Producer; Documentary Specials:

Unit 731: Nightmare in Manchuria, History Channel, 1998.

Inferno: The True Story of Dresden, History Channel, 1999.

(And segment producer) *The Bataan Death March,* History Channel, 2000.

Coney Island: America's Dreamland, The Discovery Channel, 2000.

Big Bucks: The Press Your Luck Scandal, Game Show Network, 2003.

Rage against the Machines, Sci–Fi Channel, 2004.

Decoding the Past: Prophecies of Iraq, History Channel, 2005.

Television Work; Other; Documentary Specials:

Production coordinator, *Terrors of the Deep,* CBS, 1996.

Director and additional photography, *The Bataan Death March,* History Channel, 2000.

Television Producer; Documentary Episodes:

"Mahatma Gandhi: Pilgrim of Peace," *Biography* (also known as *A&E Biography: Mahatma Gandhi*), Arts and Entertainment, 1997.

"Pyramids: Majesty and Mystery," *Modern Marvels,* History Channel, 1997.

"Mail Delivery: Erasing the Miles," *Modern Marvels,* History Channel, 1999.

"Catacomb Mummies/The Johnson Bigfoot Encounter/ The Secret of Rennes Le Chateau/Earthquake Predictions," *In Search of ...* (also known as *In Search of*), Sci–Fi Channel, 2002.

"The Death of the Red Baron," *Unsolved History,* The Discovery Channel, 2002.

"The Ghost in Mackey's Bar/Stigmata/The Haunted Hornet/Zombies," *In Search of ...* (also known as *In Search of*), Sci–Fi Channel, 2002.

"The Death of Princess Diana," *Unsolved History,* The Discovery Channel, 2003.

"JFK: The Conspiracy Myths," *Unsolved History,* The Discovery Channel, 2003.

"JFK: Death in Dealey Plaza," *Unsolved History,* The Discovery Channel, 2003.

"JFK: Beyond the Magic Bullet," *Unsolved History,* The Discovery Channel, 2004.

"The Unstoppable Wave" (also known as "Unstoppable Wave"), *Unsolved History,* The Discovery Channel, 2005.

"Stealth Technology," *Modern Marvels,* History Channel, 2006.

Television Work; Other; Documentary Episodes:

Additional camera operator, "Mahatma Gandhi: Pilgrim of Peace," *Biography* (also known as *A&E Biography: Mahatma Gandhi*), Arts and Entertainment, 1997.

Additional photography, "JFK: Death in Dealey Plaza," *Unsolved History,* The Discovery Channel, 2003.

Directed episodes of series, including *Sworn to Secrecy: Secrets of War* (documentary; also known as *Secrets of War*), History Channel; and *Talk Soup* (also known as *The Soup*), E! Entertainment Television.

Documentary Film Appearances:

Billy goat disclaimer announcer, *Chasing October* (comedic documentary; also known as *Chasing October: A Fan's Crusade*), Emerging Pictures, 2007.

American narrator, *Inside the Koran,* Juniper Entertainment/First Run, 2008.

Stage Appearances; as an Announcer:

The Ronald Reagan Freedom Award, Beverly Hills, CA, 2007.

Stand Up for a Cure 2007 (benefit), Millennium Biltmore Hotel, Los Angeles, 2007.

Stand Up for a Cure 2008 (benefit), Millennium Biltmore Hotel, 2008.

Stand Up for a Cure 2009 (benefit), Millennium Biltmore Hotel, 2009.

Radio Appearances:

Worked as a reporter in radio broadcasts.

Internet Appearances:

Network announcer for Cleanskies.tv, American Clean Skies Network. Narrator and announcer for trailers and interstitials broadcast on the Internet.

WRITINGS

Teleplays; Documentary Specials:

Coney Island: America's Dreamland, The Discovery Channel, 2000.

Big Bucks: The Press Your Luck Scandal, Game Show Network, 2003.

Teleplays; Documentary Episodes:

"Mail Delivery: Erasing the Miles," *Modern Marvels,* History Channel, 1999.

Wrote episodes of *Sworn to Secrecy: Secrets of War* (also known as *Secrets of War*), History Channel.

Writings for the Radio:

Wrote for radio broadcasts.

OTHER SOURCES

Electronic:

J. V. Martin, http://www.jvmartin.com, February 24, 2010.

MASTROGIORGIO, Danny
(Danny Mastrogeorgio, Danny Mastrogiogrio, Daniel Mastrogiorgio)

PERSONAL

Born in Mount Vernon, NY. *Education:* Attended Marin Community College and Juilliard School.

Addresses: *Agent*—Stone Manners Talent Agency, 900 Broadway, Suite 803, New York, NY 10003.

Career: Actor. Voice of Frank in commercials featuring the Budweiser lizard.

CREDITS

Film Appearances:

Vito Patrizzi, *Friends and Family,* 2001, Regent Releasing, 2003.

Jail guard, *The Producers,* Universal, 2005.

Voice of crazy dog, *Underdog* (also known as *Iron–Puppy Underdog*), Buena Vista, 2007.

(As Daniel Mastrogiorgio) Jerry, *Enchanted,* Walt Disney, 2007.

Trader Jim, *Fighting,* Rogue Pictures, 2009.

Film Appearances; as Daniel Mastrogiorgio:

Nick Davenport, *Sleepers,* Warner Bros., 1996.

Veduccio, *Dead Broke,* Polychrome Pictures, 1998.

Enzo, *Italian Lessons* (short film), Big Film Shorts, 1998.

Voice of second ram, *Brother Bear* (animated; also known as *Tierra de osos*), Buena Vista, 2003.

Andres, *Backseat,* 2005, Truly Indie, 2008.

Television Appearances; Miniseries:

(As Daniel Mastrogiorgio) Vinnie Clereuzio, *The Last Don* (also known as *Mario Puzo's "The Last Don"*), CBS, 1997.

Vinnie Clereuzio, *The Last Don II* (also known as *Mario Puzo's "The Last Don II"*), CBS, 1998.

Television Appearances; Specials:

Husband/bartender, *Contact,* PBS, 2002.

Television Appearances; Episodic:

(As Daniel Mastrogiorgio) Rescue worker, "Welcome Back Cotter," *New York News,* CBS, 1995.

(As Daniel Mastrogiorgio) Perry Behrens, "Bitter Fruit," *Law & Order,* NBC, 1995.

(As Daniel Mastrogiorgio) First reserve worker, "How to Bury a Millionaire," *Spin City,* ABC, 1999.

Stone, "Alone in a Crowd," *Third Watch*, NBC, 2000.

Bruce Valentine, "Trade This," *Law & Order*, NBC, 2000.

Earl Miller/Earl Gilmore, "Noncompliance," *Law & Order: Special Victims Unit* (also known as *Law & Order: SVU* and *Special Victims Unit*), NBC, 2000.

Michael Vaporelli, "Acceptance," *The Book of Daniel*, NBC, 2006.

Michael Vaporelli, "Assignation," *The Book of Daniel*, NBC, 2006.

Kevin Mucci, "Live Free or Die," *The Sopranos*, HBO, 2006.

Nicky Fatone, "Quit Claim," *Law & Order*, NBC, 2008.

John Testarossa, "Purgatory," *Law & Order: Criminal Intent* (also known as *Law & Order: CI*), USA Network, 2008.

Orlando McTeer, "Lunacy," *Law & Order: Special Victims Unit* (also known as *Law & Order: SVU* and *Special Victims Unit*), NBC, 2008.

Wendall Tate, "One Man Band," *The Unusuals*, ABC, 2009.

Stage Appearances:

Third outlaw, *Two Gentlemen of Verona*, New York Shakespeare Festival, Delacorte Theatre, Public Theatre, New York City, 1994.

Husband/bartender, *Contact*, Vivian Beaumont Theatre, Lincoln Center, New York City, c. 2002.

Bob, *Wintertime*, Second Stage Theatre, New York City, 2004.

Rich, *Sailor's Song*, LAByrinth Theatre Company, Susan Stein Shiva Theatre, Public Theatre, New York City, 2004.

Ike Schwecky, *Stunning*, Duke Theatre on Forty–Second Street, New York City, 2009.

Appeared in *My Italy Story* (solo show), New York City; understudy for the role of Denny, *A Steady Rain*, Gerald Schoenfeld Theatre, New York City; appeared in *The Resistible Rise of Arturo Ui*, National Actors Theatre; *The Taming of the Shrew*, Denver Theatre Center, Denver, CO, and Old Globe Theatre, San Diego, CA; *Wait until Dark*, Brooks Atkinson Theatre, New York City; also performed at City Theatre of Pittsburgh, Long Wharf Theatre, and McCarter Theatre.

RECORDINGS

Video Games:

(As Danny Mastrogeorgio) Voice, *Batman: Dark Tomorrow*, Kemco, 2003.

(As Daniel Mastrogiorgio) Voice of dealer, *The Warriors*, Rockstar Games, 2005.

(As Daniel Mastrogiorgio) Voice of Toni Cipriani, *Grand Theft Auto: Liberty City Stories* (also known as *GTA: Liberty City Stories*), Rockstar Games, 2005.

(As Daniel Mastrogiorgio) Voice of Saul Shapiro, *The Sopranos: Road to Respect*, THQ, 2006.

McCOY, LisaRaye
See LISARAYE

McGEE, Vonetta 1945–2010

PERSONAL

Original name, Lawrence Vonetta McGee, Jr.; born January 14, 1945, in San Francisco, CA; died of cardiac arrest, July 9, 2010, in Berkeley, CA. Actress. Well-known for her roles in several famous blaxploitation films of the 1970s, McGee boasted a career that spanned several decades and continents, and she is considered a pioneering African-American actress. Her career began in the 1960s while she was a pre-law student at San Francisco State College. After appearing in several community theater productions, she travelled to Italy in 1967 to star in the comedy *Faustina* and the western *Il Grande Silenzio*. In 1969 she was cast by Sidney Poitier in *The Lost Man*. After performing a small part in the John Huston film *The Kremlin Letter*, she starred in *Melinda*, the first of a series of films created exclusively by African American actors and producers. In the mid-1970s McGee played major roles in the blaxploitation movies *Blacula*, *Hammer*, *Shaft in Africa*, *Detroit 9000*, and *Thomasine & Bushrod*, many of which are considered classics of the genre. She also appeared alongside Clint Eastwood in the 1975 action film *The Eiger Sanction* and had roles in *Repo Man* in 1984 and, most recently, in the 2007 political drama *Black August*. Her television credits include short stints on *The Bill Cosby Show*; *Starsky and Hutch*; *Diffrent Strokes*; *Magnum, P.I.*; *Amen*; and *Perry Mason* and recurring roles in *Hell Town*, *Cagney & Lacey*, *Bustin Loose*, and *L.A. Law*.

PERIODICALS

Guardian, July 20, 2010.
Independent, September 23, 2010.
Los Angeles Times, July 15, 2010.
New York Times, July 16, 2010.
Washington Post, July 17, 2010.

McPHEE, Katharine 1984–

PERSONAL

Full name, Katharine Hope McPhee; born March 25, 1984, in Los Angeles, CA; daughter of Daniel (a producer) and Patricia (a cabaret singer as Peisha Arten and a vocal coach; maiden name, Burch) McPhee; married Nick Cokas (a producer and actor), February 2, 2008. *Education:* Attended Boston Conservatory of Music; also attended Broadway Theatre Project, Tampa, FL, 2004.

Addresses: *Agent*—Darren Boghosian, United Talent Agency, 9560 Wilshire Blvd., Suite 500, Beverly Hills, CA 90212. *Manager*—Schiff Co., 9465 Wilshire Blvd., Suite 480, Beverly Hills, CA 90212. *Publicist*—Jodi Gottlieb, I/D Public Relations, 8409 Santa Monica Blvd., West Hollywood, CA 90069.

Career: Actress and singer. Toured as singer, including concerts with Andrea Bocelli and with American Idols Live!, both 2006. Appeared in an infomercial for Neutrogena SkinID skin medication, 2008. McPhee Outreach, philanthropist, 2010.

Awards, Honors: Young Hollywood Award, best breakout female vocalist, 2007.

CREDITS

Television Appearances; Series:
Contestant, *American Idol: The Search for a Superstar* (also known as *American Idol* and *Idol*), Fox, 2006, 2008.

Television Appearances; Pilots:
U R Here, MTV, 2006.
Emily, *The Pink House*, NBC, 2010.

Television Appearances; Specials:
JCPenney Jam: The Concert for America's Kids, CBS, 2006.
8th Annual A Home for the Holidays with Rod Stewart, CBS, 2006.
Mother Goose Parade, 2007.
Christmas in Washington, TNT, 2007.
Macy's 4th of July Fireworks Spectacular, NBC, 2008.
"Hit Man: David Foster and Friends," *Great Performances*, PBS, 2008.
Kira Plastinina: In Her Own Words, MTV, 2008.
Chris Botti in Boston, PBS, 2009.
Kaleidoscope, 2009.
An Evening of Stars: Tribute to Lionel Richie, 2010.
Hope for Haiti Now: A Global Benefit for Earthquake Relief, multiple networks, 2010.

Television Appearances; Episodic:
The Dr. Keith Ablow Show, syndicated, 2006.
Entertainment Tonight (also known as *E.T.* and *This Week in Entertainment*), syndicated, multiple appearances, beginning 2006.

Herself, "I'm Coming Out," *Ugly Betty*, ABC, 2007.
Access Hollywood, syndicated, 2007.
Rachael Ray, syndicated, 2007, 2010.
Odessa Shaw/Dana Melton, "Prey," *CSI: NY*, CBS, 2009.
Amber, "Basic Genealogy," *Community*, NBC, 2010.
The Soup, E! Entertainment Television, 2010.
The Biggest Loser, NBC, 2010.

Television Talk Show Guest Appearances; Episodic:
Larry King Live, Cable News Network, 2006, 2007.
Live with Regis and Kelly, syndicated, 2006, 2007, 2008.
The Tonight Show with Jay Leno, NBC, 2006, 2007, 2010.
Ellen: The Ellen DeGeneres Show, syndicated, 2007.
The Morning Show with Mike & Juliet, Fox and syndicated, 2007.
"Summer in the City: Live from Orlando," *The Early Show*, CBS, 2007.
Jimmy Kimmel Live!, ABC, 2007, 2008, 2010.
The View, ABC, 2008.
The Tonight Show with Conan O'Brien, NBC, 2010.
The Bonnie Hunt Show, NBC, 2010.
The Wendy Williams Show, 2010.
Chelsea Lately, E! Entertainment Television, 2010.

Television Appearances; Awards Presentations:
Presenter, *2006 American Music Awards*, ABC, 2006.
Presenter, *The 2006 Billboard Music Awards*, Fox, 2006.
VH1 Big in 06 Awards, VH1, 2006.
2008 MTV Movie Awards, MTV, 2008.
The 2008 Teen Choice Awards, Fox, 2008.

Film Appearances:
Paramount girl, *Crazy*, Screen Media Ventures, 2008.
Harmony, *The House Bunny*, Columbia, 2008.
Masha Nikitin, *You May Not Kiss the Bride*, Hawaii Film Partners/Showcase Entertainment/Luminair Film Productions, 2010.

Stage Appearances:
Annie, Get Your Gun (musical), 2005.
Anna Muir, *The Ghost and Mrs. Muir* (musical), NoHo Arts Center, North Hollywood, CA, 2005.

Stage Work:
Coproducer, *Red Herring*, New York International Fringe Festival, 2007.

Internet Appearances; Episodic:
AOL Sessions, music.aol.com, 2006.
Random girl, "Truth or Date," *Lonelygirl15*, lg15.com, 2007.

RECORDINGS

Albums:
Katharine McPhee, RCA, 2007.
Had It All, Verve, 2009.
Say Goodbye, Verve, 2009.
I'll Be There for Christmas, Verve, 2009.
Unbroken, Verve, 2010.

Contributor to albums recorded by other artists. Singles include "Somewhere over the Rainbow/My Destiny," RCA, 2006; "Over It," BMG/RCA, 2007; "Real Love," Concord, 2008; and "I Know What Boys Like," 2008.

Videos:
Herself, *The Red Dress Collection 2007 Fashion Show,* FTC Publications, 2008.

Video Games:
(Uncredited) *Karaoke Revolution Presents: American Idol,* Konami Digital Entertainment America, 2007.
(Uncredited) *Karaoke Revolution Presents: American Idol Encore,* Konami Digital Entertainment America, 2008.
(Uncredited) *Karaoke Revolution Presents: American Idol 2,* Konami Digital Entertainment America, 2008.

WRITINGS

Songs Featured in Films:
"Beautiful Stranger," *You May Not Kiss the Bride,* Hawaii Film Partners/Showcase Entertainment/ Luminair Film Productions, 2010.

OTHER SOURCES

Periodicals:
Teen People, August, 2006, p. 70.

Electronic:
Katharine McPhee Official Site, http://www. katharinemcphee.com, June 8, 2010.

MELVILLE, J. W.
    See SHYER, Charles

MEYER, Nicholas 1945–

PERSONAL

Born December 24, 1945, in New York, NY; son of Bernard Constant (a psychoanalyst) and Elly (a concert pianist; maiden name, Kassman) Meyer; married Lauren Leigh Taylor, June 6, 1984; married Stephanie; children: Roxanne, Rachel, Madeline. *Education:* University of Iowa, B.A., theatre and filmmaking, 1968. *Politics:* Democrat. *Religion:* Jewish. *Avocational Interests:* Music, horseback riding, swimming, sailing, pets, movies, reading.

Addresses: *Agent*—WME Entertainment, One William Morris Pl., Beverly Hills, CA 90212. *Manager*—Alan Gasmer and Friends, 10877 Wilshire Blvd., Suite 1404, Los Angeles, CA 90024.

Career: Director, screenwriter, producer, actor, and novelist. Paramount Pictures Corp., New York City, associate publicist, 1968–69; Warner Bros., Inc., New York City, story editor, 1970–71.

Member: Academy of Motion Picture Arts and Sciences, Writers Guild of America, Directors Guild of America, Academy of Science Fiction, Fantasy, and Horror Films, Baker Street Irregulars.

Awards, Honors: Mystery Writers Guild Award, 1974, for *Target Practice;* Edgar Allan Poe Award nomination, best television feature, Mystery Writers of America, 1975, for *Judge Dee and the Monastery Murders;* British Crime Writers Association Gold Dagger Award, 1974, for *The Seven–Per–Cent Solution; Being a Reprint from the Reminiscences of John H. Watson, M.D.;* Emmy Award nomination, best original teleplay—special program, 1976, for *The Night That Panicked America;* Academy Award nomination, best screenplay adaptation, Writers Guild of America Award nomination, best drama adapted from another medium, 1977, for *The Seven–Per–Cent Solution;* Avoriaz Film Festival Grand Prize, and Saturn Award, best screenplay, Academy of Science Fiction, Fantasy, and Horror Films, both 1979, Edgar Allan Poe Award nomination, best motion picture, 1980, for *Time after Time;* Saturn Award, best director, 1982, for *Star Trek II: The Wrath of Khan;* Emmy Award nomination, best director of a limited series or special, 1983, for *The Day After;* George Pal Memorial Award, Academy of Science Fiction, Fantasy, and Horror Films; Anne Radcliffe Award, Count Dracula Society, for contributions to literature; Emmy Award nomination (with others), outstanding miniseries, 1997, for *The Odyssey;* Satellite Award nomination, best screenplay—adapted, 2008, for *Elegy;* Time–Machine Honorary Award, Sitges—Catalonian International Film Festival, 2008.

CREDITS

Film Work:
Unit publicist, *Love Story,* 1969.
Director, *Time After Time,* Warner Bros., 1979.

Director, *Star Trek: The Wrath of Khan* (also known as *Star Trek II: The Wrath of Khan* and *Star Trek II: The Wrath of Khan—The Director's Edition*), Paramount, 1982.

Director, *The Pied Piper*, 1984.

Director, *Volunteers*, TriStar, 1985.

Director, *The Deceivers*, Cinecom, 1988.

Director, *Star Trek VI: The Undiscovered Country*, Paramount, 1991.

Director, *Company Business*, Metro–Goldwyn–Mayer, 1991.

Executive producer, *Collateral Damage*, Warner Bros., 2002.

Film Appearances:

The Perils of Peacemaking (short documentary), 2003.

Big time producer, *Awaken the Giant* (short film), JAG Productions, 2004.

Himself, *Making "Murder on the Orient Express"* (documentary), Paramount Home Video, 2004.

Himself, *The Art of Imagination: A Tribute to Oz* (short documentary), Warner Home Video, 2005.

Himself, *H. G. Wells: The Father of Science Fiction* (short documentary), Paramount Home Entertainment, 2005.

Himself, *Villains of "Star Trek"* (short documentary), Paramount Home Entertainment, 2009.

Television Executive Producer; Miniseries:

The Odyssey (also known as *Homer's "Odyssey"*), 1997.

Television Work; Movies:

Director, *The Day After*, ABC, 1983.

Executive producer, *The Informant*, Showtime 1997.

Director, *Vendetta*, HBO, 1999.

Executive producer, *Oprheus*, CBS, 2006.

Television Work; Episodic:

"Pied Piper," *Faerie Tale Theatre* (also known as *Shelley Duvall's "Faerie Tale Theatre"*), 1985.

Television Appearances; Movies:

George Raft, *Mae West*, 1982.

Television Appearances; Specials:

"Star Trek" 25th Anniversary Special, 1991.

Commentator, *Trailer Park*, Sci–Fi Channel, 1996.

Intimate Portrait: Kim Cattrall, Lifetime, 2000.

WRITINGS

Screenplays:

Invasion of the Bee Girls (also known as *Graveyard Tramps*), Centaur, 1973.

The Seven–Per–Cent Solution (adapted from his novel of the same name), Universal, 1976.

Time after Time (based on a story by Karl Alexander and Steve Hayes), Warner Bros., 1979.

(Uncredited) *Star Trek: The Wrath of Khan* (also known as *Star Trek II: The Wrath of Khan* and *Star Trek II: The Wrath of Khan—The Director's Edition*), Paramount, 1982.

Volunteers, TriStar, 1985.

(With Harve Bennett, Steve Meerson, and Peter Krikes) *Star Trek IV: The Voyage Home* (from a story by Leonard Nimoy and Bennett; based on characters created by Gene Roddenberry), Paramount, 1986.

Fatal Attraction, Paramount, 1987.

(With Denny Martin Flinn) *Star Trek VI: The Undiscovered Country* (from a story by Nimoy, Lawrence Konner, and Mark Rosenthal; based on characters created by Roddenberry), Paramount, 1991.

Company Business, Metro–Goldwyn–Mayer, 1991.

(With Sarah Kernochan) *Sommersby* (based on the film *The Return of Martin Guerre*, screenplay by Daniel Vigne and Jean–Claude Carriere), Warner Bros., 1993.

Voices (also known as *Voices from a Locked Room*), 1995.

Dr. Dolittle, Twentieth Century–Fox, 1998.

Collateral Damage, Warner Bros., 2002.

The Human Stain, Miramax, 2003.

Elegy, Samuel Goldwyn, 2008.

The Hessen Affair, 2009.

Television Movies:

Judge Dee and the Monastery Murders (also known as *The Haunted Monastery*), ABC, 1974.

(With Anthony Wilson) *The Night That Panicked America* (also known as *Please Stand By*; based on Mercury Theatre radio adaptation of H. G. Wells's *The War of the Worlds*), ABC, 1975.

The Informant, Showtime, 1997.

Fall from the Sky, 2002.

Television Episodes:

"Pied Piper," *Faerie Tale Theatre* (also known as *Shelley Duvall's "Faerie Tale Theatre"*), 1985.

Novels:

Target Practice, Harcourt, 1974.

The Seven–Per–Cent Solution; Being a Reprint from the Reminiscences of John H. Watson, M.D., Dutton, 1974.

The West End Horror: A Posthumous Memoir of John H. Watson, M.D., Dutton, 1976.

(With Barry Jap Kaplan) *Black Orchid*, Dial, 1977.

Confessions of a Homing Pigeon, Dial, 1981.

The Canary Trainer: From the Memoirs of John H. Watson, M.D., 1993.

Nonfiction:
The "Love Story" Story, Avon, 1971.
The View from the Bridge: Memories of "Star Trek" and a Life in Hollywood, Viking Adult, 2009.

Contributor of numerous film reviews to *Daily Iowan,* 1964–68.

OTHER SOURCES

Periodicals:
Entertainment Weekly, February 17, 1995, p. 67.
Variety, September 22, 1997, p. 50.

MONTANO, Robert 1960–

PERSONAL

Born April 22, 1960, in Bayside, Queens, New York, NY. *Education:* Graduated from Adelphi University, 1983; studied dance.

Addresses: *Agent*—Cornerstone Talent Agency, 37 West 20th St., Suite 1108, New York, NY 10011.

Career: Actor and dancer. Worked as a professional jockey at horse races.

CREDITS

Stage Appearances; Musicals:
Pouncival and Mr. Mistofelees, *Cats,* Theater an der Wien, Vienna, Austria, beginning 1983, and Winter Garden Theatre, New York City, 1987.
The Chosen, Second Avenue Theatre, New York City, 1988.
Legs Diamond, Mark Hellinger Theatre, New York City, 1988–89.
Robert, *Chita Plus Two,* off–Broadway production, 1989.
Vito, *Angelina,* Cohoes Music Hall, Cohoes, NY, 1989.
Paul, *A Chorus Line,* regional production, 1991.
Aurelio, Aurora's man, prisoner, and window dresser at Montoya's, *Kiss of the Spider Woman,* Broadhurst Theatre, New York City, 1993–95.
Ozzie, *On the Town,* New York Shakespeare Festival, Joseph Papp Public Theatre, Delacorte Theatre, New York City, 1997, and George Gershwin Theatre, New York City, 1998–99.
Ralph, *Marty,* Huntington Theatre, Boston University, Boston, MA, 2002.

Himself, *A Dancer's Life* (workshop of song, dance, and anecdotes), 2004.
Pablo, *Mambo Kings,* Golden Gate Theatre, San Francisco, CA, 2005.

Appeared in dance productions.

Stage Appearances; Plays:
Honest lawyer, *How Are Things in Costa del Fuego?* (one–act play), Sixth Annual Festival of One–Act Comedies, Evening A, Manhattan Punch Line, Judith Anderson Theatre, New York City, 1990.
Rene, *Picture Perfect,* HOLA Festival (Hispanic Organization of Latin Actors), 1990.
Anibal de la Luna, *Cloud Tectonics,* Humana Festival, Actors Theatre of Louisville, Louisville, KY, 1995.
Ray, *Guyworld,* and Rolando, *The King,* both produced as part of *Young Playwrights Festival,* Joseph Papp Public Theatre, Martinson Hall, New York City, 1995.
Cal and Charles, *East of Eden,* Steinbeck: On Stage and Film, Classics in Context Festival, Actors Theatre of Louisville, Louisville, KY, 1996.
Pinch and second merchant, *The Comedy of Errors,* Bingham Signature Shakespeare, Humana Festival, Actors Theatre of Louisville, 1996.
Benito and Moon, *References to Salvador Dali Make Me Hot* (workshop), Pacific Playwrights Festival, South Coast Repertory, Costa Mesa, CA, 1999.
Reverend David Reyes, *Da Spanish Mob,* Teatro LATEA, New York City, 2000.
Waiter, Waiter, Working Theatre, American Place Theatre, New York City, c. 2001.
Sergeant Nick Harris, *One Shot, One Kill,* Primary Stages, New York City, 2002.
Miguel, *Diosa,* some sources cite workshop a workshop at Hartford Stage, Hartford, CT, c. 2002, full production at Hartford Stage, 2003.
Herve, Guy, and member of ensemble, *Fabulation, or The Re–Education of Undine,* Playwrights Horizons, Peter Jay Sharp Theatre, New York City, 2004.

Appeared in other productions, including *The Torturer's Visit.*

Major Tours; Musicals:
Bernardo, *West Side Story,* U.S. cities, 1990.

Film Appearances:
American Ballet Academy Pas De Deux class teacher, *Center Stage* (also known as *Centre Stage, City Ballet,* and *The Dance Movie*), Columbia, 2000.
Hector Gallardo, *The Yards,* Miramax, 2000.
Father Emmanuel, *Passionada,* Samuel Goldwyn, 2002.
Male dancer and member of male ensemble, *Chicago* (also known as *Chicago: The Musical*), Miramax, 2002.

Officer Bane, *It Runs in the Family* (also known as *Family Business, Family Jewels, A Few Good Years, Smack in the Kisser,* and *Smack in the Puss*), Metro–Goldwyn–Mayer, 2003.

Mike, *Second Best,* THINKFilm/Velocity Films, 2004.

(Uncredited) Member of ensemble, *The Producers* (musical; also known as *The Producers: The Movie Musical*), Universal, 2005.

(Uncredited) Attorney, *Law Abiding Citizen,* Anchor Bay Entertainment, 2009.

Normy, *Hanging Plant* (short film), 2009.

Television Appearances; Series:

Sergio Francone, *As the World Turns,* CBS, 2006.

Antonio Vega, *One Life to Live* (also known as *Between Heaven and Hell, OLTL,* and *One Life to Live: The Summer of Seduction*), ABC, 2007.

Television Appearances; Movies:

Octavio Ruiz, *Harrison: Cry of the City,* UPN, 1996.

Resto, *Undefeated* (also known as *Infamous*), HBO, 2003.

Pico, *Fresh Cut Grass,* Showtime, 2004.

Television Appearances; Awards Presentations:

America's Dance Honors, ABC, 1990.

Television Appearances; Episodic:

Rivera, "Savages," *Law & Order* (also known as *Law & Order Prime*), NBC, 1995.

Clemente, "Blood," *Law & Order* (also known as *Law & Order Prime*), NBC, 1997.

Crime scene technician, "We Like Mike," *Law & Order* (also known as *Law & Order Prime*), NBC, 1997.

Daniel Renaldo, "The Solomon Papers," *New York Undercover* (also known as *Uptown Undercover*), Fox, 1997.

"We" William, "They Shoot Single People, Don't They?," *Sex and the City* (also known as *Sex & the City, Sex and the Big City, O sexo e a cidade, Seks i grad, Sex og singelliv, Sexo en la ciudad, Sexo en Nueva York, Sinkkuelaemaeae,* and *Szex es New York*), HBO, 1999.

Father Ramon Aguerro, "Mother's Milk," *Law & Order* (also known as *Law & Order Prime*), NBC, 2000.

Mr. Barrera, "Baby Killer," *Law & Order: Special Victims Unit* (also known as *Law & Order's Sex Crimes, Law & Order: SVU,* and *Special Victims Unit*), NBC, 2000.

Jacob Wright, "Duty," *Third Watch,* NBC, 2001.

U.S. attorney Raul Menedez, "Game," *Law & Order: Special Victims Unit* (also known as *Law & Order's Sex Crimes, Law & Order: SVU,* and *Special Victims Unit*), NBC, 2005.

Gomez, *Guiding Light* (also known as *The Guiding Light*), CBS, 2005.

Eugene, "The Puncher," *Six Degrees* (also known as *6*), ABC, 2006.

Pedro Salvado (some sources cite character name as Rico Cruz), "No Man's Land," *CSI: Miami* (also known as *CSI Miami* and *CSI: Weekends*), CBS, 2007.

Paul Perez (some sources cite character name as Raul Perez), "A Dollar and a Dream," *Without a Trace* (also known as *Vanished* and *W.A.T.*), CBS, 2008.

Major Hollander, "Change of Station," *Army Wives,* Lifetime, 2010.

Major Hollander, "Over and Out," *Army Wives,* Lifetime, 2010.

RECORDINGS

Albums; with Others; Cast Recordings and Soundtracks:

Legs Diamond 1988 original Broadway cast), RCA Victor, 1990.

Kiss of the Spider Woman 1994 Broadway cast), PolyGram Records, 1995.

Chicago (film soundtrack), Sony, 2003.

The Producers (film soundtrack), Sony, 2005.

WRITINGS

Screenplays:

Under the Wire, copyrighted c. 2006.

OTHER SOURCES

Periodicals:

Dance, January, 1994.

Electronic:

Robert Montano, http://www.robertmontano.com, June 24, 2010.

MUNDT, Brennan
   See BAILEY, Brennan

MURAWSKI, Bob 1964–

PERSONAL

Full name, Robert Murawski; born June 14, 1964, in Detroit, MI; married Chris Innis (a film editor, actress, and producer), 2008. *Education:* Michigan State University, graduated.

Addresses: *Office*—Grindhouse Releasing, P.O. Box 1634, Studio City, CA 91604. *Agent*—International Creative Management, 10250 Constellation Way, 9th Floor, Los Angeles, CA 90067.

Career: Film editor and producer. Mason Releasing, Detroit, MI, intern; Grindhouse Releasing, Studio City, CA, co–owner; Box Office Spectaculars, owner and operator. Also worked as assistant film editor, third–unit director, and sound technician.

Awards, Honors: Nomination for Golden Satellite Award, best film editing, International Press Academy, 2005, for *Spider–Man 2;* Satellite Award, Boston Society of Film Critics Award, and Sierra Award, Las Vegas Film Critics Society, all 2009, Academy Award, Eddie Award, American Cinema Editors, Film Award, British Academy of Film and Television Arts, Critics Choice Award nomination, Broadcast Film Critics Association, and Online Film Critics Society Award, all 2010, all best film editing (with Chris Innis) for *The Hurt Locker.*

CREDITS

Film Editor:

Danger Zone III: Steel Horse War, Premiere Home Video, 1990.

Carnal Crimes, Axis Films International, 1991.

Army of Darkness (also known as *Army of Darkness: The Ultimate Experience in Medieval Horror* and *Bruce Campbell vs. Army of Darkness*), Universal, 1993.

Hard Target, Universal, 1993.

(Contributor) *Freaked* (also known as *Freak Show*), Twentieth Century–Fox, 1993.

Object of Obsession, Axis Films International, 1994.

Animal Instincts II, Academy, 1994.

Night of the Scarecrow, Republic, 1995.

American Hero, 1997.

Uncle Sam, A–Pix Entertainment, 1997.

From Dusk till Dawn 2: Texas Blood Money, New Films International/Amuse Pictures, 1999.

The Gift, Paramount, 2000.

Spider–Man, Columbia, 2002.

Spider–Man 2 (also known as *Spider–Man 2.1* and *Spider–Man 2: The IMAX Experience*), Columbia, 2004.

(And producer) *Alan Yates* (short film), Grindhouse Releasing, 2005.

Vic (short film), Moonblood Pictures, 2006.

Spider–Man 3 (also known as *Spider–Man 3: The IMAX Experience*), Columbia, 2007.

(With wife, Chris Innis) *The Hurt Locker,* Summit Entertainment, 2009.

Drag Me to Hell (also known as *Spell*), Universal, 2009.

(And executive producer) *Gone with the Pope,* Grindhouse Releasing, 2010.

Television Film Editor; Movies:

The Expert, HBO, 1995.

Last Lives, Sci–Fi Channel, 1997.

RECORDINGS

Video Work:

Film editor, "Wrong Way" (music video), *Sublime: Sublime,* MCA, 1997.

Executive producer, *Pieces of Juan (Piquer Simon),* Grindhouse Releasing, 2008.

Executive producer, *Paul Smith: The Reddest Herring,* Grindhouse Releasing, 2008.

Film editor for the music videos "All Night" by the Alcoholiks; "Do Ya Think I'm Sexy?" by Revco/Ministry; "Sacrifice" by Motorhead; "Substitute" by the Ramones; "Wrong Way" by Sublime; and "Zoot Suit Riot" by Cherry Poppin' Daddies.

Video Appearances:

Making the Amazing (also known as *Making the Amazing: Spider–Man 2* and *Making the Amazing: The Making of "Spider–Man 2"*), Sony Pictures Home Entertainment, 2004.

N–O

NGUYEN, Ha

PERSONAL

Born in Saigon, South Vietnam; emigrated, 1975; raised in San Diego, CA; married Dean Heyde (a writer and director). *Education:* San Diego State University, graduated; Fashion Institute of Design and Merchandising, graduate study.

Addresses: *Agent*—Gersh Agency, 9465 Wilshire Blvd., 6th Floor, Beverly Hills, CA 90212.

Career: Costume designer. Began her career as a fashion designer.

Member: Academy of Motion Picture Arts and Sciences.

Awards, Honors: Saturn Award nomination, best costumes, Academy of Science Fiction, Fantasy, and Horror Films, 1995, for *The Mask.*

CREDITS

Film Costume Designer:
Moon 44, Moviestore Entertainment, 1990.
Night Eyes, 1990, Turner Home Entertainment, 1995.
Suburban Commando, New Line Cinema, 1991.
RoboCop 3, Orion, 1993.
Heaven & Earth, Warner Bros., 1993.
The Mask, New Line Cinema, 1994.
Vampire in Brooklyn (also known as *Wes Craven's "Vampire in Brooklyn"*), Paramount, 1995.
Mortal Kombat, New Line Cinema, 1995.
The Nutty Professor, Universal, 1996.
Thinner, Paramount, 1996.
Metro, Buena Vista, 1997.

Conspiracy Theory, Warner Bros., 1997.
Lethal Weapon 4 (also known as *Lethal 4*), Warner Bros., 1998.
Payback, Paramount, 1999.
House on Haunted Hill, Warner Bros., 1999.
Sunset Strip, Twentieth Century–Fox, 2000.
Swordfish, Warner Bros., 2001.
The Last Castle, DreamWorks, 2001.
The Adventures of Pluto Nash (also known as *Pluto Nash*), Warner Bros., 2002.
Cradle 2 the Grave (also known as *Black Diamond*), Warner Bros., 2003.
In the Mix, Lions Gate Films, 2005.
Mozart and the Whale, Millennium Films, 2006.
Zoom (also known as *Zoom: Academy for Superheroes*), Columbia, 2006.
Grace Is Gone, Weinstein Company, 2007.
Shooter, Paramount, 2007.
The Maiden Heist, Sony Pictures Home Entertainment, 2009.

Television Costume Designer; Movies:
Sunset Heat, HBO, 1992.
Timescape (also known as *The Grand Tour* and *Grand Tour: Disaster in Time*), Showtime, 1993.
Norma Jean & Marilyn, HBO, 1996.
The Jack Bull, HBO, 1999.
Back When We Were Grownups, CBS, 2004.
In from the Night, CBS, 2006.
Living Proof, Lifetime, 2008.

Television Costume Designer; Pilots:
Line of Fire, ABC, 2003.
13 Graves, Fox, 2006.
Mr. and Mrs. Smith, ABC, 2007.
Drop Dead Diva, Lifetime, 2009.

RECORDINGS

Videos:
Paybacks Are a Bitch, Paramount Home Entertainment, 2007.

NIKOLAS, Alexa 1992–
(Alexa Helen Nikolas)

PERSONAL

Full name, Alexa Helen Nikolas; born April 4, 1992, in Chicago, IL; daughter of Alexandra Nikolas (a realtor). *Avocational Interests:* Animals.

Career: Actress.

Awards, Honors: Young Artist Award nomination (with others), best performance in a feature film—young ensemble cast, 2005, for *Motocross Kids;* Young Artist Awards (with others), best young ensemble performance in a television series—comedy or drama, 2006, 2007, both for *Zoey 101.*

CREDITS

Film Appearances:
Story hour girl, *Zoolander,* Paramount, 2001.
I'm Ted Kid, *Ted Bundy* (also known as *Bundy*), First Look International, 2002.
Susan Barry, *Tiptoes,* Reality Check Productions, 2003.
Katie, *Motocross Kids,* Tag Entertainment, 2005.

Television Appearances; Series:
Young Lydia, *That's Life,* CBS, 2000–2002.
Emily Barber, *Hidden Hills,* NBC, 2002–2003.
Lucy Massey, *Revelations,* NBC, 2005.
Nicole Bristow, *Zoey 101,* Nickelodeon, 2005–2006.

Television Appearances; Movies:
Nicole, *"Zoey 101": Spring Break–Up,* Nickelodeon, 2006.
Ruth, *Children of the Corn* (also known as *Stephen King's "Children of the Corn"*), SyFy, 2009.

Television Appearances; Specials:
"All That" 10th Anniversary Special, Nickelodeon, 2005.

Television Appearances; Pilots:
Nicole Bristow, *Zoey 101,* Nickelodeon, 2005.

Television Appearances; Episodic:
Little girl number one, "Trances of a Lifetime," *The Love Boat: The Next Wave,* UPN, 1999.
Little girl, "We All Scream for Ice Cream," *Charmed,* The WB, 2001.

Young Carrie, "Veiled Threat," *The King of Queens,* CBS, 2001.
Young Ren, "Band on the Roof," *Even Stevens,* The Disney Channel, 2002.
Emily Levine, "Wannabe," *Without a Trace* (also known as *W.A.T.*), CBS, 2004.
Shelly Cecil, "Happy Borthday," *Judging Amy,* CBS, 2005.
Megan Nesbitt, "You Are Here," *ER,* NBC, 2005.
Madison Reed, "8:03 AM," *Cold Case,* CBS, 2007.
Tiffany, "Miniature Golf," *The Suite Life of Zack and Cody* (also known as *TSL* and *Suite Life*), The Disney Channel, 2007.
Tiffany, "Who's the Boss?," *The Suite Life of Zack and Cody* (also known as *TSL* and *Suite Life*), The Disney Channel, 2007.
Mallary Harding, "To Kill a Predator," *CSI: Miami,* CBS, 2008.
Caitlin Mahoney—ghost, "Threshold," *Ghost Whisperer,* CBS, 2008.
Kate Carter, "Family Remains," *Supernatural,* The CW, 2009.
Angela Shaw, "Chapter Ten '1961,'" *Heroes,* NBC, 2009.
Hannah Porter, "The Magic Bullet," *Drop Dead Diva,* Lifetime, 2009.
Caitlin, "Maybe, Baby," *Raising the Bar,* TNT, 2009.
Jane McBride, "The Fight," *Criminal Minds,* CBS, 2010.

RECORDINGS

Music Videos:

Appeared in Vanessa Anne Hudgens' "Come Back to Me."

NION
See WALLACE, Ian A.

O'CONNOR, Raymond 1952–
(Raymond O'Conner)

PERSONAL

Born September 13, 1952, in New York, NY.

Career: Actor. Appeared in more than 100 television commercials, including ads for Levi's Button Fly Jeans and American Express financial services, 1999, and Swiffer cleaning products, 2007.

CREDITS

Film Appearances:

Sergeant Elgin Flowers, *Off Limits* (also known as *Saigon* and *Saigon: Off Limits*), Twentieth Century–Fox, 1988.

First drunk, *Arthur 2: On the Rocks*, Warner Bros., 1988.

Tibbs, *Traxx*, De Laurentiis Entertainment Group, 1988.

Security guard, *Halloween 4: The Return of Michael Myers* (also known as *Halloween 4*), Anchor Bay Entertainment, 1988.

Drax, *Dr. Alien* (also known as *I Was a Teenage Sex Maniac* and *I Was a Teenage Sex Mutant*), Paramount Home Video, 1988.

Dino, *My Blue Heaven*, Warner Bros., 1990.

Taylor, *Megaville*, 1990.

Yo, *Life Stinks* (also known as *Life Sucks*), Metro–Goldwyn–Mayer, 1991.

Fireman, *Pyrates*, Vestron Video, 1991.

Frank Olsen, *Mr. Nanny*, New Line Cinema, 1993.

Park Ranger Bob, *The Rock*, Buena Vista, 1996.

Eddie, *My Giant*, Sony Pictures Entertainments, 1998.

Rabo Karabekian, *Breakfast of Champions*, Buena Vista, 1999.

Father Tom Stowick, *Drowning Mona*, Destination Films, 2000.

Sergeant Ted Burns, *April's Shower*, 2003.

Jimmy, *The Bug in My Ear* (short film), Power Up Films, 2003.

Frank, *Serial Killing 4 Dummys*, Lions Gate Films, 2004.

First Heston brother, *Bananas* (short film), Big Film Shorts, 2004.

Sleazy salesman, *Careful What You Wish For* (short film), 2004.

Manager, *See This Movie*, Slamdance on the Road, 2005.

Catholic priest, *Just Like Heaven*, DreamWorks, 2005.

(As Raymond O'Conner) Charlie, *Don't Come Knocking*, Sony Pictures Classics, 2006.

Pellini, *Love Made Easy*, Columbus Film, 2006.

Frank Peadman, *Bottoms Up*, 2006.

Mr. Gretano, *Diamonds and Guns*, West Coast Film Partners, 2008.

Jimmy, *Crazy*, Screen Media Ventures, 2008.

Norman Gardy, *The Intervention*, Think Pictures, 2009.

Richard, *Off the Ledge*, Vanguard Cinema, 2009.

Television Appearances; Movies:

Joe, *The Goddess of Love*, NBC, 1988.

Tugwell, *Cast a Deadly Spell*, HBO, 1991.

Mickey Maven, *Girls in Prison*, Showtime, 1994.

Mr. Muir, *Skeletons*, HBO, 1996.

Stutts, *Prehysteria! 3*, HBO, 1998.

First minister, *Audrey's Rain*, Hallmark Channel, 2003.

Dale, *Sands of Oblivion*, Sci–Fi Channel, 2007.

George Banks, *Shark Swarm*, Hallmark Channel, 2008.

Television Appearances; Miniseries:

New York newsboy, *Kane & Abel*, CBS, 1985.

Television Appearances; Pilots:

Harrigan, *Tag Team*, ABC, 1991.

Television Appearances; Episodic:

Nate Mornath, "Suitcase," *Hill Street Blues*, 1986.

Sooky Barnes, "The Cradle Will Rock," *Hunter*, NBC, 1987.

Raymond, "The Aztec Dagger," *The Wizard*, CBS, 1987.

Rick Santini, "The Lung Goodbye," *L.A. Law*, NBC, 1987.

Dicky Rich, "Rag Doll," *J. J. Starbuck*, 1988.

Phil Marker, "Something to Bank On," *Hard Time on Planet Earth*, 1989.

Falstead, "Love Bytes," *Hooperman*, ABC, 1989.

Manny, "Five Grand," *Growing Pains*, ABC, 1989.

Frank Watson, "Jules et Joel," *Northern Exposure*, 1991.

Burly man, "Field of Screams," *Who's the Boss?*, 1991.

Immigration officer, "Good Help Is Hard to Find," *Sisters*, NBC, 1992.

"The Littlest Shoplifter," *Baby Talk*, 1992.

Charlie, "Roc and the Actor," *Roc*, Fox, 1992.

Curtis Bray, "Parental Guidance Recommended," *Beverly Hills, 90210* (also known as *Class of Beverly Hills*), Fox, 1993.

Curtis Bray, "The Child Is Father to the Man," *Beverly Hills, 90210* (also known as *Class of Beverly Hills*), Fox, 1993.

Curtis Bray, "Duke's Bad Boy," *Beverly Hills, 90210* (also known as *Class of Beverly Hills*), Fox, 1993.

Hannon, "Friday the 13th," *Sirens*, ABC, 1993.

Peter Kincaid, "Woman Trouble," *Diagnosis Murder* (also known as *Dr. Mark Sloan*), CBS, 1994.

(Uncredited) Night doorman, "The Doorman," *Seinfeld*, 1995.

Artie Gallo, "Jersey Girl," *Vanishing Son*, 1995.

Dave Katz, "The Mouse Trappers," *Fudge*, 1995.

Merchant, "The Ex–Files," *Minor Adjustments*, NBC, 1995.

Howard, "Thanksgiving in Hawaii: Parts 1 & 2," *Sister, Sister*, The WB, 1995.

Engineer Willy, "Sons and Lovers," *Wings*, NBC, 1996.

Carl Granger, "Fool's Gold," *Land's End*, syndicated, 1996.

Leo, "One for the Monet," *Hudson Street*, CBS, 1996.

Officer Dibble, "Wheels," *Boy Meets World*, ABC, 1997.

Charlie Spring, "Private Eyes," *The Sentinel*, UPN, 1997.

"Child's Play," *Silk Stalkings*, USA Network, 1997.

Frank Rizzo, "I Was En Vogue's Love Slave," *The Wayans Bros.*, The WB, 1997.

Officer Kelly, "African–American Me," *The Steve Harvey Show*, The WB, 1997.

Mack, "A View from the Gallery," *Babylon 5* (also known as *B5*), TNT, 1998.

Vice Principal Strauss, "Barricade," *Brutally Normal,* The WB, 2000.

Lenny Sinclair, "All the Rage," *Becker,* CBS, 2000.

Happy, "Jerque Du Soleil," *City of Angels,* CBS, 2000.

Harvey, "USA Toy," *The Michael Richards Show,* NBC, 2000.

"Val's on First," *V.I.P.,* 2000.

Cookie, "Heart Problems," *That's Life,* ABC, 2001.

Cab driver, *Days of Our Lives* (also known as *Days* and *DOOL*), NBC, 2001.

Charlie Cramachuck, "Laughlin' It Up," *Dead Last,* 2001.

Teeth, "Tabula Rosa," *Buffy the Vampire Slayer* (also known as *Buff, Buffy, the Vampire Slayer: The Series,* and *Nightfall*), UPN, 2001.

Man on phone, "The Plan," *Six Feet Under,* HBO, 2002.

"It's Raining Men," *Providence,* 2002.

Albert Beechem, "The Freak," *Boomtown,* NBC, 2002.

Aldo Sanfratello (The Dentist), "Nude Awakening," *NYPD Blue* (also known as *N.Y.P.D.*), ABC, 2003.

Kevin Morris, "Dirty White Collar," *The Handler,* CBS, 2003.

Clemm, "Mr. Monk and the Red Herring," *Monk,* USA Network, 2005.

Salesman, "Killer," *CSI: Crime Scene Investigation* (also known as *C.S.I.* and *CSI: Las Vegas*), CBS, 2006.

Tendell Rusk, "Would You Want Me to Tell You?," *Saving Grace,* TNT, 2007.

Also appeared as Phil, *Between Brothers,* UPN; Mr. Man, *Damon,* Fox; Carl, *Down the Shore,* Fox; Ray, *Drexell's Class,* Fox; Al, *Malcolm in the Middle,* Fox; Paul Jarrett, *To Have & To Hold,* CBS; Walter, *Two of a Kind,* ABC; and in *Frank Leaves for the Orient,* Comedy Central; according to some sources, appeared as a bus driver in an episode of *The Unit,* CBS.

OSMANSKI, Joy 1975–

PERSONAL

Full name, Joy Kathleen Osmanski; born October 29, 1975, in Seoul, South Korea; immigrated to the United States; raised in Olympia, WA; daughter of Frank (some sources cite name as Al) and Kathleen Osmanski; married Corey Brill (an actor), December 31, 2009. *Education:* Principia College, degree in creative writing and studio art (magna cum laude); University of California, San Diego, M.F.A., theatre, 2003. *Avocational Interests:* Cooking.

Addresses: *Agent*—Suzanne Wohl, TalentWorks, 3500 West Olive Ave., Suite 1400, Burbank, CA 91505; (voice work) Cunningham/Escott/Slevin & Doherty Talent Agency, 10635 Santa Monica Blvd., Suite 140, Los Angeles, CA 90025.

Career: Actress and voice artist. Appeared in advertisements. Worked as an acting coach. Worked as a graphic designer and magazine art director in Boston, MA; Open Door Design, near San Francisco, CA, founder. Volunteered as an English tutor.

Awards, Honors: San Diego *Playbill* Billie Award (with others), outstanding ensemble, 2003, for *The Three Sisters;* San Francisco Bay Area Theatre Critics Circle Award (with others), best ensemble performance, 2004, for *Major Barbara.*

CREDITS

Television Appearances; Series:

Voice, *Beverly Hills Anger Management* (animated), beginning c. 2005 (some sources cite c. 2008.

Darcy, *The Loop,* Fox, 2006–2007.

Intern Lucy, *Grey's Anatomy* (also known as *Complications, Procedure, Surgeons, Under the Knife,* and *Grey's Anatomy—Die jungen Aerzte*), ABC, 2007–2008.

Television Appearances; Episodic:

Herself, "Box Office Performance Show 1," *On the Lot,* Fox, 2007.

Herself, "13 Cut to 12 & 12 Directors Compete," *On the Lot,* Fox, 2007.

Herself, "11 Cut to 10 & 10 Directors Compete," *On the Lot,* Fox, 2007.

Tracy, "The Break Up," *Samantha Who?* (also known as *Samantha, Samantha Be Good,* and *Sam I Am*), ABC, 2007.

Tracy, "The Hockey Date," *Samantha Who?* (also known as *Samantha, Samantha Be Good,* and *Sam I Am*), ABC, 2007.

Tracy, "The Job," *Samantha Who?* (also known as *Samantha, Samantha Be Good,* and *Sam I Am*), ABC, 2007.

Tracy, "The Butterflies," *Samantha Who?* (also known as *Samantha, Samantha Be Good,* and *Sam I Am*), ABC, 2008.

File clerk, "Greatest Hits," *Numb3rs* (also known as *Numbers* and *Num3ers*), CBS, 2009.

Jackie, "The Waitress Is Getting Married," *It's Always Sunny in Philadelphia* (also known as *It's Always Sunny, It's Always Sunny on TV,* and *Sunny*), FX Network, 2009.

Lucy, "Bioshuffle," *Better Off Ted* (also known as *Untitled Victor Fresco Project*), ABC, 2009.

Miss Park, "Back to School," *True Jackson, VP* (also known as *True Fashion*), Nickelodeon, 2009.

Miss Park, "True Concert," *True Jackson, VP* (also known as *True Fashion*), Nickelodeon, 2009.

Miss Park, "My Boss Ate My Homework," *True Jackson, VP* (also known as *True Fashion*), Nickelodeon, 2010.

Miss Park, "True Drama," *True Jackson, VP* (also known as *True Fashion*), Nickelodeon, 2010.

Television Appearances; Pilots:
(Uncredited) Darcy, *The Loop,* Fox, 2006.
Judy, *Five Year Plan* (also known as *5 Year Plan*), ABC, 2008.
Lexi Miller, *Nathan vs. Nurture,* NBC, 2010.

Stage Appearances:
Irene's assistant, *The Matchmaker,* San Jose Repertory Theatre, San Jose, CA, 1999.
Margareta and Helen, *Faust Fragments,* University of California, San Diego, Mandell Weiss Center for the Performing Arts, Mandell Weiss Forum Studio, La Jolla, CA, 2001.
Member of the cheerleader chorus, *Be Aggressive,* La Jolla Playhouse, Mandell Weiss Center for the Performing Arts, Mandell Weiss Theatre, La Jolla, CA, 2001.
The Dumb Waiter, University of California, San Diego, c. 2002.
Masha, *The Three Sisters,* University of California, San Diego, Mandell Weiss Center for the Performing Arts, Mandell Weiss Forum Studio, 2003.
Jenny Hill, *Major Barbara,* San Jose Repertory Theatre, 2004.
Kim Jong Il, *The Edge of Allegiance III: Permanent Vacation, or Endless Bummer!* (also known as *The Edge of Allegiance III: Permanent Vacation*), MET Theatre, Los Angeles, 2004.
Lily Plants a Garden, Mark Taper P.L.A.Y., Los Angeles, c. 2004.
Johanna, *Baal,* Yale Cabaret Hollywood at M Bar, Hollywood, CA, 2005.
The Unbearable Truth, Mark Taper Forum P.L.A.Y., Los Angeles, c. 2005.
Juliet, *Romeo and Juliet,* A Noise Within, Glendale, CA, 2007.
Olga, *Three Sisters,* Chalk Repertory Theatre, Hollywood Forever Cemetery, Masonic Lodge, Hollywood, CA, 2009.

Appeared in other productions, including *Is Life a Dream?,* San Jose Repertory Theatre; and in a leading role in *Our Town,* San Francisco, CA area.

Film Appearances:
Receptionist, *A Fat Girl's Guide to Yoga* (short film), 2007.
Borderline (short film), 2007.
Curious cheerleader, *Fired Up!,* Screen Gems, 2009.
Mary, *White on Rice,* Variance Films, 2009.
Melanie Wynn, *A New Color* (short film), 2009.
Voice of airline representative, *Alvin and the Chipmunks: The Squeakquel* (also known as *Alvin and the Chipmunks II* and *Alvin 2*), Twentieth Century–Fox, 2009.
Jinnie Park, *Wedding Palace,* 2010.
Surrogate Valentine, Brainwave/Tiger Industry Films, 2011.

Internet Appearances:
Cohost of *Hungry? City Guides Foodie File—The Nickel Diner,* posted on *YouTube,* http://www.youtube.com. Appeared in other footage posted on the Internet.

RECORDINGS

Videos:
Thesis: Work vs. Play (short film), Twentieth Century–Fox Home Entertainment, 2007.

WRITINGS

Writings for the Stage:
Wrote plays.

Nonfiction:
Author of a cookbook with Judy Brill.

OTHER SOURCES

Periodicals:
Daily & Sunday Jeffersonian, December 31, 2009.

Electronic:
Joy Osmanski, http://joyosmanskionline.com, June 24, 2010.

P

PARISE, Vanessa

PERSONAL

Raised in RI; sister of Jeremy Parise (an actor and composer). *Education:* Harvard University, graduated (magna cum laude); attended The Second City and the Circle in the Square Theatre School.

Addresses: *Office*—Empera Pictures, 9200 West Sunset Blvd., Suite 505, West Hollywood, CA 90069.

Career: Actress, director, producer, and writer. Empera Pictures, West Hollywood, CA, principal. Participated in conventions relating to the entertainment industry.

Member: Writers Guild of America, West.

Awards, Honors: Merit Award, New England Film & Video Festival, 2000, for *Lo and Jo;* Audience Award, best feature, Rhode Island International Film Festival, 2002, Golden Starfish Award, best fictional feature film or video, Hamptons International Film Festival, 2002, Sarasota Film Festival Award, excellence in filmmaking, 2003, and special mention for Director's Award, acting category, Cinequest San Jose Film Festival, 2003, all for *Kiss the Bride.*

CREDITS

Film Appearances:
Lo and Jo (short film; also known as *lo and jo*), Empera Pictures, 1998.
Christina "Chrissy" Sposato, *Kiss the Bride,* Metro–Goldwyn–Mayer Home Entertainment, 2002.

Lucy, *Jack and Jill vs. the World* (also known as *Dick and Jane vs. the World* and *Jack and Jill vs the World*), Lantern Lane Entertainment, 2008.

Film Director and Producer:
Lo and Jo (short film; also known as *lo and jo*), Empera Pictures, 1998.
Kiss the Bride, Metro–Goldwyn–Mayer Home Entertainment, 2002.
Jack and Jill vs. the World (also known as *Dick and Jane vs. the World* and *Jack and Jill vs the World*), Lantern Lane Entertainment, 2008.

Television Appearances; Series:
Host (veejay), *Savvy,* WE: Women's Entertainment, beginning 2004.
Herself, *On Set, on Edge* (reality television series), beginning 2007.
Ali, *I'm in the Band* (also known as *Tripp's Rockband* and *Viper Slap*), The Disney Channel, beginning 2009.

Television Appearances; Episodic:
Laura Sloan Freeman, "The House on Barry Avenue," *Beyond Belief: Fact or Fiction* (also known as *Beyond Belief* and *Strange Truth: Fact or Fiction*), Fox, 1998.

Television Appearances; Pilots:
Appeared in pilots.

Television Work:
Executive producer and episode director, *On Set, on Edge* (reality television series), beginning 2007.

Stage Appearances:
Sarah, *Seascape,* Theatre 22, New York City, 1995.
Georgie, *Spike Heels,* Harbinger Theatre Company, Actors Circle Theatre, Los Angeles, 2010.

Appeared in improvisational productions at The Second City.

Stage Work:

Producer, *Spike Heels,* Harbinger Theatre Company, Actors Circle Theatre, Los Angeles, 2010.

WRITINGS

Screenplays:

Lo and Jo (short film; also known as *lo and jo*), Empera Pictures, 1998.
Kiss the Bride, Metro–Goldwyn–Mayer Home Entertainment, 2002.
(With Peter Stebbings) *Jack and Jill vs. the World* (also known as *Dick and Jane vs. the World* and *Jack and Jill vs the World*), Lantern Lane Entertainment, 2008.

With Robin Dunne, wrote the screenplay *BFF* (also known as *B.F.F.*). Author of other screenplays, including *Never Change* (based on a novel). Some sources cite work on the project *Lumiere.*

Teleplays; Pilots:

(With Robin Dunne) *Shape,* c. 2009.

Writings for the Stage:

Contributed to improvisational productions at The Second City.

OTHER SOURCES

Periodicals:

Motif, April 3, 2008.
Variety, August 15, 2005, p. 5.
Venice, April, 2008, p. 14.

Electronic:

Jack and Jill vs. the World, http://jackandjillvsthe world. com, June 24, 2010.
Script, http://www.scriptmag.com, August 9, 2010.

PARISOT, Dean

PERSONAL

Education: New York University, graduate of Tisch School of the Arts; also attended Sundance Institute.

Addresses: *Agent*—Creative Artists Agency, 2000 Avenue of the Stars, Los Angeles, CA 90067.

Career: Director, producer, and writer. Director of documentary films for various cultural institutions, including Museum of Modern Art, New York City.

Member: Directors Guild of America.

Awards, Honors: Golden Berlin Bear, best short film, Berlin International Film Festival, 1986, for *Tom Goes to the Bar;* Academy Award (with Steven Wright), best live action short film, 1988, for *The Appointments of Dennis Jennings;* Annual CableACE Award, best direction, National Cable Television Association, 1988, both for *Steven Wright in the Appointments of Dennis Jennings;* Annual CableACE Award, best direction, 1995, for "Kathy & Mo: The Dark Side," *HBO Comedy Hour;* Pegasus Audience Award, Brussels International Festival of Fantasy Film, Saturn Award nomination, best director, Academy of Science Fiction, Fantasy, and Horror Films, Silver Scream Award, Amsterdam Fantastic Film Festival, 2000, Hochi Film Award, best foreign language film, 2001, all for *Galaxy Quest.*

CREDITS

Film Director:

Tom Goes to the Bar (short film), 1985.
The Appointments of Dennis Jennings (short film), 1988, broadcast on television as *Stephen Wright in the Appointments of Dennis Jennings,* HBO, 1989, and released as a segment of the film *Two Mikes Don't Make a Wright,* 1992.
The Last Seat (short film), 1994.
At the Movies I, 1994.
At the Movies II, 1994.
Home Fries, Warner Bros., 1998.
Galaxy Quest, DreamWorks, 1999.
Fun with Dick and Jane (also known as *Alternative Career* and *Fun with Dick & Jane*), Columbia, 2005.

Television Work; Series:

Executive producer, *77 Sunset Strip,* 1996.

Television Work; Movies:

Director, *Framed,* HBO, 1990.
Director and executive producer, *A.T.F.,* ABC, 1998.
Director and executive producer, *Area 57,* 2007.
Director, *See Kate Run,* 2009.

Television Work; Pilots:

Director and producer, *Bakersfield P.D.,* Fox, 1993.
Director, *The Marshal,* The Family Channel, 1995.

Director, *The Conversation*, NBC, 1995.
Director, *The Job*, ABC, 2001.
Director, *The Heart Department*, CBS, 2001.
Director, *Monk*, USA Network, 2002.
Director, *Bad News, Mr. Swanson*, FX Network, 2002.
Director, *Sullivan's Run*, ABC, 2010.

Television Work; Specials:
Camera operator, *The Bangles Live at the Syria Mosque*, 1986.
(With others) Director, "Steven Wright: Wicker Chairs and Gravity," *HBO Comedy Hour*, HBO, 1990.
Director, "Kathy & Mo: The Dark Side," *HBO Comedy Hour*, HBO, 1995.

Television Director; Episodic:
"Health Inspector 2000," *Get a Life*, Fox, 1991.
"Things Become Extinct," *Northern Exposure*, CBS, 1992.
"Northwest Passages," *Northern Exposure*, CBS, 1992.
Likely Suspects, Fox, 1992.
"Survival of the Species," *Northern Exposure*, CBS, 1993.
Going to Extremes, ABC, 1993.
Under Suspicion, CBS, 1995.
"What Life?," *ER*, NBC, 1995.
The Marshal, ABC, 1995.
77 Sunset Strip, 1996.
L.A. Doctors (also known as *L.A. Docs*), NBC, 1998.
"Shaq," *Curb Your Enthusiasm*, HBO, 2001.
"Mr. Monk and the Candidate: Parts 1 & 2," *Monk*, USA Network, 2002.
"Arthur, Interrupted," *The Tick*, Fox, 2002.
"Mr. Monk and the Badge," *Monk*, USA Network, 2009.

Stage Director:
Directed *Kathy & Mo: The Dark Side* for the stage.

WRITINGS

Screenplays:
Still Life (also known as *Art Killer Framed* and *Still Life: The Fine Art of Murder*), 1988.

Television Specials:
"Steven Wright: Wicker Chairs and Gravity," *HBO Comedy Hour*, HBO, 1990.

PARKINSON, Katherine 1978–

PERSONAL

Born 1978, in England; married Harry Peacock (an actor). *Education:* Attended Oxford University and London Academy of Music and Dramatic Art.

Career: Actress. Appeared in commercials for Maltesers chocolates, beginning 2006.

CREDITS

Television Appearances; Series:
Pauline Lamb, *Doc Martin*, ITV, 2005—.
Jen, *The IT Crowd*, Independent Film Channel, 2006–2008.

Television Appearances; Miniseries:
Gemma, *Fear, Stress, and Anger*, BBC, 2007.
Amber, *The Old Guys*, BBC1, 2009.

Television Appearances; Movies:
Vicky Foley, *Ahead of the Class*, ITV, 2005.
Vanessa, *Christmas at the Riviera*, ITV, 2007.

Television Appearances; Specials:
Voice, *Love Triangle*, Channel 4, 2007.
Stella, *Comic Relief 2009*, BBC, 2009.

Television Appearances; Episodic:
(Uncredited) Helen Gibbons, "The Long Goodbye," *Casualty*, BBC1, 2005.
Woman in line, "Ross Kemp," *Extras*, HBO, 2005.
Nicola, "The Grinning Man," *Jonathan Creek*, PBS, 2009.

Film Appearances:
Katie, *Hard to Swallow* (short film), RSA Films, 2006.
Public relations woman, *How to Lose Friends & Alienate People*, Metro–Goldwyn–Mayer, 2008.
Marion Whittaker, *Easy Virtue*, Sony Pictures Classics, 2009.
Pirate Radio (also known as *The Boat that Rocked* and *Pirates Rock*), Focus Features, 2009.
Physics teacher, *St Trinian's 2: The Legend of Fritton's Gold* (also known as *St Trinian's II*), Ealing Studios/Fragile Films, 2009.
Voice, *Cooked*, National Film and Television School, 2010.

Stage Appearances:
Vermin (sketch show), Finborough Theatre, London, 2000.
Stephanie, *The Age of Consent*, Bush Theatre, London, and Edinburgh Festival Theatre, Edinburgh, Scotland, 2001.
Young Lynette, *Frame 312*, Donmar Warehouse Theatre, London, 2002.
Linda Lovelace, *Deep Throat Live*, Assembly Rooms, Edinburgh Festival, 2002.
Antigone, *The Riot Act*, Gate Theatre, London, 2003.

The Increased Difficulty of Concentration, Gate Theatre, 2003.

Olympe, *Camille,* Lyric Hammersmith Theatre, London, 2003.

Lilly, *Flush,* Crucible Studio Theatre, Sheffield, England, 2004.

Frank, *The Unthinkable,* Crucible Studio Theatre, 2004.

Lydia, *Other Hands,* Soho Theatre, London, 2006.

Imogen, *The Lightning Play,* Almeida Theatre, London, 2006–2007.

Masha, *The Seagull,* Royal Court Theatre, London, 2007.

Radio Appearances; Series:

Voices, *Laura Solon: Talking and Not Talking,* BBC4, 2007.

Radio Appearances; Specials:

Catherine, *A Certain Smile,* BBC4, 2004.

PARODI, Starr

PERSONAL

Born in Los Angeles, CA; married Jeff Eden Fair (a composer and musician). *Education:* Attended Interlochen Arts Academy in Michigan; Orange Coast College, graduated, 1980; attended University of California, Los Angeles, and Ecole Normale de Musique, Paris; also studied with Edith Smith.

Addresses: *Agent*—Christine Russell, Evolution Music Partners, 1680 North Vine St., Suite 500, Hollywood, CA 90028.

Career: Composer, musician, and orchestrator. Sonic Doppler–Gray Dog Studios, Los Angeles, cofounder and partner; Parodifair, partner. With husband Jeff Eden Fair, composer of music for more than 150 film trailers, including award–winning trailers for *Blown Away, Goldeneye, Hackers, Speechless, Species, Stargate, Tombstone,* and *U–Turn.* Keyboard accompanist for numerous recording artists, including Phil Collins, Celine Dion, B. B. King, Patti LaBelle, and Carlos Santana; pianist for bandleader George Howard, 1985; pianist at the inauguration of President Bill Clinton, 1993; keyboard performer for commercials and music videos. Also worked as a model.

Awards, Honors: (All with Jeff Eden Fair) BMI Cable Award, BMI Film and Television Awards, 2003, 2004, both for *The Division;* Gold Telly Award, 2004, for *Ice Age Fossils of the La Brea Tar Pits;* Telly Awards for film trailer for *Blown Away* and *Tombstone;* Chicago International Film Festival Award, London International Award, Key Art Award, and Telly Award, all for film trailer for *Goldeneye;* Chicago International Film Festival Award, Key Art Award, and Telly Award, all for film trailer for *Hackers;* Chicago International Film Festival Award and London International Award, both for film trailer for *Speechless;* New York Festivals Award and Telly Award, both for film trailer for *Species;* London International Award and Telly Award, for film trailer for *Stargate;* Chicago International Film Festival Award and Key Art Award, both for film trailer for *U–Turn;* gold record certification, Recording Industry Association of America, for the song "Best of Bond."

CREDITS

Television Appearances; Series:

Fame, NBC, 1983–86.

Synthesizer player with Michael Wolff and The Posse (house band), *The Arsenio Hall Show,* syndicated, 1988–93.

Keyboard performer for *The Fritz Coleman Show,* KNBC.

Television Work; Series:

Pianist, *The Division* (also known as *Heart of the City*), Lifetime, 2001–2003.

Television Work; Movies:

Song producer, *High Roller: The Stu Ungar Story* (also known as *Stuey*), Starz!, 2003.

Television Work; Episodic:

Musical performer for episodes of *Doogie Howser, M.D.,* ABC; *Hunter,* NBC; *L.A. Law,* NBC; *Magnum, P.I.,* CBS; *Nashville Beat; Quantum Leap,* NBC; *21 Jump Street,* Fox and syndicated; and *Wise Guy,* CBS.

Film Work:

Orchestrator, *The Eighteenth Angel,* Rysher Entertainment, 1997.

Song performer, *Becoming Bert Stern* (documentary), Magic Film Productions, 2010.

RECORDINGS

Albums:

Change, Capitol, 1991.

Common Places, 2006.

WRITINGS

Television Composer, with Jeff Eden Fair; Series:

The Edge, Fox, 1992–93.

Champs, ABC, 1996.

Malibu Shores, NBC, 1996.
Main title music, *Gottschalk,* beginning 1996.
(Including theme music) *Arsenio,* ABC, 1997.
Maggie, Lifetime, 1998–99.
The Division (also known as *Heart of the City*), Lifetime, 2001–2004.
The Starter Wife, USA Network, 2008.

Also contributor of music to the series *Fame,* NBC; composer for *The Fritz Coleman Show,* KNBC.

Television Composer, with Jeff Eden Fair; Movies:
Shame II: The Secret, Lifetime, 1995.
The Secret She Carried, NBC, 1996.
Crowned and Dangerous, ABC, 1997.
Little Girls in Pretty Boxes, Lifetime, 1997.
A Nightmare Come True (also known as *A Dream of Murder*), CBS, 1997.
I've Been Waiting for You, NBC, 1998.
The Sky's on Fire (also known as *Countdown: The Sky's on Fire*), ABC, 1998.
A Family in Crisis: The Elian Gonzales Story (also known as *The Elian Gonzales Story*), Fox Family, 2000.
Sex, Lies & Obsession, Lifetime, 2001.
High Roller: The Stu Ungar Story (also known as *Stuey*), Starz!, 2003.

Television Composer; Pilots:
Interrogation Room, Fox, 2005.

Film Composer, with Jeff Eden Fair:
Marilyn: The Last Word (documentary), Paramount, 1993.
The Eighteenth Angel, Rysher Entertainment, 1997.
Screenland Drive, Zzyzx Films, 2000.
Do You Wanna Know a Secret?, Mainline Releasing, 2001.
Ice Age Fossils of the La Brea Tar Pits (short documentary), Natural History Museum of Los Angeles County, 2004.
Conversations with Other Women, Fabrication Films, 2005.
The Cuckold, Mythological Beast Films, 2009.
5150 (short film), 2010.
(Including song "Common Places") *Becoming Bert Stern* (documentary), Magic Film Productions, 2010.

Songs Featured in Films:
"Bertha Lands," "Stargate Trailer," and "Warning," *Ghost World,* Metro–Goldwyn–Mayer, 2001.
"Tikis and Tuxedos," *Memoirs of a Teenage Amnesiac,* Toei Company, 2010.

Composer for Albums:
Change, Capitol, 1991.

With Jeff Eden Fair and Aeone, composer for music catalog collections.

OTHER SOURCES

Periodicals:
Grammy, December 2, 2002.
Mix, September 1, 1999.

Electronic:
Parodifair Web Site, http://www.parodifair.com, June 25, 2010.

PARRIOTT, James D. 1950–
   (James Parriott, Jim Parriott)

PERSONAL

Born November 14, 1950, in Denver, CO; married Diane Cary (an actress). *Education:* University of Denver, B.A., 1972; University of California, Los Angeles, M.F.A., 1974.

Addresses: *Agent*—Creative Artists Agency, 9830 Wilshire Blvd., Beverly Hills, CA 90212.

Career: Writer, producer, and director. Sometimes credited as Jim Parriott.

Member: Writers Guild of America, Directors Guild of America, Producers Guild of America.

Awards, Honors: Gemini Award nominations, best dramatic series, Academy of Canadian Cinema and Television, 1994 and 1997, for *Forever Knight;* Emmy Award nomination (with others), outstanding drama series, Writers Guild of America Award (with others), new series, Television Producer of the Year Award nomination (with others), drama—episodic, 2006, Writers Guild of America Award nominations (with others), dramatic series, 2006 and 2007, Television Producer of the Year Award (with others), drama—episodic, 2007, for *Grey's Anatomy;* Emmy Award nomination (with others), outstanding comedy series, Writers Guild of America Award (with others), new series, 2007, Television Producer of the Year Award nomination, comedy—episodic, 2008, for *Ugly Betty.*

CREDITS

Film Director:
Voyager from the Unknown, MCA Home Video, 1982.
Heart Condition, New Line Cinema, 1990.
Good, 1998.

Television Work; Series:
Producer, *The Bionic Woman,* ABC, 1976–77, then NBC, 1977–78.
Producer, *The Incredible Hulk,* CBS, 1978–82, then NBC, 1982–85.
Executive producer, *Fitz & Bones,* NBC, 1981.
Executive producer, *Voyagers!,* NBC, 1982.
Executive producer, *Hawaiian Heat,* ABC, 1984.
Executive producer and creator, *Misfits of Science,* NBC, 1985.
Executive producer, *Elvis,* ABC, 1990.
Creator and producer, *Forever Knight,* CBS, 1992–93, then syndicated, 1994–96.
Executive producer, *Dark Skies,* NBC, 1996.
Creator and executive producer, *Educating Matt Waters* (also known as *Matt Waters*), CBS, 1996.
Executive producer and creator, *The American Embassy,* Fox, 2002.
Co–executive producer, *Push, Nevada,* ABC, 2002.
Executive producer and showrunner, *MDs,* ABC, 2002.
Executive producer, *The Partners,* ABC, 2003.
(As James Parriot) Executive producer, *Grey's Anatomy,* ABC, 2005–2006.
(As James Parriot) Executive producer, *Ugly Betty,* ABC, 2006–2007.
(As Jim Parriot) Co–executive producer, *Sons of Anarchy,* FX Network, 2008.
(As James Parriot) Executive producer, *Defying Gravity,* 2009.
(As James Parriot) Executive producer, *Covert Affairs,* USA Network, 2010—.

Television Work; Movies:
Supervising producer, *The Incredible Hulk,* CBS, 1977.
Executive producer, *Island Sons,* ABC, 1987.
Executive producer, *Nick Knight,* CBS, 1989.
Executive producer, *Staying Afloat,* NBC, 1993.
Director, *Rag and Bone,* 1997.

Television Work; Miniseries:
Executive producer, *The Invaders,* The WB, 1995.

Television Work; Pilots:
Producer, *Nick and the Dobermans,* NBC, 1980.
Supervising producer, *Alex and the Doberman Gang,* NBC, 1980.
Executive producer, *The Seal,* NBC, 1981.
Director, *Voyagers!,* NBC, 1982.
Director, *Misfits of Science,* NBC, 1985.
Director and executive producer, *Bodyguards,* ABC, 1995.
Executive producer, *Educating Matt Waters* (also known as *Matt Waters*), CBS, 1996.
Executive producer, *Rag & Bone,* CBS, 1998.
Executive producer, *The Partners,* ABC, 2003.

Television Director; Episodic:
"The Haunting of Chatham Bay," *The American Girls* (also known as *Have Girls Will Travel*), CBS, 1978.

"A Child in Need," *The Incredible Hulk,* CBS, 1978.
From Here to Eternity, NBC, 1980.
Misfits of Science, NBC, 1985.
"Lights, Camera, Action," *Action,* syndicated, 1999.
"Homewrecker for the Holidays," *Tucker,* NBC, 2001.

Directed episodes of *Voyagers!,* NBC.

Television Executive Producer; Episodic:
"Natural Borne Killers," *Threat Matrix,* 2003.
Six Degrees, ABC, 2006.

WRITINGS

Screenplays:
Heart Condition, 1990.
Rag and Bone, 1997.

Television Movies:
Island Sons, ABC, 1987.
Nick Night, CBS, 1989.

Television Pilots:
The Legend of the Golden Gun, NBC, 1979.
Nick and the Dobermans, NBC, 1980.
Alex and the Doberman Gang, NBC, 1980.
The Seal, NBC, 1981.
Voyagers!, NBC, 1982.
Misfits of Science, NBC, 1985.
(As James Parriott; with Barney Cohen) "Nick Knight," *Forever Knight,* CBS, 1989.
Bodyguards, ABC, 1995.
Rag & Bone, CBS, 1998.
The American Embassy, Fox, 2002.

Television Series:
Hawaiian Heat, 1984.
Misfits of Science, NBC, 1985–86.
Forever Knight, syndicated and USA Network, 1989–96.
Matt Waters, 1996.
(As James Parriott) *Defying Gravity,* 2009.

Television Episodes:
"The Fine Art of Diplomacy," *The Invisible Man,* 1975.
"Barnard Wants Out," *The Invisible Man,* 1975.
"Pin Money," *The Invisible Man,* 1975.
"The Deadly Test," *The Six Million Dollar Man,* ABC, 1975.
"Sam Casey, Sam Casey," *Gemini Man,* 1976.
The Bionic Woman, ABC, 1976–77, then NBC, 1977–78.
"The Haunting of Chatham Bay," *The American Girls* (also known as *Have Girls Will Travel*), CBS, 1978.

"Of Guilt, Models and Murder," *The Incredible Hulk,* 1978.

"Life and Death," *The Incredible Hulk,* 1978.

From Here to Eternity, NBC, 1980.

"A Difficult Lesson," *Fitz and Bones,* NBC, 1980.

"Agents of Satan," *Voyagers,* NBC, 1982.

(With Jill Sherman) "Worlds Apart," *Voyagers,* NBC, 1982.

"The Travels of Marco Polo ... and Friends," *Voyagers,* NBC, 1982.

(With Sherman) "Voyagers of the Titanic," *Voyagers,* NBC, 1983.

(With Sara Parriott) "Jacks' Back," *Voyagers,* NBC, 1983.

"The Storm," *Elvis,* 1990.

"Mercury Rising," *Dark Skies,* NBC, 1996.

(With Gay Walch) "Ancient Future," *Dark Skies,* NBC, 1996.

"Burn, Baby, Burn," *Dark Skies,* NBC, 1996.

"The Color Of ...," *Push, Nevada,* ABC, 2002.

"China Cup," *The American Embassy,* Fox, 2002.

Threat Matrix, 2003.

(As James Parriot) "No Man's Land," *Grey's Anatomy,* ABC, 2005.

(As James Parriot) "Enough Is Enough," *Grey's Anatomy,* ABC, 2005.

(As James Parriot) "Superstition," *Grey's Anatomy,* ABC, 2006.

(As James Parriot) "I'm Coming Out," *Ugly Betty,* ABC, 2007.

(As James Parriot) "Swag," *Ugly Betty,* ABC, 2007.

(As Jim Parriot) "Patch Over," *Sons of Anarchy,* FX Network, 2008.

Also wrote episodes of *The Legend of the Golden Gun;* "Walking on the Moon," *American Embassy* (unaired), Fox; (with Leslie Stevens) "An Attempt to Save Face," *The Invisible Man* (unaired).

PASQUALE, Steven 1976–

PERSONAL

Original name, Steven J. Pasquale; born November 18, 1976, in Hershey, PA; married Laura Benanti (an actress), September 16, 2007; children: Maddie.

Addresses: *Agent*—International Creative Management, 10250 Constellation Blvd., 9th Floor, Los Angeles, CA 90067; 825 Eighth Ave., New York, NY 10019. *Manager*—Brookside Artists Management, 250 West 57th St., Suite 2303, New York, NY 10019.

Career: Actor.

Awards, Honors: Drama Desk Award nomination, outstanding featured actor in a musical, Outer Critics Circle Award nomination, outstanding featured actor in a musical, 2003, both for *A Man of No Importance.*

CREDITS

Film Appearances:

Jack Manning, *The Last Run,* New Line Cinema, 2004.

Jacob Shorter, *Aurora Borealis,* Regent Releasing, 2005.

Dallas, *AVPR: Aliens vs Predator—Requiem* (also known as *AVP: Aliens vs. Predator—Requiem, AVP: Requiem, Aliens vs. Predator 2, AvP2,* and *AvPR*), Twentieth Century–Fox, 2007.

(Uncredited) Elizabeth's date, *Arlen Faber* (also known as *The Answer Man*), Magnolia Pictures, 2009.

Television Appearances; Series:

Platinum, UPN, 2002–03.

Sean Garrity, *Rescue Me,* FX Network, 2004–10.

Television Appearances; Specials:

Presenter, *Fashion Rocks,* Fox, 2004.

Presenter, *The 63rd Annual Tony Awards,* CBS, 2009.

Television Appearances; Miniseries:

Luke, *Marry Me,* Lifetime, 2010.

Television Appearances; Episodic:

Kurt, "Crossroads," *Six Feet Under,* HBO, 2001.

Kurt, "Life's Too Short," *Six Feet Under,* HBO, 2001.

The Morning Show with Mike & Juliet, Fox and syndicated, 2009.

Stage Appearances:

Burrs and Swing, *The Wild Party,* Manhattan Theatre Club Stage I, New York City, 2000.

Greg Sullivan, *Spinning into Butter,* Mitzi E. Newhouse Theatre, New York City, 2000.

Sheriff Joe Sutter, *The Spitfire Grill,* Duke on 42nd Street Theatre, New York City, 2001.

Robbie Fay, *A Man of No Importance,* Lincoln Center Theatre, New York City, 2003.

Fabrizio, *The Light in the Piazza,* Intiman Theatre, Seattle, WA, 2003.

Isaac, *Beautiful Child,* Vineyard Theatre, New York City, 2004.

Tom, *Fat Pig,* Lucille Lortel Theatre, New York City, 2004–2005.

Captain Charles Taylor, *A Soldier's Story,* Second Stage Theatre, New York City, 2005.

(Broadway debut) *Reasons to Be Pretty,* Lyceum Theatre, New York City, 2009.

PATZWALD, Julie

PERSONAL

Career: Actress.

Awards, Honors: Leo Award, best guest actress in a dramatic series, Motion Picture Arts and Sciences Foundation of British Columbia, 2003, for "Enemy Mind," *The Dead Zone;* Leo Award, best supporting actress in a dramatic series, 2008, for "Live Free," *The Guard;* Leo Award nomination, best supporting actress in a dramatic series, 2009, for "The Hold," *The Guard.*

CREDITS

Television Appearances; Series:
Amy Vanderlee, *The Guard* (also known as *Search and Rescue*), Ion Television, 2008–2009.

Television Appearances; Movies:
Elaine, *When Danger Follows You Home,* USA Network, 1997.
Holly Simmons, *Perfect Body,* NBC, 1997.
Julie Vaccaro, *Race Against Fear* (also known as *Broken Silence, Race Against Fear: A Moment of Truth Movie,* and *Sin of Silence*), NBC, 1998.
Leigh Eversol, *Someone to Love Me* (also known as *Girl in the Backseat* and *Someone to Love Me: A Moment of Truth Movie*), NBC, 1998.
Misty, *I've Been Waiting for You,* NBC, 1998.
Young Andrea Darden, *A Murder on Shadow Mountain* (also known as *Unconditional Love*), CBS, 1999.
Counter girl, *2gether* (also known as *2GE+HER*), MTV, 2000.
Kate, *Quarantine,* ABC, 2000.
Second heartbreaker, *By Dawn's Early Light,* Showtime, 2000.
(Uncredited) Bessie Coburn, *Christy: The Movie* (also known as *Christy: Return to Cutter Gap*), PAX, 2001.
Julia, *The Secret Life of Zoey,* Lifetime, 2002.
Melinda, *The Real World Movie: The Lost Season,* MTV, 2002.
Sixth actor, *Bang, Bang, You're Dead* (also known as *Dynamite Graffiti*), Showtime, 2002.

Television Appearances; Miniseries:
Bessie Coburn, *Christy, Choices of the Heart, Part II: A New Beginning,* PAX, 2001.

Television Appearances; Pilots:
Girl who asks "When will I die?", *John Doe,* Fox, 2002.

Television Appearances; Specials:
Herself, *Camp Hollywood,* 2004.
Presenter, *The ... Annual Leo Awards,* 2008, 2009.

Television Appearances; Episodic:
Samantha Franklin, "Getting MADD," *Viper,* syndicated, 1997.
Cammi, "Black Box," *The Outer Limits* (also known as *The New Outer Limits*), Showtime, 1998.
Rachel, "The Case of the Miracle Mine," *The Adventures of Shirley Holmes,* YTV, 1998.
Vanessa, "Hypnotic," *First Wave,* Sci–Fi Channel, 1998.
Laura Wendkos, "Lullaby," *Strange World,* ABC, 1999.
Sara Winter, "Chem Lab," *The Net,* USA Network, 1999.
Tara Vanatter, "Fathers and Sons," *The Outer Limits* (also known as *The New Outer Limits*), Showtime, 1999.
Abby's granddaughter, "Handshake," *Mysterious Ways,* PAX, 2000.
Naytha, "A Hundred Days," *Stargate SG–1,* Showtime, 2000.
Adelpha, "Forest for the Trees," *The Immortal,* syndicated, 2001.
Hallie, "The Passenger List/Bokor," *Night Visions* (also known as *Nightvision*), Fox, 2001.
Monica, "T&A," *The Chris Isaak Show,* Showtime, 2001.
Jill Derr, "Enemy Mind," *The Dead Zone* (also known as *The Dark Half* and *Stephen King's "The Dead Zone"*), USA Network, 2002.
Nurse Joanie, "Healing Hands," *Beyond Belief* (also known as *Beyond Belief: Fact or Fiction*), Fox, 2002.
Lenore, "Legend of Lost Lenore," *Wolf Lake,* CBS, 2002.
Pelius, "Childhood's End," *Stargate: Atlantis* (also known as *Atlantis*), Sci–Fi Channel, 2004.
Tessa, "Be Still My Heart," *Dead like Me,* Showtime, 2004.
Crystal, "Partly Cloudy, Chance of Sex," *Life as We Know It,* ABC, 2004.
Crystal, "Natural Disasters," *Life as We Know It,* ABC, 2004.
Crystal, "With a Kiss, I Die," *Life as We Know It,* ABC, 2004.
Sally, "Lynch Pin," *The L Word,* Showtime, 2005.
Cilia, "The Alchemist," *The Collector,* CTV, 2006.
Tracey, "Champagne Kisses," *Godiva's,* Bravo, 2006.
Tracey, "Dead Flowers," *Godiva's,* Bravo, 2006.
Tracey, "The Bigger Man," *Godiva's,* Bravo, 2006.
Tracey, "The Fifth Taste," *Godiva's,* Bravo, 2006.
Jesse, "The Lady & the Tiger," *Saved,* TNT, 2006.
Charlene, "Taboos," *Alice, I Think,* CTV, 2006.
"Hollywood Babylon," *Supernatural,* The CW, 2007.
Maria, "Heart of Fire," *Blood Ties,* Lifetime, 2007.
Marsha, "Leap of Faith," *Kyle XY,* ABC Family, 2007.

Also appeared in *Beggars and Choosers,* Showtime.

Film Appearances:
Tracey, *Warriors of Virtue,* Metro–Goldwyn–Mayer, 1997.

Betty Caldicott, *Disturbing Behavior,* Metro–Goldwyn–Mayer, 1998.

Kate, *Air Bud: World Pup* (also known as *Air Bud 3*), Miramax Home Entertainment, 2000.

Becky from student council, *John Tucker Must Die,* Twentieth Century–Fox, 2006.

Female teller, *Shattered* (also known as *The Butterfly, Butterfly on a Wheel,* and *Desperate Hours*), Lions Gate Films, 2007.

April, *Sheltered Life,* Sheltered Life Productions, 2007.

Secretary, *Favourite People List* (short film), 2009.

First member of beauty staff, *Rampage,* Phase 4 Films, 2010.

Stage Appearances:

Appeared in a production of the musical *Joseph and the Amazing Technicolor Dreamcoat.*

PAUL, Aaron 1979–

PERSONAL

Original name, Aaron Paul Sturtevant; born August 27, 1979, in Emmett, ID; father a Baptist minister. *Avocational Interests:* Writing, snowboarding, bungee–jumping.

Addresses: *Agent*—International Creative Management, 10250 Constellation Way, 9th Floor, Los Angeles, CA 90067. *Manager*—Loch Powell, Leverage Management, 3030 Pennsylvania Ave., Santa Monica, CA 90404.

Career: Actor. Appeared in commercials for Pepsi soft drinks, Kellogg's Corn Pops breakfast cereal, and Pizza Hut restaurants, 1999, Juicy Fruit chewing gum, 2000, Vanilla Coke soft drinks and Burger King restaurants, 2002. Universal Studios, Hollywood, CA, worked as an usher; also performed as a singer.

Awards, Honors: Emmy Award nomination, outstanding supporting actor in a drama series, 2009, Saturn Award, best supporting actor on television, Academy of Science Fiction, Fantasy, and Horror Films, Emmy Award, outstanding supporting actor in a drama series, Satellite Award nomination, best actor in a supporting role in a series, miniseries, or motion picture made for television, and Television Critics Association Award nomination, individual achievement in drama, all 2010, all for *Breaking Bad.*

CREDITS

Television Appearances; Series:

Scott Quittman, a recurring role, *Big Love,* HBO, 2007—.

Jesse Pinkman, *Breaking Bad,* AMC, 2008—.

Television Appearances; Movies:

Even the Losers, 1998.

Owen, *Wasted,* MTV, 2002.

Monty Brant, *Perfect Opposites* (also known as *A Piece of My Heart*), Lifetime, 2004.

Television Appearances; Pilots:

Clay, *The Snobs,* Fox, 2003.

Mark Owens, *Point Pleasant,* Fox, 2005.

Jesse Pinkman, *Breaking Bad,* AMC, 2008.

Television Appearances; Specials:

Making of "Breaking Bad," AMC, 2007.

TV Guide Live at the Emmy Awards, TV Guide Channel, 2008.

The 61st Primetime Emmy Awards, CBS, 2009.

Television Appearances; Miniseries:

Stoner, *Kingpin,* NBC, 2003.

Television Appearances; Episodic:

Chad, "Fortune Cookie," *Beverly Hills, 90210* (also known as *Class of Beverly Hills*), Fox, 1999.

Second fraternity boy, "The Daughterboy," *Melrose Place,* Fox, 1999.

Student, "Dick's Big Giant Headache: Parts 1 & 2," *3rd Rock from the Sun* (also known as *Encounters of the Personal Kind* and *3rd Rock*), NBC, 1999.

Zipper, "A Day in the Life," *Suddenly Susan,* NBC, 1999.

Derek, "History Lessons," *Get Real,* Fox, 2000.

Ethan, "Eddie Loves Tori," *100 Deeds for Eddie McDowd,* Nickelodeon, 2001.

Ethan Ritter, "The Men from the Boys," *The Guardian,* CBS, 2001.

Scott, "Family Lies," *Nikki,* The WB, 2001.

Sky commander David "Winky" Winkle, "Lord of the Flies," *The X–Files,* Fox, 2001.

Tyler Petersen, "Hero," *The Division,* Lifetime, 2001.

"X–Ray" Conklin, "Crime & Puzzlement," *Judging Amy,* CBS, 2001.

Jerry, premiere episode, *Birds of Prey* (also known as *BOP*), The WB, 2002.

Marcus Denton, "Oh, Mama," *NYPD Blue* (also known as *N.Y.P.D.*), ABC, 2002.

Peter "Pete" Hutchins, Jr., "Felonious Monk," *CSI: Crime Scene Investigation* (also known as *C.S.I.* and *CSI: Las Vegas*), CBS, 2002.

"X–Ray" Conklin, "Can They Do That with Vegetables?," *Judging Amy,* CBS, 2002.

Adrian Pascal, *Guiding Light,* CBS, 2003.

Ben Gordon, "Grave Young Men," *CSI: Miami,* CBS, 2003.

Doug Hawkes, "A Saint in the City" (also known as "It's Hard to Be a Saint in the City"), *ER,* NBC, 2003.

Shane, "Natural Borne Killers," *Threat Matrix,* ABC, 2003.

Punk'd, MTV, 2003.
Drew Parkman, "Mother & Child Reunion," *Line of Fire,* ABC, 2004.
Eddie Laroche, "Silence of the Lamb," *Veronica Mars,* UPN, 2005.
Denunzio, "Secret Service," *Joan of Arcadia,* CBS, 2005.
Mark Owens, "Last Dance," *Point Pleasant,* Fox, 2005.
Mark Owens, "Waking the Dead," *Point Pleasant,* Fox, 2005.
Michael Zizzo, "The Popular Kids," *Criminal Minds,* CBS, 2005.
First teen, "Al–Faitha," *Sleeper Cell* (also known as *Sleeper Cell: American Terror*), Showtime, 2005.
Stew Ellis, "The Superhero in the Alley," *Bones,* Fox, 2006.
Link, "Fury," *Ghost Whisperer,* CBS, 2006.
The Soup, E! Entertainment Television, 2009.
Last Call with Carson Daly, NBC, 2010.

Appeared in an episode of *Costello,* NBC; also a contestant on *The Price Is Right.*

Film Appearances:
Gregor, *Locust Valley,* 1999.
Floyd, *Whatever It Takes,* Columbia, 2000.
Jonathan Warton, *Bad Girls from Valley High* (also known as *A Fate Totally Worse than Death*), 2000, Universal Home Entertainment, 2005.
Voice of Chuck, *A Fish Tale* (animated; also known as *Help, I'm a Fish* and *Hjaelp, jeg er en fisk*), A–Film, 2000.
Michael Powell at age twenty–one, *K–PAX,* Universal, 2001.
Wasted guy, *Van Wilder* (also known as *National Lampoon's "Van Wilder"* and *Van Wilder: Party Liaison*), Artisan Entertainment, 2002.
Brad Miller, *Candy Paint* (short film), School of Cinema and Television, University of Southern California, 2005.
Rick, *Mission: Impossible III* (also known as *M:i:III*), Paramount, 2006.
Jerry, *Choking Man,* International Film Circuit, 2006.
Clinton Roark, *Daydreamer,* 2007, Wellgo, 2009.
Hustler, *Leo* (short film), No Talent Films, 2007.
Victor, *Say Goodnight,* MTI Home Video, 2008.
Francis, *The Last House on the Left,* Rogue Pictures, 2009.
Rick, *Wreckage,* Camelot Entertainment Group, 2010.

Internet Appearances; Short Videos:
Weird Al, *Weird: The Al Yankovic Story,* FunnyOrDie.com, 2010.

Stage Appearances:
Appeared in *Hoodwinked,* Coronet Theatre, Hollywood, CA; also appeared in *Love, Death, and the Prom* and *The Wedding Party.*

RECORDINGS

Videos:
Appeared in the music videos "Thoughtless" by Korn, 2002, and "White Trash Beautiful" by Erik Schrody, 2004.

OTHER SOURCES

Periodicals:
Playboy, April, 2009, p. 17.
USA Today, May 1, 2009, p. 13D.

PAUL, Aislinn 1994–

PERSONAL

Born March 5, 1994, in Toronto, Ontario, Canada.

Addresses: *Agent*—Norbert Abrams, Noble Caplan Abrams, 1260 Yonge St., Second Floor, Toronto, Ontario M4T 1W6, Canada.

Career: Actress. Worked in radio. Appeared in advertisements.

Member: Alliance of Canadian Cinema, Television and Radio Artists (ACTRA), Canadian Actors' Equity Association, Screen Actors Guild.

CREDITS

Television Appearances; Series:
Hannah Woodall, *Wild Card* (also known as *Zoe Busiek: Wild Card*), Lifetime, 2003–2005.
Clare Edwards, *Degrassi: The Next Generation* (also known as *Degrassi: TNG, Degrassi: La prochaine generation,* and *Degrassi: La proxima generacion*), CTV, 2006— The N (Noggin), 2006–2009, TeenNick (new name for The N), 2009—.
Isabella, *Tell Me You Love Me* (also known as *SexLife*), HBO, 2007.

Television Appearances; Movies:
Angel, *Sister Mary Explains It All,* Showtime, 2001.
Bonnie, *Betrayed,* CBC, 2003.
Heather, *Do or Die* (also known as *Do or die*), Sci–Fi Channel, 2003.
Alexa, *Murder in the Hamptons* (also known as *Million Dollar Murder*), Lifetime, 2005.

Beth Ellen, *Harriet the Spy: Blog Wars,* The Disney Channel, 2010.

Clare Edwards, *Degrassi Takes Manhattan* (also known as *The Heat Is On* and *The Rest of My Life*), Much-More and TeenNick, 2010.

Television Appearances; Specials:

Amber, "Candles on Bay Street," *Hallmark Hall of Fame* (also known as *Hallmark Television Playhouse*), CBS, 2006.

Television Appearances; Episodic:

First girl, "Business as Usual," *The Famous Jett Jackson* (also known as *Jett Jackson*), The Disney Channel, 2000.

Chelsea, "Be True to Your School," *In a Heartbeat,* The Disney Channel, 2001.

Chelsea, "Time's Up," *In a Heartbeat,* The Disney Channel, 2001.

Lindy, "Captain Supremo: Have Tights, Will Travel," *Doc,* PAX, 2001.

Herself, *eTalk Daily* (also known as *eTalk* and *e–Talk Daily*), CTV, 2008.

Television Appearances; Pilots:

Emily Slater, *Doc,* PAX, 2001.

Hannah Woodall, *Wild Card* (also known as *Zoe Busiek: Wild Card*), Lifetime, 2003.

Isabella, *Tell Me You Love Me* (also known as *SexLife*), HBO, 2007.

Film Appearances:

Chloe, *Finn on the Fly,* Seville Pictures/Oasis International, 2008.

Third rocker girl, *Trigger,* E1 Entertainment, 2010.

Stage Appearances:

Gretl von Trapp, *The Sound of Music* (musical), Stratford Festival of Canada, Stratford, Ontario, Canada, 2001.

PAULEY, Jane 1950–

PERSONAL

Full name, Margaret Jane Pauley; born October 31, 1950, in Indianapolis, IN; daughter of Richard (a milk salesman) and Mary E. (an office clerk) Pauley; married Garry Trudeau (a cartoonist), June 14, 1980; children: Rachel and Ross (twins), Thomas. *Education:* Indiana University at Bloomington, B.A., political science, 1971. *Religion:* Presbyterian. *Avocational Interests:* Swimming, travel, reading nonfiction.

Addresses: *Agent*—International Creative Management, 825 Eighth Ave., New York, NY 10019. *Manager*—WSK Management, LLC, 888 Seventh Ave., Suite 503, New York, NY 10106.

Career: Television anchor and journalist. WISH–TV, Indianapolis, IN, reporter, 1972–73, then coanchor of midday newscasts and weekend evening anchor, 1973–75; WMAQ–TV, Chicago, IL, coanchor of evening news, 1975–76; National Broadcasting Co., New York City, member of news staff of NBC–TV, 1976–2003, Sunday evening news anchor, beginning 1980, morning news broadcast anchor for NBC–Radio, beginning 1981. Worked for Indiana Democratic Central Committee, 1972. Radio–Television News Directors Association, sponsor of Jane Pauley Internship; member of board of directors, Public Education Needs Civic Involvement in Learning; member of advisory board, Children's Health Fund and Freedom from Hunger.

Member: Society of Professional journalists (fellow; honorary chair of Jane Pauley Task Force on Mass Communications Education), Kappa Kappa Gamma.

Awards, Honors: Honorary D.Journalism, DePauw University, 1978; Media Award for television news, American Association of University Women, 1980–81; Rita V. Tishman Award, women's division, Anti–Defamation League, 1982; Spirit of Achievement Award, women's division, Albert Einstein College of Medicine, Yeshiva University, 1982; Communicator of the Year Award, New York chapter, Business/Professional Advertising Association, 1982; Humanitas Award, Human Family Educational and Cultural Institute, 1985, for "Women, Work, and Babies: Can America Cope?," *NBC White Paper;* named broadcaster of the year (with Bryant Gumbel), International Radio and Television Society, 1986; named among USO women of the year, United Service Organizations of Metropolitan New York, 1988; named "best in the business," *Washington Journalism Review,* 1990; honorary degree from Indiana University, 1996; Emmy Award (with others), general coverage of a single breaking news story, 1996, for *Dateline NBC;* Edward R. Murrow Award for feature reporting, 1997; Clarion Award, Association for Women in Communications, 1997; Wilbur Award, Religious Public Relations Council, 1997; Salute to Excellence Award, National Association of Black Journalists, 1997; Leonard Zeidenberg First Amendment Award, Radio–Television New Directors Foundation, 1997; Paul White Award, lifetime contribution to electronic journalism, Radio–Television News Directors Association, 1998; Matrix Award, Association for Women in Communications, 1998; Gracie Allen Award, outstanding achievement by an individual, American Women in Radio and Television, 1998; inducted into Broadcasting and Cable Hall of Fame, 1998; honorary degrees from Trinity College, 1998,

University of Notre Dame, and Providence College; Sol Taishoff Award, excellence in broadcast journalism, National Press Foundation; other awards include commendations from American Women in Radio and Television, Gabriel Award, Maggie Award, and Nancy Susan Reynolds Award.

CREDITS

Television Appearances; Series:
Correspondent, *NBC News*, NBC, 1976–2003.
Cohost, *Today* (also known as *The Today Show* and *NBC News Today*), NBC, 1976–89.
Reporter, *NBC Nightly News*, NBC, 1980–82.
Coanchor, *Early Today*, NBC, 1982–83.
Substitute anchor, *NBC Nightly News*, NBC, 1990–94.
Host, *Real Life with Jane Pauley*, NBC, 1990.
Coanchor, *Dateline NBC* (also known as *Dateline*), NBC, 1992–2003.
Host, *Time and Again*, MSNBC, 1999–2003.
Host, *The Jane Pauley Show*, syndicated, 2004–2005.
Contributor, "Your Life Calling with Jane Pauley", *Today* (also known as *The Today Show* and *NBC News Today*), NBC, 2010.

Television Appearances; Specials:
"Today" at Night, Volume II, NBC, 1986.
NBC's 60th Anniversary Celebration, NBC, 1986.
Anchor, *"Today"* at 35, NBC, 1987.
Host, *Some Babies Die*, PBS, 1988.
Anchor, *1988 Summer Olympic Games*, NBC, 1988.
Host, *The Eighties*, NBC, 1989.
Anchor, *Presidential Inauguration*, NBC, 1989.
Fifteen Years of MacNeil/Lehrer, PBS, 1990.
Host, *Changes: Conversation with Jane Pauley*, NBC, 1990.
Anchor, *Real Life with Jane Pauley*, NBC, 1990.
Anchor, *1990: Living on the Edge*, NBC, 1990.
Host, *42nd Annual Primetime Emmy Awards*, Fox, 1990.
Host, *The "L.A. Law" 100th Episode Special*, NBC, 1991.
Comic Relief IV, HBO, 1991.
"Today" at 40, NBC, 1992.
Presenter, *Alfred I. DuPont/Columbia University Awards in Broadcast Journalism*, PBS, 1992.
Host, *Sex, Teens and Public Schools*, PBS, 1995.
50 Years of Television: A Celebration of the Academy of Television Arts & Sciences Golden Anniversary, HBO, 1997.
Host, *Alfred I. DuPont/Columbia University Awards in Broadcast Journalism*, PBS, 1997.
Host, *Christmas in Rockefeller Center*, NBC, 1998.
Anchor, *The Greatest Generation*, NBC, 1999.
The Great American History Quiz, History Channel, 1999.
Fall in Love with a Stranger, PAX, 1999.

NBC 75th Anniversary Special (also known as *NBC 75th Anniversary Celebration*), NBC, 2002.
TV's Most Memorable Weddings, NBC, 2003.
Anchor, *Michael Jackson Unmasked*, NBC, 2003.
Host, *100 Years of Hope and Humor*, NBC, 2003.
Presenter, *The 31st Annual Daytime Emmy Awards*, NBC, 2004.
Narrator, *JFK: Breaking the News* (documentary), PBS, 2004.
Host, *Princess Diana: The Secret Tapes*, NBC, 2004.
Jane Pauley: Out of the Blue, NBC, 2004.
Generation Boom (documentary), TV Land, 2006.
Resolved (documentary), HBO, 2008.
"Take One Step: Caring for Depression with Jane Pauley," *Depression: Out of the Shadows* (documentary), PBS, 2008.

Television Appearances; Episodic:
The Tonight Show Starring Johnny Carson, NBC, 1981, 1990.
Anchor, "Women, Work, and Babies: Can America Cope?," *NBC White Paper*, NBC, 1985.
Donahue (also known as *The Phil Donahue Show*), 1985, 1989.
Anchor, "Divorce Is Changing America," *NBC White Paper*, NBC, 1986.
Voice, "Humphrey the Lost Whale: A True Story," *Reading Rainbow*, PBS, 1989.
Herself, "Monster Telethon," *The Jim Henson Hour*, 1989.
Late Night with David Letterman, NBC, 1989, 1991.
The Tonight Show with Jay Leno, NBC, 1993.
Late Night with Conan O'Brien, NBC, 1993.
Late Show with David Letterman (also known as *The Late Show* and *Letterman*), CBS, 1994.
Howard Stern, 1995.
(Uncredited) The pope, "The Weaker Sex," *Sliders*, 1995.
Voice of Rochelle, "High Crane Drifter," *Frasier*, NBC, 1996.
The Rosie O'Donnell Show, syndicated, 1996, 2000, 2002.
The View, ABC, 2002.
Correspondent, "Cold Water Survivors," *Living Dangerously*, National Geographic Channel, 2003.
Dateline NBC (also known as *Dateline*), NBC, 2004.
Larry King Live, Cable News Network, 2006.

WRITINGS

Television Series:
NBC Nightly News, NBC, 1980–82.

Television Specials:
The Eighties, NBC, 1989.
Real Life with Jane Pauley, NBC, 1990.
Changes: Conversation with Jane Pauley, NBC, 1990.

Memoir:

Skywriting: A Life Out of the Blue, Random House, 2004.

OTHER SOURCES

Books:

Newsmakers 1999, Issue 1, Gale, 1999.

Periodicals:

Entertainment Weekly, December 22, 1995, p. 86; July 10, 1998, p. 16.

New York Times, June 24, 1990.

Parade, December 13, 1998, p. 20.

Quill, November/December, 1994; March, 1995, p. 44; November, 1996, p. 18.

Saturday Evening Post, March/April, 2007, p. 52.

St. Petersburg Times, May 29, 2010, p. 1.

Time, August 30, 2004, p. 8.

TV Guide, April 13, 2002, pp. 34–38; May 10, 2003, pp. 42–46.

PAULSON, Jay

PERSONAL

Born May 29, in New York, NY; married c. July 19, 2008; wife's name, Courtney. *Education:* University of California, Los Angeles, B.A. *Avocational Interests:* Reading, playing Scrabble, distance running.

Addresses: *Agent*—Alisa Adler, Paradigm, 360 North Crescent Dr. N., Beverly Hills, CA 90210.

Career: Actor.

CREDITS

Television Appearances; Series:

Sean, *Cybill,* CBS, 1995–96.

Physical Phil, *October Road,* ABC, 2007–2008.

Eli "Root Beer" Rogers, *Happy Town,* ABC, 2010.

Television Appearances; Movies:

Paul Preston, *Trial by Fire,* ABC, 1995.

Bones, *The Apartment Complex,* Showtime, 1999.

Alan, *Stranger in My House* (also known as *Total Stranger*), Lifetime, 1999.

Stoner, *Here It Comes,* MTV, 1999.

Dave Murphy, *Rolling Kansas,* Comedy Central, 2004.

John, *Partner(s),* Lifetime, 2005.

Television Appearances; Pilots:

Blind Men, NBC, 1998.

Donnie, *Anna Says,* ABC, 1999.

Les, *Bob Patterson,* ABC, 2001.

Matthew, *Blue Skies,* NBC, 2005.

Physical Phil, *October Road,* ABC, 2007.

Television Appearances; Episodic:

"The Blue Cover," *Public Morals,* CBS, 1996.

Sam De Paul, "Three Girls and a Baby," *NYPD Blue,* ABC, 1997.

Kit, "Sweet Charity," *Just Shoot Me!,* NBC, 1997.

Carl Zernial, "Walter's Rib," *Battery Park,* NBC, 2000.

Jeffries, "Perchance to Dream," *The Invisible Man* (also known as *I–Man*), Sci–Fi Channel, 2001.

Roger, "King Corn," *The West Wing* (also known as *The White House*), NBC, 2005.

Deputy Roger Boone, "Nevada Day: Parts 1 & 2," *Studio 60 on the Sunset Strip* (also known as *Studio 60*), NBC, 2006.

Adam Whitman, "5G," *Mad Men,* AMC, 2007.

Adam Whitman, "Indian Summer," *Mad Men,* AMC, 2007.

Leo Finley/Dean James, "A Thousand Days on Earth," *CSI: Crime Scene Investigation* (also known as *C.S.I.* and *CSI: Las Vegas*), CBS, 2008.

Film Appearances:

Kirk McCormick, *Academy Boyz,* DC Productions, 1997.

Second X–phile, *Can't Hardly Wait,* Columbia, 1998.

Phoenix punk, *Permanent Midnight,* Artisan Entertainment/Live Film & Mediaworks, 1998.

Vern, *Dancing with Agnes* (short film), 1999.

Loop, *Go,* Columbia/TriStar, 1999.

Waki, *Waiting River,* American Film Institute, 2002.

Sam, *Burning Annie,* Warner Home Video, 2004.

Vern, *Imaginary Heroes,* Sony Pictures Classics, 2004.

Stuart, *Cul de Sac,* 2005.

Gerry, *The Marc Pease Experience,* Paramount Vantage, 2009.

Ron, *Red & Blue Marbles,* Don't Tread on Red, 2010.

PEACOCK, Daniel 1958–
(Danny Peacock, David Peacock)

PERSONAL

Born 1958, in London, England; son of Trevor Peacock (an actor); brother of Harry Peacock (an actor).

Addresses: *Manager*—Ed Hughes, Linda Seifert Management, 91 Berwick St., London W1F 0NE, England.

Career: Actor, director, producer, and writer. Two Hats Film and Television, partner and director with Georgia Dussaud.

Awards, Honors: Second prize, Jerwood Film Prize, c. 1998, for *Skedaddle;* BAFTA Children's Award nomination, best writer, British Academy of Film and Television Arts, 2002, for *Harry and Cosh.*

CREDITS

Film Appearances:

Danny, *Quadrophenia* (also known as *Quadrophenia: A Way of Life*), World Northal, 1979.

Rudge, *Porridge* (also known as *Doing Time* and *Porridge: The Movie*), ITC Film Distributors, 1979.

School two, *Bloody Kids* (also known as *One Joke Too Many*), Palace Pictures, 1979.

Clerk, *Riding High,* Enterprise Pictures, 1981.

Jacques Clouseau at the age of eighteen, *Trail of the Pink Panther,* Metro–Goldwyn–Mayer/United Artists, 1982.

Youth, *Gandhi* (also known as *Richard Attenborough's Film: "Gandhi"*), Columbia, 1982.

Toby, *Party Party,* Twentieth Century–Fox, 1983.

Rock promoter, *The Jewel of the Nile,* Twentieth Century–Fox, 1985.

Jim Jarvis, *The Supergrass* (also known as *The Comic Strip Presents "The Supergrass"*), Recorded Releasing, 1985, Hemdale Releasing, 1988.

Dominic, *Whoops Apocalypse,* ITC Entertainment Group, 1986, Metro–Goldwyn–Mayer, 1988.

Terence, *Eat the Rich,* New Line Cinema, 1988.

Buzzer, *I Bought a Vampire Motorcycle,* Hobo Film Enterprises, 1990.

Bull, *Robin Hood: Prince of Thieves,* Warner Bros., 1991.

(As Danny Peacock) Tonto the Torch, *Carry On Columbus,* Laurenfilm, 1992.

Waitin' for the Rocket, Edgewide Pictures/Nova Plus Entertainment, 1992 (some sources cite 1994).

(As Danny Peacock) Unfortunate man, *Small Time Obsession,* Guerilla Films, 2000.

Gielgud, *Nutcracker and the Rat King* (also known as *Nutcracker: The Curse of the Rat King, Nutcracker in 3D,* and *Nutcracker: The Untold Story*), HCC Media Group, c. 2010.

Some sources state that Peacock was involved with other film projects.

Television Appearances; Series:

Miscellaneous roles, *The Kenny Everett Television Show,* BBC, between 1983 and 1985.

Little Armadillos, Channel 4, 1984.

(Sometimes credited as David Peacock) *Assaulted Nuts,* Channel 4, 1985.

Bodie, *Valentine Park,* Central, 1987–88.

Roger Whibley, *Jackson Pace: The Great Years,* Granada Television, 1990.

Dad, *Teenage Health Freak,* Channel 4, 1991 and 1993.

Gilby Watson, *Men of the World,* BBC, 1994–95.

Freddy Argyle, *Delta Wave,* ITV, 1996.

Wendy's father, *Sister Said,* Channel 5, 1998–99.

Voice of Beeposaurus, *The Beeps* (animated), Five, 2007–2008.

Television Appearances; Specials:

Peter, "Long Distance Information," *Play for Today,* BBC, 1979.

Mr. Big, *Billy's Christmas Angels,* BBC, 1988.

(In archive footage) ... *And It's Goodnight from Him ...* (documentary), 1996.

Television Appearances; Episodic:

Lionel Pearman, "Party Line," *Shine On Harvey Moon,* ITV, 1982.

(Sometimes credited as Danny Peacock) Miscellaneous roles, *The Comic Strip Presents,* Channel 4, multiple episodes, between 1982–88.

Dying man in cabin, "Nasty," *The Young Ones,* BBC, 1984.

Guest star, "Episode 4," *The Lenny Henry Show,* BBC, 1984.

Zac, "Christmas Special 1984" (also known as "Special"), *Just Good Friends,* BBC, 1984.

Mental Mickey Magee, "It's Only Rock and Roll," *Only Fools and Horses ...* (also known as *Readies*), BBC, 1985.

Chas, "Freezeheat," *C.A.T.S. Eyes,* ITV, 1986.

Commercial actor, "Big Snogs," *Girls on Top,* ITV, 1986.

Guest star, "Neighbourhood Watch," *Lenny Henry Tonite,* BBC, 1986.

Sergeant Sparrow, "Herne's Son: Part 2," *Robin of Sherwood* (also known as *Robin Hood*), Showtime, 1986.

Alas Smith & Jones (also known as *Smith & Jones*), BBC, 1986.

Kevin, "The Price of Fame," *Pulaski* (also known as *Pulaski: The TV Detective*), BBC, 1987.

Poly Roofless, "Supergran and the Racing Cert," *Super Gran,* ITV, 1987.

"Prizegiving," *Hardwicke House,* Thames Television, 1987.

Nord, "The Greatest Show in the Galaxy: Parts 1–4," *Doctor Who* (also known as *Dr. Who*), BBC, 1988.

Sinbad, "Spook Stuff," *The Bill,* ITV, 1988.

Georgie Pearlman, "The Not So Lone Ranger," *Boon,* ITV, 1989.

Ken Playle, "Nutters," *The Bill,* ITV, 1991.

Leathers, "Pressure! What Pressure?," *Casualty* (also known as *Casual+y* and *Front Line*), BBC, 1991.

"A Just Weight," *Trainer,* BBC, 1991.

Trevor Mimms, "The Chigwell Connection," *Birds of a Feather,* BBC, 1992.

Kazanzi, "The Pit and the Pendulum," *One Foot in the Gave,* BBC, 1993.

Roger Morgan, "Publish and Be Damned," *Cluedo* (also known as *Clue*), ITV, 1993.

Vic, *Mud,* BBC, 1994.

Himself, *The Jack Docherty Show,* Channel 5, 1998.

Dad, "Boot Sale," *Billie: Girl of the Future,* Five, 2004.

Dad, "Charlotte Blain," *Billie: Girl of the Future,* Five, 2004.

Dad, "Pet Shop," *Billie: Girl of the Future,* Five, 2004.

Television Appearances; Pilots:

Wendy's father, *Sister Said,* Channel 5, 1998.

Television Work; Series:

Producer, *Ania, Fran and a Kettle of Fish,* Channel 5, 2000.

Creator, *Cave Girl* (also known as *Cavegirl*), BBC, beginning 2002.

(With Peter Duncan) Creator, *Demolition Dad* (series of silent shorts), Five, 2005.

Some sources state that Peacock was involved with other television projects.

Television Work; Movies:

Director, *Skedaddle* (short), Channel 5, 1999.

Television Work; Specials:

Director, *Stepping Out* (also known as *Steps*), ITV, 1999.

Television Director; Episodic:

Sister Said, Channel 5, multiple episodes, 1998–99.

Bang Liberty, Channel 5, multiple episodes, 1999.

Harry and Cosh, Channel 5 (later known as Five), multiple episodes, 1999–2003.

Ania, Fran and a Kettle of Fish, Channel 5, multiple episodes, 2000.

Morris 2274, Five, multiple episodes, 2003.

Billie: Girl of the Future, Five, multiple episodes, 2004–2005.

Stage Appearances:

The Alchemist, Lyric Hammersmith Theatre, London, 1985.

WRITINGS

Television Music; Series:

Main title music, *Men of the World,* BBC, 1994–95.

Teleplays; Movies:

(With Mickey Hutton) *I Hate This House,* ITV, 1996.

(Story) *The Chest,* ITV, 1997.

Teleplays; Episodic:

(With Keith Allen) "The Yob," *The Comic Strip Presents,* Channel 4, 1988.

Jackson Pace: The Great Years, Granada Television, multiple episodes, 1990.

"Double Dealing," *Very Big Very Soon,* London Weekend Television, 1991.

"Ladies Night," *Very Big Very Soon,* London Weekend Television, 1991.

"The Taxman," *Very Big Very Soon,* London Weekend Television, 1991.

"Thanks for the Memory," *Very Big Very Soon,* London Weekend Television, 1991.

Teenage Health Freak, Channel 4, multiple episodes in both 1991 and 1993.

Mud, BBC, multiple episodes, 1994.

Men of the World, BBC, multiple episodes, 1994–95.

Sister Said, Channel 5, multiple episodes, 1998–99.

Harry and Cosh, Channel 5, multiple episodes, 1999–2000.

Cave Girl (also known as *Cavegirl*), BBC, 2002.

Billie: Girl of the Future, Five, multiple episodes, 2004–2005.

Teleplays; Pilots:

(With Mickey Hutton) *For Amusement Only,* BBC, 1995.

Screenplays; with Terry Winsor:

Party Party, Twentieth Century–Fox, 1983.

Cresta Run, 1990.

OTHER SOURCES

Periodicals:

Empire, July, 1998, p. 50.

PEACOCK, Harry

PERSONAL

Son of Trevor Peacock (an actor); married Katherine Parkinson (an actress).

Career: Actor.

CREDITS

Television Appearances; Series:
Dylan Jones, *Days Like These,* ITV, 1999.
Multiple roles, *Star Stories,* BBC America, 2006–2008.

Also appeared in the series *Harry and Cosh.*

Television Appearances; Movies:
George, *Station Jim,* BBC, 2001.
John, *Judas,* ABC, 2004.

Television Appearances; Miniseries:
Ralph, *No Bananas,* BBC, 1996.
Fake German, *Band of Brothers,* HBO, 2001.

Television Appearances; Specials:
Mark, *Indian Dream,* 2003.

Television Appearances; Episodic:
Ed Martin, "Kissing the Gunner's Daughter: Part 1," *Ruth Rendell Mysteries,* PBS, 1992.
Kevin Witchell, "Out of the Mouths," *The Bill,* ITV1, 1993.
Peter, "High Score," *The Bill,* ITV1, 1995.
Mez, "The Apprentice," *Pie in the Sky,* BBC, 1997.
Young boy, "Visiting Day," *Paul Merton in Galton and Simpson's ...,* ITV, 1997.
Darren, "I'm Not a Little Baby and Daddy Hasn't Gone to Japan," *Roger Roger,* BBC, 1999.
Floyd Goodman, "The Three Gamblers," *Jonathan Creek,* PBS, 2000.
Alan Tovey, "Collateral Damage," *The Bill,* ITV1, 2001.
Mr. Bradley's grandson, "Ding Dong Merrily ...," *My Family,* BBC America, 2002.
Simon, "Horse Heir," *Keen Eddie,* Fox, 2003.
Tom Case, Jr., *Kingdom,* ITV, 2007.
Patrick Bradley, "Left for Dead," *Midsomer Murders,* Arts and Entertainment, 2008.
Proper Dave, "Forest of the Dead," *Doctor Who,* Sci–Fi Channel, 2008.
Proper Dave, "Silence in the Library," *Doctor Who,* Sci–Fi Channel, 2008.
Victor Del Angelo, "Unnatural Vices: Parts 1 & 2," *Wire in the Blood,* BBC America, 2008.
Himself, "Shadow Play," *Doctor Who Confidential,* BBC, 2008.

Film Appearances:
Mario the Magician, *Caught in the Act,* Film 2000, 1997.
Danny, *I Just Want to Kiss You* (short film), Der Kurz-FilmVerleih, 1998.

Johnny Ford, *High Adventure,* Towers of London Productions, 2001.
Crying man, *The Banker* (short film), Memory Box Films, 2004.
Voice of recruiting officer, *Valiant* (short film), Buena Vista, 2005.

PEARL, Aaron 1972–

PERSONAL

Born May 11, 1972, in Sechelt, British Columbia, Canada; married Rachel Fox, September 21, 2004; children: one. *Education:* Studied acting.

Addresses: *Agent*—Russ Mortensen, Pacific Artists Management, 685–1285 West Broadway, Vancouver, British Columbia V6H 3X8, Canada.

Career: Actor, producer, and writer. Worked as a print and runway model in New York City. Worked as a college teacher of drama and physical education.

Awards, Honors: Some sources cite awards from the New York International Talent Association.

CREDITS

Television Appearances; Series:
George Williams, *Intelligence,* CBC, 2006–2007.

Television Appearances; Miniseries:
Lookout Reginald Lee, *Titanic* (also known as *Titanic 2*), CBS, 1996.
Firefighter driver, *Atomic Train,* NBC, 1999.

Television Appearances; Movies:
Chuck, *Annie O,* Showtime, 1996.
First fraternity boy, *Home Song* (also known as *LaVyrle Spencer's "Home Song"*), CBS, 1996.
Player, *Susie Q,* The Disney Channel, 1996.
Title role at the ages of seventeen, eighteen, and twenty–five, *Ebenezer,* TNT, 1997.
Peters, *Doomsday Rock* (also known as *Cosmic Shock*), ABC Family, 1997.
Bad person, *Nobody Lives Forever* (part of the Crimes of Passion series of television movies; also known as *Crimes of Passion: Edna Buchanan's "Nobody Lives Forever,"* *Crimes of Passion: Nobody Lives Forever,* and *Edna Buchanan's "Nobody Lives Forever"*), ABC, 1998.

Fair Haristeen, "Murder She Purred: A Mrs. Murphy Mystery" (also known as "Murder, She Purred"), *The Wonderful World of Disney,* ABC, 1998.

Karl, "Noah," *The Wonderful World of Disney,* ABC, 1998.

Randy Haynes, *Voyage of Terror* (also known as *The Fourth Horseman* and *Die Schreckensfahrt der Orion Star*), The Family Channel, 1998.

Robert Singer, *Escape from Mars,* UPN, 1999.

Tom, *Heaven's Fire* (also known as *Inferno der Flammen* and *L'enfer en plein ciel*), Fox Family, 1999.

Josh Gamble, *The Spring,* NBC, 2000.

Mail carrier, *Deck the Halls,* Lifetime, 2005.

Roman, *Bloodsuckers* (also known as *Vampire Wars: Battle for the Universe*), Sci–Fi Channel, 2005.

Boston controller, *Flight 93* (also known as *Airport United 93* and *Le vol 93*), Arts and Entertainment, 2006.

Derek Woodcutter, *Engaged to Kill,* Lifetime, 2006.

Jeff Monroe, *The Accidental Witness* (also known as *The Killing of a Stranger*), Lifetime, 2006.

Sheriff, *A Little Thing Called Murder* (also known as *Dead End*), Lifetime, 2006.

(Uncredited) Tony, *Augusta, Gone* (also known as *Augusta's Battle*), Lifetime, 2006.

Blake Thompson, *Lost Holiday: The Jim and Suzanne Shemwell Story* (also known as *Christmas Miracle* and *Lost Holiday: The Jim & Suzanne Shemwell Story*), Lifetime, 2007.

Douglas Mak, *Anna's Storm* (also known as *Hell's Rain*), Lifetime Movie Network, 2007.

Nate, *Montana Sky* (also known as *Nora Roberts' "Montana Sky"*), Lifetime, 2007.

Steve Fitzgerald, *Love Notes* (also known as *Empty Arms*), Lifetime, 2007.

H. W. Tilman, *Yeti: Curse of the Snow Demon* (also known as *Yeti*), Sci–Fi Channel, 2008.

Jack Martin, *Vipers,* Sci–Fi Channel, 2008.

Kozlowski, *Past Lies,* 2008.

Milligan, *Trial by Fire* (also known as *Firejumpers, Raging Inferno, Smokejumpers,* and *Smoke Jumper*), Lifetime, 2008.

Fire lieutenant, *Fireball,* Sci–Fi Channel, 2009.

Bobby Ellis, *Growing the Big One,* Hallmark Channel, 2010.

Captain, *Stonehenge Apocalypse,* Syfy, 2010.

Television Appearances; Specials:

Kurt McPherson, *Alien Abduction: Incident in Lake County* (also known as *Alien Abduction: The McPherson Tape* and *Incident in Lake County*), UPN, 1998.

Television Appearances; Episodic:

Clark, "From Within," *The Outer Limits* (also known as *The New Outer Limits*), Showtime, Sci–Fi Channel, and syndicated, 1996.

Corman, "Manhunt," *Highlander* (also known as *Highlander: The Series*), syndicated, 1996.

Hal, "Fox Spirit," *Poltergeist: The Legacy* (also known as *Poltergeist, El legado, Poltergeist—Die unheimliche Macht, Poltergeist: El legado,* and *Poltergeist, les aventuriers du surnaturel*), Showtime and syndicated, 1996.

Harley, "Secret," *The Sentinel* (also known as *Sentinel*), UPN, 1997.

Detective Mike Olanski, "The Box," *First Wave,* Sci–Fi Channel, 1998.

Lee, "Solitude's Revenge," *The Crow: Stairway to Heaven* (also known as *The Crow, Witch Crow, El cuervo,* and *O corvo*), syndicated, 1998.

Roger Beckersly, "Monster," *The Outer Limits* (also known as *The New Outer Limits*), Showtime, Sci–Fi Channel, and syndicated, 1998.

Roosevelt, "Cadet of the Year," *Police Academy: The Series* (also known as *Police Academy*), syndicated, c. 1998.

Lieutenant George S. Hammond, "1969," *Stargate SG–1* (also known as *La porte des etoiles* and *Stargaate SG–1*), Showtime and syndicated, 1999.

Lieutenant Wingers, "Gettysburg," *The Outer Limits* (also known as *The New Outer Limits*), Showtime, Sci–Fi Channel, and syndicated, 2000.

Officer Tollin, "Maximum Byers," *The Lone Gunmen* (also known as *Lone Gunmen, Au coeur du complot,* and *Die Einsamen Schutzen*), Fox, 2001.

Sam, "Reunion," *Night Visions* (also known as *Night Terrors* and *Nightvisions*), Fox, 2001.

Raymond Paul Briner, "Dunne's Choice," *Breaking News,* Bravo (originally produced by TNT), 2002.

State trooper, "High Hopes," *Taken* (also known as *Steven Spielberg Presents "Taken"*), Sci–Fi Channel, 2002.

National Security Administration security person, "The Rising," *John Doe* (also known as *Der Fall John Doe!* and *Mies vailla nimeae*), Fox, 2003.

Team commander, "Cold Fusion," *The Twilight Zone* (also known as *Twilight Zone*), UPN, 2003.

Brett, "Last Call," *Dead Like Me* (also known as *Dead Girl, Mitt liv som doed,* and *Tan muertos como yo*), Showtime, 2004.

Glenn Burton, "Crisis," *Smallville* (also known as *Smallville Beginnings* and *Smallville: Superman the Early Years*), The WB, 2004.

Major Kearney, "Lockdown," *Stargate SG–1* (also known as *La porte des etoiles* and *Stargaate SG–1*), Sci–Fi Channel and syndicated, 2004.

Second firefighter, "Mr. Ellis Himself Woulda Been Proud," *Da Vinci's Inquest* (also known as *Coroner Da Vinci*), CBC, 2004.

(Uncredited) Cole, "The Last Goodbye," *The Dead Zone* (also known as *The Dark Half, Dead Zone, Stephen King's "Dead Zone," La morta zona, La zona morta, La zona muerta,* and *Zona smrti*), USA Network, 2005.

Cole, "Symmetry," *The Dead Zone* (also known as *The Dark Half, Dead Zone, Stephen King's "Dead*

Zone," *La morta zona, La zona morta, La zona muerta,* and *Zona smrti*), USA Network, 2006.

Ensign Abel Thornton, "The Captain's Hand," *Battlestar Galactica* (also known as *BSG, Galactica, Galactica—Estrella de combate,* and *Taisteluplaneetta Galactica*), Sci–Fi Channel, 2006.

Schell, "A Day in the Life," *Saved,* TNT, 2006.

Clinton Morrison, "Bloodletting: Part 1," *Rabbit Fall,* SPACE, 2008.

Jake, "Just Say No," *The Guard* (also known as *Search and Rescue*), Global TV, 2008.

Lieutenant Finnerty, "Lay Down the Law," *The L Word* (also known as *Earthlings, L.,* and *L Word*), Showtime, 2008.

Lieutenant Finnerty, "Let's Get This Party Started," *The L Word* (also known as *Earthlings, L.,* and *L Word*), Showtime, 2008.

Agent Tevez, "Fracture," *Fringe,* Fox, 2009.

Deputy Garrett, "Gasp," *Harper's Island,* CBS, 2009.

Deputy Garrett, "Gurgle," *Harper's Island,* CBS, 2009.

Deputy Garrett, "Thrack, Splat, Sizzle," *Harper's Island,* CBS, 2009.

Jack, "Cowgirls," *Wild Roses,* CBC, 2009.

Jack, "The Rapture," *Supernatural* (also known as *Sobrenatural*), The CW, 2009.

Some sources cite appearances in other programs, including *The Commish,* ABC.

Television Appearances; Pilots:

George Williams, *Intelligence* (also known as *Intelligence: The Movie*), CBC, 2005.

Film Appearances:

Sean Laughrea, *Wrongfully Accused* (also known as *Leslie Nielsen ist sehr verdaechtig, Sehr verdaechtig,* and *Unter falschem Verdacht*), Warner Bros., 1998.

Lou, *Little Boy Blues,* Stage 18 Pictures, 1999.

Buddy, *Duets,* Buena Vista, 2000.

Michael, *Dangerous Attraction* (also known as *Double seduction*), Remstar Distribution/Kassirer–Meyer Entertainment, 2000.

Brad, *Try Seventeen* (also known as *All I Want* and *Try 17*), Millennium Films/Nu Image Films, 2002.

Second patrol officer, *Stealing Sinatra* (also known as *Come Fly with Me*), c. 2002.

Stryker soldier, *X2* (also known as *X-Men 2, X-men 2., X-Men 2: X-Men United, X-2, X2: X-Men United,* and *X2: X-Men unis*), Twentieth Century–Fox, 2003.

Billy, *I Accuse* (also known as *J'accuse*), c. 2003.

(Uncredited) *Devour,* Sony Pictures Home Entertainment, 2005.

Bludworth, *Black Christmas* (also known as *Black X-Mas* and *Noel noir*), Metro–Goldwyn–Mayer/Dimension Films/The Weinstein Company, 2006.

K9 guard, *The Pink Panther* (also known as *The Birth of the Pink Panther* and *The Mask of the Pink Panther*), Metro–Goldwyn–Mayer, 2006.

Sergeant Miller, *The Suspect,* American Cinema International, 2006.

Team leader, *X–Men: The Last Stand* (also known as *X–Men: Final Decision, X–Men 3, X3,* and *X–men—L'engagement ultime*), Twentieth Century–Fox, 2006.

Jade agent Clark, *War* (also known as *Rogue* and *Rogue Assassin*), Lionsgate, 2007.

Stanley, *White Noise 2: The Light* (also known as *Interferences 2, White Noise: The Light,* and *White Noise 2*), Rogue Pictures/Universal/TVA Films, 2007.

Chambers, *Vice,* 41, 2008.

Helicopter pilot, *Far Cry,* Touchstone Pictures, 2008.

General Aziel, *In the Name of the King: A Dungeon Siege Tale* (also known as *Dungeon Siege, Dungeon Siege: In the Name of the King, In the Name of the Father: A Dungeon Siege Tale, In the Name of the King,* and *Schwerter des Koenigs—Dungeon Siege*), Freestyle Releasing/Vivendi Entertainment, c. 2008.

Ryan Caul, *The Seamstress,* Image Entertainment, 2009.

Father, *The Tortured* (also known as *Tortured* and *Untitled Twisted Picture*), 2010.

Reg, *Transparency* (also known as *Takedown*), American World Pictures, 2010.

Film Work:

Producer and automated dialogue replacement (ADR) director, *Little Boy Blues,* Stage 18 Pictures, 1999.

WRITINGS

Screenplays:

Little Boy Blues, Stage 18 Pictures, 1999.

PENDERGRAFT, Jason 1976–

PERSONAL

Full name, Jason David Pendergraft; born May 24, 1976, in WA; married; children: one son. *Education:* University of Washington, Seattle, graduated; trained for the stage with William Esper in New York City. *Avocational Interests:* Songwriting, carpentry, designing and building custom cabinets and furniture.

Addresses: *Manager*—Liebman Entertainment, 235 Park Ave. S., 10th Floor, New York, NY 10003.

Career: Actor.

CREDITS

Television Appearances; Series:
Lance Barton, a recurring role, *As the World Turns,* CBS, 2007.
Darren Hall, *How to Make It in America,* HBO, 2010.

Television Appearances; Episodic:
Rich Davenport, "Tomorrow," *Law & Order: Criminal Intent* (also known as *Law & Order: CI*), NBC, 2002.
Ian Duffy, "Maltese Cross," *Law & Order: Criminal Intent* (also known as *Law & Order: CI*), NBC, 2006.
Jim Morgan, "Talking Points," *Law & Order,* NBC, 2007.
Will, "Objects in the Mirror," *Six Degrees,* ABC, 2007.
Vinnie, "One Wedding and a Funeral," *CSI: NY,* CBS, 2007.
Skip Lowe, "Please Note We Are No Longer Accepting Letters of Recommendation from Henry Kissinger," *Law & Order: Criminal Intent* (also known as *Law & Order: CI*), NBC, 2008.
Publicity agent, "Reversals of Fortune," *Gossip Girl,* The CW, 2009.

Television Appearances; Pilots:
Darren Hall, *How to Make It in America,* HBO, 2010.

Film Appearances:
Homicide detective, *When Will I Be Loved,* IFC Films, 2004.
Rugger, *Press Gang* (short film), 2004.
Darryl Foreman, *Frat Brothers of the KVL,* Grayscale Productions, 2007.
Young cop, *Margaret,* Twentieth Century–Fox, 2010.

PENDLETON, Austin 1940–

PERSONAL

Born March 27, 1940, in Warren, OH; married Katina Commings (an actress), 1970; children: Audrey Christine. *Education:* Yale University, B.A., 1961; trained for the stage at Williamstown Theatre Festival, 1957–58; studied acting with Uta Hagen.

Addresses: *Manager*—Scott Hart Management, 14622 Ventura Blvd., Suite 746, Sherman Oaks, CA 91403.

Career: Actor, director, and writer. Toured with American Conservatory Theatre Company, San Francisco, CA, 1966–67; American Conservatory Theatre, San Francisco, CA, member of company, 1966–67; Studio Arena Theatre Company, Buffalo, NY, member of company, 1968–69; Long Wharf Theatre, New Haven, CT, member of company, 1971–72; Steppenwolf Theatre, Chicago, IL, affiliate, 1979—, member of ensemble company; Mirror Repertory Company, New York City, director, 1984; Riverside Shakespeare Company, New York City, associate director, 1988–89; Circle Repertory Theatre, New York City, artistic director, 1995–96; Blue Light Theatre Company, associate artist and member of advisory board. Acting teacher at Yale University, 1970s, and at Circle in the Square Theatre School and Herbert Berghof Studio.

Member: Actors' Equity Association, Screen Actors Guild, American Federation of Television and Radio Artists, Society of Stage Directors and Choreographers.

Awards, Honors: Clarence Derwent Award, 1967, for *Hail Scrawdyke!;* Obie Award, best actor, *Village Voice,* Drama Desk Award, Outer Critics Circle Award, and New York Drama Critics Poll Award, 1970, all for *The Last Sweet Days of Isaac;* Joseph Jefferson Award nomination, best director of a play, 1976, for *Misalliance;* Joseph Jefferson Award nomination, director of a play, 1980, for *Say Goodnight, Gracie;* Antoinette Perry Award nomination, best director of a drama, 1981, for *The Little Foxes;* Screen Actors Guild Award nomination (with others), outstanding performance by a cast in a theatrical motion picture, 2002, for *A Beautiful Mind;* Lucille Lortel Award nomination, outstanding play, 2005, for *Orson's Shadow;* Drama Desk Special Award, 2007; Joseph Jefferson Award nomination (with others), new work or adaptation of musical, 2009, for *A Minister's Wife.*

CREDITS

Stage Appearances:
Jonathan Rosepettle, *Oh Dad, Poor Dad, Mama's Hung You in the Closet and I'm Feelin' So Sad,* Phoenix Theatre, New York City, 1962.
Motel, *Fiddler on the Roof,* Imperial Theatre, New York City, 1964.
Irwin Ingham, *Hail Scrawdyke!,* Booth Theatre, New York City, 1966.
Leo Hubbard, *The Little Foxes,* Vivian Beaumont Theatre, Lincoln Center, New York City, then Ethel Barrymore Theatre, New York City, 1967–68.
Isaac, *The Last Sweet Days of Isaac,* Eastside Playhouse, New York City, 1970, then Cincinnati Playhouse in the Park, Cincinnati, OH, 1971.
Charles, *American Glands,* New Dramatists Theatre, New York City, 1973.
Professor Bobby Rudetsky, *An American Millionaire,* Joseph E. Levine Theatre, Circle in the Square, New York City, 1974.

Title role, *Tartuffe,* Cincinnati Playhouse in the Park, 1974.

Little Egolf, New York City, 1974.

The Government Inspector, Hartman Theatre, Stamford, CT, 1975.

Standby for Charley, *Goodtime Charley* (musical), Palace Theatre, New York City, 1975.

Frederick the Great, *The Sorrows of Frederick the Great,* American Repertory Theatre, New York City, 1976.

The Runner Stumbles, Broadway production, 1976.

Title role, *Tartuffe,* Hartman Theatre, 1977.

Tusenbach, *Three Sisters,* Brooklyn Academy of Music, Brooklyn, New York City, 1977.

Mark Antony, *Julius Caesar,* Brooklyn Academy of Music, 1977.

Estragon, *Waiting for Godot,* Brooklyn Academy of Music, 1978.

Jack, *The Office Murders,* Quaigh Theatre, New York City, 1979.

Say Goodnight, Gracie, Steppenwolf Theatre Company, Chicago, IL, 1979.

Loose Ends, Steppenwolf Theatre Company, 1982.

Bashmachkin, *The Overcoat,* Westside Mainstage Theatre, New York City, 1982.

Uncle Vanya, The Whole Theatre, Montclair, NJ, 1982.

Adam, *Up from Paradise,* Jewish Repertory Theatre, New York City, 1983.

After the Fall, Williamstown Theatre Festival, Williamstown, MA, 1984.

The Three Sisters, Steppenwolf Theatre Company, 1984.

The Sorrows of Frederick, Whole Theatre, 1985.

Arnie, *Doubles,* Ritz Theatre, New York City, 1985.

Cat on a Hot Tin Roof, Steppenwolf Theatre Company, 1986.

Shostakovich, *Master Class,* Roundabout Theatre Company, Union Square Theatre, New York City, 1986.

Frank, *Educating Rita,* Steppenwolf Theatre Company, and Westside Theatre Upstairs, New York City, 1987.

Voitski, *Uncle Vanya,* Classic Stage Company Theatre, New York City, 1987–88.

Title role, *Philoctetes,* Intar Hispanic American Theatre, New York City, 1989.

Erie Smith, "Hughie," *Serious Company: An Evening of One–Act Plays,* Apple Corps Theatre, New York City, 1989.

Title role, *Hamlet,* Riverside Shakespeare Company, 165 West 86th Street Theatre, New York City, 1989.

Ivanov, Yale Repertory Theatre, New Haven, CT, 1990–91.

Harvey, Steppenwolf Theatre Company, 1990.

Love Letters, Steppenwolf Theatre Company, 1990.

Frederick the Great, *The Sorrows of Frederick,* Kampo Cultural Center, New York City, 1991.

Harry Berlin, *What about Luv?,* York Theatre Company, Church of the Heavenly Rest Theatre, New York City, 1991–92.

Il Signor Barranco, *A Joke,* Sanford Meisner Theatre, New York City, 1992.

Inspector Carol, Steppenwolf Theatre Company, 1992.

Priest, "Show," *The Best American Short Play Series,* Evening Two, Westbeth Theatre Center, New York City, 1993.

Jeremy, *Jeremy Rudge,* Mint Theatre, New York City, 1993.

Whitey McCoy, *Sophistry,* Playwrights Horizons Theatre, New York City, 1993.

Uncle Bob, Steppenwolf Theatre Company, 1995.

Eric, *The Imposter,* Workhouse Theatre, New York City, 1995–96.

Title role, *Richard III,* New Perspectives Theatre Company, New York City, 1997.

Mr. Dussel, *The Diary of Anne Frank,* Colonial Theatre, Boston, MA, 1997, then Music Box Theatre, New York City, 1997–98.

Michael Majeski, *Valparaiso,* Steppenwolf Theatre, Chicago, IL, 2000.

King Lear, New Repertory Theatre, Newton Highlands, MA, 2000.

"Undecided," *New Cabaret Acts and Revues,* Steppenwolf Theatre Company, Players Club Theatre, New York City, 2001.

Title role, *Richard II,* West Park Auditorium, New York City, 2001.

Uncle Vanya, Steppenwolf Theatre Company, 2001.

The Chekhov Cycle, Nikos Stage, Williamstown Theatre Festival, 2003.

Lord Alfred Douglas, *The Lives of Bosie,* Hedgerow Theatre, Media, PA, then Arts Bank, Philadelphia, PA, 2004.

Chaplin, *Mother Courage and Her Children,* New York Shakespeare in the Park, 2006.

Love Song, Steppenwolf Theatre, 2006.

The Sunset Limited, Steppenwolf Theatre, 2006.

Father, *an oak tree,* Barrow Street Theatre, New York City, 2006–2007.

Judge Danforth, *The Crucible,* Steppenwolf Theatre, 2007.

Friar Laurence, *Romeo and Juliet,* Delacorte Theatre, New York City, 2007.

Also appeared in the title role, *Keats,* off–Broadway production; Otto Kringelein, *Grand Hotel* (musical), Martin Beck Theatre, New York City; in *The Loop,* off–Broadway production; *Say Goodnight, Gracie,* off–Broadway production; *The Show–Off,* off–Broadway production; *Two Character Play,* off–Broadway production; *The Exonerated,* Bleecker Street Theatre, New York City.

Major Tours:
Toured as the senator in *Finian's Rainbow.*

Stage Director:
Shelter (musical), John Golden Theatre, New York City, 1973.

The Master Builder, Long Wharf Theatre, New Haven, CT, 1973.

The Runner Stumbles, Manhattan Theatre Club, New York City, 1974.

The Scarecrow, Eisenhower Theatre, John F. Kennedy Center for the Performing Arts, Washington, DC, 1975.

The Runner Stumbles, Hartman Theatre, Stamford, CT, then John Golden Theatre, 1976–78.

Benito Cereno, American Place Theatre, New York City, 1976.

Misalliance, Academy Festival Theatre, Lake Forest, IL, 1976.

The Old Glory, American Place Theatre, 1976.

The Gathering, Manhattan Theatre Club, 1977.

Say Goodnight, Gracie, 78th Street Theatre Lab, New York City, 1979.

John Gabriel Borkman, Circle in the Square, New York City, 1980–81.

The Little Foxes, Martin Beck Theatre, New York City, 1981.

Mass Appeal, York Theatre Company, Chancel of the Church of Heavenly Rest, New York City, 1984.

After the Fall, Williamstown Theatre Festival, Williamstown, MA, 1984.

Alterations, Chelsea Playhouse, Workshop of the Players Art Theatre, New York City, 1986.

Fathers and Sons, Long Wharf Theatre, 1987–88.

Spoils of War, Second Stage Theatre, McGinn–Cazale Theatre, then Music Box Theatre, both New York City, 1988.

Who's Afraid of Virginia Woolf?, Arizona Theatre Company, Tucson, AZ, 1991–92.

Admissions, New Perspectives Theatre, New York City, 1995.

The Size of the World, Circle Repertory Theatre, New York City, 1996.

The Sea Gull, Blue Light Theatre Company, Theatre Four, New York City, 1998.

Frankie and Johnnie in the Clair de Pune, Steppenwolf Theatre Company, Chicago, IL, 2004.

The Sunset Limited, Steppenwolf Theatre Company, 2006.

Love Songs, Steppenwolf Theatre Company, 2006.

The Crucible, Steppenwolf Theatre Company, 2007.

Toys in the Attic, Pearl Theatre, New York City, 2007.

Fifty Words, Lucille Lortel Theatre, New York City, 2008.

Uncle Vanya, Classic Stage Company (CSC) Theatre, New York City, 2009.

Vieux Carre, Theatre 80 St. Marks, New York City, 2009.

Film Appearances:

(Uncredited) Intern, *Petulia,* 1968.

Fred the professor, *Skidoo,* Paramount, 1968.

Lieutenant Colonel Moodus, *Catch–22,* Paramount, 1970.

Oven 350, 1970.

Frederick Larrabee, *What's Up, Doc?,* Warner Bros., 1972.

Luther, *Every Little Crook and Nanny,* Metro–Goldwyn–Mayer, 1972.

Zukovsky, *The Thief Who Came to Dinner,* Warner Bros., 1972.

Earl Williams, *The Front Page,* Universal, 1974.

Lovesick, Warner Bros., 1974.

Guido, *The Great Smokey Roadblock* (also known as *The Last of the Cowboys*), Cinema Arts Associated, 1976.

Dr. Klein, *Diary of the Dead,* 1976.

Max, *The Muppet Movie,* Associated Film Distributors, 1979.

Paul, *Starting Over,* Paramount, 1979.

Dr. Carl Becker, *Simon,* Warner Bros., 1980.

Dr. Alexander Grade, *First Family,* Warner Bros., 1980.

Richard Patterson, *Talk to Me,* 1982.

Mr. Greenhut, *My Man Adam* (also known as *Inside Adam Swit*), TriStar, 1985.

Gun shop salesperson, *Off Beat,* Buena Vista, 1986.

Howard Marner, *Short Circuit,* TriStar, 1986.

Junior Lacey, *Hello Again,* Buena Vista, 1987.

Mr. Gadbury, *Mr. & Mrs. Bridge,* Miramax, 1990.

Lawyer Taylor, *The Ballad of the Sad Cafe,* Channel Four Films, 1991.

(Uncredited) Director of *Othello, True Identity,* 1991.

Catholic priest, *Rain Without Thunder,* Taz Pictures, 1992.

Harold Blodgett, *Charlie's Ear,* 1992.

John Gibbons, *My Cousin Vinny,* Twentieth Century–Fox, 1992.

Do You Like Women?, 1992.

Asa Hoffman, *Searching for Bobby Fischer* (also known as *Innocent Moves*), Paramount, 1993.

Dr. Bronson, *My Boyfriend's Back* (also known as *Johnny Zombie*), Buena Vista, 1993.

Alex Mason, Sr., *Mr. Nanny,* New Line Cinema, 1993.

Hotel clerk, *Greedy,* Universal, 1994.

Earl Fowler, *Guarding Tess,* TriStar, 1994.

Hamlet, *The Fifteen Minute Hamlet,* Cin–cine 19, 1995.

Peter Arnold, *Home for the Holidays,* Paramount, 1995.

Dr. Huffeyer, *Two Much* (also known as *Loco de amor*), Buena Vista, 1996.

Major Ebersole, *Sergeant Bilko* (also known as *Sgt. Bilko*), Universal, 1996.

Ralph Crupi, *Two Days in the Valley,* Metro–Goldwyn–Mayer, 1996.

Willy Kunst, *The Proprietor* (also known as *Le proprietaire*), Warner Bros., 1996.

Aesop, *The Associate,* Buena Vista, 1996.

Barry, *The Mirror Has Two Faces,* Sony Pictures Entertainment, 1996.

Himself, *The Extra,* 1996.

Bob, *Sue* (also known as *Sue Lost in Manhattan*), AMKO Productions, 1997.

Professor Gibbs, *Amistad,* DreamWorks, 1997.

Judge Paul Z. Graff, *Trial and Error,* New Line Cinema, 1997.

Billy, *A River Made to Drown In,* 1997.

Eugene Cleft, *The Fanatics* (also known as *Fumble-heads*), 1997.

Jerry Trask, *Men of Means,* Maverick Entertainment, 1998.

Harry Cedars, *Charlie Hoboken,* Northern Arts Entertainment, 1998.

Winston, *Joe the King* (also known as *Joe Henry* and *Pleasant View Avenue*), Trimark Pictures, 1998.

Lucky, *Brokendown Love Story,* 1999.

Francois Truffaut, *Skirty Winner,* 1999.

Albert Collins, *The 4th Floor,* 1999.

"Angela," *The Summer of My Deflowering* (also known as *Erotic Tales IV* and *Tagebuch einer verfuehrung*), Atlas International, 2000.

Dean, *Clowns,* DPI Entertainment, 2000.

Archie, *Broke Even,* 2000.

Bobby Austin, *The Acting Class,* 2000.

George, *Fast Food, Fast Women,* Lot 47 Films, 2001.

Alvin, *Queenie in Love,* Pyramide, 2001.

Two Digit Doyle, *Manna from Heaven,* R.S. Entertainment, 2001.

Thomas King, *A Beautiful Mind,* Universal, 2001.

Mr. Turner, *Wishcraft,* Wishcraft LLC, 2002.

Jaurice, *Sex & Violence,* Sneak Preview Entertainment, 2002.

Gus Falk, *Counting Sheep,* Oregon Creative, 2002.

Voice of Gurgle, *Finding Nemo* (animated), Buena Vista, 2003.

Mr. Mconkey, *Uptown Girls,* Metro–Goldwyn–Mayer, 2003.

Peter Pett, *Piccadilly Jim,* 2004.

Umbrella Santa/Marty, *Christmas with the Kranks,* Columbia, 2004.

Jaurice, *The Civilization of Maxwell Bright,* Grass Roots Film Distribution, 2005.

Teacher, *The Notorious Bettie Page,* Picturehouse Entertainment, 2005.

Julian, *Dirty Work* (also known as *Bad City*), Screen Media Films, 2006.

Gus Falk, *Raising Flagg,* Cinema Libre Studio, 2006.

Teacher, *Oh Boy* (short film), 2007.

Herb Lightman, *'77* (also known as *77*), 2007.

Voice of Gurgle, *"Finding Nemo" Submarine Voyage* (short film), Disneyland, 2007.

Jackson, *Lovely by Surprise,* FilmFrog Productions, 2007.

Sotirios, *Eastside Irish,* 2010.

Television Appearances; Series:

Dr. George Griscom, *Homicide: Life on the Street* (also known as *H: LOTS* and *Homicide*), NBC, 1998–99.

William Giles, *Oz,* HBO, 1998–2002.

Michael Stahl–David: Behind the Star, 2008.

Also appeared in *One Life to Live,* ABC.

Television Appearances; Miniseries:

Dr. Benjamin Rush, *Liberty! The American Revolution,* PBS, 1997.

Television Appearances; Movies:

Passenger with a moustache, *Four Eyes and Six–Guns,* TNT, 1992.

Chef Oscar, *Don't Drink the Water,* ABC, 1994.

Albert Collins, *The 4th Floor,* HBO, 1999.

Dr. George Griscom, *Homicide: The Movie,* NBC, 2000.

James Perley, *Strip Search,* HBO, 2004.

Television Appearances; Specials:

Performer, *Let's Celebrate,* ABC, 1972.

Bennie Fox, *June Moon,* PBS, 1974.

"Elizabeth Taylor": The E! True Hollywood Story, E! Entertainment Television, 1998.

Edge of Outside (documentary), TCM, 2006.

Television Appearances; Pilots:

Harry Rogers, *You're Gonna Love It Here,* CBS, 1977.

Harry Buckman, *Big City Boys,* CBS, 1978.

Dr. Arthur Ruskin, *Love, Long Distance,* 1985.

Dr. Mott, *Long Island Fever,* ABC, 1996.

Sick in the Head, Fox, 1999.

Dr. Boyd, *Cupid,* ABC, 1999.

Television Appearances; Episodic:

"Love and the Caller," *Love, American Style,* 1972.

Leo, "Love and the Pretty Secretary," *Love, American Style,* 1973.

Donald Hargrove, "The I.Q. Test," *Good Times,* 1974.

"The Film Society of Lincoln Center: A Tribute to Billy Wilder," *Live from Lincoln Center,* 1982.

White Rabbit, "Alice in Wonderland," *Great Performances,* PBS, 1983.

Bob Moran (Mr. Entertainment), "Vanity," *St. Elsewhere,* NBC, 1983.

Bob Moran (Mr. Entertainment), "Under Pressure," *St. Elsewhere,* NBC, 1983.

Hometown, 1985.

Max Rogo, "Yankee Dollar," *Miami Vice,* NBC, 1986.

Jonah, "Nightscape," *The Equalizer,* CBS, 1986.

Jonah, "Solo," *The Equalizer,* CBS, 1987.

Harold Rodman, "The Best Couple I Know," *Leg Work,* 1987.

The professor, "The Big Fight," *Spenser: For Hire,* ABC, 1988.

Danny, "Blind Chess," *B. L. Stryker,* ABC, 1989.

Jonah, "The Sins of Our Fathers," *The Equalizer,* CBS, 1989.

Mr. Kensington, "Mrs. Huxtable Goes to Kindergarten," *The Cosby Show,* NBC, 1989.

Max Templeton, "Mr. Mom," *Anything But Love,* ABC, 1990.

"Flight of the Dodo," *American Dreamer,* 1990.

Teacher, "Back to School," *21 Jump Street,* Fox, 1990.

Barney Gunderson, "Angel of Death," *Murder, She Wrote,* CBS, 1991.

Paul Kent, "Lethal Innocence" (also known as "The Vermont/Cambodia Story"), *American Playhouse,* PBS, 1991.

Maynard Caldwell, "One Day at a Time," *The Cosby Mysteries,* NBC, 1994.

"Cost of Living," *New York News,* 1995.

Dr. Orloff, "Doctor of Horror," *Tales from the Crypt,* HBO, 1995.

Dr. Dorfman, "Three Days of the Condo," *Frasier,* NBC, 1997.

(Uncredited) Sam Feldberg, "Part VI," *The Practice,* ABC, 1997.

Bobby H., "The Next Day," *Fired Up,* NBC, 1997.

Professor Kenneth Hawkins, "Age," *Tracey Takes On ...,* HBO, 1998.

Barry Haskell, "Lies, Damn Lies, and Statistics," *The West Wing* (also known as *The White House*), NBC, 2000.

"Let's Make a Night of It," *100 Centre Street,* Arts and Entertainment, 2001.

"It's Not the Wrapping, It's the Candy," *The Education of Max Bickford,* CBS, 2001.

Al Cox, "Babies," *100 Centre Street,* Arts and Entertainment, 2002.

Mr. Piltdown, "The Christmas Watch," *Touched by an Angel,* CBS, 2002.

Horace Gorman, "Control," *Law & Order: Special Victims Unit* (also known as *Law & Order: SVU* and *Special Victims Unit*), NBC, 2003.

John Manotti, "Inert Dwarf," *Law & Order: Criminal Intent* (also known as *Law & Order: CI*), NBC, 2004.

Dietrich Steinholz, "Secret Service," *Joan of Arcadia,* CBS, 2005.

Himself, "Amanda," *Character Studies,* 2005.

"Jerome Robbins: Something to Dance About," *American Masters,* PBS, 2009.

Dr. Goldman, "Revenge of Broken Jaw," *Life on Mars,* ABC, 2009.

Television Work; Specials:

Director, *Say Goodnight, Gracie,* PBS, 1983.

WRITINGS

Plays:

Booth Is Back, produced at Long Wharf Theatre, New Haven, CT, 1991–92.

Booth, produced at York Theatre Company, Theatre at St. Peter's, New York City, 1994.

Uncle Bob (two–act), produced at Mint Theatre, New York City, 1995, then Soho Playhouse, New York City, 2001.

Orson's Shadow (two–act), produced at Steppenwolf Theatre Company, Chicago, IL, then Main Stage, Williamstown Theatre Festival, Williamstown, MA, both 2000.

(Adapter) *A Minister's Wife,* produced Mitzi E. Newhouse Theatre, New York City, 2001, then Writers' Theatre, Chicago, IL, 2009.

Orson's Shadow, Barrow Street Theatre, New York City, 2005.

Television Episodes:

Wrote *Hometown.*

OTHER SOURCES

Periodicals:

Back Stage, June 12, 1998, p. 33.

PINKINS, Tonya 1963(?)–

PERSONAL

Nickname is Toni; born May 30, 1963 (some sources cite 1962), in Chicago, IL; father, a police officer and in insurance sales; mother, a postal worker and bus driver; married c. 1984 (divorced, c. 1986); married Ron Brawer (a musician and musical director), February 10, 1987 (divorced, c. 1995); married Eric Winter, July, 2009; children: Maxx, Myles, Maija, Manuel. *Education:* Columbia College Chicago, B.A., 1996; studied theatre and dance at Carnegie Mellon University; trained at William Esper Studio, a youth program with the Goodman Theatre, and with St. Nicholas Theatre Company; studied acting and voice; also attended law school. *Religion:* Agape Church of Religious Science. *Avocational Interests:* Musicals, reading, traveling.

Addresses: *Agent*—Abrams Artists Agency, 275 Seventh Ave., 26th Floor, New York, NY 10001.

Career: Actress, singer, recording artist, and writer. Appeared in advertisements. Cabaret singer; also performed the national anthem at events; affiliated with the record label Divinity to Infinity. Actorpreneur Attitude (motivational workshop series), founder and presenter; The Non–Traditional Casting Project (NTCP), member of the board of directors; Operation Z (antiviolence organization), cocreator and activist; also worked as an artist (a painter) and a teacher. Participated in several events, including workshops, benefits, conventions, and panels; lecturer, instructor, and presenter at various venues; worked at restaurants; involved in efforts for charities.

Member: Actors' Equity Association, Screen Actors Guild, American Federation of Television and Radio Artists, Writers Guild of America, West, Organization of Black Screenwriters (OBS; member of the Script Development Committee), Independent Feature Project/West, Broadcast Music, Inc. (BMI), American Federation of Teachers, United Teachers Los Angeles.

Awards, Honors: Named a National Achievement Scholar and earned college scholarships; Antoinette Perry Award, best featured actress in a musical, Drama Desk Award, outstanding featured actress in a musical, Clarence Derwent Award, most promising actor of the season, Actors' Equity Association, and Monarch Award, best actress in a musical, all 1992, and Outer Critics Circle Award, outstanding featured actress in a musical, 1993, all for *Jelly's Last Jam;* Image Award nomination, best actress in a daytime drama, National Association for the Advancement of Colored People, 1992, and *Soap Opera Digest* Award nomination, outstanding supporting actress, 1993, both for *All My Children;* Antoinette Perry Award nomination, best actress in a musical, 1997, The Eartha Kitt Award, best featured actress in a play (musical or revue), Black Theater Alliance awards, 1998, and Jeff Award nomination, best actress in a principal role in a musical, Joseph Jefferson Awards Committee, 1998, all for *Play On!;* First Annual Chutzpah Award, one of the ten women in America who will take your breath away, *O* magazine, 2004; Obie Award, performance, *Village Voice,* Lucille Lortel Award, outstanding lead actress, League of Off–Broadway Theatres and Producers, Vivian Robinson/AUDELCO Recognition awards for Excellence in Black Theatre, outstanding performance in a musical (female) and (with others) outstanding musical production of the year, Audience Development Committee (AUDELCO), Garland Award, outstanding performance, *Back Stage* magazine, Antoinette Perry Award nomination, best performance by a leading actress in a musical, Drama Desk Award nomination, outstanding featured actress in a musical, and Outer Critics Circle Award nomination, outstanding actress in a musical, all 2004, Los Angeles Drama Critics Award, best lead performance, and Los Angeles Drama Critics Award nomination (with others), best production, both 2005, Laurence Olivier Award nomination, best actress in a musical, Society of West End Theatre, and Whatsonstage.com Award nomination, best actress in a musical, both 2007, recognition from the National Association for the Advancement of Colored People (NAACP), and some sources cite other awards and honors, all for *Caroline, or Change;* Ovation Award nomination, best lead actress in a play, Los Angeles Stage Alliance, 2008, for *And Her Hair Went with Her;* named one of the alumni of the year, Columbia College Chicago, 2008; Helen Hayes Award nomination, outstanding lead actress, resident play, Washington Theatre Awards Society, 2010, for *Black Pearl Sings!*

CREDITS

Stage Appearances:

Golde, *Fiddler on the Roof* (musical), c. 1970.

Gwen Wilson, *Merrily We Roll Along* (musical), Alvin Theatre, New York City, 1981.

Little Shop of Horrors (musical), Orpheum Theatre, New York City, between c. 1982 and 1987.

Mopsa, *The Winter's Tale,* Riverside Shakespeare Company, West Park Presbyterian Church, New York City, 1983.

Charlaine and Alaine, *A ... My Name Is Alice* (musical revue), The Women's Project, Village Gate Theatre, New York City, c. 1983–84.

Eustacia Vye, *Just Say No,* Workshop of the Players Art (WPA) Theatre, New York City, 1988.

Grace, *The Piano Lesson,* Goodman Theatre, Chicago, IL, c. 1988.

Mattie Campbell, *Joe Turner's Come and Gone,* Pittsburgh Public Theater, Pittsburgh, PA, c. 1989.

Lawna, "Believing," and member of Psychocompany, "Psychoneurotic Phantasies," *Young Playwrights Festival* (also known as *The 1990 Young Playwrights Festival* and *Young Playwrights '90*), Foundation of the Dramatists Guild, Playwrights Horizons Theatre, New York City, 1990.

Ludo, doctor, lawyer, architect, chambermaid, trader, Blackshirt, and younger lady, *The Caucasian Chalk Circle,* New York Shakespeare Festival, Joseph Papp Public Theatre, Martinson Hall, New York City, 1990.

Ellie, Sylvia, and Grace, *Approximating Mother,* The Women's Project and Productions, Judith Anderson Theatre, New York City, 1991.

Sweet Anita, *Jelly's Last Jam* (musical), Center Theatre Group, Mark Taper Forum, Los Angeles, 1991, and Virginia Theatre, New York City, 1992–93.

Mistress Ford, *The Merry Wives of Windsor,* New York Shakespeare Festival, Joseph Papp Public Theatre, Delacorte Theater, New York City, 1994.

Clotilde, *Chronicle of a Death Foretold* (musical), Plymouth Theatre, New York City, 1995.

Lady Liv, *Play On!* (musical), Brooks Atkinson Theatre, New York City, 1997, and Goodman Theatre, 1998.

Kate, *The Wild Party* (musical), New York Shakespeare Festival, Virginia Theatre, 2000.

Mattie Cheeks, *No Niggers, No Jews, No Dogs,* National Playwrights Conference, O'Neill Theater Center, Waterford, CT, 2000.

Muzzy, *Thoroughly Modern Millie* (musical), La Jolla Playhouse, La Jolla, CA, 2000.

S.T.A.G.E. (benefit concert; also known as *S.T.A.G.E. LA*), The Harriet Chase and Charles Luckman Fine Arts Complex, Los Angeles, 2000.

The Vagina Monologues, Westside Theatre Downstairs, New York City, 2000.

The Diva Project (solo show), George Street Playhouse, New Brunswick, NJ, 2001.

S.T.A.G.E. Too (benefit concert; also known as *S.T.A.G.E. LA*), The Harriet Chase and Charles Luckman Fine Arts Complex, 2001.

The Vagina Monologues, produced as part of *V–Day 2001,* Madison Square Garden, New York City, 2001.

Panel participant, *Director's Lab West* (panel discussion; also known as *Lincoln Center Director's Lab West*), Pasadena Playhouse, Pasadena, CA, 2002.

Dream: The Lyrics and Music of Johnny Mercer (benefit concerts), The Harriet Chase and Charles Luckman Fine Arts Complex, 2002.

Merrily We Roll Along (benefit concert staging of musical), Fiorello H. LaGuardia High School of Music & Art and Performing Arts, New York City, 2002.

V–Day Harlem 2002, Apollo Theatre, Harlem, New York City, 2002.

Madame Fleur, *House of Flowers* (concert staging of musical), produced as part of *City Center Encores!* (also known as *Encores!, Encores! Great American Musicals in Concert,* and *New York City Center Encores!*), City Center Theatre, New York City, 2003.

Pandora's Trunk (solo show), National Black Theatre Festival, Winston–Salem, NC, 2003.

Caroline Thibodeaux, *Caroline, or Change* (musical), produced in workshops, New York Shakespeare Festival, Joseph Papp Public Theatre, Estelle R. Newman Theatre, New York City, 2003–2004, Eugene O'Neill Theatre, New York City, 2004, Center Theatre Group, Ahmanson Theatre, Los Angeles, 2004, Curran Theatre, San Francisco, CA, 2005, and National Theatre, Lyttelton Theatre, London, 2006–2007.

Children and Art (benefit), New Amsterdam Theatre, New York City, 2005.

Harold Arlen Centennial Tribute, produced as part of the American Songbook Series, Lincoln Center, Frederick P. Rose Hall, Allen Room, New York City, 2005.

Hooray for Love: A Celebration of the Music Harold Arlen (concert), The Harriet Chase and Charles Luckman Fine Arts Complex, 2005.

Mame Wilks, *Radio Golf,* McCarter Theatre Center, Matthews Theatre Auditorium, Princeton, NJ, and Cort Theatre, New York City, both 2007.

Evy, *As Much as You Can,* Celebration Theatre, West Hollywood, CA, 2008.

Jasmine and other characters, *And Her Hair Went with Her,* The Fountain Theatre, Los Angeles, 2008.

The Fabulous Miss Marie (staged readings), Cherry Lane Theatre, New York City, 2008.

Alberta "Pearl" Johnson, *Black Pearl Sings!,* Ford's Theatre, Washington, DC, 2009.

Broadway Backwards 5 (benefit), Lincoln Center, Vivian Beaumont Theatre, New York City, 2010.

Appeared in *She Said a Bad Word,* Circle Repertory, New York City; and in *Stealin',* National Playwrights

Conference, O'Neill Theater Center. Also appeared in other productions, including *Gaia, Lightning* (one–act play), *Mexican Hayride* (musical), and *An Ounce of Prevention.*

Stage Appearances; Cabaret Performances:

Live at Joe's Pub, Joseph Papp Public Theatre, Joe's Pub, New York City, 2001.

My Shining Hour: Salute to Harold Arlen (also known as *My Shining Hour*), Joseph Papp Public Theatre, Joe's Pub, 2004.

Other cabaret performances include *Live at Joe's Pub Too,* Joseph Papp Public Theatre, Joe's Pub; and performances at Sweetwater's, 1984; and at Don't Tell Mama, New York City.

Television Appearances; Series:

Heather Dalton, *As the World Turns,* CBS, 1983–86.

Olivia "Livia" Frye Cudahy, *All My Children* (also known as *All My Children: The Summer of Seduction* and *La force du destin*), ABC, 1991–95 and beginning 2003.

Nurse Mary Jenkins, *University Hospital,* syndicated, 1995.

Viola Crawford, *Army Wives,* Lifetime, beginning 2009.

Television Appearances; Miniseries:

Sharon, *Rage of Angels: The Story Continues,* NBC, 1986.

Herself, *Black in the 80s* (documentary), VH1, 2005.

Television Appearances; Movies:

Officer Janet Mazda, *Strapped,* HBO, 1993.

Sondra, *Against Their Will: Women in Prison* (also known as *Against Their Will* and *Caged Seduction: The Shocking True Story*), ABC, 1994.

Television Appearances; Specials:

Heather Dalton, *As the World Turns: 30th Anniversary,* CBS, 1986.

Herself, "Jammin': Jelly Roll Morton on Broadway," *Great Performances,* PBS, 1992.

Herself, *Happy Birthday Oscar Wilde,* Radio Telefis Eireann (RTE), 2004.

Television Appearances; Awards Presentations:

The 51st Annual Tony Awards (also known as *Fifty–First Annual Tony Awards* and *1997 Tony Awards*), CBS, 1997.

The 58th Annual Tony Awards (also known as *The 2004 Tony Awards*), CBS, 2004.

The 31st Annual Daytime Emmy Awards, NBC, 2004.

Television Appearances; Episodic:

Prostitute drug user, "Justice Hits the Skids," *Crime Story,* NBC, 1986.

Iris, "Elvin Pays for Dinner," *The Cosby Show* (also known as *Bill Cosby, Bill Cosby Show,* and *Cosby Show*), NBC, 1990.

Woman, "Subterranean Homeboy Blues," *Law & Order* (also known as *Law & Order Prime*), NBC, 1990.

Working in the Theatre, CUNY TV, 1992, 2000.

Melinda Tralins, "In Loco Parentis," *The Guardian* (also known as *El guardia, The Guardian—Retter mit Herz, Le protecteur, O allos mou eaftos, Ochita bengoshi Nick Fallin, Ochita bengoshi Nick Fallin 2,* and *Oikeuden puolesta*), CBS, 2002.

(In archive footage) Olivia "Livia" Frye Cudahy, "All My Children," *Biography* (also known as *A&E Biography: All My Children*), Arts and Entertainment, 2003.

Herself and Caroline Thibodeaux, "Production: *Caroline, or Change,*" *Working in the Theatre,* CUNY TV, 2004.

Guest, *Dennis Miller,* CNBC, 2004.

Guest, *Soap Talk,* SOAPnet, 2004, 2006.

Anita Al–Sayeed, "Family," *Sleeper Cell* (also known as *Sleeper Cell: American Terror*), Showtime, 2005.

Herself, *Bid Whist Party Throwdown,* TV One, 2005.

Angela Young, "Hindsight," *Law & Order* (also known as *Law & Order Prime*), NBC, 2006.

Detective Nora Bennett, "A Real Rain," *Criminal Minds* (also known as *Quantico, Criminal Minds—FBI tutjijat, Esprits criminels, Gyilkos elmek, Kurjuse kannul,* and *Mentes criminales*), CBS, 2006.

Dina Miller, "The River," *Cold Case* (also known as *Anexihniastes ypothesis, Caso abierto, Cold case—affaires classees, Cold Case—Kein Opfer ist je vergessen, Doegloett aktak, Kalla spaar, Todistettavasti syyllinen,* and *Victimes du passe*), CBS, 2006.

Ms. Best, "The Toot," *Unfabulous* (also known as *Allie Singer*), Nickelodeon, 2007.

Herself, "August Wilson's Legacy," *Working in the Theatre,* CUNY TV, 2007.

Donna Taft, "Split Ends," *The Closer* (also known as *L.A.: Enquetes prioritaires* and *Se apostasi anapnois*), TNT, 2008.

Alama Matobo, "Day 7: 11:00 a.m.–12:00 p.m.," *24* (also known as *Twenty Four* and *24 Hours*), Fox, 2009.

Alama Matobo, "Day 7: 12:00 p.m.–1:00 p.m.," *24* (also known as *Twenty Four* and *24 Hours*), Fox, 2009.

Alama Matobo, "Day 7: 1:00 p.m.–2:00 p.m.," *24* (also known as *Twenty Four* and *24 Hours*), Fox, 2009.

Alama Matobo, "Day 7: 2:00 p.m.–3:00 p.m.," *24* (also known as *Twenty Four* and *24 Hours*), Fox, 2009.

Appeared in other programs, including *The Charlie Rose Show* (also known as *Charlie Rose*), PBS.

Television Appearances; Pilots:
"American Dream," *American Dream,* ABC, 1981.

Film Appearances:
Carol, *Growing Up Young* (short film), Film Police, 1980.

Angela, *Beat Street* (also known as *The Perfect Beat*), Orion, 1984.

Hotshot (also known as *Football kid, Hang Tough,* and *El rey de futbol*), International Film Marketing, 1987.

Leslie, *See No Evil, Hear No Evil,* TriStar, 1989.

Mailika, *Above the Rim,* New Line Cinema, 1994.

Auntie V, *Love Hurts,* Placebo Pictures, 2002.

Mom, *Love, Mom* (short musical film), Raw Impressions, 2004.

Medic, *Romance & Cigarettes* (musical; also known as *Romance and Cigarettes*), Metro–Goldwyn–Mayer, 2005.

Herself, *Black Theater Today: 2005* (documentary), 2005.

First woman, *True Grits* (short film), Bel–Herald Pictures, 2006.

Marva, *Premium,* Codeblack Entertainment, 2006.

Herself, *Wrestling with Angels* (documentary; also known as *Wrestling with Angels: Playwright Tony Kushner*), Balcony Releasing, 2006.

Of Lesser or Greater Value (short musical film), 2006.

Phoebe Banks, *Enchanted,* Walt Disney Studios, 2007.

Herself and Caroline Thibodeaux, *ShowBusiness: The Road to Broadway* (documentary), Regent Releasing, 2007.

Mrs. Robinson, *Noah's Arc: Jumping the Broom,* New Open Door Productions, 2008.

Appeared in other films, including *Redemption* (short student film).

Film Work:
Developer of *Who Gets the Kids?* (documentary).

Internet Appearances; Episodic:
Herself, *Downstage Center* (podcast), http://americantheatrewing.org, 2004.

The Popsicle's Court, broadcast on *YouTube,* http://www.youtube.com, beginning c. 2009.

Appeared in various footage posted on the Internet.

Radio Appearances:
Herself, *All Things Considered* (also known as *ATC, Weekend All Things Considered,* and *WATC*), National Public Radio, 2007.

RECORDINGS

Albums:
Live at Joe's Pub, Divinity to Infinity, 2001.

My Shining Hour: Salute to Harold Arlen (also known as *My Shining Hour*), Divinity to Infinity, 2004.

Other recordings include *Live at Joe's Pub Too.*

Albums; with Others:

Jelly's Last Jam (original Broadway cast recording), Mercury/Decca Broadway, 1992.

Track "I Had Myself a True Love," *Dream: The Lyrics and Music of Johnny Mercer,* LML Music, 2003.

Caroline, or Change (original Broadway cast recording), Hollywood Records, 2004.

Audiobooks:

The Women of Brewster Place by Gloria Naylor, Penguin HighBridge Audio, 1993.

The Book of Virtues by William Bennett, Simon & Schuster Audio, 1994.

The Moral Compass by William Bennett (also known as *The Moral Compass: Stories for Life's Journey*), Simon & Schuster Audio, 1995.

Chocolate for a Woman's Soul by Kay Allenbaugh (also known as *Chocolate for a Woman's Soul: Stories to Feed Your Spirit and Warm Your Heart*), Simon & Schuster Audio, 1997.

The Silent Cradle by Margaret Cuthbert, Simon & Schuster Audio, 1998.

WRITINGS

Writings for the Stage:

I Married Satan and He Got Custody (monologue; also known as *Crude Awakenings* and *I Married Satan and He Got Custody: or, Crude Awakenings*), 2001.

My Shining Hour: Salute to Harold Arlen (also known as *My Shining Hour*), Joseph Papp Public Theatre, Joe's Pub, New York City, 2004.

Composer and author of book, *Le Cav* (musical); created material for *Live at Joe's Pub Too,* Joseph Papp Public Theatre, Joe's Pub, and performances at Don't Tell Mama, New York City.

Screenplays:

The Guy Gets Off, 1989.

Dangerous Players (based on *Les liaisons dangereuses,* by Pierre Choderlos de Laclos; also known as *Dangerous Games*), 2001.

In the Company of Angels, 2001.

Treatment for "Untitled" Screenplay a.k.a. Magical Child (also known as *Magical Child*), 2002.

Teleplays:

Pro Se, 2001.

Musical composer for the series *Search for Tomorrow* (also known as *Search for Happiness*), CBS and NBC.

Albums; with Others:

My Shining Hour: Salute to Harold Arlen (also known as *My Shining Hour*), Divinity to Infinity, 2004.

Contributed to other recordings, including *Live at Joe's Pub Too.*

Music:

Wrote songs.

Nonfiction:

Get over Yourself! (also known as *Get over Yourself!: How to Drop the Drama and Claim the Life You Deserve*), Hyperion, 2005.

Author of the autobiographies *The Bridges I've Burned* and *A Trial of Faith: Memoirs of a Pro Se Litigant* (also known as *Trial of Faith*). Contributor to periodicals and Internet sites. Created workshops, lectures, and other materials.

OTHER SOURCES

Periodicals:

Being Single, August/September, 2004.
Los Angeles Times, December 15, 2004.
Los Angeles Wave, May 15, 2008, pp. A1, A3.
New York Times, May 2, 2004.
Soap Opera Digest, September 14, 2004.
TV Guide, June 6, 2004, p. 61.
Washington Post, October 11, 2009.

Electronic:

Playbill.com, http://www.playbill.com, May 28, 2004;May 2, 2007.
Tonya Pinkins, http://www.tonyapinkins.com, March 18, 2010.

PINNOCK, Arnold 1961–

PERSONAL

Born March 26, 1961, in Osaka, Japan; raised in Canada.

Career: Actor. Second City (improvisation group), Toronto, Ontario, Canada, performed on Main Stage and in national touring company; also performed standup comedy at clubs in and around Toronto.

Awards, Honors: Gemini Award nominations, best ensemble in a comedy program or series, Academy of Canadian Cinema and Television, 2008, 2009, both for *Billable Hours.*

CREDITS

Television Appearances; Series:
Tyrone Meeks, *Deep in the City* (also known as *The City* and *Flesh & Blood*), CTV, 1999.
Youth pastor Dwight Gooding, *Lord Have Mercy!,* VisionTV, 2003–2004.
Toby Sayles, *Beautiful People,* ABC Family, 2005–2006.
Paul Greebie, *Life with Derek,* The Disney Channel, 2005–2009.
Vic Laghm, *Billable Hours,* Showcase, 2007–2008.
George Ryder, *The Listener,* NBC, 2009.
Voices, *Stoked* (animated), Cartoon Network, 2009.

Television Appearances; Miniseries:
Paramedic, *Undue Influence* (also known as *Steve Martini's "Undue Influence"*), CBS, 1996.
Mohammed, "We Are Circus," *Rescuers: Stories of Courage: Two Families,* Showtime, 1998.
Reggie, *Master Spy: The Robert Hanssen Story,* CBS, 2002.
Jason Marl, *Category 6: Day of Destruction,* CBS, 2004.
Dick Simon, *Covert One: The Hades Factor,* CBS, 2006.
Member of FBI staff, *The Path to 9/11,* ABC, 2006.
Simon Moody, *Riverworld,* SyFy, 2010.

Television Appearances; Movies:
Drug dealer, *Color of Justice,* Showtime, 1997.
One of the other cabbies, *Elvis Meets Nixon,* Showtime, 1997.
Second prison truck driver, *Dead Silence* (also known as *Silence de mort*), HBO, 1997.
Jackie Dee, *Naked City: A Killer Christmas,* Showtime, 1998.
Jamail, *Labor of Love,* Lifetime, 1998.
Leo, *Giving Up the Ghost,* Lifetime, 1998.
Floyd Court/Santa, *Must Be Santa,* Starz!, 1999.
Guy in convertible, *A Saintly Switch* (also known as *In Your Shoes*), ABC, 1999.
Teacher, *The Promise,* NBC, 1999.
Dickerson, *Xchange,* HBO, 2000.
Dr. Hite, *A Mother's Fight for Justice* (also known as *Crash Course*), Lifetime, 2001.
Herman Miller, *Final Jeopardy,* ABC, 2001.
Jimmy Wilmington, *After Amy* (also known as *No Ordinary Baby*), Lifetime, 2001.
Lincoln, *Bojangles,* Showtime, 2001.
Silas Bonner, *Ruby's Bucket of Blood,* Showtime, 2001.
Dr. Dean Cutler, *Tru Confessions,* The Disney Channel, 2002.
Howard Katanga, *The Brady Bunch in the White House,* Fox, 2002.

You Belong to Me (also known as *Mary Higgins Clark's "You Belong to Me"*), PAX, 2001.
Pryor, *Evel Knievel,* TNT, 2004.
Jack, *Perfect Strangers,* CBS, 2004.
David Barnes, *Twitches,* The Disney Channel, 2005.
David Barnes, *Twitches Too,* The Disney Channel, 2007.
Accidental Friendship, 2008.
Deputy, *Grey Gardens,* HBO, 2009.

Television Appearances; Pilots:
Marcus, *XPM,* CBC, 2003.
Third hiring lawyer, *Kevin Hill,* UPN, 2004.

Television Appearances; Specials:
John Willis, *The Secrets of Forensic Science: Beauty Shop Bandit/Turnbull,* The Learning Channel, 2001.

Television Appearances; Episodic:
Clyde Rodriguez, "Soul Survivor," *PSI Factor: Chronicles of the Paranormal,* syndicated, 1999.
Jones, "Self–Inflicted," *Total Recall: The Series* (also known as *Total Recall 2070*), Showtime, 1999.
Bus driver, "But I'm Too Young to Be My Dad," *The Zack Files,* Fox Family, 2000.
Dr. Stephens, "Age Old Story," *The Famous Jett Jackson,* The Disney Channel, 2000.
Neil, "Death Dish," *The War Next Door,* USA Network, 2000.
Neil, "Get a Death," *The War Next Door,* USA Network, 2000.
Souvenir shop owner, "The Put Back," *Relic Hunter,* syndicated, 2000.
Cookie man, "Little Girl Blue," *Soul Food,* Showtime, 2001.
Ray Downey, "Heroes: Part 1," *Blue Murder,* 2001.
"No Time Like the Present," *Doc,* PAX, 2001.
Music executive, "Time Out of Mind," *Odyssey 5,* Showtime, 2002.
Aneas, "Hierophant," *Witchblade,* TNT, 2002.
George, "This Is Your Life," *1–800 Missing* (also known as *Missing*), Lifetime, 2003.
Special effects guy, "Divided Kingdom," *Slings and Arrows,* The Movie Network, 2006.
Steve, "The Element of Surprise," *Flashpoint,* CBS, 2008.
Agent Cooper, "Implosion," *Warehouse 13,* SyFy, 2009.
Desmont Nbuto, "Til Death," *Cra$h & Burn,* Showcase, 2010.
Darryl, "Red Door/Paint It Black," *The Bridge,* CBS, 2010.

Appeared as Elvis Sanders in an episode of *The Hoop Life,* Showtime.

Film Appearances:
Alley officer, *Bless the Child,* Paramount, 2000.

Convict, *Bait* (also known as *Wild Chase*), Warner Bros., 2000.

Dean, *Apartment Hunting,* Alliance Atlantis Communications, 2000.

V.S.A. member, *The Ladies' Man,* Paramount, 2000.

Alan Morris, *Exit Wounds,* Warner Bros., 2001.

David Sands, *Judgment* (also known as *Apocalypse IV: Judgment*), Cloud Ten Pictures, 2001.

Joe Guy, *Down to Earth,* Paramount, 2001.

Wiry man, *Paid in Full,* Dimension Films, 2002.

Pilot in mens' room, *Cypher* (also known as *Brainstorm*), 2002.

Against the Ropes (also known as *The Jackie Kallen Story*), Paramount, 2004.

Big Shirl's male beautician, *New York Minute,* Warner Bros., 2004.

Carlyle, *Assault on Precinct 13,* Rogue Pictures, 2005.

Bruce Barnes, *Left Behind: World at War,* Columbia, 2005.

Detective, *Get Rich of Die Tryin',* Paramount, 2005.

Baxter, *Lars and the Real Girl,* Metro–Goldwyn–Mayer, 2007.

Second cop, *P2,* Summit Entertainment, 2007.

Second soldier, *The Incredible Hulk,* Universal, 2008.

Officer Cole, *The Echo,* Image Entertainment, 2009.

Detective Anderson, *The Cry of the Owl,* Myriad Pictures, 2009.

Boxed In (short film), National Film Board of Canada, 2009.

The man, *Knock Knock,* By Any Means Necessary Productions, 2010.

Stage Appearances:

Last Tango on Lombard (revue), Second City, Old Fire Hall Theatre, Toronto, Ontario, Canada, 1997.

PIPPI

     See BOECHER, Katherine

PLOTNICK, Jack 1968–

PERSONAL

Full name, Jack Stuart Plotnick; born October 30, 1968, in Columbus, OH. *Education:* Carnegie–Mellon University, degree in drama, 1991; also studied with Mel Shapiro and Marshall Mason.

Addresses: *Agent*—Stone Manners Talent Agency, 9911 West Pico Blvd., Suite 1400, Los Angeles, CA 90035. *Manager*—Principato/Young Management, 9465 Wilshire Blvd., Suite 880, Beverly Hills, CA 90212.

Career: Actor and producer. Appeared on stage with Seth Rudetsky as "Plotnick and Rudetsky," including appearance at Caroline's Comedy Club, New York City; performed and produced other live comedy shows. Appeared in commercials, including Thrifty Car Rental, 1999.

Awards, Honors: Film Discovery Jury Award (with others), best actress, U.S. Comedy Arts Festival, Grand Jury Award (with others), outstanding actor in a feature film, 2003, both for *Girls Will Be Girls.*

CREDITS

Film Appearances:

V.P. of casting, *Who's the Caboose?,* 1997.

Edmund Kay, *Gods and Monsters* (also known as *The Father of Frankenstein*), Lions Gate Films, 1998.

Zak, *Chairman of the Board,* Trimark Pictures, 1998.

Curtis, *Ground Control* (also known as *Jet*), Hard Work Productions, 1998.

Mr. Pups, *Mystery Men,* MCA/Universal, 1999.

Adam, *Forever Fabulous,* Filbert Steps Productions, 2000.

Leon Pitofsky, *Say It Isn't So,* Twentieth Century–Fox, 2001.

Steven, *Making Changes,* 2002.

Evie, *Girls Will Be Girls,* IFC Films, 2003.

David, *Taco Bender* (short film), Coppos Films, 2003.

Maurice, *Down with Love,* Twentieth Century–Fox, 2003.

Steven, *Making Changes* (short film), 2004.

Freddie Stevens, *Straight–Jacket,* Regent Releasing, 2004.

Rent–a–Car agent, *Meet the Fockers,* Universal, 2004.

(Uncredited) Mime, *Adam & Steve,* TLA Releasing, 2005.

Jack, *Radiance* (short film), 2005.

Timothy Whims, *Cook–Off!,* 2006.

Robert, *Available Men* (short film), Wolfe Video, 2006.

Dougie, *Stay* (also known as *Sleeping Dogs Lie*), Roadside Attractions, 2006.

Steve Marmella, *Reno 911!: Miami* (also known as *Reno 911!: Miami: The Movie*), Twentieth Century–Fox, 2007.

Christopher, *Feedback* (short film), 2008.

Moses, *Remarkable Power,* Dalton Pictures, 2008.

Evie, *Girls Will Be Girls: The Jizz Party* (short film), SRO Pictures, 2008.

Evie Harris, *Girls Will Be Girls: Delivering Coco, Part I* (short film), SRO Pictures, 2008.

Dog nanny, *Beverly Hills Chihuahua,* Walt Disney Studios Motion Pictures, 2008.

David, *In the Drink,* 2009.

Lonnie Del Mar, *Slate: The Teachings of Lonnie Del Mar* (short film), 2009.

Accountant, *Rubber,* Magnet Releasing, 2010.

Voice of Xandir P. Whifflebottom, *The "Drawn Together" Movie: The Movie!* (animated), Paramount Home Entertainment, 2010.

Also appeared in *Tiara Tango.*

Film Executive Producer:
Girls Will Be Girls, IFC Films, 2003.
Girls Will Be Girls: The Jizz Party (short film), SRO Pictures, 2008.
Girls Will Be Girls: Delivering Coco, Part I (short film), SRO Pictures, 2008.

Television Appearances; Series:
Slim Organbody, *Late Night with Conan O'Brien,* 1995–96.
Barrett, *Ellen* (also known as *These Friends of Mine*), ABC, 1995–98.
Various characters, *The Jenny McCarthy Show,* MTV, 1997.
Clark, *Rude Awakening,* Showtime, 1999–2000.
Stuart Glazer, *Action,* syndicated, 1999–2000.
Steve Marmella, *Reno 911!,* Comedy Central, 2003–2008.
Voice of Xandir P. Whifflebottom, *Drawn Together* (animated), Comedy Central, 2004–2008.
Sammy number two, *Joan of Arcadia,* CBS, 2004–2005.
Steve Morris, *Lovespring International,* Lifetime, 2006.
Ted, *Svetlana,* 2010.

Television Appearances; Movies:
Cop, *Clerks,* 1995.
Bad Boy Austin, *30 Days Until I'm Famous,* VH1, 2004.

Television Appearances; Specials:
The 1998 VH1 Fashion Awards, VH1, 1998.
Heroes of Comedy: Women on Top, Comedy Central, 2003.
Celebrity Autobiography: In Their Own Words, Bravo, 2005.

Television Appearances; Pilots:
Jack, *Life on Mars,* HBO, 1994.
Hey, Neighbor, Fox, 2000.
Steve Morris, *Lovespring International,* 2006.
Brett Partridge, *The Mentalist,* CBS, 2008.

Television Appearances; Episodic:
Mitch, *Madman of the People,* NBC, 1994.
Penn, "McGovern: Unclothed," *Murphy Brown,* CBS, 1995.
Button Gwinnett, "Who Let You In?," *Mr. Show with Bob and David* (also known as *Mr. Show*), 1995.
Seth, "Sit Down, You're Rockin' the Funicular," *Hope & Gloria,* NBC, 1996.

Harris, "Caroline and the Younger Man," *Caroline in the City* (also known as *Caroline*), NBC, 1996.
Sunshine Carpets crew leader, "The Checks," *Seinfeld,* NBC, 1996.
Ted, "Risky Bidness," *The Wayans Bros.,* The WB, 1997.
Ted, "Ted's Revenge," *The Wayans Bros.,* The WB, 1997.
Uncle Ralphie, "The Competition," *The Weird Al Show,* 1997.
Uncle Ralphie, "The Obligatory Holiday Episode," *The Weird Al Show,* 1997.
Deputy Mayor Allan Finch, "Homecoming," *Buffy the Vampire Slayer* (also known as *BtVS, Buffy, Buffy, the Vampire Slayer: The Series,* and *Nightfall*), The WB, 1998.
Deputy Mayor Allan Finch, "Lover's Walk," *Buffy the Vampire Slayer* (also known as *BtVS, Buffy, Buffy, the Vampire Slayer: The Series,* and *Nightfall*), The WB, 1998.
Deputy Mayor Allan Finch, "Bad Girls," *Buffy the Vampire Slayer* (also known as *BtVS, Buffy, Buffy, the Vampire Slayer: The Series,* and *Nightfall*), The WB, 1999.
Deputy Mayor Allan Finch, "Consequences," *Buffy the Vampire Slayer* (also known as *BtVS, Buffy, Buffy, the Vampire Slayer: The Series,* and *Nightfall*), The WB, 1999.
Jack, "Truth Don't Fail Me Now," *Rude Awakening,* Showtime, 2000.
Process server, "To Serve, with Love," *Dead Last,* The WB, 2001.
Mike Brandt, "Humpty Dumped," *NYPD Blue* (also known as *N.Y.P.D.*), ABC, 2002.
Andrew Waller, "Separate Ways (Worlds Apart)," *Dawson's Creek,* The WB, 2002.
Leslie, "The Helpless Hand," *For Your Love,* 2002.
Dr. Medway, "It's a Family Thing," *One on One,* UPN, 2003.
Mr. Levitch, "Nick Kicks Butt," *Complete Savages,* ABC, 2004.
Jeremiah Christopher, "Cash Springs Eternal," *Las Vegas,* NBC, 2006.
Natalie's publicist, "The Box and the Bunny," *Ugly Betty,* ABC, 2006.
Pocket elf, "I Almost Drowned in a Chocolate Fountain," *Wizards of Waverly Place,* The Disney Channel, 2007.
Dr. George, "Dawn Budge II," *Nip/Tuck,* FX Network, 2007.
Bradley Roberts, "Shaun of the Dead," *Shark,* CBS, 2007.
Eddie, "Live and Let Die," *Head Case,* Starz!, 2008.
Mike, "If My Hole Could Talk," *Two and a Half Men,* CBS, 2008.
Tommy, *Do Not Disturb,* Fox, 2008.
Ian, "It's a Terrible Lie," *Supernatural,* The CW, 2009.
Hal Connor, "Broken," *House M.D.* (also known as *House* and *Dr. House*), Fox, 2009.
Brett Partridge, "Red Sky in the Morning," *The Mentalist,* CBS, 2010.

Television Work; Series:
Supervising producer, *Lovespring International,* Lifetime, 2006.

Television Director; Episodic:
Lovespring International, Lifetime, 2006.

Stage Appearances:
Miss Industrial Northeast, *Pageant,* Blue Angel Theatre, New York City, 1991–92.
Kevin Bailey, *The Sheik of Avenue B,* Town Hall Theatre, New York City, 1992.
The News in Revue, Theatre at Del's Down Under, New York City, 1992.

Appeared off–Broadway in *Class Clown.*

WRITINGS

Screenplays:
(With others) *Feedback,* 2008.

Television Additional Material; Episodic:
Head Case, Starz!, 2007.

OTHER SOURCES

Electronic:
Jack Plotnick Website, http://www.jackplotnick.com, June 4, 2010.

PLUNKETT, Gerard
(Gerrard Plunkett)

PERSONAL

Born in Dublin, Ireland.

Addresses: *Agent*—Marcia Hurwitz, Innovative Artists Talent and Literary Agency, 1505 10th St., Santa Monica, CA 90401.

Career: Actor, voice performer, and comedian. Performed standup comedy and impersonations in and around Dublin, Ireland; performed improvisational comedy in Toronto, Ontario, Canada.

CREDITS

Television Appearances; Series:
Voice of the shadow master, *Double Dragon* (animated), syndicated, 1993–94.

Voice of Yotsuya, *Maison Ikkoku* (animated), beginning c. 1996.
Bob Kelley, *Da Vinci's Inquest* (also known as *Da Vinci's City Hall*), CBC, 1998–2005.
Multiple voices, *Aaagh! It's the Mr. Hell Show!* (animated; also known as *The Mr. Hell Show*), BBC2, 2001–2002.
Gordon Evans, *Intelligence,* CBC, 2007.

Also affiliated with the series *Darkstalkers.*

Television Appearances; Miniseries:
Fourth Officer Joseph Boxhall, *Titanic,* CBS, 1996.
Daniel, *Human Cargo,* CBC, 2004.
Dr. Richard Shwartzton, *Kingdom Hospital* (also known as *Stephen King's "Kingdom Hospital"*), ABC, 2004.
Terrence Young, *Impact,* ABC, 2009.

Television Appearances; Movies:
Diamond merchant, *Exception to the Rule,* HBO, 1997.
Sklar, *Contagious* (also known as *Virus*), USA Network, 1997.
Marcus, *Baby Monitor: Sound of Fear,* USA Network, 1998.
Mike McClary, *My Husband's Secret Life,* USA Network, 1998.
Voice of Edgar, *Futuresport,* ABC, 1998.
Dr. Leo Sardis, *Life in a Day,* UPN, 1999.
Dr. Sarkisian, *Shadow Warriors II: Hunt for the Death Merchant* (also known as *Assault on Death Mountain*), TNT, 1999.
Graham, *A Cooler Climate,* Showtime, 1999.
Griffen Bockman, *Shutterspeed,* TNT, 2000.
Trevor Hayes, *Murder at the Cannes Film Festival,* E! Entertainment Television, 2000.
Dr. Raymond Ardmore, *Devil Winds,* PAX, 2003.
Voices of Pontius Pilate, mystic, and bystander, *Ben Hur* (animated), 2003.

Television Appearances; Episodic:
Bob Bigelow, "When the Bough Breaks," *Madison,* Global TV, 1994.
Phillip Cramer, "The Lady Vanishes," *The Commish,* ABC, 1994.
Reverend Charles O'Bannen, "St. Vincent," *Neon Rider,* syndicated, 1994.
Driver, "Prince of Wails," *Sliders,* Fox, 1995.
James Bailey, "Homeland," *Highlander,* syndicated, 1995.
Stuart Harrison, "Deja Vu," *Robin's Hoods,* syndicated, 1995.
Father Jerry, "Gillian of the Spirits," *Sliders,* Fox, 1996.
Jules Morak, "Street Pirates," *Viper,* syndicated, 1996.
Roland Kantos, "Prophecy," *Highlander,* syndicated, 1996.
Dr. Calderon, "Christmas Carol," *The X–Files,* Fox, 1997.

Dr. Calderon, "Emily," *The X–Files,* Fox, 1997.

High Counselor Tuplo, "The Broca Divide," *Stargate SG–1,* Showtime, 1997.

Nem, "Fire and Water," *Stargate SG–1,* Showtime, 1997.

Quinn, "Black Widow," *Dead Man's Gun,* Showtime, 1997.

Admiral Birch, "Bodies of Evidence," *The Outer Limits* (also known as *The New Outer Limits*), Showtime, 1997.

"Pennies from Heaven," *The Sentinel,* UPN, 1997.

Voice of Scarab, "Pack to the Future," *Mummies Alive* (animated), syndicated, 1997.

Boyd, "Second Wave," *First Wave,* Sci–Fi Channel, 1998.

Dieter Imhoff, "Honest Abe," *Viper,* syndicated, 1998.

Doc Connell, "Voices," *The Crow: Stairway to Heaven,* syndicated, 1998.

Liam Conklin, "Winner Takes All," *Dead Man's Gun,* Showtime, 1998.

High Counselor Tuplo, "Enigma," *Stargate SG–1,* Showtime, 1998.

Gorsdon Kineally, "Amanda Millerd," *Cold Squad* (also known as *Files from the Past*), CTV, 1998.

Carbondale, "The Girl Who Was Plugged In," *Welcome to Paradox,* Sci–Fi Channel, 1998.

"Manimal," *Night Man,* syndicated, 1998.

"From Honey, with Love," *Honey, I Shrunk the Kids: The TV Show,* 1998.

George, "The Haven," *The Outer Limits* (also known as *The New Outer Limits*), Showtime, 1999.

Voice, "The Importance of Being Norma," *Sabrina the Animated Series* (animated; also known as *Sabrina*), ABC, 1999.

Voice, "Saturday Night Furor," *Sabrina the Animated Series* (animated; also known as *Sabrina*), ABC, 1999.

Voice, "Most Dangerous Witch," *Sabrina the Animated Series* (animated; also known as *Sabrina*), ABC, 1999.

Voice, "Harvzilla," *Sabrina the Animated Series* (animated; also known as *Sabrina*), ABC, 1999.

Maxmillian Montgomery, "Bride's Kiss," *The Immortal,* syndicated, 2000.

Bloodmist, "Its Hour Come 'Round at Last," *Andromeda* (also known as *Gene Roddenberry's "Andromeda"*), syndicated, 2001.

Bloodmist, "The Widening Gyre," *Andromeda* (also known as *Gene Roddenberry's "Andromeda"*), syndicated, 2001.

George Atzerodt, "The Brink," *Seven Days,* UPN, 2001.

Gideon Robot, "Family Values," *The Outer Limits* (also known as *The New Outer Limits*), Showtime, 2001.

Miles Davenport, "Room Service" (premiere episode), *Strange Frequency,* VH1, 2001.

Bloodmist, "Double or Nothingness," *Andromeda* (also known as *Gene Roddenberry's "Andromeda"*), syndicated, 2003.

(Uncredited) Bloodmist, "What Happens to a Rev Deferred?," *Andromeda* (also known as *Gene Roddenberry's "Andromeda"*), syndicated, 2003.

Dr. Lawrence, "Deja Voodoo," *The Dead Zone* (also known as *The Dark Half* and *Stephen King's "Dead Zone"*), USA Network, 2003.

Rudd, "A Little Help from My Friends," *The Chris Isaak Show,* Showtime, 2003.

"The Invincible Sword," *Young Blades,* I Network, 2005.

"To Heir Is Human," *Young Blades,* I Network, 2005.

Voice of Armegaddon, "Still Waters Freeze," *Dragon Booster* (animated), ABC Family, 2005.

(As Gerrard Plunkett) Dr. Hauser, "Haeckel's Tale," *Masters of Horror,* Showtime, 2006.

Harry Kram, *Three Moons over Milford,* ABC Family, 2005.

Dr. Donovan Jamison, "Prototype," *Smallville* (also known as *Smallville Beginnings*), The CW, 2007.

Dr. Donovan Jamison, "Phantom," *Smallville* (also known as *Smallville Beginnings*), The CW, 2007.

Therapist, "Echoes," *Fear Itself,* NBC, 2009.

Senator Van Horn, "Earthling," *Fringe,* Fox, 2009.

Appeared as Pat, "A Blessing in Disguise," "Duty Bound," and "Many Happy Returns," and as Richard Maitland, "Fortunes of War," all episodes of *The Campbells.*

Television Appearances; Specials:

Narrator, *Guinea Pig Club* (special), 2002.

Television Work; Episodic:

Additional voices, "Garden of Evil," *RoboCop: Alpha Commando* (animated), syndicated, 1998.

Film Appearances:

Selim Zelkha, *Bloodlines: Legacy of a Lord,* 1997.

Voice, *Lapitch the Little Shoemaker* (originally released as *Cudnovate zgode segrta Hlapica*), 1997.

Sir Robert McKintyre, *Wrongfully Accused,* Warner Bros., 1998.

Spinworthy, *Dudley Do–Right,* Universal, 1999.

Technician, *The 6th Day,* Columbia, 2000.

Voice of the oak tree, *Lion of Oz* (animated; also known as *Lion of Oz and the Badge of Courage*), Sunbow Productions, 2000.

High roller, *Rat Race* (also known as *Course folle*), Paramount, 2001.

Rod Poker, *Suddenly Naked,* 2001, Pantheon Entertainment, 2003.

Voice of Minister Eserbus, *Ark* (animated), Creative Light Worldwide, 2004.

Herbie, *Two for the Money,* Universal, 2005.

Dr. Andy Harrison, *Eight Below* (also known as *8 Below*), Buena Vista, 2006.

Paul, *Snakes on a Plane* (also known as *Snake Flight* and *SoaP*), New Line Cinema, 2006.

Engelan, *Nightwatching,* 2007, E1 Entertainment, 2009.

Isaacs, *2012,* Columbia, 2009.

Stage Appearances:
Someone Who'll Watch Over Me, c. 1996.
Henry Higgins, *My Fair Lady* (musical), Stanley Theatre, Vancouver, British Columbia, Canada, 2001–2002.

Also appeared as Richard in a production of *The Lover.*

RECORDINGS

Animated Videos; Voice Performer:
Voice of Kiba, *Green Legend Ran* (animated), Viz Video, 1992.
Voice of Toristan, *Ranma 1/2* (animated; also known as *Ranma 1/2: Nihao My Concubine, Ranma 1/2: The Movie 2, Nihao My Concubine,* and *Ranma 1/2: Kessen Togenkyo! Hanayome o torimodose!!*), Viz Video, 1993.
Happy, the Littlest Bunny, 1994.
Cinderella (also known as *La cenicienta*), 1994.
Leo the Lion: King of the Jungle (also known as *Leo Leon*), 1994.
Pocahontas (also known as *The Adventures of Pocahontas: Indian Princess*), 1994.
The Magic Gift of the Snowman (also known as *El regalo magico del muneco de nieve*), 1995.
Hercules, 1995.
Heidi, 1995.
Jungle Book (also known as *El libro de la selva*), 1995.
Curly: The Littlest Puppy, 1995.
Alice in Wonderland (also known as *Alicia en el pais de las maravillas*), 1995.
Snow White (also known as *Blancanieves*), 1995.
Black Beauty (also known as *Hermoso negro*), 1995.
The Nutcracker, 1995.
Little Red Riding Hood, 1995.
Sleeping Beauty (also known as *La bella durmiente*), 1995.
The Hunchback of Notre Dame, 1996.
Voice of Dr. Ban, *Galaxy Express 999* (anime; also known as *Galaxy Express 999: The Signature Edition* and *Ginga tetsudo Three–Nine*), Viz Video, 1996.
Mummies Alive! The Legend Begins, Buena Vista Home Video, 1998.
Voice of Turaga Dume, *Bionicle 2: Legends of Metru Nui,* Miramax Home Entertainment, 2004.

Voice of Saiyan warrior, *Dragon Ball Z: Saiyan Saga* (animated), released by Pioneer FUNimation. Some of the animated videos originally appeared as television series in Japan.

POPE, Carly 1980–

PERSONAL

Born August 28, 1980, in Vancouver, British Columbia, Canada; sister of Kris Pope (an actor). *Education:* Briefly attended University of British Columbia. *Avocational Interests:* All sports, long walks, writing poetry, reading, travel.

Addresses: *Agent*—Gersh Agency, 9465 Wilshire Ave., 6th Floor, Beverly Hills, CA 90212; Characters Talent Agency, 8 Elm St., Toronto, Ontario M5G 1G7, Canada. *Manager*—Ben Levine, Kritzer, Levine, Wilkins, Griffin Entertainment, 11872 La Grange Ave., 1st Floor, Los Angeles, CA 90025.

Career: Actress. Appeared in a commercial for Pepsi soft drinks. Also worked as a dancer.

Awards, Honors: Teen Choice Award nomination, choice television actress, 2000, for *Popular;* Leo Award, best supporting actress in a dramatic television series, Motion Picture Arts and Sciences Foundation of British Columbia, 2004, for "The Prosecutor," *The Collector;* Women in Film Award, Vancouver International Film Festival, 2005, for *The Hamster Cage;* Leo Award, best actress in a short drama, 2006, for *Sandra Gets Dumped.*

CREDITS

Film Appearances:
A Girl's Guide to Kissing and Other Nightmares in Teenland, 1996.
Abbey, *Disturbing Behavior,* Metro–Goldwyn–Mayer, 1998.
Sara Johnson, *Aliens in the Wild Wild West* (also known as *Cowboys and Aliens* and *Phantom Town*), Full Moon Entertainment/Kushner–Locke, 1999.
Fawn, *Snow Day,* Paramount, 2000.
Carla, *Finder's Fee,* Lions Gate Films, 2001.
Tasha Bess, *The Glass House,* Columbia, 2001.
Cheryth Bleyn, *Various Positions,* Telefilm Canada/British Columbia Film Commission/CanWest Western Independent Producers Fund, 2002.
Tanya, *Orange County,* Paramount, 2002.
Sara Novak, *Nemesis Game* (also known as *Paper, Scissors, Stone*), Lions Gate Films, 2003.
Sarah Calder, *Intern Academy* (also known as *White Coats*), TVA Films, 2003.
Everyone, 2004.
Angela, *Window Theory,* American World Pictures, 2004.
Rena, *Everyone,* TLA Releasing, 2005.
Title role, *Sandra Gets Dumped* (short film), Crazy 8s Film, 2005.
Candy, *The Hamster Cage,* 2005.
Anna, *The French Guy,* IndustryWorks Distribution, 2005.
Jenny, *Eighteen,* TLA Releasing, 2005.
Tammy, *Two for the Money,* Universal, 2005.
Rosie, *Break a Leg, Rosie* (short film), Like Minded Media/Two Story Productions, 2005.
Title role, *Sandra Goes to Whistler* (short film), Storycraft Pictures, 2005.
Shulamith Firestone, *Itty Bitty Titty Committee,* Power Up Films, 2007.

Vanessa, *Beneath,* Paramount, 2007.
Kris, *Young People Fucking* (also known as *Young People F*cking* and *Y.P.F.*), THINKFilm, 2008.
Crystal, *Say Goodnight,* MTI Home Video, 2008.
Voice of Zella, *Edison and Leo* (animated), TVA Films, 2008.
Roshanna, *Toronto Stories,* Christal Films, 2008.
Stacy, *Life Is Hot in Cracktown,* Lightning Media, 2009.
Karla Bravo, *Stuntmen,* Gravitas Ventures, 2009.
(Uncredited) Riley, *Kill Theory,* After Dark Films, 2010.
Simone, *Textuality,* Seville Pictures, 2010.

Film Work:
Coproducer, *Everyone,* 2003.

Television Appearances; Series:
Samantha "Sam" McPherson, *Popular,* The WB, 1999–2001.
Maya Kandinski, *The Collector,* City TV, 2004–2005.
Garbo, a recurring role, *Dirt,* FX Network, 2007.
Samantha Roth, a recurring role, *24,* Fox, 2009.

Television Appearances; Miniseries:
Young Loreto Callaghan, *Hemingway vs. Callaghan* (also known as *Hemingway: That Summer in Paris*), CBC, 2003.
Laura Malloy, *10.5: Apocalypse* (also known as *10.5*), NBC, 2006.

Television Appearances; Movies:
Student, *Principal Takes a Holiday,* ABC, 1998.
Cheerleader, *I've Been Waiting for You,* NBC, 1998.
Beth Tanner, *A Cooler Climate,* Showtime, 1999.
Mari Ferraez, *Our Guys: Outrage at Glen Ridge* (also known as *Outrage in Glen Ridge*), ABC, 1999.
Molly White, *Trapped in a Purple Haze,* ABC, 2000.
Cindy Thomas, *1st to Die* (also known as *F1rst to Die* and *James Patterson's "F1rst to Die"*), NBC, 2003.
Melissa "Mel" Rochester, *This Time Around,* ABC Family, 2003.
Beth Ann, *The Ranch,* Showtime, 2003.
Bianca, *A Tale of Two Wives* (also known as *Double Bill*), Oxygen, 2003.
J. J. Jenner, *Recipe for a Perfect Christmas* (also known as *Smothered*), Lifetime, 2005.
Sarah, *Yeti: Curse of the Snow Demon,* Sci–Fi Channel, 2008.
Samantha Roth, *24: Redemption,* Fox, 2008.

Television Appearances; Pilots:
Lucinda Pearl, *Outlaw,* NBC, 2010.

Television Appearances; Episodic:
Teresa Chase, "Manimal," *Night Man,* syndicated, 1998.
Herself, "Mommie Dearest," *Grosse Pointe,* The WB, 2000.

Voice of Amelia, "The New Ron," *Kim Possible* (animated), The Disney Channel, 2002.
Voice of Amelia, "Animal Attraction," *Kim Possible* (animated; also known as *Disney's "Kim Possible"*), The Disney Channel, 2003.
Rachel, "The Good, the Bad, and the Geeky," *Jake 2.0,* UPN, 2003.
Ronnie, "The Letter," *The Mountain,* The WB, 2004.
The enchantress, "Enchanted," *Young Blades,* PAX, 2005.
Officer Kate Wilson, "The Perfect Storm," *Tru Calling,* Fox, 2005.
"Stringers," *The Evidence,* ABC, 2006.
Kara, "Till We Have Built Jerusalem," *The 4400,* USA Network, 2007.
Bailey, "The Rules of Attachment: Part II," *Whistler,* The N, 2007.
Bailey, "Last Run," *Whistler,* The N, 2007.
Anke Vermeulen–Papathanasiou, "Cherchez la Femme," *Robson Arms,* CTV, 2008.
Annika, "Coke Dick & First Kick," *Californication,* Showtime, 2008.
Annika, "Blues from Laurel Canyon," *Californication,* Showtime, 2008.

Television Appearances; Specials:
Presenter, *The WB Radio Music Awards,* The WB, 1999.
The Teen Choice Awards 2000, Fox, 2000.
Teen People's 25 Hottest Stars under 25, ABC, 2000.

RECORDINGS

Videos:
Herself, *The Nitty Gritty behind the Itty Bitty Titty Committee,* Power Up Films, 2008.

Appeared in the music videos "Big New Shoes," 1999; and "Don't Even Try" by Jessie Farrell, 2002.

OTHER SOURCES

Periodicals:
Teen People, June, 2000, p. 95.
TV Guide, January 15, 2000, pp. 42–44.

PORTMAN, Rachel 1960–

PERSONAL

Full name, Rachel Mary Berkeley Portman; born December 11, 1960, in Haslemere, England; daughter of Berkeley Charles and Penelope (maiden name, Mowat) Portman; married Count Uberto Pasolini Dall'Onda (a producer), February 25, 1995; children: Anna Gwendolen, Giulia Ginevra, Niky Joan. *Education:* Worcester College, Oxford, B.A.

Addresses: *Agent*—Robert Messinger, First Artists Management, 4764 Park Granada, Suite 210, Calabasas, CA 91302.

Career: Composer, orchestrator, and music producer.

Awards, Honors: Named composer of the year, British Film Institute, 1988; Schneider Trophy, theme music of the year, Tric Celebrity Awards, 1989, for *Precious Bane;* Television Award nominations, best original television music, British Academy of Film and Television Arts, 1990, for *The Woman in Black,* and 1991, for *Oranges Are Not the Only Fruit;* Australian Film Institute Award nomination, best original score, 1994, for *Sirens;* Carlton TV Rank Films Labs/Creative Originality Award, Women in Film, 1996; international prize for film and media music, 1997; Academy Award, best original musical or comedy score, 1997, for *Emma;* Annie Award nomination (with Don Black), outstanding individual achievement for music in an animated feature production, International Animated Film Society, 1998, for the song "As Long As There's Christmas," *Beauty and the Beast: The Enchanted Christmas;* Golden Satellite Award nomination, best motion picture score, International Press Academy, 1999, for *Beloved;* Georges Delerue Prize, Flanders/Ghent International Film Festival, 1999, for *Ratcatcher;* Phoenix Film Critics Society Award and Golden Satellite Award nomination, both best original score, 2000, for *The Legend of Bagger Vance;* Muse Award, New York Women in Film and Television, 2000; Academy Award nomination and Chicago Film Critics Association Award nomination, both best original score, 2000, for *The Cider House Rules;* Grammy Award nomination, best score soundtrack album for a motion picture, television, or other visual media, National Academy of Recording Arts and Sciences, 2001, for *The Cider House Rules;* Academy Award nomination, best original score, and Golden Globe Award nomination, best original score for a motion picture, both 2001, for *Chocolat;* World Soundtrack Award nomination, soundtrack composer of the year, 2001, for *Chocolat* and *The Legend of Bagger Vance;* Touchstone Award, Women in Music, 2001; Grammy Award nomination, best score soundtrack album for a motion picture, television, or other visual media, 2002, for *Chocolat;* Emmy Award nomination, outstanding music direction, 2005, for "The Little Prince," *Great Performances;* Emmy Award nomination, outstanding musical score for a dramatic miniseries, movie, or special, 2009, for *Grey Gardens;* decorated officer, Order of the British Empire, 2010.

CREDITS

Film Music Orchestrator:
Where Angels Fear to Tread, Fine Line, 1991.
Used People, Twentieth Century–Fox, 1992.
Benny & Joon, Metro–Goldwyn–Mayer, 1993.
The Joy Luck Club, Buena Vista, 1993.
The Road to Wellville, Columbia, 1994.
The War of the Buttons, Warner Bros., 1994.
Only You (also known as *Him* and *Just in Time*), TriStar, 1994.
Sirens, Miramax, 1994.
To Wong Foo, Thanks for Everything! Julie Newmar, Universal, 1995.
A Pyromaniac's Love Story (also known as *Burning Love*), Buena Vista, 1995.
Smoke, Miramax, 1995.
Emma, Miramax, 1996.
Marvin's Room (also known as *My Room*), Miramax, 1996.
Palookaville, Samuel Goldwyn, 1996.
Addicted to Love (also known as *Forlorn*), Miramax, 1997.
(And song performer, "Uhuru") *Beloved,* Buena Vista, 1998.
The Other Sister, Buena Vista, 1999.
(And score producer) *The Cider House Rules* (also known as *Cider House Rule*), Miramax, 1999.
Ratcatcher, First Look Pictures Releasing, 2000.
The Legend of Bagger Vance, DreamWorks, 2000.
(And score producer) *Chocolat,* Miramax, 2000.
The Emperor's New Clothes, Paramount, 2002.
(And score producer) *The Truth about Charlie,* Universal, 2002.
The Human Stain, Miramax, 2003.
The Manchurian Candidate, Paramount, 2004.
Because of Winn–Dixie, Twentieth Century–Fox, 2005.
(And score producer) *Oliver Twist,* Sony Pictures Entertainment, 2005.
Infamous, Warner Independent Pictures, 2006.
Miss Potter, Metro–Goldwyn–Mayer/Weinstein Company, 2006.
(And score producer) *The Duchess,* Paramount, 2008.
The Sisterhood of the Traveling Pants 1, Warner Bros., 2008.

Film Work; Other:
Music director, *Privileged,* New Yorker, 1982.
Music arranger, "Tannhauser," *Meeting Venus,* Warner Bros., 1991.
Score producer, *The Adventures of Pinocchio* (also known as *Carlo Collodi's "Pinocchio," Pinocchio,* and *Die Legende von Pinocchio*), New Line Cinema, 1996.
Music producer, *Nicholas Nickleby,* Metro–Goldwyn–Mayer, 2002.

Television Work; Specials:
Musician, "Sometime in August," *Screen Two*, BBC, 1988.
Music director, *The Three Ravens*, HBO, c. 1997.
Music director, "The Little Prince" (broadcast of stage production), *Great Performances*, PBS, 2004.

Television Appearances; Specials:
The Hollywood Soundtrack Story, AMC, 1995.
The 69th Annual Academy Awards, ABC, 1997.
One Taste Is Never Enough ... The Pleasures of "Chocolat" (also known as *The Making of "Chocolat"*), 2000.
Lights! Action! Music!, 2007.

RECORDINGS

Albums:
Performer, *Benny & Joon*, Milan Records, 1993.
Orchestrator, *Only You*, Sony, 1994.
Performer, *Smoke*, Hollywood Records, 1995.
Performer and producer, *To Wong Foo, Thanks for Everything!*, MCA, 1995.
Orchestrator and producer, *Emma*, Hollywood Records, 1996.
Orchestrator, *Addicted to Love*, TVT, 1997.
Performer, orchestrator, and producer, *The Other Sister*, Hollywood Records, 1999.
Performer, *Out at the Movies*, Varese Records, 1999.
Orchestrator, *Pure Meditation*, Milan Records, 2001.
Orchestrator and producer, *The Truth about Charlie*, Sony, 2002.
Performer, *Hart's War*, Universal, 2002.

Much of this music was originally composed by Portman for films of the same name.

Video Appearances:
Twist by Polanski, Sony Pictures, 2006.

Videos Featuring Music by Portman:
The Truth about "The Truth about Charlie" (also known as *The Making of "The Truth about Charlie"*), Universal Studios Home Video, 2003.
Twist by Polanski, Sony Pictures, 2006.
It's a Happy Movie: The Children's Making–Of, Fox Pathe Europa, 2006.

WRITINGS

Composer of Film Scores:
Privileged, New Yorker, 1982.
Experience Preferred ... but Not Essential (also known as *First Love*; originally broadcast in England as a television movie), Samuel Goldwyn, 1982.

90 Degrees South, 1987.
High Hopes, Skouras, 1988.
Life Is Sweet, October Films, 1990.
Where Angels Fear to Tread, Fine Line, 1991.
(And song "Where Are the Words?") *Used People*, Twentieth Century–Fox, 1992.
Rebecca's Daughters, 1992.
The Joy Luck Club, Buena Vista, 1993.
Friends, First Run Features, 1993.
Ethan Frome, Miramax, 1993.
Benny & Joon, Metro–Goldwyn–Mayer, 1993.
The War of the Buttons, Warner Bros., 1994.
Only You (also known as *Him* and *Just in Time*), TriStar, 1994.
Sirens, Miramax, 1994.
(And songs "Laughing Song" and "The San Waltz") *The Road to Wellville*, Columbia, 1994.
To Wong Foo, Thanks for Everything! Julie Newmar, Universal, 1995.
A Pyromaniac's Love Story (also known as *Burning Love*), Buena Vista, 1995.
Smoke, Miramax, 1995.
Songwriter, *Feast of July*, 1995.
The Adventures of Pinocchio (also known as *Carlo Collodi's "Pinocchio," Pinocchio*, and *Die Legende von Pinocchio*), New Line Cinema, 1996.
Emma, Miramax, 1996.
Palookaville, Samuel Goldwyn, 1996.
Marvin's Room (also known as *My Room*), Miramax, 1996.
(And songs, including "As Long As There's Christmas," with Don Black) *Beauty and the Beast: The Enchanted Christmas* (also known as *Beauty and the Beast 2*), Walt Disney Home Video, 1997.
Addicted to Love (also known as *Forlorn*), Miramax, 1997.
Home Fries, Warner Bros., 1998.
(And songs "Little Rice, Little Bean" and "Sethe's Lullaby") *Beloved*, Buena Vista, 1998.
The Other Sister, Buena Vista, 1999.
The Cider House Rules (also known as *Cider House Rule*), Miramax, 1999.
Ratcatcher, First Look Pictures Releasing, 2000.
The Legend of Bagger Vance, DreamWorks, 2000.
The Closer You Get (also known as *American Women*), Fox Searchlight, 2000.
Chocolat, Miramax, 2000.
The Emperor's New Clothes, Paramount, 2002.
Hart's War, Metro–Goldwyn–Mayer, 2002.
(Including song "Charade d'amour") *The Truth about Charlie*, Universal, 2002.
Nicholas Nickleby, Metro–Goldwyn–Mayer, 2002.
The Human Stain, Miramax, 2003.
Mona Lisa Smile, Columbia, 2003.
The Manchurian Candidate, Paramount, 2004.
Because of Winn–Dixie, Twentieth Century–Fox, 2005.
Oliver Twist, Sony Pictures Entertainment, 2005.
Infamous, Warner Independent Pictures, 2006.
(Additional music) *Miss Potter*, Metro–Goldwyn–Mayer/ Weinstein Company, 2006.

The Lake House, Warner Bros., 2006.
The Duchess, Paramount, 2008.
The Sisterhood of the Traveling Pants 2, Warner Bros., 2008.
Never Let Me Go, Fox Searchlight, 2010.

Composer of Television Music; Miniseries:
A Little Princess, PBS, 1987.
The Storyteller (also known as *Jim Henson's "The Story-teller"*), NBC, 1987.
"Young Charlie Chaplin," *Wonderworks,* PBS, 1989.
The Storyteller: Greek Myths (also known as *Jim Henson's "The Storyteller: Greek Myths"*), HBO, 1990.
Oranges Are Not the Only Fruit, Arts and Entertainment, 1990.
Mr. Wakefield's Crusade, BBC Wales, 1991.

Composer of Television Music; Movies:
Reflections, Channel 4, 1984.
Four Days in July, BBC, 1984.
Last Day of Summer, 1984.
Sharma and Beyond, 1986.
Good As Gold, BBC, 1986.
The Short and Curlies, Channel 4, 1987.
1914 All Out, YTV, 1987.
The Falklands War: The Untold Story, YTV, 1987.
Monster Maker, 1989.
Living with Dinosaurs, 1989.
Precious Bane, PBS, 1989.
The Widowmaker, 1990.
Shoot to Kill, YTV, 1990.
The Woman in Black, Arts and Entertainment, 1991.
The Cloning of Joanna May, Arts and Entertainment, 1991.
Great Moments in Aviation (also known as *Shades of Fear*), 1993.
Grey Gardens, HBO, 2009.

Composer of Television Music; Specials:
Fearnot, NBC, 1987.
Hans My Hedgehog, NBC, 1987.
"Cariani and the Courtesans," *Screenplay,* BBC, 1987.
A Story Short, NBC, 1988.
The Luck Child, NBC, 1988.
"Sometime in August," *Screen Two,* BBC, 1988.
"Loving Hazel," *Screenplay,* BBC, 1988.
"Antonia and Jane," *Screenplay,* 1991.
"Flea Bites," *Screen Two,* BBC, 1991.
Elizabeth R: A Year in the Life of the Queen, PBS, 1992.
The Hollywood Soundtrack Story, AMC, 1995.
Songwriter, *The Real Jane Austen,* 2002.
Lard, Arte, 2004.

Television Music Compositions; Episodic:
Theme music, "Babe Ruth," *ESPN SportsCentury,* ESPN, 2000.

Television Music Compositions; Other:
Define Normal (series of five–minute episodes), 2005.

Also composer for *Charlie the Kid,* Thames; *Nice Work,* BBC; *Think of England,* BBC; and *Twice through the Heart,* BBC.

Stage Music:
The Little Prince (opera), Houston Grand Opera, Houston, TX, beginning 2003.
Little House on the Prairie: The Musical, Paper Mill Playhouse, Milburn, NJ, 2009.

Also composer for *Ourselves Alone,* Royal Court Theatre, London.

Other Compositions:
Fantasy for Cello and Piano, 1985.

ADAPTATIONS

A performance of Portman's stage opera, *The Little Prince,* was broadcast as a presentation of *Great Performances* by PBS in 2004. "Harriet's Portrait," a song composed by Portman for the 2002 television special *The Real Jane Austen* was also included in the miniseries *Lost in Austen: Behind the Scenes,* broadcast by ITV in 2008.

POTTS, Andrew Lee 1979–
(Andrew Lee–Potts, Andrew Potts, Andrew–Lee Potts)

PERSONAL

Born October 29 (some sources site August 30), 1979, in Bradford, West Yorkshire, England; son of Alan and Sara Potts; brother of Sarah–Jane Potts (an actress). *Education:* Studied performing arts in Leeds, West Yorkshire, England.

Addresses: *Agent*—Ruth Young, United Agents, 12–26 Lexington St., London W1F 0LE, England.

Career: Actor and director. Keychain Productions, cofounder, director, producer, writer, and actor in projects. Participated in conventions.

CREDITS

Television Appearances; Series:
Scott, *Children's Ward* (also known as *The Ward*), ITV, 1989.
Phillip, *WYSIWYG,* ITV, 1992.

Leo, *The Biz,* BBC, 1995.

Craig, *Lost in France,* BBC, 1998.

Toby, *Strange,* BBC, 2003.

Lee, *Ideal,* BBC3 and Independent Film Channel, beginning 2005.

(As Andrew–Lee Potts) Connor Temple, *Primeval,* ITV and BBC America, beginning 2007.

Television Appearances; Miniseries:

Mikey Carter, *Anchor Me,* ITV, 2000.

Private Eugene E. Jackson, *Band of Brothers,* HBO, 2001.

Jacob Robinson at the age of sixteen, *Stranded* (also known as *The Swiss Family Robinson*), Hallmark Channel, 2002.

Hatter, *Alice,* Syfy, 2009.

Television Appearances; Movies:

Tommy Atwell, *Night Flight,* BBC, 2002.

Nero, *Boudica,* ITV, 2003, known as *Warrior Queen* and broadcast as part of *Masterpiece Theatre* (also known as *ExxonMobil Masterpiece Theatre, Masterpiece,* and *Mobil Masterpiece Theatre*), PBS, 2003.

Jock, *Nature Unleashed: Avalanche* (also known as *Avalanche* and *Ice Hazard*), Sci–Fi Channel, 2004.

Television Appearances; Awards Presentations:

Presenter, *The British Soap Awards,* ITV, 2008.

Television Appearances; Episodic:

(As Andrew Potts) Roger Platt, "Missing," *Heartbeat* (also known as *Classic Heartbeat*), ITV, 1993.

Shane Broderick, "Fisticuffs," *Hetty Wainthropp Investigates* (also known as *Hetty Wainthropp Investigates, Series 3* and *Hetty Wainthropp Investigates III*), BBC, 1997, broadcast on *Mystery!,* PBS, 2000.

Darren Priestley, *Sunburn,* BBC, 1999.

Todd Johnson, *See How They Run,* BBC and Australian Broadcasting Corporation (ABC), 1999.

Nicholas Richmond, "Time to Go," *Dalziel and Pascoe* (also known as *Dalziel & Pascoe*), BBC, 1999, broadcast as a movie, Arts and Entertainment, 2001.

Tom Hobert, "Driven," *The American Embassy* (also known as *Emma Brody*), Fox, 2002.

Jimmy Bart, "Mr. Fox," *Absolute Power,* BBC, 2003.

Guest, *This Morning* (also known as *This Morning with Richard and Judy*), ITV, 2003.

Henry Curtis, *Buried,* Channel 4, multiple episodes in 2003.

Dan Parker, "The Funk Hole," *Foyle's War* (also known as *Foyle's War, Series II* and *Foyle's War II*), ITV, 2003, broadcast on *Mystery!,* PBS, 2004.

Jonathan Chadwick, "Eat Your Heart Out," *Fat Friends,* ITV and BBC America, 2004.

Jonathan Chadwick, "Leggs over Easy," *Fat Friends,* ITV and BBC America, 2004.

Daniel Berrington, *Rose and Maloney,* ITV, multiple episodes in 2004.

Joey, "Flat Four," *Twisted Tales* (also known as *Spinechillers, Spine–Chillers,* and *Spine Chillers*) BBC3, 2005.

(As Andrew–Lee Potts) Michael Summerby, "Sins of the Father: Parts 1 & 2," *Trial & Retribution* (also known as *Lynda La Plante's "Trial & Retribution"* and *Trial & Retribution X*), ITV, 2006.

Samuel Buckland, "Law," *Taggart,* ITV, 2006.

(As Andrew–Lee Potts) Jed Cooper, "Dead and Buried," *Cold Blood* (also known as *Cold Blood III*), ITV, 2007.

(As Andrew–Lee Potts) Guest, *Friday Night with Jonathan Ross,* BBC, 2008.

(As Andrew Lee–Potts) Jimmy Cochran, "Gently in the Blood," *Inspector George Gently* (also known as *George Gently*), BBC, 2009.

Mark, *A Passionate Woman,* BBC, 2010.

Appeared in other programs, including an appearance as Joe, *Always and Everyone* (also known as *St. Saviours*), ITV.

Film Appearances:

B–boy at the elephant, *Rage,* Metrodome Distribution, 1999.

(As Andrew Potts) Postal carrier, *Ho Ho Ho* (short film), c. 1999.

Himself, *Road to Sundance* (documentary), 2000.

Jake, *New Year's Day,* 2001.

Private Neumann, *The Bunker* (also known as *The Bunker: The Evil Is Within*), High Point Film and Television, 2001.

Rafael, *High Speed* (also known as *Highspeed*), 2002.

Rafael, *The Ride* (also known as *Joyriders* and *Joy–Rider*), 2002.

Rick, *The Poet* (also known as *Der Poet*), 2003.

(As Andrew–Lee Potts) Abe Klein, *Dead Fish,* Deadfish Distribution/Mobius International, 2004.

Title role, *Dipper* (short film), 2005.

Jake, *Rude Awakenings* (short film), 2005.

Kris, *Popcorn,* 2007.

Kyle, *Return to House on Haunted Hill* (also known as *House on Haunted Hill 2*), Warner Bros., 2007.

Mailbox person, *1408,* Metro–Goldwyn–Mayer, 2007.

Mike, *Caffeine,* 2007.

Don, *Heart of a Dragon,* Thunder Bay Films/China Film Group, 2008.

Kenneth, *Freakdog* (also known as *Red Mist*), c. 2008.

Stage Appearances; Major Tours:

Third witch, Fleance, and young Macduff, *Macbeth,* British cities, 1997.

Appeared in other stage productions.

Internet Director:
(As Andrew–Lee Potts) *Confession's of a Teenage Dad* (short film; also known as *Confessions of a Teenage Dad*), Keychain Productions, broadcast on *YouTube,* http://www.youtube.com, c. 2006.

Blood on Benefits (short film), Keychain Productions, c. 2006, broadcast on *YouTube,* http://www.youtube.com, 2007.

(As Andrew–Lee Potts) *Little Lilly* (series of short films), Keychain Productions, broadcast on *YouTube,* http://www.youtube.com, includes *Little Lilly—Colour Blind,* 2007, *Little Lilly—Chapter Two,* 2007, and *Little Lilly—Chapter Three: U–Turn,* 2008.

(And coproducer) *Pitchin* (three episodes), Keychain Productions, broadcast on *YouTube,* http://www.youtube.com, first episode, 2008, second and third episodes, both 2009.

Bubble Wrapped (short film), Keychain Productions, broadcast on *YouTube,* http://www.youtube.com, c. 2010.

Director of other projects, including *Dance!* (short documentary), Keychain Productions, broadcast on *YouTube,* http://www.youtube.com.

Internet Appearances:
Behind the Bite (documentary), Keychain Productions, broadcast on *YouTube,* http://www.youtube.com, c. 2007.

Pitchin (three episodes), Keychain Productions, broadcast on *YouTube,* http://www.youtube.com, first episode, 2008, second and third episodes, both 2009.

Host, *Through the Anomaly* (documentary), broadcast on *YouTube,* http://www.youtube.com, 2009.

WRITINGS

Writings for the Internet:
(As Andrew–Lee Potts) *Confession's of a Teenage Dad* (short film; also known as *Confessions of a Teenage Dad*), Keychain Productions, broadcast on *YouTube,* http://www.youtube.com, c. 2006.

(With Alex Moss) *Pitchin* (three episodes), Keychain Productions, broadcast on *YouTube,* http://www.youtube.com, first episode, 2008, second and third episodes, both 2009.

POWERS, Jenny 1979–
(Jennifer Powers)

PERSONAL

Full name, Jennifer Diane Powers; born August 29, 1979, in Cambridge, MA; raised in Andover, MA; daughter of David (a lawyer and bureaucrat) and Mary Ellen (a nurse practitioner and nursing professor) Powers; married Matt Cavenaugh (an actor and singer), August 23, 2009. *Education:* Northwestern University, graduated, degree in music, 2003; studied dance and voice.

Addresses: *Manager*—Meg Mortimer, Principal Entertainment, 130 West 42nd St., New York, NY 10036.

Career: Actress and singer. Sometimes known as Jennifer Powers. Performed the national anthem at various events and performed at other events. Appeared in discussions and other events. Participated in beauty pageants, awards presentations, benefits, and fundraising events. Worked at restaurants, as a lifeguard and swim instructor, and involved with activities at nursing homes.

Member: Actors' Equity Association.

Awards, Honors: Named Miss Illinois, 2000; Sarah Siddons Society Scholarship, 2001.

CREDITS

Stage Appearances; Musicals:
Betty Rizzo, *Grease,* Andover High School, J. Everett Collins Center for the Performing Arts, Andover, MA, c. 1990.

Serena, *Everything's Ducky* (later revised and known as *Lucky Duck*), Northlight Theatre, North Shore Center for the Performing Arts, Center East Theatre, Skokie, IL, 2001–2002.

Martha Jefferson, *1776,* Marriott Theatre, Lincolnshire, IL, 2002.

Boca Raton girl and member of the ensemble, *Bounce,* Goodman Theatre, Albert Theatre, Chicago, IL, and John F. Kennedy Center for the Performing Arts, Eisenhower Theater, Washington, DC, both 2003.

Petra, *A Little Night Music,* Chicago Shakespeare Theater, Chicago, IL, c. 2003.

Alice B. Toklas, *A Long Gay Book,* Northwestern University, Ethel M. Barber Theater, Evanston, IL, 2003, production later known as *Loving Repeating: A Musical of Gertrude Stein,* About Face Theatre, Museum of Contemporary Art, Chicago, IL, 2006.

Lucie Manette, *A Tale of Two Cities* (workshop production of musical), Little Shubert Theatre, New York City, 2004, also produced as a workshop production, New York City, 2005.

Meg and Clarissa, *Little Women,* Virginia Theatre, New York City, 2004–2005.

Claire, *The Secret Garden,* produced as part of *Third Annual World AIDS Day Concert* (benefit concert), Manhattan Center Studios Grand Ballroom, New York City, 2005.

Veronica Franco, *Dangerous Beauty,* New York Stage and Film, Vassar College, Powerhouse Theater, Martel Theater, Poughkeepsie, NY, 2005, produced as a reading in the Chicago, c. 2007, and as a full production by the American Music Theatre Project, Summer Music Theatre Festival, Northwestern University, Ethel M. Barber Theatre, 2008.

Bella Rose, *Desperate Measures,* New York Musical Theatre Festival, 45th Street Theatre, New York City, 2006.

Diana Devereaux, *Of Thee I Sing* (concert staging of musical), produced as part of *City Center Encores!* (also known as *Encores!, Encores! Great American Musicals in Concert,* and *New York City Center Encores!*), City Center Theatre, New York City, 2006.

Nancy Sykes, *Oliver!,* The Muny, St. Louis, MO, 2006.

The Man in the White Suit (reading of musical), Beckett Theatre, New York City, 2006.

Isabella Andreini, *The Glorious Ones,* Pittsburgh Public Theatre, Pittsburgh, PA, 2007.

Young Phyllis, *Follies* (concert staging of musical), produced as part of *City Center Encores!* (also known as *Encores!, Encores! Great American Musicals in Concert,* and *New York City Center Encores!*), City Center Theatre, 2007.

Betty Rizzo, *Grease,* Brooks Atkinson Theatre, New York City, 2007–2008.

Gina, *Happiness,* Lincoln Center, Mitzi E. Newhouse Theatre, New York City, 2009.

This Side of Paradise (reading of musical), Sunshine Series, Epic Theatre Ensemble, New York City, 2009.

Sydney Sharp, *It's a Bird ... It's a Plane ... It's Superman,* Dallas Theatre Center, AT&T Performing Arts Center, Dee and Charles Wyly Theatre, Potter Rose Performance Hall, Dallas, TX, 2010.

Little Theater, Big Dreams (benefit cabaret production), West Side YMCA, Marjorie S. Deane Little Theatre, New York City, 2010.

RATED RSO: The Music and Lyrics of Ryan Scott Oliver (concert; also known as *Rated RSO*), Joseph Papp Public Theatre, Joe's Pub, New York City, 2010.

Appeared as Rose Alvarez, *Bye Bye Birdie* (musical), Merrimack Junior Theatre; also appeared in other productions, including an appearance as Cinderella. Also cast as Rebecca and Tamar, *Masada* (musical; also known as *Imagine This*). Some sources cite that Powers was cast as the standby for Lucy Westenra, *Dracula, the Musical* (musical), Belasco Theatre, New York City, 2004–05.

Film Appearances:

First reporter, *Sexina: Popstar P.I.* (also known as *Pop Detective*), Sharkey Productions/Torino Pictures, 2007.

Irresistible fantasy woman, *I Think I Love My Wife* (also known as *Sex and the Buddy*), Fox Searchlight, 2007.

Second Borders assistant, *Confessions of a Shopaholic* (also known as *I Love Shopping*), Walt Disney Studios, 2009.

Television Appearances; Specials:

Miss Illinois, *The 80th Annual Miss America Pageant,* ABC, 2000.

Television Appearances; Episodic:

First reporter, "A Simple Twist of Fate," *Six Degrees* (also known as *6*), ABC, 2007.

Valerie Dickson, "Albatross," *Law & Order: Criminal Intent* (also known as *Law & Order: CI*), NBC, 2007.

Woman, "Tabula Rosa," *Criminal Minds* (also known as *Quantico, Criminal Minds—FBI tutjijat, Esprits criminels, Gyilkos elmek, Kurjuse kannul,* and *Mentes criminales*), CBS, 2008.

Jackie, "I'm Not That Kind of Girl," *Mercy,* NBC, 2009.

Lucretia Vanderhoven, "Identity Crisis," *Law & Order: Criminal Intent* (also known as *Law & Order: CI*), NBC, 2009.

Rude woman, "Daffodil," *Nurse Jackie* (also known as *Untitled Edie Falco Project*), Showtime, 2009.

Dr. Hines, *All My Children* (also known as *All My Children: The Summer of Seduction* and *La force du destin*), ABC, multiple episodes in 2009.

Internet Appearances:

Appeared in video footage and audio clips posted on the Internet.

RECORDINGS

Albums; with Others; Cast Recordings:

Bounce (original Goodman Theatre cast recording), Nonesuch Records, 2004.

A Tale of Two Cities (workshop cast recording), 2004.

Little Women (original Broadway cast recording), Ghostlight, 2005.

Masada (studio cast recording concept album; also known as *Imagine This*), c. 2006.

Grease (Broadway cast recording), Masterworks Broadway, 2007.

Loving Repeating: A Musical of Gertrude Stein (Chicago cast recording), Jay, 2007.

Albums; Demo Recordings; with Others:

This Side of Paradise (also known as *This Side of Paradise: The Passions of Zelda and F. Scott Fitzgerald* and *Winter Dreams: The Life and Passions of F. Scott Fitzgerald*), 2004.
Dangerous Beauty, TheJRockingRCo, 2006.

OTHER SOURCES

Periodicals:
Andover Townsman, August 1, 2007.
New York, April 12, 2009.
New York Times, April 23, 2009; August 21, 2009.

Electronic:
Playbill.com, http://www.playbill.com, August 31, 2007.

PRALGO, Robert 1966–
(Rob Pralgo)

PERSONAL

Born June 4, 1966; son of Mel Seymour Pralgo (an actor, acting teacher, musician, martial arts instructor, and business owner) and Renee Bakal. *Education:* University of Georgia, B.A., 1989; trained at HB Studio, New York City, with Joyce Davis–Smith, Sandra Dorsey, and other instructors.

Addresses: *Agent*—Brenda Pauley, People Store, 645 Lambert Dr., Atlanta, GA 30324.

Career: Actor, producer, and casting director. Appeared in advertisements; appeared in industrial films, including the series *Deadly Intent.* Also worked as a voice actor and a radio performer. Worked as a bartender. Participated in conventions.

Awards, Honors: Staten Island Film Festival (SINY Film Festival Award) nomination (with others), best dramatic short, 2009, for *The Mandala Maker;* American *Soap World* Award nomination, web series: best actor, *Time after Time/Soap World,* http://www.timeaftertime onlinedrama.webs.com, 2010, for *High Rise.*

CREDITS

Film Appearances:
Stickfighter, c. 1994.
Beat poetry master of ceremonies, *Beat Daddies,* 1996.

Mobster, *The Waterfront* (also known as *Maximum Justice*), Allied Entertainment Group/New Films International, 1998.
Jack Hess, *Blood Bath,* 2002.
Paul Trulli, *Epiphany* (short film), Framework Entertainment/Lab 601, 2002.
Leo (also known as *Leopold Bloom*), 2002, United International Pictures, 2004.
Peter Walsh, *A Conspiracy,* 2003.
Steve, *Vicious,* MTI Home Video, 2003.
Inspector Alan Goddard, *Identity Crisis* (short film), 2003, Xenon Pictures, 2006.
Chad, *Delivery Boy Chronicles,* 2004.
(As Rob Pralgo) Odesky, *Last Goodbye,* 2004.
Reporter, *Bobby Jones: Stroke of Genius,* Film Foundry Releasing, 2004.
(As Rob Pralgo) Robert Hudson, *Shooting Gallery* (also known as *Backspin, The Big Score,* and *Poolhall Prophets*), Seven Arts Pictures, 2005.
Thomas Carter, *Battaglia* (short film), 2005.
Jack Driscoll, *The Feeding,* Stormcatcher Films, 2006.
Megahertz, c. 2006.
Charles Brown, *The Promise* (short film), Kiss the Limit Productions/Visionary Films, 2007.
Jim Davis, *Blood Ties,* Media Arts International Film Corporation/Digital Film Design/My Thai Film, 2007.
Reverend, *The Honored* (short film), Lava Post, 2007.
Death Brand (also known as *Death–Brand* and *The Death Brand*), c. 2007.
Drunk man in bar, *Rex,* Cinematic Heroes/Rellim Films, 2008.
Jack, *Precious Cargo* (short film), Florida State University, 2008.
Paul Nance, *Crystal River,* Crystal River Pictures/Spring Street Films, 2008.
Rayburn, *First Kill* (short film), Florida State University Graduate Film Conservatory, 2008.
Walter, *Harvest Moon* (short film), Florida State University Graduate Film Conservatory, 2008.
Deadfall (short film; also known as *DeadFall*), Florida State University, 2008.
Tow truck driver (TTD), *Keepsake* (also known as *KeepSake*), Stormcatcher Films, c. 2008.
Art professor Wade, *The Mandala Maker* (short film), The Naoj Company, 2009.
(As Rob Pralgo) Camouflaged agent, *12 Rounds* (also known as *Shoot & Run* and *Twelve Rounds*), Fox Atomic, 2009.
Charles Galloway, *I Am the Bluebird,* Skylight Cinema, 2009.
Lemming's associate, *The Blind Side,* Warner Bros., 2009.
Stan, *Love Fever,* First Hat Productions/Dead Workers Party, 2009.
Voice, *Puppets of War* (short film featuring puppets), TBolt Pictures, 2009.

Pantheon Black, c. 2009.

Alex "The Hammer" Bayner, *The Joneses,* 2009, Roadside Attractions, 2010.

Mitchell, *Savage,* Fearmakers Studios, 2009, KOAN, 2010.

Bad lieutenant, *YardByrds* (short film), AfterLight Pictures/Fuhgawzi Entertainment Productions, 2010.

Hally's father, *Tainted Blood* (short film), 2010.

Lester Armstrong, *Kerberos,* Media Arts International Film Corporation, 2010.

Mike Ingram, *Carl,* Out of the Cage Productions, 2010.

Mr. Grove, *The Fat Boy Chronicles* (also known as *Fat Boy Chronicles*), Tin Roof Films, 2010.

Recruiter, *Upside* (also known as *Falling Up* and *This End Up*), Spyplane Films, 2010.

Exhibit A–7 (also known as *Exhibit–A7*), ARK Productions, 2010.

Zombie Invasion, c. 2010.

Appeared as Captain Parker, *Love Thy Enemy.* Appeared in other films, including *Creep, Harley White Trash, The Last Stand,* and *Shadow of the Night.*

Film Producer:

Executive producer, *Blood Ties,* Media Arts International Film Corporation/Digital Film Design/My Thai Film, 2007.

Associate producer, *The Mandala Maker* (short film), The Naoj Company, 2009.

Exhibit A–7 (also known as *Exhibit–A7*), ARK Productions, 2010.

Film Casting Director:

Blood Bath, 2002.

Blood Ties, Media Arts International Film Corporation/Digital Film Design/My Thai Film, 2007.

Digging Up Graves, Round Table Productions, 2008.

Additional casting worker, *Love Fever,* First Hat Productions/Dead Workers Party, 2009.

Television Appearances; Series:

(As Rob Pralgo) Mayor Charles Lockwood, *The Vampire Diaries,* The CW, 2009–10.

Alex Dupree, *The Gates,* ABC, beginning 2010.

Television Appearances; Movies:

Ari, *Acceptance,* Lifetime, 2009.

Ben, *My Fake Fiance* (also known as *Your Presents Required*), ABC Family, 2009.

Appeared in a sequel to *My Super Psycho Sweet 16.*

Television Appearances; Episodic:

Paul Retzke, "The Godfather," *Matlock,* ABC, 1994.

Security guard, "The Curator," *Baywatch Nights* (also known as *Detectives on the Beach, Malibu Club, Mitch Buchannon, Baywatch—A remuelet ejszakai, Los vigilantes de la noche,* and *Un prive a Malibu*), syndicated, 1996.

Vance Clarington, "The Big Padoodle," *Going to California* (also known as *On the Road Again*), Showtime, 2001.

(Uncredited) Cute man, "All Good Things ...," *Dawson's Creek* (also known as *Dawson* and *Dawsons Creek*), The WB, 2003.

(Uncredited) Cute man, "Must Come to an End ...," *Dawson's Creek* (also known as *Dawson* and *Dawsons Creek*), The WB, 2003.

Attorney, "The Lonesome Road," *One Tree Hill* (also known as *Ravens, Filoi gia panta, Les freres Scott, Tunteet pelissaa,* and *Tuti gimi*), The WB, 2005.

Agent Holdrich, "Sweet Caroline," *Prison Break* (also known as *The Break, Prison Break: Manhunt, Prison Break: On the Run, Grande evasion, I apodrasi, Pako, Pogenemine,* and *Prison Break—Em busca da verdade*), Fox, 2007.

First officer, "Club PCP," *House of Payne* (also known as *Tyler Perry's "House of Payne"*), TBS, 2007.

Sergeant George Polarski, "Goodbye Stranger," *Army Wives,* Lifetime, 2007.

Sergeant George Polarski, "Independence Day," *Army Wives,* Lifetime, 2007.

Sergeant George Polarski, "Would You Know My Name," *Army Wives,* Lifetime, 2008.

"CMT 40 Sexiest Music Videos" (also known as "40 Sexiest Music Videos"), *The Greatest* (also known as *CMT: The Greatest* and *CMT: The Greatest—Sexiest Music Videos*), Country Music Television, 2008.

Frank, "I Would for You," *One Tree Hill* (also known as *Ravens, Filoi gia panta, Les freres Scott, Tunteet pelissaa,* and *Tuti gimi*), The CW, 2009.

Prosecutor Gerron, "Dead Man Talking," *Past Life* (also known as *The Reincarnationist*), Fox, 2010.

Also appeared in episodes of *All My Children* (also known as *All My Children: The Summer of Seduction* and *La force du destin*), ABC.

Television Appearances; Pilots:

Doctor, *Drop Dead Diva,* Lifetime, 2009.

Alex Dupree, *The Gates,* ABC, 2010.

Reporter, *Franklin & Bash,* TNT, 2010.

Stage Appearances:

Member of ensemble, *Cyrano de Bergerac,* OnStage Atlanta Theatre Company, Atlanta, GA, c. 1991.

The gentleman caller, *The Glass Menagerie,* OnStage Atlanta Theatre Company, c. 1993.

Smoke Bellew, *Klondike!,* Alliance Children's Theatre, Atlanta, GA, c. 1994.

Nick, *Life beneath the Roses,* Bitter Truth Theatre, North Hollywood, CA, 1997.

Appeared as Bo Decker, *Bus Stop,* CenterStage North Theatre Company, GA; as Lieutenant Daniel Kaffee, *A Few Good Men,* Neighborhood Playhouse, Decatur, GA; and as Horatio and Laertes, *The 15 Minute Hamlet* (also known as *The Fifteen Minute Hamlet*), Dunwoody, GA.

Internet Appearances; Series:

Marcus Hunt, *High Rise* (series; also known as *HIGH RISE*), http://www.highrisetheseries.com, beginning 2009.

Himself, *The VRO,* http://www.thevro.com (online radio show), 2009, multiple appearances, 2010.

Radio Appearances:

Made appearances in radio programs.

RECORDINGS

Music Videos:

Appeared in the music video "Come to Bed," by Gretchen Wilson.

WRITINGS

Screenplays:

(Story) *Blood Ties* (screenplay by Kely McClung), Media Arts International Film Corporation/Digital Film Design/My Thai Film, 2007.

OTHER SOURCES

Electronic:

Robert Pralgo, http://robertpralgo.com, March 19, 2010.

PUSHKIN, Lesli Kay
    See KAY, Lesli

R

RANSOM, Tim 1963–

PERSONAL

Original name, Timothy Ransom Wilson; born April 19, 1963, in Binghamton, NY.

Addresses: *Manager*—Sue Leibman, Barking Dog Entertainment, 9 Desbrosses St., 2nd Floor, New York, NY 10013.

Career: Actor. Naked Angels (theatre company), founding member, 1986—, and artistic director; Our Time (theatre company), member of the advisory board. Project A.L.S., member of the executive action committee.

CREDITS

Television Appearances; Miniseries:
Robert "Bobby" Kennedy, *A Woman Named Jackie,* NBC, 1991.
Tom Custer, *Son of the Morning Star,* ABC, 1991.
Scut, *Signs and Wonders,* PBS, 1995.

Television Appearances; Movies:
Toby, *The Last to Go,* ABC, 1991.
Zeke, *Fever,* HBO, 1991.
Fred Woods IV, *They've Taken Our Children: The Chowchilla Kidnapping* (also known as *Vanished without a Trace*), ABC, 1993.
Madden, *Broken Promises: Taking Emily Back* (also known as *Broken Promises*), CBS, 1993.
Mitch Barton, *A Time to Heal* (also known as *Jenny's Story*), NBC, 1994.
Buddy, *Follow the Stars Home* (also known as *A Second Chance*), CBS, 2001.

Television Appearances; Episodic:
Brett Dillon, "Murder in White," *Murder, She Wrote,* CBS, 1993.
Stillman's attorney, "Rebels," *Law & Order,* NBC, 1995.
Whalen, "Grendlers in the Myst," *Earth 2,* NBC, 1995.
Detective Andy Sullivan, "Corruption," *Law & Order,* NBC, 1996.
George Parkins, "Evidence of Malice," *Murder, She Wrote,* CBS, 1996.
Frankie Dwyer, "Moving Target," *Nash Bridges,* CBS, 1997.
Jack, "Statistical Probabilities," *Star Trek: Deep Space Nine* (also known as *Deep Space Nine* and *DS9*), syndicated, 1997.
Jared Graham, "Con Law," *Players,* NBC, 1997.
Jack, "Chrysalis," *Star Trek: Deep Space Nine* (also known as *Deep Space Nine* and *DS9*), syndicated, 1998.
Public defender Kent Clark, "Reasons to Believe," *The Practice,* ABC, 1998.
Dan Vinton, "Two to Tango," *Providence,* NBC, 1999.
Frankie Dwyer, "Girl Trouble," *Nash Bridges* CBS, 1999.
Frankie Dwyer, "Hit and Run," *Nash Bridges,* CBS, 2000.
Frankie Dwyer, "Skin Trade," *Nash Bridges,* CBS, 2000.
Defense attorney Andrew Maynard, "Tragedy on Rye," *Law & Order,* NBC, 2002.
Michael Kenney, "The Greater Good," *Third Watch,* NBC, 2002.
Jack Kittridge, "Cold Comfort," *Law & Order: Criminal Intent,* NBC, 2003.
Attorney, "Denial," *Conviction,* NBC, 2006.
Linus Newell, "Shattered," *Without a Trace* (also known as *W.A.T*), CBS, 2006.
Nathan Engler, "Slings and Arrows," *Six Degrees* (also known as *6*), ABC, 2007.
R. C. "Robbie" Maitland, "The Book of Love," *Valentine,* The CW, 2008.
Logan Coldwell, "Lead," *Law & Order: Special Victims Unit* (also known as *Law & Order: SVU* and *Special Victims Unit*), NBC, 2009.

Also appeared in episodes of *The Lazarus Man,* TNT and syndicated; and *The X–Files,* Fox.

Television Appearances; Specials:
Virgil, *The Wide Net,* PBS, 1987.
Joel, *Love and Other Sorrows,* PBS, 1989.

Appeared in productions of *American Playhouse,* PBS.

Film Appearances:
Desperately Seeking Susan, Orion, 1985.
Wesley, *The Dressmaker,* Euro–American Pictures, 1989.
Bobby Hayes, *Vital Signs,* Twentieth Century–Fox, 1990.
Tommy Hull (some sources cite Tommy Hall), *Outbreak,* Warner Bros., 1995.
Boylar, *Courage Under Fire,* Twentieth Century–Fox, 1996.
Interviewer, *The Good Doctor,* Chesterfield Motion Pictures, 2000.
Steven, *The Learning Curve* (also known as *Dangerous Seduction*), Metro–Goldwyn–Mayer, 2001.

Also appeared in *Platypussy* and *Requiem.*

Stage Appearances:
Lesley, *Carol Mulroney,* Huntington Theatre Company, Boston, MA, 2005.

Appeared in productions of *The Bluebird Special, Gunplay, La Ronde, Naked at the Coast, Naked Rights, Nebraska,* and *Saturday Mourning Cartoons.*

Stage Work:
Producer of the plays *The Big Swing, Gunplay,* and *Signature,* all for Naked Angels Theatre Company, as well as various benefit performances.

OTHER SOURCES

Electronic:
Naked Angels, http://www.nakedangels.com, May 24, 2003.

RATNER, Brett 1969–

PERSONAL

Born March 28, 1969, in Miami Beach, FL; son of Marcia Ratner (some sources cite Marcia Presman). *Education:* Attended New York University, beginning c. 1985. *Religion:* Jewish.

Addresses: *Office*—Rat Entertainment, 100 Universal City Plaza, Building 5196, Universal City, CA 91608; Rat Television, 6715 Hollywood Blvd., Hollywood, CA 90211; Rat Press, 5555 Melrose Ave., 307 Gloria Swanson Building, Los Angeles, CA 90038. *Agent*—Creative Artists Agency, 2000 Avenue of the Stars, Los Angeles, CA 90067; (commercials and music videos) Rebecca Skinner, HSI, 3630 Eastham Dr., Culver City, CA 90232; (photography) Steven Pranica, Creative Exchange Agency, 416 West 13th St., Suite 316, New York, NY 10014; (photography syndication) Geoff Katz, Creative Photographers, Inc., 444 Park Ave. S., Suite 502, New York, NY 10016. *Publicist*—Viewpoint, Inc., 8820 Wilshire Blvd., Beverly Hills, CA 90211.

Career: Producer, director, actor, writer, publisher, photographer, and executive. Chair and chief executive officer of Rat Entertainment and Rat Television; Rat Press, chair, chief executive officer, and publisher; White Knuckle Pictures, Los Angeles, principal. Photographer, with work published in magazines, including *Heeb, Interview,* and *Vanity Fair,* and on magazine covers. Director of numerous music videos; work also includes advertising campaigns for fashion houses and others, including a commercial for New York Film Academy, 2007; appeared in an infomercial for Tony Robbins Ultimate Edge self–help system. Member of board of directors, Best Buddies and Chrysalis Foundation; We Are Family Foundation, member of board of governors; Simon Wiesenthal Center and Museum of Tolerance, member of board of trustees.

Awards, Honors: MTV Video Award, best video from a film, 1999, for "Beautiful Stranger"; Best Film Award, Sitges–Catalonian International Film Festival, 2002, for *Red Dragon;* Spirit of Chrysalis Award, Chrysalis Foundation.

CREDITS

Film Director:
(And producer) *Whatever Happened to Mason Reese* (short film), 1990, New Line Home Video, 1999.
Money Talks (also known as *Runaway*), New Line Cinema, 1997.
Rush Hour, New Line Cinema, 1998.
The Family Man, Universal, 2000.
Rush Hour 2, New Line Cinema, 2001.
Red Dragon, Universal, 2002.
After the Sunset (also known as *Diamond in Paradise*), New Line Cinema, 2004.
X–Men: The Last Stand (also known as *X–Men: Final Decision, X–Men 3,* and *X3*), Twentieth Century–Fox, 2006.
Rush Hour 3, New Line Cinema, 2007.
New York, I Love You, Vivendi Entertainment, 2009.

Film Executive Producer:
Velocity Rules (short film), American Film Institute/ Rocks and Rules Productions, 2001.
A Ribbon of Dreams, 2002.
Me and Daphne (short film), 2002.
End Game, Metro–Goldwyn–Mayer, 2006.
21 (also known as *21—The Movie*), Columbia, 2008.
Catfish (documentary), Rogue Pictures, 2010.
Skyline, Rogue Pictures, 2010.

Film Producer:
Double Take, Buena Vista, 2001.
Paid in Full, Dimension Films, 2002.
Santa's Slay, Lions Gate Films Home Entertainment, 2005.
Running Scared (also known as *Wild Bullet*), New Line Cinema, 2006.
Code Name: The Cleaner (also known as *The Cleaner*), New Line Cinema, 2007.
Mother's Day, Optimum Releasing, 2010.

Film Editor:
(English version) *Kites* (also known as *Brett Ratner Presents Kites: The Remix*), Icon Film Distribution, 2010.

Film Appearances:
(Uncredited) Boy lying on raft in pool, *Scarface,* Universal, 1983.
"Sob Story" Barry Blausteen, *The Grand,* Anchor Bay Entertainment, 2007.
Silver Street (short film), 2009.

Documentary Film Appearances:
Black and White, Screen Gems, 2000.
Los Angeles, Parallax, 2005.
The Outsider, World Film Magic Distribution, 2005.
Class Act, Morgan Spurlock Presents, 2007.
King of the B's: The Independent Life of Roger Corman, Far Hills Pictures/Stick 'n' Stone Productions, 2009.
With Great Power: The Stan Lee Story, 1821 Pictures/ Emerging Entertainment, 2010.

Television Executive Producer; Series:
Prison Break, Fox, 2005–2009.
Women's Murder Club (also known as *wmc*), ABC, 2007–2008.

Television Executive Producer and Director; Pilots:
Partners, 1999.
Prison Break, Fox, 2005.
Blue Blood, NBC, 2008.
Cop House, Fox, 2009.
Chaos, CBS, 2010.

Television Producer; Specials:
Helmut by June, Cinemax, 2007.
I Knew It Was You: Rediscovering John Cazale, HBO, 2009.

Television Director; Episodic:
Director of videos featured on the series *Making the Video,* MTV.

Television Appearances; Specials:
Canned Ham: Rush Hour, Comedy Central, 1998.
Jackie Chan, Bravo, 2001.
Inside "Red Dragon," 2002.
The Score, Trio, 2003.
Jackie Chan: The Inside Story, Channel 5, 2004.
"Reservoir Dogs" Revisited, Independent Film Channel, 2005.
AFI Life Achievement Award: A Tribute to Warren Beatty, USA Network, 2008.
Starz Inside: Fashion in Film, Starz!, 2008.
How Bruce Lee Changed the World, History Channel, 2009.
I Knew It Was You: Rediscovering John Cazale, HBO, 2009.
Presenter, *VH1 Hip Hop Honors,* VH1, 2009.

Television Appearances; Miniseries:
Heroes of Black Comedy, Comedy Central, 2002.

Television Appearances; Episodic:
"The Films of Brett Ratner," *The Directors,* Encore, 1999.
"Mariah Carey: Heartbreaker," *Making the Video,* MTV, 1999.
Nyhetsmorgon, 2001.
The Charlie Rose Show (also known as *Charlie Rose*), PBS, 2001, 2002, 2004.
Last Call with Carson Daly, NBC, 2002.
Film School, Independent Film Channel, 2004.
Inside Dish with Rachael Ray, Food Network, 2004.
Film '72, BBC, 2004.
Jimmy Kimmel Live!, ABC, 2004, 2006, 2007.
Sunday Morning Shootout (also known as *Hollywood Shootout* and *Shootout*), AMC, 2004, 2006, 2007.
"It's Like That," *Making the Video,* MTV, 2005.
Punk'd, MTV, 2006.
Himself, "The Prince's Bride," *Entourage,* HBO, 2007.
Judge of auditions, *On the Lot,* Fox, 2007.
"Rush Hour 3," *HBO First Look,* HBO, 2007.
Up Close with Carrie Keagan, ABC, 2007, 2010.
Himself, "Stay Tuned," *The Girls Next Door,* E! Entertainment Television, 2009.
Entertainment Tonight (also known as *E.T.* and *This Week in Entertainment*), syndicated, 2009, 2010.

RECORDINGS

Video Appearances:

A Piece of the Action: Behind the Scenes of "Rush Hour," New Line Home Video, 1999.

Kung Fu Choreography, New Line Home Video, 2001.

Culture Clash: West Meets East, New Line Home Video, 2001.

Language Barrier, New Line Home Video, 2001.

Attaining International Stardom, New Line Home Video, 2001.

Making Magic Out of Mire, New Line Home Video, 2001.

Shot Caller: From Videos to Features, New Line Home Video, 2002.

A Director's Journey: The Making of "Red Dragon," New Line Home Video, 2003.

Before, During, and "After the Sunset," New Line Home Entertainment, 2005.

Making of "Prison Break," Twentieth Century–Fox Home Entertainment, 2006.

X–Men: The Excitement Continues, Twentieth Century–Fox, 2006.

X–Men: Evolution of a Trilogy, Twentieth Century–Fox, 2006.

Making "Rush Hour 3," New Line Home Video, 2007.

Video Work:

Director, "Beautiful Stranger," *Madonna: The Video Collection 93:99,* Warner Reprise, 1999.

Director, "Heartbreaker," *Mariah #1's,* Sony Pictures Entertainment, 1999.

Producer, *Before, During, and "After the Sunset,"* New Line Home Video, 2005.

Executive producer, *Prison Break: The Final Break* (also known as *Prison Break: The Movie*), Twentieth Century–Fox Home Entertainment, 2009.

Director of more than 100 music videos, including "Diddy" by P Diddy, 2001; "It's like That" and "We Belong Together" by Mariah Carey, 2005; "These Boots Are Made for Walkin'" by Jessica Simpson, 2005; "Touch My Body" by Mariah Carey, 2008; "Brown Sugar" by D'Angelo; "Freek 'n You" and "Love U 4 Life" by Jodeci; "How Deep Is Your Love" by Dru Hill; "I'll Be" by Foxy Brown and Jay–Z; "Invisible Man" by 98 Degrees; "Nothin' but Love" by Heavy D; "7 Things" by Miley Cyrus; "Thank God I Found You" by Mariah Carey; and "Triumph" by Wu–Tang Clan.

WRITINGS

Film Scripts:

Whatever Happened to Mason Reese (short film), 1990, New Line Home Video, 1999.

Books:

Hilhaven Lodge: The Photo Booth Pictures, Rat Press, 2003.

OTHER SOURCES

Periodicals:

Entertainment Weekly, May 26, 2006, p. 36.

Hollywood Life, July, 2006, pp. 72–75, 107.

Premiere, November, 2002, pp. 84–89, 101.

Publishers Weekly, March 23, 2009, p. 8.

Vanity Fair, March, 2007, pp. 266–73, 300–04.

Electronic:

Brett Ratner Official Site, http://brettratner.com, June 10, 1010.

RAY, Lisa 1972–

PERSONAL

Full name, Lisa Rani Ray; born April 4, 1972, in Toronto, Ontario, Canada. *Education:* Graduated from a drama school in London; studied mime for five months in London.

Addresses: *Agent*—Innovative Artists, 1505 10th St., Santa Monica, CA 90401; United Talent Agency, 9560 Wilshire Blvd, Suite 500, Beverly Hills, CA 90212. *Manager*—Untitled Entertainment, 1801 Century Park East, Suite 700, Los Angeles, CA 90067.

Career: Actress. The 26th Annual Genie Awards, co-host, 2006. Brand ambassador for Rado Watches, Switzerland.

Awards, Honors: Vancouver Film Critics Circle, best actress—Canadian film, 2006, for *Water;* Toronto Film Festival, star of the future, 2002.

CREDITS

Film Appearances:

Simran Bhargav, *Kasoor,* Eros Entertainment, 2001.

Bhuvana, *Takkari Donga,* 2002.

Sue (Sunita) Singh, *Bollywood/Hollywood* (also known as *Bollywood/Hollywood*), Magnolia Pictures, 2002.

Saima, *Ball & Chain* (also known as *Arrangement*), Lions Gate Films, 2004.

Kalyani, *Water,* Fox Searchlight, 2005.

Nina Atwal, *Seeking Fear,* 2005.
Louise, *The Flowerman* (short film), Carpe Noctem Creatives, 2006.
Angel Matthews, *Quarter Life Crisis,* Echo Bridge Home Entertainment, 2006.
Lia, *A Stone's Throw,* THINKFilm, 2006.
Etta Parr, *All Hat,* Screen Media Ventures, 2007.
Miriam, *The World Unseen,* Regent Releasing, 2007.
Fleur, *Kill Kill Faster Faster,* Galloping Films, 2008.
Tala, *I Can't Think Straight,* Regent Releasing, 2008.
Beth, *Toronto Stories,* Christal Films, 2008.
Somnolence, 2009.
Dominique Ball, *Defendor,* Darius Films, 2009.
Maya Chopra, *Cooking with Stella,* Mongrel Media, 2009.
Eva, *Let the Game Begin,* 2010.
Star, *1 a Minute,* 2010.
Sarah, *Trader Games,* 2010.

Television Appearances; Series:
Bollywood actress, *The Standard,* 2005.

Television Appearances; Miniseries:
Rebecca Downy, "Night One" and "Night Two," *The Summit,* Ion Television, 2008.

Television Appearances; Episodic:
The Hour with George Stroumboulopoulos, CBC, 2007.
Elena, "Stone Cold," *Blood Ties,* Lifetime, 2007.
Sita, "Bollywood Homicide," *Psych,* USA Network, 2009.
(Uncredited) Herself, "Late Nights on Air," *Great Canadian Books,* 2010.

Radio Appearances:
Presenter, *Hot Breakfast Show,* BBC Asian Network, 2004.

OTHER SOURCES

Periodicals:
O, The Oprah Magazine, April, 2006, p. 51.

REASER, Elizabeth 1975–

PERSONAL

Full name, Elizabeth Ann Reaser; born June 15, 1975, in Bloomfield, MI; father, an attorney and restaurateur, later a substitute teacher; mother, a homemaker; according to some sources, stepdaughter of William Morse Davidson (a corporate executive and owner of Detroit Pistons basketball team). *Education:* Attended Oakland University; Juilliard School, B.F.A., 1999.

Addresses: *Agent*—Rhonda Price, United Talent Agency, 9560 Wilshire Blvd., Suite 500, Beverly Hills, CA 90212.

Career: Actress.

Awards, Honors: Jury Award, best actress in a feature film, Newport Beach Film Festival, 2006, and Independent Spirit Award nomination, best female lead, Independent Features Project/West, 2007, both for *Sweet Land;* Emmy Award nomination, outstanding guest actress in a drama series, 2007, Screen Actors Guild Award nomination (with others), outstanding ensemble in a drama series, 2008, and Prism Award nomination, best performance in a multi-episode dramatic storyline, Entertainment Industries Council, 2009, all for *Grey's Anatomy.*

CREDITS

Film Appearances:
Alison Holmes, *Emmett's Mark* (also known as *Killing Emmett Young*), 2002.
Young woman in class, *Thirteen Conversations about One Thing* (also known as *13 Conversations*), Sony Pictures Classics, 2002.
Malissa Zubach, *Mind the Gap,* Sky Island Films, 2004.
Athena, *Stay,* Twentieth Century–Fox, 2005.
Young Inge, *Sweet Land,* Libero, 2005.
Susannah Stone Trousdale, *The Family Stone,* Fox 2000, 2005.
Julep, *The Wedding Weekend* (also known as *Sing Now or Forever Hold Your Peace* and *Shut Up and Sing*), Strand Releasing, 2007.
Allegra, *Puccini for Beginners,* Strand Releasing, 2007.
Bernadette, *Purple Violets,* 2007.
Esme Cullen, *Twilight,* Summit Entertainment, 2008.
Liz Clarke, *Against the Current,* IFC Films, 2009.
Esme Cullen, *New Moon* (also known as *New Moon: Twilight Saga, Twilight: New Moon, The Twilight Saga: New Moon,* and *Twilight 2*), Summit Entertainment, 2009.
Esme Cullen, *The Twilight Saga: Eclipse* (also known as *Eclipse, Twilight: Eclipse, The Twilight Sage: Eclipse, the IMAX Experience,* and *Twilight 3*), Summit Entertainment, 2010.
Charlotte Howe, *Homework,* Goldcrest Pictures, 2010.

Television Appearances; Series:
Dr. Alice Alden, *Saved,* TNT, 2006.
Jane Doe/Ava/Rebecca Pope, a recurring role, *Grey's Anatomy,* ABC, 2007–2008.
Bella Bloom, *The Ex List,* CBS, 2008.

Television Appearances; Movies:
Miriam, *The Believer,* Showtime, 2001.

Television Appearances; Pilots:
Baseball Wives, HBO, 2003.
Rachel Byrnes, *The Jury,* Fox, 2004.

Television Appearances; Specials:
Ulalume: Howling at New Moon, 2009.
The Teen Choice Awards, Fox, 2009.

Television Appearances; Episodic:
Stace, "D–Girl," *The Sopranos,* HBO, 2000.
Serena Whitfield, "The Insider," *Law & Order: Criminal Intent* (also known as *Law & Order: CI*), NBC, 2002.
Elaine Jones, "Extreme Commerce," *Hack,* CBS, 2004.
Jillian Slaughter, "Proud Flesh," *Law & Order: Criminal Intent* (also known as *Law & Order: CI*), NBC, 2006.
Anya Reed, "Heroine," *Standoff,* Fox, 2006.
The Late Late Show with Craig Ferguson, CBS, 2008.
Entertainment Tonight (also known as *E.T.* and *This Week in Entertainment*), syndicated, several appearances, beginning 2008.
Made in Hollywood, 2009.
Up Close with Carrie Keagan, ABC, 2009.
Tammy Linnata, "Cleaning House," *The Good Wife,* CBS, 2010.
Tammy Linnata, "VIP Treatment," *The Good Wife,* CBS, 2010.
Tammy Linnata, "On Tap," *The Good Wife,* CBS, 2010.

Stage Appearances:
Heavenly, *Sweet Bird of Youth,* La Jolla Playhouse, La Jolla, CA, 1999.
Froggy, *Blackbird,* Performance Space 122 (P.S.122), New York City, 2000, and Bush Theatre, London, 2001.
Mimi, *The Hologram Theory,* Blue Lights Theatre Company, McGinn–Cazale Theatre, New York City, 2000.
Shaylee Ledbetter and Sharice, *Stone Cold Dead Serious,* American Repertory Theatre Company, Loeb Drama Center, Cambridge, MA, 2002.
Perdita, *The Winter's Tale,* Classic Stage Company, East Thirteenth Street Theatre, New York City, 2003.
Mr. Fox: A Rumination, O'Neill Playwrights Conference, Waterford, CT, 2003.
Patient Griselda, Nell, and Jeanine, *Top Girls,* Williamstown Theatre Festival, Williamstown, MA, 2005.

Appeared as Tatyana and title as *Tatyana in Color* (some sources spell the name "Tatjana"), Contemporary American Theatre Festival; also appeared in *Closer,* Portland Stage Center; and *A Freeman in Paris,* off–Broadway production.

Internet Appearances; Episodic:
Annie, "The Waindow," *Wainy Days,* WainyDays.com, 2008.

RECORDINGS

Videos:
The Family Stone: Behind the Scenes, Twentieth Century–Fox Home Entertainment, 2006.

OTHER SOURCES

Periodicals:
Advocate, January 30, 2007, p. 57.
TV Guide, February 12, 2007, p. 9; October 20, 2007, pp. 28–31.

REINERS, Portia 1990–

PERSONAL

Full name, Portia Sullivan Reiners; born March 8, 1990; mother is an actress.

Career: Actress.

CREDITS

Television Appearances; Series:
Lily Benton Montgomery, a recurring role *All My Children* (also known as *AMC*), ABC, 2006.
Ada Dunne, *As the World Turns,* CBS, 2006.
Britney Jennings, *One Life to Live,* ABC, 2006–2007.

Television Appearances; Movies:
Jenny Leighton at age fourteen, *Iron Jawed Angels,* HBO, 2004.
(Uncredited) April, *Loving Leah,* CBS, 2009.

Television Appearances; Episodic:
Aggie, *All My Children* (also known as *AMC*), ABC, 2000.
Nancy, "In the Wee Small Hours: Part 1," *Law & Order: Criminal Intent* (also known as *Law & Order: CI*), NBC, 2005.
Jill Sorenson, "Great Satan," *Law & Order,* NBC, 2009.

Film Appearances:
Voice of young girl, *The Grey Zone,* 2001, Lions Gate Films, 2003.
Cathy Cassady, *Neal Cassady,* IFC Films, 2008.
Mel, *Twelve Thirty,* Twelve Thirty Productions, 2010.

Stage Appearances:

Title role, *Oliver* (musical), c. 1997.

Kasia, *More Lies about Jerzy,* Vineyard Theatre, New York City, 2001.

Appeared in title role, *Annie* (musical); as Catherine, *The Children's Hour;* Lauren, *Dear Maudie;* Baby June, *Gypsy* (musical); Susan Walker, *Here's Love;* Sara Crew, *The Little Princess;* Tootie, *Meet Me in St. Louis;* and as Jenny Litnov, *The Notebook,* McGinn–Cazale Theatre, New York City.

REMINI, Leah 1970–

PERSONAL

Full name, Leah Marie Remini; born June 15, 1970, in Brooklyn, NY; daughter of George Remini (an owner of an asbestos removal company) and Vicki Marshall (a private school teacher); married Angelo Pagan (an actor, singer, and restaurant owner), July 19, 2003; children: Sofia Bella. *Education:* Studied acting at Beverly Hills Playhouse. *Religion:* Scientologist.

Addresses: *Agent*—Harry Gold, TalentWorks, 3500 West Olive Ave., Suite 1400, Burbank, CA 91505; (voice work and commercials) Tim Curtis, WME Entertainment, 9601 Wilshire Blvd., 3rd Floor, Beverly Hills, CA 90210.

Career: Actress. Columbia Broadcasting System, appeared in the public service announcement campaign *CBS Cares;* appeared in commercials, including ads for Quaker State Motor Oil, 2000–02. Worked as a telemarketer for a solar heating company, a cashier, a bill collector, and a waitress.

CREDITS

Television Appearances; Series:

Charlene "Charlie" Briscoe, *Living Dolls,* ABC, 1989.

Stacey Carosi, a recurring role, *Saved by the Bell,* 1991.

Tina Bavasso, *The Man in the Family,* ABC, 1991.

Voice of Sagan Cruz, *Phantom 2040* (animated; also known as *Phantom 2040: The Ghost Who Walks*), syndicated, 1994–95.

Dominique, *First Time Out* (also known as *Jackie Guerra*), The WB, 1995.

Terry Reynolds, *Fired Up,* NBC, 1997–98.

Carrie Heffernan, *The King of Queens,* CBS, 1998–2007.

Television Appearances; Movies:

Stephanie O'Neil, *Getting Up and Going Home* (also known as *Unfaithful*), Lifetime, 1992.

Star Witness, 1995.

Television Appearances; Specials:

ABC's Comedy Sneak Peek, ABC, 1989.

Woman on the street in New York, *The All–American Thanksgiving Parade,* 1998.

Funny Flubs & Screw–Ups III, CBS, 1999.

Voice of Vixen, *Hooves of Fire* (also known as *Robbie the Reindeer in Hooves of Fire*), BBC, 1999, then PBS, 2002.

Celebrity Profile: Leah Remini, E! Entertainment Television, 2000.

Intimate Portrait: Sharon Lawrence, Lifetime, 2000.

Funny Flubs & Screw–Ups V, CBS, 2000.

Host, *CBS and VH1: Live at the Grammys,* CBS, 2001.

(In archive footage) Carrie Heffernan, *The Victoria's Secret Fashion Show,* ABC, 2001.

I Love Lucy's 50th Anniversary Special, CBS, 2001.

Voice of Koala, *Legend of the Lost Tribe* (also known as *Robbie the Reindeer in Legend of the Lost Tribe*), CBS, 2002.

Saved by the Bell: The E! True Hollywood Story, E! Entertainment Television, 2002.

Intimate Portrait: Leah Remini, Lifetime, 2003.

VH1 Inside Out: Leah Remini, VH1, 2003.

E! Entertainer of the Year, E! Entertainment Television, 2003.

Inside Out: Leah Remini—The Baby Special, VH1, 2004.

InStyle Greatest Celebrity Weddings, VH1, 2004.

Red Carpet Confidential, CBS, 2005.

Television Appearances; Pilots:

Frankie, *Harlan & Merleen,* CBS, 1993.

Fun Jeans, Fox, 1995.

Dominique, *First Time Out* (also known as *Jackie Guerra*), The WB, 1995.

Connie, *Adam's Way,* The WB, 1996.

Carrie Heffernan, *The King of Queens,* CBS, 1998.

Jessica Keller, *Married not Dead,* ABC, 2009.

Karen Keener, *It Takes a Village,* ABC, 2010.

Television Appearances; Miniseries:

I Love the '80s, VH1, 2002.

Television Appearances; Episodic:

"Let's Rap," *Head of the Class,* 1988.

Charlie Brisco, "Life's a Ditch," *Who's the Boss?,* ABC, 1989.

Charlie Brisco, "Living Dolls," *Who's the Boss?,* ABC, 1989.

Carol, "And Baby Makes ...," *Normal Life,* 1990.

Joanne, "A Sneaking Suspicion," *Valerie's Family* (also known as *The Hogan Family* and *Valerie*), 1991.

Rose, "Out of Ashes," *Guns of Paradise* (also known as *Paradise*), 1991.

Serafina Tortelli, "Unplanned Parenthood," *Cheers,* NBC, 1991.

Ellen "E. T." Travis, "You Must Remember This," *Blossom,* NBC, 1992.

Serafina Tortelli, "Loathe and Marriage," *Cheers,* NBC, 1993.

Daisy, "She What?," *Evening Shade,* CBS, 1993.

Daisy, "Saint Bobby," *Evening Shade,* CBS, 1993.

Daisy, "The Graduation," *Evening Shade,* CBS, 1993.

Gail Ross, "Sergeant Kelly," *The Commish,* ABC, 1994.

Tina, "The King and I," *Renegade,* 1994.

Agnes Benedetto, "How to Murder Your Lawyer," *Diagnosis Murder* (also known as *Dr. Mark Sloan*), CBS, 1995.

Lydia, "The One with the Birth," *Friends,* NBC, 1995.

Angela Bohi, "Closing Time," *NYPD Blue* (also known as *N.Y.P.D.*), ABC, 1996.

Voice of Carbine, "Once upon a Time on Mars I," *Biker Mice from Mars* (animated), syndicated, 1996.

Voice of Carbine, "Once upon a Time on Mars III," *Biker Mice from Mars* (animated), syndicated, 1996.

Hollywood Squares (also known as *H2* and *H2: Hollywood Squares*), 1999.

Herself, "Who's the Boss?," *TV Tales,* 2002.

Extra (also known as *Extra: The Entertainment Magazine*), syndicated, 2003.

Entertainment Tonight (also known as *E.T.* and *This Week in Entertainment*), syndicated, multiple appearances, between 2003 and 2009.

Herself, "The Koi Effect," *Fat Actress,* Showtime, 2005.

Carrie Heffernan, *Lopez Tonight,* TBS, 2009.

Television Talk Show Guest Appearances; Episodic:

Late Show with David Letterman (also known as *The Late Show* and *Letterman*), CBS, 1999.

The Late Late Show with Craig Kilborn (also known as *The Late Late Show*), CBS, 1999, 2000, 2001.

The Rosie O'Donnell Show, syndicated, 1999, 2001, 2001.

The Howard Stern Show, E! Entertainment Television, 2001, 2003.

The Daily Show (also known as *A Daily Show with Jon Stewart* and *The Daily Show with Jon Stewart Global Edition*), Comedy Central, 2001.

Guest cohost, *The View,* ABC, 2003.

The Sharon Osbourne Show (also known as *Sharon*), syndicated, 2003.

Ellen: The Ellen DeGeneres Show, syndicated, several appearances, between 2004 and 2007.

Dennis Miller, CNBC, 2005.

The Tonight Show with Jay Leno, NBC, 2007.

"Is Leah Remini a Pushover Mom?," *Rachael Ray,* syndicated, 2008.

"Bikini Challenge," *Rachael Ray,* syndicated, 2008.

Television Appearances; Awards Presentations:

Presenter, *The 53rd Annual Primetime Emmy Awards,* CBS, 2001.

Presenter, *The ... Annual People's Choice Awards,* CBS, 2001, 2005.

Presenter, *The 59th Annual Golden Globe Awards,* NBC, 2002.

Presenter, *The 29th Annual American Music Awards,* ABC, 2002.

Television Executive Producer; Specials:

VH1 Inside Out: Leah Remini, VH1, 2003.

Film Appearances:

Theresa, *Glory Daze,* Seventh Art Releasing, 1995.

Angie, *Follow Your Heart,* DMG Entertainment, 1997.

Lara Campbell, *Old School,* DreamWorks, 2003.

Internet Appearances; Series:

Kim, *In the Motherhood,* InTheMotherhood.com, 2007–2008.

Radio Appearances; Series:

The Don and Mike Show, syndicated, beginning 2002.

RECORDINGS

Videos:

Voice of Grace Nakimura, *Gabriel Knight: Sins of the Fathers* (video game), 1994.

"*Old School*" *Orientation,* DreamWorks Home Entertainment, 2003.

OTHER SOURCES

Periodicals:

Parade, October 26, 2003, p. 20.

People Weekly, March 29, 1999, p. 133; December 1, 2003, p. 208.

Playboy, August, 2008, p. 131.

Redbook, January, 2006, p. 70.

Stuff, February, 2002, pp. 52, 55.

TV Guide, November 8, 1997, pp. 34–36; April 18, 2004, p. 46; December 4, 2006, p. 59; April 16, 2007, pp. 22–23.

Woman's Day, October 5, 2004, p. 121.

Other:

Celebrity Profile: Leah Remini (television special), E! Entertainment Television, 2000.

Intimate Portrait: Leah Remini (television special), Lifetime, 2003.

REUTHER, Steven 1951–2010

PERSONAL

Full name, Steven D. Reuther; born November 2, 1951, in St. Petersburg, FL; died of cancer, June 5, 2010, in

Santa Monica, CA. Producer. The producer of over thirty-five feature films, Reuthers most famous works include *Dirty Dancing, Pretty Woman,* and *Pay It Forward.* He began his career in late 1970s, working in the mail room of the William Morris talent agency. By the early 1980s he was an executive at Galactic Films and later at Vestron Pictures. He debuted as a producer on the 1986 Mickey Rourke and Kim Basinger film *9 1/2 Weeks.* The following year he served as executive producer of the hit film *Dirty Dancing.* In the late 1980s Reuther partnered with Arnon Milchan at New Regency Films, and the duo produced the award-winning *Pretty Woman* in 1990. Later that decade he and famed actor Michael Douglas formed Douglas/Reuther Productions, which produced the John Travolta and Nicholas Cage action movie *Face/Off* and the Frances Ford Coppola crime drama *The Rainmaker.* In 1998 Reuther developed Bel Air Entertainment, producing, among other films, the Kevin Costner drama *Message in a Bottle,* the Keanu Reeves and Gene Hackman sports comedy *The Replacements,* and the Kevin Spacey drama *Pay It Forward,* which Reuther later identified as his favorite production. His most recent film was the 2009 romantic comedy *The Ugly Truth,* starring Katherine Heigl and Gerard Butler.

PERIODICALS

Los Angeles Times, June 8, 2010.

REYNOLDS, Burt 1936–
(Buddy Reynolds)

PERSONAL

Full name, Burton Leon Reynolds, Jr.; born February 11, 1936, in Waycross, GA; son of Burton Reynolds, Sr. (a police chief) and Fern Reynolds; married Judy Carne (an actress), 1963 (divorced, 1965); married Loni Anderson (an actress), April 29, 1988 (divorced, 1994); children: (second marriage) Quinton. *Education:* Graduated from Florida State University, 1958; also attended Palm Beach Junior College.

Addresses: *Office*—Clematis Films, PO Box 3288, Tequesta, FL 33469. *Agent*—International Creative Management, 8942 Wilshire Blvd., Beverly Hills, CA 90211. *Manager*—Vox. Inc., 5670 Wilshire Blvd., Suite 820, Los Angeles, CA 90036; Kritzer Levine Wilkins Griffin Ent., 11872 La Grance Ave., 1st Floor Los Angeles, CA 90025. *Publicist*—Jeffrey Lane & Assoc., 10560 Wilshire Blvd., Suite 803, Los Angeles, CA 90024.

Career: Actor, director, producer, and writer. Drafted by the Baltimore Colts professional football team in 1955, but auto accident ended football career; Hyde Park Playhouse, New York City, actor, 1958; Burt Reynolds's Dinner Theatre, Jupiter, FL, founder and supervisor, 1979—; also stuntman in films and television; appeared in numerous television commercials, including Kodak Max Film, Elizabeth Taylor's "White Diamonds" perfume, Maaco, T–Mobile, Miller Lite, and FedEx Kinko's.

Member: Directors Guild of America.

Awards, Honors: Voted as one of the top ten box office stars, 1970–84; Golden Globe Award nomination, best television actor—drama, 1971, for *Dan August;* Golden Globe Award nomination, best motion picture actor—musical/comedy, 1975, for *The Longest Yard;* voted number one box office star, 1979–83; People's Choice Awards, all–around favorite male entertainer, 1979, 1981, 1982, 1983, and 1984; People's Choice Awards, best actor in motion pictures, 1979, 1980, 1981, 1982, 1983, and 1984; Golden Globe Award nomination, best motion picture actor—musical/comedy, 1980, for *Starting Over;* Marquee Award, American Movie Awards, 1980; Rudolph Valentino Award, 1981; Entertainer of the Year, Friars Club, 1981; Hubert H. Humphrey Memorial Award, Touchdown Club, 1984; People's Choice Award, favorite motion picture actor, 1984; Emmy Award nominations (with Bert Convy and Richard S. Kline), best game or audience participation show, 1988, 1989, 1990, all for *Win, Lose, or Draw;* Distinguished American Award, Walter Camp Football Foundation, 1989; Tuss M. McLaughr Award, American Football Coaches Association, 1990; Golden Boot Award, 1990; People's Choice Awards, best male performer in a new television program, Emmy Award and Emmy Award nomination, best lead actor in a comedy series, Golden Globe Award nomination, best actor in a comedy series, Q Award, best actor in a quality comedy series, 1991, Golden Globe Award, best performance by an actor in a television series—comedy/musical, 1992, Golden Globe Award nomination, best performance by an actor in a television series—comedy/musical, 1991 and 1993, all for *Evening Shade;* New York Film Critics Circle Award, National Society of Film Critics Award, Los Angeles Film Critics Association Award, Boston Society of Film Critics Award runner–up, all best supporting actor, 1997, Academy Award nomination, best supporting actor, Film Award nomination, best performance by an actor in a supporting role, British Academy of Film and Television Arts, Chicago Film Critics Association Award, best supporting actor, Screen Actors Guild Award nominations, outstanding performance by a male actor in a supporting role and (with others) outstanding performance by a cast, Golden Globe Award, best performance by an actor in a supporting role in a motion picture, Golden Satellite Award, best actor in a supporting role in a motion picture—drama, Online Film Critics Award, best supporting actor, Sierra Award, best supporting actor, Las Vegas Film Critics Society, Dallas–Fort Worth Film Critics Association Awards, best supporting actor, Florida Film Critics Circle Award, best ensemble cast (with others), 1998, all for *Boogie Nights;* ShoWest Award, supporting actor of the year, 1998; Lifetime Achievement Award, Crystal Reel Awards, 2002; Lifetime Achievement Award, for action movie star, World Stunt Awards, 2007; star on Hollywood Walk of Fame.

CREDITS

Film Appearances:

(Film debut) Hoke Adams, *Angel Baby,* Allied Artists, 1961.

Skee, *Armored Command,* Allied Artists, 1961.

Mark Andrews, *Operation C.I.A.* (also known as *Last Message from Saigon*), Allied Artists, 1965.

Red Hand, *Blade Rider, Revenge of the Indian Nations,* 1966.

Title role, *Navajo Joe* (also known as *Un dollaro a testa, Savage Run, A Dollar a Head,* and *Joe, el implacable*), United Artists, 1967.

Fade–In (also known as *Iron Cowboy*), 1968.

Pat Morrison, *Impasse,* United Artists, 1969.

Title role, *Sam Whiskey,* United Artists, 1969.

Yaqui Joe, *100 Rifles,* Twentieth Century–Fox, 1969.

Caine, *Shark!* (also known as *Un arma de dos filos* and *Maneater*), Excelsior, 1970.

Pat Morrison, *Impasse,* 1970.

Douglas Temple, *Skullduggery,* Universal, 1970.

Lewis Medlock, *Deliverance,* Warner Bros., 1972.

The Dangerous Wold of "Deliverance," 1972.

Switchboard, *Everything You Always Wanted to Know about Sex But Were Afraid to Ask* (also known as *Everything You Always Wanted to Know about Sex*), United Artists, 1972.

Detective Steve Carella, *Fuzz,* United Artists, 1972.

Jay Grobart, *The Man Who Loved Cat Dancing,* Metro–Goldwyn–Mayer, 1973.

Shamus McCoy, *Shamus* (also known as *Passion for Danger*), Columbia, 1973.

Gator McKlusky, *White Lightning* (also known as *McKlusky*), United Artists, 1973.

Paul Crewe, *The Longest Yard* (also known as *The Mean Machine*), Paramount, 1974.

Michael Oliver Pritchard III, *At Long Last Love,* Twentieth Century–Fox, 1975.

Lieutenant Phil Gaines, *Hustle,* Paramount, 1975.

W. W. Bright, *W. W. and the Dixie Dancekings,* Twentieth Century–Fox, 1975.

Walker, *Lucky Lady,* 1975.

Gator McKlusky, *Gator,* United Artists, 1976.

Buck Greenway, *Nickelodeon,* Columbia, 1976.

Himself, *Silent Movie,* Twentieth Century–Fox, 1976.

Billy Clyde Puckett, *Semi–Tough,* United Artists, 1977.

Bandit (Bo Darville), *Smokey and the Bandit,* Universal, 1977.

Wendell Sonny Lawson, *The End,* United Artists, 1978.

Sonny Hooper, *Hooper,* Warner Bros., 1978.

Mickey's 50, 1978.

Phil Potter, *Starting Over,* Paramount, 1979.

Jack Rhodes, *Rough Cut* (also known as *Roughcut*), Paramount, 1980.

Bandit, *Smokey and the Bandit II* (also known as *Smokey and the Bandit Ride Again*), Universal, 1980.

J. J. McClure, *The Cannonball Run,* Twentieth Century–Fox, 1981.

Buddy Evan, *Paternity,* Paramount, 1981.

Richard Babson, *Best Friends,* Warner Bros., 1982.

Sheriff Ed Earl Dodd, *The Best Little Whorehouse in Texas* (also known as *The Best Little Cathouse in Texas*), Universal, 1982.

Tom Sharky, *Sharky's Machine,* Warner Bros., 1982.

David, *The Man Who Loved Women,* Columbia, 1983.

The Real Bandit, *Smokey and the Bandit III* (also known as *Smokey Is the Bandit* and *The Real Bandit*), Universal, 1983.

Title role, *Stroker Ace,* Warner Bros., 1983.

J. J. McClure, *The Cannonball Run II,* Warner Bros., 1984.

Mike Murphy, *City Heat,* Warner Bros., 1984.

(Uncredited) Poker player, *Uphill All the Way,* 1984.

Ernest Stickley/Stick (title role), *Stick,* Universal, 1985.

Himself, *Southern Voices, American Dreams,* 1985.

American Dreamer, 1985.

Himself, *Sherman's March,* 1986.

Nick Scaliente ("Mex"), *Heat,* New Century, 1987.

Richard Malone (title role), *Malone,* Orion, 1987.

Tony Church, *Rent–a–Cop,* Kings Road Entertainment, 1988.

John L. Sullivan IV, *Switching Channels,* TriStar, 1988.

Narrator, *The Final Season,* 1988.

Voice of Charlie B. Barkin, *All Dogs Go to Heaven* (animated), United Artists, 1989.

Ernie Mullins, *Breaking In,* Samuel Goldwyn, 1989.

Joe Paris, *Physical Evidence,* Columbia, 1989.

Colonel Frank Parker, *Modern Love,* Triumph, 1990.

Picture This: The Times of Peter Bogdanovich in Archer City, Texas, 1991.

Himself, *The Player,* Fine Line, 1992.

Nick McKenna, *Cop & 1/2* (also known as *Cop and a Half*), Universal, 1993.

Roy Scudder, *The Maddening,* Trimark Pictures, 1994.

Himself, *A Century of Cinema,* 1994.

"Wacky" Jacky Jackson, *Mad Dog Time* (also known as *Trigger Happy*), Metro–Goldwyn–Mayer/United Artists, 1996.

Congressman David Dilbeck, *Striptease,* Columbia, 1996.

Les Williams, *Frankenstein and Me* (also known as *Frankenstein et moi*), 1996.

Blaine Gibbons, *Citizen Ruth* (also known as *Meet Ruth Stoops*), Miramax, 1996.

Lenny Spencer, *Meet Wally Sparks,* Trimark Pictures, 1997.

Jack Horner, *Boogie Nights,* New Line Cinema, 1997.

General Newton, *Bean* (also known as *Dr. Bean, Bean: The Movie,* and *Bean: The Ultimate Disaster Movie*), Gramercy, 1997.

The Sheriff, *Crazy Six,* Sterling Home Entertainment, 1998.

Eli Zeal, *Waterproof,* Cloud Ten Pictures, 1998.

Clayton Samuels, *The Hunter's Moon,* Entertainment Around the World, 1999.

Wolko, *Stringer,* 1999.

Judge Walter Burns, *Mystery, Alaska* (also known as *Pond Rules*), Buena Vista, 1999.

Connor, *Big City Blues,* Avalanche Home Entertainment, 1999.

Daniel Bender, *Pups,* 1999.

Joey "Bats" Pistella, *The Crew,* Buena Vista, 2000.

Carl Henry, *Driven* (also known as *A toute vitesse*), Warner Bros., 2001.

The Flamenco manager, *Hotel,* 2001.

Kage Mulligan, *The Hollywood Sign* (also known as *Der Himmel von Hollywood*), Lions Gate Films, 2001.

Larry Goldberg, *Snapshots,* 2002.

Banko, *Auf Herz und Nieren,* 2002.

Archie McGregor, *Time of the Wolf* (also known as *Animal Tales: Time of the Wolf, L'enfant et le loup, L'heure du loup,* and *The Boy from Wolf Mountain*), 2002.

Irish, *The Librarians* (also known as *Strike Force*), Lions Gate Films Home Entertainment, 2003.

Narrator, *4th and Life* (documentary), Gabriel Films, 2003.

Gumball 3000: The Movie, Universal, 2003.

Del Knox, *Without a Paddle,* Paramount, 2004.

Coach Nate Scarborough, *The Longest Yard,* Paramount, 2005.

Jefferson Davis "Boss" Hogg, *The Dukes of Hazzard,* Warner Bros., 2005.

Billy Cole, *Cloud 9,* Twentieth Century–Fox Home Entertainment, 2006.

General Montgomery, *End Game,* End Game Productions, 2006.

Sam LeFleur, *Forget About It,* Big Screen Entertainment Group, 2006.

Goldbluth, *Grilled,* New Line Cinema, 2006.

Jake Delton, *Broken Bridges,* Paramount Vantage, 2006.

(In archive footage) *I Love the '70s: Volume 2,* VH1, 2006.

King Konreid, *In the Name of the King: A Dungeon Siege Tale* (also known as *Schwerter des Konigs— Dungeon Siege*), Vivendi Entertainment, 2007.

Elmore Culpepper, *Randy and the Mob,* Vivendi Entertainment, 2007.

Tommy Vinson, *Deal,* Seven Arts Pictures, 2008.

Voice of Delgo's father, *Delgo* (animated), Key Creatives, 2008.

Jefferson Steel, *A Bunch of Amateurs,* Trademark Films, 2008.

C. J. Waters, *Not Another Not Another Movie,* 2009.

According to Dom (short documentary), Film Pharm, 2009.

Hollywood Moments (documentary), Film Pharm, 2009.

Craig Thomas, *A Fonder Heart,* Lions Gate Films, 2010.

Also appeared in *The Hermit of Amsterdam.*

Film Director:

Gator, United Artists, 1976.

The End, United Artists, 1978.

Sharky's Machine, Warner Bros., 1982.

Stick, Universal, 1985.

Film Producer:

(Uncredited) Executive producer, *Hustle,* Paramount, 1975.

Hooper, 1978.

(With others) *Big City Blues,* Avalanche Home Entertainment, 1999.

Television Appearances; Series:

Ben Frazer, *Riverboat,* NBC, 1958–60.

Quint Asper, *Gunsmoke* (also known as *Marshall Dillon* and *Gun Law*), CBS, 1962–65.

Detective Lieutenant John Hawk (title role), *Hawk,* ABC, 1966.

Detective Lieutenant Dan August (title role), *Dan August,* ABC, 1970–71.

Voice of Troy Garland of Anterias, *Out of This World,* syndicated, 1987.

Host and narrator, *The Story of Hollywood* (also known as *Talking Pictures*), TNT, 1988.

B. L. (Buddy Lee) Stryker (title role), *B. L. Stryker,* ABC, 1989–90.

Wood Newton, *Evening Shade* (also known as *Arkansas*), CBS, 1990–94.

Host, *Reel Classics with Burt Reynolds,* 2003.

Celebrity Rides: Burt Builds a Bandit, 2007.

Also appeared in *The Orson Welles Show.*

Television Appearances; Movies:

Rob, *Fade–In* (also known as *Iron Cowboy*), 1968.

L. G. Floran, *Hunters Are for Killing* (also known as *Hard Frame*), CBS, 1970.

Simon Zuniga, *Run, Simon, Run* (also known as *Savage Run* and *The Tradition of Simon Zuniga*), ABC, 1970.

Detective Lieutenant Dan August, *Double Jeopardy* (also known as *Dan August: Once Is Not Enough*), 1970.

B. L. Stryker, "Royal Gambit," *ABC Mystery Movie,* ABC, 1989.

B. L. Stryker, "The King of Jazz," *ABC Saturday Mystery,* ABC, 1989.

B. L. Stryker, "Die Laughing," *ABC Saturday Mystery,* ABC, 1989.

B. L. Stryker, "The Dancer's Touch," *ABC Mystery Movie,* ABC, 1989.

B. L. Stryker, "Blues for Buder," *ABC Mystery Movie,* ABC, 1989.

B. L. Stryker, "Blind Chess," *ABC Mystery Movie,* ABC, 1989.

B. L. Stryker, "Auntie Sue," *ABC Mystery Movie,* ABC, 1989.

B. L. Stryker, "Winner Takes All," *ABC Saturday Mystery,* ABC, 1990.

B. L. Stryker, "Plates," *ABC Saturday Mystery,* ABC, 1990.

B. L. Stryker, "Night Train," *ABC Saturday Mystery,* ABC, 1990.

B. L. Stryker, "High Rise," *ABC Saturday Mystery,* ABC, 1990.

B. L. Stryker, "Grand Theft Auto," *ABC Saturday Mystery,* ABC, 1990.

Jack Robinson, *The Man from Left Field,* CBS, 1993.

Otter Bob the Mountain Man, *The Cherokee Kid,* HBO, 1996.

Jerome "Raven" Katz, *Raven,* The Movie Channel, 1996.

Detective Logan McQueen, *Hard Time,* TNT, 1998.

Mentor/CIA Deputy Director, *Universal Soldier II: Brothers in Arms,* The Movie Channel, 1998.

Mentor/CIA Deputy Director/GR88, *Universal Soldier III: Unfinished Business,* The Movie Channel, 1998.

Detective Logan McQueen, *Hard Time: Premonition* (also known as *The Premonition*), TNT, 1999.

Detective Logan McQueen, *Hard Time: Hostage Hotel* (also known as *Hostage Hotel*), TNT, 1999.

Sonny Wexler, *The Last Producer* (also known as *The Final Hit*), USA Network, 2000.

Charlie LeBlanc, *Tempted* (also known as *Seduction fatale*), HBO, 2001.

Samuel Madison, *Miss Lettie and Me,* TNT, 2002.

John "Chill" McKay, *Hard Ground,* Hallmark Channel, 2003.

Television Appearances; Specials:
How to Handle a Woman, NBC, 1972.
Super Comedy Bowl 2, CBS, 1972.
Burt and the Girls, NBC, 1973.
Burt Reynolds' Late Show, NBC, 1973.
Host, *Dinah in Search of the Ideal Man,* NBC, 1973.
The Very First Glen Campbell Special, NBC, 1973.
The Wayne Newton Special, NBC, 1974.
At Long Last Cole (also known as *At Long Last Cole: What a Swell Party It Was!*), 1975.
Superstunt, 1977.
Barbara Walters Special, ABC, 1978.
Superstunt, 1978.
Color commentator, *The Celebrity Football Classic,* NBC, 1979.
Tonight Show Starring Johnny Carson 17th Anniversary Special, 1979.

The Orson Welles Show, 1979.
Don Siegel: Last of the Independents, 1980.
Margret Dnser, auf der Suche nach den Besonderen, 1981.
High Hopes: The Capra Years, 1981.
Jerry Reed and Special Friends, syndicated, 1982.
The Best Little Special in Texas, syndicated, 1982.
Hollywood: The Gift of Laughter, 1982.
All–Star Party for Carol Burnett, 1982.
James Bond: The First 21 Years, 1983.
Celebrity Daredevils, ABC, 1983.
Dom DeLuise and Friends, ABC, 1983.
Steve Martin's the Winds of Whoopie, NBC, 1983.
TV's Censored Bloopers, NBC, 1984.
The Screen Actors Guild 50th Anniversary Celebration, CBS, 1984.
All–Star Party for Lucille Ball, CBS, 1984.
Mike Douglas Presents, 1984.
All–Star Party for Burt Reynolds, 1984.
The Tonight Show Starring Johnny Carson: 23rd Anniversary, NBC, 1985.
Perry Como's Christmas in Hawaii, ABC, 1985.
An All–Star Party for "Dutch" Reagan, CBS, 1985.
The Spencer Tracy Legacy: A Tribute by Katharine Hepburn, PBS, 1986.
Shatters If Your Kid's on Drugs, 1986.
Ultimate Stuntman: A Tribute to Dar Robinson, ABC, 1987.
Happy Birthday, Hollywood!, ABC, 1987.
A Beverly Hills Christmas, syndicated, 1987.
Secrets Men Never Share, NBC, 1988.
Jackie Gleason: The Great One (also known as *How Sweet It Is: A Wake for Jackie Gleason*), CBS, 1988.
Walt Disney World 4th of July Spectacular, 1988.
First Person with Maria Shriver, NBC, 1990.
A Party for Richard Pryor, CBS, 1991.
Entertainers '91: The Top 20 of the Year, ABC, 1991.
Dinah Shore: A Special Conversation with Burt Reynolds, TNN, 1991.
Bob Hope and Friends: Making New Memories (also known as *Bob Hope's First Time With ...*), NBC, 1991.
Host, *The Very Best of the Ed Sullivan Show—II,* CBS, 1991.
Host, *1991 King Orange Jamboree Parade* (also known as *58th Annual King Orange Jamboree Parade*), NBC, 1991.
Benny Hill: The World's Favorite Clown, 1991.
Host, *Burt Reynolds' Conversations With ...,* CBS, 1991–94.
Hats Off to Minnie Pearl: America Honors Minnie Pearl, TNN, 1992.
Class Clowns, ABC, 1992.
Host, *Super Bowl Saturday Night,* TNT, 1992.
Wind in the Wire, ABC, 1993.
The Barbara Walters Special: What Is This Thing Called Love?, ABC, 1993.
Laughing Matters (also known as *Funny Business*), Showtime, 1993.
Good Morning America: Evening Edition, ABC, 1993.

The Andy Griffith Show Reunion, CBS, 1993.
The First Annual Comedy Hall of Fame, NBC, 1993.
The Carol Burnett Show: A Reunion, 1993.
WrestleMania X (also known as *WWF WrestleMania X*), 1994.
Smithsonian Fantastic Journey, CBS, 1996.
National Memorial Day Concert, PBS, 1996.
A Conversation with Burt Reynolds, TNN, 1997.
Himself, *The Story of Bean,* 1997.
AFI's 100 Years ... 100 Movies, CBS, 1998.
Interviewee, *The Life and Times of Tammy Wynette,* TNN, 1998.
The Barbara Walters Special, ABC, 1998.
Intimate Portrait: Marilu Henner, Lifetime, 1999.
Raquel Welch, Arts and Entertainment, 1999.
Narrator, *History vs. Hollywood,* History Channel, 2001.
Jackie Gleason: The Great One, Arts and Entertainment, 2001.
The Great Escape: Preparations for Freedom, 2001.
The Great Escape: The Flight to Freedom, 2001.
The Great Escape: A Standing Ovation, 2001.
The Great Escape: Bringing Fact to Fiction, 2001.
(In archive footage) Himself, *The Most Outrageous Game Show Moments,* NBC, 2002.
Live from New York: The First 5 Years of Saturday Night Live, NBC, 2005.
The Adventures of Errol Flynn, TCM, 2005.
Coach Nate Scarborough, *Showtime Special: The Longest Yard,* Showtime, 2005.
AFI's 100 Years ... 100 Movie Quotes: America's Greatest Quips, Comebacks and Catchphrases, CBS, 2005.
CMT Greatest Myths 3: Even More Rumors, Legends and Downright Lies, Country Music Television, 2006.
John L. Sullivan IV, *Nit vint–i–cinc,* 2008.

Television Appearances; Awards Presentations:
Copresenter, *The 45th Annual Academy Awards,* 1973.
Cohost, *The 46th Annual Academy Awards,* 1974.
The American Movie Awards, 1980.
The Golden Eagle Awards, syndicated, 1987.
The All–Star Pro Sports Awards, ABC, 1990.
The ... Annual Primetime Emmy Awards Presentation, Fox, 1991, 1992.
Host, *The 17th Annual People's Choice Awards,* CBS, 1991.
The ... Annual Golden Globe Awards, TBS, 1992, 1998.
The 4th Annual Desi Awards, syndicated, 1992.
The 19th Annual People's Choice Awards, CBS, 1993.
The First Annual Comedy Hall of Fame, 1993.
Host, *The Golden Globe's 50th Anniversary Celebration,* NBC, 1994.
The 70th Annual Academy Awards, 1998.
ESPY Awards, 2000.
World Stunt Awards, ABC, 2001.
2004 MTV Movie Awards, MTV, 2004.
Presenter, *The Southern Sports Awards,* Fox, 2005.

2007 Taurus World Stunt Awards, 2007.
Presenter, *The 14th Annual Screen Actors Guild Awards,* TBS, 2008.

Television Appearances; Miniseries:
Voice of T. Jackson, *The Great Battles of the Civil War,* 1995.
Voice of Patrick Henry, *Founding Fathers,* History Channel, 2000.
Marshal Hunt Lawton, *Johnson County War,* Hallmark Channel, 2002.

Television Appearances; Pilots:
Branch Taylor, *The Man from Everywhere,* CBS, 1961.
Pete Lassiter (title role), *Lassiter,* CBS, 1968.
The Dom DeLuise Show, syndicated, 1987.

Television Appearances; Episodic:
Playhouse 90, CBS, 1956.
Zane Grey Theater, CBS, 1956.
Chuck Blair, *Perry Mason,* CBS, 1957.
"The Teacher," *M Squad,* NBC, 1959.
"You Can't Win 'Em All," *Schlitz Playhouse of Stars,* CBS, 1959.
Ace, "The Velvet Alley," *Playhouse 90,* CBS, 1959.
"The Payoff," *Lawless Years,* NBC, 1959.
Rocky Rhodes, *The Twilight Zone,* CBS, 1959.
Latchard Duncan, "The Case of Alexis George," *Lock Up,* 1960.
Corman, "Fire Flight," *The Blue Angels,* syndicated, 1960.
"The Good Samaritan," *Pony Express,* syndicated, 1960.
Ace, "Alas, Babylon," *Playhouse 90,* CBS, 1960.
Tad Stuart, "The Stranger," *Johnny Ringo,* CBS, 1960.
Bill Davis, "Escape to Sonoita," *Alfred Hitchcock Presents,* CBS, 1960.
"The Big Swim," *The Aquanauts,* CBS, 1960.
"The Boat Caper," *Michael Shayne,* NBC, 1961.
Branch Taylor, "The Man from Everywhere," *Zane Grey Theater,* CBS, 1961.
Chuck, "Powder Puff Pilot," *The Blue Angels,* 1961.
"The Kidnap Adventure," *The Aquanauts,* 1961.
Abelard, "Bordertown," *The Brothers Brannagan,* 1961.
"Greed of the Glades," *Everglades,* 1961.
Young man, "Requiem for a Sunday Afternoon," *Naked City,* 1961.
"Friday's Children," *Everglades,* 1962.
"Love Is a Skinny Kid," *Route 66,* CBS, 1962.
Chuck Blair, "The Case of the Counterfeit Crank," *Perry Mason,* CBS, 1962.
Rocky Rhodes, "The Bard," *The Twilight Zone,* CBS, 1963.
Red Hand, "Now Join the Human Race," *Branded,* NBC, 1965.
Sergeant Chapman, "Show Me a Hero, I'll Show You a Bum," *Twelve O'Clock High,* ABC, 1965.
Michael Murtaugh, "All the Streets Are Silent," *The FBI,* ABC, 1965.

Tech Sgt. Chapman, "The Jones Boys," *Twelve O'Clock High,* ABC, 1965.

"Dolphin in Pursuit: Parts 1 & 2," *Flipper,* NBC, 1965.

Copilot, "Voice from the Wilderness," *Gentle Ben,* CBS, 1967.

The Carol Burnett Show (also known as *Carol Burnett and Friends*), 1967, 1972.

John Duquesne, "Act of Violence," *The FBI,* ABC, 1968.

Pete Lassiter, "Lassiter," *Premiere,* 1968.

You're Putting Me On, 1969.

The Match Game, 1969.

"Love and the Banned Book," *Love, American Style,* ABC, 1970.

Film '76' (also known as *Film of the Year* and *The Film Programme*), 1976.

"You've Never Seen Hollywood Like This Before," *That's Hollywood,* 1978.

Disneyland (also known as *Disney's Wonderful World, Walt Disney, Walt Disney Presents* and *The Wonderful World of Disney*), 1978.

Host, *Saturday Night Live,* NBC, 1980.

Entertainment Tonight (also known as *E.T., Entertainment This Week* and *This Week in Entertainment*), syndicated, 1981, 2007.

The 1/2 Hour Comedy Hour, 1983.

"Dom DeLuise," *This Is Your Life,* 1983.

Introducer, *Star Search,* 1984.

(Uncredited) Himself, "A Death in the Family," *Mickey Spillane's Mike Hammer,* CBS, 1984.

"Ladies of the Evening," *The Golden Girls,* NBC, 1986.

Himself, "Episode 2," *Dolly,* ABC, 1987.

Voice of Troy, *Out of This World,* NBC, 1987.

"Stand by Your Dream: The Tammy Wynette Story," *Arena,* 1987.

Win, Lose or Draw, 1987 and 1989.

"A 1000 Nights of Wogan," *Wogan,* 1991.

Himself, "She Came in through the Bathroom Window," *Beverly Hills, 90210,* Fox, 1993.

Himself, *Dame Edna's Hollywood,* 1993.

Himself, "The Grand Opening," *The Larry Sanders Show,* HBO, 1993.

Sheriff Ed Earl Dodd, *Dateline NBC,* NBC, 1994.

Himself, "Sisyphus, Prometheus, and Me," *Hope & Gloria,* NBC, 1995.

Himself, *Inside the Actors Studio,* 1995, 2001.

Himself, "The Cheese Stands Alone," *Cybill,* CBS, 1995.

Josiah Carey, *Amazing Grace,* NBC, 1995.

Himself, *Die Harald Schmidt Show,* 1996.

Voice of Judge, "Class Warfare" (also known as "Das Sub"), *Duckman,* 1997.

Voice of M. F. Thatherton, "The Company Man," *King of the Hill* (animated), Fox, 1997.

"Dolly Parton: Diamond in a Rhinestone World," *Bravo Profiles,* 1999.

"Marilu Henner," *Celebrity Profile,* 1999.

"Burt Reynolds," *E! True Hollywood Story,* E! Entertainment Television, 2000.

ESPN SportsCentury, ESPN, 2000, 2001, 2003.

Himself, "The Sidekick," *Emeril,* NBC, 2001.

Narrator, *History vs. Hollywood,* History Channel, 2001.

"Driven," *HBO First Look,* 2001.

Narrator, *Rites of Autumn,* ESPN, 2001.

Mr. Burt, "Improbable," *The X–Files,* Fox, 2002.

"Robby Benson," *Biography,* 2002.

Hollywood Squares, 2002.

Russ Burton, "The Proposal," *Ed,* NBC, 2003.

"Gilligan's Island: The Untold Tales," *ET in TV Land,* TV Land, 2003.

Russ Burton, "Pressure Points," *Ed,* NBC, 2004.

Dinner for Five, Independent Film Channel, 2004.

"Gold Dust Gasoline," *Robot Chicken* (animated), Cartoon Network, 2005.

Coach Wallcott, "Hi, School," *The King of Queens,* 2005.

Voice of Royal Serpenti, "Master & Disaster/All in the Crime Family," *Duck Dodgers* (animated; also known as *Duck Dodgers in the 24 1/2th Century*), Cartoon Network, 2005.

"The Dukes of Hazzard," *Comedy Central Canned Ham* (also known as *Reel Comedy*), Comedy Central, 2005.

Sunday Morning Shootout (also known as *Hollywood Shootout* and *Shootout*), AMC, 2005, 2006.

"The Enemy of My Enemy Is My Friend," *The Contender,* NBC, 2005.

"Betrayed," *The Contender,* NBC, 2005.

"Who's Playing the Game?," *The Contender,* NBC, 2005.

"To Be the Man, You've Got to Beat the Man!," *The Contender,* NBC, 2006.

Carl Crane Pool, "Mother of All Grandfathers," *Freddie,* 2006.

Chubby, "Jump for Joy," *My Name Is Earl,* NBC, 2006.

(Uncredited) Chubby, "Two Balls, Two Strikes," *My Name Is Earl,* NBC, 2007.

Lewis Medlock, "Movies," *TV Land Confidential,* TV Land, 2007.

John L. Sullivan IV, *Silenci?,* 2008.

Entertainment Tonight, syndicated, 2008, 2009.

Chubby, "Dodge's Dad," *My Name Is Earl,* NBC, 2009.

"Small Potatoes: Who Killed the USFL?," *30 for 30,* 2009.

Paul Anderson, "Past & Future Tense," *Burn Notice,* USA Network, 2010.

Also appeared in *General Electric Theatre,* CBS; *Route 66,* CBS; *The Sonny & Cher Comedy Hour;* as guest panelist, *The New Hollywood Squares;* himself, *Tvography.*

Television Talk Show Guest Appearances; Episodic:

The Sonny and Cher Comedy Hour, 1967, 1972.

The David Frost Show, 1969, 1971.

The Merv Griffin Show, 1970.

Guest, *The Tonight Show Starring Johnny Carson,* NBC, 1971, 1972, 1974, 1976, 1977, 1984, 1990–92.

The Virginia Graham Show, 1971.
The Flip Wilson Show, 1972.
V.I.P.–Schaukel, 1975.
The Mike Douglas Show, 1975, 1976, 1977.
The Jim Nabors Show, 1978.
The Tonight Show with Jay Leno (also known as *Jay Leno*), NBC, 1992, 1993, 1998, 2003, 2005.
The Chevy Chase Show, 1993.
Howard Stern, 1996.
The Rosie O'Donnell Show, 1996.
Himself, *Ruby Wax Meets* (also known as *The Ruby Wax Show*), Fox, 1996.
Himself, *Dennis Miller Live,* syndicated, 1998.
The Howard Stern Radio Show, 1999.
Himself, *Hollywood Squares,* 2002.
V Graham Norton, Channel 4, 2003.
Ellen: The Ellen DeGeneres Show (also known as *The Ellen Show*), syndicated, 2004.
The Daily Show (also known as *A Daily Show with Jon Stewart, Jon Stewart, The Daily Show with Jon Stewart* and *The Daily Show with Jon Stewart Global Edition*), Comedy Central, 2004.
"Shocking Maury Guests ... Where Are They Now?," *The Maury Povich Show* (also known as *Maury, Maury Povich* and *The Maury Show*), syndicated, 2004.
Live with Regis & Kelly, syndicated, 2004, 2005.
Tavis Smiley, PBS, 2005.
Corazon de ..., 2006.

Also appeared in episodes of *The Dinah Shore Show,* NBC; *The Wil Shriner Show,* syndicated.

Television Executive Producer; Series:
(With Bert Convy; and creator) *Win, Lose, or Draw,* NBC, 1987–88.
Third Degree, syndicated, 1989.
B. L. Stryker, ABC, 1989.
Evening Shade (also known as *Arkansas*), CBS, 1990–94.

Television Director; Movies:
Die Laughing, ABC, 1989.
Blues for Buder, ABC, 1989.
Night Train, ABC, 1990.
The Man from Left Field, CBS, 1993.
Harlan Merleen, 1993.
Hard Time, TNT, 1998.
The Last Producer (also known as *The Final Hit*), USA Network, 2000.

Television Executive Producer; Movies:
"Royal Gambit," *ABC Mystery Movie,* ABC, 1989.
"The King of Jazz," *ABC Saturday Mystery,* ABC, 1989.
"Die Laughing," *ABC Saturday Mystery,* ABC, 1989.
"The Dancer's Touch," *ABC Mystery Movie,* ABC, 1989.
"Winner Takes All," *ABC Saturday Mystery,* ABC, 1990.
"Plates," *ABC Saturday Mystery,* ABC, 1990.

"Night Train," *ABC Saturday Mystery,* ABC, 1990.
"High Rise," *ABC Saturday Mystery,* ABC, 1990.
"Grand Theft Hotel," *ABC Saturday Mystery,* ABC, 1990.
The Man Upstairs, CBS, 1992.
The Man from Left Field, CBS, 1993.

Television Director; Specials:
Class Clowns, ABC, 1992.
Harlan & Merleen (also known as *It's Never Too Late*), CBS, 1993.

Television Executive Producer; Specials:
Cotton Club '75, 1975.
Burt Reynolds' Conversations With ..., CBS, 1992–94.
Harlan and Merleen (also known as *It's Never Too Late*), CBS, 1993.
A Conversation with Burt Reynolds, TNN, 1997.

Television Director; Episodic:
Hawk, ABC, 1966.
"The Method Actor," *Alfred Hitchcock Presents,* NBC, 1985.
"Guilt Trip," *Amazing Stories,* NBC, 1985.
Evening Shade (also known as *Arkansas*), CBS, 1990–94.
The New WKRP in Cincinnati, syndicated, 1991.

Stage Appearances:
(As Buddy Reynolds) *Mister Roberts,* City Center Theatre, New York City, 1956.
Look: We've Come Through, Hudson Theatre, New York City, 1961.

Also appeared in *The Rainmaker,* New York City.

Major Tours:
Himself, *My Life* (one–man show), U.S. cities, 1992–93, 2002–2003.

Stage Director:
Teahouse of the August Moon, Burt Reynolds Dinner Theatre, Jupiter, FL, 1987.
Mame, Burt Reynolds Theatre, 1987.

Also director of *One Flew over the Cuckoo's Nest, The Rainmaker, Two for the See–Saw, Mass Appeal, Wrestlers,* and others, all at the Burt Reynolds Dinner Theatre.

Major Tours; Director:
(And producer) *My Life,* U.S. cities, 1992–93.

RECORDINGS

Video Games:

Voice of Avery Carrington, *Grand Theft Auto: Vice City* (also known as *GTA4*), 2002.

Videos:

Host, *Basic Football* (short documentary), 1994.

Inside "Live and Let Die," 1999.

Narrator, *Rites of Autumn: The Story of College Football* (documentary), 2002.

Interviewee, *Sex at 24 Frames Per Second* (documentary; also known as *Playboy Presents Sex at 24 Frames Per Second: The Ultimate Journey Through Sex in Cinema*), Image Entertainment, 2003.

Reflections on "The X–Files" (short documentary; featured in the season 9 DVD boxed set of *The X–Files*), Twentieth Century–Fox, 2004.

Driven: The Making of "Driven" (short documentary), Warner Home Video, 2004.

Narrator, *Legend of Frosty the Snowman,* Classic Media, 2005.

Doing Time on "The Longest Yard" (short film; featured on the Lockdown Edition DVD of *The Longest Yard*), Paramount Home Video, 2005.

Hoosiers Meets Hooters: Behind "Cloud 9" (short documentary); Twentieth Century–Fox, 2006.

Born to Controversy: The Roddy Piper Story, 2006.

Deliverance: Betraying the River (short documentary; featured on the 35th Anniversary DVD of *Deliverance*), Warner Home Video, 2007.

Deliverance: The Beginning (short documentary; featured on the 35th Anniversary DVD of *Deliverance*), Warner Home Video, 2007.

Deliverance: The Journey (short documentary; featured on the 35th Anniversary DVD of *Deliverance*), Warner Home Video, 2007.

Deliverance: Delivered (short documentary; featured on the 35th Anniversary DVD of *Deliverance*), Warner Home Video, 2007.

WRITINGS

Television Movies:

Harlan & Merleen (also known as *It's Never Too Late*), CBS, 1993.

Television Episodes:

Evening Shade, 1991–92.

Television Series:

(And creator) *Win, Lose or Draw,* NBC, 1987.

Nonfiction:

My Life (autobiography), Stoddard & Houghton, 1991.

OTHER SOURCES

Books:

Resnick, Sylvia Safran, *Burt Reynolds: An Unauthorized Biography,* St. Martin's Press, 1983.

Smith, Lisa, *Burt Reynolds,* Magic Light Productions, 1994.

St. James Encyclopedia of Popular Culture, St. James Press, 2000.

Streebeck, Nancy, *The Films of Burt Reynolds,* Citadel Press, 1982.

Whitley, Dianna, *Burt Reynolds: Portrait of a Superstar,* 1979.

Periodicals:

Entertainment Weekly, August 4, 1995, p. 7; January 23, 1998, p. 37; March 6, 1998, p. 40; May 6, 2005, pp. 46–50.

New York Times, October 1, 1989, pp. H17, H23.

New York Times Magazine, June 16, 1996.

People Weekly, September 13, 1993, pp. 80–86; December 16, 1996, p. 96.

Time, February 23, 1998, p. 91.

Variety, May 19, 1997, p. S16; November 1, 1999, p. M4.

ROBBINS, Amy 1971–

PERSONAL

Born 1971, in Bebington, Merseyside, England; father, an entertainer and comedian; mother, a singer; sister of Ted Robbins (an actor), Kate Robbins (an actress), and Jane Robbins (an actress); distant cousin of Paul McCartney (a recording artist); married Robert Daws (an actor), February, 2003; children: Elizabeth Kate, May. *Education:* Goldsmiths College, London, graduated; trained at Royal Academy of Dramatic Arts, London. *Avocational Interests:* Cooking, reading, painting, singing.

Addresses: *Agent*—ARG Talent Agency, 4 Great Portland St., London W1 8PA, England.

Career: Actress.

CREDITS

Television Appearances; Series:

Sergeant Rachel James, a recurring role, *Casualty,* BBC1, 2001.

Dr. Jill Weatherill, *The Royal,* ITV, 2003–2009.

Television Appearances; Movies:

Darla, *Nightworld: 30 Years to Life* (also known as *30 Years to Life*), UPN, 1998.

Maureen Fitzpatrick, *My Beautiful Son* (also known as *Strange Relations*), Showtime, 2001.

Television Appearances; Specials:

Robbins, ITV, 1986.

Victoria Wood with All the Trimmings, BBC, 2000.

Television Appearances; Episodic:

Isla, "Brave Heart," *Holby City,* BBC, 1999.

Shayla Connor, "The Foreign Field," *Where the Heart Is,* ITV, 2000.

Sophie Clark, "Forty," *Happiness,* BBC, 2001.

Xil, "Girlfriend," *My Hero,* BBC1, 2001.

Dr. Jill Weatherill, "Out of the Blue," *Heartbeat,* ITV, 2003.

Deborah Mattis, "Soft Touch," *Dalziel and Pascoe,* BBC, 2004.

Today with Des and Mel, ITV, 2004.

Audience member, "Soap Stars Special 3," *Stars in Their Eyes,* ITV, 2004.

GMTV, ITV, 2004.

This Morning, ITV, 2004, 2007.

Loose Women, ITV, 2007.

Film Appearances:

Molly Ward, *The Second Jungle Book: Mowgli & Baloo,* TriStar, 1997.

Bryony, *Up on the Roof,* Carlton, 1997.

Valerie Ann Platt, *All the Little Animals,* Lions Gate Films, 1999.

Sylvie, *Killing Me Softly,* Metro–Goldwyn–Mayer/Amuse Pictures, 2002.

Stage Appearances:

Appeared in the play *The Accrington Pals.*

ROBBINS, Kate 1960–

PERSONAL

Born August 21, 1960, in Liverpool, England; daughter of Mike and Bett Robbins; sister of Ted Robbins (an actor), Jane Robbins (an actress), Amy Robbins (an actress); second cousin of Paul McCartney (a musician and member of the Beatles); children: Emily Atack (an actress).

Career: Actress. Prima Donna (a band), singer.

Awards, Honors: Angel Award, best supporting actress, Monaco International Film Festival, 2006, for *Fated.*

CREDITS

Film Appearances:

Voice of the Queen, *Bullseye!,* 21st Century Pictures Group, 1990.

Blossom, *The Band Parts* (short film), 1995.

Fighting couple woman, *16 Years of Alcohol,* Palisades Tartan, 2003.

Joan, *Sex Lives of the Potato Men,* 2004.

(English version) Voice of female Gayan and Valerie, *Back to Gaya* (animated; also known as *Boo, Zino & the Snurks* and *The Snurks*), First Look International, 2004.

Female giant, Mrs. Shoe–Thing, and Chicken, *Mirror-Mask,* Samuel Goldwyn, 2005.

Clarise, *Flyboys,* Metro–Goldwyn–Mayer, 2006.

Kathleen, *Fated,* Ace Film, 2006.

Television Appearances; Series:

Kate Loring, *Crossroads,* ATV, 1980.

Impressionist, *Mike Yarwood in Person,* ITV, 1982.

Various voices, *Spitting Image,* ITV, 1984.

Various characters, *Kate and Ted's Show,* ITV, 1987.

Various characters, *The Kate Robbins Show,* ITV, 1988.

Voice of Jeremiah Wellington–Green and other characters, *Round the Bend,* ITV, 1988.

The Staggering Stories of Ferdinand De Bargos, BBC, 1989.

Voice, *Fiddley Foodle Bird,* BBC, 1991.

Voice, *The Caribou Kitchen,* ITV, 1995.

Voice of Sorceress Abigail, *The Big Knights,* BBC2, 1999.

Monkey Dust, BBC3, 2003.

Various roles, *The Impressionable Jon Culshaw,* ITV, 2004.

Prime Minister's aide, *Touch Me, I'm Karen Taylor,* BBC, 2007.

Herself, *Beyond a Joke,* ITV3, 2009.

Television Appearances; Movies:

Voice, *The Willows in Winter,* 1996.

Television Appearances; Specials:

(With Prima Donna) Competitor, *The Eurovision Song Contest,* 1980.

Various characters, *Robbins,* TIV, 1986.

Voice, *"Spitting Image": The Ronnie and Nancy Show,* NBC, 1987.

A Night of Comic Relief 2, BBC, 1989.

Voice, *Thatcherworld,* BBC, 1993.

Various, *Animal Madness,* Channel 5, 1997.

Rita Cohen, *You Are Here,* 1998.

Victoria Wood with All the Trimmings, BBC, 2000.

There's Only One Paul McCartney, BBC, 2002.

Narrator, *Dolly Parton: Platinum Blonde* (documentary), 2003.
Big Fat Documentary, BBC, 2004.
Other voices, *Shepperton Babylon,* BBC, 2005.
Best Ever "Spitting Image," ITV, 2006.
Narrator, *Queens of Heartache,* BBC, 2006.

Television Appearances; Episodic:
Saturday Gang, LWT, 1986.
You Bet, ITV, 1988.
A Question of Entertainment, BBC, 1988.
Wogan, BBC, 1991.
Voice of Miss Hackney, "The Play's the Thing," *My Little Pony Tales,* The Disney Channel, 1992.
(Uncredited) Voice of woman in film and woman in lift, "Holoship," *Red Dwarf,* BBC, 1992.
Cilla Black, *Harry Enfield's Television Programme,* BBC, 1992.
Cilla Black, "Blind Date," *Sean's Show,* Channel 4, 1992.
Voice, "Pallas 2," *Pallas,* Channel 4, 1992.
Bella White, "Once in a Lifetime," *Comedy Playhouse,* ITV, 1993.
Nurse Larkin, "Gregory: Diary of a Nutcase," *The Comic Strip Presents ...,* BBC2, 1993.
Truddles, "Those Sexciting '60s," *KYTV,* BBC, 1993.
Voiceover, *Eurotrash,* Channel 4, 1993.
Gypsy girl, "There Are Gypsies at the Bottom of Our Garden," *Last of the Summer Wine,* BBC, 1993.
Voice of Princess Anne, "Awards," *Drop the Dead Donkey,* Channel 4, 1993.
Voice of the Duchess of York, "George's Car," *Drop the Dead Donkey,* Channel 4, 1996.
Voice of Pam Ayres, "Writers," *Jack and Jeremy's Real Lives,* Channel 4, 1996.
Shooting Stars, BBC, 1997.
Alas Smith & Jones, BBC, 1997.
Bernie, *The National Lottery Big Ticket,* BBC, 1998.
Herself, "Celebrity Special 2," *Wipeout,* ABC, 1998.
Babs, "Party," *Dinnerladies,* BBC and BBC America, 1998.
Babs, "Holidays," *Dinnerladies,* BBC and BBC America, 1999.
Live Talk, ITV, 2000.
Voice of Singing Rain, *The 10th Kingdom,* 2000.
Angela Taylor, "A Good Day," *Where the Heart Is,* ITV, 2000.
Beverley Garton, "Temptation," *Where the Heart Is,* ITV, 2001.
"I Love 1985," *I Love 1980s,* BBC2, 2001.
"New Years Compilation," *I Love 1980s,* BBC2, 2001.
Leslie Harris, "Design for Living," *Holby City,* BBC, 2002.
Ladies night organiser, *Phoenix Nights,* Channel 4, 2002.
This Morning, ITV, 2004.
The Dan and Dusty Show, ITV, 2004.
Sheila Lovatt, "Wild, Wild West Midlands," *Doctors,* BBC, 2004.

Sheryl Cooper, "Wine and Roses," *Heartbeat,* ITV, 2006.
Richard & Judy, Channel 4, 2008.
Marylin Harvey, "The Hex," *Doctors,* BBC, 2008.
Baroness, "Hairwolf," *The Legend of Dick & Dom,* BBC, 2009.
Jackie, "Not Over 'Til the Fat Lady Sings," *Casualty,* BBC1, 2009.
Dancing on Ice Friday, ITV, 2010.

Stage Director:
My Bass and Other Animals (a one–man show), King's Head, Islington, England, 2006.

Radio Appearances:
Appeared in *Jammin',* BBC Radio 2; *Three Off the Tee,* BBC Radio 4.

RECORDINGS

Video Games:
Voice, *Discworld,* 1995.
Voice, *Discworld II: Missing Presumed ...!?* (also known as *Discworld II: Mortality Bytes*), Psygnosis, 1996.
Voice of Carlotta von Uberwald, Ilsa Varberg, Laredo Cronk, Mrs. Fomes, Sapphire, and various characters, *Discworld Noir,* Psygnosis, 1999.

WRITINGS

Television Episodes:
"Pallas 2," *Pallas,* Channel 4, 1992.

OTHER SOURCES

Electronic:
Kate Robbins Home Page, http://www.katerobbins.co.uk, May 26, 2010.

ROBBINS, Ted 1956–

PERSONAL

Born 1956, in Liverpool, Merseyside, England; father, an entertainer and comedian; mother, a singer; brother of Amy Robbins (an actress), Kate Robbins (an actress), and Jane Robbins (an actress); distant cousin of Paul McCartney (a recording artist).

Career: Actor.

CREDITS

Television Appearances; Series:
Presenter, *First Post,* ITV, 1983.
Cast member, *Kate and Ted's Show,* ITV, 1987.
Cast member, *The Kate Robbins Show,* ITV, 1988.
Presenter, *Quiz Night,* ITV, 1988, 1989.
Announcer, *Family Catchphrase,* The Family Channel, 1993.
Den Perry, a recurring role, *Phoenix Nights,* Channel 4, 2001–2002.
Presenter, *Boot Sale Challenge,* ITV, 2004.
Presenter, *Loose @ 5.30* (talk show), ITV, 2006.
The governor, *The Slammer,* BBC, 2006–2008.

Television Appearances; Specials:
Robbins, ITV, 1986.
Victoria Wood with All the Trimmings, BBC, 2000.
Life's a Pitch, 2000.
(Uncredited) Audience member, *An Audience with Des O'Connor,* ITV, 2001.
Big Fat Documentary, BBC, 2004.
Reader of story extracts, *The Unseen Eric Morecambe,* 2005.
The 50 Greatest Kisses, Sky Television, 2005.
Now That's Embarrassing: The 80s, Channel 5, 2006.
TV's 50 Greatest Stars, Granada Television, 2006.
The World's Greatest Comedy Characters, Channel 4, 2007.
(Uncredited) Audience member, *The Return of 'Allo 'Allo!,* BBC, 2007.
50 Greatest Comedy Catchphrases, Channel 4, 2008.

Television Appearances; Episodic:
Just a Minute, Carlton, 1994.
Presenter, *Chain Letters,* ITV, 1995.
Surprise Surprise!, ITV, 1995.
"Leonard," *That Peter Kay Thing,* Channel 4, 2000.
Tony Cluedo, "Anarchy in Royston Vasey," *The League of Gentlemen,* Comedy Central, 2000.
Tony Cisco, "Nutcase," *City Central,* BBC, 2000.
Zeppy, "Kids," *Barbara,* ITV, 2000.
D. J., *Coronation Street,* 2000.
Pete Waterman and Spud, "Rock the Blind," *Rock Profile,* 2001.
Bartender, "Home Truths," *Dalziel and Pascoe,* BBC, 2001.
Tommy Mead, "The Morning After," *Mersey Beat,* BBC, 2002.
Nick Critchley, "Judas Kiss: Part 2," *Holby City,* BBC, 2002.
Kenny Rock, "Stand–up," *Doctors,* BBC, 2002.
Bonnie, *Eyes Down,* BBC, 2003.
Restaurant customer, "Most Cigarettes in a Mouth," *Little Britain,* BBC America, 2003.
Don Dibley, "Mountains and Molehills," *Heartbeat,* ITV, 2004.

Reporter, "Hard–Boiled Egg Eating," *Little Britain,* BBC America, 2004.
Little Britain, BBC America, 2004.
Stan Tennant, "Time's Arrow," *Doctors,* BBC, 2005.
This Morning, ITV, 2005.
Tommy, "Near, Far," *Two Pints of Lager and a Packet of Crisps,* BBC3, 2005.
Tommy, "Speedycruise!," *Two Pints of Lager and a Packet of Crisps,* BBC3, 2006.
Bob Fairchild, "Allergic," *Lead Balloon,* BBC, 2006.
Richard & Judy, Channel 4, multiple appearances, 2006–2007.
Mr. Watson, *The Chase,* BBC, 2007.
Audience member, *Soapstar Superstar,* ITV, 2007.
Ken, *The Street,* ITV, 2007, 2009.
Barry, "Billy Goat," *Fair Tales,* BBC, 2008.
"Back to School," *The Legend of Dick & Dom,* BBC, 2009.
Officer McAlister, *Coronation Street,* 2009.
Mo Hallam, "Birth of the Blues," *Doctors,* BBC, 2010.

Television Appearances; Other:
Chauffeur, *This Is Personal: The Hunt for the Yorkshire Ripper* (movie), ITV, 2000.
Reverend Ward, *Trexx and Flipside* (miniseries), BBC, 2008.

Film Appearances:
Bike man, *Calendar Girls,* Buena Vista, 2003.

WRITINGS

Television Specials:
Animal Madness, Channel 5, 1997.

ROE, Channon 1969–

PERSONAL

Full name, James Channon Roe; born October 27, 1969, in Pasadena, CA; married Bianca Chiminello (an actress), October 24, 2009. *Education:* Studied acting at Joanne Barron DW Brown Studio and British Academy of Dramatic Arts at Stanford University.

Addresses: *Agent*—Harold Augenstein, Abrams Artists Agency, 9200 Sunset Blvd., Suite 1130, Los Angeles, CA 90069. *Manager*—Katie Mason, Luber Roklin Entertainment, 8530 Wilshire Blvd., 5th Floor, Beverly Hills, CA 90211.

Career: Actor.

CREDITS

Film Appearances:

Craig, *The Low Life,* Cabin Fever Entertainment, 1995.

Roach, *Bio–Dome,* Metro–Goldwyn–Mayer, 1996.

Angry guy, *Kiss & Tell,* 1996.

Surfer Joe, *Boogie Nights,* New Line Cinema, 1997.

Cab driver, *Stir,* Cintel Films, 1997.

Razor, *Full Blast,* Showcase Entertainment, 1997.

Kevin, *Girl,* Kushner–Locke Company, 1998.

Jake, *Can't Hardly Wait,* Sony Pictures Entertainment, 1998.

Steven, *Dante's View,* Showcase Entertainment, 1998.

Jimmy, *Junked,* 1999.

Wedge Riley, *Psycho Beach Party,* Strand Releasing, 2000.

Bobby Loco, *Spin Cycle,* 2000.

Younger Bobby Ray, *Mi amigo,* 2000.

Detective Jay Stanton, *Angels Don't Sleep Here,* 2000.

Testifier, *A Man Is Mostly Water,* 2000.

Jack Logan, *Stray* (short film), MeniThings, 2005.

Dave, *Rampage: The Hillside Strangler Murders,* Sony Pictures Entertainment, 2005.

Ray, *Beautiful Dreamer,* Lantern Lane Entertainment, 2006.

Zippy, *The Harsh Life of Veronica Lambert,* All Over the Place Films, 2009.

Chief Petty Officer Kevin Derricks, *Behind Enemy Lines: Colombia,* Twentieth Century–Fox Home Entertainment, 2009.

Television Appearances; Series:

Cash, *Kindred: The Embraced,* Fox, 1996.

Voice of Joey, *Spawn* (also known as *Todd McFarlane's "Spawn"*), HBO, 1997.

Jeremy Benzing, *Windfall,* NBC, 2006.

Television Appearances; Movies:

First surfer, *Sketch Artist II: Hands that See* (also known as *A Feel for Murder* and *Sketch Artist II*), Showtime, 1995.

Brophy, *Soldier Boyz,* HBO, 1995.

Mr. Pizza, *The Courtyard,* Showtime, 1995.

Lewis, *Persons Unknown,* HBO, 1996.

Johnny Toussard, *Buried Secrets,* NBC, 1996.

Skin, *Marshal Law,* Showtime, 1996.

Sun Gods, 2002.

Television Appearances; Pilots:

Nicky, *Significant Others,* Fox, 1998.

Jeremy Benzing, *Windfall,* NBC, 2006.

Jeff Stagliano, *Dirt,* FX Network, 2007.

Freddy, *Under,* Arts and Entertainment, 2008.

Television Appearances; Miniseries:

The Invaders, Fox, 1995.

Appeared as Terry, *The Genesis Files.*

Television Appearances; Episodic:

Billy, "Halloween," *My So–Called Life,* ABC, 1994.

"Stable for Transfer," *Out of Order,* 1996.

Lucas Tremaine, "Random Acts," *Touched by an Angel,* CBS, 1996.

Derek Banks, "Kaddish," *The X–Files,* Fox, 1997.

Jimmy Mosler, "Emission Impossible," *NYPD Blue* (also known as *N.Y.P.D.*), ABC, 1997.

Remy, "Cinnamon Buns," *Brooklyn South,* CBS, 1998.

Title role, "Hemeac," *Welcome to Paradox,* Sci–Fi Channel, 1998.

Pat Rush, "Parole," *The Pretender,* NBC, 1998.

Jack O'Toole, "The Zeppo," *Buffy the Vampire Slayer* (also known as *BtVS, Buffy, Buffy, the Vampire Slayer: The Series,* and *Nightfall*), The WB, 1999.

Nolan, "Moving On," *Jack & Jill,* The WB, 1999.

(Uncredited) Lucas, "Gangland: Parts 1 & 2," *Diagnosis Murder* (also known as *Dr. Mark Sloan*), CBS, 1998.

Adam Bennett, "Miles to Go," *The Fugitive,* CBS, 2000.

Steve, "What Sharp Teeth You Have," *The Division,* Lifetime, 2001.

Baggo, "Blowing Free: Part 1," *Going to California,* Showtime, 2001.

Baggo, "The Naked and the Nude," *Going to California,* Showtime, 2001.

Baggo, "Lily of the Field," *Going to California,* Showtime, 2001.

Cree, "The Eyes Have It," *Charmed,* The WB, 2002.

Brad Repkin, "Broken," *CSI: Miami,* CBS, 2002.

Tommy K, "Get Your Mack On," *Fastlane,* Fox, 2002.

"Statewide Swing," *Mister Sterling,* NBC, 2003.

"Wish List," *Mister Sterling,* NBC, 2003.

"Final Passage," *Mister Sterling,* NBC, 2003.

Drew Anderson, "Coming Home," *Without a Trace* (also known as *W.A.T.*), CBS, 2003.

Slippery Dan, "A Lie Agreed Upon: Parts 1 & 2," *Deadwood,* HBO, 2005.

Douglas Granger, "Weeping Willows," *CSI: Crime Scene Investigation* (also known as *C.S.I.* and *CSI: Las Vegas*), CBS, 2005.

Cal, "Day 5: 1:00 p.m.–2:00 p.m.," *24,* Fox, 2006.

Jake, "The Avengers," *The O.C.,* Fox, 2006.

Robber, "Chicago," *Prison Break,* Fox, 2007.

Jeff Stagliano, "Blogan," *Dirt,* FX Network, 2007.

Jeff Stagliano, "The Sexxx Issue," *Dirt,* FX Network, 2007.

Danny Fitz, "The Man in the Mud," *Bones,* Fox, 2008.

Tard, "A Tard for All Seasons," *Head Case,* Starz!, 2008.

Tard, "Best Laid Plans," *Head Case,* Starz!, 2008.

Tard, "Dreading Bells," *Head Case,* Starz!, 2008.

Tard, "Twinkle, Twinkle ...," *Head Case,* Starz!, 2009.

Greg (some sources cite Gordon) Lambro, "Caged," *Navy NCIS: Naval Criminal Investigative Service* (also known as *NCIS* and *NCIS: Naval Criminal Investigative Service*), CBS, 2009.

Kevin Henson, "A Chill Goes through Her Veins," *Castle,* ABC, 2009.

John (The Doctor) Norwood in 1963, "November 22," *Cold Case,* CBS, 2009.

William "Billy" Cline, "Betsy," *Dark Blue,* TNT, 2009.

(In archive footage) Himself, *WWF Raw,* USA Network, 2009.

William, "Fustercluck," *Terriers,* FX Network, 2010.

William, "Dog and Pony," *Terriers,* FX Network, 2010.

William, "Change Partners," *Terriers,* FX Network, 2010.

William, "Manifest Destiny," *Terriers,* FX Network, 2010.

Also appeared as Mikey, *High Incident,* ABC; Miles Crawford, *The District,* CBS.

RECORDINGS

Videos:
Voice of Brophy, *Soldier Boyz* (video game), 1997.

ROMANO, Jeanne

PERSONAL

Full name, Jeanne N. Romano.

Career: Writer, story editor, producer, and creative consultant. Seattle University, Seattle, WA, writer in residence for film studies. Participant at book readings. Some sources state that Romano and Bonnie Solomon worked on a series of toys.

Member: Writers Guild of America, West.

CREDITS

Television Work; Series:
Story editor, *His & Hers,* CBS, 1990.

Creative consultant, *Flesh 'n' Blood,* NBC, 1991.

Developer and producer, *Fish Police* (animated), CBS, 1992.

Film Work:
Producer, *My Little Pony: The Princess Promenade* (animated), Paramount Home Entertainment, 2006.

Some sources state that Romano worked as an assistant on films.

Animated Film Appearances:
Voice of Firefly, *My Little Pony: A Very Pony Place,* Paramount Home Entertainment, 2006.

WRITINGS

Teleplays; Specials:
(With others) *Before They Were Stars,* ABC, 1995.

"Me and My Hormones," *ABC Afterschool Specials,* ABC, 1996.

Teleplays; Episodic:
(With Jeanne Baruch) "An American Dream," *9 to 5* (also known as *Nine to Five*), syndicated, 1986.

(With Baruch) "Move over Millie Maple," *9 to 5* (also known as *Nine to Five*), syndicated, 1987.

(With Baruch) "The Witches of Barkley," *9 to 5* (also known as *Nine to Five*), syndicated, 1988.

(With Baruch) "Here's Looking at You, Kid," *Married ... with Children* (also known as *Married, Married with Children,* and *Not the Cosbys*), Fox, 1989.

(With Baruch) "I'll See You in Court," *Married ... with Children* (also known as *Married, Married with Children,* and *Not the Cosbys*), Fox, 1989.

"Pulling out the Weeds," *Flesh 'n' Blood,* NBC, 1991.

"The Wrath of Con," *Flesh 'n' Blood,* NBC, 1991.

"A Fish out of Water," *Fish Police* (animated), CBS, 1992.

"The Shell Game," *Fish Police* (animated), CBS, 1992.

(With others) "Como se escribe venganza?," *Matrimonio con hijos,* Cuatro, 2006.

Screenplays; Animated Films:
My Little Pony: Charming Birthday, SD Entertainment, 2003.

My Little Pony: Dancing in the Clouds, SD Entertainment, 2004.

My Little Pony: A Very Minty Christmas, Paramount Home Entertainment, 2005.

My Little Pony: Friends Are Never Far Away, SD Entertainment, 2006.

My Little Pony: Greetings from Unicornia (animated short film), SD Entertainment, 2006.

My Little Pony: The Princess Promenade, Paramount Home Entertainment, 2006.

My Little Pony: The Runaway Rainbow, SD Entertainment, 2006.

Stories:
(Contributor) Barbara Davilman and Liz Dubelman, editors, *What Was I Thinking? 58 Bad Boyfriend Stories,* St. Martin's Press, 2008.

ROSE, Jeff 1965–

PERSONAL

Born September 14, 1965, in Marietta, GA; son of Wayne and Dorrie Rose; married Tara (an actress), June

24, 2000; children: Kayla (an actress), Brody (an actor). *Education:* Attended Kennesaw State University; studied acting. *Religion:* Christian.

Addresses: *Agent*—Mystie Buice, Houghton Talent, 919 Collier Rd. NW, Atlanta, GA 30318–2533; People Store, 645 Lambert Dr., Atlanta, GA 30324.

Career: Actor, producer, casting director, and writer. Four Roses Entertainment, owner and film producer. HGTV (Home & Garden Television), host of a do it yourself tip, 2008; appeared in advertisements, infomercials, and industrial films. Public speaker at different venues.

Awards, Honors: Amazon Theater/Tribeca Short Film Competition finalist (with others), 2005, for *Battaglia;* Mason–Dixon Award, best actor, Dixie Film Festival, 2006, for *Blame Falls;* Mason–Dixon Award nomination, 2006, Secret City Film Festival Award, best family film, International Christian Film Festival Award, best dramatic film, and Southern Fried Flicks Festival, best short film: second place, all 2007, all with others, for *My Christmas Soldier;* 168 Hour Film Project and Festival Award nomination, best actor, 2010, for *The Party.*

CREDITS

Film Appearances:
Jimmy Turner, *Elysian Fields* (short film), Tapestry International, 1993.
Theodore Collins, *Sugar Creek Gang: Great Canoe Fish,* KOAN, 2004.
Theodore Collins, *Sugar Creek Gang: Swamp Robber,* KOAN, 2004.
Stanley, *Rorschach* (short film), The 48 Hour Film Project Atlanta, 2005.
Sydney Carter, *Battaglia* (short film), 2005.
Theodore Collins, *Sugar Creek Gang: Revival Villains* (also known as *Race against Nightfall*), KOAN, 2005.
Theodore Collins, *Sugar Creek Gang: Secret Hideout,* KOAN, 2005.
Theodore Collins, *Sugar Creek Gang: Teacher Trouble,* KOAN, 2005.
Captain Walker, *My Christmas Soldier* (short film), Dogwood Motion Picture Company/Four Roses Entertainment, 2006.
Man at the door, *Blame Falls* (short film), Digital Arts & Entertainment Lab, 2006.
Manny, *A Second Chance* (educational film), U.S. Department of Defense, 2007.
Preacher, *Blood Ties,* Media Arts International Film Corporation/Digital Film Design/My Thai Film, 2007.

Second young man, *Three Can Play That Game,* Sony Pictures, 2007.
Dr. Stewart, *Before I Wake* (short film), The Doorpost Film Project, 2008.
Loan officer, *The Family That Preys* (also known as *Tyler Perry's "The Family That Preys"*), Lionsgate, 2008.
Mr. Thompson, *Foreign Exchange* (short film), Creative Studies of Atlanta/Stella's Chief, c. 2008.
Frank, *No Limit Kids: Much Ado about Middle School* (also known as *Much Ado about Middle School*), Elevating Entertainment Motion Pictures/Moody Multimedia Group, 2010.
Jeremy Reece, *The Party* (short film), 168 Hour Film Project and Festival, 2010.
Dwayne Jenkins, *Goin' Green* (also known as *Going Green*), Raven Pro Media, c. 2010.

Appeared as Captain Seidel, *Astray,* Warped Wing Productions; as Sam, *The Collection Agents* (short film), Rellim Films; as Apollos, *Matinee of the Gods;* as George, *More Blessed,* Brightline Pictures; and as a police officer, *Split Second* (short film).

Film Producer:
Battaglia (short film), 2005.
Rorschach (short film), The 48 Hour Film Project Atlanta, 2005.
My Christmas Soldier (short film), Dogwood Motion Picture Company/Four Roses Entertainment, 2006.
Coproducer, *Hero* (also known as *One Good Man*), Brightline Pictures/Advent Film Group Movie One, 2010.

Film Casting Director:
My Christmas Soldier (short film), Dogwood Motion Picture Company/Four Roses Entertainment, 2006.
Hero (also known as *One Good Man*), Brightline Pictures/Advent Film Group Movie One, 2010.

Some sources state that Rose also worked as an electrician on films.

Television Appearances; Series:
Major Bryce Ogden, *Army Wives,* Lifetime, beginning 2008.
1860s minister, *God in America* (documentary), PBS, 2010.
Doug Resnick, *Drop Dead Diva,* Lifetime, beginning 2010.

Television Appearances; Miniseries:
Tommy, *Stay the Night,* ABC, 1992.

Television Appearances; Movies:
(Uncredited) Riot police officer, *Somebody Has to Shoot the Picture,* HBO, 1990.

(Uncredited) Volunteer firefighter, *Rising Son*, TNT, 1990.
(Uncredited) Member of courtroom audience, *Paris Trout* (also known as *Rage*), Showtime, 1991.
(Uncredited) Union soldier, *The Perfect Tribute*, ABC, 1991.
Benny Tarkenton, *Legal Briefs*, USA Network, 1993.
Boots Rogers, *The People v. Leo Frank*, PBS, 2009.

Television Appearances; Episodic:
Nathan Woods, "Child of Promise," *In the Heat of the Night*, NBC, 1991.
Johnny Strayhorn, "The Way Things Are," *I'll Fly Away*, NBC, 1992.
Bachelor number three, *The Dating Game*, syndicated, 1997.

Television Appearances; Pilots:
Tim (Lindsey's father), *Lindsey's Way*, c. 2009.

Stage Appearances:
First solider, *Life Is a Dream*, Actor's Express, Atlanta, GA, 1989.

Appeared as Peter Van Daan, *The Diary of Anne Frank*, as the man in white, *The House of Blue Leaves*, and as Curley, *Of Mice and Men*, all Theatre in the Square, Marietta, GA; as Tom, *Reckless*, Ramsey Actor's Canteen, Cherokee, NC; as Black Dog, *Treasure Island* (workshop), Alliance Theatre, Atlanta, GA; and in multiple roles, *Unto These Hills*, Mountainside Theatre, Cherokee, NC.

Major Tours:
Jesus, *Cotton Patch Gospel* (musical), U.S. cities, beginning 2008.

Appeared as father, *Catch'n a Dream*, European cities; and as Lucious Haggard, *Dead Man Living*, southeastern U.S. cities.

RECORDINGS

Videos:
Abusive husband and father, *Third Day Live in Concert: Live Wire*, Provident Distribution, 2004.

Host of training videos for Home Depot hardware stores and the Georgia Department of Transportation. Cohost for a recording by the North American Mission Board. Appeared in the music videos "It's a Shame," by Third Day, 2005; and as Nicolae Moldoveanu in "Break My Plants," by This Hope, 2006; producer of the music video "Cry Out to Jesus," by Third Day, c. 2005.

WRITINGS

Screenplays:
Battaglia (short film), 2005.

Teleplays; Episodic:
Some sources state that Rose wrote episodes of animated programs.

OTHER SOURCES

Periodicals:
Kennesaw State University Sentinel, January 19, 2005, p. 6.

Electronic:
Jeff Rose, http://www.jeffroseactor.com, March 19, 2010.

RUSSELL, Clive 1945–

PERSONAL

Born December 7, 1945, in Hampshire, England; raised in Fife, Scotland. *Education:* Trained as a teacher.

Career: Actor. Worked as a drama teacher, 1969–77. Appeared in commercials for Prudential insurance.

Awards, Honors: Genie Award nomination, best leading actor, Academy of Canadian Cinema and Television, 1996, for *Margaret's Museum*.

CREDITS

Television Appearances; Series:
Phil Nail, a recurring role, *Coronation Street*, ITV, between 1983 and 2006.
Tucker, *Finney*, ITV, 1994.
Archie, *Roughnecks*, 1994–95.
Bonner, *Atletico Partick*, BBC, 1995–96.
Duggie Strachen, *Heartburn Hotel*, BBC, 1998–2000.
Angus O'Connor, *Happiness*, BBC, 2001–2003.
Gordon Urquhart, a recurring role, *Rockface*, BBC America, 2002–2003.
Gary Turnbull, a recurring role, *Auf Wiedersehen, Pet*, BBC, 2004.
Jack Atwell, *According to Bex*, BBC, 2005.
MacPherson and other characters, *Mist: Sheepdog Tales*, between 2007 and 2009.

Television Appearances; Miniseries:

Jute City, BBC, 1991.

Adrian Fell, *Tell Tale Hearts,* BBC, 1992.

Caleb Garth, *Middlemarch,* PBS, 1994.

Mr. Vandemaar, *NeverWhere,* BBC, 1996.

Joe Gargery, *Great Expectations,* BBC, then PBS, 1999.

Scottish lawyer, *Oliver Twist,* ITV, 1999, then PBS, 2000.

Mark Dolby, *Hearts and Bones,* BBC, 2000.

Gorlois, Duke of Cornwall and Orkney, *The Mists of Avalon,* TNT, 2001.

Callum, *Being April,* BBC1, 2002.

Newson, *The Mayor of Casterbridge,* Arts and Entertainment, 2003.

Sheriff Brady, *The Wild West,* BBC, 2006.

Sparky, *Honest,* ITV, 2008.

Presbyterian preacher, *The Devil's Whore,* Channel 4, 2008.

Television Appearances; Movies:

Superintendent, *The Accidental Death of an Anarchist,* 1983.

(Uncredited) *The Alamut Ambush,* 1986.

Terry Knapp, *Tumbledown,* Arts and Entertainment, 1989.

Chief Inspector Ross, *Advocates I,* ITV, 1991.

Inspector Ross, *Advocates II,* 1992.

Krebs, *Fatherland,* HBO, 1994.

Prisoner, *Jolly a Man for All Seasons,* 1994.

Grazetti, *Ruffian Hearts,* BBC, 1995.

Arthur, *Lord of Misrule,* 1996.

Mick Boyd, *Crossing the Floor,* BBC, 1996.

Gordon Weir, *Flowers of the Forest,* BBC, 1996.

Station master, *The Railway Children,* PBS, 2000.

Gordon, *Faith,* BBC, 2005.

Ricky, *Heartless,* 2005.

MacPherson, *Mist: The Tale of a Sheepdog Puppy,* Channel 5, 2006.

Monsieur Roulin, *The Yellow House,* 2007.

Dave, *Joe's Palace,* BBC, 2007.

Television Appearances; Specials:

Lieutenant Ludwig von Hammerstein, "The July Plot," *The Wednesday Play,* BBC, 1964.

Mowat, "The Gift," *The Play on One,* 1989.

Alan Simpson, "Hancock," *Screen One,* BBC, 1991.

Chris Anderson, "Do Not Disturb," *Screen Two,* BBC, 1991.

Mac, "The Grass Arena," *Screen Two,* BBC, 1992.

Ronnie Black, "Seconds Out," *Screen One,* BBC, 1992.

Travis, "The Vision Thing," *Screenplay,* Granada Television, 1993.

The creature, *Frankenstein: The True Story,* Arts and Entertainment, 1994.

(In archive footage) Neil, *Weird Sex and Snowshoes: A Trek through the Canadian Cinematic Psyche,* 2004.

Coronation Street: The Grimshaw Family Album, ITV, 2007.

Television Appearances; Pilots:

Kevin Mott, *The Boss* (also known as *The Peter Principle*), BBC, 1995.

Television Appearances; Episodic:

Officer, "Consequences," *The Indian Tales of Rudyard Kipling,* BBC, 1964.

G's secretary, "Fish on the Hook," *Secret Agent* (also known as *Danger Man* and *Secret Agent aka Danger Man*), 1964.

Policeman, "Jobs for the Boys," *Boys from the Blackstuff,* BBC, 1982.

"One of Our Pigeons Is Missing," *Bulman,* ITV, 1985.

Captain Henry Stark, "Kidnapped," *Zorro,* The Family Channel, 1990.

Dave McCray, "Hiding Place," *Casualty,* BBC1, 1990.

Albie Sloeman, "Half a Ton of Heartaches," *Spender,* BBC, 1991.

Scotch Tommy, *Coronation Street,* ITV, 1991.

McReedy, "Re–Hab," *The Bill,* ITV1, 1992.

Detective Sergeant, "Joy," *Drop the Dead Donkey,* Channel 4, 1993.

Baxter, "Wheels," *Frank Stubbs Promotes,* ITV, 1993.

McVicar, "A Night Alarm," *The Tales of Para Handy,* BBC, 1994.

Mark Tabor, "Fair Exchange," *Lovejoy,* Arts and Entertainment, 1994.

William Swift, "Paying the Price," *The Bill,* ITV1, 1994.

Danny Fitzgerald, "Brotherly Love: Parts 1–3," *Cracker,* Arts and Entertainment, 1995.

Danny Fitzgerald, "Best Boys: Parts 1 & 2," *Cracker,* Arts and Entertainment, 1995.

Danny Fitzgerald, "True Romance: Parts 1 & 2," *Cracker,* Arts and Entertainment, 1995.

Tom, "The Bonny Bonny Banks," *Bad Boys,* BBC1, 1996.

Voice of Boaz, "Ruth," *Testament: The Bible in Animation,* HBO, 1996.

Detective Chief Superintendent Barratt, "Confess," *Murder Most Horrid,* BBC1, 1996.

Saddam the thug, "God Has Smiled Down on Me," *Sunnyside Farm,* BBC, 1997.

Kevin Mott, "Sex, Lies, and Videotape," *The Boss* (also known as *The Peter Principle*), BBC, 1997.

Kevin Mott, "Health Matters," *The Boss* (also known as *The Peter Principle*), BBC, 1997.

Frankie Brammer, "Wild," *Rab C. Nesbitt,* BBC, 1997.

Harry Douglas, *A Perfect Slate,* BBC, 1997.

Phil Jakes, *Hope & Glory,* BBC, 1999.

Big Eddy, "Wise Guys," *Heartbeat,* ITV, 2000.

Raymond, "White Knight," *Black Cab,* BBC, 2000.

Phil Jakes, *Hope & Glory,* BBC, four episodes, 2000.

Special Brew, " ... And a Good Slopping Out," *Lock, Stock ...,* Channel 4, 2000.

Brand Spanking New Show (also known as *Harry Enfield's Brand Spanking New Show*), Sky Television, 2000.

Damien Knox, "Change," *Spaced,* Channel 4, 2001.

Damien Knox, "Mettle," *Spaced,* Channel 4, 2001.

Damien Knox, "Help," *Spaced,* Channel 4, 2001.

Sandy Wilson, "Faith," *Where the Heart Is,* ITV, 2001.

Perry Coleman, "Burn Out: Parts 1 & 2," *Waking the Dead,* BBC, 2001.

Callum, *Being April,* BBC, 2002.

Deputy Chief Superintendent Tom Leith, "Answering Fire: Parts 1 & 2," *Silent Witness,* Arts and Entertainment, 2003.

Billy Wilson, *Shameless,* BBC America, 2004.

Innes, "Big Yin," *Still Game,* BBC, 2004.

Joe Allenson, "The Buck Stops Here," *Holby City,* BBC, 2004.

Peter Finlay, *Monarch of the Glen,* BBC America, 2005.

"Comic Relief Special," *My Family,* BBC America, 2005.

Professor Howard, "The Heart of Christmas," *My Family,* BBC America, 2006.

Billy McCabe, "The Sunny Side of the Street: Parts 1 & 2," *Casualty,* BBC1, 2006.

Victor Stone, "Blood Money," *The Bill,* ITV1, 2007.

Gary, *Secret Diary of a Call Girl,* Showtime, 2008.

Bayard, "The Poisoned Chalice," *Merlin* (also known as *The Adventures of Merlin*), NBC, 2008.

Mark, "The Old Flame," *The Old Guys,* BBC Scotland, 2009.

Barry, "Origin, Tonic," *No Heroics,* 2009.

Danny Travis, "Prodigal Son: Parts 1 & 2," *The Bill,* ITV1, 2009.

Seth Comfort, "Secrets and Spies," *Midsomer Murders,* Arts and Entertainment, 2009.

Christiano Cucci, *Hotel Babylon,* BBC America, 2009.

Jock, *Clatterford* (also known as *Jam & Jerusalem*), BBC, three episodes, 2009.

Frank Malloy, "Talk to Me," *Holby City,* BBC, 2010.

Frank Malloy, "A Glorious Reunion," *Holby City,* BBC, 2010.

Appeared in *The Shari Lewis Show,* NBC, 1960s.

Film Appearances:

Corporal Reade, *The Naked Brigade,* Universal, 1965.

Redskirts on Clydeside, 1984.

Sergeant Bormann, *The Power of One,* Warner Bros., 1992.

Clegg, *Soft Top, Hard Shoulder,* Gruber Bros., 1992.

Chief Inspector Daybury, *The Hawk,* Castle Hill, 1993.

Neil Currie, *Margaret's Museum,* Astra Cinema, 1995.

Miklos Rumbold, *For My Baby* (also known as *Goodnight Vienna*), 1997.

Theophilus Hopkins, *Oscar and Lucinda,* Fox Searchlight, 1997.

Billy Hunch, *Bodywork,* New City Releasing, 1999.

Alec the tramp, *My Life So Far,* Miramax, 1999.

Helfdane the Fat, *The 13th Warrior* (also known as *13 Warriors*), Buena Vista, 1999.

Tinker, *Out of Depth,* Steon Films, 2000.

Fraser, *Landmark,* 2001.

Mr. Michaelmas, *Mr. In-Between* (also known as *The Killing Kind*), Lions Gate Films Home Entertainment, 2002.

Sergeant Justin Bommel, *The Emperor's New Clothes,* Paramount, 2002.

Dennis Betts, *Silent Cry,* Starmedia Home Entertainment, 2002.

Thin man, *Mad Dogs,* 2002.

Angus MacKay, *The Rocket Post,* 2002, Hannover House, 2006.

Lancelot's father, *King Arthur* (also known as *King Arthur: Director's Cut*), Buena Vista, 2004.

Moon River Thompson, *Tumshie McFadgen's Bid for Ultimate Bliss* (short film), Plum Films, 2004.

Adam Penruddocke, *Ladies in Lavender,* Roadside Attractions, 2005.

Brother Mike, *Festival,* Pathe, 2005.

Cousin Finlay, *Made of Honor,* Columbia, 2008.

Hoffmeister, *Lesson 21* (also known as *Lezione 21*), RAI Cinema, 2008.

Wyburd, *Book of Blood* (also known as *Clive Barker's "Book of Blood"*), Lightning Home Entertainment, 2009.

Steve, *Beyond the Pole,* Shooting Pictures, 2009.

Captain Tanner, *Sherlock Holmes,* Warner Bros., 2009.

MacQueen, *The Wolfman,* Universal, 2010.

Mute McGill, *Cup Cake,* Wee Buns, 2010.

James Compston, *North Atlantic,* Monocle Studio, 2010.

Beame, *The Wicker Tree,* British Lion/Tressock Films, 2010.

Stage Appearances:

Harry Baylis and Bobby Cross, *The Dillen,* Royal Shakespeare Company, Other Place Theatre, Stratford-upon-Avon, England, 1985.

Ajax, *Troilus and Cressida,* Royal Shakespeare Company, Royal Shakespeare Theatre, Stratford-upon-Avon, 1985, then Barbican Theatre, London, 1986.

The Dumb Waiter, Royal Shakespeare Company, Almeida Theatre, London, 1986.

Otto, *Mephisto,* Royal Shakespeare Company, Barbican Theatre, 1986.

Edward, *Heresies,* Royal Shakespeare Company, Pit Theatre, 1986.

Alberto Fava, *Principia Scriptoriae,* Royal Shakespeare Company, Pit Theatre, 1986.

Fly, *The New Inn,* Royal Shakespeare Company, Swan Theatre, Stratford-upon Avon, 1987, then People's Theatre, Newcastle-upon-Tyne, England, 1988.

Ernst Oizermann, *A Question of Geography,* Royal Shakespeare Company, Other Place Theatre, 1987, then Gulbenkian Studio, Newcastle-upon-Tyne, 1988, later Pit Theatre, 1988.

Eric Bright, *Fashion,* Royal Shakespeare Company, Other Place Theatre, 1987, then Pit Theatre, 1988.

Macluby, *The Bite of the Night,* Royal Shakespeare Company, Pit Theatre, 1988.

Bill, *Earwig,* Royal Shakespeare Company, Pit Theatre, 1990.

Jim Rhys, *The Bright and Bold Design,* Royal Shakespeare Company, Pit Theatre, 1991.

RUSSO, James 1953–
(Jim Russo)

PERSONAL

Full name, James Vincent Russo; born April 23, 1953, in borough of Queens, New York, NY; married Bettina, 1995; children: two. *Education:* Attended New York University.

Addresses: *Agent*—United Talent Agency, 9560 Wilshire Blvd., Suite 500, Beverly Hills, CA 90212.

Career: Actor, producer, and writer. Also worked as a cab driver and gravedigger.

Awards, Honors: *Theatre World* Award, 1983, for *Extremities;* Festival Award, best actor, San Diego Film Festival, 2004, for *The Box.*

CREDITS

Film Appearances:

Robber, *Fast Times at Ridgemont High* (also known as *Fast Times*), Universal, 1982.

Ronald Thompson, *A Stranger Is Watching,* United Artists, 1982.

Nick, *Exposed,* United Artists, 1983.

Anthony Demmer, *Vortex,* B Movies, 1983.

Bugsy, *Once upon a Time in America,* Warner Bros., 1984.

Mikey Tandino, *Beverly Hills Cop,* Paramount, 1984.

Vince Hood, *The Cotton Club,* Orion, 1984.

Joe, *Extremities,* Atlantic Releasing, 1986.

Alberto "Alby" Monte, *China Girl,* Vestron, 1987.

Reno, *The Blue Iguana,* Paramount, 1988.

Frank Quinn, *Freeway,* New World Entertainment, 1988.

Vittorio de Simone, *La cintura,* 1989.

Teddy, *The Vineyard,* 1989.

Bobby, *We're No Angels,* Paramount, 1989.

(Uncredited) DeMarco, *State of Grace,* Orion, 1990.

Richard Waters, *My Own Private Idaho,* Fine Line, 1991.

Dan Corelli, *A Kiss before Dying,* Universal, 1991.

Daniel Corvin, *Cold Heaven,* Hemdale Releasing, 1992.

Bill Tanner, *Illicit Behavior* (also known as *Criminal Intent*), Prism Entertainment, 1992.

Captain Travis, *Trauma* (also known as *Dario Argento's "Trauma"*), Worldvision Home Video, 1992.

Francis Burns, *Dangerous Game* (also known as *Snake Eyes*), Metro–Goldwyn–Mayer, 1993.

Mintz, *Da Vinci's War,* Triboro Entertainment, 1993.

Kid Jarrett, *Bad Girls,* Twentieth Century–Fox, 1994.

Rodgers, *Panther,* Gramercy, 1995.

Dan Cappelli, *Condition Red,* Arrow Releasing, 1995.

Jerry, *Small Time* (also known as *Waiting for the Man*), 1995.

Eddie (some sources cite Harv), *American Strays,* A–Pix Entertainment, 1996.

Rupert Little, *Livers Ain't Cheap* (also known as *The Real Thing*), Windy City International, 1997.

Idaho, *The Postman,* Warner Bros., 1997.

Paulie, *Donnie Brasco* (also known as *Fake*), TriStar, 1997.

Tommy, *No Way Home,* Live Entertainment, 1997.

Nick the Stick, *Heist,* Trident Releasing, 1997.

Warren Erickson, *Under Oath* (also known as *Blood Money* and *Urban Justice*), Concorde/New Horizons, 1997.

Joe Massa, *BitterSweet,* Pioneer Entertainment, 1998.

Jukebox Danny, *Butter* (also known as *Never 2 Big*), Live Entertainment, 1998.

Ziggy Rotella, *Detour* (also known as *Too Hard to Die*), October Films/Shoreline Entertainment, 1998.

Max Targenville, *Charades* (also known as *Felons* and *First Degree*), York Entertainment, 1998.

Luc, *Fait Accompli* (also known as *VooDoo Dawn*), Cutting Edge Entertainment, 1998.

Otis Campbell, *Jimmy Zip,* The Asylum, 1999.

Bernie, *The Ninth Gate,* Live Entertainment, 1999, Artisan Entertainment, 2000.

(Uncredited) Damian, *Diamonds,* Miramax, 1999.

Agent Nick Halton, *Sonic Impact,* New City Releasing, 1999.

Mickey Vernon, *The Unscarred* (also known as *Everybody Dies*), Storm Entertainment, 1999.

John Rourke, *Paper Bullets* (also known as *American Samurai*), MTI Home Video, 1999.

Darryl Simmons, *Deep Core* (also known as *Deep Core 2000*), Paramount/New City Releasing, 2000.

John Tykor, *Bad Guys,* 2000.

Edward Mills, *Pendulum,* DEJ Productions, 2001.

Snake, *Double Deception* (also known as *24 Hours to Die*), Phaedra Cinema, 2001.

Sam, *Shattered Lies,* F.T.L. Films, 2002.

Carl Schmidt, *The House Next Door,* Trinity Home Entertainment, 2002.

Mr. Quinn, *My Daughter's Tears* (also known as *Against All Evidence*), Capture Film, 2002.

Roy, *A Good Night to Die,* DEJ Productions, 2003.

Leon King, *Paris,* DEJ Productions, 2003.

Frank Miles, *The Box,* Local Talent Productions, 2003.

Captain Grill, *Redemption,* 2003.
Sheriff Poole, *Open Range,* Buena Vista, 2003.
Agent, *Short* (short film), Dog Party Productions, 2003.
Donovan, *Target,* First Look International, 2004.
Fallacy, Around the Scenes Releasing, 2004.
Ryan Brannigan, *One among Us,* The Asylum, 2005.
Benny, *Come as You Are,* Eleventh Hour Productions, 2005.
Sharkey, *Confessions of a Pit Fighter,* 2005, Lions Gate Films, 2008.
Gonzo, *Cut Off,* Little Film Company, 2006.
Eddie, *Satanic,* Lions Gate Films Home Entertainment, 2006.
David Sanchez, *Shut Up and Shoot!,* IndustryWorks Distribution, 2006.
The bishop, *Blackwater Valley Exorcism,* Lions Gate Films/Barnholtz Entertainment, 2006.
Detective Defazio, *Chill,* Starmedia Home Entertainment, 2007.
Dr. Pennington, *All In,* MTI Home Video, 2007.
Sheriff Jack, *Blue Lake Massacre,* Grindstone Entertainment Group, 2007.
Butch, *Machine,* Artist View Entertainment, 2007.
Cox, *The Pink Conspiracy,* Cinema Epoch/Film Planet Entertainment, 2007.
Mr. Santucci, *The Hit,* Universal, 2007.
Janitor, *On the Doll,* Peace Arch Entertainment, 2008.
Charlie, *Dark World,* Image Entertainment, 2008.
Mr. Trundell, *Little Red Devil,* Boll World Sales, 2008, R–Squared Films, 2009.
Englehart, *Stiletto* (also known as *Velvet Spider*), First Look International, 2008.
Commander Combs, *Black Ops* (also known as *Deadwater*), First Look International, 2008.
The father, *Break,* Film Planet Entertainment, 2008.
Tom Reeser, *Born of Earth,* Lightning Home Entertainment, 2008.
McGurk, *Shoot First and Pray You Live (Because Luck Has Nothing to Do with It),* Grindstone Entertainment Group, 2008.
Ramsey, *Kings of the Evening,* Indican Pictures, 2009.
Rocco, *Charlie Valentine,* American Media Group/Gorilla Pictures, 2009.
Peter Elias, *Good God Bad Dog* (short film), Stonelock Pictures/Tripod Entertainment, 2009.
Jimmy, *Never Surrender,* Lions Gate Films, 2009.
Walter Dietrich, *Public Enemies,* Universal, 2009.
Sheriff Demming, *Dark Woods,* Nom de Plume Films, 2009.
Ramsey, *Street Poet,* Indican Pictures, 2010.
John Brunette, *Dreams and Shadows,* Synkronized, 2010.
Jimmy, *One in the Gun,* Manmade Entertainment Productions, 2010.
Larry Childs, *Boy Wonder,* Boy Wonder Films, 2010.
Lorenzo De'mon, *Love Sick Diaries,* Ola Pictures, 2010.
An American Hero, Time Factor Pictures, 2010.
Sam, *7E,* 249 Productions, 2010.
Claudius, *The One Warrior,* 2010.

Also appeared in prize–winning short film *Candy Store,* produced at New York University.

Film Producer:
The Box, Local Talent Productions, 2003.

Television Appearances; Movies:
Chicago Story, 1981.
Charlie Van, *In the Shadow of a Killer,* NBC, 1992.
Nick Ciccini, *Intimate Stranger,* Showtime, 1992.
Don Feeney, *Desperate Rescue: The Cathy Mahone Story,* NBC, 1992.
Jon Kane (some sources cite Joshua Kane), *Double Deception,* NBC, 1993.
Ted Burke, *The Secretary,* CBS, 1995.
Kliff, *The Set Up,* Showtime, 1995.
Sal Bianculli, *My Husband's Secret Life,* USA Network, 1998.
Brannagin, *The Girl Gets Moe* (also known as *Love to Kill*), HBO, 1998.
Gino Carlucci, *Laws of Deception,* Cinemax, 1999.
Matt Forman, *Hidden War,* 2000.
Frank Sinatra, Sr., *Stealing Sinatra,* Showtime, 2003.

Television Appearances; Miniseries:
Giuseppe, *Un siciliano in Sicilia,* 1987.
Captain Billy Fender, *Broken Trail,* AMC, 2006.
Jeb Dallas, *The Capture of the Green River Killer,* Lifetime, 2008.

Television Appearances; Pilots:
Victor Mura, *Falcone,* CBS, 2000.
Hate, Showtime, 2005.
Robert Franzine, *Dark Blue,* TNT, 2009.

Television Appearances; Episodic:
(As Jim Russo) Police detective, "China Rain," *The Equalizer,* 1985.
Frank Sacco, "Prodigal Son," *Miami Vice,* NBC, 1985.
Nat Martino, "Ground Zero," *Crime Story,* 1987.
Janos Korda, "Symphony in B#," *Friday the 13th,* syndicated, 1988.
Charles Crowley, "Belly of the Beast," *Gabriel's Fire,* 1991.
Frank Saretti, "Eight Pounds of Pressure," *C–16: FBI,* ABC, 1997.
Sinclair, "Getting Off," *CSI: Crime Scene Investigation* (also known as *C.S.I.* and *CSI: Las Vegas*), CBS, 2004.
Michael Krauss, "Lost and Found," *Without a Trace* (also known as *W.A.T.*), CBS, 2004.
James Karon, "Trial and Error," *Joan of Arcadia,* CBS, 2005.
Warren Pemberton, "The Story of Owe," *Las Vegas,* NBC, 2006.
Joey Salucci, "Fade Out," *CSI: Miami,* CBS, 2006.
Joey Salucci, "Wrecking Crew," *CSI: Miami,* CBS, 2008.

John Curtis, "12:01 AM," *Numb3rs* (also known as *Num3ers*), CBS, 2009.

Appeared as Tommy Bats in an episode of *Dellaventura,* CBS.

Stage Appearances:
Welcome to Andromeda, 1975.
Raul, *Extremities,* Westside Theatre Upstairs, Westside Arts Center, New York City, 1982–83.

Also appeared in productions of *Deathwatch* and *Marat/Sade.*

RECORDINGS

Videos:
(In archive footage) *Playboy: Farrah Fawcett, All of Me,* 1997.

WRITINGS

Film:
The Box, Local Talent Productions, 2003.

Author of the prize–winning short film *Candy Store.*

S

SADOSKI, Thomas 1976–
(Tom Sadoski)

PERSONAL

Born July 1, 1976, in Bethany, CT. *Education:* Trained at Circle in the Square Theatre School, New York City.

Addresses: *Agent*—United Talent Agency, 9560 Wilshire Blvd., Suite 500, Beverly Hills, CA 90212.

Career: Actor.

Awards, Honors: Drama Desk Award nomination, outstanding actor in a play, 2009, for *Reasons to Be Pretty;* Lucille Lortel Award nomination, outstanding featured actor, League of Off–Broadway Theatres and Producers, 2009, for *Becky Shaw.*

CREDITS

Film Appearances:
(As Tom Sadoski) Chris, *Loser,* Columbia, 2000.
Scott, *Happy Hour,* O'Hara/Klein Releasing, 2003.
Chris Bender, *Winter Solstice,* Paramount, 2004.
Corporal Richard Mundy, *Company K,* 2004, Indican Pictures, 2008.
Felix Canavan, *The New Twenty,* Wolfe Releasing, 2009.
Julian, *30 Beats,* Latitude 49 Production/Black Nexxus/ Worldview Entertainment, 2010.

Television Appearances; Series:
Jesse Calhoun, a recurring role, *As the World Turns,* CBS, 2007.

Television Appearances; Episodic:
Robert Barnes, "Criminal Law," *Law & Order,* NBC, 2005.
Patrick Cardell, "Lonelyville," *Law & Order: Criminal Intent* (also known as *Law & Order: CI*), USA Network, 2007.
Ryan the caterer, "Dress for Success," *Ugly Betty,* ABC, 2009.
Joe Thagard, "Anchor," *Law & Order: Special Victims Unit* (also known as *Law & Order: SVU* and *Special Victims Unit*), NBC, 2009.

Television Appearances; Specials:
The Visa Signature Tony Awards Season Celebration, CBS, 2009.
The 63rd Annual Tony Awards, CBS, 2009.

Stage Appearances:
Understudy for male roles, *This Is Our Youth,* Second Stage Theatre, McGinn–Cazale Theatre, New York City, 1998–99.
Randy Hastings, *Gemini,* Second Stage Theatre, 1999.
The Skin of Our Teeth, Williamstown Theatre Festival, Adams Memorial Theatre, Williamstown, MA, 2001.
Timothy Matlock and Pauling, *The General from America,* Alley Theatre, then Theatre for a New Audience, Lucille Lortel Theatre, New York City, 2002.
Where We're Born, Rattlestick Theatre, New York City, 2003.
Tom, Tom, Jr., and man in ski mask, *Reckless,* Manhattan Theatre Club and Second Stage Theatre, Biltmore Theatre (now Samuel J. Friedman Theatre), New York City, 2004.
Paul, *Jump/Cut,* Women's Project, Julia Miles Theatre, New York City, 2006.
Buddy, *The Mistakes Madeline Made,* Naked Angels, Forty–Five Bleecker Street Theatre, New York City, 2006.
Ty, *All This Intimacy,* Second Stage Theatre, McGinn–Cazale Theatre, 2006.

Greg, *Reasons to Be Pretty,* Manhattan Class Company, Lucille Lortel Theatre, 2008, then Lyceum Theatre, New York City, 2009.

Andrew, *Becky Shaw,* Second Stage Theatre, 2009.

Stephano, *The Tempest,* Harvey Theatre, Brooklyn Academy of Music, New York City, 2010.

Appeared in productions of *The American Clock* and *The Winter's Tale,* Circle in the Square, New York City, and in *Dissonance, Hot L Baltimore, Rodney's Wife,* and *Street Scene,* all Williamstown Theatre Festival; also appeared in *The Joke,* Studio Dante; *Left,* New York Stage and Film Theatre, New York City; *Man Measures Man,* Lark Theatre; *Moonlight and Magnolias,* Alliance Theatre Company, Atlanta, GA; *Santaland Diaries; Stay; Thunderbird,* Cherry Lane Theatre, New York City; *The Waverly Gallery,* Long Wharf Theatre, New Haven, CT.

Internet Appearances; Series:

Joe, *Circledrawers,* Poppolipictures.com, 2009.

SAMPSON, Paul

PERSONAL

Education: Earned M.B.A.; studied voice and movement with Bernard Rheele; also trained with Donald Buka, Carlton Coyer, and Liz Dixon. *Avocational Interests:* Kick–boxing, physical conditioning.

Career: Actor, producer, director, and writer. Also worked a stunt performer, casting director, and script consultant. Teacher of acting classes to children with autism spectrum disorder.

Member: Actors' Equity Association, Screen Actors Guild, American Federation of Television and Radio Artists, Writers Guild of America.

CREDITS

Film Appearances:

Club patron, *Beauty School,* Imperial Entertainment, 1993.

Gabriel's friend, *Let It Be Me,* Savoy Pictures, 1995.

(Uncredited) Pruitt, *Bullet,* New Line Cinema, 1996.

Petey, *Detour,* October Films, 1998.

Matt, *If You Only Knew,* Allumination Filmworks, 2000.

The waiter, *Enemies of Laughter,* 2000, Outrider Pictures, 2003.

Tony Cicero, *Whacked!,* THINKFilm, 2002.

Joey Pants, *Deuces Wild,* Metro–Goldwyn–Mayer/United Artists, 2002.

Himself, *Back to One* (short film), Twangy Bass Films, 2002.

Officer Danny Boblinka, *The Story of Bob* (short film), Area 51 Films, 2005.

Eric Layton, *Final Move* (also known as *Checkmate*), Imageworks Entertainment International, 2006.

Ivan, *Blonde Ambition,* First Look International, 2007.

Gordy McGraw, *Hero Wanted,* Sony Pictures Entertainment, 2008.

Paul Canales, *My Mom's New Boyfriend* (also known as *Homeland Security* and *My Spy*), Sony Pictures Home Entertainment, 2008.

Shamus the clown, *Clown* (short film), Boost Mobile, 2008.

Richie, *Wrong Turn at Tahoe,* Paramount Home Entertainment, 2009.

Lord Gregoire and Jake McCallister, *Night of the Templar,* Sampson Enterprises, 2010.

Bruku, *Tales of an Ancient Empire* (also known as *Abelar: Tales of an Ancient Empire*), KIPPJK, 2010.

Film Work:

Producer, director, and stunt coordinator, *Night of the Templar,* Sampson Enterprises, 2010.

Television Appearances; Movies:

Tony, *Laws of Deception,* Cinemax, 1999.

Matt Henderson, *Mel,* HBO, 2000.

Nathan, *Skeleton Man,* Sci–Fi Channel, 2004.

Television Appearances; Episodic:

Title role, "Bugsy Siegel," *E! Mysteries & Scandals,* E! Entertainment Television, 1998.

Driver, "No Guts, No Glory," *Hawthorne,* TNT, 2009.

Television Appearances; Series:

The Keeper Paul Sampson, *UWF Fury Hour,* 1990.

Stage Appearances:

Appeared as Lennie Small in one production of the play *Of Mice and Men,* and as George Milton in another production of the play.

WRITINGS

Screenplays:

Whacked!, THINKFilm, 2002.

Night of the Templar, Sampson Enterprises, 2010.

Other film scripts include *Victory Rose.*

OTHER SOURCES

Electronic:

Paul Sampson Official Site, http://www.paulsampson.net, June 11, 2010.

SANCHEZ, Petra
    See ERNETA, GiGi

SCARFE, Jonathan 1975–
    (Jon Scarfe)

PERSONAL

Full name, Jonathan J. Scarfe; born December 16, 1975, in Toronto, Ontario, Canada; son of Alan (an actor) and Sara (an actress; maiden name, Botsford) Scarfe; stepson of Barbara March (an actress); married Suki Kaiser (an actress), August 30, 1998; children: two. *Education:* Studied acting at Stratford Festival, Stratford, Ontario, Canada.

Addresses: *Agent*—Writers and Artists Agency, 8383 Wilshire Blvd., Suite 550, Beverly Hills, CA 90211; Greene & Associates Talent Agency, 190 N. Canon Dr., Suite 202, Beverly Hills, CA 90210. *Manager*—Jackson–Medavoy Entertainment, 9415 Culver Blvd., Culver City, CA 90232.

Career: Actor, producer, director, and writer. Sometimes credited as Jon Scarfe.

Awards, Honors: Gemini Award nomination, best performance by an actor in a leading role in a dramatic program or miniseries, Academy of Canadian Cinema and Television, 1998, for *The Morrison Murders;* Gemini Award nomination, best performance by an actor in a featured supporting role in a dramatic program or miniseries, 1998, for *White Lies;* Gemini Award, best performance by an actor in a leading role in a dramatic program or miniseries, 2000, for *The Sheldon Kennedy Story;* Leo Award nomination (with Suki Kaiser), best screenwriter, Best of Dances With Films Award (with Kaiser), short film, 2001, both for *Speak;* Gemini Award nomination, best performance by an actor in a leading role in a dramatic program, 2005, for *Burn: The Robert Wraight Story;* Gemini Award, best performance by an actor in a featured supporting role, 2007, for *Above and Beyond.*

CREDITS

Television Appearances; Movies:
First Tekkid, *TekWar: TekLab,* syndicated, 1994.
Destiny's son, *Sodbusters,* 1994.
Luke Morrison, *The Morrison Murders* (also known as *The Morrison Murders: Based on a True Story*), USA Network, 1996.

Keith, *Breaking the Surface: The Greg Louganis Story,* USA Network, 1997.
Jimmy Romeo, *Daughters* (also known as *Our Mother's Murder*), USA Network, 1997.
Jimmy, *Dead Innocent* (also known as *Eye*), HBO, 1998.
Ian McKee, *White Lies,* CBC, 1998.
Steve Fisher, *The Wrong Girl,* NBC, 1999.
Title role, *The Sheldon Kennedy Story* (also known as *Un reve abime*), CTV, 1999.
Peter Kafelnikoff (Russian mobster), *Blood Money,* The Movie Channel, 1999.
Kenny Baker, *Code Name Phoenix,* UPN, 2000.
Grant Rankin (Grunt), *100 Days in the Jungle,* 2002.
Title role, *Burn: The Robert Wraight Story* (also known as *Terres brulantes: L'histoire de Robert Wraight*), CTV, 2003.
Danny, *Mafia Doctor* (also known as *Family Doctor*), CBS, 2003.
Andrew MacDonald, *The Clinic* (also known as *Animal Clinic*), Animal Planet, 2004.
Jesus Christ, *Judas,* ABC, 2004.
Sam Buckner, *Proof of Lies,* Lifetime, 2006.
Dwight Collier, *Carolina Moon* (also known as *Nora Robert's "Carolina Moon"*), Lifetime, 2007.
Cal Taylor, *Vipers,* Sci–Fi Channel, 2008.
Kurt Warnecke, *Hidden Crimes,* 2009.

Television Appearances; Series:
R. J. Winslow, *Madison,* Global TV, 1994–95.
Chase Carter, a recurring role, *ER,* NBC, 1997–98.
Charlie Sagansky, *Raising the Bar,* TNT, 2008–2009.

Appeared as Rolf in the series *Family Passions* (also known as *Macht der Leidenschaft*), CTV.

Television Appearances; Episodic:
First Dogtown boy, "The Future of Law Enforcement: Parts 1 & 2," *Robocop* (also known as *Robocop: The Series*), syndicated, 1994.
Alan Kelly, "Courage," *Highlander: The Series* (also known as *Highlander*), syndicated, 1994.
"The Warrior," *Hawkeye,* syndicated, 1995.
Toby Finch, "Thicker Than Water," *Lonesome Dove: The Outlaw Years,* syndicated, 1995.
Jamie Carlson, "Game, Set, Murder," *Murder, She Wrote,* CBS, 1995.
"She Was," *Strange Luck,* Fox, 1995.
Charlie Walters, "Straight and Narrow," *The Outer Limits* (also known as *The New Outer Limits*), Showtime and syndicated, 1996.
Ted Manos, "Ted and Carey's Bogus Adventure," *NYPD Blue,* ABC, 1996.
Lucas Dumont, "Lives in the Balance," *Poltergeist: The Legacy,* Showtime, Sci–Fi Channel, and syndicated, 1997.
Ted Hardy, "Who's Poppa?," *Total Security,* ABC, 1997.

Lucas Dumont, "Darkside," *Poltergeist: The Legacy,* Showtime, Sci–Fi Channel, and syndicated, 1998.

Quinn Montgomery, "Murder at Midterm," *Diagnosis Murder,* CBS, 1999.

Vince, "Gettysburg," *The Outer Limits* (also known as *The New Outer Limits*), Showtime and syndicated, 2000.

Chase Carter, "Surrender," *ER,* NBC, 2001.

Chester Nolan/Uncle/Joey/Alexa/Big Steve, "The Others," *Gideon's Crossing,* ABC, 2001.

Agent Wyman, "The Grand Alliance," *Tom Stone* (also known as *Stone Undercover*), 2002.

Tommy Cabretti, "There's No Business Like No Business," *Philly,* ABC, 2002.

Arnold Milbank, "Full Moon," *The Division* (also known as *Heart of the City*), NBC, 2002.

Dean Wilder, "A Town without Pity," *The Peacemakers,* USA Network, 2003.

Matt, "Listen Up," *The L Word,* Showtime, 2004.

Matt, "Liberally," *The L Word,* Showtime, 2004.

Chase Shaw, "Legal," *CSI: Miami* (also known as *CSI: Weekends*), CBS, 2004.

Logan, "Babe in the Woods," *Dr. Vegas,* CBS, 2005.

Hank, "Shake Your Groove Thing," *Grey's Anatomy,* ABC, 2005.

Richard Laughlin, "State of the Unions," *Commander in Chief,* ABC, 2006.

Ken Scott, "Hubris," *Crossing Jordan,* NBC, 2007.

Will Paige '38, "World's End," *Cold Case,* CBS, 2007.

Robert Queen, "Veritas," *Smallville* (also known as *Smallville Beginnings* and *Smallville: Superman the Early Years*), The WB, 2008.

Also appeared as Cypher, "Mob.com," *Level 9;* Fred, "Betty," *The Atwood Stories.*

Television Appearances; Miniseries:

General George Armstrong Custer, *Into the West,* TNT, 2005.

Bill Jacobson, *Above and Beyond,* CBC, 2006.

Television Appearances; Pilots:

Earl, *Roadie,* ABC, 1996.

Charlie Sagansky, *Raising the Bar,* TNT, 2008.

Also appeared as Cole Farris, *Conspiracy,* Lifetime.

Film Appearances:

Leland, *Boogie Boy,* Sterling Home Entertainment, 1998.

Cop, *Twilight,* Paramount, 1998.

Young Derek, *The Lesser Evil,* Orion Home Entertainment, 1998.

Malcolm, *Short for Nothing,* 1998.

David "Dave" Hiatt, *Crosswalk* (short film), Shel Lar Films, 1999.

Bill Tollman, *Liberty Stands Still* (also known as *Liberty stands still–Im Visier des Moerders*), Lions Gate Films, 2002.

Skipper Day, *Slap Shot 2: Breaking the Ice,* Universal Home Entertainment, 2002.

Michael Skid, *The Bay of Love and Sorrows* (also known as *La baie de l'amour et des regrets*), Odeon Films, 2002.

Joseph Smith, *The Work and the Glory,* Excel Entertainment, 2004.

Joseph Smith, *The Work and the Glory II: American Zion,* Vineyard Distribution, 2005.

Joseph Smith, *The Work and the Glory III: A House Divided,* Excel Entertainment, 2006.

Oscar Koenig, *The Poet* (also known as *Hearts of War*), Image Entertainment, 2007.

Nicholas Brady, *Radio Free Albemuth,* 2009.

Also appeared in the film *Sodbusters.*

Film Work:

(With Sukie Kaiser) Producer and director, *Speak* (short film), Spacecake Productions, 2001.

Stage Appearances:

Gordon, *Absolution,* Los Angeles, 1999.

Billy, *The Real Thing,* Alley Theatre, Houston, TX, 2000.

Puck, *A Midsummer Night's Dream,* Alley Theatre, 2000.

Appeared as understudy for the role of Dumaine, *Love's Labour's Lost,* in *Measure for Measure,* as the reaper in *The Tempest,* and as understudy for the role of Serebreyakov, *Uncle Vanya,* all Stratford Festival, Stratford, Ontario, Canada; appeared in *King Lear, Macbeth,* and *Othello,* all Los Angeles Shakespeare Festival, Los Angeles.

WRITINGS

Screenplays:

(With Sukie Kaiser), *Speak* (short film), Spacecake Productions, 2001.

SCHREIBER, Pablo 1978–
(Pablo T. Schreiber)

PERSONAL

Full name, Pablo Tell Schreiber; born April 26, 1978, in Seattle, WA; son of Tell Schreiber (an actor); half brother of Liev Schreiber (an actor); married Jessica

Monty (an actress), 2008; children: one son. *Education:* Carnegie Mellon University, B.F.A., acting/musical theatre, 2000; once enrolled in the University of San Francisco.

Addresses: *Agent*—International Creative Management, 10250 Constellation Way, Ninth Floor, Los Angeles, CA 90067 and 825 Eighth Ave., New York, NY 10019. *Manager*—D/F Management, 270 Lafayette St., Suite 402, New York, NY 10012.

Career: Actor. Performed as a rapper at schools.

Awards, Honors: Drama Desk Award (with others), outstanding ensemble performance, and Antoinette Perry Award nomination, best featured actor in a play, both 2006, for *Awake and Sing!;* Drama League Award nomination, distinguished performance, 2007, for *Dying City;* Drama Desk Award, outstanding featured actor in a play, 2009, for *Reasons to Be Pretty.*

CREDITS

Stage Appearances:
Balm in Gilead, Carnegie Mellon University, Pittsburgh, PA, 1999–2000.

The Country Wife, Carnegie Mellon University, 1999–2000.

Three Sisters, Carnegie Mellon University, 1999–2000.

(As Pablo T. Schreiber) A cobbler, *Julius Caesar,* New York Shakespeare Festival, Joseph Papp Public Theatre, Delacorte Theatre, New York City, 2000.

(As Pablo T. Schreiber) Clinton, *Blood Orange,* Blue Heron Arts Center, New York City, 2001.

(As Pablo T. Schreiber) Patrick McSorley, *Sin (A Cardinal Deposed)* (also known as *Sin*), New Group, Clurman Theatre, New York City, 2004.

David Lewis, *Manuscript,* Daryl Roth Theatre, New York City, 2005.

Larry, *Mr. Marmalade,* Roundabout Theatre Company, Laura Pels Theatre, New York City, 2005–2006.

Peter, *The Sunday Times,* produced as part of *The 24 Hour Plays 2006* (benefit), American Airlines Theatre, New York City, 2006.

Ralph Berger, *Awake and Sing!,* Belasco Theatre, New York City, 2006.

Peter and Craig, *Dying City,* Lincoln Center, Mitzi E. Newhouse Theatre, New York City, 2007.

Jim, *Molly, Nellie, Jim and Saul,* produced as part of *The 24 Hour Plays 2008* (benefit), American Airlines Theatre, 2008.

Kent, *Reasons to Be Pretty* (also known as *reasons to be pretty*), Manhattan Class Company, Lucille Lortel Theatre, New York City, 2008.

Eben Cabot, *Desire under the Elms,* Goodman Theatre, Chicago, IL, and St. James Theatre, New York City, both 2009.

Appeared in other productions, including *Frankie and Johnny in the Clair de Lune,* Carnegie Mellon University; appeared as Benny Southstreet, *Guys and Dolls* (musical), Ragpicker, *The Madwoman of Chaillot,* Tevye, *Fiddler on the Roof* (musical), and in *Arms and the Man,* all Seattle, WA, area, all c. 1990s.

Film Appearances:
Todd, *Bubble Boy,* Buena Vista, 2001.

Eddie Ingram, *The Manchurian Candidate,* Paramount, 2004.

Kazimierz "Kaz" Malek, *Invitation to a Suicide,* 2004, Digital Shadow Films, 2008.

Sandy Manetti, *Into the Fire,* Slowhand Cinema Releasing, 2005.

Stecyk, *Lords of Dogtown* (also known as *American Knights* and *Dogtown Boys*), TriStar/Sony Pictures Entertainment, 2005.

Title role, *Jimmy Blue* (short film), Beech Hill Films, 2006.

Ben, *Vicky Cristina Barcelona* (also known as *Midnight in Barcelona* and *Woody Allen Spanish Project*), The Weinstein Company, 2008.

Brooster, *Quid Pro Quo,* Magnolia Pictures, 2008.

Charlie Torrelson, *Nights in Rodanthe,* Warner Bros., 2008.

David, *Favorite Son,* 2008, Panorama Entertainment, c. 2009.

Ricky Falcone, *It's Always Sunny in Philadelphia: A Very Sunny Christmas,* Twentieth Century–Fox Television, 2009.

Williams Bernard Cochius, *Tell Tale* (also known as *Tell–Tale*), Quality Films, 2009.

Turner, *Breaking Upwards,* Sacher Film, 2009, IFC Films, 2010.

Charlie, *happythankyoumoreplease* (also known as *HappyThankYouMorePlease*), Paper Street Films/Tom Sawyer Entertainment/Back Lot Pictures, 2010.

Christian Valentino, *After,* Girl's Gotta Eat Entertainment, 2011.

Film Work:
Coproducer, *Favorite Son,* 2008, Panorama Entertainment, c. 2009.

Television Appearances; Series:
Nickolas "Nick" Sobotka, *The Wire* (also known as *A escuta, Drot, Langalla, Oi dioktes tou eglimatos,* and *Sur ecoute*), HBO, 2003–2008.

Johnny, *Lights Out,* FX Network, beginning 2011.

Television Appearances; Movies:
Brent, *The Mudge Boy,* Showtime, 2003.
Strip Search, HBO, 2004.

Television Appearances; Specials:
Hank Spruill, "A Painted House" (also known as "John Grisham's 'A Painted House'"), *Hallmark Hall of*

Fame (also known as *Hallmark Television Play-house*), CBS, 2003.

Television Appearances; Episodic:

Ed Lang, "The Unblinking Eye," *Law & Order: Criminal Intent* (also known as *Law & Order: CI*), NBC, 2005.

Kevin Boatman, "America, Inc.," *Law & Order* (also known as *Law & Order Prime*), NBC, 2006.

Dan Kozlowski, "Haystack," *Law & Order: Special Victims Unit* (also known as *Law & Order's Sex Crimes, Law & Order: SVU,* and *Special Victims Unit*), NBC, 2007.

Mitchell Carr, "When the Door Opens," *The Black Don-nellys* (also known as *Black Donnellys* and *The Truth according to Joey Ice Cream*), NBC, 2007.

T. J. Hawkins, "Self–Made," *Law & Order: Criminal Intent* (also known as *Law & Order: CI*), NBC, 2007.

Jason Konkey, "And the Winner Is …," *Dirt* (also known as *Tabloid*), FX Network, 2008.

Jason Konkey, "Ties That (Don't) Bind," *Dirt* (also known as *Tabloid*), FX Network, 2008.

Jason Konkey, "What Is This Thing Called?," *Dirt* (also known as *Tabloid*), FX Network, 2008.

Kim Trent, "The Real Adventures of the Unreal Sam Tyler," *Life on Mars,* ABC, 2008.

Mattingley, "Eater," *Fear Itself,* NBC, 2008.

Mr. Sean Hauser, "Rumble," *Law & Order* (also known as *Law & Order Prime*), NBC, 2008.

Tim, "Payback," *Army Wives,* Lifetime, 2008.

Voice of Tim, "Great Expectations," *Army Wives,* Lifetime, 2008.

Voice of Tim, "Safe Havens," *Army Wives,* Lifetime, 2008.

Nick, "The Kindness of Strangers," *Three Rivers* (also known as *Untitled Barbee/Hanson Project*), CBS, 2009.

Officer Delaney, "Capone," *The Beast,* Arts and Enter-tainment, 2009.

Tal Feigenbaum, "Shadow Markets," *Numb3rs* (also known as *Numbers* and *Num3ers*), CBS, 2009.

Tal Feigenbaum, "Ultimatum," *Numb3rs* (also known as *Numbers* and *Num3ers*), CBS, 2009.

Jeremy Kiernan, "An Everlasting Love," *Medium* (also known as *Ghost and Crime* and *A medium*), CBS, 2010.

Television Appearances; Pilots:

Johnny, *Lights Out,* FX Network, 2010.

Internet Appearances:

Himself, *Broadway Bullet* (podcast), http://www.broadwaybullet.com, March 27, 2007.

RECORDINGS

Videos:

Himself, *The Making of "Lords of Dogtown"* (short documentary), Sony Pictures Home Entertainment, 2005.

Audiobooks:

American Psycho by Bret Easton Ellis, Brilliance Audio, 2010.

OTHER SOURCES

Periodicals:

The Villager, May 6, 2009.

SEVERANCE, Joan 1958–

PERSONAL

Full name, Joan Marie Severance; born December 23, 1958, in Houston, TX; daughter of John C. Severance (a computer systems engineer); married Eric Milan (a model), 1977 (divorced, 1984); married Rom Gemar (a cinematographer and actor). *Education:* Clayton College of Natural Health (online institution), B.N.H., 2005, graduate study, beginning 2008. *Avocational Interests:* Gourmet cooking, fashion design, writing, reading, landscape design, organic gardening, enter-taining, horses and dogs, purchasing and renovating houses, archery, shooting, hiking, cross–country skiing, volleyball.

Addresses: *Manager*—Steven Jensen, Independent Group, 6363 Wilshire Blvd., Suite 115, Los Angeles, CA 90048.

Career: Actress and producer. Elite Modeling Agency, worked as a model in the United States and abroad, 1977–95; appeared in commercials and print ads for Maybelline, Revlon, and Almay cosmetics, Clairol and L'Oreal hair care products, and others. Teacher of com-mercial acting classes in New York City, 1980–82; Good Food (catering company), New York City, co–owner, 1981–82; owner and chef of a bed and breakfast establishment in upstate New York, 1982–84; Lifestyle Enhancement (personal consulting service), founder, 2001; Canyonroadproductions.com, producer, director, and writer. Supporter of Habitat for Humanity, Smile Train, Cactus Creek Ranch, and other charities.

Member: Greater Houston Rowing Club.

CREDITS

Film Appearances:

(Uncredited) Girl in black playsuit, *Lethal Weapon,* 1987.

Samantha Moore, *No Holds Barred,* New Line Cinema, 1989.

Eve, *See No Evil, Hear No Evil,* TriStar, 1989.

Lizbette, *Worth Winning,* Twentieth Century–Fox, 1989.

Rachel Varney, *Bird on a Wire,* Universal, 1990.

Belle Washburn, *Write to Kill,* RCA/Columbia Pictures Home Video, 1991.

Maureen Mallory, *Almost Pregnant,* Columbia TriStar Home Video, 1992.

Melissa Yarnell, *Illicit Behavior* (also known as *Criminal Intent*), Prism Pictures, 1992.

Marla Stewart, *The Runestone,* Live Home Video, 1992.

Detective Melanie Hudson, *Criminal Passion* (also known as *Angel of Desire*), Vidmark, 1994.

Rose Gullerman, *Payback,* Trimark Pictures, 1995.

Caroline Everett, *Dangerous Indiscretion,* Paramount Home Video, 1995.

Madelyn Turner, *Hard Evidence,* Libra Home Entertainment, 1995.

Theresa Marsh, *Matter of Trust* (also known as *The Surgeon*), Two Sticks Productions, 1997.

Chapelle, *In Dark Places,* 1997.

Bridget Gregory, *The Last Seduction II,* PolyGram Video, 1999.

Leigh Sands, *Taylor,* Noble House Entertainment Pictures, 2005.

Lisa Wayne, *Last Sunset* (also known as *Sex & Consequences*), Maverick Entertainment Group, 2007.

Dr. Sammael, *Born,* American World Pictures, 2007.

Film Coproducer:

In Dark Places, 1997.

Matter of Trust (also known as *The Surgeon*), Two Sticks Productions, 1997.

Television Appearances; Series:

Susan Profitt, *Wiseguy,* CBS, 1988.

Camille Hunter, *Love Boat: The Next Wave,* UPN, 1998.

Anna Whitman, *Wicked Wicked Games,* MyNetworkTV, 2006–2007.

Television Appearances; Movies:

Susan Davis, *Another Pair of Aces: Three of a Kind,* CBS, 1991.

Irene, *Lake Consequence,* Showtime, 1993.

Darcy Walker (title role), *Black Scorpion* (also known as *Roger Corman Presents "Black Scorpion"*), Showtime, 1995.

Darcy Walker (title role), *Black Scorpion II: Aftershock* (also known as *Black Scorpion: Ground Zero*), Showtime, 1996.

Alison Rawlings, *Frequent Flyer,* ABC, 1996.

Dr. Hanna Carras, *Profile for Murder,* HBO, 1997.

Barbara "Babe" Paley, *Life of the Party: The Pamela Harriman Story* (also known as *Life of the Party: Pamela Harriman*), Lifetime, 1998.

Angela Carter, *Cause of Death,* Cinemax, 2000.

Mary Stenning, *Mystery Woman,* Hallmark Channel, 2003.

Television Appearances; Specials:

(Uncredited) Actress leaving limousine, "A Movie Star's Daughter," *ABC Afterschool Specials,* ABC, 1979.

Host, *Virtual World International,* Sci–Fi Channel, 1995.

Host, *Contestants Tell All … Secrets of Beauty Pageants Exposed,* UPN, 1998.

Hulk Hogan: The E! True Hollywood Story, E! Entertainment Television, 1999.

Television Appearances; Pilots:

Libby Sinclair, *Just Deserts,* ABC, 1992.

Anna Whitman, *Wicked Wicked Games,* MyNetworkTV, 2006.

Television Appearances; Episodic:

Pauline, "Lady Killer," *The New Mike Hammer* (also known as *Mickey Spillane's "Mike Hammer"* and *Mike Hammer*), CBS, 1987.

Zik–Zak hallucination girl, "Neurostim," *Max Headroom* (also known as *Max Headroom: 20 Minutes into the Future*), ABC, 1988.

Jane Ambergris/Holly, "My Enemy," *The Hitchhiker,* HBO, 1989.

Late Night with David Letterman, NBC, 1989.

Alex Kovac, "All's Wrong that Ends Wrong," *Murphy's Law,* 1989.

Norma Cheever, "Uninvited Guests," *Midnight Caller,* 1991.

Rona, "The New Arrival," *Tales from the Crypt,* 1992.

The woman, "Safe Sex," *Red Shoe Diaries,* Showtime, 1992.

Lauren Chase, "How Much Is That Bentley in the Window," *L.A. Law,* NBC, 1993.

Lauren Chase, "Foreign Co–respondent," *L.A. Law,* NBC, 1993.

Reno Hubbertson, "Lady Madonna," *Johnny Bago,* CBS, 1993.

(In archive footage) Maureen Mallory, *Joe Bob's Drive–in Theatre,* 1994.

Christine Logan, "Venom: Parts 1 & 2," *Profiler,* NBC, 1996.

Lauren Drake, "Love Kills," *She Spies,* syndicated, 2003.

Ask Rita, syndicated, 2003.

Cynthia Price, "I Shall Believe," *One Tree Hill,* The WB, 2004.

Cynthia Price, "Suddenly Everything Has Changed," *One Tree Hill,* The WB, 2004.

Sophie Townsend, "Money Plane," *CSI: Miami,* CBS, 2005.

Television Coproducer; Movies:

Black Scorpion II: Aftershock (also known as *Black Scorpion: Ground Zero*), Showtime, 1996.

RECORDINGS

Videos:
Herself, *Hulkmania 4,* 1989.

Appeared in the music video "Rhythm of Love" by Scorpions, 1988.

ADAPTATIONS

Severance's appearance in an episode of *Red Shoe Diaries* in 1992 was included in the video collection *Red Shoe Diaries 2: Double Dare,* 1993.

OTHER SOURCES

Electronic:
Joan Severance Official Site, http://www.joanseverance. com, June 28, 2010.

SHADIX, Glenn 1952–
   (Glen Shadix)

PERSONAL

Full name, William Glenn Shadix; born April 15, 1952, in Bessemer, AL. *Education:* Attended Birmingham Southern College; trained with Roy London, Ivana Chubbuck, and Groundlings (improvisation group). *Avocational Interests:* Portrait photography.

Addresses: *Agent*—Innovative Artists Agency, 1505 10th St., Santa Monica, CA 90401. *Manager*—Juliet Green Management, 445 South Beverly Dr., Suite 100, Beverly Hills, CA 90212.

Career: Actor and voice artist. Ensemble Studio Theatre, member of acting company, beginning 1986; stage actor for nearly twenty years. Appeared in commercials, including one for Post Cinna–Crunch Pebbles breakfast cereal, 1999. Worked as a waiter and house cleaner in New York City.

Member: Actors' Equity Association.

CREDITS

Film Appearances:
Twin Oaks customer, *The Postman Always Rings Twice,* Paramount, 1981.
Otho, *Beetlejuice,* Warner Bros., 1988.

Roscoe Arbuckle, *Sunset* (also known as *Catalina*), TriStar, 1988.
Father Ripper, *Heathers* (also known as *Fatal Game, Lethal Attraction,* and *Westerberg High*), New World, 1989.
Greg Samson, *Meet the Applegates* (also known as *The Applegators*), Triton Pictures, 1991.
Duke, *Bingo,* TriStar, 1991.
Mr. Fallows, *Sleepwalkers* (also known as *Sleepstalkers* and *Stephen King's "Sleepwalkers"*), Columbia, 1992.
Reader, *Earth and the American Dream,* 1992.
Associate Bob, *Demolition Man,* Warner Bros., 1993.
Voice of the mayor of Halloween Town, *The Nightmare Before Christmas* (also known as *Tim Burton's "The Nightmare Before Christmas"* and *Tim Burton's "The Nightmare Before Christmas"* in Disney Digital 3–D), Buena Vista, 1993.
Leopold Doppler, *It Runs in the Family* (also known as *My Summer Story*), Metro–Goldwyn–Mayer, 1994.
Anthony Rotundo, *Love Affair,* Warner Bros., 1994.
Leon Bennini, *Dark Side of Genius,* Paramount Home Video, 1995.
Lionel Spalding, *Dunston Checks In,* Twentieth Century Fox, 1996.
Building inspector, *Multiplicity* (also known as *Clones*), Columbia/TriStar, 1996.
Hermann Goering, *The Empty Mirror,* Lions Gate Films, 1997.
Neil, *Men,* A–Pix Entertainment, 1997.
(As Glen Shadix) The producer, *Sammy the Screenplay,* 1997.
Mr. Sweepstakes, *Sparkler,* Strand Releasing, 1998.
Larry, *Chairman of the Board,* Trimark Pictures, 1998.
Virgil Cunningham, *Red Dirt,* Sweet Tea Productions, 1999.
Geoff, *More Dogs than Bones,* Dream Entertainment, 1999.
Nate, *Storm,* 1999.
Voices of townspeople, *Bartok the Magnificent,* 1999.
Voices of Sergeant Glen Dale charity home matron, and other characters, *The World of Stainboy* (also known as *Stainboy*), 2000.
Jesse, *Fast Sofa,* Studio Home Entertainment, 2001.
Senator Nado, *Planet of the Apes,* Twentieth Century–Fox, 2001.
George, *Sol Goode,* Cutting Edge Entertainment, 2001.
Narrator, *The Day the Dolls Struck Back,* 2002.
Peter, *Shut Yer Dirty Little Mouth,* SYDLM Productions, 2002.
Sheriff Winslow, *Rose's* (also known as *Big Hopes, Little Lies* and *Confessions of a Florist*), Envisage Media Production, 2003.
Himself, *Geeks,* Post No Bills Films, 2004.
Claudius, *Trailer for a Remake of Gore Vidal's "Caligula"* (short film), Crossroads, 2005.
Karl, *To Kill a Mockumentary,* Singa Home Entertainment, 2006.

Jack Strong, *The Final Curtain* (also known as *Acts of Death*), Lightning Home Entertainment, 2007.

Tom Cool, Phoenicia Pictures, 2009.

Film Work:

Executive producer, *Sunset Tuxedo* (short film), 2004.

Television Appearances; Series:

Dr. Addington, a recurring role, *Thanks,* CBS, 1999.

Voice of Tso Lan the moon demon and Xiao Fung, *Jackie Chan Adventures* (animated), The WB, 2001–2002.

Voices of Monsieur Mallah and The Brain, *Teen Titans* (animated), Cartoon Network, 2005–2006.

Television Appearances; Movies:

Mr. Barton, *Student Exchange,* ABC, 1987.

Chet, *Parent Trap: Hawaiian Honeymoon* (also known as *Parent Trap IV: Hawaiian Honeymoon*), NBC, 1989.

Clive, *Nightlife,* USA Network, 1990.

13 Bourbon St., Fox, 1997.

Nate, *Storm* (also known as *Storm Trackers*), Fox Family, 1998.

Television Appearances; Episodic:

Musician, "Diamond in the Rough," *The Golden Girls,* 1987.

Jay, "Chicken Hearts–Chicken Hearts," *Roseanne,* ABC, 1989.

Bud Larkin, "Food for Thought," *Empty Nest,* NBC, 1991.

Harold, "The Apartment," *Seinfeld,* NBC, 1991.

Bernard, "The Beer Is Always Greener," *Cheers,* NBC, 1992.

Dermot Drake, "The 1992 Boat Show," *Night Court,* NBC, 1992.

Scorpius, "Hex and the Single Guy," *The Fresh Prince of Bel–Air,* NBC, 1993.

Walker, "Amends," *The John Larroquette Show* (also known as *Larroquette*), NBC, 1993.

Walker, "Thirty Day Chip," *The John Larroquette Show* (also known as *Larroquette*), NBC, 1993.

Leslie Loret, "Lost Weekend," *Dave's World,* CBS, 1994.

Voice of Nimbar, *Tattooed Teenage Alien Fighters from Beverly Hills,* USA Network, 1994.

Voice of monster, "Driving Miss Ethyl," *Dinosaurs* (animated), ABC, 1994.

Typhon, "Cast a Giant Shadow," *Hercules: The Legendary Journeys,* syndicated, 1995.

(As Glen Shadix) Voice, "Lake Winnibigoshish," *Life with Louie,* 1995.

Voice of Lonnie the shark, "Baby's Wild Ride," *The Mask* (animated), 1995.

Voice of Lonnie the shark, "The Green Marine," *The Mask* (animated), 1996.

Voice of Lonnie the shark, "Malled," *The Mask* (animated), 1996.

Voice of Lonnie the shark, "Convention of Evil," *The Mask* (animated), 1996.

Voice, "The Germinator," *Quack Pack* (animated), 1996.

Voice, "Pardon My Molecules," *Quack Pack* (animated), 1996.

Typhon, "Monster Child in the Promised Land," *Hercules: The Legendary Journeys,* syndicated, 1996.

Typhon, "Beanstalks and Bad Eggs," *Hercules: The Legendary Journeys,* syndicated, 1997.

Voice, *Zorro,* syndicated, 1997.

Voice of mirror demon, "The Ghostmakers," *Extreme Ghostbusters* (animated), 1997.

Voice of army leader guest, "Duckman and Cornfed in 'Haunted Society Plumbers,'" *Duckman: Private Dick/Family Man* (animated), USA Network, 1997.

Voices of Poopy the Clown, gate guard, and prisoner, "Field Trip to Folsom Prison Blues/Girls' Bathroom/I. M. Weasel: This Bridge Not Weasel Bridge," *Clown and Chicken* (animated), 1997.

Gay agent, "Agents," *Tracey Takes On ...,* HBO, 1998.

Caligula, "Salem, the Boy," *Sabrina, the Teenage Witch* (also known as *Sabrina* and *Sabrina Goes to College*), ABC, 1999.

Mr. Rook, "Aloha Christmas," *Ladies Man,* CBS, 1999.

Eldon, "Blood, Sugar, Sex, Magic," *ER,* NBC, 2001.

"The Wedding Planner," *Providence,* NBC, 2002.

Councilman Val Templeton, *Carnivale* (also known as *La feria ambulante*), HBO, 2003.

Voices, "Swirly: Experiment 383," *Lilo & Stitch: The Series* (animated), The Disney Channel, 2003.

Voices of Arthur "Artie" Brown and The Cluemaster, "Q & A," *The Batman* (animated), The WB, 2004.

Voice of giant spider, "Dangerous Minds," *Xiaolin Showdown* (animated), The WB, 2005.

Voice of Steven Mandragora, "Double Date," *Justice League* (animated; also known as *JL* and *Justice League Unlimited*), Cartoon Network, 2005.

Voices of man and King of Troy, "Never Look a Trojan in the Gift Horse," an episode of *Time Squad,* Cartoon Network; also appeared in an episode of *Great Scott!,* Fox.

Television Appearances; Pilots:

Royce Pruitt, *Locals,* Fox, 1994.

Dr. Addington, *Thanks,* CBS, 1999.

Garland Madden, *Tracey Ullman in the Trailer Tales,* HBO, 2003.

Also appeared in the pilots *Angel City,* ABC, and *Hotel Dicks,* Fox.

Television Appearances; Specials:

Clown, *In the Director's Chair: The Man Who Invented Edward Scissorhands,* 1990.

Voice of Jelly Roll, *Disney's One Saturday Morning on Friday Night,* ABC, 1999.

Stage Appearances:

Appeared as Sancho Panza in a production of the musical *Man of La Mancha,* Alliance Theatre, Atlanta, GA; appeared as Gertrude Stein in a play produced by Ensemble Studio Theatre, 1986.

RECORDINGS

Video Games:

Voice of mayor, *The Nightmare Before Christmas: Oogie's Revenge,* Buena Vista Interactive, 2004.
Voice of mayor of Halloween Town, *Kingdom Hearts II,* Square Enix, 2005.

WRITINGS

Screenplays:

Sunset Tuxedo (short film), 2004.

OTHER SOURCES

Electronic:

Glenn Shadix Official Site, http://www.glennshadix.com, June 28, 2010.

SHAIMAN, Marc 1959–

PERSONAL

Born October 22, 1959, in Newark, NJ; son of William Robert and Claire (maiden name, Goldfein) Shaiman; companion of Scott Wittman (a director and lyricist), since c. 1979. *Education:* Attended University of Illinois.

Addresses: *Agent*—The Kraft–Benjamin Agency, 345 North Maple Dr., Suite 385, Beverly Hills, CA 90210–3856.

Career: Lyricist and composer. Arranger, writer, and producer of musical shows, concerts, and albums. Began career working as music director of Bette Midler's stage shows.

Awards, Honors: Emmy Award nomination (with others), writing in a variety or music program, 1987, for *Saturday Night Live;* ASCAP Award, top box office films, American Society of Composers, Authors, and Publishers, 1990, for *When Harry Met Sally ...;* Emmy Award nomination, achievement in music direction, 1991, for *The 63rd Annual Academy Awards;* Emmy Award (with others), writing in a variety or music program, 1992, for *The 64th Annual Academy Awards;* ASCAP Award, top box office films, 1992, for *City Slickers;* ASCAP Award, top box office films, 1992, for *The Addams Family;* ASCAP Award, top box office films, 1993, for *Sister Act;* Academy Award nomination (with lyricist Ramsey McLean), best music, song, 1994, for "A Wink and a Smile," from *Sleepless in Seattle;* Film Award nomination, best score, British Academy of Film and Television Arts, 1994, for *Sleepless in Seattle;* ASCAP Award, top box office films, 1994, for *A Few Good Men;* Saturn Award nomination, best music, Academy of Science Fiction, Fantasy, and Horror Films, 1994, for *Addams Family Values;* Saturn Award nomination, best music, 1994, for *Heart and Souls;* Academy Award nomination, best music, original musical or comedy score, 1996, for *The American President;* Academy Award nomination, best music, original musical or comedy score, and ASCAP Award, top box office films, 1997, for *The First Wives Club;* ASCAP Award, top box office films, 1998, for *George of the Jungle;* Academy Award nomination, best music, original music or comedy score, 1999, and ASCAP Award, top box office films, 2000, for *Patch Adams;* Los Angeles Film Critics Association Award (with Trey Parker), best music, 1999, Online Film Critics Society Award, best original score, Chicago Film Critics Association Award, best original score, Academy Award nomination, best music, song, 2000, for *South Park: Bigger Longer & Uncut;* Hollywood Discovery Awards, outstanding achievement in music in film and outstanding achievement in production design, Hollywood Film Festival, 2002; Antoinette Perry Award (with Scott Wittman), best score, 2003, Satellite Award nomination, best original song, International Press Academy, 2007, Grammy Award nomination, best compilation soundtrack album for motion picture, 2008, for *Hairspray;* Emmy Award nomination (with Harold Wheeler), outstanding music direction, 2004, for *The 76th Annual Academy Awards.*

CREDITS

Film Music Producer:

(With Harry Connick, Jr.) *When Harry Met Sally ...,* Columbia, 1990.
Misery, Columbia, 1991.
The Addams Family, Orion, 1992.
City Slickers, Columbia, 1992.
Scenes from a Mall, Buena Vista, 1992.
(And orchestrator), *Sister Act,* Buena Vista, 1992.
A Few Good Men, Columbia, 1993.
(And score producer) *Mr. Saturday Night,* Columbia, 1993.
Addams Family Values, Paramount, 1993.
For Love or Money, Universal, 1993.
Sleepless in Seattle, TriStar, 1993.

Hocus Pocus, Walt Disney, 1993.

North, Columbia, 1994.

City Slickers II: The Legend of Curly's Gold (also known as *City Slickers II*), 1994.

The American President, Columbia, 1995.

Bogus, Warner Bros., 1996.

Ghosts of the Mississippi (also known as *Ghost from the Past*), Sony Pictures Entertainment, 1996.

Additional arrangement, "I Wish I Knew How It Would Feel To Be Free," *Ghosts of the Mississippi* (also known as *Ghost from the Past*), Sony Pictures Entertainment, 1996.

My Giant, Sony Pictures Entertainment, 1998.

Patch Adams, 1998.

The Story of Us, 1999.

Film Music Supervisor:

Divine Madness, Warner Bros., 1980.

Beaches (also known as *Forever Friends*), Buena Vista, 1988.

Big Business, Buena Vista, 1988.

When Harry Met Sally ..., Columbia, 1990.

For the Boys, Twentieth Century–Fox, 1991.

Sleepless in Seattle, TriStar, 1993.

Life with Mikey (also known as *Give Me a Break*), Buena Vista, 1993.

Sister Act 2: Back in the Habit, Buena Vista, 1993.

That's Entertainment! III, Metro–Goldwyn–Mayer, 1994.

Forget Paris, Columbia, 1995.

The First Wives Club, Paramount, 1996.

George of the Jungle, Buena Vista, 1997.

Film Work:

Arranger, *Divine Madness,* Warner Bros., 1980.

Song arranger, "Big Noise from Winnetka," *Divine Madness,* Warner Bros., 1980.

Arranger, *Big Business,* Buena Vista, 1988.

Arranger, *Beaches* (also known as *Forever Friends*), Buena Vista, 1988.

Song producer, "The Girl Friend of the Whirling Dervish," "Billy–a–Dick," and "In My Life," *For the Boys,* Twentieth Century–Fox, 1991.

Song arranger, "Billy–a–Dick," "I Remember You," "P.S. I Love You," "The Girl Friend of the Whirling Dervish," "Dixie's Dream," and "Baby It's Cold," *For the Boys,* Twentieth Century–Fox, 1991.

Orchestrator and music producer, *Scenes from a Mall,* 1991.

Orchestrator, *Sister Act,* 1992.

Song arranger, "I Put a Spell on You," *Hocus Pocus,* Walt Disney, 1993.

Music executive producer and arranger, *Sister Act 2: Back in the Habit,* Buena Vista, 1993.

Music adaptor, *Sleepless in Seattle,* 1993.

Music arranger, *Speechless,* 1994.

Music adapter and additional music arranger, *That's Entertainment! III,* Metro–Goldwyn–Mayer, 1994.

Music producer, *Stuart Saves His Family,* 1995.

Song arranger, "I Have Dreamed," *The American President* (also known as *Perfect Couple*), 1995.

Song producer, "Mrs. Robinson," *Mother,* Paramount, 1996.

Music adapter, music arranger, and additional music production, *George of the Jungle,* Buena Vista, 1997.

Song arranger, "Hail to Thee O Greenleaf High," *In & Out,* 1997.

Song producer, *That Old Feeling,* 1997.

Music producer, *South Park: Bigger Longer & Uncut* (also known as *South Park,* and *South Park: BLU*), 1999.

Music consultant, *The Wedding Planner* (also known as *Wedding Planner—verliebt, verlobt, verplant*), Columbia, 2001.

Orchestrator and music producer, *Down with Love,* 2003.

Music producer, *Marci X,* 2003.

Song producer, "America F**k Yeah," *Team America: World Police,* 2004.

Music adaptor and music producer, *Rumor Has It ...* (also known as *Rumour Has It ...*), 2005.

Executive producer, music arranger, and orchestrator, *Hairspray,* New Line Cinema, 2007.

Song producer, "Thinkin' Bee," *Bee Movie,* 2007.

Song producer, "Tush," and "La Vie En Rose," *The Bucket List,* 2007.

Song producer, "At the Nottingham Broadway Mega Resort," *Bedtime Stories,* 2008.

Film Appearances:

News theme writer, *Broadcast News,* Twentieth Century–Fox, 1987.

(Uncredited) Pianist, *Beaches,* 1988.

Piano player, *Hot Shots!* (also known as *Hot Shots: An Important Movie!*), Twentieth Century–Fox, 1991.

Conductor, *The Addams Family,* Orion, 1992.

Piano player, *Scenes from a Mall,* Buena Vista, 1992.

Lucky Zinberg, *Mr. Saturday Night,* Columbia, 1993.

Piano accompanist, *Heart and Souls,* Universal, 1993.

Piano player, *North,* Columbia, 1994.

Get Bruce (also known as *Get Bruce!*), Miramax, 1999.

How Harry Met Sally (video), 2000.

(Uncredited) Wedding pianist, *The Wedding Planner* (also known as *Wedding Planner—verliebt, verlobt, verplant*), Columbia, 2001.

The Sweatbox, 2002.

Pianist, *Down with Love,* Twentieth Century–Fox, 2003.

Talent agent, *Hairspray,* New Line Cinema, 2007.

Finding Kraftland, 2007.

Wrangler: Anatomy of an Icon, 2008.

Television Music Producer; Specials:

What's Alan Watching Now?, CBS, 1989.

Partners in Life, CBS, 1990.

(And song arranger) *The 63rd Annual Academy Awards Presentation,* ABC, 1991.

The 65th Annual Academy Awards Presentation, ABC, 1993.

Television Work; Specials:
Musical director, *Women of the Night,* HBO, 1987.
Musical director, *Bette Midler's Mondo Beyond,* HBO, 1988.
Musical director, *Billy Crystal: Midnight Train to Moscow,* HBO, 1989.
Music arranger, *The 32nd Annual Grammy Awards,* 1990.
Theme music, *Girls Night Out: Paula Poundstone and Rita Rudner,* Lifetime, 1991.
Song arranger, "A Wink and a Smile," *The 66th Annual Academy Awards Presentation,* ABC, 1994.
Special musical material, *Bette Midler—Diva Las Vegas,* HBO, 1997.
Orchestrator, *72nd Annual Academy Awards Presentation,* ABC, 2000.
Song arranger, "Wind Beneath My Wings," *A Prayer for America: Yankee Stadium Memorial,* 2001.
Music arranger, *The 63rd Annual Tony Awards,* CBS, 2009.
Music director, *The 82nd Annual Academy Awards,* 2010.

Also arranger of music, *Saturday Night Live,* NBC.

Television Work; Series:
Music director, *The Martin Short Show,* 1999–2000.

Television Music Producer; Movies:
Sessions, ABC, 1991.

Television Appearances; Series:
Skip St. Thomas, a recurring role, *Saturday Night Live* (also known as *SNL*), NBC, 1986–89.

Television Appearances; Episodic:
Saturday Night Live (also known as *SNL*), NBC, 1986.
The Tonight Show with Jay Leno, NBC, 1993 and 2009.
The Martin Short Show, NBC, 1994.
The Rosie O'Donnell Show, 1997.
Voice of Marc, "Cripple Fight," *South Park* (animated), Comedy Central, 2001.
"The Making of 'Down with Love,'" *HBO First Look,* HBO, 2003.
"Bette Midler," *Biography,* Arts and Entertainment, 2004.
"Welcome to the '60s: On the Set of 'Hairspray'," *HBO First Look,* HBO, 2007.
Late Night with Conan O'Brien, NBC, 2009.

Television Appearances; Specials:
Billy Crystal: Don't Get Me Started—The Billy Crystal Special (also known as *On Location: Billy Crystal—Don't Get Me Started*), 1986.

Billy Crystal: Don't Get Me Started—The Lost Minutes (also known as *The Lost Minutes of Billy Crystal*), 1987.
The Making of "The Addams Family," 1991.
The Hollywood Soundtrack Story, AMC, 1995.
Intimate Portrait: Better Midler, Lifetime, 1997.
The Score (documentary), Trio, 2002.
The 57th Annual Tony Awards, CBS, 2003.
The 76th Annual Academy Awards, ABC, 2004.
A–List Awards, 2008.
David Campbell on Broadway, 2010.

Stage Work:
Music, *Gotta Getaway!,* Radio City Music Hall, New York City, 1984.
Music director and orchestrator and vocal arrangements, *Haarlem Nocturne,* Latin Quarter, 1984.
Vocal arrangements, *Leader of the Pack,* Ambassador Theatre, New York City, 1985.
Conductor, *An Evening with Harry Connick, Jr., and His Orchestra,* Lunt–Fontanne Theatre, New York City, 1990.
Arrangements, *Patti LuPone on Broadway,* Walter Kerr Theatre, New York City, 1995.

Producer of numerous Broadway and off–Broadway musical shows, including *Bette Midler's Divine Madness, Peter Allen in Concert, Leader of the Pack,* and *Legends with Mary Martin and Carol Channing;* and producer of numerous concerts by various artists, including Barbara Streisand, Billy Crystal, Barry Manilow, Luther Vandross, and Raquel Welch.

Internet Appearances:
Piano player, *Prop 8: The Musical,* FunnyorDie.com, 2008.

Internet Work:
Producer, *Prop 8: The Musical,* FunnyorDie.com, 2008.

RECORDINGS

Albums:
Producer and arranger, *Bette Midler's Thighs and Whispers, Divine Madness, Beaches, When Harry Met Sally ..., We Are in Love,* and *Some Peoples Lives.*

Videos:
How Harry Met Sally, 2000.
Marc Shaiman's Musical Misery Tour, 2002.
Standing Ovations 2, 2004.
Hairspray: Inside the Recording Booth, 2007.
Playing Tracy, 2007.
The Roots of "Hairspray," 2007.

You Can's Stop the Beat: The Long Journey of "Hair-spray," 2007.

WRITINGS

Stage Music:

Gotta Getaway!, produced at Radio City Music Hall, New York City, 1984.

(With Scott Wittman) *Hairspray* (adapted from the film of the same title), produced on Broadway, 2002.

Also wrote music and/or lyrics for the off–Broadway productions *Livin' Dolls, Dementos, Trilogy of Terror,* and *The G–String Murders.* Also wrote music for *Peter Allen—Up in One, Leader of the Pack, The Tap Dance Kid, Haarlem Nocturne, Legends, Harry Connick, Jr. on Broadway,* and *Patti LuPone at Carnegie Hall.*

Film Songs:

(With Richard Wilbur and Frank Mills) "Little Ole Lady" and (with Mills) "Music Box Dancer," *Big Business,* Buena Vista, 1988.

(And lyrics) "Otto Titsling," *Beaches,* Buena Vista, 1988.

"Lady's Lunch" and (with Laura Kenyon and Scott Wittman) "The Tables Have Turned," *When Harry Met Sally ...,* Columbia, 1990.

"Dixie's Dream," *For the Boys,* Twentieth Century–Fox, 1991.

"Mamushka," "Happy Turkey Day," and "Eat Us," *The Addams Family,* 1991.

"Where Did My Heart Go," *City Slickers,* Columbia, 1992.

"I Could Love a Man (Who Uses His Head)" and "In Your Eyes," *For Love or Money,* Universal, 1993.

"Mr. Hug–A–Bug" and "My Heart and Soul," *Heart and Souls,* Universal, 1993.

"I Put a Spell on You," *Hocus Pocus,* 1993.

"When You Love Someone," *Forget Paris,* 1995.

"The American President," *Saving Ryan's Privates,* 1998.

"Dolphin Song," *Bedazzled,* 2000.

"Mountain Town," *Bowling for Columbine,* 2002.

"Annie to Empire," *How to Lose a Guy in 10 Days,* 2003.

"Everyone Has Aids," "Derka Derk," *Team America: World Police,* 2004.

"At the Nottingham Broadway Mega Resort," *Bedtime Stories,* 2008.

Film Scores:

(Lyrics) "Little Ole Lady," *Big Business,* 1988.

Misery, Columbia, 1990.

Scenes from a Mall, Buena Vista, 1991.

The Addams Family, Orion, 1991.

Father of the Bride, Buena Vista, 1991.

City Slickers, 1991.

Mr. Saturday Night, Columbia, 1992.

A Few Good Men, Columbia, 1992.

Sister Act, Buena Vista, 1993.

Heart and Souls, Universal, 1993.

(And song "A Wink and a Smile") *Sleepless in Seattle,* TriStar, 1993.

Addams Family Values, Paramount, 1993.

Speechless, Metro–Goldwyn–Mayer, 1994.

City Slickers II: The Legend of Curley's Gold, Columbia, 1994.

North, Columbia, 1994.

Speechless, 1994.

Stuart Saves His Family, Paramount, 1995.

Forget Paris, Columbia, 1995.

The American President, Columbia, 1995.

Mother, Paramount, 1996.

The First Wives Club, Paramount, 1996.

Bogus, Warner Bros., 1996.

Ghosts of the Mississippi (also known as *Ghost from the Past*), Sony Pictures Entertainment, 1996.

(And lyrics "Hail To Thee O Greenleaf High") *In & Out,* Paramount, 1997.

George of the Jungle, Buena Vista, 1997.

My Giant, Sony Pictures Entertainment, 1998.

Simon Birch (also known as *Angels and Armadillos, A Prayer for Owen Meany,* and *A Small Miracle*), Buena Vista, 1998.

Patch Adams, Universal, 1998.

(And lyrics) *South Park: Bigger, Longer and Uncut,* Paramount, 1999.

The Out–of–Towners, Paramount, 1999.

The Story of Us, Warner Bros., 1999.

The Kid (also known as *Disney's The Kid*), Buena Vista, 2000.

How Harry Met Sally ..., Metro–Goldwyn–Mayer/United Artists, 2000.

Conversations with Jon Turteltaub (also known as *Spotlight on John Turteltaub*), Buena Vista, 2000.

Get Over It (also known as *Get Over It!*), Miramax, 2001.

One Night at McCool's, USA Films, 2001.

What's the Worst That Could Happen?, Metro–Goldwyn–Mayer, 2001.

(And lyrics) *Down with Love,* Twentieth Century–Fox, 2003.

Marci X, Paramount, 2003.

(And lyrics) *The Cat in the Hat* (also known as *Dr. Seuss's "The Cat in the Hat"*), Universal, 2003.

Alex & Emma, 2003.

Rumor Has It ..., Warner Bros., 2005.

Hairspray, New Line Cinema, 2007.

The Bucket List, Warner Bros., 2007.

ShowBusiness: The Road to Broadway, 2007.

Bee Movie, 2007.

Flipped, Warner Bros., 2010.

Television Music; Specials:

The Mondo Beyondo Show (also known as *Bette Midler's Mondo Beyondo*), 1982.

Billy Crystal–Don't Get Me Started, 1986.

Billy Crystal: Don't Get Me Started–The Lost Minutes (also known as *The Lost Minutes of Billy Crystal*), 1987.

What's Alan Watching Now?, CBS, 1989.

Partners in Life, 1990.

Theme music, *Girls Night Out: Paula Poundstone and Rita Rudner,* Lifetime, 1991.

Special material writer, *The 64th Annual Academy Awards,* 1992.

Special material writer, *The 65th Annual Academy Awards,* 1993.

Song composer, "A Wink and a Smile," *The 66th Annual Academy Awards Presentation,* 1994.

Special musical material writer, *Bette Midler in Concert: Diva Las Vegas,* HBO, 1997.

Special material writer, *The 69th Annual Academy Awards,* 1997.

Special material writer, *The 70th Annual Academy Awards,* 1998.

Jackie's Back! (also known as *Jackie's Back: Portrait of a Diva*), 1999.

72nd Annual Academy Awards Presentation, ABC, 2000.

61* (also known as *61*), 2001.

76th Annual Academy Awards Presentation, 2004.

The 79th Annual Academy Awards, 2007.

A–List Awards, 2008 and 2009.

(Lyrics) *The 63rd Annual Tony Awards,* 2009.

Also writer for *The 64th Annual Academy Awards Presentation.*

Television Music; Miniseries:

"The Original Wives Club," *From the Earth to the Moon,* HBO, 1998.

Television Music; Series:

Saturday Night Live, NBC, 1986–87.

Sessions, 1991.

Bette, CBS, 2000.

Theme song, *Greg the Bunny,* Fox, 2002.

Theme music, *Charlie Lawrence,* 2003.

Television Music; Episodic:

"The Original Wives Club," *From the Earth to the Moon,* 1998.

The Tonight Show Starring Johnny Carson (also known as *The Best of Carson*), 1992.

"Mr. Hankey's Christmas Classics," *South Park,* 1999.

"In My Life," *Bette,* 2000.

(And lyrics) "Bette Midler," *Biography,* 2004.

"Derailed," *Ugly Betty,* 2007.

Loose Women, 2009.

Dancing on Ice, 2010.

Television Music; Movies:

What's Alan Watching?, 1989.

Jackie's Back (also known as *Jackie's Back: Portrait of a Diva*), Lifetime, 1999.

61* (also known as *61*), HBO, 2001.

Livin' Dolls, ABC, 2002.

Internet Scores:

Prop 8: The Musical, FunnyorDie.com, 2008.

OTHER SOURCES

Periodicals:

Entertainment Weekly, July 30, 1993, p. 36.

Electronic:

Marc Shaiman Official Site, http://shaiman.filmmusic.com, June 10, 2003.

SHAPIRO, Arnold 1941–
(Arnie Shapiro)

PERSONAL

Born February 1, 1941, in Los Angeles, CA. *Education:* University of California, Los Angeles, degree in theatre arts and television.

Addresses: *Office*—Arnold Shapiro and Allison Grodner Productions, 12925 Riverside Dr., 4th Floor, Sherman Oaks, CA 91423. *Agent*—David Tenzer, Creative Artists Agency, 9830 Wilshire Blvd., Beverly Hills, CA 90212.

Career: Producer, director, and writer. Arnold Shapiro and Allison Grodner Productions, Sherman Oaks, CA, partner. University of California, Los Angeles, teacher of extension classes. Sometimes credited as Arnie Shapiro.

Awards, Honors: Academy Award, best documentary feature, Emmy Award, outstanding informational program, and Emmy Award nomination, outstanding individual achievement in an informational program, all 1979, George Polk Memorial Award, Department of Journalism, Long Island University, Silver Gavel Award, American Bar Association, Silver Halo Award, Southern California Motion Picture Council, Award of Excellence, Film Advisory Board, Gold Cindy Award, Information Film Producers of America, CINE Golden Eagle, Committee on International Nontheatrical Events, Red Ribbon, American Film Festival, New York City, Outstanding Achievement Award, sociology category, San Francisco International Film Festival,

Chris Plaque, Columbus Film Festival, Special Judges Award, Humboldt Film Festival, Golden Camera Award, U.S. Industrial Film Festival, Award of Appreciation, International Year of the Child Film Festival of the United Nations, Silver Medal, Greater Miami International Film Festival, Special Merit Award, Athens International Film Festival, Family Life Award, National Council on Family Relations, Certificate of Appreciation, Juvenile Officers Association, National Headliners Award, outstanding documentary, John Swett Award, California Teachers Association, Banff International Film Festival Award, social and political documentary category, Television Documentary Photography Award, National Press Photographers Association, Freedoms Foundation Award, and Certificate of Merit, Gabriel Awards, all for *Scared Straight!;* Scott Newman Drug Abuse Prevention Award, 1980, for *Scared Straight! Another Story;* Emmy Award nomination (with others), outstanding technical direction, 1984, for *Jennifer Slept Here;* Emmy Award nomination (with others), outstanding informational special, 1987, for *Scared Straight! 10 Years Later;* Awards of Excellence, 1989, 1991, and President's Award, all American College of Emergency Physicians, EMS Public Education Award, Emergency Medical Services Branch, Kentucky Department for Health Services, 1990, Certificate of Appreciation, City of Santa Clarita, 1990, Media Excellence Award, Vermont Agency of Human Services, 1991, Certificate of Appreciation, Lake Mead National Recreation Area, National Park Service, 1991, Certificate of Appreciation, Maryland State Firemen's Association, 1991, Minutemen Award, community of Huntington Beach, 1992, Achievement Award, Lamar University, 1992, Certificate of Appreciation, Texas Advisory Commission on State Emergency Communications, 1992, Community Service Recognition, National Safety Council, 1992, proclamation of Rescue 911 Day, City of Los Angeles, 1992, Gold Angel awards, best action television series, 1992, 1993, Genesis Award, ongoing commitment to excellence, 1993, Emergency Medical Services Educational Award, Ambulance Association of Pennsylvania, 1993, Excellence in Journalism Award, National Marrow Donor Program, 1994, Commendation Award, Ark Trust, 1994, President's Award, National Academy of Emergency Medical Dispatch, Service Award, National Emergency Numbers Association, Presidential Leadership Award, National Association of Emergency Medical Technicians, Award of Merit, Associated Public–Safety Communications Officers, Public Education award, New York State Schools Transportation Safety Program, Certificate of Appreciation, American Red Cross, Presidential Leadership Award, Region 6, Mid–Coast Emergency Medical Services Council, and Southern Fire Command Service Award, Auckland, New Zealand, all for *Rescue 911;* Emmy Award nomination (with others), outstanding children's program, 1994, for *CBS Schoolbreak Special: Kids Killing Kids;* Humanitas Prize, special awards category for documentaries (with Melissa Jo Peltier), Human Family Educational and Cultural Institute, 1993, Humanitarian Award, Mothers against Sexual Abuse,

1997, American Legion Auxiliary awards, best television news/commentary and best in category, Silver Gavel Award, American Bar Association, Silver Effie Award, American Marketing Association, Silver Award, Houston International Film Festival, Autry Memorial Bravo Award, Birmingham International Film Festival, award from American Women in Radio and Television, For the Love of a Child Award, ChildHelp USA, Certificate of Appreciation, Los Angeles County Inter–Agency Council on Child Abuse and Neglect, Certificate of Merit, National Catholic Association for Broadcasters and Allied Communicators, and Bronze Anvil Award, Public Relations Society of America, all for *Scared Silent: Exposing and Ending Child Abuse;* Emmy Award, outstanding children's program (with others), 1994, CINE Golden Eagle, 1995, National Education Association Award, 1995, and American Library Association citation, "video for young adults," 1996, all for *Kids Killing Kids;* honorary D.F.A., University of Massachusetts, 1995; George Foster Peabody Broadcasting Award, Henry W. Grady School of Journalism and Mass Communications, University of Georgia, c. 1995, and Larry Stewart Leadership and Inspiration Award, Prism Awards, Entertainment Industries Council, 2000, both for *Break the Silence: Kids against Child Abuse;* William H. Parker Los Angeles Police Foundation Award, 1997; Humanitarian Award, Mothers against Sexual Abuse, 1997; Emmy Award, outstanding children's program (with others), 1999, for *The Teen Files: The Truth about Drinking;* Chris Plaque, 1998, CINE Golden Eagle Award and American Library Association Award, notable children's video, both 1999, Summit '99 Film Festival Award, National Network of Violence Prevention Practitioners, Governors' Award, Academy of Television Arts and Sciences, Guardian Award, National Association of Broadcasters, and Spirit of Hope Award, New Directions for Youth, all 2000, and Gold Cindy Award, all for the series *The Teen Files;* Shine Award, outstanding youth program, Media Project, 2000, for *The Teen Files: The Truth about Sex;* Humanitarian Award, Los Angeles Commission on Assaults against Women, 2000; Emmy Award (with others), outstanding children's program, 2001, for *The Teen Files: Surviving High School;* Exceptional Merit Media Award, television and radio documentary category, National Women's Political Caucus, 2001, for *Hidden Victims: Children of Domestic Violence;* New York Festivals World Medal, international television programming, 2001, for *Flipped;* commendation for Prism Award, outstanding television documentary special, 2002, for "Drugs," *Flipped;* Electronic Media Award, National Council on Problem Gambling, 2002, for "Gambling," *Flipped;* Shine Award, best youth program, 2002, for "Safe Sex," *Flipped;* Major Norman Hatch Award, Marine Corps Heritage Foundation, 2002, for *Heroes of Iwo Jima;* Albert Schweitzer Leadership Award, Hugh O'Brian Youth Foundation, 2002; National Outstanding Contribution Award (with Allison Grodner), Students against Drunk Driving, 2002.

CREDITS

Television Executive Producer; Series:
Medix, syndicated, 1974–76.
Couples, syndicated, 1982–83.
Pet Peeves, Lifetime, 1983–84.
Wish upon a Star, The Disney Channel, 1983–84.
Rescue 911, CBS, 1989–96.
L.A. Detectives, Arts and Entertainment, 1998–2000.
The Love Chronicles, Arts and Entertainment, 1999–2000.
Missing Persons, MSNBC, 2000–2001.
Flipped, MTV, 2001–2002.
Big Brother, CBS, 2001—.
Music behind Bars, VH1, 2002.
True Crime: Crimes of Passion, USA Network, 2002.
Family Business, Showtime, 2002–2004.
Minding the Stars, TBS, 2005.
The Road to Stardom with Missy Elliot, UPN, 2005.
Brat Camp, ABC, 2005.
Situation: Comedy, Bravo, 2005.
Blow Out, Bravo, 2005–2006.
Homeland Security USA, ABC, 2008–2009.

Television Executive Producer; Specials:
Happy 30th Birthday Los Angeles Television, KTLA, 1977.
The Feminine Mistake, syndicated, 1977.
The Science Fiction Film Awards, syndicated, 1978, 1979.
Gene Autry: An American Hero, 1980.
The Real Rookies, syndicated, 1981.
The Great Weight Loss Challenge, syndicated, 1983.
Samantha Smith Goes to Washington, The Disney Channel, 1984.
Return to Iwo Jima, PBS, 1985.
The Unknown Soldier, PBS, 1985.
King Kong: The Living Legend, syndicated, 1986.
Future Flight, syndicated, 1987.
P.O.W.—Americans in Enemy Hands: World War II, Korea, and Vietnam, syndicated, 1987.
Scared Straight! 10 Years Later, syndicated, 1987.
Top Flight, CBS, 1987.
"Hiroshima Maiden," WonderWorks, PBS, 1988.
Korean War—The Untold Story, syndicated, 1988.
Liberace, 1988.
Fatal Passions, syndicated, 1989.
See Dick and Jane ... Lie, Cheat, and Steal: Teaching Morality to Kids, syndicated, 1989.
The Trouble with Teachers, 1989.
The Truth about Teachers, syndicated, 1989.
The American Dream Contest, syndicated, 1990.
New and Improved Kids, syndicated, 1990.
Take Me to Your Leaders, syndicated, 1990.
True Detectives, CBS, 1990.
Over the Influence: Preventing and Recovering Our Kids from Drugs and Alcohol, syndicated, 1991.
Secret Lives of Husbands and Wives, CBS, 1992.

Best Wishes with Ringo Star, 1993.
Break the Silence: Kids against Child Abuse, CBS, 1994.
Kids Killing Kids (also known as *Kids Killing Kids/Kids Saving Kids*), CBS and Fox, 1994.
Scared Silent: Exposing and Ending Child Abuse, CBS, NBC, and PBS, 1994.
Victory over Violence, syndicated, 1994.
Everybody's Business: America's Children, NBC, 1995.
American Bounty Hunter, UPN, 1996.
(And director) *Bad Dads,* Fox, 1996.
The Story of Santa Claus (animated), CBS, 1996.
Uncommon Heroes, CBS, 1996.
What's Right with America, CBS, 1997.
Heart of Fire (also known as *The Tanker Incident*), 1997.
The Children Are Watching, PBS, 1999.
Countdown 100: Greatest Achievements of the 20th Century, The Learning Channel, 1999.
Scared Straight! 1999, MTV, 1999.
(And director) *Scared Straight! 20 Years Later,* UPN, 1999.
Teen Files: Smoking; Truth or Dare?, UPN, 1999.
Teen Files: The Truth about Drinking, UPN, 1999.
Teen Files: The Truth about Hate, UPN, 1999.
Teen Files: The Truth about Sex, UPN, 1999.
Teen Files: The Truth about Violence, UPN, 1999.
Hidden Victims: Children of Domestic Violence, Lifetime, 2000.
Hype and Glory: Sweeps Month, Arts and Entertainment, 2000.
Parole Board: Kentucky, Arts and Entertainment, 2000.
Parole Board: Nevada, Arts and Entertainment, 2000.
Parole Board: West Virginia, Arts and Entertainment, 2000.
Teen Files: Surviving High School, UPN, 2000.
Teen Files: The Truth about Drugs, UPN, 2000.
Hidden Victims: Children of Domestic Violence, 2000.
Heroes of Iwo Jima, Arts and Entertainment, 2001.
Parole Board: Kentucky State Reformatory, Arts and Entertainment, 2001.
Parole Board: Louisiana, Arts and Entertainment, 2001.
Parole Board: Montana, Arts and Entertainment, 2001.
Parole Board: New Hampshire, Arts and Entertainment, 2001.
Parole Board: New Jersey, Arts and Entertainment, 2001.
Parole Board: Oklahoma, Arts and Entertainment, 2001.
About Face: How the Military Changed My Life, 2001.
Dear Santa, ABC, 2002.
Parole Board: Missouri, Arts and Entertainment, 2002.
Small Town Ecstasy, HBO, 2002.
DNA: Guilty or Innocent?, CBS, 2002.
Blow Out: Reunion Special, Bravo, 2004.

Television Executive Producer; Episodic:
"Death Row Diary," *MSNBC Investigates,* 2001.
The Family, ABC, 2003.
"Love and Limos," *Minding the Store,* TBS, 2005.
"La Jolla," *Minding the Store,* TBS, 2005.

"A Knight of Comedy," *Minding the Store,* TBS, 2005.
"Freedom High School: Oakley, CA," *If You Really Knew Me,* MTV, 2010.

Television Producer; Specials:
(And director) *Scared Straight!,* HBO, 1978.
Scared Straight! Another Story, CBS, 1980.
The Singing Cowboys Ride Again, syndicated, 1982.
The Drug Knot, CBS, 1986.
Crimes of Violence, syndicated, 1988.

Television Executive Producer; Miniseries:
True Detectives, CBS, 1991.
Victory over Violence, 1994.
Inside America's Military Academies, The Discovery Channel, 1999.
Perfect Crimes?, History Channel, 2000–2001.
Helen of Troy, USA Network, 2002.

Television Executive Producer; Movies:
Scared Straight! Another Story, CBS, 1980.
Good Night, Sweet Wife: A Murder in Boston, CBS, 1990.
The Man with Three Wives, CBS, 1993.
Heart of Fire (also known as *The Tanker Incident*), CBS, 1997.

Television Executive Producer; Pilots:
American Heartline, syndicated, 1987.
Rescue: 911, CBS, 1989.
Best Wishes, CBS, 1993.
Ladylaw, syndicated, 1997.
Sworn Enemies, Court TV, 1999.
Family Business, Showtime, 2003.

Television Appearances; Specials:
Prism Awards 2000, syndicated, 2000.

Film Executive Producer:
Future Flight, 1987.

RECORDINGS

Video Producer:
The History Disquiz (video game), MCA, 1982.
Parents Video Magazine, Parts 1–3, Lorimar–Telepictures, 1985.
May You Live to Be 120: Jewish Homes for the Aged, 1986.
Health Champions, 1988.
How to Stop the One You Love from Drinking and Using Drugs, Paramount Home Video, 1988.
Vista Del Mar: The Future Begins Here, 1988.
Interactive Diner, 1989.
Look Who's Balking, 1990.

Somewhere to Turn: The Riess–Davis Child Study Center, 1990.
For Our Children: Parents Anonymous, 1990.
The Parent's License, 1991.
Changing Minds … Changing Times … A PETA Family Album, 1991.

WRITINGS

Television Specials:
Scared Straight!, HBO, 1978.
The Singing Cowboys Ride Again, syndicated, 1982.
The Unknown Soldier, PBS, 1985.
Future Flight, syndicated, 1987.
Kids Killing Kids (also known as *Kids Killing Kids/Kids Saving Kids*), CBS and Fox, 1994.
Scared Silent: Exposing and Ending Child Abuse, CBS, NBC, and PBS, 1994.
The Children Are Watching, PBS, 1999.
Scared Straight! 20 Years Later, UPN, 1999.
Teen Files: The Truth about Hate, UPN, 1999.
Heroes of Iwo Jima, Arts and Entertainment, 2001.

OTHER SOURCES

Electronic:
Arnold Shapiro Productions, http://www.arnoldshapiroproductions.com/, July 27, 2010.

SHAVER, Helen 1951–

PERSONAL

Born February 24, 1951, in St. Thomas, Ontario, Canada; married Steven Reuther (a producer), October 29, 1979 (divorced, 1982); married Steven Smith (a camera operator), October 9, 1988; children: Mackenzie (son). *Education:* Attended University of Victoria; Banff School of Fine Arts, A.B.

Addresses: *Manager*—Forward Entertainment, 9255 Sunset Blvd., Suite 805, Los Angeles, CA 90069.

Career: Actress, director, and producer. Began career as a stage actress in Canada.

Awards, Honors: Canadian Film Award (now Genie Award), best actress, Academy of Canadian Cinema and Television, 1978, for *In Praise of Older Women;* Bronze Leopard, Locarno International Film Festival, 1985, for *Desert Hearts;* Genie Award nomination, best actress, 1987, for *Lost!;* Gemini Award nomination, best actress in a dramatic program or miniseries, Academy of Canadian Cinema and Television, 1989, for *No Blame; Theatre World* Award, 1992, for *Jake's Women;* Annual CableACE Award, National Cable Television Association, c. 1995, for "Sandkings: Parts 1 & 2," *The Outer Limits;* Saturn Award nomination, best genre television actress, Academy of Science Fiction, Fantasy, and Horror Films, 1997, for *Poltergeist: The Legacy;* Children's Jury Award, outstanding live–action feature film, 1999, Chicago International Children's Film Festival, 1999, and Daytime Emmy Award nomination, outstanding directing in a children's special, 2000, both for *Summer's End;* Genie Award, best supporting actress, 2001, for *We All Fall Down;* Gemini Award nomination, best direction in a dramatic series, 2001, for *The Outer Limits;* Gemini Award, best direction in a dramatic series, 2003, for "Death's Details," *Just Cause;* received star on Canadian Walk of Fame.

CREDITS

Film Appearances:

Paula Lissitzen, *Shoot,* Avco Embassy, 1976.

Girl hitchhiker, *The Supreme Kid,* Cinepix, 1976.

El hombre desnudo (also known as *The Naked Man*), 1976.

Jo, *Outrageous!,* Cinema V, 1977.

Pickup, *High–Ballin',* American International Pictures, 1978.

Ann MacDonald, *In Praise of Older Women,* Avco Embassy, 1978.

Betty Duncan, *Starship Invasions* (also known as *Alien Encounter, Project Genocide, War of the Aliens,* and *Winged Serpent*), Warner Bros., 1978.

Carolyn, *The Amityville Horror,* American International Pictures, 1979.

Ruth Thompson, *Who Has Seen the Wind?,* 1077, Cinema World, 1980.

Rhonda, *Gas,* Paramount, 1981.

Catherine Tuttle, *Harry Tracy, Desperado* (also known as *Harry Tracy*), Quartet, 1982.

Virginia Tremayne, *The Osterman Weekend* (also known as *Mission CIA*), Twentieth Century–Fox, 1983.

Claire Lewis, *Best Defense,* Paramount, 1984.

Isobel, *Coming Out Alive,* TransWorld Entertainment, 1984.

Vivian Bell, *Desert Hearts,* Samuel Goldwyn, 1985.

Maria, *The War Boy,* Hollywood Home Entertainment, 1985.

Janelle, *The Color of Money,* Buena Vista, 1986.

Linda, *Lost!,* Simcom–Norstar, 1986.

(Uncredited) Sarah, *The Men's Club,* 1986.

Jessica Halliday (some sources cite Jessica Hallowell), *The Believers,* Orion, 1987.

Herself, *Walking after Midnight,* Kay Film, 1988.

Voice of Littlefoot's mother, *The Land Before Time* (animated), Universal, 1988.

Herself, *Strangers in a Strange Land: The Adventures of a Canadian Film Crew in China,* 1988.

Benet Archdale, *Innocent Victim* (also known as *Tree of Hands*), Castle Hill/Academy Home, 1990.

The Devil, *A Smile in the Dark* (also known as *California 405, A Day in L.A., Destination Unknown,* and *Jungle of Love*), 1991.

Diane, *Zebrahead* (also known as *The Colour of Love*), Triumph Releasing, 1992.

Mrs. Dowd, *Dr. Bethune* (also known as *Bethune: The Making of a Hero*), Tara Releasing, 1993.

Ann O'Connor, *That Night* (also known as *One Hot Summer*), Warner Bros., 1993.

Margaret Heller, *Born to Be Wild* (also known as *Katie*), Warner Bros., 1995.

Kate White Reilly, *Tremors 2: Aftershocks,* Universal, 1995.

Slim, *Rowing Through,* 1996.

Rachel Rowen, *Open Season,* Legacy Releasing, 1996.

Grace Downs, *The Craft,* Columbia TriStar, 1996.

Gladys, *Egg Salad,* 1996.

Narrator, *Under Wraps,* 1996.

Sherry, *We All Fall Down,* Road Cone, 2000.

Sara Bradley, *Bear with Me,* River of Stone Productions/WIC Entertainment, 2000.

Audrey, *Numb,* Scanbox Entertainment, 2007.

Herself, *The Citizen Cohl: Untold Story* (short film), Melbar Entertainment Group, 2008.

Also appeared in *Christina;* according to some sources, provided voice of Gloria Revelle for the 1984 film *Body Double.*

Film Work:

Executive producer, *We All Fall Down,* Road Cone, 2000.

Television Appearances; Series:

Dr. Liz Warren, *Search and Rescue: The Alpha Team* (also known as *Search and Rescue*), NBC, 1977–78.

Libby Chapin, *United States,* NBC, 1980.

Title role, *Jessica Novak,* CBS, 1981.

Kelby Robinson, *WIOU,* CBS, 1990–91.

Dr. Rachel Corrigan, *Poltergeist: The Legacy,* Showtime, 1996–98, Sci-Fi Channel, 1996–99.

Erica Bettis, *The Education of Max Bickford,* CBS, beginning 2001.

Also appeared in the series *Terminal City,* CBC.

Television Appearances; Movies:

Patty, *Lovey: A Circle of Children, Part II,* CBS, 1978.

Mrs. O'Mara, *Overlanders,* 1979.

Miss Beecher, *Off Your Rocker,* 1980.

Susan Frazer, *Between Two Brothers,* CBS, 1982.

Dorian Waldorf, *Countdown to Looking Glass,* HBO, 1984.

Valery Weaver, *The Park Is Mine,* HBO, 1985.
Sally Robinson, *Many Happy Returns,* CBS, 1986.
Amy Donaldson, *No Blame,* 1988.
Claire Nichols, *Mothers, Daughters, and Lovers* (also known as *American River*), NBC, 1989.
Rose, *Pair of Aces,* CBS, 1990.
Elaine Tipton, *Fatal Memories* (also known as *The Eileen Franklin Story* and *Memory of a Murder*), NBC, 1992.
Edie Ballew, *Poisoned by Love: The Kern County Murders* (also known as *Blind Angel* and *Murder So Sweet*), CBS, 1993.
Katherine Woodfield, *Trial & Error,* USA Network, 1993.
Stacy Larkin, *Survive the Night* (also known as *Endless Fear* and *Night Hunt*), USA Network, 1993.
Lula Peaks, *Morning Glory,* 1993.
Katherine Barnes, *Ride with the Wind,* ABC, 1994.
Nora Fields, *Without Consent* (also known as *Tell Laura I Love Her* and *Trapped and Deceived*), ABC, 1994.
Dr. Monique Dessier, *The Forget–Me–Not Murders* (also known as *Janek: The Forget–Me–Not Murders* and *Janek: The Wallflower Murders*), CBS, 1994.
Dr. Monique Dessier, *A Silent Betrayal* (also known as *Janek: The Brownstone Murders* and *Janek: A Silent Betrayal*), CBS, 1994.
Mary (some sources cite Ellen), *Falling for You,* CBS, 1995.
Mrs. Martin, *The Sweetest Gift,* Showtime, 1998.
Wallis Clayton, *The Wishing Tree,* Showtime, 1999.
Janet, *Common Ground,* Showtime, 2000.
Lynn Todd, *The Risen,* Women's Television Network, 2003.
Sandy Moose, *D.C. Sniper: 23 Days of Fear,* USA Network, 2003.
Ruthie, *The Keeper,* Showtime, 2004.
Rose, *A Very Merry Daughter of the Bride,* Lifetime, 2008.
Iris's mom, *Iris Expanding,* The CW, 2010.

Television Appearances; Episodic:
Bonnie, "Death Holds the Scale," *Police Surgeon* (also known as *Dr. Simon Locke*), ITV, 1972.
"Affairs of the Heart," *The Beachcombers,* CBC, 1974.
"Detroit Story," *King of Kensington,* CBC, 1976.
The Alan Hamel Show, CTV, 1977, 1978, 1979.
The Tonight Show Starring Johnny Carson, NBC, 1979.
The Alan Thicke Show (also known as *Fast Company* and *Prime Cuts*), 1981.
Teresa, "Officer of the Year," *Hill Street Blues,* NBC, 1982.
Teresa, "A Hair of the Dog," *Hill Street Blues,* NBC, 1982.
Teresa, "The Phantom of the Hill," *Hill Street Blues,* NBC, 1982.
Teresa, "No Body's Perfect," *Hill Street Blues,* NBC, 1982.
Lisa Jericho, "The Shadow of Truth," *T. J. Hooker,* ABC, 1983.

Karen, "Mirror, Mirror," *Amazing Stories* (also known as *Steven Spielberg's "Amazing Stories"*), NBC, 1986.
Belle Dellaguerra, "Spanish Blood," *Philip Marlowe, Private Eye,* HBO, 1986.
Phyllis Dayton, "The Case of the Friendly Fugitive," *The Edison Twins,* CBC, 1986.
Phyllis Dayton, "Gems and Jelly Beans," *The Edison Twins,* CBC, 1986.
Phyllis Dayton, "The Maharajah of Weston," *The Edison Twins,* CBC, 1986.
Miss Haight, "The Emissary," *Ray Bradbury Theatre,* USA Network, 1988.
Cinema 3, 1988.
Dr. Diane Decker, "The Dancer's Touch," *B. L. Stryker* (broadcast as a presentation of *ABC Mystery Movie*), ABC, 1989.
Vivian Dimitri, "Rest in Peace, Mrs. Columbo," *Columbo* (broadcast as a presentation of *ABC Saturday Mystery*), ABC, 1990.
Sarah, "Child's Play," *E.N.G.,* Lifetime, 1992.
Late Night with David Letterman, NBC, 1992.
The Tonight Show with Jay Leno, NBC, 1993.
Cathy Kress, "Sandkings: Parts 1 & 2," *The Outer Limits* (also known as *The New Outer Limits*), Showtime, 1995.
Dianna McKinney, "Next of Kin," *Dead Man's Gun,* Showtime, 1997.
Faye Buckley (some sources cite Lynn Buckley), "Luck, Next Time," *The L Word,* Showtime, 2004.
Faye Buckley (some sources cite Lynn Buckley), "Liberally," *The L Word,* Showtime, 2004.
Barbara Yates, "Becoming," *The 4400,* USA Network, 2004.
Barbara Yates, "Trial by Fire," *The 4400,* USA Network, 2004.
Herself, "In Praise of Older Women," *On Screen!,* Total Living Network, 2005.

According to some sources, also appeared in episodes of *Crusoe,* NBC, and *Terminal City,* CBC.

Television Appearances; Specials:
The Grand Knockout Tournament, 1987.
M*A*S*H, Tootsie, and God: A Tribute to Larry Gelbart, PBS, 1998.
Outer Limits Farewell Tribute, Showtime, 2000.
Narrator, *To Love, Honour, and Obey,* 2001.

Television Appearances; Pilots:
Kelby Robinson, *WIOU,* CBS, 1990.
President Marjorie Litchfield, *The First Gentleman,* CBS, 1994.

Television Work; Series:
Director, *The Outer Limits* (also known as *The New Outer Limits*), Showtime, multiple episodes, between 1998 and 2000.

Director, *Judging Amy,* CBS, multiple episodes, between 2001 and 2005.

Producer, *Judging Amy,* CBS, 2004–2005.

Television Director; Movies:

Summer's End, Showtime, 1999.

(And producer) *Due East,* Showtime, 2002.

The Stranger I Married (also known as *The Man Who Lost Himself*), Lifetime, 2005.

Television Director; Pilots:

Ultra, CBS, 2006.

Television Director; Episodic:

"The Bones of St. Anthony," *Poltergeist: The Legacy,* Showtime, 1996.

"Brother's Keeper," *Poltergeist: The Legacy,* Showtime, 1996.

"Stagecoach Marty," *Dead Man's Gun,* Showtime, 1997.

"Bulls and Bears," *The Net,* USA Network, 1998.

"Be Careful What You Wish For," *Beggars and Choosers,* Showtime, 2000.

"Fathers and Sons," *Beggars and Choosers,* Showtime, 2001.

"This Crazy Life," *Soul Food,* Showtime, 2001.

"Don't Ask Don't Tell," *The Associates,* CTV, 2001.

"Shell Game," *The District,* CBS, 2002.

"Rest in Peace," *Dead like Me,* Showtime, 2003.

"The Uncertainty Principle," *Joan of Arcadia,* CBS, 2003.

"Death's Details," *Just Cause,* PAX, 2003.

"The Proposal," *The O.C.,* Fox, 2004.

"The New and Improved Carl Morrissey," *The 4400,* USA Network, 2004.

"Divine Directions," *Close to Home,* CBS, 2005.

"Doctor's Orders," *Medium,* NBC, 2006.

"The Feed," *Vanished,* Fox, 2006.

"Borderline," *Standoff,* Fox, 2006.

"Dedication," *The Unit,* CBS, 2006.

"Natural Selection," *The Unit,* CBS, 2006.

"Every Step You Take," *The Unit,* CBS, 2007.

"Winterland," *Journeyman,* NBC, 2007.

"Black Jack," *Jericho,* CBS, 2007.

"Streetwise," *Law & Order: Special Victims Unit* (also known as *Law & Order: SVU* and *Special Victims Unit*), NBC, 2008.

"Persona," *Law & Order: Special Victims Unit* (also known as *Law & Order: SVU* and *Special Victims Unit*), NBC, 2008.

"Name of the Game," *Crusoe,* NBC, 2008.

"Nothing to Talk About," *Private Practice,* ABC, 2008.

"Slip Slidin' Away," *Private Practice,* ABC, 2009.

"Solitary," *Law & Order: Special Victims Unit* (also known as *Law & Order: SVU* and *Special Victims Unit*), NBC, 2009.

"The Hunting Party," *Crusoe,* NBC, 2009.

"One Man's Treasure," *Castle,* ABC, 2009.

"Bedtime," *Law & Order: Special Victims Unit* (also known as *Law & Order: SVU* and *Special Victims Unit*), NBC, 2010.

Shattered, 2010.

"Save the Last Dance," *Make It or Break It,* ABC Family, 2010.

"Painted Ladies," *The Bridge,* CBS, 2010.

"The Blame Game," *The Bridge,* CBS, 2010.

Also directed episodes of *The Agency* and *CSI: New York,* CBS.

Stage Appearances:

Tamara, Los Angeles, 1984.

Julia, *Ghost on Fire,* La Jolla Playhouse, La Jolla, CA, 1985.

Maggie, *Jake's Women,* Neil Simon Theatre, New York City, 1992.

Also appeared in *Are You Lookin'?; A Doll's House; The Hostage;* and *The Master Builder.*

RECORDINGS

Videos:

The Making of "We All Fall Down," 2002.

(Uncredited; in archive footage) Vivian Bell, *Sex at 24 Frames per Second,* Image Entertainment, 2003.

Alpha to Omega: Exposing "The Osterman Weekend," Anchor Bay Entertainment, 2004.

Audio Books:

Narrator, *Stories from Wilderness Tips,* by Margaret Atwood, 1992.

ADAPTATIONS

"Seduction," an episode of *Poltergeist: The Legacy* broadcast by Showtime in 1998, was based on a story by Shaver.

SHERMAN, Courtney 1946–
    (Courtney Simon)

PERSONAL

Born June 23, 1946; married Ed Easton (divorced, 1974); married Peter Simon (an actor), June 15, 1975; children: (second marriage) one.

Career: Writer and actress.

Awards, Honors: Writers Guild of America Award (with others), best writing for a daytime serial, 1985, for *Search for Tomorrow;* Daytime Emmy Award nominations, 1986, 2003, 2006, and Daytime Emmy Awards, 2001, 2002, 2004, 2005, all outstanding writing team for a drama series, Writers Guild of America Awards, 2007, 2009, and Writers Guild of America Award nomination, 2010, all best writing for a daytime serial, all (with others) for *As the World Turns;* Daytime Emmy Award nominations, 1988, 1989, and Daytime Emmy Award, 1990, all outstanding writing team for a drama series (with others), for *Santa Barbara;* Daytime Emmy Award, outstanding writing team for a drama series, 1993, and Writers Guild of America Award nomination, best writing for a daytime serial, 1996, all (with others) for *The Guiding Light;* Daytime Emmy Award, outstanding writing team for a drama series, 1997, Writers Guild of America Award, best writing for a daytime serial, 1997, and Writers Guild of America Award nomination, best writing for a daytime serial, 1998, all (with others) for *All My Children;* Daytime Emmy Award nomination, outstanding writing team for a drama series, 1998, Writers Guild of America Award, best writing for a daytime serial, 1998, and Writers Guild of America Award nomination, best writing for a daytime serial, 1999, all (with others) for *General Hospital.*

CREDITS

Television Appearances; Series:
Dinah Buckley, *The Guiding Light,* CBS, 1970–71.
Kathy Parker Phillips Taper, *Search for Tomorrow,* CBS, 1971–78, then NBC, 1983–84.
Dr. Anna Tolan, *All My Children* (also known as *AMC*), ABC, 1990–91, 1996–97.
Dr. Constance Peterson, *The City,* ABC, 1995–96.
June Reiner, *Another World,* NBC, 1999.
Dr. Lynn Michaels, a recurring role, *As the World Turns,* CBS, 2001–2005.

Television Appearances; Episodic:
The Mike Douglas Show, syndicated, 1977.

Film Appearances:
Iris McCabe, *Dirtymouth,* Superior Pictures, 1970.
Nick's mother Susan, *Roger Dodger,* Artisan Entertainment, 2002.

Stage Appearances:
Sheila McCardle, *Man Enough,* Pequod Productions, Apple Corps Theatre, New York City, 1995.

WRITINGS

Television Series:
All My Children (also known as *AMC*), ABC, 1995–96.
(As Courtney Simon) *One Life to Live,* ABC, 2010.

Television Episodes:
As the World Turns, CBS, 1984 and (as Courtney Simon) 2005.
(As Simon) *Santa Barbara,* NBC, 1985, 1988.
Loving, ABC, 1991.
(As Simon) *The Guiding Light,* CBS, 1993.
(As Simon) *General Hospital,* ABC, 1998.

Also writer for *Another World,* NBC.

SHYER, Charles 1941–
(J. W. Melville)

PERSONAL

Full name, Charles Richard Shyer; born October 11, 1941, in Los Angeles, CA; son of Melville (a film director and production executive) and Lois (maiden name, Jones) Shyer; married Nancy Meyers (a screenwriter, director, and producer), July 28, 1995 (divorced), married Deborah Lynn (an actress), 2004; children: (first marriage) Annie, Hallie; (second marriage) two. *Education:* Attended University of California, Los Angeles.

Addresses: *Agent*—International Creative Management, 8942 Wilshire Blvd., Beverly Hills, CA 90211.

Career: Writer, director, and producer. Began career as assistant director and production manager.

Member: Academy of Motion Picture Arts and Sciences, Writers Guild of America, American Society of Composers, Authors, and Publishers, Directors Guild of America, Writers Guild of America–West.

Awards, Honors: Writers Guild of America Award nomination (with others), best comedy writing, c. 1979, for *House Calls;* Academy Award nomination and Writers Guild of America–West Award (both with Nancy Meyers and Harvey Miller), both best original screenplay, 1981, for *Private Benjamin;* Humanitas Prize (with Meyers), Human Family Educational and Cultural Institute, 1989, for "Guilt," *Baby Boom.*

CREDITS

Film Producer:
(With Nancy Meyers), *Private Benjamin,* Warner Bros., 1980.

(With Meyers) *Baby Boom,* United Artists, 1987.
(With Meyers) *Father of the Bride,* Buena Vista, 1991.
The Parent Trap (also known as *Disney's "The Parent Trap"*), Buena Vista, 1998.
The Affair of the Necklace, Warner Bros., 2001.
Alfie, Paramount, 2004.
Eloise in Paris, 2010.

Film Director:
Irreconcilable Differences, Warner Bros., 1984.
Baby Boom, United Artists, 1987.
Father of the Bride, Buena Vista, 1991.
I Love Trouble, Buena Vista, 1994.
Father of the Bride Part II, Buena Vista, 1995.
The Affair of the Necklace, Warner Bros., 2001.
Alfie, Paramount, 2004.
Eloise in Paris, 2010.

Film Work; Other:
Second unit director, *The Parent Trap* (also known as *Disney's "The Parent Trap"*), Buena Vista, 1998.

Television Director; Episodic:
(Assistant director) "Everybody Wants to Be a Writer," *The Mothers–in–Law,* 1967.
"Two Men on a Hoarse," *The Odd Couple,* ABC, 1975.
Baby Boom, NBC, 1988.

Television Director; Movies:
Him and Us, ABC, 2006.

Television Producer; Pilots:
(With Alan Mandel), *Cops,* CBS, 1973.

Television Producer; Series:
Love, American Style, 1969.

Television Executive Producer; Series:
(With Nancy Meyers), *Baby Boom,* NBC, 1988.

Television Appearances; Episodic:
"'The Affair of the Necklace': The Making of a Scandal," *HBO First Look,* HBO, 2001.
Film (also known as *Film of the Year* and *The Film Programme*), BBC, 2004.
"Lindsay Lohan," *E! True Hollywood Story,* E! Entertainment Television, 2005.

Television Appearances; Specials:
Movie News Hot Summer Sneak Preview, CBS, 1994.

WRITINGS

Screenplays:
(With James Lee Barrett and Alan Mandel) *Smokey and the Bandit,* MCA/Universal, 1977.

(With Mandel, Max Shulman, and Julius J. Epstein) *House Calls* (based on a book by Shulman and Epstein), Universal, 1978.
(With Mandel, John Herman Shanner, and A. Ramrus) *Goin' South* (based on a story by Shanner and Ramrus), Paramount, 1978.
(With Nancy Meyers and Harvey Miller) *Private Benjamin,* Warner Bros., 1980.
(With Meyers) *Irreconcilable Differences,* Warner Bros., 1984.
Protocol, Warner Bros., 1984.
(As J. W. Melville) *Jumpin' Jack Flash,* 1986.
(With Meyers) *Baby Boom,* United Artists, 1987.
(With Meyers, Frances Goodrich, and Albert Hackett; and composer of the song "I'm Your Man") *Father of the Bride,* Buena Vista, 1991.
(With Meyers and others) *Once upon a Crime,* Metro–Goldwyn–Mayer, 1992.
(With Meyers) *I Love Trouble,* Buena Vista, 1994.
(With Meyers) *Father of the Bride Part II,* Buena Vista, 1995.
The Parent Trap (also known as *Disney's "The Parent Trap"*), Buena Vista, 1998.
The Affair of the Necklace, Warner Bros., 2001.
(And composer of songs "Darkness of Your Love" and "That Friend of Mine") *Alfie,* Paramount, 2004.
Eloise in Paris, 2010.

Television Episodes:
"You Gotta Have Soul," *Barefoot in the Park,* 1970.
"Nothin' But the Truth," *Barefoot in the Park,* 1970.
"Bunny Is Missing Down by the Lake," *The Odd Couple,* ABC, 1971.
"Jenny, Jenny," *Getting Together,* ABC, 1971.
"A Man Called Snake," *The Partridge Family,* 1971.
"The Muckrackers," *Happy Days* (also known as *Happy Days Again*), 1976.
"Benjamin to the Rescue," *Private Benjamin,* 1981.
(With Nancy Meyers) "Guilt," *Baby Boom,* NBC, 1988.
"The Right School for Elizabeth," *Baby Boom,* NBC, 1988.

Also writer for episodes of *All in the Family.*

Television Writing; Other:
(With Alan Mandel and Dean Hargrove) *Lady Luck* (pilot), NBC, 1973.
Baby Boom (pilot), NBC, 1988.

ADAPTATIONS

The television series *Private Benjamin,* broadcast by CBS in 1981, and *Baby Boom,* broadcast by NBC in 1988, were based on characters created by Shyer and Nancy Meyers for their screenplays of the same titles.

SIMON, Courtney
    See **SHERMAN, Courtney**

SMITH, Danny 1973–

PERSONAL

Full name, Daniel Arthur Smith; born October 2, 1973, in Montreal, Quebec, Canada; raised in Pickering, Ontario, Canada. *Education:* Studied improvisational comedy at Second City, Toronto, Ontario.

Career: Actor and composer. Singer, guitarist, pianist, and songwriter for the band City Drive; appeared in commercial for Canadian McDonald's restaurants, 2009. 1888 (clothing company and environmental fundraiser), founder, 2006.

Awards, Honors: *Montreal Mirror* Awards, best actor and most desirable male, 2001.

CREDITS

Television Appearances; Series:
Who Rules?, YTV, 1995.
Jonovision, CBC, 1996–97.
Merton J. Dingle, *Big Wolf on Campus,* Fox Family, 1999–2002.

Television Appearances; Movies:
Buck Greene, *Open Season,* HBO, 1995.
Stagehand, *Sugartime,* HBO, 1995.
Khaki kid, *White Lies,* CBC, 1998.
Ensign Mac, *Deadliest Sea,* Discovery Channel, 2009.
Tim, *Harriet the Spy: Blog Wars,* The Disney Channel, 2010.

Television Appearances; Episodic:
Student, "Howie Farr Is Too Far," *Class of '96,* Fox, 1993.
Sketch performer, *It's Alive!,* YTV, 1993, 1994.
Contestant, *The Price Is Right,* 2001.
Entertainment Tonight Canada (also known as *ET Canada*), Global TV, 2005, 2010.

First poker player, "Missing," *The Listener,* NBC, 2009.

Appeared in an episode of *Open Mike with Mike Bullard* (also known as *The Mike Bullard Show* and *Open Mike*), Global TV.

Television Appearances; Other:
Merton J. Dingle, *Big Wolf on Campus* (pilot), Fox Family, 1999.
Himself, *Camp Hollywood,* 2004.

Film Appearances:
(Uncredited) Superguy, *PCU,* Twentieth Century–Fox, 1994.
Barry "Virus" Kremmer, *Senior Trip* (also known as *National Lampoon's "Senior Trip"*), New Line Cinema, 1995.
Video store kid, *The Big Hit* (also known as *Warheads*), TriStar, 1998.
Groundhog, *Strike!* (also known as *All I Wanna Do, Girl Power,* and *The Hairy Bird*), Miramax, 1998.
Boy Meets Girl, ARTO–pelli Motion Pictures III, 1998.
Benji Berg, *The Bail* (also known as *Fizzy Bizness*), Regent Entertainment, 2002.
Jerry, *Suck,* Alliance Films/Equinoxe Films, 2009.

RECORDINGS

Albums; With City Drive:
Always Moving Never Stopping, 2006.
Egocentral, 2007.

WRITINGS

Television Music; Series:
Theme song, *Big Wolf on Campus,* Fox Family, 1999–2002.

Songs Featured in Films:
"Bring Me Everything" and "Defeated," *American Pie Presents "Band Camp,"* Universal, 2005.

SOBIESKI, Leelee 1982–

PERSONAL

Full name, Lilane Rudabet Gloria Elsveta Sobieski; born June 10, 1982, in New York, NY; daughter of Jean (an artist and painter) and Elizabeth (a novelist and screenwriter) Sobieski; married Adam Kimmel (a menswear designer), May 28, 2009. *Education:* Attended Brown University, c. 2001. *Avocational Interests:* Tae kwon do, movies, music, painting, ceramics, poetry, horseback riding.

Addresses: *Agent*—William Morris Agency, 151 El Camino Dr., Beverly Hills, CA 90212; United Talent Agency, 9560 Wilshire Blvd., Suite 500, Beverly Hills, CA 90212. *Manager*—Magnolia Entertainment, 9595 Wilshire Blvd., Suite 601, Beverly Hills, CA 90212. *Publicist*—Kane and Associates, Pinnacle Public Relations, 8265 Sunset Blvd., Suite 201, Los Angeles, CA 90046.

Career: Actress and producer.

Awards, Honors: Chicago Film Critics Association Award nomination, most promising actress, and Young Artist Award nomination, best performance in a feature film by a leading young actress, both 1999, for *A Soldier's Daughter Never Cries;* YoungStar Award nomination, best performance by a young actress in a comedy film, *Hollywood Reporter,* 1999, for *Never Been Kissed;* Emmy Award nomination, outstanding lead actress in a miniseries or a movie, and YoungStar Award, best young actress in a miniseries or television movie, both 1999, Golden Globe Award nomination, and Golden Satellite Award nomination, both best actress in a miniseries or motion picture made for television, 2000, all for *Joan of Arc;* Young Hollywood Award, female superstar of tomorrow, *Movieline,* 2000; Teen Choice Award nomination, choice breakout performance, 2000, for *Here on Earth;* Golden Globe Award nomination, best actress in a miniseries or motion picture made for television, 2002, for *Uprising.*

CREDITS

Film Appearances:
Karen Kempster, *Jungle 2 Jungle* (also known as *Un Indien a New York*), Buena Vista, 1997.
Charlotte Anne "Channe" Willis at age fourteen, *A Soldier's Daughter Never Cries* (also known as *La fille d'un soldat ne pleure jamais*), October Films, 1998.
Sarah Hotchner Beiderman, *Deep Impact,* Paramount/DreamWorks, 1998.
Milich's daughter, *Eyes Wide Shut* (also known as *EWS*), Warner Bros., 1999.
Aldys Martin, *Never Been Kissed,* Twentieth Century–Fox, 1999.
Samantha "Sam" Cavanaugh, *Here on Earth,* Twentieth Century–Fox, 2000.
Jennifer "J" Anne Wilson, *My First Mister,* Paramount, 2001.
Venna, *Joy Ride* (also known as *Road Kill*), Twentieth Century–Fox, 2001.

Ruby Baker, *The Glass House,* Columbia, 2001.
Sarah Silver, *L'idole* (also known as *The Idol*), 2002.
Liselore Von Peltz, *Max,* Lions Gate Films/Alliance Atlantis Motion Picture Distribution, 2002.
Sarah, *Lying,* Arthouse Films, 2006.
Victoria Price, *Heavens Fall,* Allumination Filmworks, 2006.
Anna Veigh, *In a Dark Place,* Arsenal Pictures, 2006.
Sister Honey, *The Wicker Man* (also known as *Wicker Man—Ritual des Boesen*), Warner Bros., 2006.
Narrator, *Coven* (short film), 2006.
Lolita, *The Elder Son,* Peace Arch Home Entertainment, 2006.
Muriella, *In the Name of the King: A Dungeon Siege Tale* (also known as *Schwerter des Koenigs—Dungeon Siege*), Freestyle Releasing, 2007.
Lauren Douglas, *88 Minutes* (also known as *88* and *88: 88 Minutes*), Columbia, 2007.
Alberta, *Walk All Over Me,* Genius Products, 2007.
Olivia Flyn, *Acts of Violence,* I.L. Films, 2008.
Jody Balaban, *Finding Bliss,* 2009.
Chloe White, *Night Train,* National Entertainment Media, 2009.
Polly Hamilton, *Public Enemies,* Universal, 2009.
Stalker, *The Last Film Festival,* 2009.
Abby Gibbons, *The Mad Cow,* 2009.

Film Producer:
Two Other Dreams (short film), Psycho Kitty, 2009.

Also produced *Acts of Violence.*

Film Executive Producer:
Finding Bliss, 2009.

Television Appearances; Movies:
Anna Yates, *Reunion,* CBS, 1994.
Danielle "Danny" Fortuna, *A Horse for Danny,* ABC, 1995.
Deianeira, *Hercules,* NBC, 2005.

Television Appearances; Miniseries:
Title role, *Joan of Arc* (also known as *Jeanne d'Arc*), CBS, 1999.
Tosia Altman, *Uprising,* NBC, 2001.
Cecile de Volanges, *Les liaisons dangereuses* (also known as *Dangerous Liaisons*), Women's Entertainment Television, 2002.

Television Appearances; Series:
Jenny Grace, *Charlie Grace,* ABC, 1995.

Television Appearances; Episodic:
Lucy, "Positively Hateful," *Grace under Fire,* ABC, 1996.

Leslie, "Love, Death, and Soda," *The Home Court,* NBC, 1996.

Girl, "Arcade," *NewsRadio,* NBC, 1996.

Tanya, "Evil Eye," *F/X: The Series,* syndicated, 1998.

Voice of Sheila, "Enemy at the Gate," *Frasier,* NBC, 2002.

Entertainment Tonight (also known as *E.T., ET Weekend, Entertainment This Week* and *This Week in Entertainment*), syndicated, 2007.

Samantha Colby, "A Mother's Secret," *Drop Dead Diva,* Lifetime, 2010.

Television Talk Show Guest Appearances; Episodic:

Late Night with David Letterman, 1999.

The Tonight Show with Jay Leno, 1999, 2000, 2006.

The Rosie O'Donnell Show, syndicated, 1999, 2000.

The Daily Show (also known as *A Daily Show with Jon Stewart, Jon Stewart, The Daily Show with Jon Stewart* and *The Daily Show with Jon Stewart Global Edition*), 2000.

The Late Late Show with Craig Ferguson, CBS, 2005.

Last Call with Carson Daly, NBC, 2008.

Television Appearances; Specials:

Come Together: A Night for John Lennon's Words and Music, 2001.

Presenter, *AFI Life Achievement Award: A Tribute to Al Pacino,* USA Network, 2007.

Television Appearances; Awards Presentations:

The 51st Annual Primetime Emmy Awards, 1999.

The Teen Choice Awards, Fox, 2000.

Presenter, *The 6th Annual Blockbuster Entertainment Awards,* Fox, 2000.

Presenter, *The 7th Annual Screen Actors Guild Awards,* TNT, 2001.

The 2002 IFP/West Independent Spirit Awards, 2002.

Young Hollywood Awards, Independent Film Channel, 2003.

RECORDINGS

Videos:

Breaking Down the Walls: The Road to Recreating the Warsaw Ghetto Uprising, 2001.

Appeared in the music video "Where You Are" by Jessica Simpson.

OTHER SOURCES

Books:

Newsmakers, Issue 3, Gale, 2002.

Periodicals:

Interview, September, 1998, pp. 158–61.

Los Angeles, September, 2000, p. 114.

Movieline, March, 1999, p. 11; March, 2000, pp. 54–60, 103.

People Weekly, October 5, 1998, p. 147; November 12, 2001, pp. 79–80.

Premiere, September, 1999, pp. 94–96; October, 2001, pp. 82–83.

Seventeen, December, 1998, p. 106; October, 1999, pp. 130–34.

Teen People, February, 1999, p. 71.

Time Out New York, August 30, 2001, pp. 34–35.

TV Guide, May 15, 1999, pp. 38–42.

W, September, 1998, pp. 272, 274.

SOWERBY, Jane
(Jayne Sowerby)

PERSONAL

Raised in Kelowna, British Columbia, Canada. *Education:* Attended the American Academy of Dramatic Arts, New York City.

Addresses: *Agent*—Linda Saint, The Saint Agency, 18 Gloucester Lane, Toronto, Ontario M4Y 1L5, Canada; Jamie Levitt, Lauren Levitt & Associates, 1525 Eighth Ave. West, Vancouver, British Columbia V6J 1T5, Canada; Robyn Friedman, Artist Management, Inc., 550 Queen St. East, Suite 315, Toronto, Ontario M5A 1V2, Canada.

Career: Actress, director, producer, editor, writer, singer, and songwriter. As a singer, performed in a Tribute to Janis Joplin, performed at various venues, and performed as an opening act for various artists. Affiliated with R. Pumpkin Productions.

Awards, Honors: Leo Award, short drama: best performance—female, and Leo Award nominations, best short film (with Richard Zwic), best director of a short film, and best screenwriter (short), all Motion Picture Arts & Sciences Foundation of British Columbia, 2003, for *Jane Post.*

CREDITS

Film Appearances:

Pink Chiquita, *The Pink Chiquitas,* Cinesphere/Shapiro Entertainment, 1987.

(As Jayne Sowerby) Joyce, *Ski School 2* (also known as *Crazy Ski School*), Cinepix Film Properties, 1994.

Sheila's friend, *Devotion,* Northern Arts Entertainment, 1995.

Hostess, *Shoes Off!* (short film), AtomFilms, 1998.

Bookstore manager, *The Rememberer* (short film), Cracked Pot Films, 1999.

Julie Beston, *MVP: Most Valuable Primate* (also known as *Snapshot*), Red Sky Entertainment/Keystone Family Pictures, 2000.

Mary Singer, *A Twist of Faith* (also known as *Beyond Redemption, Crack in the Mirror,* and *Au–dela du mal*), Prophecy Entertainment, 2000.

Becky, *Beautiful Joe* (also known as *My Beautiful Joe*), Comstock/New Films International, 2001.

Julie, *MVP: Most Vertical Primate* (also known as *MVP: Most Vertical Primate, MVP 2: Most Vertical Primate,* and *Mon primate adore II*), Keystone Entertainment, 2001.

Woman in the powder room, *Out Cold* (also known as *Cool Border, Snowbiz!, Snow, Sex and Sun, Ten to One,* and *10 to 1*), Buena Vista, 2001.

Woman, *Cheats* (also known as *Cheaters* and *Chea+ers*), Destination Films/New Line Cinema, 2002.

Title role, *Jane Post* (short film), 2002, CineClix Distribution, 2004.

Madame X, *How It All Went Down,* The Asylum, 2003.

The woman, *Arbor Vitae* (short film), Stage 18 Pictures, 2003.

Aunt Lydia, *11:11* (also known as *11:11: The Gate, Hell's Gate,* and *Hell's Gate 11:11*), Screen Media Ventures, 2004.

Loni Lipvanchuck, *The Life and Hard Times of Guy Terrifico* (also known as *La vie trepidante de Guy Terrifico*), Alliance Atlantis Communications/THINKFilm, 2004.

Jan, *Ill Fated,* Prehumous Productions/Ocule Films, 2005.

Title role, *Eugeena Yart* (short film), R. Pumpkin Productions, 2009.

Trashy woman, *You Might as Well Live,* E1 Entertainment, 2009.

Film Work; Short Films:

Director and (with Richard Zwic) producer, *Jane Post,* 2002, CineClix Distribution, 2004.

Coproducer and film editor, *Eugeena Yart,* R. Pumpkin Productions, 2009.

Worked on other projects, including the feature film *Myrtle the Turtle.*

Internet Appearances:

Polina Popopolinskie, *Cows & Ducks* (short film), R. Pumpkin Productions, broadcast on *YouTube,* www.youtube.com, c. 2009.

Internet Work; Short Films:

Director, *The Drawstring,* R. Pumpkin Productions, broadcast on *YouTube,* www.youtube.com, c. 2008.

Director, cinematographer, and editor, *The Card Sharks,* R. Pumpkin Productions, broadcast on *YouTube,* www.youtube.com, c. 2009.

Director, producer (with Zwic), camera operator, editor, and sound technician, *Cows & Ducks,* R. Pumpkin Productions, broadcast on *YouTube,* www.youtube.com, c. 2009.

Television Appearances; Series:

Peggy Cates, *Mentors,* Family Channel (Canada), 2000–2002.

Victoria Harrison, *Instant Star,* CTV and The N, 2004–2006.

Diana Vink, *Cra$h & Burn* (also known as *Lawyers, Guns and Money*), Showcase, beginning 2009.

Television Appearances; Movies:

(As Jayne Sowerby) Debi, *Voices from Within* (also known as *Silhouette*), NBC, 1994.

Chrissie Hynde, *The Linda McCartney Story* (also known as *L'histoire de Linda McCartney*), CBS, 2000.

Q. T.'s mother, *2gether* (also known as *2GE+HER*), MTV, 2000.

Waitress, *Mermaid,* Showtime, 2000.

Mrs. Futerman, *Hostage Negotiator,* USA Network, 2001.

Mother, *Cabin Pressure* (also known as *Autopilot* and *Hijack'd*), PAX, 2001.

Roxanne Du Bois, *Anatomy of a Hate Crime,* MTV, 2001.

Linda Markham, *Christmas on Chestnut Street* (also known as *The Competition*), Lifetime, 2006.

Aunt Susan, *Booky and the Secret Santa* (also known as *Booky & the Secret Santa*), CBC, 2007.

Max Macauley, *Secrets of an Undercover Wife* (also known as *Undercover*), Lifetime, 2007.

Woman, *Wide Awake,* Lifetime, 2007.

Television Appearances; Specials:

Morning Man at 88.0, CanWest Global Television, 1993.

Party girl, *The Sports Pages,* Showtime, 2001.

Television Appearances; Episodic:

Claire, "Epitaph for Tommy," *Highlander* (also known as *Highlander: The Series*), syndicated, 1993.

Nancy Snyder, "Eastbridge Boulevard," *The Commish,* ABC, 1993.

Alice Burke, "Lullaby," *Poltergeist: The Legacy* (also known as *Poltergeist, El legado, Poltergeist—Die unheimliche Macht, Poltergeist: El legado,* and *Poltergeist, les aventuriers du surnaturel*), Showtime and syndicated, 1997.

Ruth, "Promised Land," *The Outer Limits* (also known as *The New Outer Limits*), Showtime, Sci–Fi Channel, and syndicated, 1998.

Vivian, "Sisters of Mercy," *Dead Man's Gun,* Showtime, 1998.
Aleztra, "Honey, the Future's Coming Back on Me," *Honey, I Shrunk the Kids: The TV Show* (also known as *Disney's "Honey, I Shrunk the Kids: The TV Show"* and *Honey, I Shrunk the Kids*), syndicated, 1999.
Farnsworth, "Girls' Night Out, Boys' Night In," *Cold Feet,* NBC, 1999.
Farnsworth, "How Much Is That Sex Act in the Window," *Cold Feet,* NBC, 1999.
Farnsworth, "The Strange Loves of Shelley Bumstead," *Cold Feet,* NBC, 1999.
Kate Mizlowski, "Blues in A–Minor," *Da Vinci's Inquest* (also known as *Coroner Da Vinci*), CBC, 1999.
Fran, "Crazy," *Mysterious Ways* (also known as *One Clear Moment, Anexegeta phainomena, Les chemins de l'etrange, Mysterious ways—les chemins de l'etrange, Rajatapaus,* and *Senderos misteriosos*), NBC, 2000.
Lisa MacIntosh, "Death by Intent: Parts 1 & 2," *Cold Squad* (also known as *Files from the Past, Cold Squad, brigade speciale,* and *Halott uegyek*), CTV, 2000.
Servant (some sources cite role as concubine), "Reunion," *Harsh Realm,* FX Network, 2000.
Clair, "Reunion," *Night Visions* (also known as *Night Terrors* and *Nightvisions*), Fox, 2001.
Gem, "Bad Words, Good Business," *Big Sound,* CanWest Global Television, 2001.
Gem, "Sutton Killed the Radio Star," *Big Sound,* CanWest Global Television, 2001.
Misty, "Dances with Squirrels," *The Sausage Factory* (also known as *MTV's "Now What?," Much Ado about Whatever, Now What?,* and *Special Ed*), MTV and The Comedy Network, 2001.
Wife, "Proof of Purchase," *Dark Angel* (also known as *James Cameron's "Dark Angel"*), Fox, 2001.
Mary Reed, "Here There Be Monsters," *The Dead Zone* (also known as *The Dark Half, Dead Zone, Stephen King's "Dead Zone," La morta zona, La zona morta, La zona muerta,* and *Zona smrti*), USA Network, 2002.
Susan, "Dark Child," *The Outer Limits* (also known as *The New Outer Limits*), Showtime, Sci–Fi Channel, and syndicated, 2002.
Jane Smith, "Deep Cover," *Missing* (also known as *1–800–Missing* and *Porte disparu*), Lifetime, 2004.
Marcy, "The Old Man," *The Collector,* Citytv and SPACE, 2004.
Monica Bennett, "Hit and Run," *Sue Thomas: F.B.Eye* (also known as *Sue Thomas—FBI, Sue Thomas, FBI,* and *Sue Thomas, l'oeil du FBI*), PAX, 2004.
Catherine Doyle, "Betrayed," *72 Hours: True Crime,* CBC, 2005.
Baby lady, "That's How You Wave a Towel," *At the Hotel* (also known as *Hotel* and *Hotel Metropolitan*), CBC, 2006.

Television Appearances; Pilots:
Krista, "My Generation," *Strange Frequency,* VH1, 2001.

RECORDINGS

Songs:
Performed songs, and some have been posted on the Internet, including "Mary Ann," "Money Changes Ev'rythang," "On an Angel's Wing," "One Lucky Break from Lucky," "Ride with the Wind," "What Do You Say," and "Ya Gotta Have Faith."

WRITINGS

Screenplays; Short Films:
Jane Post, 2002, CineClix Distribution, 2004.
Eugeena Yart, R. Pumpkin Productions, 2009.

Wrote screenplays for feature films, including *Jane Post* (based on her short film of the same name), *Ballroom Bev,* and *Elmer the Angel.* Worked on other projects, including *Myrtle the Turtle.*

Screenplays; Internet Short Films:
The Drawstring, R. Pumpkin Productions, broadcast on *YouTube,* www.youtube.com, c. 2008.
The Card Sharks, R. Pumpkin Productions, broadcast on *YouTube,* www.youtube.com, c. 2009.
Cows & Ducks, R. Pumpkin Productions, broadcast on *YouTube,* www.youtube.com, c. 2009.

Television Music; Specials:
Cowrote songs appearing in television specials.

Teleplays; Pilots:
Wrote pilots.

Songs:
Wrote the song "On an Angel's Wing," posted on the Internet. With Richard Zwic, wrote other songs posted on the Internet, including "Mary Ann," "Money Changes Ev'rythang," "One Lucky Break from Lucky," "Ride with the Wind," and "Ya Gotta Have Faith."

OTHER SOURCES

Electronic:
Jane Sowerby, http://www.janesowerby.com, March 16, 2010.

SPENCE, Jennifer 1977–

PERSONAL

Born January 22, 1977, in Toronto, Ontario, Canada.

Career: Actress.

CREDITS

Television Appearances; Series:
Suko, *Northern Town,* CBC, 2006.
Joanna, *The 4400* (also known as *4400* and *Los 4400*), USA Network and Sky One, 2007.
Devin, *Exes and Ohs* (also known as *Exes & Oh's* and *The Rules: A Lesbian Survival Guide*), Logo and Showcase, 2009.
Dr. Lisa Park, *Stargate Universe* (also known as *SGU Stargate Universe, SG.U Stargate Universe,* and *SGU: Stargate Universe*), Syfy, beginning 2009.

Television Appearances; Movies:
Gate attendant, "Mr. St. Nick" (also known as "Mr. Saint Nick" and "Monsieur St–Nick"), *The Wonderful World of Disney,* ABC, 2002.
Gwen Stathis, *A Decent Proposal,* Lifetime, 2006.
Cathy, *Write & Wrong* (also known as *And She Was*), Lifetime, 2007.

Television Appearances; Episodic:
Witness, "It's Backwards Day," *Da Vinci's Inquest* (also known as *Coroner Da Vinci*), CBC, 2001.
Kimmy, "Twenty–Five Dollar Conversation," *Da Vinci's Inquest* (also known as *Coroner Da Vinci*), CBC, 2003.
Tricia, "Thanks for the Toaster Oven," *Da Vinci's Inquest* (also known as *Coroner Da Vinci*), CBC, 2003.
Kimmy, "Out of the Bag and All over the Street," *Da Vinci's Inquest* (also known as *Coroner Da Vinci*), CBC, 2004.
Kimmy, "Wash the Blood out of the Ring," *Da Vinci's Inquest* (also known as *Coroner Da Vinci*), CBC, 2004.
Nurse's aide, "Mercy," *Touching Evil,* USA Network, 2004.
Stephanie Brandis, "The Longest Day," *Tru Calling* (also known as *Heroine, Tru,* and *True Calling*), Fox, 2004.
Detective Burch, "Game Over," *Killer Instinct* (also known as *Deviant Behavior, The Gate,* and *Pahuuden jaeljillae*), Fox, 2005.
Evelyn, "1993," *Reunion,* Fox, 2005.
Dr. Monroe, "Shower the People," *Eureka* (also known as *EUReKA* and *A Town Called Eureka*), Syfy, 2009.

Appeared as Detective Burch in "Love Hurts," an un-aired episode of *Killer Instinct* (also known as *Deviant Behavior, The Gate,* and *Pahuuden jaeljillae*), Fox.

Television Appearances; Pilots:
Third nurse, *The Heart Department,* CBS, 2001.
Monique, *Huff* (also known as *!Huff*), Showtime, 2004.

Dr. Lisa Park, "Air," *Stargate Universe* (also known as *SGU Stargate Universe, SG.U Stargate Universe,* and *SGU: Stargate Universe*), Syfy, 2009.

Film Appearances:
Girl in the park, *Blind Spot* (short film), 1997.
Zimsky's assistant, *The Core* (also known as *Core* and *Fusion—The core*), Paramount, 2003.
Second woman, *The Truth about Miranda,* Wheelbarrow Films, 2004.
Comforting friend, *Catch and Release* (also known as *Catch & Release*), Columbia, 2007.

Internet Appearances:
Dr. Lisa Park, *SGU Stargate Universe Kino* (webisodes; also known as *Kino* and *Kino Webisodes*), http://stargate.mgm.com, beginning 2009.

STAITE, Jewel 1982–
(Jewel Straite)

PERSONAL

Full name, Jewel Belair Staite; born June 2, 1982, in White Rock, British Columbia, Canada; mother, in advertising; married Matt Anderson, April 25, 2003. *Education:* Trained at Vancouver Youth Theatre, Vancouver, British Columbia, Canada. *Avocational Interests:* Travel, writing.

Addresses: *Manager*—Elements Entertainment, 1635 N. Cahuenga Blvd., 5th Floor, Santa Monica, CA 90403. *Publicist*—Nicole Nassar Public Relations, 1111 Tenth St., Suite 104, Santa Monica, CA 90403.

Career: Actress. Performed as a singer; worked as a model; appeared in commercials. Children with AIDS Project, teen spokesperson.

Awards, Honors: Gemini Award nomination, best performance in a children's or youth program or series, Academy of Canadian Cinema and Television, 1998, for "Presents," *Flash Forward;* Gemini Award nomination, best performance by an actress in a continuing leading dramatic role, 2008, and Leo Award nomination, best lead performance by a female in a dramatic series, 2009, both for *Stargate: Atlantis.*

CREDITS

Television Appearances; Series:
Catalina, *Space Cases,* Nickelodeon, 1996.

Rebecca "Becca"/"Beck" Fisher, *Flash Forward*, ABC, 1996–97.

Gabriella Da Vinci, *Da Vinci's Inquest* (also known as *Coroner Da Vinci*), CBC, 1998–2001.

Daisy Lipenowski, *Higher Ground*, Fox, 2000.

Laurel, *Just Deal*, NBC, 2002.

Kaywinnit Lee "Kaylee" Frye, *Firefly* (also known as *Joss Whedon's "Firefly"* and *Firefly: The Series*), Fox, 2002–2003.

Dr. Jennifer Keller, *Stargate: Atlantis*(also known as *La porte d'Atlantis*), Sci–Fi Channel, 2005–2009.

Television Appearances; Movies:

Jennifer Lanahan, *Posing: Inspired by Three Real Stories* (also known as *I Posed for Playboy*), CBS, 1991.

Liar, Liar (also known as *Liar, Liar: Between Father and Daughter* and *Daddy's Little Secret*), CBC and CBS, 1993.

Alexandra Carlisle, *The Only Way Out*, ABC, 1993.

Theresa, *Prisoner of Zenda, Inc.* (also known as *Double Play*), Showtime, 1996.

Susan Olivia Clemens, *Roughing It* (also known as *Mark Twain's "Roughing It"*), Hallmark Channel, 2002.

Bryanna, aged 15–20, *Damaged Care*, Showtime, 2002.

Jenny Cavanaugh, *Widow on the Hill*, Lifetime, 2005.

Television Appearances; Episodic:

Labelia, "The Believers," *The Odyssey*, CBC, 1992.

Labelia, "The Prophecy," *The Odyssey*, CBC, 1994.

Kelly, "The Tale of Watcher's Woods," *Are You Afraid of the Dark?*, Nickelodeon, 1994.

Cody, "The Tale of the Unfinished Painting," *Are You Afraid of the Dark?*, Nickelodeon, 1995.

Amy Jacobs, "Oubliette," *The X–Files*, Fox, 1995.

Julia, *Super Dave's All Stars*, syndicated, 1997.

Tiara Vanhorn, "Honey, I Know What You're Thinking," *Honey, I Shrunk the Kids: The TV Show*, syndicated, 1997.

Tiara Vanhorn, "Honey, You're Living in the Past," *Honey, I Shrunk the Kids: The TV Show*, syndicated, 1997.

Tiara Vanhorn, "Honey, I'm in the Mood for Love," *Honey, I Shrunk the Kids: The TV Show*, syndicated, 1998.

Tiara Vanhorn, "Honey, You're So Transparent," *Honey, I Shrunk the Kids: The TV Show*, syndicated, 1998.

Tiara Vanhorn, "Honey, It's Gloom and Doom," *Honey, I Shrunk the Kids: The TV Show*, syndicated, 1999.

Sally Prentiss, "Fools for Love," *Nothing Too Good for a Cowboy*, CBC, 1999.

Sally Prentiss, "Happy Trails," *Nothing Too Good for a Cowboy*, CBC, 1999.

Callie Snow, "Siren," *So Weird*, The Disney Channel, 1999.

Voice, "You Said a Mouse–ful," *Sabrina the Animated Series* (animated; also known as *Sabrina*), 1999.

Voice, "Harvzilla," *Sabrina the Animated Series* (animated; also known as *Sabrina*), 1999.

Voice, "Saturday Night Furor," *Sabrina the Animated Series* (animated; also known as *Sabrina*), 1999.

Voice, "The Importance of Being Norma," *Sabrina the Animated Series* (animated; also known as *Sabrina*), 1999.

Danielle Jenkins, "Learning Curve," *The Immortal*, syndicated, 2001.

Josie, "Kiss," *2gether: The Series*, MTV, 2001.

Molly, the psychic, "Empty Quiver," *Seven Days* (also known as *Seven Days: The Series*), UPN, 2001.

Carly and Shannon, "Second Sight," *Beyond Belief: Fact or Fiction* (also known as *Beyond Belief*), Fox, 2002.

Goth girl, "Rest in Peace," *Dead Like Me*, Showtime, 2003.

Heidi Gotts, "Safety Canary," *Wonderfalls*, Fox, 2004.

Heidi Gotts, "Lying Pig," *Wonderfalls*, Fox, 2004.

Heidi Gotts, "Cocktail Bunny," *Wonderfalls*, Fox, 2004.

Heidi Gotts, "Cage Bird," *Wonderfalls*, Fox, 2004.

Thora Andrews, "Girlfriend in a Closet," *Cold Squad*, CTV, 2004.

Film '72 (also known as *Film of the Year* and *The Film Programme*), BBC, 2005.

"Two of Six Voted Off," *So You Think You Can Dance*, Fox, 2009.

Loretta, "Mild Mannered," *Warehouse 13*, SyFy, 2010.

Television Appearances; Specials:

The ABC Saturday Morning Preview Party, ABC, 1996.

Interviewee, *Sci Fi Inside: Serenity*, Sci–Fi Channel, 2005.

07 Spaceys, SPACE, 2007.

Voice for the Japanese miniseries *The Shintotsukawa Story*.

Television Appearances; Pilots:

(As Jewel Straite) Carolyn, *Huff*, Showtime, 2004.

Television Work; Series:

Provided additional voices for the series *Mummies Alive!*, syndicated.

Film Appearances:

Samantha, *Gold Diggers: The Secret of Bear Mountain*, Universal, 1995.

Soap opera actress, *Carpool*, Warner Bros., 1996.

Teddy Blue, the curser, *Cheats* (also known as *Chea+ers*), New Line Cinema, 2002.

Kaylee Frye, *Serenity*, Universal, 2005.

Liz, *The Forgotten Ones*, 2009.

Dr. Jennifer Keller, *Stargate: Extinction* (also known as *Stargate Atlantis Movie*), 2009.

Katharine, *Mothman*, 2010.

Debbie, *P5Ych*, 2010.

Also appeared in *The Tribe*.

Film Work:
Additional voices, *Mummies Alive! The Legend Begins,* Buena Vista Home Video, 1998.

Stage Appearances:
Appeared in productions of *Magical Rock/Arts Club* and *10th Anniversary Retrospective,* both Ensemble Vancouver Youth Theatre, Vancouver, British Columbia, Canada; and in *You're a Good Man, Charlie Brown,* Ensemble Arts Club Showcase.

Major Tours:
Kids Writes/93 Tour, Ensemble Vancouver Youth Theatre, Canadian cities, 1993.

RECORDINGS

Videos:
Here's How It Was: The Making of "Firefly" (short documentary), Twentieth Century–Fox, 2003.
Re–Lighting the Firefly (short documentary; featured on the DVD release of *Serenity*), 2005.
A Filmmaker's Journey (short documentary), Universal, 2006.
Done the Impossible: The Fans' Tale of "Firefly" and "Serenity" (documentary), Done the Impossible, 2006.

OTHER SOURCES

Electronic:
Firefly, http://www.fireflyfans.net, July 31, 2002.
Jewel Staite: Official Web Site, http://jewelstaite.com, July 28, 2010.

STERLING, Leslie Kay
    See KAY, Lesli

STEVENSON, Jessica
    See HYNES, Jessica

STIMELY, Brett

PERSONAL

Born in WA; father, a former Air Force pilot; mother's name, Merle Stimely. *Education:* Attended University of Washington, Seattle; studied acting with Harry Mas-

trogeorge, Margie Haber, and George Gilbert. *Avocational Interests:* Equestrian activities.

Addresses: *Manager*—Studio Talent Group, 1328 12th St., Santa Monica, CA 90401.

Career: Actor and producer. Also worked as assistant director. Appeared in more than 100 television commercials, including ads for Budget Suites of America motels, Budweiser beer, J. C. Penney department stores, Subway sandwich shops, European appearances and precision driving jobs for auto company ads. Volunteer with civic and charitable organizations, including Airport Marina Counseling Service, Boys and Girls Clubs of Santa Monica, Good News Foundation, and Olive Crest Homes and Services for Abused Children.

Member: Academy of Television Arts and Sciences, Screen Actors Guild, American Federation of Television and Radio Artists, Actors' Equity Association, Academy of Magical Arts.

CREDITS

Television Appearances; Series:
Jay Garvin, a recurring role, *The Bold and the Beautiful* (also known as *Belleza y poder*), CBS, 1992.
Joshua Sloane, a recurring role, *Sunset Beach,* NBC, 1999.
Host, *Real Conspiracies,* 2000.

Television Appearances; Movies:
John, *My First Love,* ABC, 1988.
Robert, *Deconstructing Sarah,* USA Network, 1994.

Television Appearances; Episodic:
Messenger, *The Young and the Restless* (also known as *Y&R*), 1986.
Bellman, "The Mothers," *Dynasty,* ABC, 1987.
Patrolman, "Class Act," *Murder, She Wrote,* CBS, 1989.
Porter Stevenson, "End Game," *Equal Justice,* ABC, 1991.
Brian O'Keefe, "Bebe's Wedding," *Flesh 'n' Blood,* NBC, 1991.
Chapman, "Blue Fiber: Part 2," *FBI: The Untold Stories,* ABC, 1992.
Avery at 35, "One," *Murphy Brown,* CBS, 1993.
Steve, "The Penthouse," *Getting By,* NBC, 1993.
Marty Green, "Pretty Woman," *Step by Step,* CBS, 1994.
Dr. Julian Morgan, "Love! Valor! Deception!," *Kirk,* The WB, 1995.
Bill Seenis, "Family Val's," *High Society,* CBS, 1995.
Reed, "Goodbye, Mr. Chip," *High Tide,* syndicated, 1996.

Man in restaurant, "The Fifth Wheel," *The Nanny*, CBS, 1997.

Mark, "Laundromat," *Red Shoe Diaries* (also known as *Zalman King's "Red Shoe Diaries"*), Showtime, 1997.

Paramedic, "There Was an Old Woman," *Cybill*, CBS, 1997.

Eric Burns, "Family Ties," *Providence*, NBC, 2000.

Robert Jones, "Dominoes Falling," *The Shield*, FX Network, 2003.

Public Defender Greg Saunders, "The Fritz and Williamson Case," *Guilty or Innocent?*, The Discovery Channel, 2005.

Dan Wisner, "California College Conservative Union Caucus," *Party Down*, Starz!, 2009.

John Edwards impersonator, *Jimmy Kimmel Live!*, ABC, 2009.

Television Appearances; Other:

Larry, *Unhappily Ever After* (pilot), The WB, 1995.

Frederick Albert Cook, *Race for the Poles* (special), The Learning Channel, 2000.

Also appeared in a miniseries titled *The Adventurous Travels of Lord Glenarvan* and the program *What Should You Do?*

Film Appearances:

Sandy McVey, *Bloodstone,* Omega Pictures, 1988.

Jean–Pierre, *Cannibal Women in the Avocado Jungle of Death* (also known as *Jungle Heat* and *Piranha Women in the Avocado Jungle of Death*), Paramount Home Video, 1989.

Last Chance Saloon (short film), 1990.

Disco Years (short film), 1991.

Bernd, *Greshnitsa v maske,* 1993.

Steven, *Last Chance Love,* Lau Film International, 1997.

Prescott, *Citizens of Perpetual Indulgence,* 2000.

John, *The Whisper,* 2003.

Dr. Steve, *Rene Turns 40* (short film), Mortimer Olive Productions, 2006.

John F. Kennedy, *Watchmen* (also known as *Watchmen: The IMAX Experience*), Warner Bros., 2009.

Appeared as Colonel James Mallory in the military film *Operation Safeguard;* also appeared in the film *Faust's Roulette.*

Film Work:

Producer, *Citizens of Perpetual Indulgence,* 2000.

RECORDINGS

Video Games:

Voice of first commentator, *Mech Commander 2,* 2001.

OTHER SOURCES

Electronic:

Brett Stimely Official Site, http://www.brettstimely.com, June 8, 2010.

STONE, Paul
See LOGAN, Paul

STOWE, Madeleine 1958–
(Madeline Stowe)

PERSONAL

Original name, Madeleine Marie Stowe Mora; born August 18, 1958, in Los Angeles, CA; daughter of Robert (a civil engineer) and Mireya (maiden name, Mora) Stowe; married Brian Benben (an actor), August 8, 1986; children: May, one son. *Education:* Studied cinema and journalism at University of Southern California.

Addresses: *Agent*—David Schiff, United Talent Agency, 9560 Wilshire Blvd., Suite 500, Beverly Hills, CA 90212; The Gersh Agency, 9465 Wilshire Blvd., 6th Floor, Beverly Hills, CA 90212. *Manager*—Cynthia Pett–Dante, Brillstein–Grey Entertainment, 9150 Wilshire Blvd., Suite 350, Beverly Hills, CA 90212.

Career: Actress. Solari Theatre, Beverly Hills, CA, worked as volunteer early in her career. Co–owner of a cattle ranch near Fredericksburg, TX.

Awards, Honors: National Society of Film Critics Award, best supporting actress, 1993, Volpi Cup (with others), best ensemble cast, Venice Film Festival, 1993, and Golden Globe Special Award (with others), best ensemble cast, 1994, all for *Short Cuts;* Universe Reader's Choice Award, best actress in a genre motion picture, *Sci–Fi Universe,* Saturn Award nomination, best actress, Academy of Science Fiction, Fantasy, & Horror Films, 1996, for *Twelve Monkeys;* ALMA Award nomination, outstanding actress in a feature film, and Blockbuster Entertainment Award nomination, favorite supporting actress in a suspense film, both 2000, for *The General's Daughter.*

CREDITS

Film Appearances;:

Ruth Lasker, *Gangster Wars,* 1981.

Maria McGuire, *Stakeout,* Buena Vista, 1987.

Marina, *Tropical Snow* (also known as *Nieve tropical*), PSM Entertainment, 1989.

Veronica Briskow, *Worth Winning,* Twentieth Century–Fox, 1989.

Mireya Mendez, *Revenge,* New World, 1990.

Lillian Bodine, *The Two Jakes,* Paramount, 1990.

The woman, *Closet Land,* Universal, 1991.

Cora Munro, *The Last of the Mohicans,* Twentieth Century–Fox, 1992.

Karen Carr, *Unlawful Entry,* Twentieth Century–Fox, 1992.

Sherri Shepard, *Short Cuts* (also known as *L.A. Shortcuts*), Fine Line, 1993.

(Uncredited) Maria, *Another Stakeout* (also known as *House of Cops, The Lookout,* and *Stakeout 2*), Buena Vista, 1993.

Emma Brody, *Blink,* New Line Cinema, 1994.

Rachel Munro, *China Moon,* Orion, 1994.

Cody Zamora, *Bad Girls,* Twentieth Century–Fox, 1994.

Dr. Kathryn Railly, *Twelve Monkeys,* Universal, 1995.

Eleanor Barret, *The Proposition* (also known as *Shakespeare's Sister* and *Tempting Fate*), PolyGram Filmed Entertainment, 1998.

Gracie, *Playing by Heart* (also known as *Intermedia*), Miramax, 1998.

If They Only Knew (also known as *Dancing about Architecture*), 1998.

Maya Olham, *Impostor,* Dimension Films, 1999.

Warrant Officer Sarah Sunhill, *The General's Daughter* (also known as *Wehrlos—Die Tochter des Generals*), Paramount, 1999.

Julie Moore, *We Were Soldiers* (also known as *Wir waren Helden*), Paramount, 2002.

Jennifer Barrett Allieghieri, *Avenging Angelo* (also known as *Mafia Love*), Warner Bros., 2002.

Senga Wilson, *Octane* (also known as *Pulse*), Overseas FilmGroup, 2003.

Television Appearances; Movies:

Hetty Hutter, *The Deerslayer,* NBC, 1978.

(As Madeline Stowe) Mary, *The Nativity,* ABC, 1978.

Dr. Sharon Fields, *Amazons,* ABC, 1984.

Isabel Amberson Minafer, *The Magnificent Ambersons,* Arts and Entertainment, 2002.

Milly Kondracke, *Saving Milly,* CBS, 2005.

Charlotte, *Southern Comfort,* Fox, 2006.

Patricia Addison, *The Christmas Hope,* Lifetime, 2009.

Television Appearances; Miniseries:

Selma Kendrick Davis, *Beulah Land,* NBC, 1980.

(As Madeline Stowe) Hester Ashley Murdoch, *Blood and Orchids,* CBS, 1986.

Television Appearances; Series:

Dr. Samantha Kohl, *Raines,* NBC, 2007.

Television Appearances; Specials:

The American Film Institute Salute to Jack Nicholson, CBS, 1994.

Herself, *Luck, Trust & Ketchup: Robert Altman in Carver County* (also known as *Luck, Trust, and Ketchup*), Bravo, 1994.

Presenter, *The 66th Annual Academy Awards Presentation,* ABC, 1994.

Cora Munro, *Twentieth Century Fox: The Blockbuster Years,* 2000.

The WIN Awards, PAX, 2005.

Television Appearances; Episodic:

(As Madeline Stowe) Anna, "The Marker," *Baretta,* ABC, 1978.

Maria Calderon, "Escort to Danger," *The Amazing Spider–Man* (also known as *Spiderman*), CBS, 1978.

Diane, "School of Terror," *Barnaby Jones,* 1979.

(As Madeline Stowe) Annie Crane, "Portrait of Love," *Little House on the Prairie* (also known as *Little House: A New Beginning*), NBC, 1980.

(As Madeline Stowe) Cassie, "Creepy Time Gal," *Trapper John, M.D.,* 1981.

The Tonight Show with Jay Leno (also known as *Jay Leno*), NBC, 1992.

Late Show with David Letterman (also known as *Late Show Backstage, Letterman* and *The Late Show*), 1994.

The Rosie O'Donnell Show, syndicated, 1999.

"The Films of Terry Gilliam," *The Directors,* 2001.

"The Films of Michael Mann," *The Directors,* 2001.

"Cannes Festival 2002," *Leute heute,* ZDF, 2002.

"Kevin Costner," *Biography,* Arts and Entertainment, 2003.

Also appeared as Ruth Lasker in *The Gangster Chronicles* (also known as *The Gangster Chronicles: An American Story.*

Stage Appearances:

Appeared in *The Tenth Man,* Solari Theatre, Beverly Hills, CA.

RECORDINGS

Videos:

(Uncredited) *The Hamster Factor and Other Tales of Twelve Monkeys* (documentary; featured on the DVD release of *Twelve Monkeys*), 1997.

The General's Daughter: Behind the Secrets (short documentary), 1999.

We Were Soldiers: Getting It Right (short documentary), 2002.

Making "Avenging Angelo," (short documentary), Columbia TriStar Home Video, 2003.

Obsession: The Sex and Violence of Revenge (short documentary; featured on the Director's Cut DVD of *Revenge*), Sony Pictures Home Entertainment, 2007.

OTHER SOURCES

Books:
Notable Hispanic American Women, Book 2, Gale, 1998.

Periodicals:
Cosmopolitan, December, 1995, p. 168.
Empire, Issue 60, 1994, pp. 50–51.
Entertainment Weekly, February 4, 1994, p. 26.
Evening Standard Hot Tickets, March 8, 2002, p. 2.
Harper's Bazaar, February, 1994, p. 178.
Interview, May, 1990.
Los Angeles Times, January 30, 1994.
Madison, May, 1999, pp. 88–93.
Movieline, February, 1998.
People Weekly, May 9, 1994, p. 120; May 16, 1994, p. 126; November 14, 1994, p. 152; January 15, 1996, p. 106.
Texas Monthly, June, 1999, p. 130.
Time, February 7, 1994, p. 75.
Town & Country Monthly, March, 1996, p. 92.
W, June, 1999, p. 52.

STRAITE, Jewel
See STAITE, Jewel

STRICKLAND, Jen 1983–

PERSONAL

Born April 17, 1983, in St. Marys, OH. *Education:* Attended New Village School of Drama, New York City. *Avocational Interests:* Karate.

Career: Actress. Appeared in commercials, including ads for Subway sandwich shops.

CREDITS

Television Appearances; Movies:
Theatre patron, *Alchemy,* ABC, 2005.
(Uncredited) Laura, *Murder 101,* Hallmark Channel, 2006.

Television Appearances; Miniseries:
Running girl, *Kidnapped,* BBC, 2005.

Television Appearances; Episodic:
(Uncredited) Receptionist, "The Domino Effect," *Sex and the City* (also known as *S.A.T.C.* and *Sex and the Big City*), HBO, 2003.

Hannah Campbell, *Port Charles,* ABC, four episodes, 2003.
Lizzy Barnes, "Now I Lay Me Down to Sleep," *The Division,* Lifetime, 2004.
Lizzy Barnes, "Acts of Desperation," *The Division,* Lifetime, 2004.
Lena, "My Boyfriend's Back," *North Shore,* Fox, 2004.
Malena, "Hawaiian Justice," *Hawaii,* NBC, 2004.
Malena, "Underground," *Hawaii,* NBC, 2004.
Faith, "Natural Disasters," *Life as We Know It,* ABC, 2004.
(Uncredited) Trish Parker, "Changing Partners," *Windfall,* NBC, 2006.
(Uncredited) Trish Parker, "Answered Prayers," *Windfall,* NBC, 2006.
(Uncredited) Trish Parker, "The Myth of More," *Windfall,* NBC, 2006.
(Uncredited) Trish Parker, "Crash into You," *Windfall,* NBC, 2006.
Kathie Ann, "All about Eva," *The Nine,* ABC, 2006.

Film Appearances:
(Uncredited) Cheerleader, *Bring It On Again,* Universal Home Entertainment, 2004.
(Uncredited) Rachel, *Trust the Man,* Fox Searchlight, 2006.
Pizza patron, *Rattle Basket,* May Contain Nuts/T–Street Productions, 2007.

Stage Appearances:
Appeared in stage productions of *Take a Number Darling* and *'Tis Pity She's a Whore.*

SUCHANEK, Michal 1987–
(Michael Suchanek)

PERSONAL

Born October 27, 1987, in Slovakia; son of Michal (an actor and acting coach) and Yveta (a computer animation and multimedia entrepreneur). *Avocational Interests:* Computers, playing tennis, swimming, chess, skiing.

Career: Actor. Appeared in numerous television commercials, including Shamrock Farms.

Awards, Honors: Daytime Emmy Award nomination, outstanding performer in a children's special, 1999, for *Edison: The Wizard of Light;* YoungStar Award nomination, best young actor/performance in a miniseries/made–for–television film, Young Artist Award nomination, best performance in a television movie or pilot—young actor age ten or under, 2000, both for *Aftershock:*

Earthquake in New York; Young Artist Award, best performance in a television drama series—guest starring young actor, 2001, for *Mysterious Ways.*

CREDITS

Film Appearances:
Ten–year–old boy, *Dudley Do–Right,* Universal, 1999.
Mitch Dobson, *Big Brother Trouble,* Mainline Releasing, 2000.
Tzvi Szchevisky, *Various Positions,* 2002.
Voice, *Joe* (animated short film), National Film Board of Canada, 2003.
Nick, *AVPR: Aliens vs Predator—Requiem* (also known as *AVP: Aliens vs. Predator—Requiem, AVP: Requiem, Aliens vs. Predator 2, AvP2,* and *AvPR*), Twentieth Century–Fox, 2007.

Television Appearances; Miniseries:
(As Michael Suchanek) Danny Thorell, *Aftershock: Earthquake in New York,* CBS, 1999.
The boy, *Fallen,* ABC Family, 2006.
Lance Stone, *The Andromeda Strain,* Arts and Entertainment, 2008.

Television Appearances; Movies:
Boy number one, *Convictions,* Lifetime, 1997.
Charlie Ramer, *Dirty Little Secret,* USA Network, 1998.
Benny Waters, *Noah,* ABC, 1998.
Kurt Traynor, *A Murder on Shadow Mountain,* CBS, 1999.
Donny Cromwell, *Y2K* (also known as *Countdown to Chaos* and *Y2K: The Movie*), NBC, 1999.

Television Appearances; Specials:
Young Jack Maloney, *Edison: The Wizard of Light,* HBO, 1998.

Television Appearances; Episodic:
Keith Gilpin, "Night Terrors," *Sleepwalkers,* NBC, 1997.
Young Jeffrey Spender, "The Red and the Black," *The X–Files,* Fox, 1998.
Young Jeffrey Spender, "Two Fathers," *The X–Files,* Fox, 1998.
Cory, "Twenty Sailors Around a Buttonhole," *Hope Island,* PAX, 2000.
Kevin, "Camp Sanopi," *Mysterious Ways,* NBC, 2000.
Todd, "Partly Cloudy, Chance of Sex," *Life As We Know It* (also known as *life as we know it*), ABC, 2004.
Doug, "You Promised Me a Celebrity," *Da Vinci's Inquest,* CBC, 2004.
Larry Jameson, "Pelts," *Masters of Horror,* Showtime, 2006.

Stage Appearances:
The Nutcracker, 1999.

SULIEMAN, Sterling
(J. Sterling Sulieman)

PERSONAL

Born in Oakland, CA; raised in CA and HI; brother of Yasmeen Sulieman (a singer). *Education:* Attended school in HI; University of California, Los Angeles, B.A. *Avocational Interests:* Hiking and other outdoor activities, photography.

Addresses: *Manager*—Pallas Management, 12535 Chandler Blvd., Suite 1, North Hollywood, CA 91607.

Career: Actor and dancer. Appeared in Disney 411 segments (later known as Disney 365 segments), The Disney Channel.

Awards, Honors: Winner of talent competitions in the state of Hawaii.

CREDITS

Television Appearances; Series:
Dre Woods, *All My Children* (also known as *All My Children: The Summer of Seduction* and *La force du destin*), ABC, 2007–2008.
Harper, *The Vampire Diaries,* The CW, beginning 2010.

Television Appearances; Specials:
(As J. Sterling Sulieman) Dancer, *High School Musical: The Concert,* The Disney Channel, 2007.

Television Appearances; Episodic:
Marcus, "The Big Days of Wine & Neuroses Episode" (also known as "The Big Days of Wine & Neuroses"), *Half & Half,* UPN, 2005.
Chris, *The Bold and the Beautiful* (also known as *Glamour, Rags, Top Models,* and *Belleza y poder*), CBS, 2007.
Craig, "Security Briefs," *Entourage,* HBO, 2009.
Dwight, "You Gotta Lose This Job," *Hannah Montana* (also known as *Secret Idol Hannah Montana*), The Disney Channel, 2009.
Nest technician, "The Science in the Physicist," *Bones* (also known as *Brennan, Bones—Die Knochenjaegerin, Dr. Csont,* and *Kondid*), Fox, 2009.
Dwight, "Got to Get Her out of My House," *Hannah Montana* (also known as *Secret Idol Hannah Montana*), The Disney Channel, 2010.
Jim (CTU agent), "Day 8: 12:00 a.m.–1:00 a.m.," *24* (also known as *Twenty Four* and *24 Hours*), Fox, 2010.

(Uncredited) Jim (CTU agent), "Day 8: 3:00 a.m.–4:00 a.m.," *24* (also known as *Twenty Four* and *24 Hours*), Fox, 2010.

Jim (CTU agent), "Day 8: 5:00 a.m.–6:00 a.m.," *24* (also known as *Twenty Four* and *24 Hours*), Fox, 2010.

Jim (CTU agent), "Day 8: 6:00 p.m.–7:00 p.m.," *24* (also known as *Twenty Four* and *24 Hours*), Fox, 2010.

TAC agent, "Day 8: 7:00 p.m.–8:00 p.m.," *24* (also known as *Twenty Four* and *24 Hours*), Fox, 2010.

NCIS special agent Emil Mineoux, "Patriot Down," *Navy NCIS: Naval Criminal Investigative Service* (also known as *Naval CIS, Navy CIS, Navy NCIS, NCIS,* and *NCIS: Naval Criminal Investigative Service*), CBS, 2010.

Television Appearances; Pilots:
Reed Armstead, *Ibanker,* c. 2007.
Raffi, *Limelight,* ABC, 2009.

Film Appearances:
Game player, *Apocalypse Oz,* MeniThings, 2006.

Stage Appearances:
John Proctor, *The Crucible,* Punahou School, Punahou Theatre, Honolulu, HI, c. 2001.

Major Tours:
Member of dance ensemble, *High School Musical* (also known as *Disney's "High School Musical," Disney's "High School Musical National Tour,"* and *High School Musical National Tour*), U.S. and Canadian cities, c. 2006–2007.

RECORDINGS

Videos:
Dancer, *High School Musical: The Concert—Extreme Access Pass,* Walt Disney Home Entertainment, 2007.

SUMATRA, Aristide
     See ELFMAN, Richard

SUMATRA, Mahatma Kane
     See ELFMAN, Richard

SYDOW, Jack 1921–2010

PERSONAL

Original name, John David Sydow; born October 7, 1921, in Rockford, IL; died May 28, 2010, in Los Angeles, CA. Actor and director. A major figure in American theater, Sydow earned a Tony award nomination in 1967 for his direction of a Broadway revival of *Annie Get Your Gun.* Sydow began his career in the 1940s, directing and acting in community theater productions. At the time he was working towards a masters degree at the Yale School of Drama. After directing at New York Citys Hunter College and Woodstock Playhouse throughout the early 1950s, he garnered a 1958 Obie Award for his adaptation of *The Brothers Karamazov.* He also acted in several productions at the Woodstock Playhouse in the early 1950s, including *You Never Can Tell, An Inspector Calls,* and *Invitation to a Murder.* In 1959 Sydow directed Buster Keaton in a national tour of *Once Upon a Mattress.* During the 1960s he worked on Broadway plays, directing *The Crucible, Annie Get Your Gun,* and *A Touch of the Poet,* among others. Sydow headed the directing program at the University of Washington from 1970 to 1986, and in 1994 he appeared in the Frank Mosvold short film *Forsaken.* He played roles on numerous television series throughout the 1990s, including *Frasier, Touched by an Angel,* and most recently *Brothers & Sisters.* Towards the end of his career, Sydow was a regular performer at the South Coast Repertory in Los Angeles.

PERIODICALS

Los Angeles Times, July 7, 2010.
Variety, June 28, 2010.

T

TALALAY, Rachel 1958–

PERSONAL

Born July 16, 1958, in Chicago, IL; raised in Baltimore, MD; daughter of Paul and Pamela J. (maiden name, Samuels) Talalay. *Education:* Yale University, B.A., 1980.

Addresses: *Agent*—Charlotte Kelly, Casarotto Ramsay and Associates Ltd., Waverly House, 7–12 Noel St., London W1F 8GQ, England. *Manager*—Fineman Entertainment, 8250 Wilshire Blvd., Suite 300, Beverly Hills, CA 90212.

Career: Director, producer, and executive. New Line Cinema, vice president for production and executive in charge of production, 1986–90; Talalay Films, producer and director; previously worked as production associate, script supervisor, apprentice film editor, assistant director, assistant production manager, location manager, and line producer. Director of promotional documentaries and public service announcements, including work on behalf of Fund for Animals. Originally worked as a computer analyst in Baltimore, MD; became an accountant and software supplier for films; P.M. Software, Los Angeles, president, 1985; Computer Access Center, member of board of directors. Los Angeles Council on Assaults Against Women, counselor, 1985–86.

Member: Directors Guild of America, Directors Guild of Canada, Directors and Producers Rights Society, Academy of Television Arts and Sciences, Women in Film.

Awards, Honors: Independent Spirit Award nomination, best feature, Independent Features Project/West, 1989, for *Hairspray;* Sitges–Catalonian International Film Festival Award nomination, best film, 1991, for *Freddy's Dead: The Final Nightmare;* Alexander Korda Award nomination (with others), best British film, British Academy of Film and Television Arts, 1998, for *The Borrowers;* Leo Award, best direction in a dramatic series, Motion Picture Arts and Sciences Foundation of British Columbia, 2006, for *Terminal City;* Leo Award, best direction in a youth or children's program or series, 2007, for *The Wind in the Willows;* West Coast Emmy Award nomination for work related to Computer Access Center.

CREDITS

Television Director; Miniseries:
(Contributor) *Band of Gold* (also known as *Gold*), HBO, 1995.
Dice, 2001.
Terminal City, The Movie Network and Movie Central Network, 2005.
Durham County, Ion Television, 2009.
Bloodletting & Miraculous Cures, Movie Central Network, 2010.

Television Director; Movies:
A Tale of Two Wives (also known as *Double Bill*), Oxygen, 2003.
The Wind in the Willows (movie), PBS, 2006.

Television Director; Episodic:
"Turkey Day Blues," *To Have & to Hold,* CBS, 1998.
"Saving Santa," *Ally McBeal,* Fox, 1999.
"Prime Suspect," *Ally McBeal,* Fox, 2000.
"Two's a Crowd," *Ally McBeal,* Fox, 2000.
"Mental Apparition Disorder," *Randall & Hopkirk (Deceased),* BBC, 2000.
"A Blast from the Past," *Randall & Hopkirk (Deceased),* BBC, 2000.
"Chapter Five," *Boston Public,* Fox, 2000.
"Eve of Discussion," *State of Grace,* Fox Family, 2001.

"Miracle at the Cucina," *That's Life,* ABC, 2001.

"Tastes like Chicken," *Wolf Lake,* CBS, 2001.

"Blowin' in the Wind," *Ally McBeal,* Fox, 2002.

"Four Fathers," *Crossing Jordan,* NBC, 2002.

"He Saw, She Saw," *Without a Trace* (also known as *W.A.T.*), CBS, 2002.

"Shaman," *The Dead Zone* (also known as *The Dark Half* and *Stephen King's "Dead Zone"*), USA Network, 2002.

Girls Club, Fox, 2002.

"Castaways," *The Division,* Lifetime, 2003.

"Sherry Darlin'," *Cold Case,* CBS, 2003.

"Y Me," *Touching Evil,* USA Network, 2004.

"Natural Disasters," *Life as We Know It,* ABC, 2004.

"The Perfect Couple," *Unfabulous,* Nickelodeon, 2005.

Sex, Love & Secrets, UPN, 2005.

"In the Air," *Whistler,* The N, 2006.

"After the Fall," *Whistler,* The N, 2006.

"Scratching the Surface," *Whistler,* The N, 2006.

"Meltdown," *Whistler,* The N, 2006.

"Symmetry," *The Dead Zone* (also known as *The Dark Half* and *Stephen King's "Dead Zone"*), USA Network, 2006.

"Ego," *The Dead Zone* (also known as *The Dark Half* and *Stephen King's "Dead Zone"*), USA Network, 2007.

"Hunted," *Supernatural,* The CW, 2007.

"Separation Anxiety," *Greek,* ABC Family, 2007.

"Hands on a Hybrid," *Kyle XY,* ABC Family, 2007.

"Leap of Faith," *Kyle XY,* ABC Family, 2007.

"The Betty and Veronica Syndrome," *jPod,* CBC, 2008.

"Fine China," *jPod,* CBC, 2008.

"Blame," *Flash Gordon,* Sci–Fi Channel, 2008.

"Of Papers and Patois," *Da Kink in My Hair,* Global TV, 2009.

"Playing Social," *Da Kink in My Hair,* Global TV, 2009.

"Honesty the Best Policy," *Da Kink in My Hair,* Global TV, 2009.

"Lawyers, Guns & Money," *Cra$h & Burn,* Showcase, 2010.

"Bond Blame Baptize," *Cra$h & Burn,* Showcase, 2010.

Also directed episodes of *South Beach,* UPN; *State of Grace; Touching Evil* (also known as *Mystery! Touching Evil II*), PBS; *What about Brian,* ABC; and *Wildfire,* ABC Family.

Television Work; Series:

Co–executive producer, *Touching Evil,* USA Network, 2004.

Television Work; Pilots:

Producer, *Space Rangers,* CBS, 1993.

Co–executive producer, *Touching Evil,* USA Network, 2004.

Television Appearances; Specials:

The Making of "Nightmare on Elm Street IV" (also known as *Elm Street USA: A Halloween Nightmare*), 1989.

Television Appearances; Episodic:

Showbiz Today, 1991.

Film Director:

Freddy's Dead: The Final Nightmare (also known as *A Nightmare on Elm Street 6*), New Line Cinema, 1991.

Ghost in the Machine (also known as *Deadly Terror*), Twentieth Century–Fox, 1993.

Tank Girl, United Artists, 1995.

Film Producer:

Hairspray, New Line Cinema, 1988.

A Nightmare on Elm Street 4: The Dream Master, New Line Cinema, 1988.

Book of Love, New Line Cinema, 1990.

Cry–Baby, Universal, 1990.

The Borrowers, PolyGram Filmed Entertainment, 1997.

Film Appearances:

Terrapol in landing party, *Android,* New Line Cinema, 1982.

Science of Horror (documentary), Totho, 2008.

RECORDINGS

Videos:

Welcome to Primetime, 1999.

It Came from Baltimore, Universal Home Entertainment, 2005.

Never Sleep Again: The Elm Street Legacy, 1428 Films, 2010.

Fred Heads: The Ultimate Freddy Fans, 1428 Films, 2010.

Director of the music video "2 Cents" by *Beowolf.*

ADAPTATIONS

The 1991 film *Freddy's Dead: The Final Nightmare* (also known as *A Nightmare on Elm Street 6*) was based on a story by Talalay.

OTHER SOURCES

Periodicals:

Starlog, May, 1995.

Electronic:
TalalayFilms, http://www.talalayfilms.com, May 24, 2010.

TAYLOR, Roberta 1948–

PERSONAL

Born 1948, in London, England; married Peter Guinness (an actor).

Career: Actress. Appeared as Inspector Gina Gold in a commercial for the television program *The Bill,* 2003.

CREDITS

Television Appearances; Series:
Irene, *EastEnders,* BBC, 1997–2000.
Rachel Whiting, a recurring role, *Doctors,* BBC, 2001.
Inspector Gina Gold, *The Bill,* ITV1, 2002–2008.

Television Appearances; Miniseries:
Mrs. Golden, *Wolcott,* ITV, 1981.
Aggie, *Sharman,* 1996.
Jane, *The Passion,* BBC, 1999.
Mrs. Pardiggle, *Bleak House,* BBC1, 2005, then PBS, 2006.

Television Appearances; Specials:
Mother, *Eye Contact,* Channel 4, 1991.
It Shouldn't Happen to a ... Soapstar, ITV, 2002.
Test the Nation: The Great British Test, BBC, 2004.
Presenter, *The British Soap Awards,* ITV, 2007.
The Bill Made Me Famous, ITV1, 2008.

Television Appearances; Episodic:
"Betrayal of Trust," *Crown Court,* ITV, 1979.
Roberta Martin, "Lucky, Lucky Thirteen!," *Lady Killers,* Granada Television, 1980.
Sheila Williams, "The Wolvercote Tongue," *Inspector Morse,* PBS, 1987.
Athene, "One Way Out," *Screen One,* BBC, 1989.
Angie Purser, "Market Force," *The Bill,* ITV1, 1990.
Pat Norris, "The Loneliness of the Long Distance Entrepreneur," *Minder,* ITV, 1991.
(Uncredited) Ray's landlady, "Guess Who's Coming to Dinner?," *Minder,* ITV, 1991.
Liz Turner, "Getting Through," *The Bill,* ITV1, 1992.
Mrs. Reid, "Care in the Community," *The Bill,* ITV1, 1993.
Violette Kaye, "The Boaster," *In Suspicious Circumstances,* ITV, 1994.

Mrs. Weatherall, "The Call Girl," *Dangerfield,* BBC, 1995.
Dr. de Groot, "Cease upon the Midnight: Parts 1 & 2," *Silent Witness,* BBC, 1997.
Ms. Gardiner, *The Knock,* ITV, 1997.
Herself, *Blankety Blank,* ITV, 2001.
Karen Lake, "Fathers and Sons," *Holby City,* BBC, 2002.
Inspector Gina Gold, "Moving Targets," *M.I.T.: Murder Investigation Team* (also known as *Murder Investigation Team*), Arts and Entertainment, 2003.
Interviewee, "Miranda Richardson," *A Taste of My Life,* BBC, 2007.
(Uncredited) *TV Burp,* ITV, 2008.

Television Talk Show Guest Appearances; Episodic:
Loose Women, ITV, 2000, 2005, 2009.
Today with Des and Mel, ITV, 2004.
GMTV, ITV, 2004.
The Paul O'Grady Show, ITV, between 2004 and 2009.
Guest panelist, *The Wright Stuff,* Channel 5, 2005, 2009.
This Morning, ITV, 2006.
Richard & Judy, Channel 4, 2007.

Film Appearances:
Witch chef, *The Witches,* Warner Bros., 1990.
Ottoline Morrell, *Tom & Viv,* Miramax, 1994.
Aggie, *The Turnaround,* 1995.

RECORDINGS

Audio Books:
Too Many Mothers by Roberta Taylor (memoir), abridged audio edition, Orion Publishing Group, 2006.

WRITINGS

Memoirs:
Too Many Mothers: A Memoir of an East End Childhood, Atlantic Books, 2005.

OTHER SOURCES

Books:
Taylor, Roberta, *Too Many Mothers: A Memoir of an East End Childhood,* Atlantic Books, 2005, abridged audio version released as *Too Many Mothers,* by Roberta Taylor, Orion Publishing Group, 2006.

Periodicals:
Radio Times, August 24, 2002, p. 13.

TENA, Natalia 1984–
(Nat Gastiain Tena)

PERSONAL

Full name, Natalia Gastiain Tena; born November 1, 1984, in London, England.

Addresses: *Agent*—Curtis Brown Group, Ltd., Haymarket House, 28–29 Haymarket, London SW1Y 4SP, England.

Career: Actress.

CREDITS

Film Appearances:
(As Nat Gastiain Tena) Ellie, *About a Boy* (also known as *About a Boy oder: Der Tag der toten Ente* and *Pour un garcon*), Universal, 2002.
Peggy, *Mrs. Henderson Presents* (also known as *Mrs. Henderson* and *Mrs Henderson Presents*), The Weinstein Company, 2005.
Vera, *The Fine Art of Love: Mine Ha–Ha* (also known as *The Grooming, Laughing Water (Mine Ha–Ha),* and *L'educazione fisica delle fanciulle*), 01 Distribuzione, 2005.
Thomson, *Lezione 21* (also known as *Lecture 21* and *Lesson 21*), Rai Cinema, 2008.
Rose, *Womb,* 2010.

Film Appearances; as the Character Nymphadora Tonks:
Harry Potter and the Order of the Phoenix (IMAX version known as *Harry Potter and the Order of the Phoenix: The IMAX Experience;* also known as *Order of the Phoenix, The Order of the Phoenix, Tip Top, Hari Poter i Red Feniksa, Harry Potter e a Ordem da Fenix, Harry Potter e l'ordine della Fenice, Harry Potter en de orde van de feniks, Harry Potter es a Foenix Rendje, Harry Potter et l'ordre du phenix, Harry Potter i l'orde del Fenix, Harry Potter ja feeniksin kilta, Harry Potter och fenixordern, Harry Potter og foniksordenen, Harry Potter und der Orden des Phoenix,* and *Harry Potter y la orden del Fenix*), Warner Bros., 2007.
Harry Potter and the Half–Blood Prince (IMAX version known as *Harry Potter and the Half–Blood Prince: An IMAX 3D Experience;* also known as *The Half–Blood Prince, HP and the HBP,* and *HP6*), Warner Bros., 2009.
Harry Potter and the Deathly Hallows: Part I (also released in an IMAX version; also known as *The Deathly Hallows*), Warner Bros., 2010.
Harry Potter and the Deathly Hallows: Part II (also released in an IMAX version; also known as *The Deathly Hallows*), Warner Bros., 2011.

Television Appearances; Specials:
Herself, *The Hidden Secrets of Harry Potter* (also known as *Harry Potter: The Hidden Secrets*), Arts and Entertainment, 2007.

Television Appearances; Episodic:
Amy Emerson, "Boundaries," *Doctors,* BBC, 2005.
Gemma, "Mirrorball," *Afterlife,* ITV and BBC America, 2006.

Stage Appearances:
Zelda, *Sitting Pretty,* Watford Palace Theatre, Watford, England, and New Wolsey Theatre, Ipswich, England, both 2005.

Major Tours:
Hazel, *Gone to Earth,* British cities, 2004.
Cathy and Bertha, *Bronte,* British cities, 2005.
Fevvers, *Nights at the Circus,* British cities, 2006.
Matilde, *The Clean House,* British cities, 2008.
Desdemona, *Othello,* Royal Shakespeare Company, British cities, 2009.

RECORDINGS

Videos:
Herself, *Trailing Tonks* (short documentary), Warner Home Video, 2007.

Video Games:
Voice of Nymphadora Tonks, *Harry Potter and the Order of the Phoenix,* Electronic Arts, 2007.

THARP, Twyla 1941–

PERSONAL

Born July 1, 1941, in Portland, IN; married Peter Young (divorced); married Robert Hout; children: (second marriage) Jesse. *Education:* Attended Pomona College; Barnard College, B.A., art history, 1963; studied with Richard Thomas, Merce Cunningham, Igor Schwezoff, Louis Mattox, Paul Taylor, Margaret Craske, and Erick Hawkins.

Career: Dancer and choreographer. Paul Taylor Dance Company, New York City, dancer, 1963–65; Twyla Tharp Dance Company, New York City, choreographer,

1965–87; American Ballet Theatre, New York City, artistic associate and resident choreographer, 1987–89; regrouped Twyla Tharp Dance, 1999—; Twyla Tharp Productions, founder; Robert Joffrey Ballet, choreographer; toured frequently with American Ballet Theatre. Resident at colleges and universities, including University of Massachusetts, Oberlin College, Walker Art Center, and Boston University; Twyla Tharp Dance Foundation, New York City, founder.

Awards, Honors: Guggenheim Foundation Fellowship, John S. Guggenheim Memorial Foundation, 1971; Creative Arts Award, Brandeis University, 1972; *Dance Magazine* Award, 1981; Emmy Award nomination, best choreography in a single episode of a regular or limited series or special, 1983, for *Catherine Wheel;* Directors Guild of America Award (with others), outstanding directorial achievement in musical/variety, Emmy Awards, outstanding achievement in choreography and outstanding individual achievement—classical music/dance programming—directing (with Don Mischer), Emmy Award nomination (with Peter Elbeing), outstanding individual achievement—classical music/dance programming—writing, 1985, all for *Dance in America;* Medal of Excellence, Columbia University, 1987; Lion of the Performing Arts Award, New York Public Library, 1989; Samuel H. Scripps/American Dance Festival Award, 1990; Wexner Foundation Award, Ohio State University Wexner Center for the Arts, 1991; Laurence Olivier Theatre Award, outstanding achievement in dance, Society of West End Theatre, 1991, for *The Upper Room;* Golden Plate Award, American Academy of Achievement, 1993; named Woman of Achievement, Barnard College, 1993; American Academy of Arts and Sciences, inductee, 1993; Arts Award, Dickinson College, 1996; Distinguished Artist Award, International Society for the Performing Arts, 1996; American Academy of Arts and Letters, named honorary member, 1997; MOCA Award to Distinguished Women in the Arts, Museum of Contemporary Art, 1999; Doris Duke Award for New Work, 1999; Laurence Olivier Theatre Award nomination, outstanding achievement in dance, 1999, for *BITE:98;* Antoinette Perry Award, best choreographer, Antoinette Perry Award nomination, best director of a musical, Drama Desk Award, outstanding choreography, Drama Desk Award nomination, outstanding director of a musical, 2003, all for *Movin' Out;* National Medal of Arts, 2004; Touring Broadway Award, 2005, for *Movin' Out;* Kennedy Center Honors, John F. Kennedy Center for the Performing Arts, 2008; Antoinette Perry Award nomination, best choreography, Drama Desk Award, outstanding choreography, 2010, both for *Come Fly Away.* Honorary degrees include D.Performing Arts from California Institute of the Arts, 1978, Brown University, 1981, and Bard College, 1981; L.H.D. from Indiana University—Bloomington, 1987, D.F.A. from Pomona College, 1987, Hamilton College, 1988, Skidmore College, 1988, Marymount Manhattan College, 1989, Ball State University, 1996.

CREDITS

Stage Ballet Choreographer:
Push Comes to Shove, American Ballet Theatre, Uris Theatre, New York City, 1976.
Nine Sinatra Songs, 1982, then Metropolitan Opera House, New York City, 1990.
The Little Ballet (also known as *Once Upon a Time*), Northrop Auditorium, Minneapolis, MN, 1983.
(With Jerome Robbins) *Brahms/Handel,* City Center Theatre, New York City, 1984.
At the Supermarket, American Ballet Theatre, 1984.
Ballare, Brooklyn Academy of Music Theatre, New York City, 1987.
Stations of the Crossed, Soho's Ohio Theatre, New York City, 1988.
Brief Fling, War Memorial Opera House, San Francisco, CA, 1990, then New York State Theatre, New York City, 1990.
The Upper Room, American Ballet Theatre, 1990.
Grand Pas: Rhythm of the Saints, Paris Opera Ballet, 1991.
Deuce Coupe II, City Center Theatre, 1992.
Men's Piece, City Center Theatre, 1992.
Waterbaby Bagatelles, Boston Ballet, 1994.
BITE:98, 1998.
Known by Heart, American Ballet Theatre, City Center Theatre, 1998.
The Beethoven Seventh, New York City Ballet, State Theatre, New York City, 2000.
Variations on a Theme by Haydn, American Ballet Theatre, Kennedy Center, Washington, DC, 2000.

Stage Choreographer:
Tank Dive, 1965.
Re–Moves, 1966.
Forevermore, 1967.
Generation, 1968.
Medley, 1969.
Fugue, Delacorte Theatre, New York City, 1970.
Eight Jelly Rolls, 1971.
The Raggedy Dances, 1972.
As Time Goes By, 1974.
Sue's Leg, 1975.
Once More Frank, New York State Theatre, New York City, 1976.
Mud, 1977.
Baker's Dozen, 1979.
When We Were Very Young, 1980.
Twyla Tharp and Her Dancers, Winter Garden Theatre, New York City, 1981.
The Catherine Wheel, Winter Garden Theatre, 1981.
Nine Sinatra Songs, Queen Elizabeth Theatre, Vancouver, British Columbia, Canada, 1982.
Sinatra Suite, Queen Elizabeth Theatre, 1982.
Bach Partrita, Kennedy Center for the Performing Arts, Washington, DC, 1983.
Amadeus, 1984.

White Nights, 1985.

Sorrow Floats (musical), Broadway production, 1985.

Singin' in the Rain (musical), George Gershwin Theatre, New York City, 1985–86.

In the Upper Room, Ravinia Festival, Highland Park, IL, 1986.

Bum's Rush, Civic Opera House, Chicago, IL, 1989.

Everlast, War Memorial Opera House, San Francisco, CA, 1989.

Quartet, Jackie Gleason Theatre of the Performing Arts, Miami Beach, FL, 1989.

Demeter and Persephone, 1993.

American We, Metropolitan Opera House, New York City, 1995.

Jump Start, Metropolitan Opera House, 1995.

How Near Heaven, Kennedy Center for the Performing Arts, 1995.

The Elements, Metropolitan Opera House, 1996.

Moondog, Twyla Tharp Dance Foundation, Stanford, CA, 1998.

Yemaya, Miami, FL, 1998.

Diabelli, Twyla Tharp Dance Foundation, Palermo, Italy, 1998.

Hammerklavier, Twyla Tharp Dance Foundation, Duke University, Durham, NC, 1999.

Mozart Clarinet Quintet K581, Twyla Tharp Dance Foundation, Duke University, 2000.

Surfer at the River Styx, Twyla Tharp Dance Foundation, Duke University, 2000.

Westerly Round, 2001.

Movin' Out, Shubert Theatre, Chicago, IL, 2002, then Richard Rogers Theatre, New York City, 2002–2005.

Even the King, 2003.

The Time They Are A–Changin', Brooks Atkinson Theatre, New York City, 2006.

Come Fly with Me, Alliance Theatre at Woodruff, Atlanta, GA, 2009, then Marquis Theatre, New York City, 2010.

Also choreographed *Deuce Coupe,* Joffrey Ballet, City Center Theatre, New York City.

Stage Director:

The Catherine Wheel, Winter Garden Theatre, New York City, 1981.

Movin' Out, Shubert Theatre, Chicago, IL, 2002, then Richard Rogers Theatre, New York City, 2002–2005.

The Time They Are A–Changin', Brooks Atkinson Theatre, New York City, 2006.

Come Fly with Me, Alliance Theatre at Woodruff, Atlanta, GA, 2009, then Marquis Theatre, New York City, 2010.

Stage Concept:

The Time They Are A–Changin', Brooks Atkinson Theatre, New York City, 2006.

Stage Creator and Developer:

Come Fly with Me, Alliance Theatre at Woodruff, Atlanta, GA, 2009, then Marquis Theatre, New York City, 2010.

Major Tours:

Producer and choreographer, *Cutting Up,* 1992–93.

Choreographer, *Tharp!,* 1996.

Choreographer, *Twyla Tharp Dance,* U.S. and world cities, 2002–2003.

Film Choreographer:

Tank Dive: Excerpts, 1965.

Hair, United Artists, 1979.

Ragtime (also known as *Love and Glory*), Paramount, 1981.

Amadeus (also known as *Peter Schaffer's "Amadeus"* and *Amadeus: The Director's Cut*), Orion, 1984.

(With Roland Petit and Mikhail Baryshnikov) *White Nights,* Columbia, 1985.

Valmont, Orion, 1989.

I'll Do Anything, 1994.

Film Appearances:

Tank Dive: Excerpts, 1965.

Voice, *Zorn's Lemma,* 1970.

Herself, *The Making of "Amadeus,"* 2002.

Television Work; Specials:

Choreographer, "Sue's Leg," *Twyla Tharp and Dancers,* 1976.

Choreographer and director, *The Catherine Wheel,* PBS, 1982.

Choreographer, "Zoetrope," *Great Performances' 20th Anniversary Special,* PBS, 1992.

Choreographer, "In the Upper Room," *Twyla Tharp: Oppositions,* PBS, 1996.

Television Work; Episodic:

Choreographer and (with Don Mischer) director, "Baryshnikov by Tharp with American Ballet Theatre," *Dance in America* (also known as *Great Performances: Dance in America*), PBS, 1984.

Television Appearances; Specials:

Twyla Tharp and Dancers, 1976.

Great Performances' 20th Anniversary Special, PBS, 1992.

"The Individual and Tradition," *Dancing,* PBS, 1993.

A Century of Women, TBS, 1994.

Twyla Tharp: Oppositions, PBS, 1996.

The 57th Annual Tony Awards, CBS, 2003.

The Kennedy Center Honors: A Celebration of the Performing Arts (also known as *The 31st Annual Kennedy Center Honors*), PBS, 2008.

The 64th Annual Tony Awards, CBS, 2010.

Television Appearances; Episodic:
Charlie Rose (also known as *The Charlie Rose Show*), PBS, 1995.

WRITINGS

Stage Musical Books:
Come Fly with Me, Alliance Theatre at Woodruff, Atlanta, GA, 2009, then Marquis Theatre, New York City, 2010.

Television Episodes:
(With Peter Elbling) "Baryshnikov by Tharp with American Ballet Theatre," *Dance in America,* PBS, 1984.

Autobiographies:
Push Comes to Shove, 1992.

Nonfiction:
The Creative Habit: Learn It and Use It for Life: A Practical Guide, 2005.
The Collaborative Habit: Life Lessons for Working Together, 2009.

OTHER SOURCES

Periodicals:
Dance Magazine, January, 2000, p. 44; March, 2001, p. 44; April, 2001, p. 36; February, 2003, p. 47; January, 2007, p. 86; December, 2009, p. 98.
Los Angeles Times, November 22, 1992.
Nation, March 28, 1987, p. 410.
Newsweek, November 6, 2008, p. 68.
New York Times, January 1, 1989.
Playbill, November 30, 2002.
The Progressive, January, 2005, p. 41.
U.S. News & World Report, November 1, 2009, p. 62.

Electronic:
Twyla Tharp Home Page, http://www.twylatharp.org, June 16, 2010.

THORNE, Bella 1997–

PERSONAL

Full name, Annabella Avery Thorne; born October 8, 1997, in Hollywood, FL; sister of Dani Thorne (an actress and model), Kaili Thorne (an actress), and Remy

Thorne (an actor). *Education:* Studied at Dolphin Entertainment, at various institutions, and with various instructors. *Avocational Interests:* Hiking, swimming, snorkeling, surfing, in–line skating, dancing, playing soccer, painting, spending time with pets.

Addresses: *Agent*—Innovative Artists, 1505 10th St., Santa Monica, CA 90401. *Manager*—Kritzer Levine Wilkins Griffin Entertainment, 11872 La Grange Ave., 1st Floor, Los Angeles, CA 90025. *Publicist*—Anderson Group Public Relations, 8060 Melrose Ave., 4th Floor, Los Angeles, CA 90046.

Career: Actress. Worked as a model; appeared in several advertisements and served as a spokesperson; model for the covers of books. Supporter of charities.

Member: Screen Actors Guild.

Awards, Honors: Young Artist Award nominations, best performance in a television series—guest starring young actress, Young Artist Foundation, 2008, for *The O.C.,* 2009, for *October Road,* and 2010, for *Mental;* Young Artist Award, best performance in a television series—supporting young actress, 2009, for *My Own Worst Enemy.*

CREDITS

Film Appearances:
Sideline fan, *Stuck on You,* Twentieth Century–Fox, 2003.
Extra, *Finishing the Game: The Search for a New Bruce Lee* (also known as *Finishing the Game*), IFC Films/IFC First Take, 2007.
Julia, *Craw Lake* (short film; also known as *Crawlake*), In Broad Daylight Films, 2007.
Young Claire, *The Seer,* Nuragic Films, 2007.
Annabella, *Blind Ambition,* Subcontinent Films, 2008.
Viola: The Traveling Rooms of a Little Giant (short film; also known as *Viola*), University of Southern California, c. 2008.
Psych out girl, *Water Pills* (short film), Hildour Films, 2009.
Young Angela, *Forget Me Not,* Fries Film Group, 2009.
Danielle, *Under the Influence,* Just Make It Happen Productions, 2010.
Messenger, *One Wish,* One Wish Productions, 2010.
Sarah Patterson, *Raspberry Magic,* 2010.
Jennie, *Buttermilk Sky,* Hometown Studio & Distribution Company, c. 2011.
Mallory, *Corpse,* Fright Flix Productions, c. 2011.
Skylar, *Taxidermist,* Talmarc Productions, c. 2011.

Appeared in the short films *Little Boy Blue* and *This Old Man.* Some sources cite appearances in other films.

Television Appearances; Series:
Ruthy Spivey, *My Own Worst Enemy*, NBC, 2008.
Annie, *In the Motherhood*, ABC, 2009.
CeCe Jones, *Shake It Up!* (also known as *Dance Dance Chicago*), The Disney Channel, beginning 2010.
Tancy "Teenie" Henrickson, *Big Love*, HBO, beginning c. 2010.

Television Appearances; Episodic:
Kid, "I Wanna Be Sedated," *Entourage*, HBO, 2006.
Jess, *Jimmy Kimmel Live!* (also known as *Jimmy Kimmel* and *The Jimmy Kimmel Project*), ABC, 2006.
Performer in Keith Richards skit, *Jimmy Kimmel Live!* (also known as *Jimmy Kimmel* and *The Jimmy Kimmel Project*), ABC, 2006.
Margaux Darling, "The Chiavennasca," *Dirty Sexy Money* (also known as *Sexy Money*), ABC, 2007.
Young Taylor Townsend, "The Case of the Franks," *The O.C.* (also known as *California Teens, Newport Beach, O.C., O.C., California, Orange County, A Narancsvidek, O.C.—Um estranho no paraiso,* and *Zycie na fali*), Fox, 2007.
Angela Ferilli, "Stand Alone by Me," *October Road* (also known as *October Road.*), ABC, 2008.
Herself, "Sit Down with 12 Year Old Actress Bella Thorne," *The View from the Bay*, ABC Channel 7, 2008.
Margaux Darling, "The Family Lawyer," *Dirty Sexy Money* (also known as *Sexy Money*), ABC, 2008.
Margaux Darling, "The Silence," *Dirty Sexy Money* (also known as *Sexy Money*), ABC, 2008.
Margaux Darling, "The Summer House," *Dirty Sexy Money* (also known as *Sexy Money*), ABC, 2008.
Nancy Lueke, "Max's Secret Girlfriend," *Wizards of Waverly Place* (also known as *The Amazing Hannigans, The Amazing O'Malleys,* and *Disney Wizards*), The Disney Channel, 2010.

Appeared in other programs, including *When We Were Girls*, Women's Network.

Television Appearances; Pilots:
Ruthy Spivey, "Breakdown," *My Own Worst Enemy*, NBC, 2008.
Emily, *Mental*, Fox, 2009.
CeCe Jones, *Shake It Up!* (also known as *Dance Dance Chicago*), The Disney Channel, 2010.

Internet Appearances; Series:
Wendy, *Little Monk*, broadcast on *USA Network*, http://www.usanetwork.com/series/littlemonk, 2009.

RECORDINGS

Video Games:
Voice of ant kid, *Ant Bully*, Warner Bros./Midway Games, 2006.

OTHER SOURCES

Periodicals:
Buzzine, November, 2008.

Electronic:
The Star Scoop.com, http://www.thestarscoop.com, October 6, 2008.
Thorne Kids, http://www.thornekids.net, March 2, 2010.

THORNE, Remy 1995–

PERSONAL

Full name, Remington Hunter Thorne; born December 22, 1995, in Miami, FL; brother of Dani Thorne (an actress and model), Kaili Thorne (an actress), and Bella Thorne (an actress). *Education:* Trained with Simmons & Scott Entertainment, Burbank, CA, Dolphin Entertainment, Miami, FL, and Joey Paul Jensen. *Avocational Interests:* Improvisational comedy, his pets, hiking, biking, skateboarding, reading, video games.

Addresses: *Agent*—AKA Talent Agency, 6310 San Vicente Blvd., Suite 200, Los Angeles, CA 90048. *Manager*—Adam Griffin, Kritzer Levine Wilkins Entertainment, 11872 La Grange Ave., 1st Floor, Los Angeles, CA 90025.

Career: Actor. Worked as a model; appeared in commercials and several print advertisements; also appeared in industrial films and Internet broadcasts. Involved with a fashion show, Otis School of Design and the Cirque du Soleil. Involved with charities, including Nomad Charities, UNICEF, and World Vision.

Member: Screen Actors Guild.

Awards, Honors: Young Artist Award nomination, best performance in a television series (comedy or drama)—guest–starring young actor, Young Artist Foundation, 2007, for *Las Vegas*; Young Artist Award, best performance in a short film—young actor, 2008, for *Bad*; Young Artist Award nomination, best performance in a television series—guest–starring young actor, 2008, for *Criminal Minds*; Young Artist Award nomination, best performance in a television series—guest–starring young actor, 2009, for *October Road*.

CREDITS

Film Appearances:
(Uncredited) Sidelines fan, *Stuck on You*, Twentieth Century–Fox, 2003.

Abused child and child in happy memories, *Down with Memories* (short film), New York Film Academy, c. 2006.

Extra, *Finishing the Game: The Search for a New Bruce Lee* (also known as *Finishing the Game*), IFC Films/ IFC First Take, 2007.

(Uncredited) Young Gary, *Captivity,* Lionsgate/After Dark Films, 2007.

Young Matt, *Even If* (short film), Black Hole Films, 2007.

John Read, *Bad* (short film), 2008.

Tommy, *St. California* (short film), Blood and Whiskey Films, 2008.

Bo Tyler, *First Strike,* 2009.

Child Baxter, *Orgies and the Meaning of Life* (also known as *O and the Meaning of Life*), Cinema Epoch, 2009.

Young Tucker, *Miss March* (also known as *Miss February, Miss March: Generation Penetration,* and *Playboys*), Fox Searchlight, 2009.

Zach, *Rubber,* Magnet Releasing/Elle Driver, c. 2009.

11:11, Hourglass Pictures, c. 2010.

Television Appearances; Series:
Appeared in the programs *Sabado gigante,* Telemundo; and *Tarzan,* MTV.

Television Appearances; Episodic:
Kevin, "White Christmas," *Las Vegas* (also known as *Casino Eye*), NBC, 2006.

Kid, "Meaning," *House M.D.* (also known as *Doctor House, Dr House, Dr. House, Dr. [H]ouse, Dr. House—Medical Division, Dr. House: Medical Division,* and *House*), Fox, 2006.

Milo, "Scoop and Run," *ER* (also known as *Emergency Room* and *E.R.*), NBC, 2006.

(In archive footage) Himself, *Today* (also known as *NBC News Today* and *The Today Show*), NBC, 2006.

Young Reid, "Revelations," *Criminal Minds* (also known as *Quantico, Criminal Minds—FBI tutjijat, Esprits criminels, Gyilkos elmék, Kurjuse kannul,* and *Mentes criminales*), CBS, 2007.

Young Eddie, "Stand Alone by Me," *October Road* (also known as *October road* and *October Road.*), ABC, 2008.

Television Appearances; Pilots:
Young Bobby, *Four Kings,* NBC, 2006.

Mike Borelli, Jr., *Protect and Serve,* CBS, 2007.

Joshua, *Mental,* Fox, 2009.

OTHER SOURCES

Periodicals:
Entertain Your Brain!, January 9, 2006, p. 1.

Young Stars News, June 13, 2006, p. 1; October 12, 2006.

Electronic:
Thorne Kids, http://www.thornekids.net, March 16, 2010.

TIERNAN, Andrew 1965–
(Andy Tiernan)

PERSONAL

Born November 30, 1965, in Birmingham, England. *Education:* Trained at Drama Centre, London.

Addresses: *Agent*—Dallas Smith, United Agents, 12–26 Lexington St., London W1F 0LE, England; (personal appearances) Michael Brooks, Innovative Artists Talent and Literary Agency, 1505 10th St., Santa Monica, CA 90401. *Manager*—Paula Rosenberg, ICA Talent Management, 818 12th St., Suite 9, Santa Monica, CA 90403.

Career: Actor and producer. Performed with Birmingham Youth Theatre, Birmingham, England, and National Youth Theatre.

CREDITS

Film Appearances:
Mark, *Proper Seasons* (short film), 1988.

(As Andy Tiernan) Tramp's follower, *Dead Cat* (short film), 1989.

Dog, *Sweet Nothing,* 1990.

The man, *The End of the Road* (short film), 1991.

Piers Gaveston, *Edward II,* 1991, Fine Line, 1992.

Orlando and Oliver, *As You Like It,* Walt Disney, 1992.

Berthold, *The Trial,* Angelika Films, 1993.

Cyprian's man, *Being Human,* Warner Bros., 1994.

Paris vampire, *Interview with the Vampire: The Vampire Chronicles* (also known as *Interview with the Vampire*), Warner Bros., 1994.

Mark, *Some Kind of Life,* Granada, 1995.

The hooligan, *Awayday* (short film), Big Pond Productions, 1995.

Captain Jorgu, *Two Deaths,* Castle Hill, 1996.

Chris, *Face,* New Line Cinema, 1997.

Cyril, *Playing God* (also known as *Playing Hero 14 April 1999*), Buena Vista, 1997.

Corporal Muller, *The Scarlet Tunic,* Marie Hoy Film and Television, 1998.

Mohammed, *The Protagonists,* Medusa Distribuzione, 1998.

Map of the Scars, 1998.

(As Andy Tiernan) Man in pub, *Lock, Stock, and Two Smoking Barrels* (also known as *Two Smoking Barrels*), Gramercy, 1999.

Mr. Page, *Small Time Obsession,* Guerilla Films/J&M Entertainment, 2000.

Harris, *The Criminal,* Paramount, 2000.

Mark, *Checkout Girl* (short film), Company 342 Limited, 2000.

Art critic, *Brilliant!* (short film), BBC Bristol, 2000.

(As Andy Tiernan) John, *Left Turn* (short film), RSA Films, 2001.

Squeegee merchant, *Lava,* 2001.

Andy, *Mr. In–Between* (also known as *The Killing Kind*), Enterprise Films, 2001.

Lance Corporal Schenke, *The Bunker,* Millennium Pictures, 2001.

La sirene rouge (also known as *The Red Siren*), Haut et Court, 2002, Lions Gate Films, 2004.

Szalas, *The Pianist,* 2002.

The Earl of Richmond, *Richard III,* 2005.

Bruce, *Snuff–Movie,* Lions Gate Films, 2005.

Reverend Carmichael, *The Man Who Sold the World,* Man Who Films/Snakehair Productions, 2006.

Ephialtes, *300* (also known as *300: The IMAX Experience*), Warner Bros., 2006.

Zavodsky, *Bathory,* Tatrafilm, 2008.

John, *Rough Cut* (short film), McMartin Productions, 2010.

Alan Marcuson, *Mr. Nice,* Contender Entertainment Group, 2010.

Stanni, *Freight,* Icon Film Distribution, 2010.

Chekha, *Dead Cert,* Momentum Pictures, 2010.

Martin Stone, *War of the Dead* (also known as *Stone's War*), Scanbox Entertainment, 2010.

Film Work:

Producer, *Rough Cut,* McMartin Productions, 2010.

Associate producer, *Dead Cert,* Momentum Pictures, 2010.

Television Appearances; Miniseries:

Deputy Chief Rosper, *Prime Suspect* (also known as *Prime Suspect 1*), PBS, 1990.

Deputy Chief Rosper, *Prime Suspect 2,* PBS, 1992.

Leo, *The Guilty,* 1992.

Dagley, *Middlemarch,* PBS, 1994.

Gary O'Brien, *The Sculptress,* PBS, 1996.

Johnny Starkie, *Four Fathers,* ITV, 1999.

Freddie, *Hawk,* BBC, 2000.

Gary, *In a Land of Plenty,* BBC, 2001.

Gary Shale, *M.I.T.: Murder Investigation Team* (also known as *Murder Investigation Team*), Arts and Entertainment, 2005.

Richard Vaugh, *Murphy's Law,* BBC America, 2005.

Television Appearances; Movies:

Davey Royce, *Thacker,* 1992.

Scar, *Snow White: A Tale of Terror* (also known as *Snow White*), Showtime, 1997.

Bunting, *Hornblower: The Examination for Lieutenant* (also known as *Horatio Hornblower: The Fire Ship*), Arts and Entertainment, 1998.

Dean, *Rehab,* BBC, 2003.

Dave, *Whose Baby?* (also known as *Whose Baby Is It Anyway?*), Granada Television, 2004.

Roy Slater, *The Rotters' Club,* BBC, 2005.

(As Andy Tiernan) Victor Carroon, *The Quatermass Experiment,* BBC, 2005.

(Uncredited) Colin Feather, *Cold Blood,* Granada Television, 2005.

Colin Feather, *Cold Blood 2,* 2007.

Television Appearances; Specials:

Duggie, "Safe," *Screenplay,* Granada Television, 1993.

Banquo, "Macbeth on the Estate," *Performance,* BBC, 1997.

Ben Jonson, *A Waste of Shame: The Mystery of Shakespeare and His Sonnets,* BBC, 2005.

Prison Officer Bennett, "Pieces of a Silver Lining," *The Afternoon Play,* BBC, 2007.

Blue, *Harvest* (also known as *Coming Up: Harvest*), BBC, 2009.

Television Appearances; Episodic:

Dog, "Sweet Nothing," *Screen One,* BBC, 1990.

David Panter, "Watching the Detectives," *Between the Lines,* BBC, 1992.

Sean, "To Say I Love You: Parts 1–3," *Cracker,* ITV (later broadcast by Arts and Entertainment), 1993.

Billy Pink, "Doing the Business," *99–1,* ITV, 1994.

Billy Pink, "The Cost of Living," *99–1,* ITV, 1994.

"Fall," *Capital Lives,* ITV, 1994.

Andy Sturgeon, "The Enforcer," *Space Precinct,* syndicated, 1994.

John Campbell, "Black Orchid," *Taggart,* ITV, 1995.

Eddie Gilmour, "Man of Honour," *Ellington,* YTV, 1996.

Guy Walsh, "The Lions Den," *The Bill,* ITV1, 1997.

Psycho, "Out," *Soldier Soldier,* ITV, 1997.

John Isles, "Road Rage," *Thief Takers,* ITV, 1997.

Alan Dodds, "Out and About," *The Bill,* ITV1, 1999.

Lenny Spearfish, "The Curious Tale of Mr. Spearfish," *Jonathan Creek,* BBC1, 1999, BBC America, 2000.

Ray Nixon, "The Seven Year Itch," *Heartbeat,* ITV, 2000.

Gerard Ridley, "Everything Must Go," *City Central,* BBC, 2000.

Nick Cross, "Obsessions," *McCready and Daughter,* BBC, 2001.

Tom Jordan, premiere episode, *William and Mary,* Showtime, 2003.

Mike Wilder, "089," *The Bill,* ITV1, 2003.

Sergeant Charlie Fleckner, "Friendly Fire," *Red Cap,* BBC, 2004.

Don Keech, "Anger Management: Part 1," *Waking the Dead,* BBC1, 2004.

Owen Forster, *Spooks* (also known as *MI–5*), Arts and Entertainment, 2005.

Kim Trent, *Life on Mars,* BBC America, 2006.

Jake McNally, "Fallen Angel: Parts 1 & 2," *Dalziel and Pascoe,* BBC, 2006.

Steve Bright, "Picture of Innocence," *Midsomer Murders,* Arts and Entertainment, 2007.

Crixus, "Spartacus," *Heroes and Villains,* 2008.

Sergeant Major Sharratt, "Mad Dogs," *New Tricks,* BBC, 2008.

Gavin, *Survivors,* BBC America, 2008.

O'Neill, "Shields," *Casualty,* BBC1, 2009.

Craig Middleton, "Live by the Sword," *The Bill,* ITV1, 2009.

Craig Middleton, "Die by the Sword," *The Bill,* ITV1, 2009.

Whitaker, "Carrie's Story," *Murderland,* 2009.

Whitaker, "Hain's Story," *Murderland,* 2009.

Whitaker, "Carol's Story," *Murderland,* 2009.

Richard Henley, *Luther,* 2010.

Steven Dukes, *Whitechapel II,* ITV, 2010.

Mr. Purcell, "What Are Little Boys Made Of?," *Doctor Who,* 2011.

Appeared as Robin Sheppard in an episode of *Hawkins,* BBC; Raymond Wilcox in the series *Nice Work,* BBC.

Stage Appearances:

Bong and Nigel, *The Walking Class,* Midlands Art Center, 1983, then Birmingham Repertory Theatre, Birmingham, England, 1984, later Shaw Theatre, London, 1985.

Azor, *The Dispute,* Crucible Theatre, Sheffield, England, 1990.

Matt, *Noise,* Soho Theatre, London, 1997.

Mike, *The Bullet,* Donmar Warehouse Theatre, London, 1998.

Mike, *A Lie of the Mind,* Donmar Warehouse Theatre, 2001.

Austin, *True West,* Bristol Old Vic Theatre, London, 2003.

Vincent, *Flesh Wound,* English Stage Company, Royal Court Theatre, London, 2003.

Pacha, *A Couple of Poor Polish–Speaking Romanians,* Soho Theatre, 2008.

Also appeared in *The Geography of a Horse Dreamer,* Royal Court Theatre, London.

RECORDINGS

Videos:

Bring Something Back: The Making of "The Quatermass Experiment," DD Home Entertainment, 2005.

OTHER SOURCES

Electronic:
Andrew Tiernan Official Site, http://www.web.mac.com/andytiernan, May 20, 2010.

TILLING, Roger 1971–

PERSONAL

Born October 17, 1971.

Career: Voice artist; worked as a narrator and announcer; wrote scripts for such work. Worked for various radio and television networks, including live work; head of on–air continuity and voice for European markets for the Hallmark Channel; voices for promotional trailers; provided voice work for radio commercials and corporations. Also provided voice work for satellite navigation systems.

CREDITS

Television Appearances; Series:
Announcer, *University Challenge,* BBC2, beginning 1997.

Announcer, *Family Fortunes,* ITV, beginning 2002.

Announcer, *University Challenge: The Professionals,* BBC2, beginning 2003.

Television Appearances; Documentary Series:
French scientist, *Days That Shook the World,* BBC, History Channel, Discovery Channel, and Viasat History, beginning 2003.

Narrator, *Naked Science* (also known as *Superscience*), National Geographic Channel, beginning 2004.

British series narrator, *Mega Disasters,* History Channel, 2006–2008.

British narrator, *Jetman,* National Geographic Channel, beginning c. 2009.

Narrator for other programs, including *Head for the Med,* Travel Channel; *Man Eaters,* Five; and *When ... Goes Wrong,* Sky Television.

Television Appearances; Documentary Specials:
Narrator, *Case Reopened: The Black Dahlia,* History Channel, 1999.

Announcer, *40 Years of University Challenge,* BBC, 2002.

Narrator, *DNA: Guilty or Innocent?*, CBS, 2003.

Narrator, *The Battle of Tripoli*, History Channel, 2004.

(In archive footage) Announcer, *University Challenge: The Story So Far*, BBC, 2006.

Narrator, *Cannibalism: Extreme Survival*, History Channel, 2006.

Narrator, *Sahara*, History Channel, 2006.

Narrator, *Skeletons on the Zahara* (also known as *Skeletons on the Sahara*), History Channel, 2006.

Newsreader and racing commentator, *To Kidnap a Princess* (docudrama), Granada Television, 2006.

Narrator, *Caught on Safari: Battle at Kruger* (also known as *Caught on Safari*), National Geographic Channel, 2008.

Narrator, *Hubble's Amazing Universe*, National Geographic Channel, 2008.

Narrator, *The Lost Pyramid*, History Channel, 2008.

British narrator, *Bizarre Dinosaurs*, National Geographic Channel, 2009.

Narrator, *Underwater Universe*, History Channel, 2009.

Television Appearances; Episodic:

Newsreader, *Children's Ward* (also known as *The Ward*), ITV, 1997.

Voice–over, "Blair's University Challenge," *Panorama*, BBC, 2003.

Himself, *GMTV* (also known as *GMTV Today*), ITV, 2006.

Narrator, "Aryan Brotherhood," *Gangland*, History Channel, 2007.

Narrator, "Bear," *Prehistoric Predators*, National Geographic Channel, 2007.

Narrator, "Sabertooth Cat," *Prehistoric Predators*, National Geographic Channel, 2007.

Narrator, "Wolf," *Prehistoric Predators*, National Geographic Channel, 2007.

British narrator, "The Whale That Exploded," *Wild*, National Geographic Channel, 2008.

British narrator, "Frogs: The Thin Green Line," *Nature*, PBS, 2009.

Narrator, "Alaska's Extreme Machines," *Man–Made* (also known as *Man Made* and *Man Made: Alaska's Extreme Machines*), National Geographic Channel, 2009.

Voice–over, "Banks Behaving Badly?," *Panorama*, BBC, 2009.

Documentary Film Appearances:

British narrator, *Case Reopened: The Zodiac with Lawrence Block*, Film Garden Entertainment, 1999.

Narrator, *Singing in the Shadow: The Children of Rock Royalty*, Film Transit, 2003.

Narrator, *Dean Martin: A Reflection* (with accompanying CD), WHE International, 2006.

Film Appearances:

Television announcer, *Heart*, Feature Film Company, 1999.

RECORDINGS

Video Games:
Provided voices for video games.

WRITINGS

Teleplays; Episodic:
Product descriptions, *Family Fortunes*, ITV, beginning 2002.

Wrote scripts for his work as an announcer.

OTHER SOURCES

Electronic:
Roger Tilling, http://www.rogertilling.com, March 2, 2010.

TUNNEY, Robin 1972–

PERSONAL

Born June 19, 1972, in Chicago, IL; father, an auto salesman; mother, a bartender; married Bob Gosse (an actor, producer, and director), October 4, 1997 (divorced January 26, 2006); married Andrew Dominik (a director), November 15, 2007. *Education:* Attended Chicago Academy for the Performing Arts; also trained with Second City Players Workshop, Chicago, IL.

Addresses: *Agent*—The Gersh Agency, 9465 Wilshire Blvd., 6th Floor, Beverly Hills, CA 90212; Special Artists Agency, 9465 Wilshire Blvd., Suite 470, Beverly Hills, CA 90212. *Manager*—Hyler Management, 25 Sea Colony Dr., Santa Monica, CA 90405. *Publicist*—I/0 Public Relations, 8409 Santa Monica Blvd., West Hollywood, CA 90069.

Career: Actress. Also worked as a model.

Awards, Honors: MTV Movie Award, best fight (with Fairuza Balk), 1997, for *The Craft*; Volpi Cup, best actress, Venice Film Festival, 1997, and Independent Spirit Award nomination, best female lead, 1999, both for *Niagara, Niagara*; Blockbuster Entertainment Award nomination, favorite actress in an action film, 2001, for *Vertical Limit*; Festival Prize, best actress, Boston Film Festival, 2006, for *Open Window*.

CREDITS

Film Appearances:

Ella, *Encino Man* (also known as *California Man*), Buena Vista, 1992.

Debra, *Empire Records* (also known as *Empire* and *Rock & Fun*), Warner Bros., 1995.

Sarah Bailey, *The Craft,* Columbia, 1996.

Sarah, *Julian Po* (also known as *The Tears of Julian Po*), Fine Line, 1997.

Marcy, *Niagara, Niagara* (also known as *Niagra, Niagra*), Artisan Entertainment, 1997.

Christine York, *End of Days,* MCA/Universal, 1999.

Danika Lund, *Supernova,* Metro–Goldwyn–Mayer/United Artists, 2000.

(Uncredited) Party guest, *Bread and Roses* (also known as *Brot und Rosen* and *Pan y rosas*), Lions Gate Films, 2000.

Annie Garrett, *Vertical Limit,* Columbia, 2000.

Zoe, *Investigating Sex* (also known as *Intimate Affairs* and *Investigating Sex–Auf der Suche nach dem perfekten Orgasmus*), Janus Films/Kingsgate Films, 2001.

Zoe, *Cherish,* Fine Line, 2002.

Laura, *The Secret Lives of Dentists,* Manhattan Pictures International, 2002.

Herself, *Abby Singer* (*Abby Singer 2007*), Wembly Hall Theatre Company, 2003.

Angela Harris, *The In–Laws* (also known as *Ein ungleiches Paar* and *Wild Wedding—Ein ungleiches Paar*), Warner Bros., 2003.

Wynn French, *Shadow of Fear,* Mainline Productions, 2004.

Abby Laramie, *Paparazzi,* Twentieth Century–Fox, 2004.

Carly, *Runaway,* E1 Entertainment, 2005.

Laura Parish, *The Zodiac,* THINKFilm, 2005.

Zoe, *The Darwin Awards,* Metro–Goldwyn–Mayer, 2006.

Leonore Lemmon, *Hollywoodland,* Focus Features, 2006.

Melanie Hanson, *August* (also known as *Landshark*), First Look International, 2008.

Laura, *The Burning Plain* (also known as *Camino a la redencion*), Magnolia Pictures, 2008.

Theresa, *Passenger Side,* 2009.

Television Appearances; Series:

Veronica Donovan, *Prison Break* (also known as *Prison Break: On the Run*), Fox, 2005–2006.

Teresa Lisbon, *The Mentalist,* CBS, 2008—.

Television Appearances; Movies:

Hannah, *Frogs!,* PBS, 1992.

Sandra Turner, *Perry Mason: The Case of the Reckless Romeo,* NBC, 1992.

Elizabeth "Bess" Erne, *Riders of the Purple Sage,* TNT, 1996.

Kitty, *Montana* (also known as *Nothing Personal*), HBO, 1998.

Merri Coffman, *Naked City: Justice with a Bullet,* Showtime, 1998.

Melvina "Malka" Csizmadia, "Malka Csizmadia," *Rescuers: Stories of Courage: Two Families,* Showtime, 1998.

Izzy Fieldston, *Open Window,* Showtime, 2006.

Nancy Kissel, *The Two Mr. Kissels,* Lifetime, 2008.

Television Appearances; Episodic:

Mary, "Corky's Travels," *Life Goes On,* ABC, 1990.

Linda Miller, "They Shoot Baskets, Don't They," *Class of '96,* 1993.

Linda Miller, "Midterm Madness," *Class of '96,* 1993.

Linda Miller, "When Whitney Met Linda," *Class of '96,* 1993.

Linda Miller, "The Best Little Frat House at Havenhurst," *Class of '96,* 1993.

Marybeth, "Silent Night, Holy Cow," *Dream On,* 1993.

Jill Templeton, "Mayhem," *Law & Order,* NBC, 1994.

The Rosie O'Donnell Show, syndicated, 2000 and 2002.

"Surviving 'Vertical Limit,'" *HBO First Look,* HBO, 2000.

Edie (some sources cite Eve) Durant, "Developing," *The Twilight Zone,* UPN, 2003.

The Late Late Show with Craig Kilborn, 2004.

Last Call with Carson Daly, NBC, 2006.

"Tournament 8, Game 5," *Celebrity Poker Showdown,* Bravo, 2006.

"Tournament 8 Championship," *Celebrity Poker Showdown,* Bravo, 2006.

Fame Can Be a Killer: The Making of "Hollywoodland," *HBO First Look,* HBO, 2006.

Voice of Madame Razz/Entrapta/Carole Demas/skin graft patient, "Slaughterhouse on the Prairie," *Robot Chicken* (animated), Cartoon Network, 2007.

Ellen: The Ellen DeGeneres Show (also known as *The Ellen Show*), syndicated, 2009.

Also appeared as Deborah Hart, *Cutters,* CBS.

Television Appearances; Specials:

Brooke, the best friend, "But He Loves Me," *CBS Schoolbreak Special,* CBS, 1991.

2000 Blockbuster Entertainment Awards, 2000.

Prison Break: Season 2 Special, Fox, 2007.

Presenter, *The 35th Annual People's Choice Awards,* CBS, 2009.

Television Appearances; Miniseries:

Kathleen "Kick" Kennedy, *JFK: Reckless Youth,* ABC, 1993.

Herself, *The Witching Hour,* 1996.

Television Appearances; Pilots:

Linda Miller, *Class of '96,* 1993.

Nicole, *Profiles,* ABC, 1994.

Rebecca Adler, *House M.D.* (also known as *House*), Fox, 2004.

Veronica Donovan, *Prison Break* (also known as *Prison Break: On the Run*), Fox, 2005.

Teresa Lisbon, *The Mentalist,* CBS, 2008.

Stage Appearances:

Appeared in *Agnes of God, Bus Stop,* and *The Effect of Gamma Rays on Man–in–the–Moon Marigolds,* all Chicago, IL.

RECORDINGS

Videos:

End of Days: The Beginnning (short documentary; also known as *Spotlight on Location: End of Days;* released on the DVD version of *End of Days*), 2000.

Conjuring "The Craft" (short documentary), 2000.

Abby Laramie, *The Making of "Paparazzi"* (short film; released on the DVD version of *Paparazzi*), Twentieth Century–Fox Home Entertainment, 2004.

Cut, Good: The Making of "Runaway" (short documentary), E1 Entertainment, 2009.

OTHER SOURCES

Periodicals:

Details, November, 1999, pp. 122–26.

Detour, February, 1998, pp. 50–52.

Esquire, October, 1997, pp. 90–92.

Femme Fatales, February, 2000, pp. 8–11; January, 2001, pp. 20–23.

Harper's Bazaar, January, 1998, p. 49.

Interview, March, 1998, pp. 178–80.

Movieline, July, 1997.

New York Times, March 22, 1998, p. 24.

TURNBULL, Ann

(Anne Turnbull, Annie Turnbull)

PERSONAL

Canadian. *Education:* Ryerson University, graduated.

Career: Actress.

Member: Alliance of Canadian Cinema, Television, and Radio Artists, Canadian Actors' Equity Association.

CREDITS

Television Appearances; Movies:

Bluffing It, ABC, 1987.

Joan, *The Ann Jillian Story,* NBC, 1988.

The Defenders: Payback, Showtime, 1997.

Nurse Thompson, *A Day in a Life,* 2000.

Alex's mom, *Model Behavior,* ABC, 2000.

Wife at party, *Unstable,* Lifetime, 2009.

Ms. Finch, *Harriet the Spy: Blog Wars,* The Disney Channel, 2010.

Betty, *When Love Is Not Enough: The Lois Wilson Story,* CBS, 2010.

Television Appearances; Miniseries:

Cheryl and Mom, *Hotbox,* Comedy Network, 2009.

Television Appearances; Episodic:

Second nurse, "Our Selena Is Dying," *The Twilight Zone,* CBS, 1988.

Female guard, "Last Rites: Part 1," *Street Legal,* CBC, 1994.

Paula O'Connor, "The Perfect School: Parts 1 & 2," *Goosebumps* (also known as *Ultimate Goosebumps*), Fox, 1997.

Mrs. Toole, "Amy to the Rescue: The Amy Toole Story," *Real Kids, Real Adventures,* Global TV, 1999.

(As Annie Turnbull, "Leslie Franklin, "Homeless," *Blue Murder,* Global TV, 2001.

Laura Comrie, "Lover's Lane," *Blue Murder,* Global TV, 2003.

Dr. Geller, "Rage," *Odyssey 5,* Showtime, 2003.

Counselor, "Dearly Beloved," *Wild Card* (also known as *Zoe Busiek: Wild Card*), Lifetime, 2003.

Martha Caldwell, "Family Reunion," *Blue Murder,* Global TV, 2004.

Detective Cara McMillan, "Hustler," *72 Hours: True Crime,* CBC, 2005.

"Hit Delete," *The Eleventh Hour* (also known as *Bury the Lead*), CTV, 2005.

First Republican lady, *Queer as Folk* (also known as *Q.A.F.*), Showtime, 2005.

Mrs. Magnussen, "Chapter Seven," *Living in Your Car,* HBO Canada, 2010.

Also appeared in episodes of *Check It Out* and *Jonovision,* CBC.

Film Appearances:

(As Anne Turnbull) Minor talent contest audience member, *The Ballad of Little Roger Mead* (short film), AtomFilms, 2001.

Sandy, *Man v. Minivan* (short film), Canadian Film Centre, 2009.

Stage Appearances:
Appeared as Lily, *As Is,* Shaw Festival, Niagara–on–the–Lake, Ontario, Canada, and Toronto Free Theatre, Toronto, Ontario; Eve, *Back to Methusaleh,* Shaw Festival; mother, *Bedtimes and Bullies,* Citadel Theatre; Barbara, *Black Coffee,* Shaw Festival; Cleo, *Bravado,* Magnus Theatre; Pat Green, *Breaking the Code,* Cleveland Playhouse, Cleveland, OH; Faye, *Chapter Two,* Port Mansion Theatre; Avdotya, *The Government Inspector,* Theatre Plus; Mrs. Braddock, *The Graduate,* Theatre New Brunswick; Helen, *Helen's Necklace,* Thousand Islands Playhouse, Gananoque, Ontario; soothsayer, *Julius Caesar,* Citadel Theatre; Kate Keller, *The Miracle Worker,* Citadel Theatre; Patricia, *Sight Unseen,* Ford Centre Theatre; maid, *The Singular Life of Albert Nobbs;* Annelle, *Steel Magnolias,* Canadian production; Kate, *Sylvia,* Globe Theatre; Mrs. Peachum, *The Threepenny Opera,* Bathurst Street Theatre, Toronto; second old hag, *Tropical Madness,* Shaw Festival; Tamara, *The Women,* Shaw Festival; and Norah, *Wrong for Each Other,* Case Theatre.

U–V

UNGER, Billy 1995–

PERSONAL

Full name, William Brent Unger; born October 15, 1995, in Palm Beach County, FL; brother of Eric Unger (an actor).

Addresses: *Agent*—The Osbrink Agency, 4343 Lankershim Blvd., Suite 100, Universal City, CA 91602.

Career: Actor.

Awards, Honors: Young Artist Award, best performance in a DVD film, Young Artist Foundation, 2009, for *Cop Dog;* Young Artist Award nomination, best performance in a television series—guest starring young actor, 2009, for *Medium.*

CREDITS

Film Appearances:

Charles Gates, *National Treasure: Book of Secrets* (also known as *National Treasure 2* and *National Treasure 2: Book of Secrets*), Walt Disney Studios Motion Pictures, 2007.

Frankie, *Seven's Eleven: Sweet Toys* (short film; also known as *Yahoo! Kids: Seven's Eleven*), Yahoo!, 2007.

Robby North, *Cop Dog* (also known as *Marlowe*), Marvista Entertainment, 2008.

(Uncredited) Voice of screaming boy, *Changeling,* Universal, 2008.

Sammy Benson, *Opposite Day,* TVA Films, 2009.

Voice of hatchling Sammy, *Sammy's Adventures: The Secret Passage* (animated; also known as *Around the World in 50 Years 3D*), 2009.

Young Chev Chelios, *Crank: High Voltage* (also known as *Adrenaline: High Voltage, Crank: High Voltage—Fully Charged, Crank 2, Crank 2—High Voltage, Crank 2: High Voltage,* and *High Voltage*), Lions Gate Films, 2009.

Young version of title character, *Rock Slyde* (also known as *Rock Slyde: Private Eye*), Monarch Home Video, 2009.

Ben, *You Again,* Walt Disney Studios Motion Pictures/ Touchstone Pictures, 2010.

Billy Stone, *The Lost Medallion: The Adventures of Billy Stone,* MeThinx Entertainment/Downes Brothers Entertainment, 2010.

Prince Charming, *Jack and the Beanstalk,* Avalon Family Entertainment, 2010.

Zack Taylor, *Monster Mutt,* 2010.

Film Additional Voices:

Alabama Moon, Myriad Pictures, 2009.

Bride Wars (also known as *Bridal Wars*), Twentieth Century–Fox, 2009.

The Invited (also known as *The Conjuring* and *Untitled Ryan McKinney Project*), Relativity Media, 2010.

Television Appearances; Animated Series:

Voice of Eric, *Can You Teach My Alligator Manners?,* Playhouse Disney, The Disney Channel, beginning 2008.

Voice of Michael, *Special Agent Oso* (also known as *Agent Special Oso* and *Special–agent Oso*), The Disney Channel, beginning c. 2009.

Television Appearances; Episodic:

Chad, "Gossip," *Desperate Housewives* (also known as *Beautes desespereees, Desperate housewives—I segreti di Wisteria Lane, Desupareto na tsuma tachi, Esposas desesperadas, Frustrerte fruer, Gotowe na wszystko, Kucanice, Meeleheitel koduperenaised, Mujeres desesperadas, Noikokyres se apognosi, Szueletett felesegek,* and *Taeydelliset naiset*), ABC, 2007.

Devin, "My Turf War," *Scrubs* (also known as *[scrubs]*, *Scrubs: Med School, Foersta hjalpen, Helt sykt, Klinika, Meditsinskaya akademiya, Scrubs—Die Anfaenger, Toubib or not toubib,* and *Tuho–osasto*), NBC, 2007.

Jeff Reed, "Stalker," *Cold Case* (also known as *Anexihniastes ypothesis, Caso abierto, Cold case—affaires classees, Cold Case—Kein Opfer ist je vergessen, Doegloett aktak, Kalla spaar, Todistettavasti syyllinen,* and *Victimes du passe*), CBS, 2007.

Jeremy McMullin, "Something's Coming," *Desperate Housewives* (also known as *Beautes desespereees, Desperate housewives—I segreti di Wisteria Lane, Desupareto na tsuma tachi, Esposas desesperadas, Frustrerte fruer, Gotowe na wszystko, Kucanice, Meeleheitel koduperenaised, Mujeres desesperadas, Noikokyres se apognosi, Szueletett felesegek,* and *Taeydelliset naiset*), ABC, 2007.

Second kid/transfat kid, *The Tonight Show with Jay Leno* (also known as *Jay Leno* and *Jay Leno Show*), NBC, 2007.

Marty Bedell, "Goodbye to All That," *Terminator: The Sarah Connor Chronicles* (also known as *The Sarah Connor Chronicles* and *Terminator: S.C.C.*), Fox, 2008.

Teddy Carmichael and the young Joey, "Being Joey Carmichael," *Medium* (also known as *Ghost and Crime* and *A medium*), NBC, 2008.

Voice of handicapped kid, "Tales of a Third Grade Nothing," *Family Guy* (animated; also known as *Padre de familia* and *Padre del familia*), Fox, 2008.

Conor Stephens, "Manic at the Disco," *Mental,* Fox, 2009.

Sam, "Yielding," *Hawthorne* (also known as *HawthoRNe* and *Time Heals*), TNT, 2009.

Pete Murphy, "The Children's Parade," *Ghost Whisperer,* CBS, 2010.

Television Appearances; Pilots:
Brad, *Billion Dollar Freshmen,* Disney XD, 2011.

Television Work; Movies:
Additional voices, *Children of the Corn* (also known as *Stephen King's "Children of the Corn"*), Syfy, 2009.

UNGER, Eric 1998–

PERSONAL

Full name, Eric William Unger; born November 22, 1998, in Palm Beach County, FL; brother of Billy Unger (an actor).

Addresses: *Agent*—The Osbrink Agency, 4343 Lankershim Blvd., Suite 100, Universal City, CA 91602.

Career: Actor.

CREDITS

Film Appearances:
Security guard and kid pedestrian, *Opposite Day,* TVA Films, 2009.

Son walking with father, *Reconciliation,* 100 to 1 Productions, 2009.

Student, *Hip–Hop Headstrong* (short film), 2009.

Voice of Bader, *Gift of the Hoopoe* (animated short film), Saudi Aramco, 2009.

Voice of first hatchling, *Sammy's Adventures: The Secret Passage* (animated; also known as *Around the World in 50 Years 3D*), 2009.

Boy, *Monster Mutt,* 2010.

Student in locker room, *The Lost Medallion: The Adventures of Billy Stone,* MeThinx Entertainment/ Downes Brothers Entertainment, 2010.

Film Additional Voices:
Alabama Moon, Myriad Pictures, 2009.

Unstoppable (also known as *8888* and *Runaway Train*), Twentieth Century–Fox, 2010.

Television Appearances; Episodic:
Jeremy, "No Complaints," *'Til Death* (also known as *Eddie & Jeff*), Fox, 2009.

(Uncredited) Kid in child labor skit, *The Jay Leno Show,* NBC, 2009.

Second boy in skit, *The Tonight Show with Jay Leno* (also known as *Jay Leno* and *Jay Leno Show*), NBC, 2009.

Son, "Means and Ends," *Medium* (also known as *Ghost and Crime* and *A medium*), CBS, 2010.

Van Der BEEK, James 1977–

PERSONAL

Full name, James William Van Der Beek, Jr.; born March 8, 1977, in Cheshire, CT; son of James William (a cellular phone company executive and former professional baseball pitcher) and Melinda (a gymnastics studio manager and former dancer) Van Der Beek; married Heather McComb, July 5, 2003. *Education:* Studied English at Drew University. *Avocational Interests:* Sports, writing, playing guitar.

Addresses: *Agent*—Paradigm, 360 N. Crescent Dr., Beverly Hills, CA 90210. *Manager*—Brillstein Entertainment Partners, 9150 Wilshire Blvd., Suite 350, Beverly

Hills, CA 90212. *Publicist*—Cindy Guagenti, Baker/ Winokur/Ryder, 9100 Wilshire Blvd., 6th Floor, West Tower, Beverly Hills, CA 90212.

Career: Actor.

Awards, Honors: Selected one of the fifty most beautiful people in the world, *People Weekly,* 1998; Teen Choice Award nomination, TV—choice actor, 1999, for *Dawson's Creek;* MTV Movie Award nomination, best breakthrough male performance, 1999, Teen Choice Award, film—breakout performance, 1999, and Blockbuster Entertainment Award nomination, favorite new actor, 2000, both for *Varsity Blues;* MTV Movie Award, best cameo in a movie, 2001, for *Scary Movie;* San Diego Film Festival Award, best actor, 2009, for Formosa Betrayed.

CREDITS

Film Appearances:
Rick Sandford, *Angus* (also known as *Angus—Voll Cool*), New Line Cinema, 1995.

Tony, *I Love You, I Love You Not,* Avalanche Releasing, 1997.

Jonathan "Mox" Moxon, *Varsity Blues,* Paramount, 1999.

James Peterson, *Harvest* (also known as *Cash Crop* and *A Desperate Season*), Artisan Entertainment, 1999.

(Uncredited) Dawson Leery, *Scary Movie,* Dimension Films, 2000.

Lincoln Rogers Dunnison, *Texas Rangers,* Miramax/ Dimension Films, 2001.

(Uncredited) Himself, *Jay and Silent Bob Strike Back,* Dimension Films, 2001.

Sean Bateman, *The Rules of Attraction* (also known as *Die Regeln des Spiels*), Lions Gate Films, 2002.

(English version) Voice of Pazu, *Laputa, Castle in the Sky* (animated; also known as *Castle in the Sky* and *Tenku no shiro Rapyuta;* Japanese–language version originally released in 1986, 2003.

Simon, *Standing Still,* Freestyle Releasing, 2005.

James Van Der Beek, *Danny Roane: First Time Director,* Lionsgate, 2006.

Tom Russell, *The Plague* (also known as *Clive Barker's "The Plague"*), Sony Pictures Home Entertainment, 2006.

Paul Twist, *Final Draft,* 2007.

Diploma/Roggiani, *Stolen Lives,* Code Entertainment, 2009.

Jake Kelly, *Formosa Betrayed,* Screen Media Films, 2009.

Television Appearances; Series:
Dawson Leery, *Dawson's Creek,* The WB, 1998–2003.

Television Appearances; Movies:
Dan Leland, *Eye of the Beast,* Sci–Fi Channel, 2007.

Tony Zappa, *Taken in Broad Daylight,* Lifetime, 2009.

Debbie Macomber's "Mrs. Miracle," Hallmark Channel, 2009.

Television Appearances; Episodic:
Paulie, "Alter Ego," *Clarissa Explains It All* (also known as *Clarissa*), 1993.

Ethan, "You Don't Have a Pet to Be Popular," *Aliens in the Family,* 1996.

Himself, *The Panel,* Ten Network, 1999.

Host, *Saturday Night Live,* NBC, 1999.

"The Rules of Attraction," *Anatomy of a Scene,* 2002.

"Kids of Dawson Creek," *E! True Hollywood Story,* E! Entertainment Television, 2005.

Voice of pager bag/time traveller, "Rodigitti," *Robot Chicken* (animated), Cartoon Network, 2006.

Jonathan 'Mox' Moxon/Bush's aide/doctor, "Massage Chair," *Robot Chicken* (animated), Cartoon Network, 2006.

Raphael/Tobias Hankel, "The Big Game," *Criminal Minds,* CBS, 2007.

Tobias Hankel, "Revelations," *Criminal Minds,* CBS, 2007.

Luke Carnes, "Grin and Bear It," *Ugly Betty,* ABC, 2007.

Simon, "Sandcastles in the Sand," *How I Met Your Mother* (also known as *H.I.M.Y.M*), CBS, 2008.

Reese Dixon, "You Have to Be Joking," *One Tree Hill,* The WB, 2008.

"The Temp," *Free Radio,* VH1, 2008.

Entertainment Tonight (also known as *E.T.,* ET Weekend, *Entertainment This Week,* and *This Week in Entertainment*), syndicated, 2008.

Reese Dixon, "We Change, We Wait," *One Tree Hill,* The WB, 2009.

Reese Dixon, "Screenwriter's Blues," *One Tree Hill,* The WB, 2009.

Reese Dixon, "Searching for a Former Clarity," *One Tree Hill,* The WB, 2009.

Dylan Hoyt, "All in the Family," *Medium,* CBS, 2009.

Dr. Jonathan Kirk, "The Storm: Parts 1 & 2," *The Storm,* NBC, 2009.

Judd Shaw, "Lucky John," *The Forgotten,* ABC, 2009.

Also appeared as Stephen Anderson, *As the World Turns.*

Television Talk Show Guest Appearances; Episodic:
The Rosie O'Donnell Show, syndicated, 1998, 2000, and 2001.

The Howie Mandel Show, 1999.

Late Night with Conan O'Brien, 1999.

The Daily Show (also known as *A Daily Show with Jon Stewart,* Jon Stewart, The Daily Show with Jon Stewart and The Daily Show with Jon Stewart Global Edition), Comedy Central, 2001.

TRL, 2002.
Himself, *Total Access 24/7,* Fox, 2002.
The Tonight Show with Jay Leno, NBC, 2002.
The Late Late Show with Craig Kilborn, 2002.
''Katie Holmes,'' *Revealed with Jules Asner* (also known as *Revealed*), 2002.
V Graham Norton, Channel 4, 2003.
T4, Channel 4, 2003.
Last Call with Carson Daly, NBC, 2003.

Television Appearances; Specials:

Interviewee, *Dawson's Creek: Behind the Scenes,* E! Entertainment Television, 1998.
(Uncredited; in archive footage) *Seventeen: The Faces for Fall,* The WB, 1998.
Host, *True Life: No Money, Mo' Problems,* MTV, 1998.
Saturday Night Live: 25th Anniversary (also known as *Saturday Night Live 25* and *SNL25: 25 Years of Laughs*), NBC, 1999.
(In archive footage) Dawson Leery, *Songs from Dawson's Creek,* 1999.
(In archive footage) *Saturday Night Live: The Best of Tom Hanks,* NBC, 2004.
(In archive footage) *100 Greatest Teen Stars,* VH1, 2006.
(In archive footage) Voice of Bush's aide, *Robot Chicken: Star Wars* (animated), Cartoon Network, 2007.

Television Appearances; Awards Presentations:

Presenter, *The 50th Emmy Awards,* NBC, 1998.
The 1999 MTV Movie Awards, MTV, 1999.
Presenter, *The 51st Annual Primetime Emmy Awards,* Fox, 1999.
The Teen Choice Awards, Fox, 2000.
Presenter, *The 6th Annual Blockbuster Entertainment Awards,* Fox, 2000.
Presenter, *2000 MTV Movie Awards,* MTV, 2000.
Presenter, *Nickelodeon's 14th Annual Kids' Choice Awards,* Nickelodeon, 2001.

Television Appearances; Pilots:

Dawson Leery, *Dawson's Creek,* The WB, 1998.

Also appeared in the following unaired pilots: as John–O, *Three;* as Ozzie, *Sex, Power, Love & Politics;* as Connor Strikes, *Eva Adams,* Fox; as Brian Reynolds, *Football Wives,* ABC.

Stage Appearances:

Fergus, "Finding the Sun," *Sand* (three one–act plays), Signature Theatre Company, Kampo Cultural Center, New York City, 1993.
Shenandoah (musical), Goodspeed Opera House, East Haddam, CT, 1994.

My Marriage to Earnest Borgnine, off–Broadway production, 1997.
Rain Dance, off–Broadway production, 2003.

Music Videos:

Appeared in "Run" by Collective Soul.

OTHER SOURCES

Periodicals:

Big, January 6, 1999, pp. 22–23; March 3, 1999, pp. 22–25; May 12, 1999, pp. 26–29.
Cosmopolitan, November, 2002, p. 54.
Empire, June, 1999, pp. 78–79.
Entertainment Weekly, January 15, 1999, p. 18.
Film Review, June, 1999, pp. 70–71.
Heat, May 8, 1999, p. 68.
Interview, July, 1998, pp. 70–75.
J17, April, 1999, pp. 52–55.
Movieline, February, 1999, pp. 76–77.
People Weekly, March 23, 1998; May 11, 1998, p. 168.
Premiere, April, 2000, pp. 90–92.
Teen Celebrity, February, 1999, pp. 14–17.
Teen People, September, 1998, pp. 68–73.
TV Guide, March 7, 1998, pp. 18–23.
TV Zone, March, 1999, pp. 12–13.
USA Today, January 20, 1998.

Van PATTEN, Timothy 1959–
(Tim Van Patten, Timmy Van Patten)

PERSONAL

Original name, Christopher Van Patten; born June 10, 1959, in Brooklyn, NY; half–brother of Dick Van Patten (an actor) and Joyce Van Patten (an actress); married Wendy Rossmeyer, May 23, 1996; children: two.

Addresses: *Agent*—Cassell–Levy, Inc., 843 North Sycamore Ave., Hollywood, CA 90038; Creative Artists Agency, 9830 Wilshire Blvd., Beverly Hills, CA 90212. *Contact*—c/o 7461 Beverly Blvd., #400, Los Angeles, CA 90036; 13920 Magnolia Ave., Sherman Oak, CA 91423.

Career: Actor, director, producer, and writer.

Awards, Honors: Emmy Award nomination, outstanding directing for a drama series, 2001, for episode "Amour Fou," Emmy Award nomination (with Terence Winter), outstanding writing for a drama series, 2001, Writers Guild of America Award (with Winter), episodic drama, and Edgar Award (with Winter), best television episode, both 2002, all for episode "Pine Barrens," Emmy Award nomination, outstanding directing for a drama series, 2002, and Directors Guild of America Award nomination, outstanding directorial achievement in dramatic series—night, both for episode "Whoever Did This," Emmy Award nomination, outstanding directing for a drama series, 2003, and Directors Guild of America Award nomination, outstanding directorial achievement in dramatic series—night, 2005, both for episode "Long Term Parking," Emmy Award nomination, outstanding directing for a drama series, 2006, and Directors Guild of America Award nomination, outstanding directorial achievement in dramatic series—night, 2007, both for episode "Members Only," and Directors Guild of America Award nomination, outstanding directorial achievement in dramatic series—night, 2008, for episode "Soparnos Home Movies," all for *The Sopranos;* Directors Guild of America Awards (with others), outstanding directorial achievement in a comedy series, 2004, for episode "Boy Interrupted," and 2005, for episode "An American Girl in Paris: Part Deux," both for *Sex and the City.*

CREDITS

Film Appearances:
Peter Stegman, *Class of 1984,* United Film Distribution Company, 1982.
The Silence, 1982.
Pauli, *Escape from El Diablo* (also known as *California Cowboys*), 1983.
Private Joey Verona, *Zone Troopers,* Empire Pictures, 1986.
J. T., *The Wrong Guys,* New World Pictures, 1988.
Father John Durham, *Catacombs* (also known as *Curse IV: The Ultimate Sacrifice*), Epic Pictures, 1988.
Narrator, *Water with Food Coloring,* 2001.

Television Appearances; Series:
Mario "Salami" Pettrino, *The White Shadow,* CBS, 1978–81.
Max Keller, *The Master* (also known as *Master Ninja*), NBC, 1984.
Sergeant Andy Wojeski, *True Blue,* NBC, 1989.

Television Appearances; Movies:
Bill Reed, *High Powder,* 1982.

Television Appearances; Specials:
(As Tim Van Patten) *Reinventando Hollywood,* Canal+ Espana, 2008.

Television Appearances; Miniseries:
(As Tim Van Patten) Lugar, *Dress Gray,* NBC, 1986.

Television Appearances; Pilots:
Mario "Salami" Pettrino, *The White Shadow,* CBS, 1978.
Mike, Frankie's assistant, *Johnny Garage,* CBS, 1983.
Sergeant Andy Wojeski, *True Blue,* NBC, 1989.

Television Appearances; Episodic:
(As Timmy Van Patten), "The Lost Weekend," *Eight Is Enough,* 1978.
Dean, "Saving Face," *St. Elsewhere,* NBC, 1985.
Dean, "Give the Boy a Hand," *St. Elsewhere,* NBC, 1985.
Dean, "Any Portrait in a Storm," *St. Elsewhere,* NBC, 1985.
Danny Rivera, "Fighting Back," *Night Heat,* 1986.
Greg, "Tell Me a Story," *Night Heat,* 1987.

Television Director; Episodic:
"Nothing Personal," *Homicide: Life on the Street* (also known as *H:LOTS* and *Homicide*), NBC, 1995.
"Dear God," *Touched by an Angel,* CBS, 1996.
"Homecoming," *Promised Land* (also known as *Home of the Brave*), CBS, 1996.
"The Road Home: Part 1," *Touched by an Angel,* CBS, 1997.
"Hubris," *New York Undercover* (also known as *Uptown Undercover*), Fox, 1997.
"The Trial," *The Visitor,* Fox, 1998.
"Rat Trap," *New York Undercover* (also known as *Uptown Undercover*), Fox, 1998.
"Undercover Granny," *Promised Land* (also known as *Home of the Brave*), CBS, 1998.
(As Tim Van Patten) "When Darkness Falls," *Promised Land* (also known as *Home of the Brave*), CBS, 1998.
"A Case of Do or Die," *Homicide: Life on the Street* (also known as *H:LOTS* and *Homicide*), NBC, 1999.
(As Tim Van Patten) *The Sopranos,* HBO, 1999–2007.
(As Tim Van Patten) "Opposites Distract," *Ed* (also known as *Stuckeyville*), NBC, 2001.
(As Tim Van Patten) "Changes," *Ed* (also known as *Stuckeyville*), NBC, 2001.
(As Tim Van Patten) "The Test," *Ed* (also known as *Stuckeyville*), NBC, 2001.
(As Tim Van Patten) "Neighbors," *Ed* (also known as *Stuckeyville*), NBC, 2002.
(As Tim Van Patten) "Puppy Love," *Pasadena,* 2002.
(As Tim Van Patten) "Sentencing," *The Wire,* HBO, 2002.
(As Tim Van Patten) "Second Chances," *Ed* (also known as *Stuckeyville*), NBC, 2003.
"The Amazing Larry Dunn," *Keen Eddie,* Fox, 2003.
(As Tim Van Patten) "Stray Rounds," *The Wire,* HBO, 2003.

"A Woman's Right To Shoes," *Sex and the City,* HBO, 2003.

"Boy, Interrupted," *Sex and the City,* HBO, 2003.

(As Tim Van Patten) "Back Burners," *The Wire,* HBO, 2004.

"An American Girl in Paris: Parts Une & Deux," *Sex and the City,* HBO, 2004.

(As Tim Van Patten) "Childish Things," *Deadwood,* HBO, 2005.

"Pharsalus," *Rome,* HBO, 2005.

"Passover," *Rome,* HBO, 2007.

Also directed episodes of *The Road Home,* CBS; *Matt Waters,* CBS; *The American Embassy;* "Out on Bail," *Central Park West* (also known as *C.P.W.*), CBS; "Love and Guns," *The Sentinel,* UPN; "Vendetta," *The Sentinel,* UPN; "Nothing to Fear, but Nothing to Fear," *Now and Again,* ABC.

Television Director; Miniseries:

"Casualties of War," *Into the West,* TNT, 2005.

The Pacific, HBO, 2010.

Television Work; Pilots:

Director, *Untitled Paul Simms Pilot,* 2002.

Executive producer, *Boardwalk Empire,* HBO, 2009.

Also worked as director and producer, *Russo,* CBS.

RECORDINGS

Videos:

The White Shadow: More Than Basketball (short documentary; featured on the first season DVD release of *The White Shadow*) Twentieth Century–Fox Home Entertainment, 2005.

The White Shadow: The Shadow of Bruce Paltrow (short documentary; featured on the season two DVD release of *The White Shadow*), Twentieth Century–Fox Home Entertainment, 2006.

The White Shadow: Director's Debut (short documentary; featured on the season two DVD release of *The White Shadow*), Twentieth Century–Fox Home Entertainment, 2006.

The White Shadow: A Series of Memories Preview (short documentary; featured on the season two DVD release of *The White Shadow*), Twentieth Century–Fox Home Entertainment, 2006.

WRITINGS

Film Music:

"Stegman's Concerto," *Class of 1984,* United Film Distribution Company, 1982.

Television Episodes:

(As Tim Van Patten; with Terence Winter) "Pine Barrens," *The Sopranos,* HBO, 2001.

W–Y

WAGNER, Helen 1918–2010

PERSONAL

Full name, Helen Losee Wagner; born September 3, 1918, in Lubbock, TX; died of cancer, May 1, 2010, in Mount Kisco, NY. Actress. Wagner played the role of the matronly Nancy Hughes on the CBS soap opera *As the World Turns* for over fifty years, the longest-running continuous performance of a single character in the history of television. After graduating from Monmouth College in 1938, she acted with the St. Louis Municipal Opera Company then earned her first Broadway roles in the musicals *Sunny River, Oklahoma!* and *The Winters Tale* in the mid-1940s. In 1952 Wagner appeared briefly on the soap opera *The Guiding Light* and subsequently played parts on *Valiant Lady, Inner Sanctum,* and the sitcom *The World of Mr. Sweeney. Guiding Light* creator Irna Phillips sought her for the role of Nancy Hughes in her new soap opera *As the World Turns* in 1956, and Wagner spoke the series first lines. She was twice fired from the program, once in the mid-1950s and again in the 1980s, only to be reinstated after fans of the show demanded her return. In 2004 Wagner was presented with a Lifetime Achievement Award by the National Academy of Television Arts and Sciences.

PERIODICALS

Independent, May 22, 2010.
Los Angeles Times, May 4, 2010.
New York Times, May 3, 2010.
Washington Post, May 6, 2010.

WALKER, Crystal
See KEYMAH, T'Keyah Crystal

WALKINSHAW, Alex 1974–

PERSONAL

Full name, Alex Newcombe Walkinshaw; born October 5, 1974, in Barking, Essex, England; married Sarah Trusler (a makeup artist), June 20, 2009; children: Flora, Jack. *Education:* Trained at Sylvia Young Theatre School and London Dance Studios.

Addresses: *Agent*—Christian Hodell, Hamilton Hodell Ltd., 66–68 Margaret St., 5th Floor, London W1W 8SR, England.

Career: Actor. Appeared in a public safety announcement for safe driving, 1997, and in other commercials.

Awards, Honors: National Television Award nomination, outstanding drama performance, 2008, for *The Bill.*

CREDITS

Television Appearances; Series:
Terry Shane, *Side by Side,* BBC, c. 1992.
Deputy Superintendent Small, *McCallum,* STV, 1995–98.
Inspector Dale Smith, *The Bill,* ITV1, 1999–2010.

Television Appearances; Miniseries:
Boy mugger, *To Play the King,* PBS, 1993.
Troy Daly, *Crown Prosecutor,* 1995.
Tommy, *Stan the Man,* ITV, 2002.

Television Appearances; Specials:
Older boy, *Death in Venice* (opera), 1990.

(Uncredited; in archive footage) Sergeant Dale Smith, *The Bill Uncovered: Des and Reg,* ITV, 2004.
Himself, *The Bill Made Me Famous,* ITV1, 2008.

Television Appearances; Episodic:
Steven Murray, "Fair Play," *The Bill,* ITV1, 1992.
Alan, "Money Talks," *Casualty,* BBC1, 1992.
Danny, "Pig Boy," *Scene,* BBC, 1993.
Lee Tarrant, "Deadly Weapon," *The Bill,* ITV1, 1993.
"Back to Basics," *Nelson's Column,* BBC, 1994.
Kevin, "Requiem," *Anna Lee,* ITV, 1994.
Cockney man, "O Mary This London," *Screen Two,* BBC, 1994.
Party crasher, *Harry Enfield and Chums,* BBC, 1994.
Pearce, "Appropriate Adults," *A Touch of Frost,* ITV, 1995.
Andy Franklin, "Flora and Fauna," *The Bill,* ITV1, 1995.
Stevo, "Sandman," *Urban Gothic,* Channel 5, 2001.
Mickey, "Starting Over," *Holby City,* BBC, 2001.
Richard & Judy, Channel 4, 2004.
GMTV, ITV, 2006.
"Goodies and Baddies," *The Weakest Link,* BBC, 2007.
(Uncredited) *TV Burp,* ITV, 2008.
Loose Women, ITV, 2008.
The Paul O'Grady Show, ITV, 2009.

Appeared in "Breed of Heroes," an episode of *Screen One,* BBC.

Television Appearances; Other:
Ed Darvas, *A Question of Guilt* (movie), 1993.

Appeared in *Crime and Punishment,* BBC.

Stage Appearances:
Arthur Wellesley, *The Judas Kiss,* Playhouse, London, 1998.

Appeared as a youth, *Death in Venice* (opera), Glyndebourne Opera Festival, Glyndebourne, England; as Tone, *Lift Off,* Royal Court Theatre, London; and as Lee, *Sing Yer Heart Our for the Boys,* Royal National Theatre, London.

WALLACE, Amber 1987–
   (Amber Brooke, Amber Brooke Wallace)

PERSONAL

Born May 14, 1987, in Atlanta, GA. *Education:* Studied English, creative writing, and film at Georgia State University; studied acting, camera work, and dance with various instructors.

Addresses: *Manager*—Five Star Talent Management, 3544 White Sands Way, Suwanee, GA 30024.

Career: Actress, singer, and songwriter. Appeared in industrial films. Announcer for Boomerang (television channel) in Latin America. Also known as Amber Brooke and performer with the Amber Brooke Band. Affiliated with merchandise associated with her music career.

Awards, Honors: Horizon Artist, Just Plain Folks Music awards, 2002; National Christian School Association Songwriting Competition, first place and fourth place designations, MOVA Arts Festival first place, John Lennon Songwriting Contest, runner–up, 2002, and Pontiac Vibe Summer Sound Off Contest finalist, all for "So Small"; winner of the MakeAStar.com contest, and Just Plain Folks Music Award nomination (with Richard Wallace), pop song nomination, 2002, both for "These Games"; winner of the MakeAStar.com contest, International Songwriting Competition honorable mention, 2002, and USA Songwriting Competition finalist, 2003, all for "Michelle's Song"; first place designations, Rocket to Fame, female vocals, acoustic and soft rock/pop categories, 2003; Windrift Music Songwriting Competition finalist, International Songwriting Competition runner–up, teen category, and *Lady Six String* Songwriting Contest fourth place, all 2003, all for "Spacin' Out"; named AOL Music and Tonos Entertainment musician of the week, 2003; Rock Solid Pressure grand Champion, 2003; International Songwriting Competition semifinalist, 2003, MOVA Arts Festival first place and best of show designations, and Just Plain Folks Music Award nomination, punk song of the year, 2004, all for "Slacker"; Just Plain Folks Music Award second place (with others), punk song of the year, 2004, for "Paper Doll"; Just Plain Folks Music Award third place, album of the year, 2004, for *Don't Label Me;* Just Plain Folks Music Award fourth place (with others), alternative song of the year, 2004, and MOVA Arts Festival second place designation, both for "Nobody"; Just Plain Folks Music Award sixth place (with others), alternative song of the year, 2004, for "Confinement"; *Creative Loafing* Reader's Choice Award, best local vocalist, 2005; Emergenza Finals designation, best singer, 2006; Just Plain Folks Music Award second place (with the Amber Brooke Band), album of the year, 2006, for *Destructive Behavior.*

CREDITS

Television Appearances; Series:
Glenda Farrell, *One Tree Hill* (also known as *Ravens, Filoi gia panta, Les freres Scott, Tunteet pelissae,* and *Tuti gimi*), The WB, 2006, The CW, 2006–2007.
Lila, *90210* (also known as *Beverly Hills 90210: The Next Generation* and *90210: The Next Generation*), The CW, 2009—.

Appeared as Swoozie in the series *Grandpa's Garage*, TBS.

Television Appearances; Miniseries:
(Uncredited) Baby, *Oldest Living Confederate Widow Tells All*, CBS, 1994.

Television Appearances; Movies:
(Uncredited) Malone's sister, *Passing Glory*, TNT, 1999.
Isabel, *Pop Rocks* (also known as *Head Rush* and *Rockstars Forever*), ABC Family, 2004.
(As Amber Brooke Wallace) Vita, *The Initiation of Sarah*, ABC Family, 2006.

Television Appearances; Episodic:
Summer, "Lost Girls," *The Vampire Diaries*, The CW, 2009.
Summer, "You're Undead to Me," *The Vampire Diaries*, The CW, 2009.

Television Appearances; Pilots:
Young Eileen, *Angels: The Mysterious Messengers* (also known as *Angels, Our Mysterious Messengers*), NBC, 1994.

Television Song Performer; Movies:
(As Amber Brooke; as a member of the Amber Brooke Band) "Nobody," "Paper Doll," "Paralyzed," "Slacker," and "So Small," *The Initiation of Sarah*, ABC Family, 2006.

Film Appearances:
(Uncredited) Wendy girl, *Happy Campers*, New Line Cinema, 2001.
Young Casey, *Saudade* (short film), Florida State University, 2001.
Young Molly, *Good Neighbor* (also known as *The Killer Next Door*), Creative Light Worldwide, 2001.
Tammy at the age of twelve, *Run Ronnie Run* (also known as *Run Ronnie Run! The Ronnie Dobbs Story: A Mr. Show Movie*), New Line Cinema, 2002.
Emily, *Black Oasis* (short film), SkyChase Pictures, 2006.
Ilona, *The Marc Pease Experience*, Paramount Vantage, 2008.
Second student, *One Missed Call* (also known as *Don't Pick Up the Cell Phone!* and *Toedlicher Anruf*), Warner Bros., 2008.
Violet, *Mean Girls 2*, Paramount Famous Productions, 2011.

Some sources cite appearances in other projects.

Internet Appearances:
Jen, *IQ–145* (series), http://www.iq-145.com, beginning c. 2008.

Appeared in contests broadcast on *MakeAStar.com*, http://www.makeastar.com and *Fuse.tv*, http://www.fusetv.

Stage Appearances:
Appeared as Alyssa, *Dream Maker* (also known as *Dreammaker* and *Dream Makers*), as Sunshine, *A Play on Words*, and as Tessie, *Rewind*, all musicals at the Atlanta Workshop Players, Alpharetta, GA; appeared as a townsperson, *Happily Ever After*, and as Penny, *Transcendental Ultimate Reality Tour*, both Galloway Kids; also appeared as a reindeer, *Magical Nights of Lights*, Lake Lanier Islands, Lake Lanier, GA.

RECORDINGS

Albums; as Amber Brooke:
Shades of Amber (includes "Gone," "I Don't Care," "Michelle's Song," "So Small," and "These Games"), c. 2002.

Other albums include *Beanie Tunes*, Avid Productions; and *Bookin' It*, Bennett Productions.

Albums; as Amber Brooke; with the Amber Brooke Band:
Don't Label Me (includes songs "Confinement," "Nobody," "Paper Doll," "Slacker," "So Small," and "Spacin' Out"), Naughty Lizard Records, 2003, Sound Decision Studios, 2004.
Destructive Behavior (includes song "Paralyzed"), Naughty Lizard Records, 2006.

Albums; with Others as Amber Brooke; with the Amber Brooke Band:
(Track "Michelle's Song") Various artists, *Make a Star.com Volume One* (also known as *Make a Star.com Volume 1*), MakeaStar Records, 2002.
(Track "These Games") Various artists, *Make a Star.com Volume Three* (also known as *Make a Star.com Volume 3*), MakeaStar Records, 2003.

Other albums include *Dream Maker* (also known as *Dreammaker* and *Dream Makers*), EB Productions.

WRITINGS

Television Music; Songs for Movies:
(With others; performed the songs as a member of the Amber Brooke Band) "Nobody," "Paper Doll," "Paralyzed," "Slacker," and "So Small," *The Initiation of Sarah*, ABC Family, 2006.

Albums; as Amber Brooke:
Shades of Amber (includes "Gone," "I Don't Care," "Michelle's Song," "So Small," and "These Games"), c. 2002.

Other albums include *Beanie Tunes,* Avid Productions; and *Bookin' It,* Bennett Productions.

Albums; as Amber Brooke; with the Amber Brooke Band:
Don't Label Me (includes songs "Confinement," "Nobody," "Paper Doll," "Slacker," "So Small," and "Spacin' Out"), Naughty Lizard Records, 2003, Sound Decision Studios, 2004.
Destructive Behavior (includes song "Paralyzed"), Naughty Lizard Records, 2006.

Albums; with Others: as Amber Brooke; with the Amber Brooke Band:
(Track "Michelle's Song") Various artists, *Make a Star.com Volume One* (also known as *Make a Star.com Volume 1*), MakeaStar Records, 2002.
(Track "These Games") Various artists, *Make a Star.com Volume Three* (also known as *Make a Star.com Volume 3*), MakeaStar Records, 2003.

OTHER SOURCES

Electronic:
Amber Brooke, http://www.amberbrooke.com, March 15, 2010.

WALLACE, Ian A. 1944–
 (Nion, Ian Wallace)

PERSONAL

Born July 4, 1944, in Edinburgh, Scotland; immigrated to Canada, 1951. *Education:* Graduated from the University of Alberta; studied at Atelier Pochinko; studied film with Marushka Stankova (some sources spell name as Maruska Stankova), National Film Board of Canada; also studied art in Vancouver and with Susan Sarbach.

Addresses: *Agent*—JR Talent, 1080 Mainland, Suite 413, Vancouver, British Columbia V6B 2T4, Canada.

Career: Actor. West End Public Theatre. Clown and mask performer; performed as the character Nion; worked with Richard Pochinko to develop the Pochinko Mask Technique. Theatre Resource Centre, Ottawa,

Ontario, Canada and Toronto, Ontario, Canada, cofounder; instructor of clown and other disciplines; presenter of clown/mask and other workshops. Worked as a graphic artist and produced batik paintings; worked as a teacher in Edmonton, Alberta, Canada.

Member: Canadian Actors' Equity Association, Union of British Columbia Performers/Alliance of Canadian Cinema, Television and Radio Artists (UBCP/ACTRA).

Awards, Honors: Nominations for various awards, including the Dora Mavor Moore Award, Toronto Alliance for the Performing Arts, and the Genie Award, Academy of Canadian Cinema and Television, all for projects featuring his character Nion.

CREDITS

Stage Appearances:
The Comedy of Errors, Stratford Young Company, Stratford Shakespearean Festival of Canada, Stratford, Ontario, Canada, 1975.
Madame Zaza, *Elizabeth,* Theatre Resource Centre, Toronto, Ontario, c. 1975.
Nion, *Nion in the Kabaret de la Vita,* multiple productions, including a Montreal, Quebec, Canada, venue, then Theatre Quatre–Sous, Montreal, both c. 1980, then the Rivoli, Toronto, 1981.
(As Nion) Title role, *American Demon,* Rhubarb!, Nightwood Theatre, Toronto, 1982.
The Supermale, 1984, and Theatre Passe Muraille, Toronto, 1986.
(As Nion) *The Beavers* (clown musical), Native Earth Theatre, Theatre Resource Centre, 1990.

Appeared in *Asylum* (clown show), *The Maids, Passages* (ritual mask performance), and *Red Noses,* all Theatre Resource Centre; in *The License* and *Woman with a Flea in Her Mouth,* both St. John's Church, Vancouver, British Columbia, Canada; as Mr. Hardcastle, *She Stoops to Conquer,* Gastown Actors Studio, Vancouver; as Yves, *Head a Tete;* in *Andre's Mother,* Theatre Positive, Vancouver; in *Vital Signs,* The Cavern, Vancouver; and in *Winter Solstice* (mummer's production), St. John's, Newfoundland, Canada. As Nion, appeared as the General, *Auto–da–fe,* Dancemakers, Toronto; as the character Nion, performed in other venues, including Central Park, New York City, 1984; and the Caravan Farm Theatre, Armstrong, British Columbia, Canada, 2003. Performer in other productions, including the outdoor circuses *Circus Bizarro,* Toronto; and *Cyrc en Bicycle,* Ottawa, Ontario. Appeared in productions with the Buddies in Bad Times Theatre, Factory Theatre, Tarragon Theatre, and The Theatre Centre, all Toronto; with the Citadel Theatre, Edmonton, Alberta, Canada; with the Neptune Theatre, Halifax, Nova Scotia, Canada; with the Theatre Hour Company; and in various productions in Montreal and Toronto.

Major Tours:
Appeared as Nion, *Nion—Birth of a Clown* (also known as *Birth of a Clown*), Canadian cities.

Stage Work:
Worked as a set designer.

Television Appearances; as Ian Wallace; Miniseries:
Raynz, *Tin Man*, Sci–Fi Channel, 2007.
Klegg, *Knights of Bloodsteel* (also known as *Dragon Eye, Dragons of Black Roc, Dragonsteel,* and *Mirabilis*), Sci–Fi Channel, 2009.

Television Appearances; Movies:
Ira Deeks, *Whispers and Lies* (also known as *Ashes to Ashes*), Lifetime Movie Network, 2008.

Television Appearances; Specials:
Russian spy, *The Canadian Conspiracy,* CBC and HBO, 1985.

Television Appearances; Episodic:
Nion, "Elephant's Doctor," *Sharon, Lois & Bram's "Elephant Show"* (also known as *The Elephant Show*), CBC, 1984.
Frankie, "Guns at Cyrano's," *Philip Marlowe, Private Eye* (also known as *Marlowe* and *Philip Marlowe*), HBO, 1986.
Nurse Swanson, "An Now the News," *Freddy's Nightmares* (also known as *Freddy's Nightmares: A Nightmare on Elm Street: The Series, Freddy, le cauchemar de vos nuits, Freddyn painajaiset, Las pesadillas de Freddy,* and *Les cauchemars de Freddy*), syndicated, 1988.
Mathematics teacher, "The Fair Haired Child," *Masters of Horror,* Showtime, 2006.
(As Ian Wallace) Curate (shaman of the blue people), "Secrets and Lies," *Flash Gordon,* Sci–Fi Channel, 2007.
Homeless man, "The Trader," *Traveler,* ABC, 2007.
(As Ian Wallace) Fire creature, "Sanctuary for All: Part 1," *Sanctuary,* Sci–Fi Channel, The Movie Network, and other channels, 2008.
(Uncredited) Ferryman, "Know Thy Enemy," *Caprica,* SyFy, 2010.

Film Appearances:
Title role, *Nion,* 1984.
Nion, *Nion in the Kabaret de la Vita* (short film; also known as *Nion in the Kabaret de LaVita*), 1986.
(Uncredited) NS4 robot and NS5 robot, *I, Robot* (also known as *Hardwired*), Twentieth Century–Fox, 2004.
(As Ian Wallace) Priest, *Wind Chill,* TriStar, 2007.
(As Ian Wallace) Prior, *Stargate: The Ark of Truth* (also known as *The Ark of Truth*), Metro–Goldwyn–Mayer, 2008.

Bald lunatic, *Case 39,* Paramount, 2009.
(As Ian Wallace) Third monk, *The Imaginarium of Doctor Parnassus* (also known as *Dr. Parnassus, The Imaginarium of Dr. Parnassus, The Mirror of Doctor Parnassus, Parnassus,* and *L'imaginarium du Docteur Parnassus*), Sony Pictures Classics/Lionsgate, 2009.

Appeared as a background performer.

WRITINGS

Nonfiction:
Contributor to periodicals, including *Impact.* Author of material posted on the Internet.

WALTERS, Lucia

PERSONAL

Raised in Athabasca, Alberta, and Squamish, British Columbia, Canada; daughter of an Anglican minister. *Education:* Earned nursing diploma and a university degree (with distinction). *Avocational Interests:* Dance, decorating, writing, yoga.

Addresses: *Agent*—Jennifer Goldhar, Characters Talent Agency, 8 Elm St., Toronto, Ontario M5G 1G7, Canada. *Manager*—Lena Lees, Play Management, Inc., 825 Powell St., Suite 220, Vancouver, British Columbia V6A 1H7, Canada.

Career: Actress. Appeared in commercials. Worked as a registered nurse for several years. Also worked as a commercial model.

CREDITS

Television Appearances; Movies:
First sassy lady, *The Right Connections,* Showtime, 1997.
Yacht girl, *Unwed Father,* ABC, 1997.
Miss Baram, *In the Doghouse,* Showtime, 1998.
Nurse, *The Inspectors,* Showtime, 1998.
Tasha, *Sweetwater* (also known as *Sweetwater: A True Rock Story*), VH1, 1999.
Lavender Rose, *The Ranch,* Showtime, 2004.
Janelle, *Fighting the Odds: The Marilyn Gambrell Story,* Lifetime, 2005.
Paige Holloway, *Home for the Holidays,* Lifetime, 2005.
Claire, *Fatal Reunion,* Lifetime, 2005.

Detective Miller, *Double Cross,* Lifetime, 2006.
Abbey Noonan, *A Job to Kill For,* Lifetime, 2006.
Livingstone, *Safe Harbor,* Lifetime, 2006.
Monica Strauss, *Center Stage: Turn It Up,* Oxygen, 2009.

Television Appearances; Series:
Fern, *Life Unexpected,* The CW, 2010.

Television Appearances; Miniseries:
Adreanna, *Tin Man,* Sci–Fi Channel, 2007.

Television Appearances; Episodic:
Paramedic, "Moving On: Part 2," *Neon Rider,* syndicated, 1994.
(Uncredited) Receptionist, "522666," *Millennium,* Fox, 1996.
(Uncredited) Emergency medical technician, "Leonard Betts," *The X–Files,* Fox, 1997.
Receptionist, "Death of an Angel," *The Net,* USA Network, 1998.
Disciple, "Seth," *Stargate SG–1,* Showtime, 1999.
Sheila Harden, "Promises Made in a Storm Are Forgotten on a Calm Sea," *Hope Island,* PAX, 2000.
Nurse, "Blah Blah Woof Woof," *Dark Angel* (also known as *James Cameron's "Dark Angel"*), Fox, 2000.
Karen, "The Fortunate One," *The Fearing Mind,* Fox Family, 2000.
Belinda Jenkins, "Jitters," *Smallville* (also known as *Smallville Beginnings*), The WB, 2001.
Cop, "Date Night," *Black Sash,* The WB, 2003.
Evelyn Jackson, "Day 1,370: Part 1," *The Days,* ABC, 2004.
Tipinski, "Before They Twist the Knife," *Da Vinci's Inquest,* CBC, 2005.
Tara Kendrick, "Weight of the World," *The 4400,* USA Network, 2005.
Lara, "The Intruder," *Stargate: Atlantis* (also known as *Atlantis*), Sci–Fi Channel, 2005.
Candace, "Wine and Die," *The Evidence,* ABC, 2006.
Shante, "All that Glitters," *Da Kink in My Hair,* Global TV, 2007.
(Uncredited) Mom, "Lesson Number One," *The L Word,* Showtime, 2007.
Mom, "Lexington and Concord," *The L Word,* Showtime, 2007.
Camilla, "LGB Tease," *The L Word,* Showtime, 2008.
Ms. Wahl, "Double Felix," *The Troop,* Nickelodeon, 2010.

Television Appearances; Other:
(Uncredited) *Supervolcano* (special), The Discovery Channel, 2005.
(Uncredited) Nurse, *Psych* (pilot), USA Network, 2006.

Film Appearances:
Second pretty girl, *Mission to Mars* (also known as *M2M*), Buena Vista, 2000.

Angel Cat (short film), 2005.
Lisa Wilcox, *Crossed,* Infinite Reality Productions, 2006.

Internet Appearances; Episodic:
Belinda Jenkins, "Chronicle 1," *Smallville: Chloe Chronicles,* America Online and The WB.com, 2003.
Belinda Jenkins, "Chronicle 4," *Smallville: Chloe Chronicles,* America Online and The WB.com, 2003.

OTHER SOURCES

Electronic:
Lucia Walters Official Site, http://www.luciawalters.com, June 11, 2010.

WANAMAKER, Zoe 1949–

PERSONAL

Born May 13, 1949, in New York, NY; raised in London, England; British citizenship, 2000; daughter of Sam (an actor and director) and Charlotte (an actress; maiden name, Holland) Wanamaker; married Gawn Grainger (an actor and writer), 1994. *Education:* Attended Central School of Speech and Drama, London.

Addresses: *Contact*—Conway Van Gelder Ltd., 18–21 Jermyn St., London SW1Y 6HP, England. *Agent*—Innovative Artists, 1505 10th St., Santa Monica, CA 90401.

Career: Actress. Manchester 69 Theatre Company, member of company, 1970; Royal Lyceum Theatre, member of repertory company, 1971–72; Oxford Playhouse, member of repertory company, 1974–75; member of a repertory company in Nottingham, England, 1975–76. Also former member of repertory company, Royal Shakespeare Company; Globe Theatre, London, member of board of trustees and honorary president. Appeared in television commercials, including Marks & Spencer, 2003, and HSBC Banks, 2008. Voluntary Euthanasia Society, vice president and spokesperson.

Awards, Honors: Laurence Olivier Award, best actress in a revival, Society of West End Theatre, 1979, for *Once in a Lifetime;* Antoinette Perry Award nomination, best actress in a featured role in a play, 1981, for *Piaf;* Laurence Olivier Award nominations, 1982, for

The Importance of Being Earnest, 1983, for *Comedy of Errors, The Time of Your Life,* and *Twelfth Night,* and 1984, for *Mother Courage; Drama* Magazine Award, 1985, for *Mother Courage;* Antoinette Perry Award nomination, best actress in a featured role in a play, 1986, for *Loot;* Laurence Olivier Award nominations, 1986, for *The Bay at Nice* and *Wrecked Eggs,* and 1990, for *The Crucible;* Television Award nomination, best actress, British Academy of Film and Television Arts, 1992, for *Prime Suspect;* Royal Television Society Award, best actress, and Television Award nomination, best actress, British Academy of Film and Television Arts, both 1993, for *Love Hurts;* Laurence Olivier Award nominations, 1993, for *The Last Yankee,* and 1995, for *The Glass Menagerie;* honorary doctor of letters, South Bank University, 1995; Film Award nomination, best performance by a supporting actress, British Academy of Film and Television Arts 1998, for *Wilde;* Laurence Olivier Award, best actress, 1998, and Antoinette Perry Award nomination, best performance by a leading actress in a play, 1999, both for *Electra;* honorary doctor of letters, Richmond American International University, 1999; honorary Commander, Order of the British Empire, 2000; Laurence Olivier Award, best actress, 2001, for *Boston Marriage;* Golden Rose Award, best sitcom actress, Rose d'Or Light Entertainment Festival, 2005, for *My Family;* Antoinette Perry Award nomination, best performance by a featured actress in a play, and Drama Desk Award (with others), outstanding ensemble performance, 2006, for *Awake and Sing!.*

CREDITS

Stage Appearances:

Hermia, *A Midsummer Night's Dream,* Manchester 69 Company, England, 1970.

The Cherry Orchard, Stables Theatre Club, 1970, then Royal Lyceum Theatre, Edinburgh, Scotland, 1971.

Viola, *Twelfth Night,* Leeds Playhouse, Leeds England, 1971, then Cambridge Theatre Company, 1973–74, later Royal Shakespeare Company, Royal Shakespeare Theatre, Stratford–upon–Avon, England, 1983, then Theatre Royal, Newcastle–upon–Tyne, England, and Barbican Theatre, London, 1984.

Dick Whittington, Royal Lyceum Theatre, 1971–72.

Guys and Dolls, Manchester 69 Company, 1972.

Bellinda, *The Provok'd Wife,* Palace Theatre, Watford, England, 1973.

Cabaret, Farnham Theatre, 1974.

Fears and Miseries of the Third Reich, Oxford Playhouse, Oxford, England, 1974.

Kiss Me Kate, Oxford Playhouse, 1974.

Tom Thumb, Young Vic Theatre, London, 1974.

Much Ado about Nothing, Young Vic Theatre, 1974.

Kate, *The Taming of the Shrew,* New Shakespeare Company, Regent's Park Open Air Theatre, London, 1975.

Clara, *The Widowing of Mrs. Holyrood,* Nottingham Playhouse, Nottingham, England, 1975.

Lucy and Mrs. Vixen, *The Beggar's Opera,* Nottingham Playhouse, 1975–76.

Stella, *A Streetcar Named Desire,* Nottingham Playhouse, 1975–76.

Pygmalion, Nottingham Playhouse, 1975–76.

Trumpets and Drums, Nottingham Playhouse, 1975–76.

Essie, *The Devil's Disciple,* Royal Shakespeare Company, Aldwych Theatre, London, 1976.

Jane, *Wild Oats; or, The Strolling Gentleman,* Royal Shakespeare Company, Aldwych Theatre, 1976, then Royal Shakespeare Theatre, and Piccadilly Theatre, London, 1977, later Theatre Royal, 1979.

Babakina, *Ivanov,* Royal Shakespeare Company, Aldwych Theatre, 1976.

Catherine Wintour, *Winter's Tale,* Royal Shakespeare Company, The Other Place, Stratford–upon–Avon, 1978.

Bianca, *The Taming of the Shrew,* Royal Shakespeare Company, Royal Shakespeare Theatre, 1978, then Theatre Royal, and Aldwych Theatre, 1979.

Gemma Beech, *Captain Swing,* Royal Shakespeare Company, The Other Place, 1978, then Gulbenkian Studio, Newcastle–upon–Tyne, and Donmar Warehouse Theatre, London, 1979.

Toine, *Piaf,* Royal Shakespeare Company, The Other Place, 1978, then Gulbenkian Studio, Donmar Warehouse Theatre, and Aldwych Theatre, 1979, later Wyndhams Theatre, London, and Piccadilly Theatre, 1980, then (Broadway debut) Plymouth Theatre, 1981.

Mary Daniels, *Once in a Lifetime,* Royal Shakespeare Company, Aldwych Theatre, 1979, then Piccadilly Theatre, 1980.

Gwendoline, *The Importance of Being Earnest,* Royal National Theatre, London, 1982.

Kitty Duval, *The Time of Your Life,* Royal Shakespeare Company, The Other Place, 1983, then Gulbenkian Studio, and Pit Theatre, London, 1984.

Adriana, *The Comedy of Errors,* Royal Shakespeare Company, Royal Shakespeare Theatre, 1983, then Theatre Royal, and Barbican Theatre, 1984.

Katrin, *Mother Courage,* Royal Shakespeare Company, Barbican Theatre, 1984.

Grace, *Wrecked Eggs,* Royal National Theatre, 1986–87.

Sophia, *The Bay at Nice,* Royal National Theatre, 1986–87.

Fay, *Loot,* Manhattan Theatre Club Stage I, then Music Box Theatre, both New York City, 1986.

Made in Bangkok, Mark Taper Forum, Los Angeles, 1988.

Paula, *Mrs. Klein,* Royal National Theatre, 1988, then Apollo Theatre, London, 1989.

Emilia, *Othello,* Royal Shakespeare Company, 1989.

Elizabeth Proctor, *The Crucible,* Royal National Theatre, 1990–91.

Patricia, *The Last Yankee,* Young Vic Theatre, then New York City production, 1993.

Eleanor, *Dead Funny,* Hampstead Theatre and Vaudeville Theatre, both London, 1994.
Amanda, *The Glass Menagerie,* Donmar Warehouse Theatre, then Comedy Theatre, London, 1995.
Title role, *Sylvia,* Apollo Theatre, 1996.
Jolly, *The Old Neighbourhood,* Royal Court Theatre, London, 1998.
Title role, *Electra,* Chichester Festival and Donmar Warehouse Theatre, 1997, then McCarter Theatre, Princeton, NJ, later Ethel Barrymore Theatre, New York City, 1998–99.
Battle Royal, Royal National Theatre, 1999–2000.
Anne, *Boston Marriage,* Donmar Warehouse Theatre and New Ambassadors Theatre, London, 2001.
Hildy, *His Girl Friday,* Royal National Theatre, 2003.
Bessie Berger, *Awake and Sing!,* Belasco Theatre, New York City, 2006.
Serafina, *The Rose Tattoo,* Royal National Theatre, 2007.
Beatrice, *Much Ado about Nothing,* Royal National Theatre, 2007–2008.

Also appeared as chorus member, *Henry V,* Globe Theatre; Eva, *Jug,* Nottingham Playhouse; in *She Stoops to Conquer,* Cambridge Theatre Company.

Major Tours:
Toine, *Piaf,* 1981.

Toured U.K. cities in *Twelfth Night,* Cambridge Theatre Company.

Film Appearances:
Elle, *The Raggedy Rawney,* Island, 1988.
Mary Foster, *Swept from the Sea* (also known as *Balaye par la mer, Amy Foster,* and *Amy Foster: Swept from the Sea*), TriStar, 1997.
Ada Leverson, *Wilde* (also known as *Oscar Wilde*), Sony Pictures Classics, 1997.
Madam Hooch, *Harry Potter and the Sorcerer's Stone* (also known as *Harry Potter and the Philosopher's Stone*), Warner Bros., 2001.
Voice of Tooth Fairy, *The Dark* (animated short film), 2001.
Martha, *Five Children and It* (also known as *5 Children & It* and *Cinq enfants et moi*), Warner Home Video, 2004.
Narrator, *Ochberg's Orphans* (short documentary), Rainmaker, 2008.
Muse of Fire: A Documentary (documentary), Chocolate Milk, 2010.
It's a Wonderful Afterlife, Bend It Films, 2010.

Television Appearances; Series:
Charlotte "Charlie" Titmuss, *Paradise Postponed,* PBS, 1986.
Tessa Piggott, *Love Hurts,* BBC, 1992–94.

Susan Harper, *My Family,* BBC1 and BBC America, beginning 2000.

Television Appearances; Miniseries:
Pearl Craigie, *Jennie: Lady Randolph Churchill,* 1975.
Annemarie Kempf, *Inside the Third Reich,* ABC, 1982.
Clementine "Clemmy", *Edge of Darkness,* BBC and syndicated, 1986.
Jean Kennerly, *Poor Little Rich Girl: The Barbara Hutton Story,* NBC, 1987.
Charlotte Collard, *The Blackheath Poisonings,* PBS, 1993.
Audrey Maclintick, *A Dance to the Music of Time,* 1997.
Narrator, *Conjuring Shakespeare,* 1997.
Mary Muldoon, *The Magical Legend of the Leprechauns* (also known as *Leprechauns* and *Kampf der Kobolde*), NBC, 1999.
Clarice, *Gormenghast,* BBC and BBC America, 2000.
Tania Braithwaite, *Adrian Mole: The Cappuccino Years,* BBC, 2001.
Narrator, *Someone to Watch over Me,* BBC, 2004.

Television Appearances; Specials:
Enemy of the State, 1981.
Toine, *Piaf,* The Entertainment Channel, 1982.
Lady Anne, *The Tragedy of Richard the Third* (also known as *The Complete Dramatic Works of William Shakespeare: "The Tragedy of Richard the Third"* and *"Richard III"*), BBC, 1983.
May Daniels, *Once in a Lifetime,* PBS, 1988.
Moyra Henson, *Prime Suspect* (also known as *Prime Suspect 1* and *Prime Suspect 1: A Price to Pay*), PBS, 1992.
Herself, *Comic Relief: The Invasion of the Comic Tomatoes,* 1993.
Narrator of prologue, *Henry V at Shakespeare's Globe,* 1997.
Narrator, *Norman Ormal: A Very Political Turtle,* 1998.
The Man Who Saw the Future, PBS, 1999.
Miss Murdstone, *David Copperfield,* BBC1, 1999, then PBS, 2000.
The 53rd Annual Tony Awards, 1999.
Narrator, *Adolf Eichamnn—Begegnungen mit einem Moerder* (also known as *I Met Adolf Eichmann*), 2003.
Narrator, *Cinema Sex Politics: Bertolucci Makes "The Dreamers"* (also known as *Bertolucci Makes "The Dreamers"*), 2003.
Richard II, 2003.
The Evening Standard Theatre Awards 2003, ITV, 2003.
Narrator, *Seven Days That Shook the Weathermen,* Channel 4, 2005.
The Evening Standard British Film Awards, ITV3, 2005.
Narrator, *The 50 Greatest Documentaries,* 2005.
Narrator, *The Real Amityville Horror,* Channel 4, 2005.
Behind the Scenes: Agatha Christie's "Poirot," ITV, 2006.

(Uncredited; in archive footage) Emma Pickford, *The Music of Morse,* ITV, 2007.

Television Appearances; Movies:
Corinna, *The Confederacy of Wives,* 1975.
Belle, *A Christmas Carol,* 1977.
Strike: The Birth of Solidarity, 1981.
Sophie, *Baal,* 1982.
Bildebeck, *The Dog It Was That Died,* 1989.
Sarah Marriot, *Ball–Trap on the Cote Sauvage* (also known as *Screen One: Ball–Trap on the Cote Sauvage*), 1989.
Emilia, *Othello,* 1990.
Olive Mannering, *Memento Mori,* PBS and BBC, 1992.
Connie, *The Countess Alice,* PBS, 1993.
Caroline Griveau, *The English Wife,* 1995.
Letitia Blacklock, *Marple: A Murder Is Announced* (also known as *Miss Marple: A Murder Is Announced*), PBS, 2005.
Countess of Pembroke, *A Waste of Shame: The Mystery of Shakespeare and His Sonnets,* 2005.
Mrs. Tachyon, *Johnny and the Bomb* (also known as *Terry Pratchett's "Johnny and the Bomb"*), BBC, 2006.
Mrs. Jarley, *The Old Curiosity Shop,* ITV and PBS, 2007.

Television Appearances; Episodic:
Ada Abbott, "The Silver Mask," *Between the Wars,* 1973.
Muriel, "Sale of Work," *Spy Trap,* 1973.
Shirley Chatsfield, "Miss Health and Beauty," *Village Hall,* 1975.
Joan Carmichael, "Marathon," *Crown Court,* 1975.
Dorinda, "The Beaux Stratagem," *BBC Play of the Month,* 1978.
Lucille, "Danton's Death," *BBC Play of the Month,* 1978.
Berengaria of Navarre, "Bolt from the Blue," *The Devil's Crown* (also known as *La Couronne du diable*), 1978.
(Uncredited) Villager, "State of Decay: Part 2," *Doctor Who,* BBC1 and Sci–Fi Channel, 1980.
Margaret Smythe, "Skeleton in the Cupboard," *Tales of the Unexpected* (also known as *Roald Dahl's "Tales of the Unexpected"*), syndicated, 1987.
Emma Pickford, "Fat Chance," *Inspector Morse,* CTV, 1991.
Voice of Lady Macbeth, "Macbeth," *Shakespeare: The Animated Tales* (animated), 1992.
Mrs. Holroyd, "The Widowing of Mrs. Holroyd," *Performance,* 1995.
Narrator, "The Outcasts," *Q.E.D.,* 1996.
Narrator, *Creatures Fantastic,* 1997.
Richard and Judy, Channel 4, 2001, 2003.
The Kumars at No. 42, BBC2 and BBC America, 2005.
Voice of Cassandra, "The End of the World," *Doctor Who,* BBC1 and Sci–Fi Channel, 2005.

Ariadne Oliver, "Cards on the Table," *Agatha Christie: Poirot* (also known as *Agatha Christie's "Poirot"* and *Poirot*), PBS, 2005.
Cassandra, "New Earth," *Doctor Who,* BBC1 and Sci–Fi Channel, 2006.
(Uncredited; in archive footage) Voice of Cassandra, *This Morning,* ITV, 2006.
"A Funny Thing Happened on the Way to the Studio," *Imagine,* BBC, 2006.
"Eugene O'Neill: A Documentary Film," *The American Experience,* PBS, 2006.
"Actors on Performing," *Working in the Theatre,* 2006.
Ariadne Oliver, "Mrs. McGinty's Dead," *Agatha Christie: Poirot* (also known as *Agatha Christie's "Poirot"* and *Poirot*), PBS, 2008.
Ariadne Oliver, "Third Girl," *Agatha Christie: Poirot* (also known as *Agatha Christie's "Poirot"* and *Poirot*), PBS, 2008.
"Zoe Wanamaker," *Who Do You Think You Are?,* BBC, 2009.
"The Enemies," *Doctor Who Greatest Moments,* BBC, 2009.
Ariadne Oliver, "Hallowe'en Party," *Agatha Christie: Poirot* (also known as *Agatha Christie's "Poirot"* and *Poirot*), PBS, 2009.

Radio Appearances:
The Golden Bowl, 1979.
Plenty, 1979.
Bay at Nice, 1987.
A February Morning, 1990.
Carol (book reading), 1990.
Such Rotten Luck, 1991.
Mrs. Boston, BBC Radio 4, 2005.

RECORDINGS

Videos:
2nd Annual Directors Guild of Great Britain DGGB Awards, Director's Guild of Great Britain, 2005.

Video Games:
Voice of Theresa, *Fable 2,* Microsoft, 2008.

OTHER SOURCES

Periodicals:
Interview, April, 1999.
Los Angeles Times, March 16, 1999, pp. F1, F8.
Radio Times, March 11, 1995, p. 6; March 4, 2006, pp. 6–8.
Telegraph, March 30, 2007; December 14, 2007.

WASHINGTON, Dennis
(J. Dennis Washington)

PERSONAL

Born in Santa Monica, CA. *Education:* Trained in architectural design and theatre.

Addresses: *Agent*—Ann Murtha, Murtha Agency, 4240 Promenade Way, Suite 232, Marina del Rey, CA 90292.

Career: Production designer and art director. Also worked as second unit director and aerial unit director.

Member: Directors Guild of America.

Awards, Honors: New Zealand Screen Award (with Robert Gillies), best production design, 2006, for *The World's Fastest Indian.*

CREDITS

Film Production Designer:
(As J. Dennis Washington) *Victory,* Paramount, 1981.
Hysterical, Embassy Pictures, 1983.
Prizzi's Honor, Twentieth Century–Fox, 1985.
Stand by Me, Columbia, 1986.
No Way Out, Orion, 1987.
The Dead (also known as *John Huston's "The Dead"*), Vestron, 1987.
Off Limits (also known as *Saigon* and *Saigon: Off Limits*), Twentieth Century–Fox, 1988.
Chances Are, TriStar, 1989.
Another You, TriStar, 1991.
White Men Can't Jump, Twentieth Century–Fox, 1991.
(As J. Dennis Washington) *Nowhere to Run* (also known as *Ganar o morir*), Columbia, 1993.
The Fugitive, Warner Bros., 1993.
(As J. Dennis Washington) *Angels in the Outfield,* Buena Vista, 1994.
Speechless, Metro–Goldwyn–Mayer, 1994.
The Net (also known as *The Internet*), Columbia, 1995.
High School High, TriStar, 1996.
Dante's Peak, Universal, 1997.
Paulie, DreamWorks, 1998.
The General's Daughter (also known as *The General's Daughter: Elizabeth Campbell*), Paramount, 1999.
Thirteen Days, New Line Cinema, 2000.
Life as a House, New Line Cinema, 2001.
(As J. Dennis Washington) *Dark Blue,* Metro–Goldwyn–Mayer/United Artists, 2002.
(As J. Dennis Washington) *Twisted,* Paramount, 2004.
(As J. Dennis Washington) *The World's Fastest Indian,* Magnolia Pictures, 2005.

Premonition (also known as *Shuffle*), Metro–Goldwyn–Mayer/Sony Pictures Entertainment, 2007.
(As J. Dennis Washington) *Shooter,* Paramount, 2007.
The Resident, Spitfire Pictures, 2010.
(As J. Dennis Washington) *The Hungry Rabbit Jumps,* Endgame Entertainment, 2010.

Film Art Director:
(As J. Dennis Washington) *Convoy,* United Artists, 1978.
(As J. Dennis Washington) *The Electric Horseman,* Columbia, 1979.
(As J. Dennis Washington) *The Ninth Configuration,* Warner Bros., 1980.
Rocky III, Metro–Goldwyn–Mayer/United Artists, 1982.
(As J. Dennis Washington) *To Be or Not to Be,* Twentieth Century–Fox, 1983.
(As J. Dennis Washington) *Finders Keepers,* Warner Bros., 1984.

Film Appearances:
Frankenstein, *Another You,* TriStar, 1991.

Television Production Designer; Pilots:
Big Love, HBO, 2006.
(As J. Dennis Washington) *Blue Blood,* NBC, 2008.

Television Art Director; Episodic:
"Beast in View," *Alfred Hitchcock Presents,* NBC, 1986.
"The Creeper," *Alfred Hitchcock Presents,* NBC, 1986.

Television Work; Other:
According to some sources, production designer for the miniseries *My Life and Times,* ABC, 1991.

RECORDINGS

Videos:
(As J. Dennis Washington) *From the Ground Up,* New Line Home Video, 2001.
Bringing History to the Silver Screen, New Line Home Video, 2001.
(As J. Dennis Washington) *Blue Code,* Metro–Goldwyn–Mayer Home Entertainment, 2003.
(As J. Dennis Washington) *Glimpses of the Future: Making "Premonition,"* Sony Pictures Home Entertainment, 2007.

WASIKOWSKA, Mia 1989–
(Mia Wasikoska)

PERSONAL

Born October 14, 1989, in Canberra, Australian Capital Territory, Australia. *Education:* Studied dance.

Addresses: *Agent*—William Morris Endeavor Entertainment (WmEE2), One William Morris Place, Beverly Hills, CA 90212; RGM Associates, 64–76 Kippax St., Suites 202 & 206, Level 2, Surry Hills 2010, New South Wales, Australia. *Publicist*—WKT Public Relations, 335 North Maple Dr., Suite 351, Beverly Hills, CA 90210.

Career: Actress. Also known as Mia Wasikoska.

Awards, Honors: Young Actor's Award nomination, Australian Film Institute, 2006, for *Suburban Mayhem;* named one of the top ten actors to watch, *Variety* magazine, 2008; International Award nomination, best actress, Australian Film Institute, 2009, for *In Treatment;* Special Jury Award (with others), best ensemble cast, SXSW Film Conference and Festival, 2009, and Independent Spirit Award nomination, best supporting female, Independent Feature Project/West, 2010, both for *That Evening Sun;* named a star for the new year, 2010, *Entertainment Weekly* magazine.

CREDITS

Film Appearances:

Girl, *Lens Love Story* (short film), New South Wales Film & Television Office, 2006.

Lilya, *Suburban Mayhem,* Icon Film Distribution, 2006.

Amelia Hamilton, *September,* Hopscotch Productions, 2007.

Title character, *Cosette* (short film), Australia Film, Television and Radio School (AFTRS), 2007.

Emma, *Skin* (short film), The Australian Film Commission, 2007.

Sherry, *Rogue* (also known as *Rogue Crocodile, Solitaire,* and *Territory*), Roadshow Entertainment, 2007, Third Rail Releasing, 2008.

Chaya Dziencielsky, *Defiance,* Paramount Vantage, 2008.

Kara, *Summer Breaks* (short film), Colour in Pictures, 2008.

Sarah Jane, *I Love Sarah Jane* (short film), Aquarius Films/Blue–Tongue Films/The Last Picture Company, 2008.

Elinor Smith, *Amelia* (also known as *Amelia Earhart*), Fox Searchlight, 2009.

Pamela Choat, *That Evening Sun* (also known as *I Hate to See That Evening Sun Go Down*), Freestyle Releasing, 2009.

Alice, *Alice in Wonderland* (also known as *Alice;* IMAX version released as *Alice in Wonderland: An IMAX 3D Experience*), Walt Disney Studios, 2010.

Joni, *The Kids Are All Right,* Focus Features, 2010.

Title character, *Jane Eyre,* 2010, Focus Features, 2011.

Teenager, *Restless* (also known as *Untitled Gus Van Sant Project*), Columbia, 2011.

Television Appearances; Series:

Sophie, *In Treatment,* HBO, 2008.

Television Appearances; Episodic:

Lily Watson, "Out on a Limb," *All Saints* (also known as *All Saints: Medical Response Unit*), Seven Network, 2004.

Lily Watson, "Sins of the Mothers," *All Saints* (also known as *All Saints: Medical Response Unit*), Seven Network, 2005.

Herself, "2010 Academy Awards Spotlight," *Made in Hollywood,* syndicated, 2010.

Herself, *Cinema 3* (also known as *Cinema tres* and *Informatiu cinema*), Televisio de Catalunya, 2010.

Herself, *Entertainment Tonight* (also known as *Entertainment This Week, E.T., ET Weekend,* and *This Week in Entertainment*), syndicated, multiple episodes in 2010.

Herself, *Late Night with Jimmy Fallon,* NBC, 2010.

Herself, *Late Show with David Letterman* (also known as *The Late Show, Late Show Backstage,* and *Letterman*), CBS, 2010.

Herself, *Made in Hollywood,* syndicated, 2010.

Herself, *The 7PM Project,* Ten Network, 2010.

Herself, *Sunrise,* Seven Network, 2010.

Herself, *Up Close with Carrie Keagan,* 2010.

Herself, *The View,* ABC, 2010.

Herself, *Xpose,* Televisio de Catalunya, 2010.

WATKINS, Micaela 1971–

PERSONAL

Full name, Michaela Suzanne Watkins; born December 14, 1971, in Syracuse, NY; father, a university professor of mathematics; mother, a Latin teacher. *Education:* Boston University, B.F.A.

Addresses: *Agent*—Meredith Wechter, International Creative Management, 10250 Constellation Blvd., 9th Floor, Los Angeles, CA 90067. *Manager*—Flutie Entertainment, 9300 Wilshire Blvd., Suite 333, Beverly Hills, CA 90212.

Career: Actress and comedienne.

CREDITS

Television Appearances; Series:

Snobby stylist, *$25 Million Dollar Hoax,* NBC, 2004.

Jennifer, *7 Deadly Hollywood Sins,* E! Entertainment Television, 2006.

Lucy, *The New Adventures of Old Christine* (also known as *Old Christine*), CBS, 2008–2009.

Various characters, *Saturday Night Live* (also known as *The Albert Brooks Show,* The Best of Saturday Night Live, NBC's "Saturday Night," *Saturday*

Night, Saturday Night Live '80, Saturday Night Live 15, Saturday Night Live 20, Saturday Night Live 25, SNL, and *SNL 25*), NBC, 2008–2009.

Television Appearances; Episodic:

Andrea (Davidson's assistant), "Death Takes a Halliwell," *Charmed,* The WB, 2001.

Marla, "Maple Street," *Without a Trace* (also known as *Vanished* and *W.A.T.*), CBS, 2003.

Susan Scott, "Divorce Happens," *Miss Match* (also known as *Miss Kohting*), NBC, 2003.

Julia, "Bleeding Heart," *Strong Medicine,* Lifetime, 2004.

Amanda, "Give 'til You Learn," *Modern Men* (also known as *Men Behaving Better* and *The Evolution of Man*), The WB, 2006.

Clerk, "Allison Wonderland," *Medium* (also known as *Ghost and Crime* and *A medium*), NBC, 2006.

Clerk, "Sweet Child o' Mine," *Medium* (also known as *Ghost and Crime* and *A medium*), NBC, 2006.

Nikki Ratlin, "Superstition," *Grey's Anatomy* (also known as *Complications, Procedure, Surgeons, Under the Knife,* and *Grey's Anatomy—Die jungen Aerzte*), ABC, 2006.

Receptionist, "Hal's Dentist," *Malcolm in the Middle* (also known as *Fighting in Underpants*), Fox, 2006.

(Uncredited) Executive, "Coke Dick & First Kick," *Californication* (also known as *Untitled David Duchovny Series* and *Untitled Tom Kapinos Project*), Showtime, 2008.

Executive, "Going Down and Out in Beverly Hills," *Californication,* Showtime, 2008.

Julia Roberts, *Frank TV* (also known as *The Frank Show*), TBS, 2008.

Judge Leigh Rappaport, "Sonoma," *Eli Stone,* ABC, 2009.

Carla, "Time of Death," *Miami Medical* (also known as *Miami Trauma* and *Untitled Bruckheimer/Lieber Project*), CBS, 2010.

Lucy Estman, "Team Braverman," *Parenthood,* NBC, 2010.

Herself, *Entertainment Tonight* (also known as *Entertainment This Week,* E.T., *ET Weekend,* and *This Week in Entertainment*), syndicated, 2010.

Television Appearances; Pilots:

Amanda, *Modern Men* (also known as *Men Behaving Better* and The Evolution of Man), The WB, 2006.

Mary–Louise, *Revenge,* Fox, 2007.

Various characters, *Man Stroke Woman,* 2008.

Film Appearances:

Marcy, *Inconceivable,* The Asylum/Curb Entertainment, 1998.

Jill Goering, *Yoga Matt* (short film), FilmPhobia/Metra Entertainment, 2008.

Herself, *Funny: The Documentary,* 2010.

Miss LaFleur, *The Prankster,* Prankster Entertainment, 2010.

Mona, *The Back–Up Plan* (also known as *Plan B*), CBS Films, 2010.

Stage Appearances:

Elma Duckworth, *Bus Stop,* Portland Center Stage, Portland, OR, 2000.

Jehanne D'Alcy, *Laura Comstock's Bag–Punching Dog* (musical), Circle X Theatre Co., Twenty–Fourth Street Theatre, Los Angeles, 2002.

Nia, *Fighting Words,* Vineyard Playhouse, Martha's Vineyard, MA, 2003.

Marie Antoinette, *Sperm,* Circle X Theatre Co., Twenty–Fourth Street Theatre, 2004.

The Groundlings, Los Angeles, member of the company; also performer of stand–up comedy at the Hollywood Improv, the Laugh Factory, and other venues.

Internet Appearances:

Herself, *Live! from the Future … with Stuart Paap!* (also known as *Live! from the Future*), www.livefromthefuture.com, c. 2008.

Appeared as Jane in the short video clip *Tight* (also known as *Tight w/ Michaela Watkins*), posted on *Funny or Die,* www.funnyordie.com.

RECORDINGS

Videos:

Mother, *Wacky Spoof Commercials,* Hip how hang Productions, 2007.

WRITINGS

Writings for the Stage:

The Groundlings, Los Angeles, member of the company; created comedic material to perform at the Hollywood Improv, the Laugh Factory, and other venues.

OTHER SOURCES

Periodicals:

TV Guide, April 20, 2009, pp. 36–37; September 21, 2009, p. 16.

WEAVER, Brett 1966–

PERSONAL

Born November 16, 1966, in Lafayette, LA. *Avocational Interests:* Music, cooking, computers, hockey, paintball.

Career: Actor and voice artist.

CREDITS

Television Appearances; Voices for English–Language Versions; Animated Series:

Voice of Kane Smith, *Bubblegum Crisis: Tokyo 2040* (also known as *Bubblegum Crisis 2040;* originally released in Japan in Japanese, 1998–99, The Anime Network and Encore Action, 1999.

Blue Seed (also known as *Aokushimitama Blue Seed;* originally released in Japan in Japanese, 1994–95, 1999–2000.

Voices of Gai Daigoji (original name Jiro Yamada) and Tsukomo Shiratori, *Martian Successor Nadesico* (also known as *Mobile Battleship Nadesico, Nadesico, Kido senkan Hadeshiko, Kido senkan Nadesico,* and *Kidou senkan Nadeshiko;* originally released in Japan in Japanese, Bandai Channel and TV Tokyo, 1996–97, The Anime Network, Sci–Fi Channel, and Cartoon Network, 2003.

Voices of Captain "Axe–Hand" Morgan, Mr. 1, and Daz Bones, *One Piece* (also known as *Shonen Jump One Piece* and *Wan pisu: One Piece;* originally released in Japan in Japanese, Fuji Television, 1999, FoxBox programming block on Fox, 2004–2005, 4KidsTV programming block on Fox, 2004–2006, YTV, 2005–2006, Cartoon Network, 2005–2008.

Voice of Ryu, *Street Fighter II: V* (also known as *Street Fighter II Victory* and *Street Fighter II: Victory;* originally released in Japan in Japanese, Yomiuri Telecasting Corporation, 1995, Super Channel, 2007, Independent Film Channel Canada, 2008.

Voice of Akira Nakata, *Witchblade* (originally released in Japan in Japanese, Tokyo Broadcasting System and Chubu–Nippon Broadcasting Communication, 2006, Independent Film Channel, 2008.

Voice of Kamina, *Gurren Lagann* (also known as *Heavenly Breakthrough Crimson Face, Heavenly Breakthrough Gurren Lagann, Maiking Break–Through Gurren–Lagann, Tengen toppa Gurren–Lagann,* and *Tengen toppa Gurren Lagann;* originally released in Japan in Japanese, AT–X, TV Tokyo, and BS Japan, 2007, Sci–Fi Channel and Super Channel, 2008, Animax Asia and Animax India, 2009.

Voice of Roy Focker, *The Super Dimension Fortress Macross* (includes *Dangerous Divisions, Fallen Angels, When Worlds Collide,* and *Eve of Destruction;* also known as *Battle City Megaload, Macross, Robotech: The Macross Saga, Space Fortress Macross, Super Dimension Fortress Macross, Super Dimensional Fortress Macross, Trans Time Space Fortress Macross, Chojiku yosai Macross,* and *Cho jiku yosai Macross;* originally released in Japan in Japanese, Mainichi Broadcasting, 1982–83), The Anime Network; voices of manager and Mafia don, *Dirty Pair OAV* (includes *Dirty Pair OAV 1, Dirty Pair OAV 2, Dirty Pair OAV 3,*

Dirty Pair OAV 4, and *Dirty Pair OAV 5;* also known as *Original Dirty Pair;* originally released in Japan in Japanese, 1989), Showtime Beyond; voices of Shinichi, delinquent on roof, and teenager with glasses, *All Purpose Cultural Cat Girl Nuku Nuku* (also known as *Cat Girl Nuku Nuku, Nuku Nuku, Super Catgirl Nuku Nuku, Super Cat Girl Nuku Nuku, Banno bunka neko-musume,* and *Bannou bunka neko–musume;* originally released in Japan in Japanese, 1992), The Anime Network; voice of Tora, *Ushio and Tora* (also known as *Ushio & Tora;* originally released in Japan in Japanese, 1992–93), The Anime Network; voices of president, Semolina, copilot, and stud, *Dirty Pair Flash* (includes *Dirty Pair Flash 1, Dirty Pair Flash 2,* and *Dirty Pair Flash 3;* originally released in Japan in Japanese, Bandai Channel, 1994); voices of Gill and Miguel, *Ruin Explorers* (also known as *Ruin Explorer Fam & Ihrlie, Ruin Explorers: Quest for the Ultimate Power,* and *Hikyou Tanken Fam & Ihrlie;* originally released in Japan in Japanese, 1995), Animax Asia; voice of Carrot Glasse, *Sorcerer Hunters* (includes *Of Inhuman Bondage, Fires of Passion, Phantoms of Love, Forbidden Desires,* and *Arcane Revelations,* as well as *2 Beauties and a Beast* and *Magical Encounters;* also known as *The Sorcerer Hunters, Spell War: Sorcerer Hunters Revenge, Spell Wars: Sorcerer Hunter's Revenge Vol. 1,* and *Bakuretsu Hunter;* originally released in Japan in Japanese, TV Tokyo, 1995–96), The Anime Network; voices of Hans, Semolina, copilot, president, geek, and others, *Dirty Pair Flash 3* (also known as *Dirty Pair Flash: Mission 3, Dirty Pair Flash: Mission 3 Act 1,* and *Dirty Pair Flash: Random Angels;* originally released in Japan in Japanese, Bandai Channel, 1995–96), Showtime Behind; voice of first terrorist, *Burn Up W* (also known as *Burn Up W!* and *Burn Up Warrior;* originally released in Japan in Japanese, 1996), The Anime Network; voice of Pirate Hammerhead, *Those Who Hunt Elves* (also known as *Elf o karu mono–tachi* and *Elf wo karu mono-tachi;* originally released in Japan in Japanese, TV Tokyo, 1996), The Anime Network; voice of Akira (Devilman), *Cutey Honey Flash* (also known as *Cutey Honey F* and *Kyutei Hani Flash;* originally released in Japan in Japanese, TV Asahi, 1997–98); voice of Ranbert, *Getter Robo: Armageddon* (also known as *Change!! True Getter Robo: The Final Days of the World, Getter Robo Armageddon, Getter Robo—The Last Day, Change!! Shin Getter Robo: Sekai Saishuu no Hi, Chenji! Getta robo: sekai saigo no hi, Shin Getta robo,* and *Shin Getter Robo;* originally released in Japan in Japanese, 1998), The Anime Network; voice of Kiyoharu Gowa, *Gasaraki* (originally released in Japan in Japanese, Animax, 1998–99) The Anime Network; voice of Nabeshin, *Excel Saga* (also known as *Anime Experimental Anime Excel Saga, Excel saga, Quack Experimental Anime Excel Saga, Weird Anime Excel Saga,* and *Heppoko jikken animeshon excel saga;* originally released in Japan in Japanese, TV Tokyo, 1999–2000), The Anime Network; voice of Hines, *Zone of the Enders* (also known as *Dolores, i, Z.O.E. Dolores, i, Zone of Enders,* and *Zone of the Enders: Dolores, I;* originally released in Japan in Japanese, AT–X, 2001), The Anime

Network; voice of Ricardo Kidel, *Najica: Blitz Tactics* (also known as *Najica* and *Najika dengeki sakusen;* originally released in Japan in Japanese, KIDS STATION, Television Kanagawa, Television Saitama, and Chiba Television, 2001), The Anime Network; voice of Vodka, *Jing: King of Bandits* (also known as *Bandit King Jing, King of Bandit Jing, O dorobo Jing,* and *Ou dorobou Jing;* subtitled version broadcast by iaTV, originally released in Japan in Japanese, Nippon Housou Kyoukai (NHK) BS2, 2002), The Anime Network; voice of Goh Saruwatari, *Godannar* (also known as *God and Spirit Combination Godannar!!, Marriage of God & Soul Godannar!!, Shinkon Gattai Godannar!!,* and *Shinkon Gattai Godannar!! Second Season;* originally released in Japan in Japanese, AT–X and Bandai Channel, 2003–04), The Anime Network; voice of Akitoshi, *Gantz* (originally released in Japan in Japanese, AT–X and Fuji Television, 2004), The Anime Network; voice of Vincent Greco, *Solty Rei* (also known as *SoltyRei;* originally released in Japan in Japanese, TV Asahi, 2005), FUNimation Channel, Anime Selects, Animax Asia, Animax India, and Animax South Africa; voice of man, *Ouran High School Host Club* (also known as *Ouran Koukou Host Club;* originally released in Japan in Japanese, Nippon Television, Chukyo Television, and Yomiuri Telecasting Corporation, 2006); voice of rental man, *Nerima Daikon Brothers* (also known as *The Freshly–Grated Musical Nerima Daikon Brothers* and *Oroshitate Musical Nerima Daikon Brothers;* originally released in Japan in Japanese, TV Tokyo and AT–X, 2006); mysterious voice, *The Wallflower* (also known as *Perfect Girl Evolution, Wallflower, Yamato nadeshiko shichihenge,* and *Yamato nadeshiko shichi henge;* originally released in Japan in Japanese, TV Asahi and TV Tokyo, 2006–07, also broadcast by TV5, 2008).

Television Appearances; Voices for English–Language Versions; Animated Miniseries:

Blue Seed Beyond (also known as *Blue Seed OAV, Blue Seed 2, Blue Seed 2: Operation Mitama,* and *Aokushimitama blue seed 2;* originally released in Japan in Japanese, 1996, The Anime Network, 2003.

Voice of Syusai, *Samurai 7* (also known as *Akira Kurosawa's "Samurai 7";* originally released in Japan in Japanese, SKY PerfecTV!, 2004, Independent Film Channel, 2006.

Voice of manager, *Dirty Pair OAV 5* (also known as *Original Dirty Pair Vol. 5;* originally released in Japan in Japanese, 1988), Showtime Beyond; voice of Joe Takagami, *Dark Warrior* (originally released in Japan in Japanese, 1991); voice of Damaramu, *Dragon Half* (originally released in Japan in Japanese, 1993); voices of Rasha and flight announcer, *Battle Angel* (also known as *Battle Angel Alita, Gunn–Dream Gunnm, Gunnm, Hyper Future Vision GUNNM,* and *Tsutsu Yume Gunnm;* originally released in Japan in Japanese, 1993); voice of Julian, *Fire Emblem* (originally released in

Japan in Japanese, 1995); voices of the young Kageyama, an adjutant, and others, *Super Atragon* (also known as *The New Submarine Battleship, Super Atragon 1 & 2,* and *Shin kaitei gunkan;* originally released in Japan in Japanese, 1995), The Anime Network; voice of Jonathan Washington, *Gunsmith Cats* (also known as *GSC, Gunsmith Cat's,* and *Gun Smith Cats;* originally released in Japan in Japanese, 1995–96), The Anime Network and Encore Action; voice of Carrot Glasse, *Sorcerer Hunters OAV* (also known as *The Original Sorcerer Hunters, Bakuretsu hunter OAV,* and *Ganso bakuretsu hunter;* originally released in Japan in Japanese, 1996), The Anime Network; voices of Jeffrey, Goldias, and old man, *Slayers Special* (also known as *Slayers Book of Spells, Slayers: Book of Spells, Slayers: The Book of Spells, Slayers Dragon Slave, Slayers Explosion Array, Slayers OVA 1,* and *Sureiyazu supesharu;* originally released in Japan in Japanese, 1996); voices of lead hero and Sato, *Spectral Force* (originally released in Japan in Japanese, 1998); voice of Genmi, *Sorcerer on the Rocks* (also known as *Chivas 1–2–3;* originally released in Japan in Japanese, 1999), The Anime Network; voice of Nabeshin, *Puni puni poemi* (originally released in Japan in Japanese, 2001), The Anime Network; *Claymore* (also known as *Kureimoa;* originally released in Japan in Japanese, Nippon Television and NittelEPlus, 2007); *Gunslinger Girl—Il Teatrino* (also known as *Gansuringa garu: Iru teatorino;* originally released in Japan in Japanese, Tokyo MX Television, TV Osaka, Chukyo Television, and BS11 Digital, 2008).

Television Appearances; Voices for English–Language Versions; Animated Movies:

Voice of Mughi, *Dirty Pair: Affair of Nolandia* (also known as *Dirty Pair: Mystery of Norlandia, Dirty Pair: Norandia no Nazo, Original Dirty Pair: Affair of Nolandia, Original Dirty Pair #5: Affair of Nolandia,* and *Dati pea: Norandia no nazo;* originally released in Japan in Japanese, 1985, The Anime Network, c. 2003.

Voice of Toji Suzuhara, *Neon Genesis Evangelion: Death & Rebirth* (also known as *Evangelion: Death & Rebirth, Shin seiki Evangelion Gekijoban: Death & Rebirth—Shi to shinsei,* and *Shin seiki Evangelion Gekijo–ban: Shito shinsei;* originally released in Japan in Japanese, 1997, SBS Channel, 2004, Encore Action, 2005.

Voice of Toji Suzuhara, *Neon Genesis Evangelion: The End of Evangelion* (also known as *The End of Evangelion, The End of Evangelion: Episode 25: Love Is Destructive/One More Final: I Need You, New Century Evangelion Theatrical Edition: Air/Sincerely Yours, Shin seiki Evangelion Gekijoban: The End of Evangelion: Air/Magokoro o, Kimi ni,* and *Shin seiki Evangelion Gekijo–ban: Air/Magokoro wo, kimi ni;* originally released in Japan in Japanese, 1997, SBS Channel, 2004, Encore Action, 2005.

Voice of Mughi, *Dirty Pair Flight 005 Conspiracy* (also known as *Dirty Pair: Flight 005 Conspiracy* and *Dirty*

Pair: Bouryaku no 005–bin; originally released in Japan in Japanese, 1990), The Anime Network; voice of militia leader, *Plastic Little* (also known as *Plastic Little: The Adventures of Captain Tita* and *Purasuchikku ritoru;* originally released in Japan in Japanese, 1994), The Anime Network; voice of Osamu, *Ki*Me*Ra* (also known as *Kimera;* originally released in Japan in Japanese, 1996), The Anime Network; voices of Mr. Sugisawa and new ABCB owner, *Kimagure Orange Road: Summer's Beginning* (also known as *New Kimagure Orange Road: And Then, the Beginning of That Summer, New Kimagure Orange Road: Summer's Beginning, Shin Kimagure Orange Road—Soshite, Ano Natsu no Hajimari,* and *Shin Kimagure orenji rodo: Soshite, ano natsu no hajimari;* originally released in Japan in Japanese, 1996), The Anime Network; voice of classmate, *Supurigan* (also known as *Spriggan;* originally released in Japan in Japanese, 1998, Tokyo Broadcasting System, 2000), The Anime Network; voice of Hines, *Zone of the Enders: Idolo* (also known as *Idolo, Z.O.E. Idolo, Zone of the Enders 2167 Idolo,* and *Zone of the Enders: 2167 Idolo;* originally released in Japan in Japanese, 2001), The Anime Network.

Television Appearances; Voices for English–Language Versions; Animated Episodes:

Voices of Hadrian and Hamilton, "Akaoni Village Fire Festival Murder Case," *Case Closed* (also known as *Case Closed: One Truth Prevails, Detective Conan, O Detective Conan,* and *Meitantei Conan;* originally broadcast in Japan in Japanese, Animax, Nippon Television, and Yomiuri Telecasting Corporation, 1996, Cartoon Network, 2004, YTV, 2006.

Voices of Hadrian and Hamilton, "Missing Corpse Murder Case," *Case Closed* (also known as *Case Closed: One Truth Prevails, Detective Conan, O Detective Conan,* and *Meitantei Conan;* originally broadcast in Japan in Japanese, Animax, Nippon Television, and Yomiuri Telecasting Corporation, 1996, Cartoon Network, 2004, YTV, 2006.

Voice of Mark Newman, *Case Closed* (also known as *Case Closed: One Truth Prevails, Detective Conan, O Detective Conan,* and *Meitantei Conan;* originally broadcast in Japan in Japanese, Animax, Nippon Television, and Yomiuri Telecasting Corporation, 1996, Cartoon Network, 2004, YTV, 2006.

Voice of Toji Suzuhara, *Neon Genesis Evangelion* (also known as *Evangelion, New Century Evangelion,* and *Shin seiki evangerion;* originally released in Japan in Japanese, TV Tokyo and Animax, 1995, also BS11 Digital, as well as WoWow, 2003, Cartoon Network, 2005–2006.

Voice of Dagao, *The Super Dimension Fortress Macross* (includes *Dangerous Divisions, Fallen Angels, When Worlds Collide,* and *Eve of Destruction;* also known as *Battle City Megaload, Macross, Robotech: The Macross Saga, Space Fortress Macross, Super Dimension Fortress Macross, Super Dimensional Fortress Macross, Trans*

Time Space Fortress Macross, Chojiku yosai Macross, and *Cho jiku yosai Macross;* originally released in Japan in Japanese, Mainichi Broadcasting, c. 1983), The Anime Network; voices of various characters, including Professor Kaps, elder Kaps, Overlord Kaps, little boy Kaps, little girl Kaps, Hans the cyberjunkie, copilot, a eunuch, and Kaps villagers, *Dirty Pair Flash* (includes *Dirty Pair Flash 1, Dirty Pair Flash 2,* and *Dirty Pair Flash 3;* originally released in Japan in Japanese, Bandai Channel, 1994); voices of Prince Jeffrey, Jeffrey's father, and old man, "Angry? Lina's Furious Dragon Slave!," *Slayers* (also known as *Reena & Gaudi, The Slayers,* and *Sureiyazu;* originally released in Japan in Japanese, AT–X and TV Tokyo, 1995), International Channel, The Anime Network, and Colours TV; voice of Akira, *New Cutey Honey* (also known as *Cutey Honey, Cutey Honey–1, Go Nagai's "New Cutey Honey," New Cutie Honey, New Super Android Cutey Honey, Shin Cutey Honey,* and *Shin Kyutei Hani;* originally released in Japan in Japanese, c. 1995), The Anime Network; voice of Ishimaru, *Princess Nine* (also known as *Princess Nine: Kisaragi Girls' High School Baseball Team, Princess Nine—Kisaragijoshikou Yakyuubu,* and *Princess Nine kisaragi joshi kou yakuu–bu;* originally released in Japan in Japanese, NHK, multiple episodes in 1998), The Anime Network; voice of director, *Excel Saga* (also known as *Anime Experimental Anime Excel Saga, Excel saga, Quack Experimental Anime Excel Saga, Weird Anime Excel Saga,* and *Heppoko jikken animeshon excel saga;* originally released in Japan in Japanese, TV Tokyo, c. 1999), The Anime Network; voice of old man, *Najica: Blitz Tactics* (also known as *Najica* and *Najika dengeki sakusen;* originally released in Japan in Japanese, KIDS STATION, Television Kanagawa, Television Saitama, and Chiba Television, 2001), The Anime Network; voice of Andy, "The Rising Wind in the Homeland: Pat 1," *Full Metal Panic!* (originally released in Japan in Japanese, WoWow and BS11 Digital, 2002), The Anime Network and Animax Asia; voice of Nabeshin, "Pioneer! The Animation Company That Invites Storms," *Nurse Witch Komugi* (also known as *Nurse Witch Komugi–chan Magikarte* and *Nurse Witch Komugi–chan Magi Karte;* originally released in Japan in Japanese, Television Kanagawa, c. 2002), The Anime Network; voice of green delinquent, *The Wallflower* (also known as *Perfect Girl Evolution, Wallflower, Yamato nadeshiko shichihenge,* and *Yamato nadeshiko shichi henge;* originally released in Japan in Japanese, TV Asahi and TV Tokyo, c. 2006).

Television Appearances; Voices for English–Language Versions; Animated Pilots:

Voice of Joe Takagami, *Dark Warrior: First Strike* (also known as "First Strike," *Dark Warrior* and *Makyuu Senjou;* originally released in Japan in Japanese, 1991, 1996.

Television Additional Voices; Voices for English–Language Versions; Animated Series:

Princess Nine (also known as *Princess Nine: Kisaragi Girls' High School Baseball Team, Princess Nine—*

Kisaragijoshikou Yakyuubu, and *Princess Nine kisaragi joshi kou yakuu-bu;* originally released in Japan in Japanese, NHK, 1998), The Anime Network; *Najica: Blitz Tactics* (also known as *Najica* and *Najika dengeki sakusen;* originally released in Japan in Japanese, KIDS STATION, Television Kanagawa, Television Saitama, and Chiba Television, 2001), The Anime Network.

Television Additional Voices; Voices for English–Language Versions; Animated Miniseries:
Sol Bianca (also known as *Taiyou no Fune Sol Bianca;* originally released in Japan in Japanese, 1990 and c. 1992); *Super Atragon* (also known as *The New Submarine Battleship, Super Atragon 1 & 2,* and *Shin kaitei gunkan;* originally released in Japan in Japanese, 1995), The Anime Network.

Television Additional Voices; Voices for English–Language Versions; Animated Movies:
Plastic Little (also known as *Plastic Little: The Adventures of Captain Tita* and *Purasuchikku ritoru;* originally released in Japan in Japanese, 1994), The Anime Network; *Supurigan* (also known as *Spriggan;* originally released in Japan in Japanese, 1998, Tokyo Broadcasting System, 2000), The Anime Network.

Television Additional Voices for English–Language Versions; Animated Episodes:
Martian Successor Nadesico (also known as *Mobile Battleship Nadesico, Nadesico, Kido senkan Hadeshiko, Kido senkan Nadesico,* and *Kidou senkan Nadeshiko;* originally released in Japan in Japanese, Bandai Channel and TV Tokyo, c. 1996–97, Cartoon Network.
"Shito, shurai" (also known as "Angel Attack" and "An Angel's Attack"), *Neon Genesis Evangelion* (also known as *Evangelion, New Century Evangelion,* and *Shin seiki evangerion;* originally released in Japan in Japanese, TV Tokyo and Animax, 1995, also BS11 Digital, and WoWow, 2003, Cartoon Network, 2005.

Dirty Pair Flash 3 (also known as *Dirty Pair Flash: Mission 3, Dirty Pair Flash: Mission 3 Act 1,* and *Dirty Pair Flash: Random Angels;* originally released in Japan in Japanese, Bandai Channel, 1995–96), Showtime Behind; *Gasaraki* (originally released in Japan in Japanese, Animax, 1998–99), The Anime Network.

Animated Film Appearances; Voices for English–Language Versions:
Voice of second thief, *Slayers: The Motion Picture* (also known as *Slayers Perfect* and *Sureiyazu;* originally released in Japan in Japanese, Toei Animation, 1995, released on video, 1997, ADV Films, 2000.
Voices of Bruno and Mughi, *Original Dirty Pair: Project Eden* (also known as *Dirty Pair, Dirty Pair: The*

Movie, Daati pea Gekijou–ban, and *Dati pea Gekijo–ban;* originally released in Japan in Japanese, c. 1986, and Shochiku Company, 1987, c. 2003.
Voices of head dragon knight and lizard henchman, *Dragon Knight* (originally released in Japan in Japanese, 1991, c. 2003.
Voice of operator, *Martian Successor Nadesico: The Motion Picture—Prince of Darkness* (also known as *Martian Successor Nadesico: The Motion Picture, Nadesico Martian Successor—Prince of Darkness, Nadesico: Prince of Darkness,* and *Kido Senkan Nadeshiko: Prince of Darkness;* originally released in Japan in Japanese, 1998, c. 2003.
Voice of commissioner, *Burst Angel: Infinity* (animated short film; also known as *Bakuretsu tenshi: Infinity;* originally released in Japan in Japanese, Gonzo, 2007, FUNimation Entertainment, 2007.
Voices of Mr. 1 and Daz Bones, *One Piece: The Desert Princess and the Pirates—Adventure in Alabasta* (also known as *One Piece: The Desert Princess and the Pirates—Adventure in Alabasta (Movie 8), One Piece the Movie: Adventures in Alabasta, One Piece the Movie: Episode of Arabasta—The Desert Princess and the Pirates,* and *One Piece: Episode of Alabaster—Sabaku no Ojou to Kaizoku Tachi;* originally released in Japan in Japanese, 2007, 2008.

Voice of Tora, *Ushio and Tora: Comically Deformed Theater* (originally released in Japan in Japanese, 1993); voices of head bad person and Masaru, *Suikoden Demon Century* (also known as *Suikoden, Suikoden: Demon Century,* and *Youseiki Suikoden;* originally released in Japan in Japanese, 1993), ADV Films/Madman Entertainment; voice of Kane Smith, *Bubblegum Crisis Tokyo 2040: Shadow War* (originally released in Japan, c. 1999).

Live Action Film Appearances; Voices for English–Language Versions:
Voices of scientific assistant and a news anchor, *Gamera* (also known as *Gamera Defender of the Universe, Gamera: Giant Monster Midair Showdown, Gamera: The Guardian of the Universe, Gamera 2: Assault of the Legion,* and *Gamera daikaiju kuchu kessen;* originally released in Japan in Japanese, 1995, 1997.

Animated Film Additional Voices; Voices for English–Language Versions:
Slayers: The Motion Picture (also known as *Slayers Perfect* and *Sureiyazu;* originally released in Japan in Japanese, Toei Animation, 1995, released 1997, ADV Films, 2000.

RECORDINGS

Video Games:
Voice of Bernard Montgomery, *Axis & Allies* (also known as *Axis & Allies RTS*), Atari, 2004.

Voice, *Kohan II: Kings of War,* Global Star Software/G. O.D., 2004.

Videos:
Provided voices for English–language versions of anime videos originally released in Japanese.

Albums; with Others:
Various artists, *Voices for Tolerance* (fundraising album for charity), 2008.

OTHER SOURCES

Electronic:
Brett's Site of Destiny, http://www.siteofdestiny.com, July 22, 2002.

WEBER, Leyna
(Leyna Juliet Weber)

PERSONAL

Born in New York, NY. *Education:* Hunter College of the City University of New York, B.A. (summa cum laude); trained in sketch comedy and improvisation at Acme Comedy Club, Los Angeles.

Addresses: *Agent*—Bobby Ball Agency, 4605 Lankershim Blvd., Suite 721, North Hollywood, CA 91602; (voice work and commercials) Atlas Talent Agency, 15 East 32nd St., New York, NY 10016. *Manager*—Steven Buchsbaum, Ad Astra Management, Los Angeles, CA.

Career: Actress, writer, and producer. Working Bug Media, cofounder, partner, producer, and writer of short films, some of which have been broadcast by the Web site FunnyOrDie.com, 2008–; Leyna Snaps (photography business), founder; Acme Comedy Club, Los Angeles, member of company. Commercials include work for DayQuil cold medication and Sony Cybershot digital cameras; public service announcements include the anti–smoking ad "Left Behind," 2008.

Member: Screen Actors Guild, American Federation of Television and Radio Artists, Actors' Equity Association.

CREDITS

Film Appearances; Short Films:
Beth, *Getaway* (also known as *Getaway ... Another Weekend with the Old Battleaxe*), Absolute Motion, 2002.

Susan, *The Other Woman,* Quantock Group, 2007.
Nurse, *The Line,* Sleeper Productions, 2007.
Mandy, *Speeding Ticket,* Working Bug Media, 2008.
Whitney, *Taboo,* Working Bug Media, 2008.
Alex, *The Passenger,* School of Cinematic Arts, University of Southern California, 2009.
Kelly Hightower, *Veiled,* Clara Luna Productions, 2009.
Wife, *Looking at Animals,* Oota Productions, 2009.
Summer, *Donation,* Working Bug Media, 2009.
Summer, *Parking Spot,* Working Bug Media, 2009.

Film Producer; Short Films:
Speeding Ticket, Working Bug Media, 2008.
Taboo, Working Bug Media, 2008.
Donation, Working Bug Media, 2009.
Parking Spot, Working Bug Media, 2009.

Television Appearances; Series:
Nurse, *As the World Turns,* CBS, several episodes, 1999–2004.
Voices, *Kenny the Shark,* The Discovery Channel, 2003.
Narrator, *Assignment Discovery,* The Discovery Channel, 2006–2007.

Television Appearances; Specials:
Dawn, *Cost of Living,* 2009.

Television Appearances; Episodic:
Wife, "DR 1–102," *Law & Order,* NBC, 2002.
(Uncredited) Bar patron, *All My Children* (also known as *AMC*), ABC, 2002.
(As Leyna Juliet Weber) Bartender Molly, "Lowdown," *Law & Order: Special Victims Unit* (also known as *Law & Order: SVU* and *Special Victims Unit*), NBC, 2004.
(As Leyna Juliet Weber) Dee Dee, "A Coat of White Primer," *Six Feet Under,* HBO, 2005.

Internet Appearances; Series:
Rochelle Shapiro, *Road to the Altar,* 2009.

Internet Appearances; Episodic:
Live! from the Future, LiveFromTheFuture.com, 2006.

Stage Appearances:
Appeared as Grace, *The Beat Goes On,* Pulse Ensemble Theatre in New York; Jennifer, *The Ferry,* CAC Second Stage, New York City; Patsy Ann and Catherine, *The Girl at the Dance,* Blank Theatre, Los Angeles; Ophelia, *Hamlet,* Manhattan Playhouse, New York City; and Stella, *A Streetcar Named Desire,* Sylvia and Danny Kaye Playhouse, New York City.

RECORDINGS

Videos:

Voice of Amy Scheckenhausen, *Grand Theft Auto: Vice City* (video game; also known as *Vice City*), Rockstar Games, 2002.

(As Leyna Juliet Weber) Voice of Gina, *Midnight Club II* (video game), Rockstar Games/Take2 Interactive, 2003.

Appeared in the music video "Everybody" by Kanye West, Fonzworth Bentley, and Andre, 2000.

WRITINGS

Film Scripts; Short Films:

Speeding Ticket, Working Bug Media, 2008.
Taboo, Working Bug Media, 2008.
Donation, Working Bug Media, 2009.
Parking Spot, Working Bug Media, 2009.

Internet Series:

Road to the Altar, 2009.

OTHER SOURCES

Electronic:

Leyna Weber Official Site, http://www.leynaj.com, June 11, 2010.
Working Bug Media, http://www.workingbug.com, June 11, 2010.

WEBSTER, Derek

PERSONAL

Education: California Institute of the Arts, B.F.A., 1993.

Addresses: *Agent*—Progressive Artists Agency, 1041 North Formosa Ave., Suite 194, West Hollywood, CA 90046. *Manager*—Main Title Entertainment, 8383 Wilshire Blvd., Suite 408, Beverly Hills, CA 90211.

Career: Actor and voice performer. Neurotic Young Urbanites, member of acting company, beginning c. 1994.

CREDITS

Television Appearances; Series:

Rollie Jordan, *NightMan,* syndicated, 1997–98.
Jigsaw, 2001.
Dr. Carl Belle, *Mental,* Fox, 2009.

Television Appearances; Movies:

The Return of Ironside, NBC, 1993.
Lowell, *Childhood Sweetheart?,* CBS, 1997.
Steve James, *Ring of Death,* Spike TV, 2008.

Television Appearances; Pilots:

Lieutenant Brown, *Stargate SG–1: Children of the Gods* (also known as *Stargate SG–1*), c. 1997.
Raleigh Jordan, *NightMan,* syndicated, 1997.
Deputy Jaffe, *Supernatural,* The WB, 2005.
Charlie Pratt, *K–Ville,* Fox, 2007.
Dr. Carl Belle, *Mental,* Fox, 2009.
Richard Tunick (some sources cite Eugene Tunick), *Edgar Floats,* ABC, 2010.

Television Appearances; Episodic:

Derek, "The Accused," *Class of '96,* 1993.
Lieutenant Sanders, "Gambit: Part 1," *Star Trek: The Next Generation* (also known as *Star Trek: TNG*), syndicated, 1993.
Corbett, "Whale Song," *SeaQuest DSV* (also known as *SeaQuest 2032*), NBC, 1994.
Richard Scott, "The Sea Wasp," *M.A.N.T.I.S.,* Fox, 1995.
Client, "Just Say No," *Party Girl,* Fox, 1996.
Reporter, "Fashion Show," *The Nanny,* CBS, 1996.
Dr. Tarloff, "Sleeping Beauty," *The Sentinel,* UPN, 1997.
David, "Mirror Image," *Promised Land,* CBS, 1998.
Oscar Parrish, "The Local Weather," *Sports Night,* ABC, 2000.
Officer Kenny Grant, "Survival of the Fittest," *ER,* NBC, 2001.
Gunnery Sergeant Smith, "Dog Robber: Part 2," *JAG,* CBS, 2001.
"Zol Zein Gezint," *Strong Medicine,* Lifetime, 2001.
"Eye of the Storm," *Providence,* NBC, 2002.
Cord, "Untouchables," *Hunter,* NBC, 2003.
Captain Hanson, "Doctor Germ," *Threat Matrix,* ABC, 2003.
FBI agent, "Family Dynamics," *Everwood,* The WB, 2004.
Calvin Parker, "Colonel Knowledge," *NYPD Blue* (also known as *N.Y.P.D.*), ABC, 2004.
Major Joe Sacco, "Missing," *Navy NCIS: Naval Criminal Investigative Service* (also known as *NCIS* and *NCIS: Naval Criminal Investigative Service*), CBS, 2004.
Captain Stanley Ellis, "This Just In from Baghdad," *JAG,* CBS, 2004.
Captain Stanley Ellis, "Death at the Mosque," *JAG,* CBS, 2005.
Art Gadway, "Of Mice and Lem," *The Shield,* FX Network, 2006.
Marine Captain Stengel, "Dead and Unburied," *Navy NCIS: Naval Criminal Investigative Service* (also known as *NCIS* and *NCIS: Naval Criminal Investigative Service*), CBS, 2006.
Lawyer, "Aftermath," *Criminal Minds,* CBS, 2006.

Wendell Sutherland, "Reefer," *Nip/Tuck,* FX Network, 2006.

Uniformed cop, "The Killer in the Concrete," *Bones,* Fox, 2007.

Dave Rosso, "Crash," *Crossing Jordan,* NBC, 2007.

Detective Cooper, "You're Being Watched," *The Nine,* ABC, 2007.

Charlie Pratt, "No Good Deed," *K–Ville,* Fox, 2007.

Charlie Pratt, "Flood, Wind, and Fire," *K–Ville,* Fox, 2007.

Dr. Derek Taylor, *Days of Our Lives* (also known as *Cruise of Deception: Days of Our Lives, Days,* and *DOOL*), NBC, 2008.

Paul Miller, "Waiting for That Day," *Eli Stone,* ABC, 2008.

Dr. Giles Bromfield, "The Mighty Rogues," *Boston Legal,* ABC, 2008.

Dr. Robert Langley, "Bombshell," *CSI: Miami,* CBS, 2008.

Eric Barnett, "Hair Apparent," *Raising the Bar,* TNT, 2009.

Mr. Anderson, "Invest in Love," *Grey's Anatomy,* ABC, 2009.

Appeared as Jared Everett, *Family Law,* CBS; voice of the commander, "Snoot's New Squat," *Snoot;* also voice performer in *2 Stupid Dogs* (animated).

Film Appearances:

(Uncredited) Venarius's man, *Enter the Ninja* (also known as *Ninja I*), Warner Bros., 1981.

Croupier, *Strapless,* Miramax, 1990.

Black and White, 1992.

One of Joe Robbins's pals, *Short Cuts,* Fine Line, 1993.

Lieutenant Brown, *Stargate,* Metro–Goldwyn–Mayer, 1994.

Sky crane pilot, *Independence Day* (also known as *ID4*), Twentieth Century–Fox, 1996.

Darryl, *Sweet Jane,* Phaedra Cinema, 1998.

Utah captain, *Godzilla,* TriStar, 1998.

First police officer, *Kids in America,* Launchpad Releasing/Slowhand Cinema Releasing, 2006.

Long Shot, *Flight of the Living Dead: Outbreak on a Plane,* New Line Home Video, 2007.

Cal Dunning, *Extraordinary Measures,* CBS Films, 2010.

Stage Appearances:

Appeared in the title role, *Othello,* and as Prospero, *The Tempest;* also appeared in *Alone at the Beach, The Boys Next Door, Etta Jenks, The Myth of More, Private Eyes, Rope,* and *Twelfth Night,* all Neurotic Young Urbanites, Powerhouse Theatre, Santa Monica, CA.

RECORDINGS

Videos:

Dr. Zoetrope, *Josh Kirby ... Time Warrior: Chapter 1, Planet of the Dino–Knights* (also known as *Dino Knights: Josh Kirby ... Time Warrior!*), Full Moon Entertainment/Kushner–Locke/Paramount, 1995.

Dr. Zoetrope, *Josh Kirby ... Time Warrior: Chapter 2, the Human Pets,* Full Moon Entertainment, 1995.

Dr. Zoetrope, *Josh Kirby ... Time Warrior: Chapter 3, Trapped on Toyworld,* Full Moon Entertainment, 1995.

Dr. Zoetrope, *Josh Kirby ... Time Warrior: Chapter 4, Eggs from 70 Million B.C.,* Paramount Home Video, 1995.

Dr. Zoetrope, *Josh Kirby ... Time Warrior: Chapter 5, Journey to the Magic Cavern,* Paramount Home Video, 1995.

Dr. Zoetrope, *Josh Kirby ... Time Warrior: Chapter 6, Last Battle for the Universe,* Paramount Home Video, 1996.

(English–language version) Voice of Captain Harlock, *Queen Emeraldas* (animated), Selecta Vision, 1998.

WEIXLER, Jess 1981–
(Jessica Weixler)

PERSONAL

Full name, Jessica Weixler; born June 8, 1981, in Louisville, KY; father, an art retoucher. *Education:* Graduated from The Juilliard School, 2003; attended A Guthrie Experience for Actors in Training, Guthrie Theater, 2002.

Addresses: *Agent*—Rhonda Price, The Gersh Agency, 41 Madison Ave., 33rd Floor, New York, NY 10010. *Manager*—Mimi DiTrani, Schiff Company, 9465 Wilshire Blvd., Suite 480, Beverly Hills, CA 90212. *Publicist*—Melissa Raubvogel, Baker Winokur Ryder, 825 Eighth Ave., Worldwide Plaza, New York, NY 10019.

Career: Actress and writer. Former member of Chamber Singers.

Awards, Honors: Named most talented, Atherton High School, Louisville, KY, c. 1999; Special Jury Prize, dramatic category, Sundance Film Festival, and Breakthrough Award nomination, Gotham awards, Independent Feature Project, both 2007, for *Teeth;* named the new indie queen and one of the fourteen New Yorkers you need to know, *New York* magazine, 2009.

CREDITS

Film Appearances:

Cowgirl, *Little Manhattan,* Twentieth Century–Fox, 2005.

Jordan Gallagher, *The Big Bad Swim,* Four Act Films, 2006.

Dawn O'Keefe, *Teeth,* Roadside Attractions, 2007.

Denise, *Goodbye Baby,* Gigantic Pictures/Renart Films/Cinevolve Studios, 2007.

Alex, *Alexander the Last,* IFC Films, 2009.

Amy, *As Good as Dead* (also known as *Dark Side*), Eclectic Pictures/Major Motion Pictures/First Line Entertainment/Millennium Films, 2009.

Carrie, *Today's Special* (also known as *The Nosferatu Project, 7 to the Palace,* and *The Untitled Aasif Mandvi Feature Project*), Inimitable Pictures/Sweet180, 2009.

Sophie Sullivan, *Welcome to Academia,* 2009.

Vandy, *Peter and Vandy,* Strand Releasing, 2009.

Clover, *The Lie,* Perception Media, 2010.

Julie, *A Woman,* Bidou Pictures, 2010.

Madison, *Periphery,* Red Elephant Films/Matinee Productions, 2010.

Tammy, *Audrey the Trainwreck,* Zero Trans Fat Productions, 2010.

Television Appearances; Awards Presentations:

The 17th Annual Gotham Awards, Documentary Channel, 2007.

Television Appearances; Episodic:

Martha Skulnick, "Blind Faith," *Hack,* CBS, 2003.

Caroline Boyle, *Guiding Light* (also known as *The Guiding Light*), CBS, 2003.

Nikki, "Do or Die," *Everwood* (also known as *Our New Life in Everwood*), The WB, 2004.

Amy Buckley, "In the Wee Small Hours: Part 2," *Law & Order: Criminal Intent* (also known as *Law & Order: CI*), NBC, 2005.

Rose, *One Life to Live* (also known as *Between Heaven and Hell, OLTL,* and *One Life to Live: The Summer of Seduction*), ABC, 2006.

Herself, *Up Close with Carrie Keagan,* 2008, 2009.

Herself, "Good Hair/Peter and Vandy," *Moving Pictures Live* (also known as *Moving Pictures Live!*), 2009.

Laura Green, "The Glory That Was ...," *Law & Order: Criminal Intent* (also known as *Law & Order: CI*), NBC, 2009.

Carrie Newton, "Brilliant Disguise," *Law & Order* (also known as *Law & Order Prime*), NBC, 2010.

Mandy Sutton, "An Everlasting Love," *Medium* (also known as *Ghost and Crime* and *A medium*), CBS, 2010.

Stage Appearances; as Jessica Weixler:

Angela, *The King Stag,* The Juilliard School, Drama Theatre, New York City, 2003.

Chorus member, *The Trojan Women,* The Juilliard School, Studio 301, New York City, 2003.

Appeared in various productions of The Juilliard School; member of Atherton High School's River City Players, c. 1990s.

Stage Work:

House staff member, *Beckett Shorts,* XO Projects and Division 13, The Old American Can Factory, Brooklyn, New York City, 2003.

RECORDINGS

Video Games:

Voice of Amy Buckley, *Law & Order: Criminal Intent* (also known as *Law & Order: Criminal Intent—The Video Game*), Legacy Interactive, 2005.

WRITINGS

Screenplays; with Others:

Alexander the Last, IFC Films, 2009.

The Lie (based on a short story by T. Coraghessan Boyle), Perception Media, 2010.

OTHER SOURCES

Periodicals:

New York, January 11, 2009.

New York Daily News, January 12, 2008.

Electronic:

Under the Radar, http://www.undertheradar.com, October 9, 2009.

WHALEY, Frank 1963–
(Frank Whalley)

PERSONAL

Born July 20, 1963, in Syracuse, NY; son of Robert W. and Josephine (maiden name, Timilione) Whaley; brother of Robert Whaley (a musician, composer, and actor); married Heather Bucha (a playwright and actress), May 5, 2001; according to some sources, divorced); children: two. *Education:* State University of New York at Albany, B.A., 1985; trained for the stage at Actors Studio, New York City.

Addresses: *Agent*—Jeff Witjas, Agency for the Performing Arts, 405 South Beverly Dr., Beverly Hills, CA 90212.

Career: Actor, musician, director, and writer. Naked Angels (theatre company), New York City, founding member of company; Malaparte Theatre Company, founding member. The Niagras (band), cofounder and drummer.

Awards, Honors: Young Artist Award nomination (with others), outstanding youth ensemble in a motion picture, 1994, for *Swing Kids;* nomination for Grand Jury Prize, dramatic category, and Waldo Salt Screenwriting Award, both Sundance Film Festival, and nomination for Open Palm Award, Gotham Awards, all 1999, for *Joe the King;* Feature Film Award, best actor, New York International Independent Film and Video Festival, 2001, for *Pursuit of Happiness;* Festival Achievement Award, Stony Brook Film Festival, 2002.

CREDITS

Film Appearances:

Young Francis Phelan, *Ironweed,* TriStar, 1987.

Younger Archie "Moonlight" Graham, *Field of Dreams* (also known as *Shoeless Joe*), Universal, 1989.

Boy, *Little Monsters* (also known as *Little Ghost Fighters*), Metro–Goldwyn–Mayer, 1989.

Timmy, *Born on the Fourth of July,* Universal, 1989.

Steve Bushak, *The Freshman,* TriStar, 1990.

Michael Latchmer, *Cold Dog Soup,* 1990.

Robby Kreiger, *The Doors,* TriStar, 1991.

Jim Dodge, *Career Opportunities* (also known as *One Wild Night*), Universal, 1991.

Lee Harvey Oswald imposter (in director's cut only), *JFK,* Warner Bros., 1991.

Archer Sloan, *Back in the U.S.S.R.,* Twentieth Century–Fox, 1992.

Paul "Father" Mundy, *A Midnight Clear,* InterStar Releasing, 1992.

Young kid, *Hoffa,* Twentieth Century–Fox, 1992.

Arvid, *Swing Kids,* Buena Vista, 1993.

Brett, *Pulp Fiction,* Miramax, 1994.

Guy, *Swimming with Sharks* (also known as *The Boss, The Buddy Factor, The Director,* and *The Producer*), Trimark Pictures, 1994.

Frank, *I.Q.,* Paramount, 1994.

Archie Landrum, *Homage,* Arrow Releasing, 1995.

(As Frank Whalley) *Cannes Man* (also known as *Canne$ Man, Cannes Player,* and *Con Man*), Rocket Pictures Home Video, 1996.

Giles Prentice, *Broken Arrow,* Twentieth Century–Fox, 1996.

(In archive footage) Brett, *You're Still Not Fooling Anybody,* 1997.

Skee–ball Weasel, *Went to Coney Island on a Mission from God ... Be Back by Five,* Phaedra Cinema, 1998.

Brett Conway, *Curtain Call* (also known as *Later Life*), Ardustry Home Entertainment, 1999.

(Uncredited) Angry guy who Bob Henry owes money to, *Joe the King* (also known as *Joe Henry* and *Pleasant View Avenue*), Trimark Pictures, 1999.

(Uncredited) Narrator, *Two Family House,* Lions Gate Films, 2000.

Franky Syde, *Glam,* Storm Entertainment, 2001.

Alan Oliver, *Pursuit of Happiness,* Showcase Entertainment, 2001.

Jimmy O'Brien (title role), *The Jimmy Show,* First Look Pictures, 2002.

Lynny Barnum, *Chelsea Walls* (also known as *Chelsea Hotel*), Lions Gate Films, 2002.

(Uncredited) Ralph Mandy, *Red Dragon,* Metro–Goldwyn–Mayer, 2002.

Chad, *A Good Night to Die,* Regent Entertainment, 2003.

(Uncredited) Battle of the Bands director, *The School of Rock,* Paramount, 2003.

Prison guard, *The System Within,* First Look International, 2006.

Chuck Sereika, *World Trade Center,* Paramount, 2006.

Himself, *'Tis Autumn: The Search for Jackie Paris* (documentary), Kinosmith, 2006, Outsider Pictures, 2007.

Harris, *The Hottest State,* THINKFilm, 2007.

Brent Sykes, *Crazy Eights* (also known as *6+*), After Dark Films, 2007.

Wade Chandling, *Cherry Crush,* First Look International, 2007.

Mason, *Vacancy,* Screen Gems, 2007.

Les, *New York City Serenade* (also known as *NYC Serenade*), Anchor Bay Entertainment, 2007.

Jittery bodyguard, *Drillbit Taylor* (also known as *Drillbit Taylor: Budget Bodyguard*), Paramount, 2008.

Duncan, *The Cell 2,* New Line Home Video, 2009.

Aaron, *As Good as Dead,* VVS Films, 2010.

Film Director:

Joe the King (also known as *Joe Henry* and *Pleasant View Avenue*), Trimark Pictures, 1999.

The Jimmy Show, First Look Pictures, 2002.

New York City Serenade (also known as *NYC Serenade*), Anchor Bay Entertainment, 2007.

Film Work; Other:

Associate producer, *Homage,* Arrow Releasing, 1995.

Television Appearances; Series:

Bob Jones, *Buddy Faro,* CBS, 1998.

Christopher Wey and future guy, *The Dead Zone* (also known as *The Dark Half* and *Stephen King's "Dead Zone"*), USA Network, 2003–2004.

Television Appearances; Movies:

Arnie Woods, *Unconquered* (also known as *Invictus*), CBS, 1989.

Joey, *Flying Blind,* NBC, 1990.

James, "To Dance with the White Dog," *Hallmark Hall of Fame,* CBS, 1993.

Lee Harvey Oswald/Alik, *Fatal Deception: Mrs. Lee Harvey Oswald,* NBC, 1993.

Walter Cooper, *The Desperate Trail,* TNT, 1995.

Mickey Jelke, *Cafe Society,* Showtime, 1995.

Joey, *The Winner,* The Movie Channel, 1996.

Malcolm Garvey, *Bombshell,* Sci–Fi Channel, 1996.

Cole, "My Brother's Keeper" segment, *Dead Man's Gun,* Showtime, 1997.

Brian, *Retroactive* (also known as *Reverse*), HBO, 1997.

Medic Chamberlain, *When Trumpets Fade* (also known as *Hamburger Hill 2*), HBO, 1998.

Bishop, *The Wall,* Showtime, 1998.

Brew master, *Detective* (also known as *Arthur Hailey's "Detective"*), Lifetime, 2005.

George Bolen, *Mrs. Harris,* HBO, 2005.

Richie Greene, *Where There's a Will,* Hallmark Channel, 2006.

Bill Nack, *Ruffian,* ABC, 2007.

Television Appearances; Specials:

Jeff Dillon, "Seasonal Differences," *ABC Afterschool Specials,* ABC, 1987.

Scott McNichol, "Soldier Boys," *CBS Schoolbreak Specials,* CBS, 1987.

Voice of Alexander Graham Bell, "The Telephone," *The American Experience,* PBS, 1997.

Outer Limits Farewell Tribute, Showtime, 2000.

Sun Gods, ABC, 2002.

(Uncredited; in archive footage) *"Pulp Fiction" on a Dime: A 10th Anniversary Retrospect,* Independent Film Channel, 2004.

(In archive footage) Brett, *Boffo! Tinseltown's Bombs and Blockbusters,* HBO, 2006.

(In archive footage) Brett, *Dialogos de cine,* 2008.

Television Appearances; Pilots:

Sonny Day, *Life on the Flipside* (also known as *Homeward Bound* and *Pop Rock*), NBC, 1988.

Bad News Mr. Swanson, FX Channel, 2001.

Marriage, HBO, 2004.

Television Appearances; Miniseries:

Allen Kogan, *Shake, Rattle, and Roll: An American Love Story* (also known as *Shake, Rattle, and Roll*), CBS, 1999.

Television Appearances; Episodic:

Evicted boy, "The Road Back," *Spenser: For Hire,* 1987.

Press, "The Child Broker," *The Equalizer,* 1988.

Himself, "Super Robby," *The State,* 1995.

Henry Marshall, "The Conversion," *The Outer Limits* (also known as *The New Outer Limits*), Showtime, 1995.

Oddville, MTV, 1997.

Zig Fowler and Cliff Unger, "Zig Zag," *The Outer Limits* (also known as *The New Outer Limits*), Showtime, 2000.

"Time Is on My Side," *Strange Frequency,* VH1, 2001.

John McDowell, "Access Nation," *Law & Order,* NBC, 2002.

Martin Donner, "Future Trade," *The Twilight Zone,* UPN, 2002.

Mitch Godel, "Eosphoros," *Law & Order: Criminal Intent* (also known as *Law & Order: CI*), NBC, 2004.

Jeffrey White, "Chained," *Navy NCIS: Naval Criminal Investigative Service* (also known as *NCIS* and *NCIS: Naval Criminal Investigative Service*), CBS, 2004.

Pete Hagen, "Lewis Needs a Kidney," *Curb Your Enthusiasm,* HBO, 2005.

Robert, "Who Ya Gonna Call?," *Psych,* USA Network, 2006.

Frankie Cox, "Brotherly Love," *Boston Legal,* ABC, 2007.

Mr. X, "Mirror Mirror," *House M.D.* (also known as *Dr. House* and *House*), Fox, 2007.

Navy Commander Grant Marcus, "PTSD," *Law & Order: Special Victims Unit* (also known as *Law & Order: SVU* and *Special Victims Unit*), NBC, 2008.

Miles, "Disarmed and Dangerous," *CSI: Crime Scene Investigation* (also known as *C.S.I.* and *CSI: Las Vegas*), CBS, 2009.

Mr. Sparks, "Blackout!," *Ugly Betty,* ABC, 2010.

Stage Appearances:

Cob, *Tigers Wild,* Playhouse 91, New York City, 1986.

Andrew, *The Years,* Manhattan Theatre Club Stage I, New York City, 1993.

Jimmy Bonaparte, *Veins and Thumbtacks,* Malaparte Theatre Company, Theatre Row Theatre, New York City, 1994.

Jacob, *Hesh,* Malaparte Theatre Company, Theatre Row Theatre, 1994.

Tom Casey, *The Great Unwashed,* Malaparte Theatre Company, Theatre Row Theatre, 1994.

Peter Hogancamp, *The Size of the World,* Circle Repertory Company, Circle in the Square, New York City, 1996.

Benny, "Crazy Eights," *The 24 Hour Plays 2003,* American Airlines Theatre, New York City, 2003.

Mike, *A Lie of the Mind,* New Group, Acorn Theatre, New York City, 2010.

Also appeared in a production of *Good Evening.*

Stage Director:

Gin–Jazz–Love–Drama, Rich Forum Theatre, Stamford, CT, 2003.

RECORDINGS

Videos:

Himself, *The Road of Excess,* 1997.

Field of Dreams: Passing Along the Pastime, Universal, 2004.

Con Man with a Heart of Gold, Echo Bridge Home Entertainment, 2006.

Audio Books:
Born to Steal: When the Mafia Hit Wall Street, by Gary Weiss, Warner Books, 2003.

WRITINGS

Screenplays:
Joe the King (also known as *Joe Henry* and *Pleasant View Avenue*), Trimark Pictures, 1999.
The Jimmy Show, First Look Pictures, 2002.
New York City Serenade (also known as *NYC Serenade*), Anchor Bay Entertainment, 2007.

OTHER SOURCES

Periodicals:
Back Stage, April 5, 1996, p. 5.
Entertainment Weekly, April 25, 1997, p. 81.
Madison, October, 1999, pp. 32–33.

WHALLEY, Joanne 1964–
(Joanne Whalley–Kilmer)

PERSONAL

Born August 25, 1964, in Salford, Manchester, England; married Val Kilmer (an actor), February 28, 1988 (divorced February 1, 1996); children: Jack, Mercedes.

Addresses: *Agent*—Creative Artists Agency, 9830 Wilshire Blvd., Beverly Hills, CA 90212; ICM, Oxford House, 76 Oxford St., London W1N OAX, England. *Publicist*—PYR PR, 139 S. Beverly Dr., Suite 230, Beverly Hills, CA 90212. *Manager*—Catch 23 Management, 100 N. Crescent Dr., Suite 323, Beverly Hills, CA 90210.

Career: Actress. Member of the group Cindy & The Saffrons, early 1980s.

Awards, Honors: Olivier Award nomination, best actress, 1985; TV Award nomination, best actress, British Academy of Film and Television Arts, 1986, for *Edge of Darkness; Theatre World* Award, 1989, for *What the Butler Saw.*

CREDITS

Film Appearances:
Groupie, *Pink Floyd—The Wall* (also known as *The Wall*), Metro–Goldwyn–Mayer/United Artists, 1982.

Christine, *Dance with a Stranger,* Twentieth Century–Fox, 1985.
Mary Hall, *The Good Father,* Skouras Pictures, 1986.
Cheryl, *No Surrender,* Norstar, 1986.
Sorsha, *Willow,* Metro–Goldwyn–Mayer/United Artists, 1988.
(As Joanne Whalley–Kilmer) Anna, *Popielusko* (also known as *To Kill a Priest, Zabic ksiedza,* and *Le complot*), Columbia, 1989.
(As Joanne Whalley–Kilmer) Christine Keeler, *Scandal,* Miramax, 1989.
(As Joanne Whalley–Kilmer) Fay Forrester, *Kill Me Again,* Metro–Goldwyn–Mayer/United Artists, 1989.
(As Joanne Whalley–Kilmer) Claire Varrens, *Navy SEALS,* Orion, 1990.
(As Joanne Whalley–Kilmer) Beth Scoular, *The Big Man: Crossing the Line* (also known as *The Big Man* and *Crossing the Line*), Miramax, 1991.
(As Joanne Whalley–Kilmer) Jenny Scott, *Shattered* (also known as *Plastic Nightmare*), 1991.
(As Joanne Whalley–Kilmer) Natalie Tate, *Storyville,* Twentieth Century–Fox, 1992.
(As Joanne Whalley–Kilmer) Celia Adekunle, *A Good Man in Africa,* Gramercy, 1994.
(As Joanne Whalley–Kilmer) Colleen "Callie" Harland, *Mother's Boys* (also known as *Kodliche Absichten*), Dimension Films, 1994.
(As Joanne Whalley–Kilmer) Katherine Coleridge, *The Secret Rapture,* Castle Hill, 1994.
(As Joanne Whalley–Kilmer) Valerie Alston, *Trial by Jury,* Warner Bros., 1994.
Lorelei 'Lori,' *The Man Who Knew Too Little* (also known as *Agent Null Null Nix*), Warner Bros., 1997.
Natalie Crane, *The Guilty,* 2000.
Caroline Henshow, *Breathtaking,* IAC Film, 2000.
Mary, *Before You Go,* Capitol, 2002.
Jessie Eastwood, *Virginia's Run,* Virginia's Run Productions, 2002.
Luna, *The Californians,* Fabrication Films, 2005.
Maggie, *Played,* Lions Gate Films, 2006.
Liz, *44 Inch Chest,* Image Entertainment, 2009.
Agatha McNaughton, *Golf in the Kingdom,* Lightning Entertainment, 2010.

Television Appearances; Series:
Angela Read, *Emmerdale Farm* (also known as *Emmerdale*), YTV, 1977.
Sarah Hughes, *How We Used to Live,* 1978–79.
Ingrid Rothwell, *A Kind of Loving,* 1982.

Television Appearances; Movies:
Molly McLeod, *Joby,* 1975.
Doris, *The One and Only Phyllis Dixey* (also known as *Peek–A–Boo*), 1978.
Mary, *Noddy,* 1981.
Fan, *A Christmas Carol,* CBS, 1984.

Jackie, *Will You Love Me Tomorrow* (also known as *Screen Two: Will You Love Me Tomorrow*), 1987.

(As Joanne Whalley–Kilmer) Beatrice, *A TV Dante: The Inferno Cantos I–VIII* (also known as *A TV Dante* and *Dante: The Inferno*), 1989.

Miranda, *A Texas Funeral*, Starz!, 1999.

Ruby Miller, *Run the Wild Fields*, Showtime, 2000.

Jess, *40,* Channel 4, 2003.

Tess Palmer, *Child of Mine*, 2005.

Katy Adair, *Life Line*, BBC, 2007.

Marion Price, *Diverted*, 2009.

Also appeared in *A Quiet Life.*

Television Appearances; Miniseries:

Emma Craven, *Edge of Darkness*, BBC and syndicated, 1985.

Nurse Mills, *The Singing Detective*, BBC1, then *Channel Crossings*, PBS, 1988.

(As Joanne Whalley–Kilmer) Scarlett O'Hara (title role), *Scarlett*, CBS, 1994.

Title role, *Jackie Bouvier Kennedy Onassis*, CBS, 2000.

Queen Mary, *The Virgin Queen* (also known as *Elizabeth I: The Virgin Queen*), PBS, 2005.

Patricia Nash, *The Flood*, Ion Television, 2007.

Television Appearances; Specials:

(As Joanne Whalley–Kilmer) *CBS Sneak Peek II*, CBS, 1994.

Willow: The Making of an Adventure, 1988.

Television Appearance; Episodic:

Customer in Sylvia's Separates, *Coronation Street* (also known as *Corrie* and *The Street*), CBC and ITV, 1976.

Janice Scott, "The Right of Every Woman," *Crown Court*, Granada Television, 1976.

Linda Mason, "A Man with Everything," *Crown Court*, Granada Television, 1978.

Madge, "Words Fail Me," *Omnibus*, 1979.

Little Red Riding Hood, "The Brothers Grimm," *Omnibus*, 1979.

Maureen Maskell, "Shot Gun," *Juliet Bravo*, BBC, 1980.

Lindsey, "Too Close to the Edge," *ITV Playhouse*, 1980.

"And Mum Came Too," *Scene*, 1980.

Nancy, "The Trouble with Women," *The Gaffer*, 1981.

Assistant travel agent, *Coming Home*, 1981.

Dany, "Dany," *The Gentle Touch*, 1982.

Ulla, "The Visiting Fireman," *Reilly: Ace of Spies*, PBS, 1983.

Christine Bolton, "Always Leave Them Laughing," *Bergerac*, BBC, 1983.

Laura Fox, "Jobs for the Girls," *Hold the Back Page*, 1986.

(Uncredited) *Troldspejlet* (also known as *Magic Mirror*), 1989.

(As Joanne Whalley–Kilmer), *The Word*, 1990.

Karen Donovan, "Extreme Aggressor," *Criminal Minds*, CBS, 2005.

Voice of Sarya/Emerald Empress/Tinya Wazzo/Phantom Girl, "Far from Home," *Justice League* (animated; also known as *JL* and *Justice League Unlimited*), Cartoon Network, 2006.

Carolyn, "If You're Seeing This Tape," *Unknown Sender*, 2008.

Television Appearances; Pilots:

Travel agent, *Coming Home*, 1981.

Television Appearances; Other:

Appeared in *Save Your Kisses.*

Stage Appearances:

Maria, *Bows and Arrows*, Young Writers' Festival, Royal Court Theatre, London, 1982.

Rita, *Rita, Sue, and Bob Too*, Young Writers' Festival, Royal Court Theatre, 1982.

Gilly Brown, *The Genius*, English Stage Company, Royal Court Theatre, 1983.

Title role, *Kate*, Bush Theatre, London, 1983.

Coquart and Esther van Gobseck, *The Crimes of Vautrin*, Joint Stock Theatre Company, Almeida Theatre, London, 1983.

June, *The Pope's Wedding*, Royal Court Theatre, 1984.

Pam, *Saved*, Royal Court Theatre, 1984.

Dewey Dell, *As I Lay Dying*, National Theatre Company, Cottesloe Theatre, London, 1985.

Bianca, *Women Beware Women*, Royal Court Theatre, 1986.

Masha, *Three Sisters*, Greenwich Theatre, London, 1987.

(As Joanne Whalley–Kilmer) Geraldine Barklay, *What the Butler Saw*, Manhattan Theatre Club, City Center Theatre, New York City, 1989.

Also appeared in *The Lulu Plays.*

RECORDINGS

Taped Readings:

Provided voice of unnamed narrator, *The Historian* by Elizabeth Kostova.

Singles:

As a member of Cindy & The Saffrons, recorded "Past, Present and Future" by the Sangri–Las, 1982, and "Terry" by Twinkle, 1983.

OTHER SOURCES

Periodicals:

People Weekly, August 7, 1995, p. 42.

Premiere, March, 1991.

Time, July 31, 1995, p. 71.
TV Guide, November 12, 1994, p. 14.
Vanity Fair, November, 1994, p. 146.

WHATELY, Kevin 1951–
(Kevin Whateley, Kevin Whatley)

PERSONAL

Born February 6, 1951, in Newcastle–upon–Tyne, England; son of Richard and Mary (maiden name, Pickering); married Madelaine Newton (an actress), April 30, 1984; children: Catherine (Kitty), Kieran. *Education:* Trained at Central School of Speech and Drama. Additional interests: Charity golf events; cricket.

Addresses: *Contact*—c/o CDA, Apartment 9, 47 Courtfield Road, London SW7 4DB, England.

Career: Actor. Appeared in television commercials, including voice work for Tesco Insurance, 2003–04, and Kellogg's Bran Flakes, 2007. Sometimes credited as Kevin Whatley or Kevin Whateley.

Awards, Honors: Pye Comedy Performance of the Year Award, 1983; Variety Club Northern Personality of the Year Award, 1990; honorary doctorate, University of Northumberland.

CREDITS

Television Appearances; Series:
Neville Hope, *Auf Wiedersehen, Pet,* Central, 1984–86, then BBC, 2002, 2004.
Detective Sergeant Lewis, *Inspector Morse,* Central and PBS, 1987–93, 1995–97, 2000.
Ray Hilton, *Look and Read,* 1988.
Dr. Jack Kerruish, *Peak Practice,* Central, 1993–95.
James "Jimmy" Griffin, *The Broker's Man,* 1997–98.
Detective Inspector Robert Lewis, *Lewis* (also known as *Inspector Lewis*), ITV and PBS, 2007—.

Also appeared in *Kevin Whately: Morse & Me,* ITV.

Television Appearances; Specials:
(Uncredited) *An Audience with Ken Dodd,* 1994.
Christmas Glory with Kiri Te Kanawa, PBS, 1998.
Interviewee, *The Last Morse,* PBS, 2001.
Interviewee, *John Thaw: An Appreciation,* Carlton, 2002.
The John Thaw Story, 2002.
Presenter, *The BAFTA TV Awards 2002,* ITV, 2002.

(In archive footage) Lewis, *Total Cops,* BBC, 2003.
Wolf, *The Legend of the Tamworth Two,* BBC, 2004.
ITV 50 Greatest Shows, ITV, 2005.
ITV 50: The Golden Years, ITV, 2005.
TV's Greatest Stars, Granada Television, 2006.
(In archive footage) Detective Inspector Robert Lewis, *Lewis ... Behind the Scenes,* ITV3, 2007.
There's Something About ... Morse, ITV, 2007.
Narrator, *The Music of Morse,* ITV, 2007.
50 Greatest TV Endings, Sky Television, 2008.
(And in archive footage) *Top of the Cops,* ITV, 2009.

Television Appearances; Movies:
Jameson Adams, *Shackleton* (also known as *Icebound in the Antarctic*), BBC, 1982.
Detective Sergeant Fletcher, *A Murder Is Announced* (also known as *Miss Marple: A Murder Is Announced*), PBS and Arts and Entertainment, 1985.
Neil Baldwin, *Night Voice,* 1990.
Steve Shepherd, *B & B,* Thames, 1992.
Ian Armstrong, *Trip Trap,* BBC, 1995.
Colin Worsfold, *Gobble,* 1996.
Geoff Meadows, *Pure Wickedness,* BBC1, 1998.
Dr. Philip Carr, *What Katy Did* (also known as *La revanche de Katy*), 1999.
Judas, *The People's Passion,* 1999.
David Bruce, *Plain Jane,* Carlton, 2001.
Neville Hope, *Comic Relief 2003: The Big Hair Do,* BBC, 2003.
Major Nigel Hurst, *Promoted to Glory,* ITV, 2003.
Jacob Copplestone, *Belonging,* ITV, 2004.
Oliver James, *Dad,* BBC, 2005.
Kevin Hill, *Footprints in the Snow,* ITV, 2005.
Jack Evans, *Who Gets the Dog?,* BBC, 2007.

Television Appearances; Episodic:
Bobby Treen, "The Partnership," *Shoestring,* 1979.
Bob Smith, "The Dig," *BBC2 Playhouse,* BBC2, 1980.
Norman Pollard, *Angels,* 1980.
Michael Hobb, "Retribution," *Strangers,* 1980.
PC Chris Evans, "Coming Back," *Juliet Bravo,* 1980.
Kevin, *Coronation Street* (also known as *Corrie* and *The Street*), Granada Television, 1981.
Alas Smith & Jones (also known as *Smith & Jones*), 1987.
Hugo Mansell, "A Bit Prickly in the Morning," *You Must Be the Husband,* 1988.
Aspel & Company, 1991.
Narrator, "Food Fights," *Q.E.D.,* 1994.
"Ooh Doctor, I Feel a Bit Peaky," *Light Lunch,* 1997.
Whatever Happened to ... Clement and La Frenais?, 1997.
Songs of Praise, 2001.
Mr. Liddy, "Neighbours," *Murder in Mind,* BBC and BBC America, 2001.
Philip Kitchener, "Crying Out Loud," *Mersey Beat,* BBC, 2001.

Philip Kitchener, "What Goes Around," *Mersey Beat,* BBC, 2001.

GMTV, ITV, 2003, 2004, 2005.

Richard & Judy, Channel 4, 2004.

This Morning (also known as *This Morning with Richard and Judy*), ITV, 2004.

Who Wants to Be a Millionaire, syndicated, 2004.

"Auf Wiedersehen, Pet," *Drama Connections,* BBC, 2005.

Today with Des and Mel, ITV, 2006.

Andrew Simson, "Congratulations," *New Tricks,* BBC, 2006.

Bus driver, *Dogtown,* 2006.

Cameron Miller, *The Children,* ITV, 2008.

The Alan Titchmarsh Show, ITV, 2008.

"Colin Dexter," *Profiling,* ITV, 2008.

"Kevin Whately," *Who Do You Think You Are?,* BBC, 2009.

Also appeared as narrator, "David and Goliath," *Bible Mysteries;* as voice of Dr. Matthews, *Hilltop Hospital* (also known as *Hopital Hilltop* and *Klinik Huegelheim*).

Film Appearances:

Hostile soldier's mate, *The Return of the Soldier,* European Classics Video, 1982.

Sam Hopkins in *Skallagrigg,* 1994.

Sergeant Hardy, *The English Patient,* Miramax, 1996.

Clive, *Paranoid,* Portman Entertainment, 2000.

Mr. Caird, *Purely Belter,* Channel Four Films, 2000.

Neville Hope, *Sunday for Sammy,* Mauron and Wareham, 2000.

Dr. Richard Herd, *Silent Cry,* Screen Media Ventures, 2002.

Voice of Akela, *Little Wolf's Book of Badness* (animated short film), 2003.

Narrator, *The Fourth King* (also known as *Der vierte Koenig*), 2005.

Stage Appearances:

Tom, *A Quaker in Cullercoats,* People's Theatre, Newcastle, England, 1972.

The Rivals, Prospect Theatre Company, Old Vic Theatre, London, 1978.

Prince Hal, *Henry IV Part 1,* Newcastle, 1981.

Andy, *Accounts,* Edinburgh, Scotland, and London, 1982.

Bad Language, Hampstead Theatre, London, 1983.

John Proctor, *The Crucible,* Leicester, England, 1989.

Daines, *Our Own Kind,* Bush Theatre, London, 1991.

Twelve Angry Men, Comedy Theatre, London, 1996.

Ray Lucas, *Snake in the Grass,* Sir Peter Hall Company, Old Vic Theatre, 1997.

Uncle Peck, *How I Learned to Drive,* Donmar Warehouse Theatre, London, 1998.

Major Tours:

Title role, *Billy Liar,* U.K. cities, 1983.

RECORDINGS

Videos:

Sergeant Lewis, *Inspector Morse: Rest in Peace,* 2000.

Taped Readings:

Appeared on the recordings *The Way through the Woods, The Jewel That Was Ours, The Daughters of Cain,* and *Death Is Now My Neighbour,* all published by Macmillan.

OTHER SOURCES

Periodicals:

Independent, January 12, 2006; April 15, 2008, p. 8.

Radio Times, January 28, 2006, pp. 14–17.

WHEATLEY, Thomas 1951–

PERSONAL

Born August, 1951, in Chelmsford, Essex, England.

Addresses: *Agent*—Evan & Reiss, 100 Fawe Park Rd., London SW15 2EA, England.

Career: Actor.

CREDITS

Television Appearances; Movies:

James Fletcher, *Honest, Decent & True,* 1986.

Joseph Mills, *Harry's Kingdom,* 1987.

Sandra's Stephen, *First and Last,* 1989.

Malcolm Turner, *Just Another Secret,* USA Network, 1989.

Stuart Whittaker, *Bambino mio* (also known as *Mon enfant*), BBC America, 1994.

Anthony, *The Vacillations of Poppy Carew,* 1995.

Half the Picture, 1996.

Inspector Groves, *The Colour of Justice,* 1999.

Superintendent Lawson, *Second Sight: Parasomnia* (also known as *Parasomnia*), PBS, 2000.

Superintendent Lawson, *Second Sight: Hide and Seek* (also known as *Hide and Seek*), PBS, 2000.

Superintendent Lawson, *Second Sight: Kingdom of the Blind* (also known as *Kingdom of the Blind*), PBS, 2000.

Francis Chibnall, *Fields of Gold,* BBC, 2002.

Patrick Lamb/James Blitz, *Justifying War: Scenes from the Hutton Enquiry,* BBC4, 2004.

Assistant Commissioner Harkness, *The Murder Room,* BBC and PBS, 2004.

Television Appearances; Specials:
Working with Pinter, 2007.

Television Appearances; Series:
Reg, *Les Girls,* 1988.

Television Appearances; Miniseries:
Registrar, *The Singing Detective,* PBS and BBC, 1988.
Francis Salk, *Campaign,* 1988.
Jan Hensmann, *Selling Hitler,* 1991.
Dickie Bird, *A Perfect Hero,* PBS, 1992.
Dr. Canivet, *Madame Bovary,* PBS, 2000.

Television Appearances; Episodic:
James Buchanan, "Man of Property," *Bust,* 1987.
Farris, "Bad Vibrations," *A Very Peculiar Practice,* 1988.
Farris, "Values of the Family," *A Very Peculiar Practice,* 1988.
Farris, "The Big Squeeze," *A Very Peculiar Practice,* 1988.
Heimi Henderson, "Mr. Jolly Lives Next Door," *The Comic Strip Presents,* 1988.
Doctor, "Visiting Time," *A Gentleman's Club,* 1988.
Doctor, "A Memorial Service," *A Gentleman's Club,* 1988.
Andrew Barker, "In It for the Monet," *Boon,* 1989.
Dennis Parker, "Trouble in Mind," *Heartbeat* (also known as *Classic Heartbeat*), 1994.
Mr. Virgil, "Blue Heaven," *Love Hurts,* 1994.
Harding, "The End User: Parts 1 & 2," *Between the Lines* (also known as *Inside the Line*), 1994.
Berens, "Damage," *The Bill,* ITV, 1995.
Sean Duncan, *The Governor,* 1995.
Dangerfield, "A Case of Coincidence: Parts 1 & 2," *Ruth Rendell Mysteries,* 1996.
Drake, "Hollow Man," *Bugs,* 1997.
Professor Hare, "The Eagle Has Landed," *Aquila,* 1997.
Professor Hare, "New #1," *Aquila,* 1998.
Douglas Fleming, "Out of Bounds," *Taggart,* 1998.
Priest, "The Pox," *Let Them Eat Cake,* 1999.
Walter Haworth, "Diminished Responsibility," *Dangerfield,* 1999.
Chief constable, "Appendix Man," *A Touch of Frost,* 1999.
Lawson, "The White Feather," *Foyle's War,* ITV and PBS, 2002.
Gleeson, "Britannia Waives the Rules," *Auf Wiedersehen, Pet,* BBC, 2004.
Robin Carr QC, "So Long, Samantha," *The Brief,* ITV, 2004.
Oliver Currie, "Another Country," *Holby City* (also known as *Holby*), BBC, 2007.
Judge Grant O'Connor, "Conviction: Judgment Day," *The Bill,* ITV, 2009.

Also appeared as Professor Hare, "Comprehension Exercise," *Aquila.*

Film Appearances:
Saunders, *The Living Daylights,* United Artists, 1987.
Mr. Kingcroft, *Where Angels Fear to Tread,* 1991.
The Reverend, *Death at a Funeral* (also known as *Sterben fuer Anfaeger*), Metro–Goldwyn–Mayer, 2007.

WIDDOWS, Connor 1992–
    (Conner Widdows, Conor Widdows)

PERSONAL

Born January 27, 1992, in Vancouver, British Columbia, Canada; son of Kathleen Widdows (a casting director); brother of Sarah Widdows (an actress).

Career: Actor.

Awards, Honors: Leo Award nomination, best supporting actor in a feature–length drama, Motion Picture Arts and Sciences Foundation of British Columbia, 2002, for *Mile Zero.*

CREDITS

Film Appearances:
Little shirtless boy, *A Feeling Called Glory* (short film), 1999.
Anthony, *Beautiful Joe* (also known as *My Beautiful Joe*), Columbia/TriStar Home Video, 2000.
Andy Malloy, *Freddy Got Fingered,* Twentieth Century–Fox, 2001.
Boy, *Say It Isn't So,* Twentieth Century–Fox, 2001.
Robbie Tyson, *Liberty Stands Still* (also known as *Sniper*), Lions Gate Films, 2002.
Will Ridley, *Mile Zero,* Cinemavault Releasing, 2002.
Young Aaron Fitz, *Go–Go Boy (Prelude)* (short film), Karma2000, 2002.
Alex Banks, *Agent Cody Banks,* Metro–Goldwyn–Mayer, 2003.
Brandon, *La La Wood,* Gold Circle Productions, 2003.
Jones, *X2* (also known as *X–Men 2, X–Men 2: X–Men United,* and *X2: X–Men United*), Twentieth Century–Fox, 2003.
Alex Banks, *Agent Cody Banks 2: Destination London,* Metro–Goldwyn–Mayer, 2004.
Kid, *The Harp* (short film), 2005, One Media, 2007.
Jones, *X–Men: The Last Stand* (also known as *X–Men: Final Decision, X–Men 3,* and *X3*), Twentieth Century–Fox, 2006.

Freshman at beach, *John Tucker Must Die,* Twentieth Century–Fox, 2006.

Television Appearances; Miniseries:

(As Conner Widdows) Jesse Keys as a child, *Taken* (also known as *Steven Spielberg Presents "Taken"*), Sci–Fi Channel, 2002.

Young James Van Praagh, *Living with the Dead* (also known as *Talking to Heaven*), CBS, 2002.

Boxey, *Battlestar Galactica* (also known as *Battlestar Galactica: The Miniseries*), Sci–Fi Channel, 2003.

Television Appearances; Movies:

Dylan Nicholson, *First Target,* TBS, 2000.

Brian Foley, *The Hostage Negotiator,* USA Network, 2001.

Bryan Peeno, *Damaged Care,* Showtime, 2002.

Television Appearances; Episodic:

Calvin Scranton, "Saturn Dreaming of Mercury," *Millennium,* Fox, 1999.

Danny, "Nightmare," *So Weird,* The Disney Channel, 1999.

Younger Cabot son, "Leviathan," *Harsh Realm,* Fox, 1999.

(As Conor Widdows) Patrick and the fourth Francis Jeffries, "The Flight of Francis Jeffries," *First Wave,* Sci–Fi Channel, 2000.

Bugler, "Bag 'Em," *Dark Angel* (also known as *James Cameron's "Dark Angel"*), Fox, 2001.

John, "A Town without Pity," *Peacemakers,* USA Network, 2003.

Boxey, "Bastille Day," *Battlestar Galactica* (also known as *BSG*), Sci–Fi Channel, 2004.

First bully, "Prey," *Smallville* (also known as *Smallville Beginnings*), The CW, 2008.

Television Appearances; Pilots:

Emile Hewitt, *The Warden,* TNT, 2001.

Kendall Ross, *The Funkhousers,* ABC, 2002.

WILLIAMS, Jim Cody

PERSONAL

Education: University of Arizona, B.F.A., 1984.

Addresses: *Agent*—House of Representatives, 1434 Sixth St., Suite 1, Santa Monica, CA 90401.

Career: Actor and stunt performer.

CREDITS

Film Appearances:

Bearded cowboy, *Bill & Ted's Excellent Adventure,* Orion, 1989.

Charlie Bacchas, *Steel Frontier,* PM Entertainment Group, 1995.

Heavy lowlife, *Trial and Error,* New Line Cinema, 1997.

(Uncredited) FBI agent (FBI Two), *Traffic,* USA Films, 2000.

Redneck, *Italian Ties* (also known as *Face to Face*), Giants Entertainment, 2001.

Billy Floydd, *The Creature of the Sunny Side Up Trailer Park,* Plaster City Productions, 2003, M.I.B., 2006.

Earl, *Torque,* Warner Bros., 2003.

Suspect, *Dark Blue,* United Artists, 2003.

Weird guy with monster truck, *Dodgeball: A True Underdog Story* (also known as *Dodgeball*), Twentieth Century–Fox, 2004.

Truck driver, *Grand Theft Parsons,* Swipe Films, 2004.

Farmer at gas station, *Species III,* Metro–Goldwyn–Mayer Home Entertainment, 2004.

Monster truck driver, *Herbie Fully Loaded,* Buena Vista, 2005.

Security guard Chip, *The Dukes of Hazzard,* Warner Bros., 2005.

Earl, *Puff, Puff, Pass,* Sony Pictures Home Entertainment, 2005.

Junior, *Confessions of an Action Star* (also known as *Sledge: The Untold Story*), 2005, Lightyear Entertainment, 2009.

BoBo, *Lies & Alibis* (also known as *The Alibi*), Sony Pictures Home Entertainment, 2006.

Cowboy, *I'm Red Fish,* Screen Media Films, 2006.

Fisherman in montage, *Pirates of the Caribbean: Dead Man's Chest* (also known as *Pirates 2* and *P.O.T.C. 2*), Buena Vista, 2006.

Ticket taker, *Dark Ride,* Lions Gate Films, 2006.

Vince the engineer, *Rails & Ties,* Warner Bros., 2007.

Salamander, *The Comebacks,* Fox Atomic, 2007.

Leslie's John, *Gardens of the Night,* City Lights Pictures, 2008.

Dougie, *Garden Party,* Roadside Attractions, 2008.

Bo, *Good Intentions,* Phase 4 Films, 2010.

Rusty Whyte, *Huntin'* (short film), 2010.

Television Appearances; Movies:

Lou Ormsby, *Desert Rats,* NBC, 1988.

Merle (some sources cite Earl), *Desperado: Badlands Justice,* NBC, 1989.

(Uncredited) Undercover police officer, *Overkill: The Aileen Wuornos Story,* ABC, 1992.

Hillbilly, *Knight Rider 2010,* UPN, 1994.

Billy Ray, *The Cherokee Kid,* HBO, 1996.

First drinker, *Blackout* (also known as *A.K.A.* and *Midnight Heat*), HBO, 1996.

Hippie store clerk, *On the Edge of Innocence,* NBC, 1997.

Rancher Sid, *Alien Avengers II* (also known as *Aliens Among Us, Roger Corman Presents "Alien Avengers II,"* and *Welcome to Planet Earth II*), The Movie Channel, 1997.

Wyatt, *Los Locos* (also known as *Los Locos: Posse Rides Again*), The Movie Channel, 1997.

Sonny, *McBride: Murder Past Midnight,* Hallmark Channel, 2005.

Tunes, *Our House,* Hallmark Channel, 2006.

Tyler, *Big Stan,* HBO, 2007.

Earl, *Hallowed Ground,* Sci–Fi Channel, 2007.

(Uncredited) Curse man, *Lower Learning,* Starz!, 2008.

Jed, *Infestation* (also known as *Big Bugs Panic*), SyFy, 2009.

Television Appearances; Pilots:
Big Jim, *1%,* HBO, 2008.

Television Appearances; Episodic:
Otis, "Fall from Grace," *The Young Riders,* ABC, 1990.

Calib, "Judgment Day," *The Young Riders,* ABC, 1991.

Jack, "A Tiger's Tale," *The Young Riders,* ABC, 1991.

Murphy, "Moody River," *Renegade,* USA Network and syndicated, 1993.

First biker, "The Houseguest," *Ellen* (also known as *These Friends of Mine*), ABC, 1994.

Roy, "The Psychic and the C–Cup," *Bakersfield P.D.,* Fox, 1994.

"Freudian Slip," *Silk Stalkings,* USA Network, 1994.

First thug, "Ceremonies of Light and Dark," *Babylon 5* (also known as *B5*), syndicated, 1996.

Grease monkey, "Stand by Your Man," *California Dreams,* NBC, 1996.

Hippie bus rider, "Nobody Walks in El Camino," *High Incident,* ABC, 1996.

Biker, "The Last Ride," *Pacific Blue,* USA Network, 1997.

Burly man, "The Church Supper," *The Simple Life,* CBS, 1998.

Contractor, "The Remodeling Show," *The Simple Life,* CBS, 1998.

Contractor, "Sara's Ex," *The Simple Life,* CBS, 1998.

Farmer, "One Day Out West," *The Magnificent Seven,* CBS, 1998.

Mr. Partridge, "Green Justice," *L.A. Heat,* TNT, 1999.

Cal Jeppy, "Invocation," *The X–Files,* Fox, 2000.

Gosny, "Games of Chance," *18 Wheels of Justice,* The Nashville Network, 2000.

Boudreau, "One Can Only Hope" (also known as "The Lottery"), *ER,* NBC, 2002.

Ed, "O Brother, Who Art Thou?," *The Drew Carey Show,* ABC, 2002.

Man, "Shades of Gray," *The District,* CBS, 2002.

Roy Peters, "Wild Ride" (also known as "Zero Disrespect"), *Robbery Homicide Division* (also known as *R.H.D./LA: Robbery Homicide Division/Los Angeles*), CBS, 2002.

Terrence, "Bullock Returns to the Camp," *Deadwood,* HBO, 2004.

Terrence, "Suffer the Little Children," *Deadwood,* HBO, 2004.

Preston, "Strays," *The Shield,* FX Network, 2004.

B–Dub, "Old Cherry Blossom Road," *Carnivale* (also known as *La feria ambulante*), HBO, 2005.

Toulouse, "Show Ghouls," *Charmed,* The WB, 2005.

Captain Happy Jack, "Pirates of the Third Reich," *CSI: Crime Scene Investigation* (also known as *C.S.I.* and *CSI: Las Vegas*), CBS, 2006.

Calvin Oats, "Traffic," *Numb3rs* (also known as *Num3ers*), CBS, 2006.

Uncle Vinky, "Fun Town," *Sons of Anarchy,* FX Network, 2008.

Modesto Bull, "Catching Out," *Criminal Minds,* CBS, 2008.

Al, "Mirror Ball," *Life,* NBC, 2009.

RECORDINGS

Videos:
Himself, *Odds & Ends,* Home Box Office Home Video, 2009.

WILLIAMS, Rosalyn Coleman
See COLEMAN, Rosalyn

WILLIAMS, Tam 1971–

PERSONAL

Full name, Tamlyn Williams; born 1971 in England; son of Simon Williams and Belinda Carroll; married Dr. Serena Bourke, September 1999. *Education:* Trained at Guildford School of Acting.

Addresses: *Agent*—Creative Artists Management, 1st Floor, 55–59 Shaftesbury Ave., London W1D 6UD, England.

Career: Actor.

CREDITS

Television Appearances; Movies:
Tony Gregg, *Cold Enough for Snow,* 1997.
Eric Spate, *Anorak of Fire,* 1998.

Television Appearances; Miniseries:
Scott Miller, *Killer Net* (also known as *Lynda La Plante's "Killer Net"*), 1998.

Television Appearances; Specials:
Todgers' Lodger, *Martin Chuzzlewit* (also known as *Charles Dickens' "Martin Chuzzlewit"*), PBS, 1995.

Television Appearances; Episodic:
(Uncredited) Schoolboy, "Remembrance of the Daleks: Part 1," *Doctor Who,* 1988.
Harry, "Sins of the Fathers: Part 1," *Silent Witness,* 1996.
Budd, "The Twenties," *A Dance to the Music of Time,* 1997.
Alex Arroyan, "Heir and the Spare," *Starhunter,* syndicated, 2004.
Charles Maltravers, "Precious Stones," *Heartbeat* (also known as *Classic Heartbeat*), ITV, 2004.
Michael/Michele, "In the Public Interest," *A Touch of Frost,* ITV, 2004.
Charles Nebley, "Enter Two Gardeners," *Rosemary & Thyme,* ITV, 2006.
Nat Adams, "About Face," *Doctors,* BBC, 2006.
Adam Bowden, "The Hands That Rock the Cradle: Parts 1 & 2," *Holby City* (also known as *Holby*), BBC, 2009.

Film Appearances:
Thomas, *Il tempo dell'amore* (also known as *Les saisons de l'amour* and *A Time to Love*), Eurozoom, 1999.
Private Eddie Macfarlane, *The Trench* (also known as *La tranchee*), Somme Productions, 1999.
James, *Friday Night In* (short film), UK Film Council, 2003.

Stage Appearances:
Rutland, son, and lieutenant, *Henry VI: The Battle for the Throne,* The Other Place, Stratford–upon–Avon, England, 1994.
Man 1 and boy 1, *The Park,* Pit Theatre, London, 1995.
Birdy, Comedy Theatre, London, 1997.
Jimmy, *Remember This,* Royal National Theatre, London, 1999.
Lucentio, *The Taming of the Shrew* and *Twelfth Night,* Courtyard Theatre, Stratford–upon–Avon, 2006.

Major Tours:
Rutland, son, and lieutenant, *Henry VI: The Battle for the Throne,* 1994.

WILLIAMSON, Felix

PERSONAL

Son of David (a writer) and Kristen (a journalist, writer, and researcher; maiden name, Loefven; different sources spell first name as Kristin and surname as Lofven) Williamson. *Education:* Graduated from the National Institute of Dramatic Art (Australia), 1991.

Addresses: *Agent*—Don Buchwald & Associates, 6500 Wilshire Blvd., Suite 2200, Los Angeles, CA 90048. *Manager*—Beth Holden–Garland, Untitled Entertainment, 1801 Century Park East, Suite 700, Los Angeles, CA 90067.

Career: Actor.

CREDITS

Film Appearances:
Alex, *Dust off the Wings,* Bombshell Films, 1997.
Wozzle, *Thank God He Met Lizzie* (also known as *The Wedding Party*), REP Distribution/First Look International, 1997.
Jerome, *Welcome to Woop Woop* (also known as *The Big Red*), Samuel Goldwyn, 1998.
(Uncredited) Private Drake, *The Thin Red Line,* Twentieth Century–Fox, 1998.
Raider, *Babe: Pig in the City* (also known as *Babe in Metropolis* and *Babe 2*), Universal, 1998.
Neil, *Strange Planet,* New Vision Films, 1999.
Geoff, *Me Myself I* (also known as *La chance de ma vie*), Hollywood Pictures/Sony Pictures Classics, 2000.
Rats, *Mr. Accident,* Metro–Goldwyn–Mayer/United Artists/Pathe, 2000.
Scott, *WillFull,* Showtime Australia/Cinemavault Releasing, 2001.
Sal Cassela, *Dirty Deeds* (also known as *Knocking Mr. Big* and *Sacre boulot*), Hoyts Distribution/DEJ Productions/Momentum Pictures, 2002, Paramount Home Video, 2003.
Bill Gennaro, *The Wannabes* (also known as *Criminal Ways*), Cinemavault Releasing, 2003.
Sinclair, *Ned,* Becker Entertainment/Ocean Pictures Pty Limited/Icon Entertainment International, 2003.
Lift man, *The Rage in Placid Lake* (also known as *Placid Lake*), Moviehouse Entertainment/Palace Films, 2004.
Commentator, *A Family Legacy* (short film), Hulahoop Films, 2005.
Father, *In a Pickle* (short film), Hulahoop Films, 2005.
Member of live action cast, *Happy Feet* (animated and live action; also released as *Happy Feet: The IMAX Experience*), Warner Bros./Village Roadshow Entertainment, 2006.
Kenneth Monk, *Haunted Echoes* (also known as *Darkness Visible*), Lightning Media, 2008.
Father, *Shock* (short film), Tropfest, 2010.

Television Appearances; Series:
Dr. John Bourke, *RAN: Remote Area Nurse,* SBS (Special Broadcasting Service), beginning 2006.

Television Appearances; Miniseries:
Murray, *A Difficult Woman,* Australian Broadcasting Corporation, 1998.
Sam Burlington, *My Brother Jack,* Ten Network, 2001.

Television Appearances; Movies:
Milton, *The Road from Coorain,* Australian Broadcasting Corporation and broadcast as part of *Masterpiece Theatre* (also known as *ExxonMobil Masterpiece Theatre, Masterpiece,* and *Mobil Masterpiece Theatre*), PBS, both 2002.
Miles Dobbie, *Go Big,* Ten Network, 2004.
Paul Keating, *Hawke,* Ten Network, 2010.

Television Appearances; Episodic:
Max Blair, "A Kiss before Dying: Parts 1 & 2," *A Country Practice,* Seven Network, 1992.
Wallis, "Speeding," *Police Rescue,* Australian Broadcasting Corporation, 1993.
Alberto Latarza, "Import/Export," *Water Rats,* Nine Network, 1997.
Alberto Latarza, "Jilted," *Water Rats,* Nine Network, 1997.
Martin Carlisle, "Short Circuit," *Murder Call,* Nine Network, 1998.
Justin Lemont, *Wildside,* Australian Broadcasting Corporation, 1998.
Bogdan Lukawski, "Vicki in Love," *Dog's Head Bay,* Australian Broadcasting Corporation, 1999.
Prince Clavor, "Look at the Princess, Part 1: A Kiss Is but a Kiss," *Farscape* (also known as *Space Chase* and *Farscape—Verschollen im All*), Sci–Fi Channel, Nine Network, and BBC, 2000.
Prince Clavor, "Look at the Princess, Part 2: I Do, I Think," *Farscape* (also known as *Space Chase* and *Farscape—Verschollen im All*), Sci–Fi Channel, Nine Network, and BBC, 2000.
Prince Clavor, "Look at the Princess, Part 3: The Maltese Crichton," *Farscape* (also known as *Space Chase* and *Farscape—Verschollen im All*), Sci–Fi Channel, Nine Network, and BBC, 2000.
David Callahan, *Home and Away,* 7 Network, multiple episodes in 2003.
Michael Stakis, "A Mere Formality," *Blue Heelers* (also known as *Boys in Blue*), Seven Network, 2004.
Dr. Ian McVay, "?," *Lost,* ABC, 2006.
Garry, "The Mole," *Stupid Stupid Man,* TV1, 2006.

Stage Appearances:
Steve Shetlebaum, *The Virgin Mim,* Wharf Theatre, Sydney, New South Wales, Australia, 2002.

WILSON, Owen 1968–
   (Owen C. Wilson)

PERSONAL

Full name, Owen Cunningham Wilson; born November 18, 1968, in Dallas, TX; son of Robert (an advertising executive and operator of a public television station) and Laura (a photographer) Wilson; brother of Andrew Wilson (an actor) and Luke Wilson (an actor, director, producer, and writer). *Education:* Attended University of Southern California; University of Texas at Austin, B.A., 1991.

Addresses: *Office*—116 North Robertson Blvd., Los Angeles, CA 90048. *Agent*—United Talent Agency, 9560 Wilshire Blvd., Suite 500, Beverly Hills, CA 90212. *Publicist*—Ina Treciokas, Slate Public Relations, 8322 Beverly Blvd., Suite 201, Los Angeles, CA 90048.

Career: Actor, producer, and writer. American Empirical Pictures, partner. Performed radio commercials for Michelob Lite beer, 2004, and for Heineken beer.

Awards, Honors: Special Award (with Wes Anderson and Luke Wilson), debut of the year, Lone Star Film and Television Awards, 1996, for *Bottle Rocket;* Lone Star Film and Television Award, 1999, and Chlotrudis Award nomination, 2000, both best screenplay (with Anderson), for *Rushmore;* Blockbuster Entertainment Award nomination, favorite supporting actor in a horror film, 2000, for *The Haunting;* Blockbuster Entertainment Award nomination, favorite supporting actor in a comedy, 2001, for *Meet the Parents;* Golden Satellite Award nomination, best supporting actor in a comedy or musical role, International Press Academy, 2001, and Blockbuster Entertainment Award nomination (Internet poll only; with Jackie Chan), favorite action team, both 2001, for *Shanghai Noon;* Academy Award nomination, Film Award nomination, British Academy of Film and Television Arts, Writers Guild of America Award nomination, Chicago Film Critics Association Award nomination, Phoenix Film Critics Society Award nomination, and Online Film Critics Society Award nomination, all best original screenplay (with Anderson), Phoenix Film Critics Society Award nomination (with others), best acting ensemble, and Golden Satellite Award nomination, best supporting actor in a comedy or musical, all 2002, for *The Royal Tenenbaums;* MTV Movie Award nomination (with Ben Stiller), best onscreen team, 2002, for *Zoolander;* MTV Movie Award nomination (with Jackie Chan), best onscreen team, 2003, for *Shanghai Knights;* Critics Choice Award nomination (with others), best acting ensemble, Broadcast Film Critics Association, 2005, for *The Life Aquatic with Steve Zissou;* Teen Choice Award nomination, choice movie actor in a comedy film, MTV Movie Award (with Carmen Electra and Amy Smart), best kiss, and MTV Movie Award nomination (with Stiller), best onscreen team, all 2004, Teen Choice Award nomination, 2004, and People's Choice Award nomination, 2005, both favorite onscreen chemistry (with Stiller), Proctor & Gamble Productions, all for *Starsky & Hutch;* MTV Movie Award nomination, best comedic performance, Teen Choice Award nomination (with Rachel McAdams), choice kiss in a movie, MTV Movie Award and People's Choice Award, both best onscreen team (with Vince Vaughn), all 2006, for *Wedding Crashers.*

CREDITS

Film Appearances:

Dignan, *Bottle Rocket* (short film), 1994.

(As Owen C. Wilson) Dignan, *Bottle Rocket,* Columbia, 1996.

Robin's date, *The Cable Guy,* Columbia/TriStar, 1996.

Gary Dixon, *Anaconda,* Columbia, 1997.

Nicky, *Permanent Midnight,* Artisan Entertainment, 1998.

Oscar Choi, *Armageddon,* Buena Vista, 1998.

(Uncredited) Edward Applebee, *Rushmore,* Buena Vista, 1998.

Vann Siegert, *The Minus Man,* Artisan Entertainment, 1999.

Monte Rapid, *Breakfast of Champions,* Buena Vista, 1999.

Luke Sanderson, *The Haunting* (also known as *La maldicion*), DreamWorks, 1999.

Roy O'Bannon, *Shanghai Noon,* Buena Vista, 2000.

Kevin Rawley, *Meet the Parents,* Universal, 2000.

Hansel McDonald, *Zoolander,* Paramount, 2001.

Eli Cash, *The Royal Tenenbaums,* Buena Vista, 2001.

Lieutenant Chris Burnett, *Behind Enemy Lines,* Twentieth Century–Fox, 2001.

Alex Scott, *I Spy,* Columbia, 2002.

Roy O'Bannon, *Shanghai Knights,* Buena Vista, 2003.

Wilbur Wright, *Around the World in 80 Days,* Buena Vista, 2004.

Ken "Hutch" Hutchinson, *Starsky & Hutch,* Warner Bros., 2004.

Jack Ryan, *The Big Bounce,* Warner Bros., 2004.

Ned Plimpton, *The Life Aquatic with Steve Zissou* (also known as *Life Aquatic*), Buena Vista, 2004.

Kevin Rawley, *Meet the Fockers,* Universal, 2004.

Neil King, *The Wendell Baker Story,* THINKFilm, 2005.

John Beckwith, *Wedding Crashers,* New Line Cinema, 2005.

Voice of Lightning McQueen, *Cars* (animated), Buena Vista, 2006.

Randy Dupree, *You, Me, and Dupree,* Universal, 2006.

(Uncredited) Jedediah, *Night at the Museum* (also known as *Night at the Museum: The IMAX Experience* and *Night Museum*), Twentieth Century–Fox, 2006.

Title role, *Drillbit Taylor* (also known as *Drillbit Taylor: Budget Bodyguard*), Paramount, 2008.

John Grogan, *Marley & Me,* Twentieth Century–Fox, 2008.

Jedediah, *Night at the Museum: Battle of the Smithsonian* (also known as *Night at the Museum: Battle of the Smithsonian—The IMAX Experience, Night at the Museum 2,* and *Night Museum 2*), Twentieth Century–Fox, 2009.

Voice of Coach Skip, *Fantastic Mr. Fox* (animated), Twentieth Century–Fox, 2009.

Voice of Marmaduke, *Marmaduke,* Twentieth Century–Fox, 2010.

Manny, *Everything You've Got,* Columbia, 2010.

Kevin Rawley, *Little Fockers,* Paramount, 2010.

Film Work:

Associate producer, *As Good As It Gets* (also known as *Old Friends*), 1997.

Executive producer, *Rushmore,* Buena Vista, 1998.

Executive producer, *The Royal Tenenbaums,* Buena Vista, 2001.

Producer, *You, Me, and Dupree,* Universal, 2006.

Television Appearances; Specials:

"I Spy," *Reel Comedy* (also known as *Comedy Central Canned Ham*), Comedy Central, 2002.

Bar Mitzvah Bash! (also known as *Comedy Central's Bar Mitzvah Bash!*), Comedy Central, 2004.

"Starsky & Hutch," *Reel Comedy* (also known as *Comedy Central Canned Ham*), Comedy Central, 2004.

"Wedding Crashers," *Reel Comedy* (also known as *Comedy Central Canned Ham*), Comedy Central, 2005.

Starz on the Set: The Life Aquatic with Steve Zissou, Starz!, 2005.

The Road to Cars, ITV, 2006.

CMT: The Greatest—Sexiest Southern Men, Country Music Television, 2006.

Comic Relief 2009, BBC, 2009.

Television Appearances; Pilots:

Voices of Heat Vision and Doug, *Heat Vision and Jack,* Fox, 1999.

Television Appearances; Episodic:

HBO First Look, HBO, multiple appearances, between 1999 and 2005.

Voice of Rhett van der Graaf, "Luanne Virgin 2.0," *King of the Hill* (animated), Fox, 2001.

Tinseltown TV, International Channel, 2004.

"Impin' with a Pippin!," *Player$,* TechTV, 2004.

4Pop, 2004.

Getaway, Nine Network, 2005, (in archive footage) 2006.

Magacine, 2005.

(Uncredited) "Here's Looking at You, Hef," *The Girls Next Door,* E! Entertainment Television, 2006.

HypaSpace (also known as *HypaSpace Daily* and *HypaSpace Weekly*), SPACE, 2006.

Corazon de ..., 2006.

Senkveld med Thomas og Harald, 2006.

Entertainment Tonight (also known as *E.T.* and *This Week in Entertainment*), syndicated, multiple appearances, beginning 2007.

Access Hollywood, syndicated, 2008.

(In archive footage) *The O'Reilly Factor,* Fox News Channel, 2008.

Le grand journal de Canal+, 2009.

TV total, 2009.

Quelli che ... il calcio, 2009.

Leader of other study group, "Investigative Journalism," *Community*, NBC, 2010.
Made in Hollywood, 2010.

Television Talk Show Guest Appearances; Episodic:
Late Night with Conan O'Brien, NBC, 1996, 2004, 2005, 2006.
Nyhetsmorgon, 1998.
Rove Live, 2000.
The Daily Show with Jon Stewart (also known as *The Daily Show* and *The Daily Show with Jon Stewart Global Edition*), Comedy Central, 2001, 2006.
"Ben Stiller and Parents," *Ruby Wax With ...*, BBC, 2003.
TRL, 2003.
Friday Night with Jonathan Ross, BBC America, 2004.
The Tonight Show with Jay Leno, NBC, 2004, 2005, 2006, 2008.
Ellen: The Ellen DeGeneres Show, syndicated, 2005.
Charlie Rose (also known as *The Charlie Rose Show*), PBS, 2005.
Richard & Judy, Channel 4, 2005.
Live with Regis and Kelly, syndicated, 2005, 2006.
Late Show with David Letterman (also known as *The Late Show* and *Letterman*), CBS, 2009.
Wetten, dass ...?, 2009.

Television Appearances; Awards Presentations:
The 2000 Blockbuster Entertainment Awards, Fox, 2000.
Presenter, *The ... Annual Academy Awards*, ABC, 2002, 2004, 2006, 2008.
Presenter, *Brit Awards 2003*, 2003.
Presenter, *The MTV Movie Awards*, MTV, 2004, 2006.
The MTV Movie Awards MTV, 2005.
Nickelodeon Kids' Choice Awards, Nickelodeon, 2009.

Television Work; Pilots:
Executive producer, *Bert & Dickie*, HBO, 2006.

RECORDINGS

Videos:
The Making of "The Haunting," 1999.
The Making of "Rushmore," 2000.
Behind the Scenes: Behind Enemy Lines, 2002.
Yeah Right!, Girl Skateboard Co., 2003.
Starsky & Hutch: A Last Look, Warner Bros., 2004.
This Is an Adventure, Criterion Collection, 2005.
Voice of Lightning McQueen, *Mater and the Ghostlight* (animated), Buena Vista Home Entertainment, 2006.
Voice of Lightning McQueen, *Cars* (video game), THQ, 2006.
Producer, *Becoming Icizzle*, Paramount, 2009.

Appeared in the music videos "God's Gonna Cut You Down" by Johnny Cash and "Start the Commotion" by the Wiseguys.

WRITINGS

Screenplays:
Bottle Rocket (short film), 1994.
(As Owen C. Wilson; with Wes Anderson) *Bottle Rocket*, Columbia, 1996.
(With Anderson) *Rushmore*, Buena Vista, 1998.
(With Anderson) *The Royal Tenenbaums*, Buena Vista, 2001.
(With Anderson) *Behind Enemy Lines*, Twentieth Century–Fox, 2001.

Television Pilots:
Bert & Dickie, HBO, 2006.

OTHER SOURCES

Books:
Newsmakers, Issue 3, Gale, 2002.

Periodicals:
Chicago Tribune, November 5, 2008.
Details, March, 1999.
Empire, September, 2000.
Entertainment Weekly, June 16, 2000, pp. 36–37.
Interview, May, 2000, p. 112.
Los Angeles, July, 1998; December, 2001, p. 90.
Los Angeles Times, December 2, 2001.
Maxim, July, 2006, pp. 112–13.
Newsweek, December 7, 1998, p. 72.
New York Post, November 25, 2001.
New York Times, January 31, 1999.
Parade, February 2, 2003, p. 8.
People Weekly, July 24, 2006, p. 70.
Playboy, July, 2005, pp. 55–60, 144.
Premiere, December, 2002, pp. 54–60, 128.
Rolling Stone, July 28, 2005, pp. 50–56.
Texas Monthly, June, 2003.
Time, December 3, 2001, p. 68; March 8, 2004, p. 70.
USA Today, May 26, 2000; August 29, 2007, p. 2D; December 9, 2008.
Us Weekly, June 19, 2000.

WINNER, Michael 1935–
    (Arnold Crust, Arnold Crust, Jr.)

PERSONAL

Full name, Michael Robert Winner; born October 30, 1935, in London, England; son of George Joseph (a company director) and Helen (maiden name, Zloty)

Winner; engaged to Geraldine Lynton–Edwards, 2008. *Education:* Downing College, Cambridge, M.A. (law and economics; with honors), 1956. *Religion:* Jewish.

Addresses: *Office*—Scimitar Films Ltd., 6–8 Sackville St., London W1X 1DD, England.

Career: Producer, director, film editor, and writer. Film and restaurant critic and columnist for British newspapers and magazines, beginning 1951; Scimitar Films Ltd., London, chair, 1957—. Michael Winner Ltd., principal. Police Memorial Trust, chair, 1984. Appeared in advertisements, including Doritos, Kenco Coffee, eSure Car Insurance, and Books for Schools.

Member: Directors Guild of Great Britain (member of council and board of trustees and chief censorship officer, 1983).

Awards, Honors: Venice Film Festival Award, 1971, for *The Nightcomers;* special award, School of Visual Arts, 1976, for contributions to education; Saturn Award nomination, best writing, Academy of Science Fiction, Fantasy, & Horror Films, 1978, for *The Sentinel;* First Prize, Cologne Film Festival, 1990; awards from San Francisco and other film festivals.

CREDITS

Film Director:
Climb Up the Wall, 1960.
Shoot to Kill, Border, 1961.
(And associate producer) *Some Like It Cool,* 1961.
(And associate producer) *Old Mac,* 1961.
Play It Cool, Allied Artists, 1962.
(And producer) *Out of the Shadow* (also known as *Murder on the Campus*), 1962.
The Cool Mikado, United Artists, 1962.
Behave Yourself, 1962.
The System (also known as *The Girl Getters*), American International Pictures, 1963.
West Eleven, Associated British, 1963.
You Must Be Joking!, Columbia, 1965.
The Jokers, Universal, 1967.
(And producer) *I'll Never Forget What's 'is Name,* Regional, 1967.
(And producer) *Hannibal Brooks,* United Artists, 1968.
The Games, Twentieth Century–Fox, 1969.
(And producer) *Lawman,* United Artists, 1970.
(And producer) *The Nightcomers,* Avco–Embassy, 1971.
(And producer) *Chato's Land,* United Artists, 1971.
Scorpio, United Artists, 1972.
The Mechanic (also known as *Killer of Killers*), United Artists, 1972.
(And producer) *The Stone Killer* (also known as *L'assassino di pietra*), Columbia, 1973.

(And producer) *Death Wish,* Paramount, 1974.
(And producer) *Won Ton Ton, the Dog That Saved Hollywood* (also known as *Won Ton Ton*), Paramount, 1975.
(And producer) *The Sentinel,* Universal, 1977.
(And producer) *The Big Sleep,* United Artists, 1978.
(And producer) *Firepower,* Associated Film Distributors, 1979.
Death Wish II, Warner Bros., 1982.
The Wicked Lady, Metro–Goldwyn–Mayer/United Artists, 1983.
(And producer) *Scream for Help,* Lorimar, 1984.
(And producer) *Death Wish 3,* Cannon, 1985.
(And producer) *Dirty Weekend,* 1987, Scimitar Films, 1992.
(And producer) *Appointment with Death,* Cannon, 1988.
(And producer) *A Chorus of Disapproval,* South Gate, 1989.
(And producer) *Bullseye!,* RCA/Columbia Pictures Home Video, 1991.
(And producer) *Parting Shots,* Michael Winner Ltd./Scimitar Films, 1998.

Also director (and producer) of *Behave Yourself, Girls, Girls, Girls, It's Magic,* and *Swiss Holiday.*

Film Producer:
Claudia (also known as *Claudia's Story*), 1985.

Film Editor; as Arnold Crust or Arnold Crust, Jr.:
The Nightcomers, Avco–Embassy, 1971.
(Uncredited) *Chato's Land,* United Artists, 1971.
(Uncredited) *Scorpio,* United Artists, 1972.
The Mechanic (also known as *Killer of Killers*), United Artists, 1972.
Firepower, Associated Film Distributors, 1979.
Death Wish II, Warner Bros., 1982.
The Wicked Lady, Metro–Goldwyn–Mayer/United Artists, 1983.
Scream for Help, 1984.
Death Wish 3, Cannon, 1985.
Dirty Weekend, 1987, Scimitar Films, 1992.
Appointment with Death, Cannon, 1988.
A Chorus of Disapproval, South Gate, 1989.
Bullseye!, 1990.
Parting Shots, 1999.

Film Appearances:
(Uncredited) *The Cool Mikado,* 1963.
Omnibus: The Last Moguls, 1986.
The director, *Calliope,* 1993.
Member of entourage, *Decadence,* 1994.
Neighbor, *Shelf Life,* H30 Films Ltd., 2000.
Vivienne Gibson–Forbes: Portrait of a Film Extra, 2002.

Stage Producer:
Nights at the Comedy, Comedy Theatre, London, 1960.
The Silence of St. Just, Gardner Centre Theatre, Brighton, England, 1971.
The Tempest, Wyndham's Theatre, London, 1974.
A Day in Hollywood/A Night in the Ukraine, Mayfair Theatre, London, 1978.

Television Work; Series:
Associated with *Dick and the Duchess,* CBS, 1957–58; and with the British series *White Hunter.*

Television Appearances; Series:
Narrator, *True Crimes* (also known as *Michael Winner's "True Crimes"*), London Weekend Television, 1990–94.

Television Appearances; Episodic:
Film Night, 1971.
The Kenny Everett Television Show, 1982.
"Oooh Er, Missus! The Frankie Howerd Story, or Please Yourselves," *Arena,* 1990.
Clive Anderson Talks Back, 1993.
Danny Baker After All, 1993.
Interviewee, *Entertainment UK,* 1993.
Notes and Queries with Clive Anderson, 1993.
The Danny Baker Show, 1994.
"Christmas in Dreamland," *Birds of a Feather,* 1994.
Have I Got News for You (also known as *HIGNFY*), BBC, 1995, 2005.
The Mrs. Merton Show, BBC, 1997.
"Crime," *Brass Eye* (also known as *Trip TV*), Channel 4, 1997.
TFI Friday (also known as *Thank Four It's Friday*), 1997.
Question Time, BBC, 1998, 1999, 2000, 2005, 2006, 2009.
Bang, Bang, It's Reeves and Mortimer, BBC2, 1999.
Casting Couch, 1999.
"Rolls–Royce Silver Shadow," *The Car's the Star,* 1999.
Clarkson, 1999.
Meet Ricky Gervais, Channel 4, 2000.
"Comic Relief's Weakest Link," *The Weakest Link,* BBC and Seven Network, 2001.
Celebrity Sleepover, 2001.
"Burt Lancaster," *The Hollywood Greats* (also known as *Hollywood Greats*), BBC1, 2002.
Shooting Stars, BBC, 2002.
God Almighty, 2003.
Liquid News, BBC, 2004.
Star Sale, 2004.
Room 101, BBC, 2004.
The Dan and Dusty Show, 2004.
Kelly, UTV, 2004.
GMTV, ITV, 2004.
The Paul O'Grady Show (also known as *The New Paul O'Grady Show*), ITV, 2004.
Breakfast with Frost, BBC1, 2004.

"The Films That Shocked Britain," *X–Rated,* Channel 5, 2004.
"The Scenes They Tried to Ban," *X–Rated,* Channel 5, 2004.
Richard and Judy, Channel 4, 2004, 2006, 2007.
This Week, BBC, 2004, 2006, 2007.
"Apprentice Celebrities," *The Apprentice,* NBC, 2005.
Calendar, 2006.
How Do You Solve a Problem Like Maria, 2006.
"Magic, Murder and Monsters: The Story of British Horror and Fantasy," *Birtish Film Forever,* BBC, 2007.
Parkinson, BBC, 2007.
Loose Women, ITV, 2007.
Happy Hour (also known as *Al Murray's Happy Hour*), Fox, 2008.
"Michael Winner," *Cash in the Celebrity Attic,* 2008.
ITV Lunchtime News, ITV, 2009.
Hotel Babylon, BBC1 and BBC America, 2009.
Al Murray's Multiple Personality Disorder, 2009.

Also appeared as a film director in an episode of *I, Camcorder;* appeared in *Legends.*

Television Appearances; Specials:
(Uncredited) *One More Audience with Dame Edna Everage,* 1988.
Sir Randolph Spence, *For the Greater Good,* 1991.
Interviewee, *The Fame Factor: The Battersea Bardot,* 1994.
(Uncredited) *Happy Birthday Shirley,* 1996.
James Bond: Shaken and Stirred, 1997.
Annie Goes to Hollywood, BBC, 2001.
Night of a Thousand Faces, BBC, 2001.
Presenter, *The British Soap Awards,* Granada Television, 2005.
Death of Celebrity, Channel 4, 2005.
Play It Again: The Panel Game, BBC, 2005.
Greatest Ever Comedy Movies, 2006.
Comic Relief: The Apprentice (also known as *Comic Relief Does the Apprentice*), 2007.
Greatest Ever Romantic Movies, Channel 5, 2007.
Brando, TCM, 2007.
Memoirs of a Cigarette, Channel 4, 2007.
Most Shocking Celebrity Moments of the 80s, 2007.
Truly, Madly, Cheaply!: British B Movies, BBC, 2008.

RECORDINGS

Videos:
Presenter, *The Diary of Jack the Ripper: Beyond Reasonable Doubt?* (documentary), 1993.
Dennis Pennis R.I.P., 1997.
Master of ceremonies, *1st Annual Directors Guild of Great Britain DGGB Awards,* 2004.
Have I Got News For You: The Best of the Guest Presenters—Volume 2, Hat Trick Productions, 2005.

WRITINGS

Screenplays:
Man with a Gun, 1958.
Climb Up the Wall, 1960.
Some Like It Cool, 1961.
Shoot to Kill, Border, 1961.
(With Maurice Browning and Lew Schwartz) *The Cool Mikado,* United Artists, 1962.
Out of the Shadow (also known as *Murder on the Campus*), 1962.
Behave Yourself, 1962.
(With Alan Hackney) *You Must Be Joking!,* Columbia, 1965.
The Jokers, Universal, 1967.
(With Tom Wright) *Hannibal Brooks,* United Artists, 1968.
(With Jeffrey Konvitz) *The Sentinel,* Universal, 1977.
The Big Sleep, United Artists, 1978.
Firepower, Associated Film Distributors, 1979.
(With Leslie Arliss) *The Wicked Lady,* Metro–Goldwyn–Mayer/United Artists, 1983.
Claudia (also known as *Claudia's Story*), 1985.
(With Anthony Shaffer and Peter Buckman) *Appointment with Death* (based on the novel by Agatha Christie), Cannon, 1988.
(With Alan Ayckbourn) *A Chorus of Disapproval* (based on the play by Ayckbourn), South Gate, 1989.
(With L. Marks and M. Gran) *Bullseye!,* 1990.
(With Helen Zahari) *Dirty Weekend,* Scimitar Films, 1992.
(With N. Mead) *Parting Shots* (based on a story by Winner), Michael Winner Ltd./Scimitar Films, 1998.

Also author of *Girls, Girls, Girls, It's Magic,* and *Swiss Holiday.*

Nonfiction Writings:
Winner's Dinners, 1999, revised edition, 2000.
Winner Guide to Whining and Dining, 2002.
Winner Takes All (autobiography), 2004.
Michael Winner's Fat Pig Diet, 2006.

Contributor to books, including *Directing the Film,* American Film Institute, 1974. Also contributor of articles to periodicals, including *Daily Express, Evening Standard, Spectator,* and *Sunday Times* (London).

ADAPTATIONS

The film *Bullseye!* was based on a story by Winner.

OTHER SOURCES

Books:
Contemporary Authors, Volume 137, Gale, 1992.

Harding, Bill, *The Films of Michael Winner,* Frederick Muller, 1978.

Periodicals:
Empire, November, 1993, pp. 88–94; June, 1999, pp. 95–101.

WINTHER, Michael 1962–

PERSONAL

Born February 1, 1962, in San Francisco, CA; son of Joern H. (a television producer and director) and Rosemary E. (a writer; maiden name, Farmer) Winther. *Education:* Attended Hotchkiss School, Lakeville, CT; Williams College, B.A., theatre, 1985; studied acting with David Kaplan, Alice Spivak, and J. B. Bucky; studied stage fighting with John Waller; studied movement and historic dance with Sue Lefton, jazz and modern dance with Sandra Burton, Blondel Cummings, and Gary Restifo, and mime technique with Ben Benison and Jon Torel. *Religion:* Buddhist.

Career: Actor.

Member: Screen Actor Guild, Actors' Equity Association, American Federation of Television and Radio Artists, Association of Canadian Television and Radio Artists.

Awards, Honors: Los Angeles Outer Critics Drama Award (with others), best ensemble, 1985, for *Berlin to Broadway;* Drama Desk Award nomination, outstanding solo performance, 2006, for *Songs from an Unmade Bed.*

CREDITS

Stage Appearances:
(Stage debut) Rolf Gruber, *Sound of Music,* Sharon Playhouse, Sharon, CT, 1979.
(New York debut) Tracy Everett, *Vicki's Valentine Thing,* Ballroom Theatre, New York City, 1987.
Tracy Everett, *A Very Vicki Christmas,* Ballroom Theatre, 1987–88.
Donny Dulce, *Tony 'n' Tina's Wedding,* Washington Square Church, New York City, 1988.
The Virgin Mary, *The Council of Love,* Home for the Contemporary Arts, New York City, 1988.
Young Donner, *Artist Descending a Staircase,* Helen Hayes Theatre, New York City, 1989.

Gordon, *Dangerous Corner,* Syracuse Stage, Syracuse, NY, 1989–90.

Ozzie, *Damn Yankees,* Marquis Theatre, New York City, 1994.

Maggs, *Hapgood,* Mitzi E. Newhouse Theatre, New York City, 1994–95.

James Wilson, *1776,* Roundabout Theatre, New York City, 1997–98.

Berlin to Broadway, Triad Theatre, New York City, 2000.

Jamie deRoy & Friends Benefit for Variety: The Children's Charity, Florence Gould Hall, New York City, 2000.

Looking Forward, An Evening of New Theatre Music, Triad Theatre, 2000.

Bound for Broadway, Merkin Concert Hall, New York City, 2001.

Frankie, *Forever Plaid,* Pasadena Playhouse, Pasadena, CA, 2001.

"Hear & Now: Contemporary Lyricists with Michael Winther," *American Songbook,* Stanley Kaplan Penthouse, New York City, 2002.

Michael Winther, Ars Nova Theatre, New York City, 2002.

Reverend Hale, *The Crucible,* Virginia Theatre, New York City, 2002.

Various characters, *Radiant Baby,* Joseph Papp Public Theatre, Newman Theatre, New York City, 2003.

Harry Bright, *Mama Mia!,* Cadillac Winter Garden Theatre, New York City, 2003.

Songs from an Unmade Bed, New York Theatre Workshop, 2005.

Ensemble member and understudy Anton Diabelli and Ludwig van Beethoven, *33 Variations,* Eugene O'Neill Theatre, New York City, 2009.

Also appeared as Benny, *The Desert Song,* Light Opera of Manhattan, New York City; the lightbulb, *Dr. Faustus Lights the Lights,* Ensemble Studio Theatre, Los Angeles; the tenor, *Berlin to Broadway,* Zephyr Theatre, Los Angeles; Sammy, *Gorilla,* Dorset Theatre Festival, VT; Nanki–Poo, *The Mikado,* Green Mountain Guild, VT; Finch, *How to Succeed ...,* Green Mountain Guild; Horatio, *Hamlet,* University of London Theatre, London; Puck, *Midsummer Night's Dream,* University of London Theatre; Jerry, *The Zoo Story,* University of London Theatre; Pip, *Great Expectations,* Goodspeed Playhouse, East Haddam, CT.

Film Appearances:

Head novice, *We're No Angels,* Paramount, 1989.

Technician, *Universal Soldier,* TriStar, 1992.

Coworker number three, *Independence Day* (also known as *ID4*), Twentieth Century–Fox, 1996.

The roach chorus, *Joe's Apartment,* Warner Bros., 1996.

Rocco, *The Tag,* 2001.

Investment banker number two, *Mr. & Mrs. Smith,* Twentieth Century–Fox, 2005.

Shutment singer, *The Wedding Weekend* (also known as *Shut Up and Sing* and *Sing Now or Forever Hold Your Peace*), Strand Releasing, 2006.

Tone ranger, *The Break–Up,* Universal, 2006.

Day bank manager, *Jumper,* Twentieth Century–Fox, 2008.

Tourist, *Meet Dave,* Twentieth Century–Fox, 2008.

Television Appearances; Movies:

Job interviewer, *Mary and Rhoda,* NBC, 2000.

Television Appearances; Episodic:

Billy, "Next Victim," *21 Jump Street,* Fox, 1989.

Vern, "New York News," *New York News,* CBS, 1995.

Reporter, "School Daze," *Law & Order,* NBC, 2001.

Chaplain, "Uninvited," *One Life to Live,* ABC, 2008.

Also appeared as singer, *Remote Control,* syndicated.

WISDOM, Robert 1953–
(Bob Wisdom)

PERSONAL

Born September 14, 1953, in Washington, DC. *Education:* Graduated from Columbia University. *Avocational Interests:* International music, playing percussion instruments, world travel.

Addresses: *Agent*—Todd Eisner, Agency for the Performing Arts, 405 South Beverly Dr., Beverly Hills, CA 90212. *Manager*—Ben Levine, Kritzer, Levine, Wilkins, Griffin Entertainment, 11872 La Grange Ave., 1st Floor, Los Angeles, CA 90025. *Publicist*—Nicole Nassar, Nicole Nassar Public Relations, 1111 10th St., Suite 104, Santa Monica, CA 90403.

Career: Actor, producer, and artistic director. WKCR–FM Radio, New York City, jazz and program director, beginning 1972; National Public Radio, associate producer of *All Things Considered,* beginning 1979, and contemporary arts editor of *Sunday Show.* The Kitchen, Soho, New York City, music and performance curator, beginning 1984; Institute of Contemporary Art, London, head of performing arts program, beginning 1987. New Music America Festival, Washington, DC, artistic director, 1983; Media and Democracy Conference, director, 1984; Los Angeles Festival, associate artistic director. Competed in the 1976 Summer Olympics in track and field events.

CREDITS

Film Appearances:

Mort, *Clean Slate,* Metro–Goldwyn–Mayer, 1994.

Bobby Washington, *That Thing You Do!,* Twentieth Century–Fox, 1996.

Colonel Jessie Pratt, *Invader* (also known as *Lifeform*), Live Entertainment, 1996.

Motel manager, *No Easy Way,* 1996.

Detective Williams, *Stir,* 1997.

Inspector Sterling, *Jamaica Beat,* 1997.

Second Office of Emergency Management staff member, *Volcano,* Twentieth Century–Fox, 1997.

Tito Biondi, *Face/Off,* Paramount, 1997.

Kweli, *Mighty Joe Young* (also known as *Mighty Joe*), Universal, 1998.

Leroy Jasper, *Three Businessmen,* 1998.

Quonset Jones, *How to Get Laid at the End of the World,* 1999.

Slim, *The Heist* (also known as *The Metal Box*), 1999.

(As Bob Wisdom) Michael Jones, *Rocky Road,* 1999, Quality Entertainment, 2001.

The Dutchman, *Hollywood Palms,* Moonstone Entertainment, 2001.

Eddie, *Dancing at the Blue Iguana,* Lions Gate Films, 2001.

Miles, *D.C. Smalls* (short film), 2001.

Bob Johnson, *Coastlines,* IFC Films, 2002.

Mr. Gary Scott, "Fiction," *Storytelling,* Fine Line, 2002.

Lucius, *Masked and Anonymous,* Sony Pictures Classics, 2003.

Officer Dan, *Duplex* (also known as *Our House*), Miramax, 2003.

Alderman Lalowe Brown, *Barbershop 2: Back in Business,* Metro–Goldwyn–Mayer, 2004.

Carl Dayton, *The Forgotten* (also known as *Stranger*), Columbia, 2004.

Jack Lauderdale, *Ray,* Universal, 2004.

Mr. Sterling, *Haven,* 2004, Freestyle Releasing/Yari Film Group, 2006.

Moker, *Killer Diller* (also known as *Rockin' the House*), 2004, Freestyle Releasing, 2006.

Freak Weather, Sparring Partners I, 2005.

Sheriff Roy Fowler, *Crazy like a Fox,* Innovation Film Group, 2005.

Billy Bob, *The Hawk Is Dying,* Strand Releasing, 2006.

Blume, *Mozart and the Whale,* Millennium Films, 2006.

Dr. Carl Cohn, *Freedom Writers,* Paramount, 2007.

Alpha, *Sex and Death 101,* Anchor Bay Entertainment, 2007.

Officer Perkins, *Ball Don't Lie,* Night and Day Pictures, 2008.

Roy, *The Collector,* Freestyle Releasing, 2009.

Film Work:

Additional voices, *Osmosis Jones* (live–action and animated), Warner Bros., 2001.

Television Appearances; Series:

Detective Danny Watlington, *Cracker* (also known as *Cracker: Mind over Murder, Cracker: The Complete Series,* and *Fitz*), ABC, 1997–99.

Major Howard "Bunny" Colvin, *The Wire,* HBO, 2003–2008.

Lechero (some sources spell the name "Luchero"), *Prison Break,* Fox, 2007–2008.

Roger Hobbs, *Happy Town,* ABC, 2010.

Television Appearances; Miniseries:

Police officer, *If These Walls Could Talk,* HBO, 1996.

Rolando, *Kingpin,* NBC, 2003.

Television Appearances; Movies:

Sergeant Tambul, *Sahara* (also known as *Desert Storm*), Showtime, 1995.

Oscar Valdez, *For Love or Country: The Arturo Sandoval Story* (also known as *The Arturo Sandoval Story*), HBO, 2000.

Bernard Shaw, *Live from Baghdad,* HBO, 2002.

Television Appearances; Specials:

The 21st Annual Tony Awards, 1967.

The Wire: It's All Connected, HBO, 2006.

Television Appearances; Pilots:

Professor James, *Wasteland,* ABC, 1999.

Bonds, *Lie to Me,* Fox, 2009.

Television Appearances; Episodic:

(As Bob Wisdom) Waiter, "The Adventure of the Egyptian Tomb," *Agatha Christie's "Poirot"* (also known as *Poirot*), broadcast on *Mystery!,* PBS, 1993.

Lieutenant Williams, "The Debt," *The Sentinel,* UPN, 1996.

Daniel Euwara, "Spirit Thief," *Poltergeist: The Legacy,* Showtime, 1997.

(In archive footage) Daniel Euwara, "The Choice," *Poltergeist: The Legacy,* Showtime, 1997.

Daniel Euwara, "The Darkside," *Poltergeist: The Legacy,* Showtime, 1998.

Prospero, "It Takes a Village," *Dharma & Greg,* ABC, 1998.

"His Name Is Arliss Michaels," *Arli$$,* 1998.

Daniel Euwara, "Possession," *Poltergeist: The Legacy,* Showtime, 1999.

Dr. Hammond, "Piece of Mind," *ER,* NBC, 2001.

Mr. Ronald Broyles, "To Serve and Protect," *The District,* CBS, 2001.

Eric Green, "Safari, So Good," *NYPD Blue* (also known as *N.Y.P.D.*), ABC, 2002.

Daryl C. Norcott (Chronic), "Execution," *Boomtown,* NBC, 2003.

District Attorney Matthews, "Tricks of the Trade," *Judging Amy,* CBS, 2003.

Mr. Banga, "Absolute Bastard," *The Agency* (also known as *CIA: The Agency*), CBS, 2003.

Reverend Scofield, "Eminent Domain," *Close to Home,* CBS, 2007.

Clarence Jones, "Man of the Year," *The Nine,* ABC, 2007.

Uriel, "It's the Great Pumpkin, Sam Winchester," *Supernatural,* The CW, 2008.

Uriel, "I Know What You Did Last Summer," *Supernatural,* The CW, 2008.

Uriel, "Heaven and Hell," *Supernatural,* The CW, 2008.

Uriel, "On the Head of a Pin," *Supernatural,* The CW, 2009.

Warden Gene Halsey, "Caged," *Navy NCIS: Naval Criminal Investigative Service* (also known as *NCIS* and *NCIS: Naval Criminal Investigative Service*), CBS, 2009.

McCraken, "Murtaugh," *How I Met Your Mother* (also known as *H.I.M.Y.M.*), CBS, 2009.

Father Theo Burdett, "Hell," *Law & Order: Special Victims Unit* (also known as *Law & Order: SVU* and *Special Victims Unit*), NBC, 2009.

Vaughn, "Friends and Enemies," *Burn Notice,* USA Network, 2010.

Vaughn, "Fast Friends," *Burn Notice,* USA Network, 2010.

According to some sources, appeared (credited as Bob Wisdom) as Johnny Olina–Olu in "Street Smart," an episode of the British series *The Bill,* 1990.

Stage Appearances:
Brace Up!, Wooster Group, London, c. 1993.

Appeared in *Hapgood,* London.

RECORDINGS

Video Games:
Voice of Luke Cage, *Spider–Man: Web of Shadows,* Activision, 2008.

Voice of second Uruk–Hai officer, *Lord of the Rings: Conquest,* Electronic Arts, 2009.

WORTHINGTON, Wendy 1954–

PERSONAL

Born September 17, 1954, in Memphis, TN. *Education:* Temple University, B.A. (summa cum laude), radio/ television/film. *Avocational Interests:* Reading, traveling, going to horse races and baseball games.

Career: Actress. Theatre Neo, cofounder; also a theater director and singer. Appeared in television commercials, including Chex Party Mix, 1997–2004, and H&R Block, 1999. Also worked as an arts administrator; CineKye, cofounder; The Clay Studio, executive director; held managerial jobs at People's Light and Theatre Company.

Member: Screen Actors Guild.

Awards, Honors: Dramalogue Award, for *Lulu;* Dramalogue Award, for *Gynecomedy;* *LA Weekly* Award nomination, for *The Women.*

CREDITS

Film Appearances:
Tour guide, *Mannequin: On the Move* (also known as *Mannequin 2: On the Move* and *Mannequin Two: On the Move*), Twentieth Century–Fox, 1991.

Lady customer, *The Life and Times of Charlie Putz,* 1994.

Prostate nurse, *Father of the Bride Part II,* Buena Vista, 1995.

Demented Hills nurse, *Good Burger,* Paramount, 1997.

Jowly clerk, *Trojan War* (also known as *Rescue Me*), Warner Bros., 1997.

Bank manager, *Best Men* (also known as *Risky Bride*), Orion, 1997.

First bar–goer, *Sparkler,* Strand Releasing, 1997.

Secretary, *Krippendorf's Tribe,* Buena Vista, 1998.

Receptionist, *Carnival of Souls* (also known as *Wes Craven Presents "Carnival of Souls"*), Trimark Pictures, 1998.

Connie Mahoney, M.D., *Every Night and Twice on Sundays,* IndieDVD, 1998.

Arlette, *The Quantum Project,* 2000.

Nurse Bates, *Teacher's Pet* (also known as *Devil in the Flesh 2* and *Teacher's Pet*), 2000.

Wendy Larson, *Cast Away,* Twentieth Century–Fox, 2000.

Joannie Wodinski, *On Edge,* KBK Entertainment, 2001.

Receptionist, *Catch Me If You Can,* DreamWorks, 2002.

Barbara, *Connecting Dots,* 2003.

Marilyn, *L.A. Twister,* Indican Pictures, 2004.

Customer, *Win a Date with Tad Hamilton!,* DreamWorks, 2004.

Bizarre woman, *Breaking Dawn,* Lions Gate Films Home Entertainment, 2004.

Nurse Cetnik, *Love Comes to the Executioner,* Velocity Home Entertainment, 2006.

Oregon woman, *The Great Buck Howard,* Magnolia Pictures, 2008.

Maria, *Man Maid,* Marvista Entertainment, 2008.

Reception nurse, *Changeling,* Universal, 2008.

Motel manager, *The Canyon,* Truly Indie, 2009.

Mary Renfrew, *Rock Bottom* (short film), 2010.

Television Appearances; Series:
Margaret Camaro, *Ally McBeal* (also known as *Ally My Love*), Fox, 1999.

Ellen Westmore, *So Little Time,* 2001.
Nurse, *Ghost Whisperer,* CBS, 2008–2009.

Television Appearances; Movies:
Mrs. Gifford, *Norma Jean & Marilyn* (also known as *Norma Jean and Marilyn*), HBO, 1996.
Emeline Partridge, *Tower of Terror,* ABC, 1997.
Jury forewoman, *Breast Men,* HBO, 1997.
Nurse Bates, *Devil in the Flesh 2,* HBO, 2000.

Television Appearances; Episodic:
Woman number three, "Be Careful What You Wish For," *Murphy Brown,* CBS, 1994.
Heloise, "Freezer Burn," *Picket Fences,* CBS, 1995.
Woman, "Let's Call the Whole Thing Off," *Wings,* NBC, 1995.
Louise, "The Kiss Hello," *Seinfeld,* NBC, 1995.
Woman, "Two Men and a Baby," *The Wayans Bros.,* The WB, 1995.
Yvonne, "Pal Joey," *Picket Fences,* CBS, 1995.
Heloise, "Freezer Burn," *Picket Fences,* CBS, 1995.
Muu–muu woman, "Murder on the Run: Part 1," *Diagnosis Murder* (also known as *Dr. Mark Sloan*), CBS, 1996.
Alcatraz tour guide, "The Code," *Dangerous Minds,* ABC, 1996.
Evelyn, "The Foosball Connection," *Life with Roger,* The WB, 1996.
Judge, *Arli$$,* HBO, 1996.
Cotton candy lady, "Love Triangles," *Family Matters,* ABC, 1997.
Officer Donna, "Past Tense," *Suddenly Susan,* NBC, 1997.
Mrs. Cooper, "Again with the Laser Surgery," *Alright Already,* The WB, 1997.
Scrub nurse, "The Adventures of Baron Von Munchausen ... by Proxy," *Chicago Hope,* CBS, 1997.
Second woman, "The Player," *Between Brothers,* 1997.
Mrs. Poupiepenz, "Inna–Gadda–Sabrina," *Sabrina, the Teenage Witch* (also known as *Sabrina* and *Sabrina Goes to College*), ABC, 1997.
Jury foreperson number one, "Dog Bite," *The Practice,* ABC, 1997.
Female shadow, *The Visitor,* Fox, 1997.
Chef, *Party of Five,* Fox, 1997.
Officer Donna, "Car Trouble," *Suddenly Susan,* NBC, 1998.
DMV tester, "Rent," *The Steve Harvey Show,* The WB, 1998.
First customer, "Eric's Buddy," *That '70s Show,* Fox, 1998.
Queen Victoria, "Saving Mr. Lincoln," *The Secret Diary of Desmond Pfeiffer,* 1998.
Mrs. Baker, "See Dharma Run," *Dharma & Greg,* ABC, 1999.
Nurse number one, "Veronica Falls Hard," *Veronica's Closet,* NBC, 1999.
The lunch lady, "Earshot," *Buffy, the Vampire Slayer* (also known as *BtVS, Buffy, Buffy, the Vampire Slayer: The Series,* and *Nightfall*), The WB, 1999.

Mrs. Gower, "Bad to the Bone," *The Parkers,* UPN, 2000.
Elsa Scholtz, "Foodzilla," *Even Stevens,* ABC, 2000.
Nurse, "Primrose Empath," *Charmed,* The WB, 2000.
Waitress at tea house, *Reba,* The WB, 2001.
Unemployment clerk, "Welcome to the Rest of Your Life," *Nikki,* The WB, 2002.
Mailwoman God, "Touch Move," *Joan of Arcadia,* CBS, 2003.
Dog Lady, "The Doghouse," *Happy Family,* NBC, 2003.
Amy Bernstein, "Let's Spend the Night Together," *The Guardian* (also known as *Ochita bengoshi Nick Fallin*), CBS, 2003.
Cindy, "Assault with a Lovely Weapon," *The Drew Carey Show,* ABC, 2004.
Mrs. Velsey, "Still Decorating," *Still Standing,* CBS, 2006.
Cheryl, "Bomb Shelter," *Malcolm in the Middle,* Fox, 2006.
Helga, "California Girl," *One on One,* UPN, 2006.
Jean, "Sticks & Stones," *My Name Is Earl,* NBC, 2006.
Nurse Parker, "Nice She Ain't," *Desperate Housewives,* ABC, 2006.
(Uncredited) Nurse Parker, "Children and Art," *Desperate Housewives,* ABC, 2006.
Nurse Parker, "The Little Things You Do Together," *Desperate Housewives,* ABC, 2007.
Drugstore clerk, "Mars, Bars," *Veronica Mars,* 2007.
The Secret Life of the American Teenager, ABC Family, 2007.
Bettina, "Hug & Tell," *Back to You,* Fox, 2008.
Annie, "The Test of My Love," *Hannah Montana* (also known as *Secret Idol Hannah Montana*), The Disney Channel, 2008.
Brenda, "Sonny at the Falls," *Sonny with a Chance,* The Disney Channel, 2009.
Woman auditioning, "Dream On," *Glee,* Fox, 2010.

Also appeared as woman, *The Home Court.*

Stage Appearances:
Appeared in *Lulu,* Hollywood Moguls; *All about Steve; My Secretary; Bookkeeping; Gynecomedy,* Improv, Los Angeles; *Van Gough on Prozac; Cementville; Queen of Swords; Our Town; The Odd Couple; The Matchmaker; South Pacific; Gypsy; Hay Fever; Cabaret; Blithe Spirit; One Flew over the Cuckoo's Nest; The Dining Room; A Doll's House; Candida; Funny Girl; The Pirates of Penzance; A Little Night Music; The Philadelphia Show;* as Countess de Lage, *The Women,* Theatre Neo.

WYATT, Lisa K.

PERSONAL

Addresses: *Manager*—Rothman, Patino, Andres Entertainment, 4370 Tujunga Ave., Suite 120, Studio City, CA 91604.

Career: Actress.

CREDITS

Film Appearances:
Desert Princess, *Visceral Matter* (short film), 1997.
Linda Connie, *Donnie Darko* (also known as *Donnie Darko: The Director's Cut*), Newmarket Films, 2001.
Jail house guard, *Legally Blonde* (also known as *Cutie Blonde*), Metro–Goldwyn–Mayer, 2001.
Necklace admirer, *Intermission* (short film), 2004.
Amanda, *50 Ways to Leave Your Lover* (also known as *How to Lose Your Lover*), New Line Cinema, 2004.
Aunt Edna, *American Dreamz*, Universal, 2006.
Teri Riley, *Southland Tales*, Destination Films, 2006.
Housewife, *Mr. Woodcock,* New Line Cinema, 2007.
Rhonda Martin, *The Box,* Warner Bros., 2009.
Peggy Hamill, *The Crazies,* Overture Films, 2010.
The Eater (short film), 2010.

Television Appearances; Series:
Lynn, *The Office,* NBC, 2009.

Television Appearances; Episodic:
Madeline, "The Joint," *Clueless,* UPN, 1998.
Any Day Now, Lifetime, 1998.
Transpo technician, "Middle of Nowhere," *ER,* NBC, 1999.
Aunt Ruby, "The Good, the Bad and the Luau," *Sabrina, the Teenage Witch* (also known as *Sabrina*), ABC, 1999.
Hannah, "The Loud Solomon Family: A Dickumentary," *3rd Rock from the Sun* (also known as *3rd Rock* and *Encounters of the Personal Kind*), NBC, 2000.
Olivia Cassidy, "Veronica Loses Her Olive Again," *Veronica's Closet,* NBC, 2000.
Trailer trash woman, "The Shocking Possession of Harrison John," *Popular,* The WB, 2001.
Francine the Sonics fan, "Hooping Cranes," *Frasier,* NBC, 2001.
Joyce, "An Aborted Dinner Date," *That's My Bush!,* Comedy Central, 2001.
Mindy, "Subject: Sunrise at Sunset Streams," *Freaky-Links,* Fox, 2001.
Pam, Kroehner mortician, "Crossroads," *Six Feet Under,* 2001.
Pam, Kroehner mortician, "The New Person," *Six Feet Under,* 2001.
Darlene the receptionist, "The Big Leagues," *The Tick,* Fox, 2001.
Customer, "The Gamble," *The O.C.,* Fox, 2003.
Minnie, "After the Ball Is Over," *Carnivale* (also known as *La feria ambulante*), HBO, 2003.
(Uncredited) Doris, "Cinderella in Scrubs," *Strong Medicine,* Lifetime, 2004.

Madonna Louise, "Written in the Stars," *Gilmore Girls,* The WB, 2004.
Bunny, "Class Reunion," *My Wife and Kids,* ABC, 2004.
Doris, "Jump for Joy," *My Name Is Earl,* NBC, 2006.
Doris, "The Trial," *My Name Is Earl,* NBC, 2007.
Janet, copy editor, "Sofia's Choice," *Ugly Betty,* ABC, 2007.
"Reunion," *Big Love,* HBO, 2007.
Caitlin, "Trust Never Sleeps," *The Riches,* FX Network, 2008.
Helga Von Lempke, "Move On Cartwrights," *Greek,* USA Network, 2008.
Mrs. Walker, "iCarly Saves Television," *iCarly,* Nickelodeon, 2008.
Ranger Stone, "Unshockable," *CSI: Crime Scene Investigation* (also known as *CSI: Las Vegas* and *C.S.I.*), CBS, 2010.

YUAN, Eugenia
(Eugenia Yuen)

PERSONAL

Original name sometimes cited as Eugenia Yuen Lai–Kei; daughter of Cheng Pei Pei (an actress, martial artist, and producer; also known as Cheng Pei–Pei, Cheng Pei–pei, and Pei–pei Cheng); sister of Marsha Yuen (an actress). *Education:* Studied dance and gymnastics.

Career: Actress. Gymnast and member of the U.S. Olympic Team.

Awards, Honors: Hong Kong Film Award, best new performer, and Hong Kong Film Award nomination, best supporting actress, 2003, both for *Saam gaang;* named a rising star/screen acting discovery, Hamptons International Film Festival, 2004, for *Mail Order Wife;* Golden Horse Film Festival Award nomination, best supporting actress, 2004, *Gin gwai 2;* was ranked the fourth best rhythmic gymnast in the world.

CREDITS

Film Appearances:
Hai'er, "Going Home" segment, *Saam gaang* (includes three segments; also known as *Three, Three ... Extremes, Three ... Extremes II, Three Extremes 2, 3 Extremes II,* and *San geng*), Bac Films/Lionsgate, 2002.
Lori, *charlotte sometimes* (also known as *Duplex* and *Sex or Lunch*), Visionbox Pictures, 2002.
Xiao Xia, *Flying Dragon, Leaping Tiger* (also known as *Dragon Soaring, Tiger Leaping, Long teng hu yue,* and *Lung tung fu yuek*), Deltamac Entertainment, 2002.

Irina, *My Name Is Modesty: A Modesty Blaise Adventure* (also known as *Modesty Blaise, Modesty Blaise: The Beginning,* and *My Name Is Modesty*), Buena Vista Home Video, c. 2003.

Yuen Chi–Kei, *Gin gwai 2* (also known as *The Eye 2, Jian gui 2,* and *Khon hen phi 2*), Applause Pictures/Mediacorp Raintree Pictures, 2004.

Lichi, *Mail Order Wife* (also known as *Mail Order Bride* and *Untitled Mail Order Bride Project*), Dada Films, 2004, First Independent Pictures, 2005.

Cora (Manilla nurse), *The Great Raid,* Miramax, 2005.

Korin, *Memoirs of a Geisha* (also known as *Geisha*), Columbia, 2005.

Amy, *Choking Man,* International Film Circuit, 2006.

Kate O'Connor, *Locked,* Mandorla Pictures, 2006.

Kwan's wife, *Zhan. gu* (also known as *The Drummer* and *Die Reise des chinesischen Trommlers*), Emperor Motion Pictures, 2007, Film Movement, 2009.

Jenny, *Wu* (also known as *Fog*), 408 Films/Bears Productions, 2009.

Yin Yin, *Shanghai Hotel,* Cornucopia Productions, 2009.

Slaughter, c. 2009.

Lucy Galland, *Will's Diaries,* Quercus Productions, 2010.

Alex, *Strangers,* c. 2010.

Grace, *Jasmine,* c. 2010.

Television Appearances; Awards Presentations:
2007 AZN Asian Excellence Awards, AZN Television, 2007.

Television Appearances; Episodic:
(As Eugenia Yuen) Girl, "Everything's Coming Up Roses," *Beverly Hills 90210* (also known as *Beverly Hills, Beverly Hills, 90210, Beverly Hills 90210 Classic, Class of Beverly Hills,* and *L.A. Beat*), Fox, 1995.

Sun Yi, "Promised Land," *Baywatch* (also known as *Baywatch Hawaii* and *Baywatch Hawai'i*), syndicated, 1995.

Maya Chu, "Final Conflict: Parts 1 & 2," *Martial Law* (also known as *Le flic de Shanghai, Ley marcial,* and *Piu forte ragazzi*), CBS, 2000.

Jenny Chin, "Everyone into the Poole," *NYPD Blue* (also known as *New York Blues, New York Cops—NYPD Blue, New York Police, New York Police Blues, New York Police Department, N.Y.P.D,* and *N.Y.P.D.*), ABC, 2001.

"Evil Twin," *Arrest & Trial* (also known as *Arrest and Trial*), syndicated, 2001, Five, 2002.

Kim Lee, "Clowning Glory," *Glory Days* (also known as *CSL—Crime Scene Lake Glory, Demontown,* and *Demon Town*), The WB, 2002.

Theresa Chu, "Hello, Henry," *My Own Worst Enemy,* NBC, 2008.

Theresa Chu, "That Is Not My Son," *My Own Worst Enemy,* NBC, 2008.

WRITINGS

Writings for the Internet:
Author of a blog posted at *alive not dead,* http://www.alivenotdead.com/eugeniayuan.

OTHER SOURCES

Periodicals:
Femme Fatales, December, 2001, pp. 41–47.

Cumulative Index

To provide continuity with *Who's Who in the Theatre*, this index interfiles references to *Who's Who in the Theatre*, 1st–17th Editions, and *Who Was Who in the Theatre* (Gale, 1978) with references to *Contemporary Theatre, Film and Television*, Volumes 1–109.

References in the index are identified as follows:

CTFT and volume number—*Contemporary Theatre, Film and Television*, Volumes 1–109
WWT and edition number—*Who's Who in the Theatre*, 1st–17th Editions
WWasWT—*Who Was Who in the Theatre*

B

C

E

G

J

Cumulative Index

M

O

Q

Cumulative Index

Z

Cumulative Index